CONTEMPORARY

AMILIES

CONTEMPORARY FAMILIES

A SOCIOLOGICAL VIEW

Richard J. Gelles

PHOTOGRAPHS BY JUDY S. GELLES

SAGE Publications
International Educational and Professional Publisher
Thousand Oaks   London   New Delhi

For information address:

SAGE Publications, Inc.
2455 Teller Road
Thousand Oaks, California 91320

SAGE Publications Ltd.
6 Bonhill Street
London EC2A 4PU
United Kingdom

SAGE Publications India Pvt. Ltd.
M-32 Market
Greater Kailash I
New Delhi 110 048 India

Printed in the United States of America

Library of Congress Cataloging-in-Publication Data

Gelles, Richard J.
  Contemporary families: A sociological view / Richard J. Gelles.
    p. cm.
  Includes bibliographical references and indexes.
  ISBN 0-8039-3419-X (cl). — ISBN 0-8039-5821-8 (pb)
  1. Family—United States.   I. Title.
HQ536.G435   1995
306.85′0973—dc20   94-16439

95 96 97 98 99 10 9 8 7 6 5 4 3 2 1

Sage Production Editor: Diane S. Foster

To my brother, Bob

■■ Contents in Brief

■ Detailed Contents

CHAPTER 2   FAMILY STUDIES: THEORETICAL AND METHODOLOGICAL APPROACHES   33

CHAPTER 6   LOVE, COURTSHIP, AND MATE SELECTION   165

CHAPTER 10 CHILD SOCIALIZATION   289

CHAPTER 11 WORK AND FAMILY   319

■ Acknowledgments

The germ of the idea that I should actually write a Sociology of the Family text came from Judy Greissman, who edited our Social Problems text and was then with Harcourt Brace. Judy has left college textbook publishing, but I would never even have thought of undertaking this text without her push. I took so long to write this book that many people at Sage Publications were involved. Al Goodyear believed in the idea of this text and signed me to my contract. C. Terry Hendrix guided the book for a year or so until Mitchell Allen returned from his foray into managing a folk dance company. Mitch provided the editorial guidance and spiritual motivation during most of the journey. He, too, went through a number of significant personal and family changes during the time I was writing the book. Mitch has an incredible touch. He knows when to be compassionate and when to be tough and demanding. He has a gifted insight into family studies and combines that with nearly the perfect temperament to be an editor. Mitch has also become a valued personal friend. The book would never have been completed without him. Sara Miller McCune and George McCune have published my books for more than 20 years. I can never repay Sara for her support over the years. I deeply regret that George is not alive to see this project come to fruition.

Quite a number of my students aided in this undertaking. Diane Hanscom, Margaret Rauch, and Lani Dingman served as assistants during parts of this project. Heidi Reckseik was my assistant for the majority of the work done on the book. Heidi was an invaluable aid, in addition to being one of the most gifted students with whom I have every worked.

Ann Levine did not actually write any of this book, but she has been my coauthor on so many books that I owe her one of my most important debts. Ann, more than anyone, taught me how to actually write. Of course, since she did not coauthor this book she is not responsible for any of the lessons I did not learn nor for any of the errors in the book.

Roz Sackoff was the developmental editor for the book. Roz brought me down the home stretch and added a great deal to the final product.

Like any text author, I owe a major debt to the hundreds (probably thousands by now) of my students. They were the final arbitrators of which ideas, concepts, and materials work and of those that do not. Their individual contributions to my ideas and approaches are innumerable and helped to mold this book.

Finally, my own intimate environment has provided me help and, most of all, nurturance for this project. My wife Judy was my partner, providing nearly all the photographs for the text. My sons Jason and David grew up with this book. My love of all three is unending. I finished the book during a 6-month period when Jason was in college, David worked in Washington as a Senate page, and Judy taught three courses.

A number of reviewers read and criticized my manuscript in various drafts. I sincerely appreciate the contributions of the following people in the shaping of this book: Tricia Dyk, University of Kentucky; Keith Farrington, Whitman College; Roma Hanks, University of South Alabama; Rudy Ray Seward, University of North Texas; and Maxi Szinovacz, Old Dominion University.

■ Preface

The family, as I say in the first sentence of Chapter 1, is both obvious and elusive. The family is an intimate environment as well as a social institution. This book is about families and the family. I present some material that seems obvious and some that penetrates the elusive nature of families. I will also go back and forth between families as intimate environments and the family as a social institution.

The Preface is supposed to tell students why they should read the text. Of course, one reason is because it is the basis of the course in which you are enrolled. I am going to take a more unconventional path to explain why I think you should read this text.

My first contact with the Sociology of the Family was as a sophomore in college. I had recently declared a major in sociology, having changed from history. The Bates College sociology department was small, and having taken both "Introduction to Sociology" and "Social Problems," the only course offered that I could take was "Marriage and the Family." The course was not entirely memorable. The instructor had not completed his doctorate and was not entirely familiar with the subject matter. The text was a bit dry—no photographs, tables, or "boxes." I remember two things about the course. First, I received a B+ and thought I deserved an A. Second, although I do not remember much of the actual course content, I vividly remember my surprise that the course discussed issues and problems that I had thought were unique to me and my family. The course provided me a view or perspective that I had never had into my own life and my own family.

I had no further contact with the "Sociology of the Family" or family studies for a number of years. I never enrolled in a family sociology course of any type in either my M.A. program or even during the first two years of my doctoral program. Quite by chance, in my fourth year in graduate school, I began a working relationship with my then major professor, Murray Straus, that would span more than two decades. Murray was in the first stages of his research on family violence. I was a fourth-year student in search of a dissertation topic. I was intrigued by the topic of family violence, although I knew nothing about child abuse or wife abuse (and had never even considered the issue of elder abuse).

My studies of family violence provided me a new and different window into understanding families and the family as a social institution. Studying the darker side of family relations not only uncovered family secrets, it helped illuminate my understanding of how families actually worked.

I began my teaching career at the University of Rhode Island in 1973 and taught my first family sociology course. My goals were to take my students beyond their knowledge and understanding of their own families and to place their own experience in a larger social, cultural, and historical context. "Don't generalize from an N of 1," I repeatedly told my students. "Don't assume that you know everything there is to know about even your own family." And finally, "Remember that social structures affect people." Everything that goes on in families is not the result of individual acts or individual motivations. Social class, race, age, and gender affect families and family life. Other social institutions influence the family. The family as a social institution has a history. Finally, family life both varies and is consistent across cultures and time. To understand the family, one needs to recognize the consistencies and the differences.

Somewhere around 1979 I got the idea of writing a textbook on the Sociology of the Family. I had just completed the first edition of my text *Sociology: An Introduction* (with Michael Bassis and Ann Levine), and I thought the next logical step would be to write a family sociology text. My own text would allow me to not only fashion my own course the way I wanted it, it would provide me a chance to contribute to how my colleagues approached and taught a topic to which I had grown deeply committed.

The project began in fits and starts. I actually began to write in earnest in 1982. Eleven years later, almost to the day, I finished the book. The delay was not due entirely to lack of time or lack of interest. I actually completed three more editions of my introductory sociology text and a number of other book projects during this time.

There were many reasons why it took me so long to write this book, and many of the reasons reflect some fundamental truths and insights about families. When I started to write the book I was married and had two sons, 8 and 5 years old. I was an Associate Professor of Sociology and Anthropology. Over the years, I was promoted, served one year as Associate Dean of Arts and Sciences, served six years as Dean of Arts and Sciences, and coached Little League baseball and youth soccer. I spent two years as a "househusband" when my wife returned to graduate school. My father died after a short but difficult illness. I aged from a young man to what I thought was a middle-aged man—my brother cruelly pointed out that since no one in our family had lived to be 90, I am older than middle-aged. In short, I went through many of the family developmental stages and crises that I talk about in this book. Each change, each stress, each new opportunity not only delayed the book but gave me more insight into the family as a changing intimate environment.

During the same 11 years, the family as a social institution changed. There were consistent claims that the family was declining, but real changes happened as well. The divorce rate peaked the year I began to think about writing this text. At the time, many of us thought the divorce rate would continue to climb—it did not. Child abuse and wife abuse went from being deviant acts committed behind closed doors to public issues and social problems so significant that they are discussed in major political addresses. Childbirth and marriage became increasingly disconnected, and the proportion of children who live in single-parent homes increased. The war on poverty was lost, and more and more families, and especially children, lived below the poverty line. Racial and gender issues took a more central position in the national conversation. Progress was made, backlash fired up, and there were times of retrenchment in efforts to achieve equity for women and ethnic minorities. AIDS became an important facet of dating and intimate relations. Homosexuality was also an issue that received more attention—some good and accepting, some vindictive and harmful.

It was clear to me as the years unfolded, and as my editors called in anguish about how little progress I was making with the text, that a major facet of this book had to be the notion of change and families—both as intimate environments and as a social institution.

A second thing happened during the 11-year effort. I began the book as a faithful and loyal sociologist. However, as I continued my research on family violence, I began to realize that sociology and sociological variables could not fully explain why intimates abused and hurt those they professed they loved. I began to look beyond my discipline and read more psychology—especially developmental psychology and clinical psychology. Freud, who had been the straw man target in many of my lectures, became more relevant to me as I looked deeper into the roots of physical and sexual abuse. I conducted cross-cultural research, and so the writings and findings of anthropologists became relevant. Finally, I returned to my original roots as a history major to try to uncover more about the historical roots of family violence.

As I applied each of these disciplines to my research, the disciplines became more relevant to this text. I would not, I decided, strictly limit this text to research and theories of sociologists. The text is still primarily a "sociological view" of "contemporary families," but that view is complemented, when appropriate, by the work and thoughts of psychologists, anthropologists, and historians. And while I focus on contemporary intimate environments and the contemporary family as a social institution, I also bring to bear historical and cross-cultural evidence and comparisons to illuminate what we know about families and the family.

■ Notes to the Instructor

The course you teach on families has a lasting effect on your students' lives. Almost all of your students come from families of their own and many will have fiancés, spouses, and their own children when they take your class. We know from research that a large number will have already experienced divorce, stepfamilies, family violence, family stresses, and other subjects discussed in depth in this book firsthand. Thus your class on families will be inherently interesting to your students. I have prepared this text with you and your students in mind, trying to capture this inherent fascination with families in the pages of the textbook to reinforce the excitement you generate in the classroom.

Traditionally, courses on families and the family have been divided into one of two kinds: institutional or functional. The institutional course is generally offered in sociology departments. This course, often titled "Sociology of the Family," stresses the family as a social institution and applies a sociological perspective to studying families. The functional course is usually offered in colleges or departments of family studies or human development. Although in many ways similar to the institutional course, it includes more material and advice about "how to have a good marriage." This textbook is designed for the institutional course. I place a great deal of emphasis on social science research findings related to the important dimensions of family life but spend little time on issues such as contraception techniques, how to communicate better with your spouse, or proper child-rearing techniques.

I have kept in mind that there are a variety of paths that students take into this course and various paths that they follow when they complete it. Many students enroll in a family course after having taken "Introduction to Sociology" or "General Sociology" classes. However, a number of colleges and universities, including my own, offer "Family Sociology" or "The Family" without a prerequisite course in sociology. Thus I have not presumed that your students are well acquainted with theories, methods, and basic terminology of sociology or psychology and have included a detailed glossary to help them.

For many of your students, your class will be their only exposure to the social-scientific study of families. I have aimed at providing these students a thorough overview of the main topics and issues in family studies. A smaller number of students may enroll in additional family studies courses and these students will receive a firm foundation for their future study of families from reading this book.

Let me point out to you *special features* I have included in the book:

■ As I indicate in the Preface, I began writing this book a decade ago as a sociologist and completed writing the book from the more interdisciplinary perspective of a sociologist/psychologist. Although I retain my discipline's roots, I did not want to pigeonhole all the material in this book into a strict sociological framework. When appropriate, I introduce psychology (e.g., Chapter 10: Child Socialization). I have also drawn on the disciplines of anthropology and history (Chapter 3: Families Across Time and Cultures), as well as introducing a biosocial perspective (Chapter 9: Parents and Parenthood).

■ I chose *three major themes* to run throughout the book. Each is highlighted in a boxed format:

1. *The Family Over Time.* There is a historical box in almost every chapter. I begin many of the chapters with historical perspectives on the topic of the chapter. My goal is to provide the students with a *historical* understanding of the important family issues that concern students today.

2. *The Global View.* I also want students to see the broad trends of similarities and differences in families as intimate environments and the family as a social institution *across cultures.* Many chapters have global boxes that examine specific issues cross-culturally.

3. *Diverse Families.* I also want students to know about and understand *multicultural differences* within American society. Thus many chapters contain multicultural boxes that examine in depth family issues within and between specific ethnic and racial groups in the United States.

■ Two additional boxes, *What the Research Shows* and *Thinking About Families,* afford students an in-depth look at current research on and theoretical issues addressed in family studies. Almost all of the chapters contain a research box, and several offer a theory box.

■ The book examines families across the *entire life span*. Although the primary consumers of this book may be students 18 to 24 years of age, colleges and universities have increased enrollments of what we used to call "nontraditional students." Because of the wider age span of students, and because I believe students can only understand families if they know how issues affect families across the entire life course, the book includes more discussion of the later part of the life span than many other texts in this field.

■ I focus on the different levels at which families are experienced—*institutions, intimate environments,* and by *individuals.* I repeatedly emphasize in this text that there is an interface between the family as an institution in society, families as intimate environments in which people interact, and individuals and their relationships to their families. As a sociologist, I believe that structures affect people, and I have attempted to illustrate how the main social structures in our society—social institutions, social stratification, gender stratification, racial and ethnic stratification, and age stratification—affect families and individuals. Within the broad macrostructural context, I examine the structures, processes, and interactions between individuals within families. I feel it is important for students to study all three structural levels—and how they intersect—to gain a full understanding of this crucial social institution.

■ I have organized the text somewhat *developmentally.* The first two chapters set the stage for the student of families—terms, issues, theories, and methods. The following three chapters examine families across time, across cultures, and in terms of structural variations and similarities in the United States. Chapters 6 through 12 follow the important stages of the life course. The family issues of divorce, stress, and family violence are examined in a three-chapter sequence toward the end of the volume. The book concludes with a discussion of the future of families. I have not divided the book into specific sections or parts because I assume that most instructors, like me, have a specific sequence of topics or issues they like to follow and that sequence might differ from the one I use for this book.

■ I have worked closely with a colleague and experienced teacher, Patricia Hyjer Dyk of the University of Kentucky, in developing a comprehensive and useful Instructor's Manual. The manual contains descriptive information about the textbook, well-designed test questions in a variety of formats, and ideas to assist you in preparing for class. It also contains numerous suggested writing assignments to give to your students, in line with the increased emphasis on writing-across-the-curriculum that is a feature in most contemporary colleges and universities. The Instructor's Manual, which is available at no charge from the publisher for teachers who adopt this textbook for their class, should enhance your use of this book with your students and improve your students' mastery of the material in the course.

▪ Finally, I have endeavored to present what sociologists know about families. I have drawn on some of the *best social science research* to paint a portrait of what families are like in contemporary society, across cultures and groups, and over time. I have included both exemplary contemporary studies as well as classic research and theoretical analyses on the topic.

Although many of my colleagues might know me best for my research and writings on family violence, I have also been passionately concerned about teaching and improving the quality of teaching over my entire career. I edited the journal *Teaching Sociology* for 10 years. I was deeply involved with those in the American Sociological Association who worked to raise the importance of teaching in the profession and to improve the quality of sociologists' teaching. Finally, I have coauthored two other sociology texts through multiple editions.

I have tried to bring my passion and commitment to teaching to the textbook. My goal was to make the text accessible, interesting, and informative for students without violating the basic rules of evidence for social theory and research. I hope that you, the instructor, share my passion and commitment for teaching and will find this text a useful foundation for your own course on families.

Richard J. Gelles

Richard J. Gelles

. . . is Professor of Sociology and Psychology and Director of the Family Violence Research Program at the University of Rhode Island. His book *The Violent Home* was the first systematic empirical investigation of family violence and continues to be highly influential. He is author or co-author of 15 books and more than 90 articles and chapters on family violence. His most recent books are *Intimate Violence* (Simon & Schuster, 1988), *Physical Violence in American Families: Risk Factors and Adaptations in 8,145 Families* (Transaction Books, 1990), *Intimate Violence in Families* (Sage, 1990), *Current Controversies on Family Violence* (Sage, 1993), and, with Ann Levine, the fifth edition of *Sociology: An Introduction* (McGraw-Hill, 1995).

Gelles received his A.B. degree from Bates College (1968), an M.A. in sociology from the University of Rochester (1971), and a Ph.D. in sociology from the University of New Hampshire (1973). He edited the journal *Teaching Sociology* from 1973 to 1981 and received the American Sociological Association, Section on Undergraduate Education, "Outstanding Contributions to Teaching Award" in 1979. Gelles has presented innumerable lectures to policy-making groups and media groups, including *The Today Show, CBS Morning News,* and *Good Morning, America.* In 1984, *Esquire* named him one of the men and women under the age of 40 who are "changing America."

CHAPTER 1

■■ Understanding Families

The family is both obvious and elusive. Virtually everyone spends at least part of his or her life in families. When people talk about family life and family problems, they draw from personal experience. Most of us either have firsthand experience with such family topics as divorce and unwanted pregnancy, or know about them through friends, neighbors, and relatives. Given this intimate knowledge, we should all be experts on the family.

In fact, no other social institution is as poorly understood as the family. Most of us are ill-informed, even about our own families. How many people can construct a family tree from memory, beginning with their great-grandparents and filling in all of their cousins? Most people know little about their own parents' marriage. How old were they when they met? Did they have sexual intercourse with each other before they were married? Has either ever had an extramarital affair? Did they ever think about getting divorced, or, if they are divorced, have they seriously considered getting back together? Most people know very little about their parents' lives. How much does their father earn? Their mother? What exactly do they do at work? What would they like to be doing? Few people can answer all of these questions about their own families.

Discussions of the family nearly always stir controversy. During the 1992 national presidential election, families and family values were among key campaign issues and images. Hillary Rodham Clinton stirred controversy during a television interview when she noted that she was *not* someone who "stayed home and baked cookies." She was later attacked as someone who advocated allowing children to sue their parents. Vice President Dan Quayle stirred up a hornet's nest when he criticized television character "Murphy Brown," who was having a baby both out of wedlock and without any intention of having a husband or father to help raise the child.

Ask a group of people what makes for a happy family and you will get nearly as many answers as there are members of the group. Sharp disagreements are almost certain. Tune into one TV talk show and you will find guests deploring the decay of modern life. Turn the dial and you will find another commentator extolling the virtues of variation and change in today's families. Even experts who have years of experience in studying families draw different conclusions. Sixteen years ago, while historian Christopher Lasch (1977) was arguing that the modern family could no longer fulfill essential functions and had ceased to be a "haven in a heartless world," sociologist Mary Jo Bane (1976) was reporting that the family was "here to stay." Analyzing the same statistics, experts sometimes take opposite positions on what those numbers mean. Paul Glick (1979), former senior demographer of the U.S. Bureau of the Census, saw data on the change in family size, decreases in the number of children born, and the growing tendency of individuals to delay marriage well past age 20 as evidence that the family was healthy and viable. Looking at the same numbers, sociologist Amitai Etzioni (1977), then of Columbia University, concluded, with some exaggeration, that not one family would be left by 1990 (see also Chapter 16)! Of course, Etzioni was wrong—there are families in the 1990s. But he was also right—the family is a much more troubled social institution than Glick had portrayed it in 1979.

BARRIERS TO UNDERSTANDING FAMILIES

How can something with which everyone has extensive, personal experience be so mystifying? How can something as mundane as family life be so controversial? Sometimes, the very qualities that make families special block understanding. Barriers to understanding the family include the bias of personal involvement, the private nature of the family, the "sacredness" or sanctity of family life, and variation and change in families.

Personal Involvement

We are born into families, and more than 90% of us will go on to be married at least once. Our values, beliefs, goals, and even thought patterns are rooted in our family experience. Sometimes, we may see our own family through rose-colored glasses and think that it is ideal—the "best" type of family. Other times, we may think the grass is greener in every other yard and think our own family is the most dysfunctional. But in every case, our personal involvement tends to lead us to make generalizations based on a single case—our own family. To a certain extent, our experience becomes a set of blinders that biases how we think about families in general.

The first bias is that we are personally involved in families. In some instances, this bias takes the form of generalizing from our own family experiences to all other families. We may expect that other families are like ours or should be like ours. In other instances, the bias can take the form of assuming that our family is dysfunctional and that *all other* families are more functional. Last, the bias can result from the lack of knowledge we have about our own families. We may have an image of what our family is like, but this may be quite different from reality—recall for a moment how many of the questions posed on the first page of this chapter about your own parents and family you could answer accurately.

Privacy

The family today is an exceptionally private institution (Laslett 1973). This was not always so. In the Middle Ages, family members worked and played together, took their meals together, and slept in the same room. Children were not sheltered from the facts or the fun of adult life. Often, nonfamily members (servants, lodgers, and others) were part of the household. Married couples handled economic matters in the open. Although sexual intercourse did not take place in the open, it was not confined to a separate bedroom either. There was little privacy—both from the external world and within the home.

In contrast, much of modern family life takes place behind closed doors. There is both privacy from the outside world and privacy within the home. Outsiders knock before they enter. Homes have separate rooms for separate functions. (Eating in the living room or bedroom is often forbidden.) It is nearly impossible to find a household that does not have a lock on at least the bathroom door.

The modern family is what sociologist Erving Goffman (1959) calls a *backstage* area: a place where people can remove the masks they wear in public and be themselves. To a certain extent, everyone "performs" in public. We play the roles of teacher or student, executive or secretary, according to social scripts; we try to look and act the part. Backstage, in the privacy of the home, these pretenses can be dropped. Thus the smiling couple sees their dinner guests to the door and, as soon as the door is closed, resumes the bitter quarrel they were having when the guests arrived. Everyone knows that the way their family group acts in public is different from the way members behave in private. But we rarely, if ever, see other people's families backstage. And although most of us judge our own families in terms of their backstage behavior, we judge other families in terms of their onstage, public performances.

Family members often try to maintain high degrees of privacy within the family. A teenager shuts the door when conferring with her best friend; a parent may suppress a guilty urge to look at his son's diary; parents wait for the children to go to bed to quarrel. It is not uncommon for the youngest child in a family to go off to college and then, when she returns for Thanksgiving, to learn that her parents are getting a divorce—and that they had been planning to for years but had waited until the children were grown.

The realities of family life are hidden behind this double layer of privacy—privacy from the outside world and privacy from the other members of the family group. We have superficial knowledge of other people's families and limited knowledge of our own.

Privacy also limits what social scientists can learn about family life. Unlike scholars who study other areas of social behavior, students of the family rarely, if ever, are allowed to make firsthand observations of backstage behavior. Thus our knowledge about sexual relations and practices, violence, abuse, sexual abuse, and stress is limited to what individual family members are willing to tell scholars in interviews or questionnaires (although some social scientists do collect information by observing families—see Chapter 2).

Privacy was one of the reasons why sexual abuse and child and wife battering were not recognized as extensive social problems until recently. Privacy also obscures the true nature of marital sexual behavior.

The high emotional value invested in the family, the considerable emotional energy expended on the family, and the reverence in which the family is held constitute the third barrier to understanding. The family is a sacred institution. Family and family life are often idealized in personal, public, media, and political discussions. We tend to create an ideal image of what the family *was like, is like,* and *should be like.* Discussions about what families were like a hundred years ago tend to idealize the virtues of the extended family—a family type that exists in our idealizations but rarely existed in practice (see Chapter 4). Similarly, discussions of families in the 1950s recreates the image of another "Golden Age" of family life and values (Coontz 1992; Skolnick 1991). Current discussions of family problems and pathologies also tend to be measured against these often inaccurate idealizations.

Because the family is sacred, people often deny their own deviations from the ideal. A husband and wife who are having sexual difficulties or who hit one another try to hide this from other family members, friends, and professionals in order to publicly measure up to ideals of family life. People also practice *self*-deception about their families. A wife who has been abused repeatedly convinces herself that it won't happen again or that she "asked for it" and carries on as if nothing were wrong. The sacred ideals are maintained, often in direct contradiction to reality.

Sanctity

The search for the "perfect marriage" and the "perfect family" obscures a wide range of variations in families. We tend to see the nuclear family, formed by love and attraction, with a husband, wife, and children living under one roof, as both the cultural ideal and the most advanced form of family life. Other family forms and structures, such as arranged marriages and **polygamous** (multiple spouse) marriages, are thought by many to be primitive.

By overlooking family variation, we fail to know and appreciate that in some cultures a man does not feel he has achieved full adult status until he has acquired several wives **(polygyny)**. Women in polygynous societies may also feel unfulfilled if their husbands do not have more than one wife. Wives may

Variations

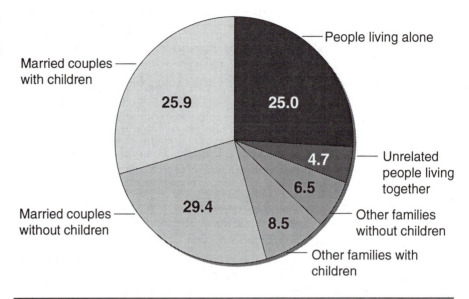

Figure 1-1 Family arrangements: Percentages of all U.S. households in 1991

People living alone

Married couples with children

25.9

25.0

4.7 — Unrelated people living together

6.5

29.4

8.5 — Other families without children

Married couples without children

Other families with children

SOURCE: U.S. Bureau of the Census (1992).
NOTE: Children refer to a family's own child or children under 18 years of age.

motivate their husbands to take other wives because they have no co-wives to share their work and leisure time. Our experience with family life in the modern United States causes us to assume that monogamy is the most widespread form of family. In fact, polygamous marriage is the cultural ideal in the majority of the world's societies (see Chapter 3).

In some cultures, married couples never dream of having a home of their own. They expect and want to live with either parents in a three-generation household. In our society, the ideal family is a **nuclear family:** a married couple and their children, who are economically independent and run their own household. This is what most young people want for themselves and what most parents hope for their children. We tend to think of other family forms, such as a single parent who chooses to live as a single parent, a childless couple, or a divorced parent and child, as deviant or temporary arrangements. In fact, the majority of Americans do not conform to the nuclear ideal. The most common household is a married couple with no children at home (see Figure 1-1).

The nuclear family is a moral or normative ideal type, an abstraction that captures the essential features of how we think families ought to be. In reality, there is, however, no one single type of family. There are at least five types of households classified by the U.S. Bureau of the Census (1991): (1) families; (2) unrelated subfamilies (households with subgroups of persons who are related to one another but not to the head of the household); (3) related subfamilies; (4) married couples without children; and (5) unrelated individuals.

Moreover, people go through different types of family arrangements, depending on what stage in their marriage they are in. Many working-class couples start out by living with their parents until they get their financial feet on the ground. Anthropologist Carol Stack (1974) has described the pattern of sharing and exchange among black families, where children are taken in and raised by relatives during hard times.

Thus, when we speak of family, we are speaking of a variety of patterns of living arrangements and household organization.

A fourth barrier to understanding families is change—both rapid and steady. Our wish to see the family as a stable unit and as an enduring social institution can blind us to the changes our own families go through over their lifespan and to changes in the institution of the family. We tend to see the family as suspended in time and immune to historical forces. As Mary Jo Bane (1976) has pointed out, "In technology, progress is the standard." People welcome innovations in transportation, communications, and the like. In the family, however, "continuity is the standard, and when change occurs it is seen as decline rather than advance" (p. 4). Indeed, almost every generation imagines that families were happier and healthier in their grandparents' day (Goode 1963; Skolnick 1991).

Change

Families are changing. For instance, married couples with a child or children under age 18 living in the home have declined dramatically just in the past two decades (Figure 1-2). Households with a wife in the labor force have increased dramatically in the past three decades.

Sometimes, individuals exaggerate changes in families, as if to prove that the current family is decaying, disintegrating, or collapsing. Public discussions of divorce often point to a continuing increase in the divorce rate. The divorce rate, however, while increasing dramatically in the 1960s and 1970s, has actually leveled off and is no longer increasing (see Chapter 15). Similarly, advocates on behalf of battered women and children talk about epidemic-like increases in child abuse and wife abuse. Yet some research actually shows a decrease in both forms of abuse since the 1970s (see Chapter 14).

Privacy, sanctity, variations, and change are why what should be obvious eludes us when we consider the family. We know some of what goes on in our own families, but the veil of privacy masks some of our own family's secrets and keeps us from knowing more than the public performance of other families. We might be able to measure our own family against cultural ideals or

Breaking Through the Barriers: The Sociological Perspective

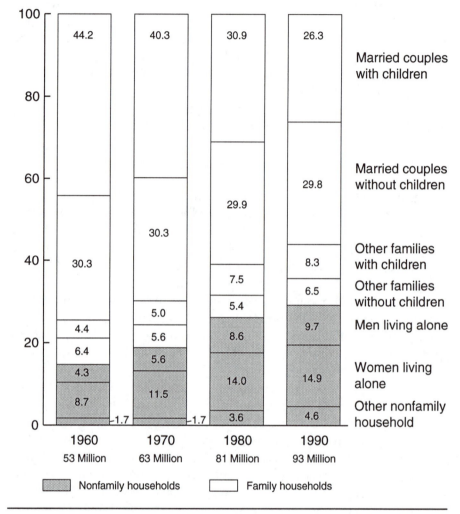

Figure 1-2 Household composition, 1960–1990

SOURCE: U.S. Bureau of the Census (1989, p. 10; 1991, p. 2).

statistical norms, but we know little about the interior of other families. The idealization of family life, the variation of family form, and change also blind us to fully understanding families in our own and other cultures. The study of the family is not merely an exercise in "belaboring the obvious," wasting time discovering what everyone already knows. In reality, the study of families is an exploration into the unknown.

A useful road map or guidebook in the trip through the unknown is the **sociological perspective.** What is the sociological perspective? Sociologist Peter Berger (1963) claims that the sociological perspective is a consciousness, a way of viewing the world allowing us to see through the illusions of the present *status quo* and also through the illusions concerning possible futures (p. 9). The sociological perspective allows us to break through myths and reconstructions of history and see through the illusions of the past.

An important part of the sociological perspective is what Berger calls the "debunking motif." Sociologists are driven to question what is taken for granted, to explode myths and conventional wisdoms, to question the "obvious," what everyone else believes to be true. Sociologists want to get in behind the closed doors of the family and see what really goes on. They delight in finding out what others do not know. They frequently are motivated to explore the seamier side of family life, the unrespectable, the taboo topics that are not discussed in public or sometimes even in private.

Chapter 2 fully explores the sociological perspective by examining the theoretical and methodological tools that sociologists use to examine and analyze families and family relations.

BOX 1-1: WHAT THE RESEARCH SHOWS

Public Objections to the Sociological Perspective

There are some real drawbacks to applying a sociological perspective to something as taken for granted as the family. Although there are indeed limitations and biases of familiarity and obstacles to truly understanding families, most people do not consider these biases or obstacles—they believe they know about family life because they have experienced it. When sociologists announce a new finding or the results of a detailed study on family life, they risk what sociologist Robert Merton (1959) has called the "quadruple bind."

If, after detailed scientific investigation, a sociologist confirms a finding that people widely accept as true—that there is a double standard in sexual behavior in marriage—then the sociologist is viewed as a bore, laboring uselessly to find the obvious. Should the sociologist find the opposite, that a widely believed fact is in fact untrue—that children do not hold marriages together—then he or she is likely to be seen as a heretic, someone who refuses to

accept what everyone knows is true. The methods of the study and the values or the intelligence of the sociologist are likely to be called into question. What if a study reveals that something that people believed to be false is in fact true? Here, then, our sociologist can be labeled a charlatan, claiming obvious falsehoods. Finally, our sociologist could investigate something that all intelligent people view as false (for instance, abusing children does them no harm) and indeed finds that this claim is false. Here again, the sociologist is ridiculed for wasting effort to study something that everyone already knew was untrue.

So, no matter what topic or issue a family sociologist may choose to study, no matter how hard a sociologist may try to demystify the family, he or she inevitably will run into criticism and even ridicule. Thus the sociological perspective can at times confirm common sense and at other times challenge common sense.

Table 1-1
Definitions of
What Constitutes
a Family

Definition	Percentage Agreeing[a]
A married couple living with their children	98
A man and a woman who are married but have no children	87
A divorced mother living with her children	84
A divorced father living with his children	80
A never-married mother living with her children	81
A never-married father living with his children	73
A man and a woman who have lived together for a long time and are not married but are raising children	77
A man and woman who have lived together for a long time and are not married	53
Two lesbians living with children they are raising	27
Two gay men committed to each other and living together	20

SOURCE: Roper Starch Worldwide, Inc. (1992). Reprinted with permission.
a. Percentages reflect responses by Americans surveyed in February 1992.

WHAT IS A FAMILY?

Everyone knows what a family is—or thinks one knows. Most readers will propose that a family consists of people who are related by blood or marriage, live together, share numerous economic and social responsibilities, and have or plan to have children.

The U.S. Census Bureau defines family as "a group of two or more persons related by birth, marriage, or adoption and residing together in a household. A family includes among its members the householder" (U.S. Bureau of the Census 1992).

One of the earliest definitions of the family in the field of family studies was proposed by Ernest Burgess (1926), who defined the family as "a unity of interacting personalities each with its own history" (p. 3). Harold Christensen (1964) introduced his *Handbook of Marriage and the Family* by defining family as *marriage plus progeny* (children).

A national opinion poll by the Roper Organization in February 1992 found a wide variation in the public's definitions of what constitutes a family (Table 1-1). Although 98% of those surveyed identified a married couple living with their children as a family, one in five also identified two gay men committed to each other and living together as a family.

My own definition of **family** is that the family is a social group and a social institution that possesses an identifiable structure made up of positions (e.g., breadwinner, child rearer, decision maker, nurturer) and interactions among those who occupy the positions. The structure typically carries out specialized functions (e.g., child rearing), is characterized by biologically and socially defined kinship, and often involves sharing a residence.

I concede that my definition of "family" is a bit broad and somewhat complex. One reason for this is that the job of defining "family" is much more difficult than one would first realize. Is a family a couple with children, or can a couple without children be a family? Does "family" include grandparents, uncles, aunts, cousins, relatives by marriage? What about the father of your stepmother—is he a member of your family? What are gay and lesbian couples—are they a family? What about a lesbian women who has a child by artificial insemination?

Some textbook writers avoid the issue of defining a family completely. It is not uncommon to pick up a textbook on marriage and the family, examine the index, and find that nowhere in the book has the author attempted to

Although the U.S. Census Bureau's definition of "family" would not include a gay or lesbian couple, sociologists' definitions of "family" would.

define "family." He or she may take for granted that readers will know a family when they see one. Perhaps the author tried to define "family" and gave up in frustration.

In this section, I want to go beyond our definition of family and consider in some detail the characteristics commonly thought of as being part of the definition of "family." I want to note carefully the family organizations and structures that differ from conventional understandings of what a family is, as well as draw distinctions between family and nonfamily organizations.

Residence: A House Is Not a Home

Common residence is one of the characteristics of families that people take for granted. Suppose you heard that a couple had an extravagant, traditional wedding, went to Bermuda for a two-week honeymoon, and then she returned to the apartment she shares with a roommate and he went back to his parents' house. You would be sure that something was wrong with their marriage. But the rule of common residence should not be taken too literally. The fact that people live together does not make them a family, nor does the fact that members live apart destroy a family.

Roommates are a clear example of people who live together but are not a family. They may share domestic chores and expenses, but they do not feel

---

BOX 1-2: THINKING ABOUT FAMILIES

The Family as an Ideal Type

Throughout this book I will use terms like *family*, *nuclear family*, *extended family*, *monogamous relations*, *patriarchal family organization*, and many more. Sociologists refer to these concepts and constructs as "ideal types."

In our everyday language, "ideal" frequently means valued, good, perfect, the best. And indeed, some concepts used by family sociologists imply a moral judgment. People often think of the nuclear family (father, mother, and child living under one roof) as the best form of family—female-headed households are thought of as less than ideal.

Sociologists have a different meaning for the term "ideal type." The German sociologist Max Weber ([1922] 1968) coined the concept ideal type to mean a stereotyped, abstract, "pure" model of a concept, with which reality can be compared for purposes of objective study. An ideal type is a theoretical abstraction. Ideal types are abstractions, and no phenomenon exists in the real world that can perfectly match the ideal type. Thus a husband, wife, and children can live under one roof, but they may continue to have considerable contact and exchange with other members of their family. Men can have the power in societies, but that does not necessarily mean that women are completely oppressed and powerless.

Thus, when we speak of the American family throughout this book or even when we try to define the concept "family," it is important to keep in mind that we are defining an ideal type.

the emotional ties and long-term obligations of family members. Their household is based more on convenience than commitment. In some groups, married couples establish a separate household but feel stronger ties to their parents and brothers and sisters than they do to one another (Schneider and Smith 1973). The boundaries of their household do not coincide with their emotional and social commitments. Cohabitating couples who live together and have a sexual relationship fall somewhere between roommates and established families. Some see their relationships as a temporary convenience; others as a trial marriage. (And in some cases the two partners disagree about what living together means.)

On the other hand, there are people who do not live together but nevertheless are a family. In some New Guinea tribes, for example, all the men in a village live together in a central house, visiting their wives and children for meals and other activities (see Chapter 3). Even children may live away from home. In some types of Israeli *kibbutzim,* children do not live with their parents. In England, upper-class families traditionally send their sons to boarding school at age 7 or 8. But one need not travel abroad to find families with separate residences. Naval personnel who ship out to sea for months at a time do not share a common residence with their families year round (Mederer and Weinstein 1992). Actors and musicians may spend as many nights in hotel rooms as they do at home with their spouses and children. And commuter marriages—couples who work in different cities and maintain two residences that they share only on weekends and holidays—have become more common, especially with the increase of married women in the workplace. One example of this is the experience of Isabell Sawhill, family researcher and coauthor of *Time of Transition: The Growth of Families Headed by Women* (Ross and Sawhill 1975), who lived in Washington, D.C. for a time while her husband John, president of New York University, lived in New York City.

In short, residence does not make—or break—a family. The distinction between households and families is an important one. A household is a group of people who are bound to a *place* (Ball 1972). A family is bound not to the residence itself but by ties of kinship (Ball 1972; Turner 1970). As the saying goes, "Home [the family] is where the heart is."

Kinship: Flesh and Blood

Most people think of the family as resting on a firm genetic foundation. What makes the family different from other social groups is the sexual bond between husband and wife and the genetic ties of parents and children. Children are their parents' "flesh and blood." In other words, what sets families apart is **kinship**: relationships based on birth and the birth cycle.

To some extent this is true, but kinship is determined not only by genetics. It is a matter of social definition. Who people consider kin depends more on social norms than on genetic closeness. Not infrequently, the social facts override the genetic facts of family life. An example of this is the incest taboo that prohibits biological members of the same family from having sexual relations with one another. In many jurisdictions in the United States and in many countries around the world, a stepfather who has sexual relations with his stepdaughter has violated the incest taboo, even though he and his step-daughter have only social ties, not genetic ones. Comedian and film director Woody Allen was the center of a controversy around this issue in 1992 when, in the course of a custody battle, he announced that he'd had an affair with the adopted daughter of his lover Mia Farrow. The media, public, and some social scientists debated whether the relationship between Allen and Farrow's adopted daughter was incest, tacky, or acceptable.

Definitions of kinship differ from one culture to the next. The ancient Chinese, for example, defined the family as a chain of fathers and sons, extending back to distant ancestors and forward to unborn sons (Wolfe 1972). This is considered **patrilineal descent** (see Chapter 3). Of course, women were necessary to provide links in the chain of fathers and sons. They were members of their fathers' households as children and of their husbands' households as adults. But they were not counted as family or recorded in family genealogies. Similarly, traditional Navajo defined the family as the long line of mothers and daughters, in which men played only a peripheral role. This is an example of **matrilineal descent** (see Chapter 3). The emphasis in these cultures is on lines of descent, or **consanguine (blood) relationships.** In our society, the emphasis is on marital ties, or the **conjugal relationship.**

However the family is defined, most individuals are able to recognize their kin. In our society, most people can identify their parents, siblings, grandparents, uncles, aunts, and cousins. The status of these people as kin is clearly defined. But there are complications to even the clear and ordinary kinship system. Social convention in our society has created the status of **fictive kin** (Ball 1972; Kessing 1958). Fictive kin, or pretend relatives, include close friends of a child's parents who come to be called "Uncle Willie" or "Aunt Jeannette" (Liebow 1967; Stack 1974). There are also **discretionary kin.** These are individuals who are ordinarily distant in normal kinship terms and may or may not be included in the family based on a member's inclination (Ball 1972). The husband of a married man's sister may or may not be considered a brother-in-law. When the father of an adult child remarries, the parents and/or children of the new wife may or may not be considered step-grandparents, stepbrothers, and stepsisters. An example of this type of discretionary kin involves one of my colleagues whose father remarried shortly after the death of his first wife. The new wife had two grown sons. On one occasion, one of the sons, a successful attorney, was introduced to me by my colleague as his stepbrother. Later, when the stepbrother was out of the room, my colleague noted that his stepbrother had a younger brother who was constantly unemployed and had recently moved in with his mother and her new husband. When I asked him if he would have introduced this son as his stepbrother, my colleague said, "Never, he's an idiot—I wouldn't have him as a relative!" Fictive and discretionary relatives underline the social nature of kinship.

The main socially approved reason for getting married and starting a family in our society is love. (Most people would not admit to marrying for money, for example.) The notion of marrying for love is not universal. In most societies and times, marriage has been viewed as a contract between families, not between two individuals; marriages have been arranged by kin, not by the bride and groom; and love has been considered irrelevant, if not abnormal and disruptive (Linton 1936). In traditional Japan, for example, a young person was not introduced to his or her future spouse until the marriage contract had been sealed. Young men were encouraged to seek sexual adventure, companionship, and entertainment from "professionals" or geishas. What we call love was deliberately separated from marriage in traditional Japan. In India, many marriages are still arranged. To Americans and other Westerners, this may seem "cruel and unusual." But a close look at love and marriage in the United States today suggests that the free choice of mates is in part an illusion (see Chapter 6). All available evidence indicates that love is far from blind. Most people happen to fall in love with someone who is of the same race, religion, social status, generation, and marital status (single or divorced) as themselves. As a general rule, women marry men who are taller, better educated, better paid, and a few years older than they are (see Chapter 6). It is highly unusual for a woman to marry a man who is 10 years younger or 40 years older than she is. To do so might invite ridicule. But the point is that most people never even consider breaking the rules. The thought never occurs to them. They want to do what society expects of them.

Marriage legitimizes sex and parenthood (see below). Sex outside marriage is more socially acceptable in the United States today than it was in the past. Nevertheless, we still use the terms **pre**marital and **extra**marital sex, implying that the *proper* setting for sexual relations is the marriage bed. Although Americans have increased in their willingness to approve of premarital sex, most Americans disapprove of extramarital affairs (Smith 1992). Whereas traditional norms had proscribed (or forbidden) sex outside marriage, today's norms prescribe (or require) sex within marriage and, sometimes, before.

Love, Sex, and Marriage: The Defining Components of Marriage

It has only been in the past decade or so that the wedding ceremony stopped including the bride's promise to "love, honor, and obey her husband."

Marriage manuals in the 1930s described sex as the key to a happy marriage. Infrequent or indifferent sexual relations between a husband and wife are still seen as symptoms of marital problems today. Whereas couples used to worry that they were the only ones "doing it," now they may worry that they are the only ones who are not. Thus sex, like love, is something less than free.

Domestic Relations: The Defining Substance of Marriage

As recently as 25 years ago, as part of the traditional wedding ceremony, a bride vowed to "love, honor, and *obey*" her husband. A husband was legally responsible for supporting his wife and children, whether or not she had an income of her own. A wife was held responsible for housekeeping and child rearing. Once married, a wife had no legal identity of her own. She was required by law to live where her husband lived; she could be denied credit, even if she earned more than her husband; and so on. The division of labor in the family was clear-cut: The husband earned the bread and the wife baked it (Tavris and Offir 1977). Much has changed. Many couples write their own marriage ceremonies today. Most like to think of marriage as an equal partnership. The laws have been changed and reinterpreted to give both sexes more equal rights. Perhaps most significant, a vast majority of married women hold jobs.

What is surprising is that, although so much has changed outside the home, so little has changed inside. Domestic relations are still governed by the division of labor by sex. Women's (and men's) liberation seems to have stopped at the front door. One might expect that with so many wives working, husbands would be doing more around the house. They are not. Studies show that the average American husband devotes only a few hours a week to domestic chores (Koorman and Kapteyn 1987; Pleck 1985; see also Chapter 11). In contrast, the wives do about 80% of all housework (Beckett and Smith 1981; Berardo, Sheehan, and Leslie 1987; Kooreman and Kapteyn 1987). In effect, she holds two jobs (Hochschild and Machung 1989). When husbands do contribute to housekeeping, their contribution usually is defined as "helping out." Ultimate responsibility for the home and for children belongs to the wife.

Parenthood

With modern birth control and legal abortions, parenthood has become a matter of choice. Sexual intercourse does not inevitably lead to pregnancy, although unplanned pregnancies do occur. Thus the question is whether the definition of what is a family requires that there be children.

Statistics indicate that, given a choice, most American couples do decide to have children. The overall birth rate in the United States has plunged since the peak in the 1950s (Cherlin 1990). The reason is not that fewer couples are having children but that couples are having fewer children (one or two instead of three or four). There has been an increase in voluntary childlessness in recent years, but this has been met in part by a decrease in involuntary childlessness (because of improvement in the medical treatment of infertility) and an increase in "late" births to women in their 30s.

The rights and responsibilities of parenthood are the subject of much debate and confusion these days. Should a woman quit her job and devote herself full-time to being a mother, at least while her child is small? Is a child who is left with a baby-sitter or in a day care center all day deprived? Underlying these questions is the assumption that only the family (and especially the child's mother) can provide **nurturant socialization**: the combination of care and instruction with emotional support and responsiveness (Reiss 1980). The notions that parents are wholly responsible for their children and that the parent-child bond cannot be replaced without risk are not universal. In traditional Samoan society, for example, children were free to wander from one relative's household to another's, as they wished. In effect, they had many parents to choose from and the choice was left to them (Mead 1928).

The issues of parenthood multiply as children approach their teenage years. How can parents possibly compete with the influence of the mass media? Of teachers? Of peers and the closed, secret adolescent society? If, for example, a teenage daughter becomes pregnant, are her parents to blame? Should she be allowed to decide for herself whether to inform her parents and whether to have the baby or have an abortion? These questions reflect the impact of social forces on the family. For example, the invention of the automobile and the prosperity that enabled many American families to have at least one car freed young people from parental surveillance. At the same time, the requirement that young people attend school until age 16 and declining job opportunities for those who do not complete high school—and some college—have increased the number of years that children are financially

---

BOX 1-3: THE FAMILY OVER TIME

Family Change:
Your Parents' Marriage and Yours

One way of seeing the changes that have occurred in the modern American family is to consider the changes that have occurred since the time your parents were married. Assuming that the average student reading this text is in his or her early 20s (with apologies to older students), then your parents were probably married in the early to mid 1970s. Richard M. Nixon was about to resign as President of the United States and be replaced by Gerald Ford. Gasoline was 55 cents a gallon—for high-test (there was no unleaded gas). American troops had recently departed Vietnam, and prisoners of war had returned home. The Beatles were among those seeking spiritual guidance from the Maharishi in the Himalayas. Michael Jackson was 12 years old. *Dallas*, *The A-Team*, and *Charlie's Angels* were the top-rated television shows. Tennis star Jimmy Connors was 20 years old.

There are 14.6 million more families in the United States today than there were in 1970. In 1970, the average age at first marriage for a woman was 20.6 years; for a man, it was 22.5 years. Today, men marry about 3.5 years later, women nearly 3.3 years later. The average family was 3.33 people when your parents were married, today the typical family is smaller—less than 3 people per home. Marriage has become more popular in the past decade and a half—in 1970, 7.6% of those over 65 years of age had never married; by 1989, the percentage is down to about 5%. There were no official statistics for unmarried couples who lived together in 1970—today the U.S. Bureau of the Census reports that the number is nearly 3 million and growing each year.

In summary, chances are that you will get married at an older age than your parents were, you are more likely to have lived with a member of the opposite sex prior to your marriage than your parents were, and that you will have fewer children than your parents did.

dependent on their parents. These and other social changes have extended and complicated parenthood.

In review, there is considerably more to the family than meets the eye. Many of the things we take for granted as normal and natural are not universal. In societies that allow a man to have many wives, for example, a devoted husband is one who works hard to acquire additional wives. A woman who tries to hold her husband's undivided attention is considered as odd as a woman who encourages her husband to have lovers would be in our society.

Thus, although I began this chapter with a working definition of what a family is, it is important to realize the difficulty and sometimes the futility of trying to simply define something as complex as "a family" or "the family." Indeed, families do seem to have common structures and functions. But structures—such as living arrangements and residence—vary within cultures and over time. Kinship is an important and universal aspect of families, but the determination of who is kin and how kin are recognized also varies. To insist on a rigorous, precise definition of "families," set in stone for all times, all cultures, and all families is to omit the dynamic variation of families.

I have tried to capture the main and unique characteristics of families in this section, and I think this does more justice to understanding families than would a simple dictionary definition. I continue my examination of families in the next section by examining the family as a social institution and an intimate environment.

THE FAMILY AS AN INSTITUTION AND INTIMATE ENVIRONMENT

When people discuss and debate the future of "the family," they are not concerned about what will become of the Smiths, now that Mr. Smith has lost his job, nor are people talking about whether Mr. and Mrs. Jones will decide to have a third child. The debate over the future of the family focuses on a larger reality of "family" than the goings on in a single household. There are two levels of reality when considering the family. The first, the future of the Smith family, or the child-rearing decisions of the Jones family is the *microlevel approach*. Here the focus is on the interpersonal relationships of the people who make up the small group we label "a family." The second approach, the more global concern that might examine the future of all families, is a *macrolevel approach*. Here the concern is with the family as a social institution. In

Table 1-2 Statistics on Family Composition, 1992

U.S. population	252,688,000
Number of households	94,312,000
Number of families	66,322,000
Average family size	3.23
Average age at first marriage	
Men	25.5 years
Women	23.7 years
Percentage never married	
65 years old	4.7
25-29 years old	45.9
Unmarried couples living together	2,764,000

SOURCE: U.S. Bureau of the Census (1992).

this section, I examine the two realities of families: (1) the family as a *social institution* and (2) the more microlevel concern with the family as an *intimate environment*.

A key point here is the distinction between the family as a social institution and families as social groups. When social scientists talk about the *family*, they are referring to the institution: the blueprint that guides individuals in love, sex, and marriage, defines kinship, transforms a house into a home, and shapes relationships between the sexes and the generations in the family. When social scientists talk about *families*, they are referring to a wide range of social groups and to the way people actually live their lives (Table 1-2).

The Family as a Social Institution

The family is one of society's social institutions, along with education, economics, religion, and politics. A *social institution* is defined as an established pattern of social relationships and behavior that structures a particular area of social life. One might think of the institution of the family as a blueprint. Just as a blueprint tells a builder how to construct a house from truckloads of loose, unconnected bricks and boards, so the institution of the family directs individuals in constructing a family out of their different personalities and skills.

The institution of the family rests on a firm foundation of custom and tradition. The basic structure is built with positions and roles. The term **position** (or status) refers to the place a person occupies in the family or another social group, to where he or she fits in with others. The position of son, for example, defines a person's relationship to other family members. The position of wife or aunt establishes other relationships. The term **role** refers to the set of rights, obligations, and expectations that accompany a particular role. A mother, for example, has the right to order her daughter to go to her room (a right the daughter does not have over her mother) and the obligation to support her while she is young. Positions and roles make up the basic family structure. **Values** (shared ideas about what is right and good), **norms** (guidelines for behavior in specific situations), and **sanctions** (rewards for conformity to norms and punishments for nonconformity) provide the wiring and plumbing, making the family structure habitable on a daily basis.

The institutional blueprint provides only the skeleton of a family, however. The occupants of this structure—the Smiths and Joneses—determine the final design. Members of a society start with a basic blueprint; all families are in some respects alike. But the blueprint varies by age, gender, race, and ethnicity. In addition, because each family's members have unique personalities and skills and their own way of interpreting their assigned roles, each family is in some respects unique.

Social institutions like the family have enormous impact on individuals' attitudes, feelings, and behaviors. The best way to illustrate this is to suggest alternatives to established norms and values. A science fiction writer, designing an imaginary society of the future, might invent any number of new ways for men and women to get together. In this fictional society, individuals might be assigned mates by lottery; women (or men) might be awarded as prizes for winning a sports contest. But anyone in our society who seriously proposed setting up marital sweepstakes or sexual Olympics would be branded a hopeless cynic, or worse. Romantic courtship has been institutionalized in our society.

Science fiction writers have invented societies that produce new generations without families (see *Walden II, Brave New World,* or *The Handmaid's Tale*). Babies would be conceived in test tubes, brought to birth in artificial wombs, and raised in state nurseries under "scientific" conditions. Most of this is now technically possible. But such a revolution in childbearing and rearing is highly unlikely. Scientifically produced children runs counter to our values. It would deprive adults of the social roles of mother and father and, later, grandparent; it would deprive children of the social identity of being Mary Smith's son and John Smith's brother. Mate selection by lottery and laboratory babies seem inhumane to us because the institution of the family shapes our internal hopes and desires as well as our external social world. Drastic changes are virtually unthinkable.

The institution of the family is closely connected with the other social institutions: education, religion, politics, and economics. Changes in one invariably produce changes in the others. For example, the decline in the birth rate over the past two decades reduced the number of school-aged children, which then caused teachers to be laid off, schools to be closed, and college programs in education to be cut back. The decline in the birth rate was stimulated by changes in the economy that encouraged more women to work outside their homes, which in turn led women to have fewer children (Cherlin 1990; Glick 1979). Politics has both direct and indirect effects on families.

Civil rights legislation may have created new job opportunities for women, indirectly contributing to the lower birth rate. Politicians who seek to please special interest groups, such as the pro-life movement, are attempting to pass laws that would limit or outlaw abortions. This might lead to more unwanted children being born and to more babies put up for adoption. Government cutbacks in food stamps, social security, and other social services have direct impact on millions of families.

The Family as an Intimate Environment

The modern family is a special type of small group. It is different from most small groups you will ever belong to. To begin with, the family is an *intimate environment* (Skolnick 1992). An important aspect of the family as an intimate environment is the deep sexual and personal attachment between husband and wife and the deep emotional attachment of all family members (Skolnick 1992). Social scientists focus on the interactions between individuals in this intimate environment.

The contemporary family is a unique small group because of a number of distinguishing characteristics.

Time Together. We are born into families as dependent infants. Our earliest days and months are spent almost exclusively with family members. As we grow older and venture out to day care centers, preschools, and finally formal education, we spend less and less time with our family. When we fall in love, one aspect of love is wanting to be with our love object as much as possible. In forming our new family, or what family sociologists call our **family of procreation,** we spend more time with our partner and our children and less time with our parents, our **family of orientation.** Over the entire life course, the ratio of time we spend with our families of orientation and procreation far exceeds the ratio of time we spend with others. This ratio does vary with stages of the life cycle (college students generally spend more time away from family members, preschoolers may spend all of their time with family members). However, in general, the family demands and gets more of our time and attention than any other group.

Range of Activities. Not only do we spend a great deal of time with our families, but the range of activities and interests we share with family members covers a much wider spectrum than contacts with friends, fellow workers, and other groups we may belong to. Eating, bathing, recreation, education, fighting, hugging, punishing, sex, sleeping, and more are all done with family members. Again, the range of activities will vary from person to person and according to

The "right to influence" in a family sometimes extends to a wife selecting what her husband will wear to work.

age and stage in the life course, but it is *expected* that families will participate in wide-ranging activities together and that people want to do this.

Intensity of Involvement. The investment in family contact, the degree of emotional commitment to the family typically exceeds that devoted to other groups. If a friend or co-worker is fat, has bad breath, or cannot spell, this may be a cause for concern among those who know the person or it may be a cause of ridicule and behind-the-back comments. However, if a family member is fat, has bad breath, or cannot spell, this would most likely cause deep concern among other family members, probably because they see these shortcomings as reflections on them. A spouse whose husband wears a tie that clashes with his jacket might think that people will think she is a bad wife for letting him out of the house in such a condition. Parents of a child doing poorly in school often invest great energy in the child because they see the child's shortcomings as their own.

Right to Influence. Membership in the modern family carries with it the implicit right to influence the values, attitudes, and behaviors of other members. We might try to influence a friend or fellow worker as to what politician to vote for or whether abortion is morally right or wrong. But we *expect* that children will listen to their parents, that husbands and wives will heed one another. Not only do we feel we have the ability to influence, but there is a moral rightness of influencing family members and demanding allegiance to the family that distinguishes families from other social groups.

Age and Sex Differences. Although this may seem obvious, the family is unique because it is one of the few social groups that includes both sexes and a wide span of ages of the members. Although some small groups may be mixed-sex (school, work, etc.), few such groups contain members from infancy to elderly. A feature of modern living is the segregation of age cohorts (e.g., housing for the elderly, day care for infants). The family is the last bastion of mixed-sex and mixed-aged groupings.

Assignment of Tasks. Families are also special because tasks and responsibilities are almost always assigned based on sex and age. Most social groups make these assignments based on experience, interest, or ability. But the typical family assigns work roles, child-care tasks, cooking, cleaning, and problem solving based on age and sex.

Involuntary Membership. Families are exclusive organizations. Birth relationships are involuntary and cannot be terminated. There may be ex-husbands and ex-wives, but there are no ex-children and ex-parents (Rossi 1968). Belonging to a family involves personal, social, legal, and material commitment and sometimes entrapment.

Extensive Knowledge of Social Biographies. The intimacy and emotional involvement of family relations reveals a full range of identities to members of families. Strengths, vulnerabilities, fears, weaknesses, loves, and hates are all known to family members.

FAMILY VALUES

From the 1960s through the 1980s and into the 1990s there has been considerable debate over what government could do to "shore up" the "fragile" family. In the late 1960s, liberals in the U.S. Congress advanced programs that they saw as supportive of the family—including the Comprehensive Child Development Bill that would have provided an expansive range of services and assistance to children and their families. The Presidential Commission on Population Growth (1972) proposed that making contraceptive information and services available to teenagers would help deal with the problems of unwanted pregnancy, teenage pregnancy, and population growth. Both the Comprehensive Child Development Bill and the Commission on Population Growth's proposals were seen by many as helping the family. Yet the Child Development Bill was vetoed by then President Richard Nixon, who stated that such a bill would "Sovietize" the American family. The Commission on Population Growth's recommendations were also rejected by President Nixon, who saw the dissemination of contraceptive services to teenagers as weakening the family.

Controversy over family values was not limited to the Nixon administration. Jimmy Carter called for a White House Conference on the Family during his presidential campaign of 1976. It was not until 1980 that the conference was held. By then, its name had been changed to the White House Conference on Families, and so much controversy over the conference had been generated that the original plan to hold the conference in Washington, D.C. was changed, and three conferences were held—one in Baltimore, one in Minneapolis, and another in Los Angeles. The controversy began when Patsy Fleming, a black divorcee and mother of three teenaged children, resigned as executive director of the conference, before her appointment could be confirmed. Mrs. Fleming had learned that the Secretary of Health, Education, and Welfare, apparently bowing before pressure from groups that resented that a divorcee would lead a conference on "the family," intended to appoint a white male, head of an intact family, as codirector of the conference.

The selection of delegates for the conference turned into a wholesale moral crusade over the rightful definition of a "family" and what families should be. Conservatives, organizing first and fast, captured early elections for state delegates to the conference. State governors were then lobbied by liberals to balance the delegations with their appointees.

The very first regional conference in Baltimore saw 30 self-styled "pro-family" delegates storm out of the conference when the meeting voted down anti-Equal Rights Amendment and antihomosexual rights motions. A liberal motion to define the family as "two or more persons who share resources, responsibility for decisions, values, and goals and have a commitment to one another over time" was also defeated. Each session of the conference was greeted by protestors and pickets for or against some proposal or position. The family conference had become a family feud.

The family values debate heated up further in the 1980s. With the election of Ronald Reagan in 1980 and the growing public pronouncements of the

One of the major flashpoints of the battle over family values is the ongoing debate over abortion.

moral majority, the family became one of the focal points of conservative legislation. The Family Protection Act was first introduced for consideration in the 97th Congress, and although parts of the bill were enacted, the entire Act was never voted into law. A multifaceted piece of legislation, the Act was intended to preserve and protect the institution of the American family. The Act contained numerous sections and covered a wide range of programs and steps that supporters saw as necessary for protecting the family. One such section provided for parents to be notified when an unmarried minor child receives contraceptive devices or abortion-related services—a number of states have enacted this provision. The definition of child abuse was to *exclude* corporal punishment. The use of federal funds for abortion was prohibited—this provision was enacted by Congress and approved by President Reagan. Parents were to be given a right to review textbooks that are to be used in schools. One section of the Act prevented the use of federal funds for promoting educational material that "denigrates the role of women as it has been historically understood."

The Family Protection Act was debated well into the 1980s, and although the entire bill was not enacted, it served as yet one more point of confrontation for people holding differing views on family and families.

The debate over the family and family values continued into the 1990s. Just prior to the election campaign of 1992, Vice President Dan Quayle was critical of the decision of television character "Murphy Brown" to have a baby and raise the child on her own. Quayle argued that children need to have a father present and that "Murphy Brown" was a poor role model for young girls. During the campaign, the Republicans argued film actor Woody Allen's relationship with Mia Farrow's adopted daughter was typical of the Democrats' approach to family values. The more substantive debates over the family in the early 1990s concerned legislation regarding parental leave and child care. Government officials also canceled a proposed national survey of sexual behaviors, designed to help prevent AIDS, because of the explicit wording of some of the questionnaire items. The survey was ultimately carried out, funded by private foundations.

Just the words "family" and "families" are social issues. Current discussions of families are almost always heated and political. There is debate and discussion about whether modern families are in trouble or what the trouble actually is.

One thing is for certain: When it comes to families as a social issue, there are few uninvolved or neutral parties. Politicians, special interest groups, social scientists, and the public are all ready and waiting to jump into any debate over families, ranging from the impact of abortion to the decline and fall of Western civilization.

From the preceding discussion, it is clear that at the top of the list of important family issues are two questions:

Issues and Concerns

Will the family (families) survive?

Do rising divorce rates, perceived changes in sexual mores and behavior, and increases in the number of working mothers signal the demise of what we know and recognize as the modern family?

From the general concern with the current status and future of families arise questions concerning which changes and policies will help or harm families:

Will increased equality for women undermine the structure and functions of families, or will equality at home, work, and in other institutions strengthen families?

Will liberalized attitudes and laws concerning homosexuals destroy the moral fabric of the family, or are these changes unrelated to families?

Will sex education programs and increased dissemination of contraceptive information and devices lead to wholesale promiscuity and collapse of families, or will it prevent AIDS or cut back on teenage pregnancy and unwanted children, thus strengthening families?

There are issues other than those that are moral and political in nature. Individuals embarking on marriage ask,

Who should I marry?

How can I have a "good" marriage?

Married couples consider whether or not they should have children, and if they want children, when should they have them? The birth of the first child raises several questions:

How should I raise my child?

What is best for my child?

Should we have another child? When?

Troubled couples ask,

Should we seek marriage therapy?

Is a divorce the best solution for my (our) troubles?

Family issues range from global-political-moral considerations about the future of the institution to private, intimate concerns, worries, and troubles over family matters. These issues and concerns are not far removed from one another. Private troubles are nearly always inextricably linked to larger social issues and structures (Mills 1959). Individual concerns do not arise in a social vacuum. As we will see throughout this book, answering questions about private troubles is often dependent on analyzing large social issues. Answers to both public and private questions are neither obvious nor straightforward nor readily available.

The family is perhaps the central and most important social institution in society. It is also the most intimate, intense, social group most of us belong to. The family is the source of our greatest joys, our deepest sorrows, and our most painful hurts (Skolnick 1991). The centrality and importance of the family and the intimacy of the family environment often blind us to the reality of family life and the family as a social institution.

SUMMING UP

There are five major barriers that obscure our ability to objectively examine families: our personal involvement in families, the private nature of families, the sanctity of families and family relations, the variation in family forms over time and across our society, and the changes that have occurred in families. The sociological perspective helps us break through these barriers and examine marriages and families more clearly and more objectively.

Given the variability and change that characterize families, developing a definition of "family" proves to be a much greater challenge than one would expect. Although the definition of "family" will vary depending on the purpose for which the definition is used—researchers use different definitions than do social workers or politicians—for the purpose of this text, we define "family" as a social group and a social institution that possesses an identifiable structure made up of positions (e.g., breadwinner, child rearer, decision maker, nurturer), and interactions among those who occupy the positions. The structure typically carries out specialized functions (e.g., child rearing), is characterized by biologically and socially defined kinship, and often involves sharing a residence.

Families, however, are more than a neat and simple definition. The family is a social institution and a social group. Families are a special kind of social group because they are intimate environments. There are a number of distinguishing characteristics of families as intimate environments, including the time members spend together, the range of activities, the intensity of involvement, the right of family members to influence one another, age and sex differences of the members, how tasks are assigned to members, the fact that membership (especially for children) is involuntary, and the extensive knowledge of social biographies.

We often sentimentalize families, conjuring up nostalgic images of the self-sufficient nuclear family or the golden age of the "Ozzie and Harriet" family of the 1950s. Debates over "family values" often create idealized images of what families were like, or should be like, as if there were one "best" form of family that would enrich and better all of society.

As an institution, the family is dynamic, fluid, and variable. The dynamic and variable nature of family form and family function applies both to our own society and across societies. As an intimate environment, the family is also dynamic and variable. Many people grew up in families that had a structure, norms, and values that are quite different from the structure, norms, and values today's families have. Given the variation and change, "families" is perhaps a much better term to use than the singular "family."

In the following chapters, this text will use various social science theoretical frameworks (to be discussed in the next chapter) and report on research findings based on studies of families in the United States and around the world in order to illuminate and expand our understanding of "families."

REFERENCES

Ball, Donald W. 1972. "The 'Family' as a Sociological Problem: Conceptualization of the Taken-for-Granted as Prologue to Social Problems Analysis." *Social Problems* 19(3):295-305.

Bane, Mary J. 1976. *Here to Stay: American Families in the Twentieth Century.* New York: Basic Books.

Beckett, Joyce O. and Audry D. Smith. 1981. "Work and Family Roles: Egalitarian Marriage in Black and White Families." *Social Service Review* 55(June): 314-26.

Berardo, Donna Hodgkins, Constance L. Sheehan, and Gerald R. Leslie. 1987. "A Residue of Tradition: Jobs, Careers, and Spouses' Time in Housework." *Journal of Marriage and the Family* 49(May): 381-90.

Berger, Peter L. 1963. *An Invitation to Sociology: A Humanistic Perspective.* New York: Doubleday.

Burgess, Ernest. 1926. "The Family as a Unity of Interacting Personalities." *The Family* 7:3-9.

Cherlin, Andrew. 1990. "Recent Changes in American Fertility, Marriage, and Divorce." *Annals of the American Academy of Political and Social Sciences* 510(July): 145-55.

Christensen, Harold T. 1964. *Handbook of Marriage and the Family.* Chicago: Rand McNally.

Coontz, Stephanie. 1992. *The Way We Never Were: American Families and the Nostalgia Trap.* New York: Basic Books.

Etzioni, Amitai. 1977. "The Family: Is It Obsolete?" *Journal of Current Social Issues* 14(Winter): 4-9.

Glick, Paul C. 1979. "Future American Families." *Coalition of Family Organizations Memo* 2(3).

Goffman, Erving. 1959. *The Presentation of Self in Everyday Life.* Garden City, NY: Anchor/Doubleday.

Goode, William J. 1963. *World Revolution and Family Patterns.* New York: Free Press.

Hochschild, Arlie and Anne Machung. 1989. *The Second Shift.* New York: Viking.

Kessing, Felix M. 1958. *Cultural Anthropology: The Science of Custom.* New York: Rinehart.

Kooreman, Peter and Arie Kapteyn. 1987. "A Disaggregated Analysis of the Allocation of Time Within the Household." *Journal of Political Economy* 95(21):223-49.

Lasch, Christopher. 1977. *Haven in a Heartless World: The Family Besieged.* New York: Basic Books.

Laslett, Barbara. 1973. "The Family as a Public and Private Institution: An Historical Perspective." *Journal of Marriage and the Family* 35(3):480-92.

Liebow, Elliot. 1967. *Tally's Corner.* Boston: Little, Brown.

Linton, Ralph. 1936. *The Study of Man.* New York: Appleton-Century-Crofts.

Mead, Margaret. 1928. *Coming of Age in Samoa.* New York: William Morrow.

Mederer, H. J. and L. Weinstein. 1992. "Choices and Constraints in a Two-Person Career." *Journal of Family Issues* 13(September):334-50.

Merton, Robert K. 1959. "Notes on Problem-Finding in Sociology" Pp. xv-xvi in *Sociology Today: Problems and Perspectives,* edited by Robert K. Merton, Leonard Brown, and Leonard S. Cottrell, Jr. New York: Basic Books.

Mills, C. Wright. 1959. *The Sociological Imagination.* New York: Oxford University Press.

Pleck, Joseph H. 1985. *Working Wives, Working Husbands.* Beverly Hills, CA: Sage.

Presidential Commission on Population Growth. 1972. *Report.* Washington, DC: Government Printing Office.

Reiss, Ira L. 1980. *Family Systems in America.* 3rd ed. New York: Holt, Rinehart & Winston.

Roper Organization. 1992. Survey conducted, February. Storrs, CT: Roper Center for Public Opinion Research.

Ross, Heather L. and Isabell V. Sawhill. 1975. *Time of Transition: The Growth of Families Headed by Women.* Washington, DC: Urban Institute.

Rossi, Alice. 1968. "Transition to to Parenthood." *Journal of Marriage and the Family* 30 (February):26-39.

Schneider, Daniel M. and Raymond T. Smith. 1973. *Class Differences and Sex Roles in American Kinship and Family Structure.* Englewood Cliffs, NJ: Prentice Hall.

Skolnick, Arlene S. 1991. *Embattled Paradise.* New York: Harper Collins.

———. 1992. *The Intimate Environment: Exploring Marriage and the Family.* 5th ed. New York: Harper Collins.

Smith, Tom W. 1992. "Attitudes Toward Sexual Permissiveness: Trends Correlations, and Behavioral Connections." Paper presented at the MacArthur Foundation Research Network on Successful Midlife Development Conference, New York.

Stack, Carol B. 1974. *All Our Kin.* New York: Harper &Row.

Tavris, Carol and Carole Offir. 1977. *The Longest War: Sex Dif-*

ferences in Perspective. New York: Harcourt Brace Jovanovich.

Turner, Ralph. 1970. *Family Interaction.* New York: John Wiley.

U.S. Bureau of the Census. 1989. *Changes in American Family Life.* Current Population Reports: Special Studies, Series P-20, No. 450. Washington, DC: Government Printing Office.

———. 1991. *Marital Status and Living Arrangements: March 1990. Current Population Reports: Population Characteristics,* Series P-23, No. 163. Washington, DC: Government Printing Office.

———. 1992. *Statistical Abstracts of the United States.* Washington, DC: Government Printing Office.

Weber, Max. [1922] 1968. *Economy and Society.* Translated by Ephraim Fischoff et al. New York: Bedminster Press.

Wolfe, Margery. 1972. *Women and the Family in Rural Taiwan.* Stanford, CA: Stanford University Press.

CHAPTER **2**

▉▉ Family Studies: Theoretical and Methodological Approaches

Drive down the typical suburban street in America. If it is a weekday morning in the fall or spring, you may find the street more or less deserted. Children are at school, a few blocks or sometimes miles from home. Husbands have left for work, either driving, car pooling, or, in the rarest of cases, walking. More than half of the wives have also left for work. Infants or preschool children have been deposited at a day care center, left with a friend, relative, or baby-sitter, or perhaps someone has come into the home to watch the children. Preschoolers who are at home are watching television, playing inside, or behind the house in a fenced-in yard. Infants either toddle around the house; clutch at the top of their playpens, looking for all the world like they want to get out; or are mercifully tucked in for a morning nap. Those men and women who do not work are probably pouring a second cup of coffee. The remnants of family life lie around the inside of the home. Outside, a tricycle is overturned in the driveway. Balls, bats, and doll carriages are littered across the front lawn. By afternoon, the children are home. Ball games begin, dirt bikes tear down driveways, the television is clicked on—either to the favorite electronic baby-sitter, *Sesame Street,* or, perhaps without the parents' permission, to the afternoon movie, reruns of *Happy Days,* whatever is showing on cable, or a movie on the VCR. Nightfall brings home one or both workers. Dinner begins, followed by homework, and by 9 p.m., one can usually detect the bluish glow of the television lighting the homes lining the streets.

These homes, these scenes, are the settings for marriage and family life. The scene and setting may vary—instead of tree-lined streets, the scene may be the stoops and windows of city tenements. The space between houses may be close, as in the middle- or working-class development, or acres, as in the upper-class compounds. But the streets, houses, and apartments and what goes on in the homes are the prime concern of the family social scientist.

Sociologist Lillian Rubin drove those streets, dressed as she thought a college professor should dress and carrying her pens, pencils, and tape recorder. She visited 75 homes and conducted hundreds of hours of interviews to learn about marriage and family life in working-class homes (Rubin 1976).

What Rubin found in those homes surprised her. Although she herself was the product of a working-class home—her mother had been a sewing machine operator in a factory—the lives of the working-class families were in many ways foreign to her current experiences. Money problems, scrambling to pay bills, and intermittent unemployment and work, frequently barren of joy or fulfillment, were the substance of many interviews. Alcoholism, violence, and brief glimpses of happiness were also discussed. Women, 25 or 30 years old, recalled their times as young girls whose parents fought—physically and verbally. As girls, they spent time dreaming of a better life, fostered by photographs of beautiful homes in glossy magazines and television programs where all the problems were solved inside of 30 or 60 minutes. Escape from the poverty, alcohol, and violence was through marriage, they thought. And then came reality. Young girls, children themselves, became pregnant, married, and began to live the same cycle they had grown up in. Old before their time at age 27 or 28, they looked back and recalled life when they were young.

From these interviews, Lillian Rubin began to develop a portrait of life in working-class homes, homes that she labeled as either "hard living" or "settled in." Her task of making sense out of thousands of hours of interviews and thousands of pages of interview transcriptions was quite difficult. To make sense out of the nearly infinite variety of families, family experiences, and family behaviors, she employed the approach used by social scientists in their study of family life using frames of reference called **conceptual frameworks.** Conceptual frameworks are defined as clusters of interrelated but not as yet interdefined concepts for viewing the phenomenon of marriage and family behavior and classifying its parts (Hill 1966, p. 11). Frameworks operate like a "cognitive lens" or a pair of prescription glasses. They allow social scientists to focus in on certain issues and ideas while leaving other ideas or issues to be studied at another time.

In family social science, there are a number of different conceptual frameworks or competing schools of thought about marriage and family behavior. The first part of this chapter examines the major conceptual frameworks that are used to study marriage and family. The section begins by examining an important nonscientific perspective—common sense. This is followed by reviewing the five historically dominant conceptual frameworks that are used by family social scientists. The second part of the chapter considers the research methods that are used to gather information and data about marriage and family life. The method used by Lillian Rubin, in-depth interviewing, is one of a number of possible strategies that a social scientist could use in seeking to understand families and to answer questions about family life. The chapter concludes with a discussion of the science of family studies.

COMMON SENSE

Much of what we know about marriage and family is based on our own experiences (see Chapter 1) and common sense. Commonsense conceptions of the world are a mixture of our personal observations (using our senses), opinions, beliefs, attitudes, hearsay, media reports, folklore, logic, and intuition. Our common sense is influenced by numerous social forces that surround us—our sex, age, race, education, occupation, friends, what television programs we watch, what newspapers and magazines we read. Lillian Rubin found that magazine stories and pictures that idealized family life played a major role in the view of marriage and family developed and nurtured by working-class girls. Surprisingly, their own experiences, their own sensory input of what marriage and family life was all about, played a somewhat diminished role in their commonsense view of what their own lives would be like when they were married. Marriage, however, brought a new view, as explained by one woman:

> The dream I had about getting married, in my own house and having a storybook life didn't exactly work out. . . . The first thing was my own little family, in my own house, and everything pretty and shiny and new, like in magazine pictures. Life sure doesn't match the dreams, does it? Here I am living in this old, dumpy house and the furniture is a grubby mess. I still have those pictures of the storybook life in my head, but I have a lot more sense now than when I was young. (Rubin 1976, p. 72)

The common sense of the magazine pictures gave way to the common sense of experience. Both, however, can be wrong.

The topic of divorce abounds with commonsense wisdom. For example, consider the following statements:

- The divorce rate in the United States has been rising continuously and is now the highest in history.
- The current divorce rate in the United States is higher than the divorce rate in every other country in the world.
- Most divorces occur during the seventh year of a marriage and that is why people call this the "Seven Year Itch."
- Children hold marriages together.

Surprisingly, these statements are not accurate. The divorce rate in the United States peaked in the late 1970s and has actually fallen since then. Even at the peak, U.S. divorce rates never challenged the rate of divorce in Japan in 1880—300 divorces per 1,000 existing marriages. Most divorces take place in the first year or two of marriage. As for children holding the marriage together, more than half of those who get divorced have children.

I could continue with an even longer list of commonsense understandings about marriage and family life that are believed by many and supported by little or no factual information. In fact, presenting long lists of commonsense beliefs and then exploding them as myths is a tradition among sociologists, who are, as Peter Berger (1963) notes, driven time and time again to debunk the social system they are studying.

Substituting a theoretical framework and data derived from research is frequently considered superior to relying on commonsense beliefs or understandings. But—be cautious. For one thing, much commonsense thinking is actually correct (see Box 2-1). Social science frequently ends up matching and supporting common sense (Pease 1981). Even when common sense is wrong, it still may contain a grain of truth.

Using a theoretical framework and research data does not always guarantee finding the "truth." In fact, social scientists frequently disagree with one another's theories, research strategies, and research findings. It is not surprising to find that two different social scientists, looking at the same data on families, will come up with two completely different conclusions. One of the main reasons why the conclusions differ is that different conceptual frameworks are being used.

PERSPECTIVES ON FAMILIES

One of Lillian Rubin's subjects, a 34-year-old truck driver, looked back over his childhood and described his father and mother:

> My father was an alcoholic, so I don't know. My mother probably should have gotten a divorce, but I think she stayed married because of the kids, and probably because she didn't have any job skills and everything like that. I remember my mother going down to the bar after he got paid when I was twelve, thirteen, fourteen and pleading for money to go pay the bills. But once she got down there to the bar, she'd go in and sit with him and drink beer, too. But I don't want you to get the idea she was an alcoholic, because she wasn't. She'd just sit there and drink beer with him, that's all.
>
> When I was a lot younger—a real little kid—I remember sitting in the car outside the bar for a long time waiting for them to come out. Sometimes I remember we would go in and ask them when they were coming home, and they'd give us a nickel or a dime to get rid of us. Then we'd go back and sit in the car. It got cold out there, and we'd be so hungry.
>
> We didn't know any better; it was okay. I suppose the worst part was having to sit down there when you're a little kid and you're cold and hungry, and your mother and father are still sitting in the bar. That's the worst part. Sometimes, though, they'd let us come in and we'd sit in a corner and drink Coke, and we'd

try to be quiet so nobody would see us or notice us. Those times were better. At least we could be close to them and see what was going on. (Rubin 1976, p. 28)

There are numerous observations and questions that arise out of this one brief part of the interview. Why didn't his mother get a divorce? Certainly, life with an alcoholic who spent money on beer and had little left to pay the bills could not have been that pleasant. Why do women stay married to men like that? What about the children? What was the impact of this kind of a family life on them? Another line of thought might notice that the mother and not the father pays the bills in the family. Is this common in all families? Is it unique to working-class families? Was it unique to just this household? Who decides what responsibilities family members have?

Just as there are different ways to view this quote and the situation the man found himself in as a child, there are also different ways to look at families. The formalized different approaches to looking at families, assumptions about families, and questions asked about families are the conceptual frameworks used by social scientists who study families and family life.

BOX 2-1: WHAT THE RESEARCH SHOWS

When Common Sense Is Correct

In the effort to distinguish the scientific approach to social behavior from common sense, textbook authors frequently provide students with a list of commonsense assumptions about social behavior and then use the results of social research to show how common sense can be wrong (just as I have done in this text).

Actually, attacking common sense is somewhat easy, but it can be quite misleading. It is easy because students tend to sit up and take notice when a long-cherished belief is challenged and proven wrong. Now, many students may reject the attack and continue to believe that their initial commonsense beliefs were correct. Others may take great joy in being able to debunk their friends' and relatives' common sense by repeating the findings learned in class or read in their textbook.

What makes debunking common sense misleading is that in many instances, common sense is correct and accurate. Surprisingly, when

sociologists support common sense, they come in for the greatest criticism.

Sociologists Phillip Blumstein and Pepper Schwartz published the results of one of the largest and most ambitious studies of American families to date in their 1983 book *American Couples.* Blumstein and Schwartz collected 12,000 questionnaires and conducted 600 interviews to learn about American couples. They studied married couples, gay and lesbian couples, and couples who cohabitated. They examined the role of money, power, and sex in the relationships. Among some of their conclusions were the following:

• Money establishes the balance of power in relationships, except among lesbians.
• Men who did the least housework were the most satisfied with their relationship.
• Married couples who have more extramarital affairs are more deceptive than any other kinds of couples.

CONCEPTUAL FRAMEWORKS

A number of conceptual frameworks have been brought to bear on marriage and families over the years. In 1960, Reuben Hill and Donald Hansen identified five main frameworks: structural functional, developmental, interactional, situational, and institutional. Other frameworks have been developed and applied to family studies since 1966, including the family process framework (Broderick 1990) and a feminist framework (Ferree 1990; Kaufman 1990).

As new research and theory building are carried out, certain perspectives wax and wane in popularity and applicability to students of family relations (Thomas and Wilcox 1987). Choosing which conceptual framework to examine in detail is a difficult task, one which, by necessity, will leave out someone's favorite approach and emphasize another perspective that the same person might consider less worthy.

These and other findings are certainly neither surprising nor shocking. In large part, they confirm our commonsense understandings about relationships.

For the "sin" of uncovering what everyone thought they already knew about relationships, Blumstein and Schwartz were taken to task by reviewers of their book. Writing in the November 1983 issue of *Ms.* magazine, Christine Doudna said that Blumstein and Schwartz went on a giant fishing expedition but served up fish stew. Such are the perils of social scientists confirming common sense.

One of the commonsense findings reported by Blumstein and Schwartz in their study of American couples was that men who did the least housework were the most satisfied with their relationships.

In choosing which frameworks to present, I was guided by Carlfred Broderick's (1970) analysis of Hill and Hansen's five conceptual frameworks. Reviewing the development of family theory that took place in the 1960s, Broderick concluded that only three frameworks had emerged as viable: structural functional, symbolic interactional, and developmental. In the 1970s, two additional frameworks took hold and emerged as legitimate and popular perspectives: conflict theory and social exchange theory (sometimes referred to as choice theory; see Nye 1979). These then are the five theoretical perspectives that are reviewed here.

Structural Functionalism

Firmly rooted in psychology, sociology, and anthropology (Malinowski 1939; Parsons 1951; Radcliffe-Brown 1952), the structural functional framework emphasizes the interrelationships between parts of a social system and the whole. As a general sociological perspective, the structural functional outlook uses an organic analogy to examine how society operates and how social order is possible. An organism, like the human body, has a **structure** made up of specialized parts (the brain, the heart, the circulatory system, the central nervous system, etc.). Each part has a specific task or **function** that contributes to the overall functioning and well-being of the body. When one part is injured or slows down, other parts may have to adjust to restore equilibrium to the system and maintain the overall balance and functioning of the system.

Just as the heart has a function to play in maintaining the body, parts of society have functions that maintain the social system and make social order possible.

From a **macrosocial perspective,** the family is viewed as a part of the social system, and the structure of the family is viewed as existing to maintain the social system. Bearing and raising children is considered one of the central functions of the family in society.

But the family can also be examined at a **microsocial level** as a small society, and the parts of a family can be studied in terms of how they relate to the ongoing operation of a family. These parts can be the **positions** people occupy in families (e.g., father, mother, son, daughter) and the **roles** they enact.

Central Assumptions

There are a number of key assumptions made by those who employ the structural functional framework:

1. They propose that *all social systems function*. Functioning means to operate and to be task or goal oriented (Levy 1952).

2. *Structures influence functions*. When examining social systems, **social structure** is defined as the orderly and patterned ways in which people or groups interact with one another. From a societal point of view, this may mean the way social institutions interact. At a more individual level, social structure emerges out of the pattern of interactions that develop among individuals, as in a group. This assumption means that the social order (function) of a society is dependent on the structure of the institutions. Looking at a particular family, how that family functions may be dependent on the structure—large families may function differently than small families.

3. *Functions require particular structures*. In brief, this means that if a function is to be performed, then a certain structure must exist. For some time, sociologists believed that the absence of men in black families meant that black male children could not be properly socialized into the male role (see Chapter 5). This proposition assumes that because the structure of the mother-led family is different, it must have some consequence for the functions performed in households with that structure.

4. There are *functional prerequisites* that are required for society to exist. There are problems that must be solved or activities that must be performed for the survival of the social order on a given level. Functional prerequisites are thought to be *universal;* that is, every society requires structures to meet the minimal level of functioning to survive. For example, at a macrosocial level, societies need to ensure the replacement of their members. The following universal structures are thought to be the main social institutions that exist in societies: family, education, economics, political-legal, and religion. The fourth assumption is that the family is a universal institution and that there is a minimum definition of what a family is from the standpoint of the functions the family must perform.

5. The fifth assumption is that *all systems, social and organic, seek to maintain their equilibrium or balance*. Thus any disturbance to the system triggers functions to bring the system back into balance.

Key Concepts

For those who apply the structural functional framework to the study of society and the family, there are a number of key concepts:

■ *Society*. A society is a large, independent collection of people who interact within socially structured relationships. Societies survive their original members, replacing them through biological reproduction, and are typically self-sufficient (Winch 1966). Societies also tend to have a common culture.

■ *Culture*. A culture is a society's entire way of life, including all the material and nonmaterial products that are passed from generation to generation. The major elements of nonmaterial culture are *norms,* rules about what people should or should not do, say, or think in specific situations; *values,* broad, abstract, shared standards of what is considered right, desirable, and worthy of respect; and *sanctions,* a system of rewards and punishments by which people are encouraged to adhere to norms.

■ *Institutions.* Within societies are institutions. Institutions are relatively stable sets of social relationships, norms and values, groups, and organizations that provide structure for behavior in particular areas of social life. Most sociologists recognize five major social institutions: the family, education, religion, politics, and economics. Other stable sets of social relationships, such as the military, health care systems, and legal systems, are also considered social institutions.

■ *Groups.* A social group is a set of individuals whose relationship is characterized by a continuing pattern of interaction, a structure of positions and roles, and a feeling of interconnectedness (i.e., agreement that they belong to a group).

■ *Position and Role.* A position is a location or place occupied by an individual or category of people within a system of social relationships. A role is the behavior expected of a person occupying a particular position.

This list of concepts begins with the highest level of abstraction, "society," and works down to the individual actions of people in a society. If society is the sum of the parts, as is believed by structural functionalists, then all the concepts that follow after "society" are the key parts of structures that, analogous to the parts of the human body, make up the entire social system.

Questions Asked by Structural Functionalists

With these key assumptions and defined concepts, structural functionalists have a particular view of the family both as a social institution and as a social group.

Among the first questions a structural functionalist asks are

Why does the institution of family exist?

Why are there families in virtually every known society?

To answer these questions, the structural functionalist searches for functions that families perform in societies. Considerable work has been done trying to isolate the universalistic functions of the family (see, e.g., Murdock 1949; Reiss 1965; also see Chapter 3). A second set of key questions asks:

What structures have to exist for a family to exist?

Do families require two parents?

Is it necessary for the partners to have a division of labor where one performs some functions (hunting, working, paying the bills) while the other performs other functions (cooking, cleaning, raising the children)?

Sociologists have examined the pattern of the two-parent family (Zelditch 1955) and have looked at the division of labor between husband and wife. Sociologists Talcott Parsons and Robert Bales (1955) made the distinction between instrumental or task-oriented roles in families and expressive roles. They proposed that in the typical family the husband/father performs the instrumental roles while the wife/mother is the expressive leader of the family.

Critiques of the Structural Functional Framework

As previously noted, the structural functional approach has a long tradition in sociology and family studies. It offers a perspective for studying the broader issues concerning the interface of family and society but is also applicable to microlevel issues, such as the impact of birth order on IQ, self-concept, and behavior. But such a long tradition also means that this perspective has been subject to considerable criticism. The main criticism of the framework arises from the proposition that all systems, social and organic, seek to maintain their equilibrium. This vision of society and family life is considered too static and unable to deal with issues of social change. If a body loses a major organ—say, the heart—it ceases to function and dies. But society and families seem to be much more flexible and adaptable. If a father dies or abandons his family, the family persists. The history of the relationship between the family and society is one that demonstrates that the family has changed and developed without dying or without killing society.

Another important criticism of the structural functional perspective is that it tends to ignore the conflict that exists in families. Conflict, viewed by a structural functionalist, would be something dysfunctional to families. But, as we see in the next framework, many scholars see conflict as a core part of family relations.

Yet another criticism of the structural functional perspective focuses on Parson's and Bales's notions of instrumental and expressive functions. This notion of the division of labor in families is now seen as outdated and out of touch with current notions about male and female roles. Specifically, critics reject the idea that females are oriented toward expressive roles and males toward instrumental roles and that such a division of labor is necessary for a family to function.

The Conflict
Framework

Lillian Rubin's examination of working-class families is anything but a portrait of a harmonious, balance-seeking social group. Conflict is a daily part of the marriage and family life of the couples Rubin interviewed. One view of the early years of a marriage is provided by a 31-year-old painter:

> I didn't know how to handle her when we were first married. I couldn't understand what she was screaming about all the time. I guess I used to think she was too possessive and too jealous, like she wanted to own me. (Rubin 1976, p. 79)

The picture does not change much as marriage moves along after the first few years. Thus, rather than seeing families as loving harmonious units, families can be viewed as "a confrontation between individuals with conflicting interests in their common situation" (Sprey 1969, p. 702).

Conflict theory developed from the thinking and writings of Karl Marx. Marx was not specifically interested in family relations; rather, he was concerned with the broad historical dimensions of social relations. He and colleague Friedrich Engels laid out a series of propositions concerning economic organization (Marx and Engels [1849] 1967). First, the history of all existing societies is the history of class struggle. Second, human societies function under conditions of perpetual scarcity. No society has ever succeeded in meeting the material needs of all its members. Thus a fundamental aspect of societies is confrontation over scarce resources. Finally, when a group succeeds in gaining control over resources and thereby obtains both social and political power, it tends to use its power in an exploitive way, taking advantage of those with less power (Sprey 1979, p. 132).

Central Assumptions

Marx and Engels's view of the social order (or conflict in society) can be applied to family relations. There are four central assumptions of the framework:

1. The family, like all other social institutions, can be viewed as a *system directed toward the regulation of conflict* (Dahrendorf 1965, p. 165).

2. There is an *underlying competitive structure that is part of all marriage and family systems* (Sprey 1979, p. 145).

3. *Family relations are characterized by a struggle to control the scarce social, psychological, and economic resources of the family system.* Typically, men tend to control the economic resources, as was clearly pointed out by one of Lillian Rubin's respondents:

I had to work from the time I was thirteen and turn over most of my pay to my mother to help pay the bills. By the time I was nineteen, I had been working all those years and I didn't have anything—*not a thing.* I used to think a lot about how when I got married, I would finally get to keep my money for myself. I guess that sounds a little crazy when I think about it now because I have to support the wife and kids. I don't know *what* I was thinking about, but I never thought about that then. But even so, my wife doesn't get it all, you can bet on that. (Rubin 1976, pp. 56-57)

4. A final assumption is that *conflict is not necessarily bad or harmful to family relations.* In fact, conflict theorists see conflict and continuous confrontations as a necessary condition for growth and social change (Sprey 1979, p. 132).

Key Concepts

Conflict theorists have developed a specific vocabulary to capture the essence of their approach to the family system:

■ *Competition.* The essential part of the definition of competition as applied by conflict theorists is that in competition one person or party wins and another loses. Gains for one always produce losses for the other. This has been referred to as a *zero sum* process. Practically applied, if a family has one color television and one person wants to watch a football game while the other wants to watch *Murphy Brown,* then whatever show is chosen, one person wins and the other person loses. The same goes for using the bathroom, choosing a vacation, and raising children.

■ *Conflict.* Conflict behavior in families can range from the use of violence to litigation (Sprey 1979, p. 134). In families, just as in other institutions, conflict can arise over a wide range of issues.

■ *Consensus.* Conflict theorists also employ the term consensus. Rather than being antithetical to a conflict approach, the notion of consensus helps to deal with the question of how social order is possible—even with conflict being a fundamental part of human existence (Sprey 1979, p. 135). Consensus can mean common awareness of knowledge of a given issue, unanimous agreement, and seeing things the same way.

Conflict theorists also employ the concepts of *negotiation* and *bargaining, power* and *influence,* and *force* and *aggression* when examining family relations.

Questions Asked By Conflict Theorists

Conflict theorists ask essentially the same key question as is asked by structural functionalists: "How is orderly cooperation between families possible?"

(Sprey 1969, p. 703). Of course, the main difference between the theories is how the frameworks are used to answer the question. With this question as a starting point, conflict theorists concern themselves with the types of conflicts in families, the consequences of the conflicts, and how the conflicts are managed. The issue of family violence, child abuse, and wife abuse was illuminated by applying a conflict perspective to families. Without a conflict orientation, violence appeared to be the exception to the rule in family life. With a conflict perspective, sociologists found that violence was much more widespread in families than anyone imagined (see Chapter 15). The conflict perspective also allowed the focus on violence to change from one of individual pathology to one of power and the use and abuse of power in intimate relationships.

Critiques of the Conflict Framework

The main criticism of conflict theory is that it tends to overemphasize conflict and coercion in families and underplay the order, stability, and agreement in families. The assumption that differences always lead to conflicts is also considered a weakness of the theory. Conflict theory seems to be an overly negative and pessimistic view of human behavior in general and family life in particular. Finally, because the family is a private institution, much of the conflict that is presumed by conflict theorists to exist in families is often out of sight and difficult for researchers to study.

Symbolic Interaction

The **symbolic interaction framework** is widely used by family theorists (Klein, Schvanevelt, and Miller 1977) and is the only perspective to be considered a major framework in each of the past four decades (Broderick 1970; Holman and Burr 1980; Thomas and Wilcox 1987). The symbolic interaction view of human behavior grew and prospered as a reaction against psychological theories that proposed that human behavior was guided by instinct or deterministic reactions to various stimuli. Symbolic interactionists are concerned with everyday behavior and interpersonal relationships. Symbolic interactionism begins with the assumption that much of human behavior is guided not by instinct or stimuli but by the meanings that people ascribe to social situations. For example, throughout her analysis of working-class families, Lillian Rubin found that the process by which people shaped their own self-concepts played a crucial role in structuring their lives and marriages. As a 33-year-old truck driver (not the same man discussed earlier or later in this chapter) noted,

In the kind of life I lived, you didn't think about tomorrow. I didn't know where I'd be tomorrow, so how could I plan for it? In fact, I don't think I knew how to make plans. I wasn't even so sure about today. Tomorrow just didn't exist; it didn't have any reality. (Rubin 1976, p. 39).

What looks to be a thoughtless process of not planning for tomorrow is actually quite a rational approach based on the meaning that the words "plans" and "tomorrow" had for these families. It is the process by which these meanings arise and are derived that is the main concern of symbolic interactionists.

Central Assumptions

Symbolic interaction is a social psychological perspective. Those who employ this orientation concern themselves with the *process* of social interaction. The key to understanding this process involves three assumptions about human behavior:

1. Humans act toward things on the basis of the "meanings" that the things have for them.
2. Meanings arise and are derived from social interaction.
3. Meanings are handled and modified in an interaction process used by persons in dealing with things they encounter.

The tool that people use to develop and modify "meanings" is symbolic language. For a symbolic interactionist, nothing is self-evident. Everything needs to be identified and labeled for it to have meaning.

From these basic assumptions arise additional assumptions. Human beings are viewed as being born "tabula rasa," or with a clean slate. At birth, infants are seen as having tremendous potential, and their lives and basic nature will be shaped by what they encounter and their reactions to what they encounter—rather than by instincts or biological inheritance.

Because of the importance of language and interaction to symbolic interactionists, these researchers tend to focus on marriage and family only among humans. Apes, rats, dogs, and other animal family systems hold no clues to human behavior because these species either are not able to use symbols or use symbols at a level that is not nearly as advanced as humans' (although symbol use has been found among some chimpanzees, and some researchers also believe that dolphins can use symbols).

Key Concepts

A core concept for symbolic interaction is "self."

- *Self.* The "self," the individual's sense of identity and awareness of being a separate person, is dependent on social interaction. Sociologist Charles Cooley (1902) observed that individuals tend to develop self-images based on how they think others see them. In other words, we use society as a mirror to find out about who and what we are.

- *Role Taking.* The actual process by which we develop a sense of self is *role taking,* which has three basic stages: play, role, and organized game. First is the *play* stage. Young children begin to develop self-concepts by playing at being Mommy, Daddy, Superman, doctors, firemen, or the Ninja Turtles. This apparent child's play is the first step of the process by which we develop the capacity of having different perspectives on human behavior. The second stage, according to one of the founding fathers of the symbolic interactionist perspective, George Herbert Mead (1934), is actual *role* taking. This involves "taking the role of another," or putting oneself into another person's shoes. This is a crucial process because it allows us to see ourselves as other people see us. The final stage, again according to Mead, is the *organized game.* This involves engaging in reciprocal relationships with others. At this stage, a child moves from the specifics of role taking ("Mommy wants me to eat with a knife and fork") to a more general perspective ("People are supposed to eat food with utensils").

- *Generalized Other.* A generalized other is an image of the structure and norms and values of a society as a whole. As a part of the self, the generalized other guides behavior in socially acceptable directions.

Symbolic interactionists also use concepts employed by structural functionalists—position and role being of major importance to both frameworks. However, rather than looking at how positions and roles fit into a larger structure, the symbolic interactionist is concerned with the actual behavior of a small group of people. Whereas **socialization,** defined as the lifelong process of social interaction that shapes and reshapes us as social beings, is of concern to structural functionalists because it is the central function that makes society possible, its major interest for symbolic interactionists is with the actual social acts of socialization—the actions of the agents (e.g., parents) and the actions and reactions of the recipients (children).

Questions Asked by Symbolic Interactionists

If a symbolic interactionist were to examine the families interviewed by Lillian Rubin, he or she might ask

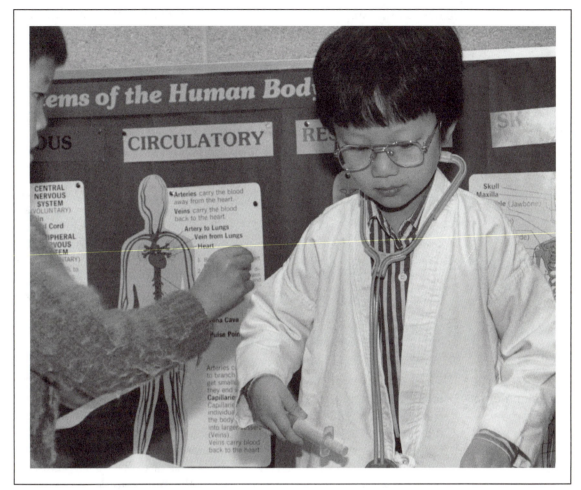

One of the key concepts in the symbolic interactionist perspective is the role taking—such as when a child plays at a role; for example, being a doctor.

How do husbands and wives define what it means to have a good marriage?

What is a "good" husband, a "good" wife?

How do the socialization experiences of these people affect their definitions of good marriage, good husband, and so forth?

What impact do their friends and neighbors have on their view of marriage?

A symbolic interactionist who was interested in premarital sexual behavior would ask questions about the impact of people's friends or the impact of an individual's **reference group**. A reference group describes groups or social categories that individuals use as a guide in developing their values, attitudes, behavior, and self-image. It can be a group that people belong to or do not belong to. Always of concern for symbolic interactionists are the meanings that events and things have for individual family members and how these individual meanings are shaped through a process of interaction.

Critiques of Symbolic Interaction

Because the symbolic interaction framework is so focused on social acts and behavior of individuals, it has been criticized as being poorly related to broader social processes. The lack of a historical context and the weak links made between social interaction and social institutions cause some to think that symbolic interactionists fail to see the forest because of their concern for the trees. But the widespread applicability of this framework and the fact that it has endured in family studies for so many years seem to indicate that these are but minor and perhaps inappropriate criticisms.

The Developmental Framework

When Lillian Rubin had completed her interviews and was organizing her findings for presentation in a book, she chose a traditional presentation strategy—she examined working-class marriage by looking at various stages of family life. The analysis began by looking at the childhood experiences of the individuals she interviewed. Then she proceeded to courtship and the reasons why they married. The next chapter dealt with the early years of the marriage, and the following chapter covered the middle years.

Rubin's stages were a convenient organizational strategy. Those who employ the **developmental framework** to study marriage and family relations go well beyond simply organizing families into a developmental stage or category. Those who use the developmental framework have systematically tried to assess the family life cycle by examining the growth and development of families.

One task for those using the developmental framework is to categorize the family life cycle into discrete stages. Evelyn Duvall's (1967) 8-stage framework and Roy Rodgers's (1962) 10-stage framework have been the most widely used categorizations in the field (see Table 2-1). Rubin used only four stages: childhood, beginning marriage, the early years, and the middle years. Of course, this was in great part due to the fact that she interviewed couples in the middle years of their marriages, and she was not primarily concerned with a precise categorization of family stages. Others have divided the family

Rubin's (1976) 4 stages of the family life cycle[a]	**Table 2-1**
1. Childhood	Three Views
2. Beginning marriage	of the Stages
3. The early years	of Family Life
4. The middle years	

Rubin's (1976) 4 stages of the family life cycle[a]
1. Childhood
2. Beginning marriage
3. The early years
4. The middle years

Duvall's (1967) 8 stages of the family life cycle[b]
1. Couples without children
2. Oldest child younger than age 30 months
3. Oldest child from age 30 months to 6 years
4. Oldest child from age 6 to 13 years
5. Oldest child from age 13 to 20 years
6. When first child leaves until last child is gone
7. Empty nest until retirement
8. Retirement until death of one or both spouses

Rodgers' (1962) 10 stages of family development[c]
1. Childless couple
2. All children younger than age 36 months
3. Preschool children, with (a) oldest aged 3-6 years and youngest under 3 years of age or (b) all children aged 3-6 years
4. School-aged family, with (a) infants, (b) preschoolers, (c) school-agers, or (d) all children aged 6-13 years
5. Teenaged family, with (a) infants, (b) preschoolers, (c) school-agers, (d) teenagers, or (e) all children aged 13-20 years
6. Young adult family, with (a) infants, (b) preschoolers, (c) school-agers, (d) teenagers, or (e) all children over age 20 years
7. Launching family, with (a) infants, (b) preschoolers, (c) school-agers, (d) teenagers, or (e) youngest child over age 20 years
8. When all children have been launched until retirement
9. Retirement until death of one spouse
10. Death of first spouse until death of survivor

SOURCES: [a]From Rubin, L. B. 1976. *Worlds of Pain: Life in the Working Class Family,* New York: Basic Books.
            [b]From Family Development, Third Edition by Evelyn Millis Duvall. Copyright © 1957, 1962, 1967, 1971 by HarperCollins Publishers, Inc. Copyright Renewed. Reprinted by permission of HarperCollins Publishers, Inc.
            [c]Reprinted by permission of Roy Rogers.

life cycle up into as few as 4 (Kirkpatrick, Cowles, and Tough 1934; Sorokin, Zimmerman, and Galpin 1931) to as many as 24 (Rodgers 1962) stages or categories.

Central Assumptions

The main assumption made by developmentalists is that family relations can be looked at in terms of definable *stages* or at least in terms of a process of development. Earliest applications of the developmental perspective used each particular stage of a marriage to explain other behaviors—for example, level of marital satisfaction was found to be related to the stage of a marriage (Hill and Rodgers 1964). A second assumption is that success in family relations is dependent on complex interactions within the family as its members deal with **developmental tasks** (Duvall 1967). Developmental tasks are those that arise at particular points in an individual's life. Successful achievement of these tasks leads to happiness and success in later tasks. Failure leads to unhappiness, later failure, and disapproval by society (Havinghurst 1953). Popular writer Gail Sheehy (1976) applied the notion of developmental tasks when she analyzed the process of adult development in her best-selling book *Passages*.

Key Concepts

- *Family Life Cycle.* The major concept used by developmentalists is family life cycle—the notion that families go through life cycle stages.

- *Developmental Tasks.* A developmental task is one that arises at or about a certain period in the life of an individual or family. A developmental task can originate as a result of physical maturation—for instance, puberty—or is the result of cultural pressures and privileges. Developmental tasks are those tasks that must be successfully accomplished in order to move from one developmental stage to the next.

- *Family Careers.* The concept of family career was developed by sociologist Joan Aldous (1978). A family career consists of the timing, sequence, and occurrence of family structural changes over time.

- *Stage.* A stage is defined as a division within the lifetime of a family that is distinctive enough from those that precede or follow it to constitute a separate period (Aldous 1978).

- *Transitions.* Developmentalists are concerned with the various transitions from one stage to another. Alice Rossi (1968) noted these transitions in her examination of the change from being a married couple without children to having the first child. Ralph LaRossa (1977) found that the transition to parenthood actually began during the wife's pregnancy (see Chapter 7).

Questions Asked by Developmentalists

Obviously, the first questions asked by developmentalists are

What are the stages of the family life cycle?

How does a particular stage influence marriage and family life?

The concern with developmental tasks causes those employing this framework to ask

> What factors influence success or failure in meeting these varied developmental tasks?

The life cycle approach to families allows sociologists to consider issues and ideas that they might have overlooked. Alice Rossi (1979), for instance, found important issues and problems facing middle-aged parents that were distinct from the issues and concerns they faced when they were younger. Without a developmental approach, one might be lulled into thinking that issues of parenthood did not change once the children were born.

Critiques of the Developmental Framework

There are a number of important limitations and problems with the developmental framework that may explain why it tends to be used in organizing books but has a more limited use in the field of family studies. First, the framework is designed to study the "normal" or "average" type of family. Typically, this is a married couple, who have children and live independently. Although this is the "ideal" type family, it actually is not even the major form of family organization in the United States today (see Chapters 1 and 4). The developmental framework is not always applicable to studying or even understanding alternative family forms. Developmentalists have little or nothing to offer about childless couples. A second criticism of the framework is that it is essentially a descriptive framework. Although the listing of stages or categories is interesting and illuminating, the framework tends not to lead to theoretical propositions about family relations.

Social Exchange

The **social exchange approach** to human behavior has a long history in both sociology and anthropology (Nye 1979). Nevertheless, this approach to behavior was infrequently applied to family relations until recently. The explanation of family relations as a process of exchange involving costs and rewards has become an important conceptualization of family relations in the past 10 years, and this framework is perhaps the fastest growing perspective in the field.

Earlier, we presented Lillian Rubin's interview with a 34-year-old truck driver whose father was an alcoholic but whose mother never sought a divorce. In the earlier quote, the truck driver explained that his mother stayed married because of the kids and because she had no job skills. Someone using the social exchange framework would probably find the mother's behavior quite reasonable. She had assessed the advantages (or rewards) of a divorce, balanced them against the costs (having to support the children and having no job skills), and had found that staying married to an alcoholic was, as least for her, the least costly alternative.

Central Assumptions

There are four major assumptions of the social exchange perspective:

1. Social behavior is a series of exchanges.
2. In the course of these exchanges, individuals attempt to maximize their rewards and minimize their costs.
3. Under certain circumstances, a person will accept certain costs in exchange for other rewards.
4. When we receive rewards from others, we are obliged to reciprocate and supply benefits to them in return (from Homans 1961; see also Blau 1964; Nye 1979).

Key Concepts

■ *Rewards.* Rewards are defined as pleasures, satisfactions, and gratifications (Thibaut and Kelley 1959). Rewards also include a gain in status, relationships, interaction, experiences other than interaction, and feelings that provide gratification to people (Nye 1979, p. 2).

■ *Costs.* Costs are defined as any loss in status, loss of a relationship or milieu, or feeling disliked by an individual or group (Nye 1979, p. 2). There are two types of costs—punishments and losing out on some reward because another alternative was chosen (missing a good movie because you chose to go to a concert).

■ *Reciprocity.* The key to social exchange is reciprocity. In brief, people are expected to help those who help them and not injure those who have helped them (Gouldner 1960).

Questions Asked by Social Exchange Theorists

Perhaps one reason for the growth in popularity of the social exchange framework among family scholars is the wide applicability of the perspective to family relations. Exchange theorists examine mate selection and ask

Why did that couple marry?

Did he exchange his good looks for her status and money?

Looking at premarital sex, exchange theorists ask

Why do engaged women have higher rates of premarital sex than other women?

Are they exchanging sex for commitment?

Nye (1979) has considered why women choose to go back to work at particular times and has found social exchange theory to be a useful framework for pursuing this question. He proposes that mothers will seek and secure employment outside the home when they see work as providing more monetary and intrinsic rewards than remaining a full-time housewife and caregiver for children. Why people marry at a particular time, why violence occurs in families, and many other questions are all asked within the framework offered by social exchange.

Critiques of the Social Exchange Framework

Detractors of the social exchange approach to family relations note that the perspective is indeed useful for studying the courtship process and the kinds of marriages seen in marriage therapy. But the more complex relations in the exchange process are more complicated and less amendable to a short-term cost/reward analysis (Holman and Burr 1980; Murstein, Cerreto, and MacDonald 1977).

One interesting facet of the review of the five major schools of thought in family studies is that it reveals that no one unifying general theory of marriage and family life is used by all students of family relations. Also, it is quite clear that the field still has not moved any closer to such an integrating general theory (Klein 1979; Thomas and Wilcox 1987). What is available are a number of major and minor perspectives that help guide investigation into the complex area of marriage and family and serve to organize the questions asked and findings and conclusions about how families function and operate. The newer perspectives in family studies include feminist theory (see Box 2-2), radical critical theory (Osmond 1987), and biosocial theory (see Chapter 3). Sometimes, insights derived from one school of thought complement ideas

A Brief Review

from other frameworks. Other times, we find major contradictions between the perspectives.

The theoretical frameworks provide numerous assumptions and guidelines for thinking about family relations. Testing these assumptions and developing new propositions is central to sociological inquiry. The strategies for carrying out research on family life are examined in the next section.

STUDYING FAMILIES

Conceptual frameworks serve to guide the development of questions social scientists ask about families. The questions are answered by collecting information. Social scientists use a number of different methods to investigate

---

BOX 2-2: THINKING ABOUT FAMILIES

Feminist Theory and Method

One of the most significant recent developments in family studies is the development of feminist theory and methods for studying and analyzing family relations. Feminist scholars stress that families are not separate from wider systems of male domination (Ferree 1990). Early conceptualizations of feminist theory explained women's subordination in the family and in society by examining sex roles and socialization. Current feminist approaches to women and families employ *gender theory*, which argues that male dominance within families is part of a wider system of male domination. This domination is neither natural nor inevitable.

Feminist theory is not limited to examining the costs that women pay as a result of male domination. The theoretical framework "opens up" the examination of women and families by linking gender roles in the family to gender roles in other social institutions (Ferree 1990).

Feminist theory and method is activist- or "praxis"-driven research that is "on, by, and for women" (Stacy 1988). Women are at the center of feminist scholarship as both the subjects of inquiry and gatherers of knowledge.

In addition to feminist theory, there is feminist methodology. Although there is not total agreement on what feminist research methods are, it is generally agreed that feminist researchers hope to sensitize people to the reality of womens' lives, including sexism and social injustice (Thompson 1992). Research is *for* women and is aimed at emancipating them and enhancing their lives. There is some debate about the way the research should be done, and some feminist researchers reject social surveys as positivist research that divorces data about women from the context and process of behavior and their lives. The Conflict Tactics Scales (see the following section on Social Surveys) are especially targeted by feminist researchers as an example of a research method that separates behavior (e.g., violence) from the process and context of the experience.

Feminist methodology often employs qualitative research, such as used by Rubin (1976), to capture the essence of womens' social experiences. Unstructured interviews, ethnographies, and personal histories are methods often used by feminist researchers.

Step	Description
1	Formulate the problem or question you want to answer or address.
2	Examine the relevant literature—other studies or theories related to this topic.
3	Construct a research design. Select the techniques that will be used to collect information or data.
4	Decide on the population and sample. Who will you collect data from? To what larger group do you want to generalize your findings?
5	Gather data.
6	Analyze data.
7	Interpret the data.
8	Verify the data. Compare your findings to other research in this area.
9	Present findings in a public report.

Table 2-2 Steps of the Research Process

SOURCE: The Scientific Approach by Carlo Lastrucci, 1967, Cambridge, MA: Schenkman. Copyright © 1967 by Schenkman Books, Inc. Adapted by permission.

marriage and family life. The most common approach is the *social survey,* but *field studies* and *experiments* are also used to learn about various facets of family life. The choice of what research method to use depends on the questions that one wants to answer. Irrespective of what method is being employed, social scientists tend to pursue their research by following the same steps (see Table 2-2).

Understanding the research methods used by family social scientists is important for two reasons. First, it is impossible to appreciate the nature of the facts and findings about the family that will follow in this text without having some sense of how these findings were arrived at. Second, numerous facts, findings, and conclusions about family life are presented on television and radio and in newspapers, journals, books, and everyday conversations. Knowledge of the methods used, and of the advantages and disadvantages of each method, will make you a more intelligent consumer of the information about family relations that you attain outside a course on marriage and family.

Field Studies

The portrait of working-class family life painted by Lillian Rubin in her 1976 book *Worlds of Pain* was derived from interviews with 50 white working-class families. Families for the study were located in many ways. Friends of Rubin suggested possible families. PTA members, ministers, women at a beauty shop, and the families themselves provided suggestions of others to interview. Rubin, however, notes that the interviews were not the only source of data for her study. Because she herself had grown up in a working-class home, her own past and present were sources of information for her examination (p. 12). Rubin presented her findings with long quotes and anecdotes. No statistics, tables, or charts were used to capture life in working-class homes.

Experiments, such as observing how a family goes about solving a puzzle or completing a task, are one of the three main methods of collecting data on families.

Rubin's research can be categorized as a type of **field study.** Field studies typically are studies that seek to obtain in-depth information about the issues or questions studied. Field studies can be observational, or they can use unstructured, in-depth interviewing to collect data. In Rubin's research, in-depth information was obtained by conducting interviews with a small number of subjects—less than 100. Sometimes, the number of people interviewed can be greater than 100, but the main thrust is to gather more information than could be gathered by interviewing someone for 30 minutes or an hour—as is typically done in surveys.

Another type of fieldwork is **observational research** or **participant observation research.** Here, information is collected by observing actual behavior rather than asking people to report their behavior in an interview. When anthropologist Carol Stack wanted to examine family life in a black community, she chose to spend time in the community as a participant observer. The life histories she reported in her 1974 book *All Our Kin* were based on long periods of observing behavior in homes and on the street corners of the black community of a mid-western city. In *Talley's Corner,* Elliot Liebow (1967) examined friendships and adaptations to poverty and discrimination. In addition, he analyzed marital relations and child-rearing practices among the lower-class blacks he observed and interacted with.

Stack and Liebow actually participated in their subjects' daily lives. Other examples of fieldwork are more observational in nature. Some family sociologists simply observe and record behavior. In a number of cases, researchers have observed family behavior in its natural setting (the home) or have brought families into a laboratory (Hartup 1978; Lerner and Spanier 1978; Riskin and Faunce 1968, 1970, 1972).

Finally, some researchers have observed families without the families knowing it, as was the case when Bruce Brown (1979) observed and recorded incidents of parents spanking children in public.

Strengths and Weaknesses of Fieldwork

The major advantage of gathering data through fieldwork is that this technique allows researchers to make observations, uncover social regularities in family relations, and generate hypotheses about marriage and family. Depth interviewing in the subject's home, participant observation, and observation allow researchers to observe subtleties of attitudes and behaviors that are not revealed in a mailed questionnaire or a highly structured interview. Fieldwork is the only way to study people in their natural setting. Interaction between family members is best studied by observing it rather than having people provide retrospective accounts that may be biased by their desire to give a good impression of themselves and their families to an interviewer. It is more useful for observers to see child-rearing behavior rather than to rely on a parent's self-report. As Rubin (1976) says,

> We need work that takes us inside family dynamics, into the socio-emotional world in which people are born, live, and die—real people with flesh, blood, bones, and skeletons. (p. 14)

But there are trade-offs. For one, fieldwork takes much more time than surveys or experiments. Some studies take years to carry out and complete. Second, the field-worker can conduct only a limited number of in-depth interviews and can observe only a limited number of people. The number of subjects involved in a field research study is typically small, and because they are not randomly chosen, they are of questionable representativeness. Generalizing beyond these small samples is risky, even if the researcher believes he or she has uncovered "universal" social regularities. Another problem, one that also is problematic for generalizing from the group observed to a wider universe, is that the researcher may become overly involved with the subjects and become more of a friend than an impartial observer (anthropologists call this over-identification "going native"). Carol Stack spent three years in the "Flats." She not only observed, she became a full-scale participant. Her car became a community resource. Throughout the fieldwork, she tried to remain objective and record what she saw. Yet she was part of what was happening. Just by being there, field-workers may actually alter what is happening. To what degree does the behavior being observed get changed by the observer? This is a question that is constantly being considered by field-workers as they collect their data.

Social Surveys

In the early 1970s when very little was known about wife abuse and family violence, I used the field study method, similar to that employed by Rubin, to conduct 80 in-depth interviews on the topic of violence between husbands and wives (Gelles 1974). The study produced descriptive accounts of wife abuse and violence, suggested how extensive violence might be, and led to the generation of a number of hypotheses about the causes of violence in the home. The drawbacks of the study were obvious. Eighty families in New Hampshire were in no way reflective of families in the United States, and the number of families, or *sample,* was far too small to do sophisticated analyses of the data.

My next step was to conduct a study that had a large enough sample to test hypotheses and a sample that was *representative* of families in the United States. This research required using a method called the **social survey.**

Social surveys typically use standardized questions to collect information from people (see Figure 2-1 for an example of the standardized questions used to collect information on violence between husbands and wives).

To learn about the extent of family violence in the United States and the causes of family violence, I joined with Murray Straus to conduct a survey that used a sample of families representative of families in the United States (some of the results of this survey are presented in Chapter 15). Because one of the important objectives was to answer the question "How extensive is family violence in the United States?" we needed to conduct a study that was generalizable. The key to this and to most survey research is sampling. A **sample** is a portion of the population about which the researcher wants to generalize. There are two general types of samples: representative and nonrepresentative. A **representative** sample is one in which each member of a population

35. No matter how well a couple gets along, there are times when they disagree, get annoyed with the other person, or just have spats or fights because they're in a bad mood or tired or for some other reason. They also use many different ways of trying to settle their differences. I'm going to read some things that you and your partner might do when you have an argument. I would like you to tell me how many times [READ EACH ITEM] in the past 12 months you [READ LIST].

36. Thinking back over the past 12 months you've been together, was there ever an occasion when (your spouse/partner) [READ ITEM]? [READ ACROSS]

(IF EITHER "NEVER" OR "DON'T KNOW" ON ITEM FOR BOTH Q.35 AND Q.36, ASK Q.37 FOR THAT ITEM, THEN CONTINUE WITH LIST FOR Q.35.)

37. Has it ever happened?

[READ LIST]	Q.35 Respondent								Q.36 Spouse								Q.37 Ever Happen		
	Once	Twice	3-5 Times	6-10 Times	11-20 Times	More Than 20 Times	[DO NOT READ] Don't Know	[DO NOT READ] Never	Once	Twice	3-5 Times	6-10 Times	11-20 Times	More Than 20 Times	[DO NOT READ] Don't Know	[DO NOT READ] Never	Yes	No	[DO NOT READ] Don't Know
a. Discussed an issue calmly	-1 (60(	-2	-3	-4	-5	-6	-8	-0	-1 (61(	-2	-3	-4	-5	-6	-8	-0	-1 (62(	-0	-8
b. Got information to back up your/his/her side of things	-1 (63(	-2	-3	-4	-5	-6	-8	-0	-1 (64(	-2	-3	-4	-5	-6	-8	-0	-1 (65(	-0	-8
c. Brought in or tried to bring in someone to help settle things	-1 (66(	-2	-3	-4	-5	-6	-8	-0	-1 (67(	-2	-3	-4	-5	-6	-8	-0	-1 (68(	-0	-8
d. Insulted him or swore at him/her/you	-1 (69(	-2	-3	-4	-5	-6	-8	-0	-1 (70(	-2	-3	-4	-5	-6	-8	-0	-1 (71(	-0	-8
e. Sulked or refused to talk about an issue	-1 (72(	-2	-3	-4	-5	-6	-8	-0	-1 (73(	-2	-3	-4	-5	-6	-8	-0	-1 (74(	-0	-8
f. Stomped out of the room or house or yard	-1 (75(	-2	-3	-4	-5	-6	-8	-0	-1 (76(	-2	-3	-4	-5	-6	-8	-0	-1 (77(	-0	-8
g. Cried	-1 (78(	-2	-3	-4	-5	-6	-8	-0	-1 (79(	-2	-3	-4	-5	-6	-8	8	-1 (80(	0	8
h. Did or said something to spite him/her/you	-1 (3*8(	-2	-3	-4	-5	-6	-8	-0	-1 (9(	-2	-3	-4	-5	-6	-8	-0	-1 (10(	-0	-8
i. Threatened to hit him/her/you or throw something at him/her/you	-1 (11(	-2	-3	-4	-5	-6	-8	-0	-1 (12(	-2	-3	-4	-5	-6	-8	-0	-1 (13(	-0	-8
j. Threw or smashed or hit or kicked something	-1 (14(	-2	-3	-4	-5	-6	-8	-0	-1 (15(	-2	-3	-4	-5	-6	-8	-0	-1 (16(	-0	-8
k. Threw something at him/her/you	-1 (17(	-2	-3	-4	-5	-6	-8	-0	-1 (18(	-2	-3	-4	-5	-6	-8	-0	-1 (19(	-0	-8
l. Pushed, grabbed, or shoved him/her/you	-1 (20(	-2	-3	-4	-5	-6	-8	-0	-1 (21(	-2	-3	-4	-5	-6	-8	-0	-1 (22(	-0	-8
m. Slapped him/her/you	-1 (23(	-2	-3	-4	-5	-6	-8	-0	-1 (24(	-2	-3	-4	-5	-6	-8	-0	-1 (25(	0	8
n. Kicked, bit or hit him/her/you with a fist	-1 (26(	-2	-3	-4	-5	-6	-8	-0	-1 (27(	-2	-3	-4	-5	-6	-8	-0	-1 (28(	-0	-8
o. Hit or tried to hit him/her/you with something	-1 (29(	-2	-3	-4	-5	-6	-8	-0	-1 (30(	-2	-3	-4	-5	-6	-8	-0	-1 (31(	-0	-8
p. Beat him/her/you up	-1 (32(	-2	-3	-4	-5	-6	-8	-0	-1 (33(	-2	-3	-4	-5	-6	-8	-0	-1 (34(	-0	-8
q. Choked him/her/you	-1 (35(	-2	-3	-4	-5	-6	-8	-0	-1 (36(	-2	-3	-4	-5	-6	-8	-0	-1 (37(	-0	-8
r. Threatened him/her/you with a knife or gun	-1 (38(	-2	-3	-4	-5	-6	-8	-0	-1 (39(	-2	-3	-4	-5	-6	-8	-0	-1 (40(	-0	-8
s. Used a knife or fired a gun	-1 (41(	-2	-3	-4	-5	-6	-8	-0	-1 (42(	-2	-3	-4	-5	-6	-8	-0	-1 (43(	-0	-8

Figure 2-1 Measuring Violence Between Spouses

(e.g., all families in the United States) has (a) a chance and (b) the *same* chance of being selected. Because Lillian Rubin conducted her research in the San Francisco area, every family in the United States did not have a chance to be included. Because she obtained families through friends and referrals, not every family had the same chance to be in the study. Thus her study used a **nonrepresentative** sample.

For our two national surveys on family violence, we sampled 2,143 families across the United States in 1976 and 6,002 families in 1985 (Gelles and Straus 1988; Straus and Gelles 1986, 1990; Straus, Gelles, and Steinmetz 1980). There are two sources of sampling error in social surveys that use representative sampling. First is the size of the sample. The smaller the sample, the greater the chance of error. In a sample of 50 families, one individual quirk might bias the whole study. With a sample of 2,000 or 6,000, a single quirky person or family has less of an impact on the entire study. A second source of error is **response rate.** Imagine if I had arrived at the front door of the houses and told the person answering that I was studying wife abuse. The abusers might have slammed the door in (or on) my face, whereas the nonviolent couples might have been more willing to let me in. Had this occurred (it did not—we introduced ourselves as conducting a survey on family relations) it would surely have *underestimated* the extent of violence in American families. Similarly, if a researcher wants to conduct a survey on working women and only goes to homes during the day, then the number of "not at homes" will be high. The response rate will be low and the results biased. In other words, the resulting sample will not be truly representative of the total population of working women. The smaller the response rate (the percentage of all eligible subjects who agree to participate in and complete the study), the greater the chance of error and bias.

Our national surveys on family violence involved interviewing individual family members. In 1975, we interviewed people in their own homes for about an hour. In 1985, we conducted telephone interviews and interviewed each person for about 35 minutes. Because we wanted to increase the chances of getting truthful, or *valid,* reports of violence, we took great care in wording our questions and ordering them in the interview. Figure 2-1 shows how we began with the least sensitive questions and worked our way toward the most sensitive.

In-person interviews are but one type of social survey. Murray Straus (1974) studied family violence by administering *questionnaires* to college students. He had also mailed questionnaires home to students' parents. Mailed questionnaires are typically a quick and inexpensive way of conducting social research, but they typically result in response rate of around 30%-60%. *Telephone interviews,* a third method of survey, are more expensive than questionnaires but less expensive than in-person interviewing. Because 95% of all households have telephones and because telephone interviewing provides anonymity to the subjects, telephone surveys using computer-generated telephone numbers have become a major technique of social research.

One major source of survey data on families is the National Survey of Families and Households that was conducted during 1987 and 1988. The survey involved interviews with 13,017 respondents, including a national cross section of 9,643 persons aged 19 and over plus an oversample of minorities and households containing single parents, stepfamilies, recently married couples, and cohabiting couples. In each household, a randomly selected adult was interviewed on a wide range of issues about American family life (Sweet, Bumpass, and Call 1988). Another important source of survey data is the National Opinion Research Center's annual General Social Survey of a national cross section of 1,250 respondents. This survey contains a number of items that relate to marriage and family life.

Although university-based researchers gather considerable data about families using social surveys, the majority of data about families comes from surveys conducted by the federal government. The U.S. Bureau of the Census conducts a census of the entire population every 10 years (as mandated by the U.S. Constitution). The Census Bureau also conducts surveys using samples of the population to provide yearly updates on the state of the American family. We will be referring to information from these Bureau of the Census surveys throughout the entire book.

Strengths and Weaknesses of Social Surveys

The chief advantage of social surveys is the savings of time and money. This may explain why social surveys are the most common form of research method used by family social scientists. The majority of published research on marriage and family relations—nearly 70%—uses social surveys to collect the data (Nye 1988; Nye and Bayer 1963). Information can be collected on a great number of people in a short amount of time. Carol Stack spent three years in the "Flats" studying black families. The in-person interviews I conducted on family violence took four months. The telephone survey we conducted on family violence took but a month to complete.

A second advantage of surveys is standardization. Each respondent is asked the same question, and, if the survey uses a closed-end question format, each respondent has to choose from a standard set of answers (as in Figure 2-1). Findings from standardized interviews can be quantified and subjected to rigorous statistical testing.

Social surveys also have numerous drawbacks. Thirty-minute telephone interviews, 1-hour in-person interviews, and 20-page questionnaires provide but the slimmest amount of data on family relations. Surveys provide a brief glimpse into family life—sacrificing depth for breadth of coverage. Standardized questions and answers are also a drawback. Researchers frequently are accused of oversimplifying complex issues in the struggle to precisely word standardized questions and answers.

The last and most significant drawback of a social survey is that it is a step removed from actual human behavior. Surveys depend on people's self-reports of their behavior. Researchers learn about what people say they do rather than seeing what they actually do. Because most people want other people to think well of them, subjects in social surveys may often give *socially desirable* answers rather than tell the truth.

When we completed our survey of family violence and totaled up the extent of violence, we were surprised at how large the numbers were. While we wanted a study of the true level of family violence, we knew we had a study of what people would be willing to admit to. Our surprise came from how much violence people would admit to!

BOX 2-3: WHAT THE RESEARCH SHOWS

College Students, Couples, and Family Research

The family is a complex and difficult social institution to study. For one thing, families are made up of a number of individuals occupying multiple statuses and roles. Thus a researcher who interviews a family member is collecting data from someone at the intersection of many and varied roles (mother, wife, worker, daughter, sister, and the like). Second, "family" as a group or social institution is more than one person. Social researchers are used to collecting data from individuals, but a family is a father, mother, son, daughter, and others, and each of these individuals is likely to have a unique subjective perception of what things are like in the family (Laing 1971).

If the number of different people do not make things sufficiently complicated, the fact that the family is a private, intimate, and sacred social group makes entry into the family difficult for social researchers. One reason why less than 1% of all published family research employs observational methods (Larzelere and Klein 1987; Nye 1988; Nye and Bayer 1963) is that the private nature of the family makes it difficult for a researcher to employ standard participant observational methods within the home. Few researchers have ever actually moved in with families and observed their behavior (the most noted exception is Jules Henry's 1971 study of families with psychotic children).

Last, most behavior in families cannot be simulated or manipulated in an experimental laboratory (see following section on Experiments). It would be difficult to experimentally simulate dating, mating, premarital sex,

A true experimental design allows researchers to assess the impact of one factor or variable while holding all other factors constant. There are two conditions of a true experiment. First, at least two groups are involved. One is the **experimental group**—the group that is exposed to the experimental treatment. The other is the **control group**—one that is put through the experimental design but is *not* exposed to the experimental treatment. The control group makes it possible to measure the results effects of a treatment against no treatment at all. The second condition of a true experiment is that people are randomly assigned to the two groups. Random assignment means that all participants have an equal chance of being assigned to the treatment group or no treatment (control) group, so the only factor that is varied is the experimental treatment. The key to an experiment is that the experimental group is randomly chosen from the same population of possible subjects as the control group, and any differences that arise after the experiment must be a result of exposure to the treatment (Miller 1986).

Experiments are perhaps the most advantageous method of determining causal relations. Yet experiments are rarely used in family research. This is

Experiments

divorce, and other important family issues, let alone manipulate them in the real world.

The complex, private, and intimate nature of family relations has resulted in social researchers making some compromises in studying families. A number of social researchers have criticized family research for relying too heavily on college student populations (Berardo 1976; Landis 1957).

College students are readily accessible subjects for many family researchers, and many researchers believe that students are articulate "informants" on various aspects of family life. But students are clearly an unrepresentative sample of the population—they are more affluent than noncollege students and college student populations have lower percentages of Blacks, Latinos, and other ethnic minorities than are found in the general population.

Furthermore, it is possible that many aspects of students' own families have been shielded or hidden from them (witness the surprise of a college student when his or her parents decide to get divorced).

When family researchers have gone beyond the walls of their colleges or institutions in search of families to study, all too often they choose to study a single member of a family. Lillian Rubin's decision to interview both husbands and wives for her study was atypical. An analysis of published research on families found that only 30% of all survey studies (and surveys are the most commonly used research strategy) used two or more members of the same family (Klein 1982). Family researchers are sometimes criticized for obtaining data on families from only one perspective—wives, because they are the most available for research (Safilios-Rothschild 1969, 1971).

Maximiliane Szinovacz (1983) has shown that there is much to be gained in gathering information from husbands *and* wives in the same family. Husbands and wives do have differing opinions about what is going on in families, and these differences provide important data for those interested in learning about how families actually function.

A substantial number of studies of family life are based on survey data collected from college.

probably due to the fact that few of the significant aspects of family relations can be ethically experimentally manipulated. One could not approve of an experiment that manipulated factors to see what influenced mate selection or divorce. Few people would tolerate an experiment that assessed what factors caused child abuse, as one would have to passively stand by while children are abused for experimental purposes.

Some experiments attempt to simulate behavior that occurs in homes. Murray Straus and Irving Tallman (1971) developed a unique laboratory experiment to assess the impact of crises on family problem-solving ability. While the control group was made to believe they were successful, the experimental group experienced a "crisis of failure."

In the "ball and pusher" task, families consisting of a husband, wife, and child entered the laboratory, or the court (see Figure 2-2). At the front of the room were three pairs of red and green lights mounted on a single board. One pair was for the husband, one for the wife, and one for the child. When the family entered the room, a white band was placed on the husband's wrist, a yellow one on the wife's, and a blue one on the child's. The family was then

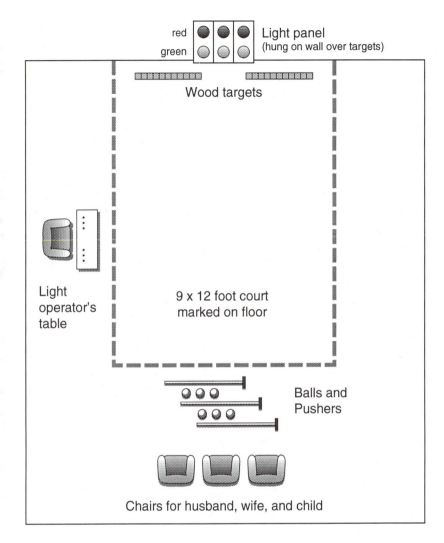

Figure 2-2
Laboratory Setup
for Straus and
Tallman's "Ball
and Pusher"
Family Crisis Sim-
ulation Experiment

SOURCE: Figure from *Family Problem Solving: A Symposium of Theoretical, Methodological, and Substantive Concerns* by Joan Aldous and Thomas Condon, copyright © 1971 by the Dryden Press, reproduced by permission of the publisher.

told "the problem to be solved is to figure out how to play this game." They were told that if what they did was correct, a green light would flash, and if what they did was incorrect, a red light would flash. Finally, the family was shown a scoreboard (Figure 2-3). On top were the game numbers (eight 3-minute innings or trials). The next row showed supposed average family

Figure 2-3 Score-board for Straus and Tallman's "Ball and Pusher" Family Crisis Simulation Experiment

Game number	1	2	3	4	5	6	7	8
Average family's score	21	40	55	90	122	156	191	218
Your score	—	—	—	—	—	—	—	—

SOURCE: Figure from *Family Problem Solving: A Symposium of Theoretical, Methodological, and Substantive Concerns* by Joan Aldous and Thomas Condon, copyright © 1971 by the Dryden Press, reproduced by permission of the publisher.

scores. Beneath that would be posted the score achieved by the family participating in the experiment. In the experiment, the red and green lights flashed so fast that no family could actually keep track of their score. The experimental treatment was to manipulate the family's score in comparison to the "average family's score." The experimenters felt they could simulate a crisis by making it impossible for a family to get green lights and a good score after the fifth session of the game. No matter what a family did, they would get red lights and their own score would be considerably lower than the average score. Control families continued to get green lights and their scores progressed right through the game. Thus experimental families were put through a "crisis of failure," whereas controls believed they were doing well.

By simulating a crisis, Straus and Tallman were able to study the impact of a family crisis on family power, support, communication patterns, problem-solving ability, and creativity.

Experimental designs are a particularly effective means of studying variations in family interaction, family power, and decision making.

Strengths and Weaknesses of Experiments

The major advantage of experimental designs is control. Straus and Tallman, by randomly assigning couples into "crisis" and "noncrisis" conditions, were able to control all other possible influences on the outcome factors they wanted to measure (e.g., power, communication). Experiments are also easier to replicate than surveys or field studies. Last, there are techniques that can be used in the experiment to prevent the experimenter from biasing the outcome (in the ball and pusher study, the experimenters could have been kept "blind" to whether or not the families they were observing were in the "crisis" condition).

The disadvantage of experiments is their artificiality. Typically, controlled experiments are conducted in a laboratory. Subjects know they are being observed and may behave self-consciously. An important question, especially in family studies, is whether the laboratory condition adequately represents the same events in the real world. Is a poor score on the ball and pusher task really a good representation of a crisis, such as a death or unemployment, on the family? Straus and Tallman say yes, but others frequently see experiments as too artificial to fully capture the complex nuances of family life.

SUMMING UP

The knowledge that family sociologists obtain and generate about marriage and family life is derived from integrating theoretical frameworks and research methods. The frameworks serve to help generate the questions, define the terms or concepts that will be used, and guide the collection of data and the interpretation of the findings.

This chapter reviewed the five most widely used conceptual frameworks: structural functionalism, the conflict framework, symbolic interaction, the developmental framework, and social exchange theory. Feminist theory and methods were also discussed. Each framework was examined in terms of its major assumptions, key concepts, the questions asked by theorists who use the framework, and finally, its strengths and weaknesses.

The development of a foundation of knowledge about family life depends on sound research methods. Adequate sampling, accurate measurement, and replication of findings are the core of sociological knowledge about the family. Generalizations from a study can be made only by considering the representativeness of the sample. The accuracy of the study depends in large part on the researcher's ability to develop measurement techniques that accurately measure the major concepts of a study. Imagine the confusion if one researcher measured "working mother" by restricting the measure to only women who work more than 35 hours a week, while a second researcher measured the concept by including any woman who worked outside the home, and a third researcher included women who worked for any wage inside and outside the home—if these three studies resulted in different findings about the effect of working mothers on family life, who would be surprised? The final test of sound research is whether another investigator can replicate the original study and obtain the same results. Many acceptable ideas that arose from one study failed to find acceptance in the scientific community because no one else could replicate the study and find the same things.

This chapter reviewed the three major methods of studying families: field studies, social surveys, and experiments. Field studies allow researchers to study behavior in its natural setting. Given the privacy and intimacy of families, field studies are often difficult to conduct. Social surveys enable researchers to gather data on large populations and to quantify the results. Surveys, however, can only measure what people say or are willing to report. Experiments are the most useful in studying limited, clearly defined questions. They enable researchers to isolate independent and dependent variables. Experiments, however, can often produce artificial results because the behavior studied may not be the same behavior that would occur in a natural family setting.

REFERENCES

Aldous, Joan. 1978. *Family Careers: Developmental Change in Families.* New York: John Wiley.

Berardo, Felix. 1976. "Beyond the College Student: An Editorial Comment." *Journal of Marriage and the Family* 38 (May): 211.

Berger, Peter. 1963. *Invitation to Sociology.* New York: Anchor/Doubleday.

Blau, Peter M. 1964. *Exchange and Power in Social Life.* New York: John Wiley.

Blumstein, Philip and **Pepper Schwartz.** 1983. *American Couples: Money, Work, and Sex.* New York: Morrow.

Broderick, Carlfred B. 1970. "Beyond the Five Conceptual Frameworks: A Decade of Development in Family Theory." Pp. 3-14 in *A Decade of Family Research and Action, 1960–1969,* edited by Carlfred B. Broderick.

Minneapolis: National Council on Family Relations.

———. 1990. "Family Process Theory." Pp. 171-206 in *Fashioning Family Theory: New Approaches,* edited by Jetse Sprey. Newbury Park, CA: Sage.

Brown, Bruce. 1979. "Parents' Discipline of Children in Public Places." *Family Coordinator* 28 (January):67-71.

Cooley, Charles H. 1902. *Social Organization.* New York: Charles Scribner's Sons.

Dahrendorf, Ralf. 1965. *Gessellschaft und Demokratie in Deutschland.* München: Piper Verlag.

Duvall, Evelyn M. 1967. *Family Development.* 3rd ed. Philadelphia: J. B. Lippencott.

Ferree, Myra Marx. 1990. "Feminism and Family Research." *Journal of Marriage and the Family* 52(November):866-84.

Gelles, Richard J. 1974. *The Violent Home.* Beverly Hills, CA: Sage.

Gelles, Richard J. and **Murray A. Straus.** 1988. *Intimate Violence.* New York: Simon & Schuster.

Gouldner, Alvin W. 1960. "The Norm of Reciprocity." *American Sociological Review* 25:(April) 161-78.

Hartup, William W. 1978. "Perspectives on Child and Family Interaction: Past, Present, and Future." In *Child Influences on Marital and Family Interaction: A Life Span Perspective,* edited by R. M. Lerner and G. B. Spanier. New York: Academic Press.

Havinghurst, Robert J. 1953. *Human Development and Education.* New York: Longmans, Green.

Henry, Jules. 1971. *Pathways to Madness.* New York: Vintage.

Hill, Reuben. 1966. "Contemporary Developments in Family

Theory." *Journal of Marriage and the Family* 28(February): 10-25.

Hill, Reuben and Donald A. Hansen. 1960. "The Identification of Conceptual Frameworks Utilized in Family Study." *Marriage and Family Living* 22(November):299-311.

Hill, Reuben and Roy H. Rodgers. 1964. "The Developmental Approach." Pp. 171-211 in *Handbook of Marriage and the Family,* edited by Harold T. Christensen. Chicago: Rand McNally.

Holman, Thomas B. and Wesley R. Burr. 1980. "Beyond the Beyond: The Growth of Family Theories in the 1970s." *Journal of Marriage and the Family* 42(November):729-41.

Homans, George. 1961. *Social Behavior: Its Elementary Forms.* New York: Harcourt Brace Jovanovich.

Kaufman, Debra Renee. 1990. "Engendering Family Theory: Toward a Feminist-Interpretive Framework." Pp. 107-35 in *Fashioning Family Theory: New Approaches,* edited by Jetse Sprey. Newbury Park, CA: Sage.

Kirkpatrick, Ellis L., Mary Cowles, and Roselyn Tough. 1934. "The Life Cycle of the Farm Family." *University of Wisconsin Experiment Station Bulletin No. 121.*

Klein, David M. 1979. "A Social History of a Grass-Roots Institution: The Case of the NCFR Workshop on Theory Construction and Research Methodology." Paper presented to the

Theory Construction and Research Methodology Workshop, Boston.

———. 1982. "The Problems of Multiple Perception in Families." Unpublished manuscript, University of Notre Dame.

Klein, David M., Jay D. Schvanevelt, and Brent C. Miller. 1977. "The Attitudes of Contemporary Family Theorists." *Journal of Contemporary Family Studies* 8(Spring):5-27.

Laing, R. D. 1971. *The Politics of the Family.* New York: Vintage.

Landis, Judson T. 1957. "Values and Limitations of Family Research Using Student Subjects." *Marriage and Family Living* 19(February):100-5.

LaRossa, Ralph. 1977. *Conflict and Power in Marriage: Expecting the First Child.* Beverly Hills, CA: Sage.

Lastrucci, Carlo. 1967. *The Scientific Approach.* Cambridge, MA: Schenkman.

Larzelere, Robert E. and David M. Klein. 1987. "Methodology." Pp. 125-55 in *Handbook of Marrige and the Family,* edited by Marvin B. Sussman and Suzanne K. Steinmetz. New York: Plenum.

Lerner, Richard M. and Graham B. Spanier, eds. 1978. *Child Influences on Marital and Family Interaction.* New York: Academic Press.

Levy, Marion J. 1952. *The Structure of Society.* Princeton, NJ: Princeton University Press.

Liebow, Elliot. 1967. *Talley's Corner.* Boston: Little, Brown.

Malinowski, Bronislaw. 1939. "The Group and the Individual in Functional Analysis." *American Journal of Sociology* 44 (May):938-64.

Marx, Karl and Friedrich Engels. [1849] 1967. *The Communist Manifesto.* Translated by S. Moore. Baltimore: Penguin.

Mead, George H. 1934. *Mind, Self, and Society.* Chicago: University of Chicago Press.

Miller, Brent C. 1986. *Family Research Methods.* Beverly Hills, CA: Sage.

Murdock, George P. 1949. *Social Structure.* New York: Macmillan.

Murstein, Bernard I., Mary Cerreto, and Marcia B. MacDonald. 1977. "A Theory and Investigation of the Effects of Exchange-Orientation on Marriage and Friendship." *Journal of Marriage and the Family* 39 (August):543-48.

Nye, F. Ivan. 1979. "Choice, Exchange, and the Family." Pp. 1-41 in *Contemporary Theories About the Family,* Vol. 2, edited by Wesley R. Burr, Reuben Hill, F. Ivan Nye, and Ira L. Reiss. New York: Free Press.

———. 1988. "Fifty Years of Family Research: 1937–1987." *Journal of Marriage and the Family* 50(May):305-16.

Nye, F. Ivan and Alan Bayer. 1963. "Some Recent Trends in Family Research." *Social Forces* 41(March):290-301.

Osmond, Marie. 1987. "Radical-Critical Theories." Pp. 103-24 in *Handbook of Marriage and the Family,* edited by Marvin B.

Sussman and Suzanne K. Steinmetz. New York: Plenum.

Parsons, Talcott. 1951. *The Social System.* Glencoe, IL: Free Press.

Parsons, Talcott and Robert F. Bales, with James Olds and Morris Zelditch, Jr., eds. 1955. *Family, Socialization, and the Interaction Process.* Glencoe, IL: Free Press.

Pease, John. 1981. "Sociology *and* the Sense of the Commoners." *American Sociologist* 16 (November):257-71.

Radcliffe-Brown, Alfred R. 1952. *Structure and Function in Primitive Society.* Glencoe, IL: Free Press.

Reiss, Ira L. 1965. "The Universality of the Family: A Conceptual Approach." *Journal of Marriage and the Family* 27 (November):443-53.

Riskin, Jules and Elaine E. Faunce. 1968. *Family Interaction Scales Scoring Manual.* Published privately.

———. 1970. "Family Interaction Scales, III: Discussion of Methodology and Substantive Findings." *Archives of General Psychiatry* 22(June):527-37.

———. 1972. "An Evaluative Review of Family Interaction Research." *Family Process* 11(4):365-455.

Rodgers, Roy. 1962. *Improvements in the Construction and Analysis of Family Life Style Categories.* Kalamazoo: Western Michigan University Press.

Rossi, Alice S. 1968. "Transition to Parenthood." *Journal of Marriage and the Family* 30(February):26-39.

———. 1979. "The Middle Years of Parenting." Unpublished manuscript.

Rubin, Lillian B. 1976. *Worlds of Pain: Life in the Working Class Family.* New York: Basic Books.

Safilios-Rothschild, Constantina. 1969. "Family Sociology or Wives' Family Sociology? A Cross-Cultural Examination of Decision Making." *Journal of Marriage and the Family* 31 (May):290-301.

———. 1971. "The Study of Family Power Structure: A Review, 1960–1969." Pp. 79-90 in *A Decade Review of Family Research and Action, 1960–1969,* edited by Carlfred Broderick. Minneapolis: National Council on Family Relations.

Sheehy, Gail. 1976. *Passages.* New York: E. P. Dutton.

Sorokin, P. A., Carle C. Zimmerman, and C. J. Galpin. 1931. *A Systematic Sourcebook in Rural Sociology,* Vol. 2. Minneapolis: University of Minnesota Press.

Sprey, Jetse. 1969. "The Family as a System in Conflict." *Journal of Marriage and the Family* 31 (November):699-706.

———. 1979. "Conflict Theory and the Study of Marriage and the Family." Pp. 130-59 in *Contemporary Theories About the Family,* Vol. 2, edited by Wesley R. Burr, Reuben Hill, F. Ivan Nye, and Ira L. Reiss. New York: Free Press.

Stack, Carol B. 1974. *All Our Kin.* New York: Harper & Row.

Stacy, Judith. 1988. "Can Theory Be a Feminist Ethnography?" *Women's Studies International Forum* 11(1):21-27.

Straus, Murray A. 1974. "Leveling, Civility, and Violence in the Family." *Journal of Marriage and the Family* 36(February):13-29.

Straus, Murray A. and Richard J. Gelles. 1986. "Societal Change and Change in Family Violence From 1975 to 1985 as Revealed in Two National Surveys." *Journal of Marriage and the Family* 48(August):465-79.

———. 1990. *Physical Violence in American Families: Risk Factors and Adaptations to Violence in 8,145 Families.* New Brunswick, NJ: Transaction.

Straus, Murray A., Richard J. Gelles, and Suzanne K. Steinmetz. 1980. *Behind Closed Doors: Violence in the American Family.* Garden City, NY: Anchor/Doubleday.

Straus, Murray A. and Irving Tallman. 1971. "SIMFAM: A Technique for Observational Measurement and Experimental Study of Families." Pp. 380-438 in *Family Problem Solving,* edited by Joan Aldous, Thomas Confon, Reuben Hill, Murray A. Straus, and Irving Tallman. Hinsdale, IL: Dryden.

Sweet, James A., Larry L. Bumpass, and Vaughan R. A. Call. 1988. *The Design and Content of the National Survey of Families and Households.* NSFH Working Paper No. 1. Madison: University of Wisconsin, Center for Demography and Ecology.

Szinovacz, Maximiliane E. 1983. "Using Couple Data as a Methodological Tool: The Case of Marital Violence." *Journal of Marriage and the Family* 45 (August):633-44.

Thibaut, John W. and Harold H. Kelley. 1959. *The Social Psychology of Groups.* Morristown, NJ: General Learning Press.

Thomas, Darwin L. and Jean E. Wilcox. 1987. "The Rise of Family Theory: A Historical and Critical Analysis." Pp. 81-102 in *Handbook of Marriage and the Family,* edited by Marvin B. Sussman and Suzanne K. Steinmetz. New York: Plenum.

Thompson, Linda. 1992. "Feminist Methodology for Family Studies." *Journal of Marriage and the Family* 54(February): 3-18.

Winch, Robert. 1966. *The Modern Family.* 3rd ed. New York: Holt, Rinehart & Winston.

Zelditch, Morris, Jr. 1955. "Role Differentiation in the Nuclear Family: A Comparative Study." Pp. 307-51 in *Family Socialization and Interaction Process,* edited by Talcott Parsons and Robert F. Bayles, with James Olds and Morris Zelditch, Jr. Glencoe, IL: Free Press.

CHAPTER 3

▪▪ Families Across Time and Cultures

The child abuse team at a hospital in the Northeast was confronted with a difficult problem. They were discussing the case of a family in which four of the children—all of whom were younger than 10 years old—were suffering from lead poisoning. This posed a significant health risk to the children and had the potential, if not properly treated, of permanently impairing the children's physical and intellectual development. The cause of the poisoning was lead paint chips that were crumbling off the window sills of the family's apartment and being eaten by the children. There was also lead-contaminated soil on the playground near the house. The playground was beneath a bridge that was often repainted. Lead paint chips fell from the bridge every time workers sand-blasted the bridge before applying a new coat of paint. The lead got into the childrens' systems from the contaminated dirt.

The child abuse team did not blame the mother for the lead poisoning. Clearly both sources of lead contamination were beyond her control. The team, however, was troubled by certain facts that had emerged during the assessment of the family. The mother reported that she and the children lived in a one-bedroom apartment in a poorer section of the city. The family had been on welfare for the past six years and the mother reported that she and the four children all slept in the same bed. This alerted the child abuse team to the possibility of sexual abuse in the home. Their major focus was the fact that the mother and the children slept in the same bed. A number of the team members felt that such a sleeping arrangement was neglectful and harmful to the children and that it might be in the best interests of the children if the mother was reported for child neglect to the Department of Social Services. A few members of the team believed that the children might be better off if they were placed in a foster home until the mother found a more suitable apartment, one that had at least two bedrooms and a bed for each child.

Coincidentally, a cultural anthropologist who had an interest in child maltreatment was observing the meeting of the child abuse team. At the end of the meeting she voiced concern about the team's judgment that four children sleeping in the same bed with their mother could constitute child neglect. The anthropologist said she once described American child-rearing patterns to the !Kung San, a hunting and gathering society that lived on the Kalahari Desert in a remote corner of the African country of Botswana. She noted that most American parents put their children, even newborns, in a separate room each evening. Some parents turn off all the lights in the room, while others leave on only a dim night light. She went on to tell the !Kung San that "experts" on babies in the United States advise parents that when the babies are older than six months of age, they should be allowed to cry themselves to sleep in the dark room. The !Kung San could only shake their heads in disbelief about such barbaric and abusive ways of raising children. !Kung San offspring sleep in the same room and often the same "bed" with their parents. A !Kung San child abuse team, if one existed, would never consider a mother who slept with her four children as abusive. She would be thought of as caring and nurturing.

This chapter examines variation in family organization and function across time and cultures. The main objective of the chapter is to provide a broad overview of the social history of families, family organization, and family functions. Second, the chapter examines the major ways families are organized and differ across societies. Because most of the readers of this text are college students in the United States, one subtle objective of this chapter is to challenge the taken-for-granted ethnocentrism that we bring to an examination of family organizations other than ones we experience in our day-to-day lives. **Ethnocentrism** is the tendency to evaluate other cultures in terms of one's own and to conclude that the other culture is inferior.

The chapter concludes by examining families in hunting and gathering societies. In his book *Future Shock,* Alvin Toffler (1970) divided the past 50,000 years of human existence into lifetimes of approximately 62 years each. Thus, Toffler concludes, there have been 800 lifetimes up to 1970. Toffler illustrates modern social change by pointing out that for 650 of the 800 lifetimes, men and women lived in caves. Writing and communications across lifetimes was developed during the 750th lifetime. Mass distribution of the printed word has been available for the past 6 lifetimes. The precise measurement of time has been available for the past 4 lifetimes. Most material goods that we use today, televisions, VCRs, radios, automobiles, airplanes, processed foods, and so forth were developed during the 800th lifetime. For 90% to 99% of human existence (720 to 792 lifetimes) men, women, and families lived in hunting and gathering societies. Thus our examination of family life among hunters and gatherers provides us with an important look into the form of family life that humans have lived in for most of their time on earth.

THE ORIGINS OF THE FAMILY

The first **hominid,** or member of the human family, lived between 1 and 6 million years ago (Haviland 1990; Hill, Ward, Deino, Curtis, and Drake 1992). The early hominids were not as large as modern humans, but they were more muscular. Early hominids walked erectly but did not have a highly developed or enlarged brain. Hominids used animal flesh as a food source rather than foraging for food in the forest. *Homo sapiens* evolved out of the early hominids between 60,000 and 2½ million years ago. The precise dating is difficult because anthropologists continue to discover fossil and skeletal evidence of early humans and each discovery sets the earliest date of the evolution of the human-type, or **homo,** species further back in time. In addition, anthropologists often disagree about what each new discovery means, especially because they are working with only fragments of body parts. Sometimes, anthropologists question the scientific techniques used to date the new fossils.

Theories of Family Origin

There are a number of theories about the origins of the family. The biblical story of creation is one explanation. In the Bible, the first family was made up of Adam and Eve and their children. Early social scientists proposed evolutionary models of the origins of the family (Bachofen 1861; Briffault 1932; Engels 1884, 1962; Lang 1903; McLennan 1896; Maine 1885; Morgan 1878; Westermarck 1921) that speculated about a series of evolutionary steps through which the family must have passed until it evolved into its highest, modern form. The common thread in the various theories was that the family evolved from a primitive form in conjunction with human civilization's evolution into its "highest" modern form (Lee 1982).

More recent discussions of the origin of the family consist of two major competing theories: One argues that the earliest humans lived in conditions of "original promiscuity," and the other argues that the family is a universal institution formed by all humans. There are, of course, no hard data that can be used to answer this question—writing and measuring time were not developed until long after the human species evolved. The question is answered using speculation, fossil records left behind by our ancestors, and studies of nonhuman primates as well as current hunter and gatherer societies like the !Kung San.

Original Promiscuity

Nineteenth-century scholars of the family presumed that the earliest humans lived in a state of "original promiscuity," where there were no social regulations placed on sexual relations (Bachofen 1861; Morgan 1878). The earliest men and women had no permanent relationships, and no institutionalized methods or norms were developed to sanction or maintain permanent relationships. Love did not exist, and early humans were thought not to have enduring relationships between the sexes. Because there were no permanent relationships, the social concept of paternity did not exist, nor did the social role of "father." Thus the theory of original promiscuity proposed that the earliest form of family was the "pair bond" between mother and child.

The major assumption of the theory of original promiscuity was that social rules concerning sexual relationships either did not exist or were relaxed enough to allow completely promiscuous sexual relationships. This means that there were also no rules about an appropriate age at which to begin sexual relations, nor were there rules regarding permissible sex partners.

The original promiscuity theory of early humans is both a product of the times when the authors were writing and symbolic of a linear way of thinking about families that has its beginning point with primitive and promiscuous behavior and its end point with the developed, modern, and socially regulated family (Lee 1982).

The Original Family

Kathleen Gough (1971) begins her examination of the origins of the family with the qualification that no one really knows for sure when and how the family first evolved.[1] Fossil evidence suggests that the family originated between 2 million and 100,000 years ago. Although most anthropologists and sociologists argue that the use of language is the accepted criteria of humanness, it is not clear whether the family developed before or after the development of language.

Gough uses three sources of information and data to develop her theory of the origin of the family. First, she draws on studies of the social and physical lives of our evolutionary ancestors, nonhuman primates, especially New and Old World monkeys and the great apes. Second, she examines the physical and fossil record of tools and homesites of prehistoric humans. Last, she draws from modern studies of hunters and gatherers.

One major characteristic that all primates share, human and nonhuman alike, is that their offspring are born relatively helpless. The erect posture of primates—human and nonhuman— requires a pelvic structure that produces a relatively narrow birth canal. For the newborn to pass through the birth canal, the skull and brain cannot develop fully prior to birth. Newborns and infants suckle for months, need protection for long periods of time after they are weaned, and have a longer childhood period than other species. A second major characteristic of primates is that monkeys, apes, and humans can mate during all months of the year, not just during one fertility period.

Nonhuman primates are found to have sexual bonds and restrictions as well as rudimentary "incest" prohibitions. Among gibbons, single males and females live together as couples with their young. Young juveniles are expelled from the living place by the same-sex parent and find a mate elsewhere. This

One of the major characteristics of human and nonhuman primates is that their infants are born relatively helpless.

pattern undermines the theory of original promiscuity among humans, for if all monkeys are not promiscuous, then it is unlikely that humans began their existence promiscuous.

Although evidence of families can be found in some prehuman species, the family, according to Gough (1971), is not found totally in any prehuman species. The family became desirable in humans because of the need for prolonged child care and the need for hunting with weapons over large terrains. Gough explains that hunting became an important form of subsistence for early humans when indigestible grasses spread over the open savannahs of Africa. Hunters had to range several miles each day to find food. However, given that human offspring were dependent and required nursing, nursing women could hunt only small game close to home. This produced a division of labor on which the human family was founded.

ARE THERE FAMILY UNIVERSALS?

Kathleen Gough and other social scientists believe that some kind of family exists in all known human societies, although the possibility exists that some prehistoric human groups did not have a family. In addition, even if the family is a universal social institution, clearly everyone in every society does not live in a family (Lee 1982).

Kathleen Gough (1971) approaches the issue of universals without focusing on functions. She argues that there are four universals regarding families across cultures and over time:

1. Rules or incest taboos exist that forbid sexual relations and marriage between close relatives.

2. Men and women in a family cooperate though a division of labor.

3. Marriage exists as a socially durable social institution, although not necessarily a lifelong relationship between individual men and women.

4. Men in general have higher social status and authority over the women of their families.

Anthropologist George Murdock (1949) examined the records of 250 societies and concluded that the nuclear family is a universal in all human social groupings. Moreover, he argued that there are four *universal* functions of the nuclear family: sexual, reproductive, educational, and economic. Although families in some societies have more than these four functions, these were seen as the basic family functions across all known societies. Families regulate sex, produce offspring, educate and socialize the offspring, and have basic economic functions, including a division of labor between men and women.

Social scientists have found exceptions to Murdock's four basic family functions. For example, Kathleen Gough (1959) cites research on the Nayar of South India. Nayar adults of both sexes continue to live in their mother's households for their entire lives. Married couples do not live together. Even though there is a ritualistic marriage ceremony for a man and a woman conducted near the time of puberty, the husband has no official or meaningful role in the life of the woman or her children. Thus the nuclear family has neither an educational function nor a division of labor and economic function (Reiss 1965). A more modern exception is the Israeli kibbutz system. The Israeli kibbutzim are small, self-contained collectives. In some kibbutzim (not all), children do not live with their parents but live collectively. At about four days of age the children are placed in a "Children's House" where they are fed, clothed, housed, and educated. Children and parents visit after work and on Saturdays, but the parents and family do not have an educational function in the lives of their children. Also, at least in ideology, there is no division of labor by sex.

There has been fairly spirited debate about whether Murdock was correct in concluding that there are four universal functions performed by families. On the one hand, social scientists supporting Murdock have argued that the societies cited as exceptions are not exceptions and that there are different ways to interpret the data on those societies. On the other hand, some cogent criticisms have been leveled at the four universals. Sociologist Ira Reiss (1965) argues that there is at least one society in the world, the Nayar of India, in which sexual gratification, reproduction, and economic cooperation is not tied to any kind of family relationship (see Box 3-1). Reiss also points to the kibbutz as an example of a society where education/socialization is not a function of the family. Reiss, however, does not totally overthrow the notion of universal family functions. He argues that the family institution is a small kinship-structured group with the key function of **nurturant socialization**

BOX 3-1: THE GLOBAL VIEW

The Nayar

The Nayar of South India are a culture often alluded to in discussions of family organization, structure, and function because they appear to be an exception to many of the postulated "universals" of family function and because their form of family organization is so different from the modern Western family's. Kathleen Gough (1959) carried out extensive research on the Nayar. A summary of her findings follows.

The Nayar are a matrilineal and matrifocal society. Nayar girls between the ages of 7 and 12 are "married" to men (boys) of approxi-

mately the same age. The ritual marriage ceremony includes four days of celebration, during which the first sexual intercourse between the bride and groom is permitted. After the first sexual intercourse, the groom leaves the bride's home and has no further obligation to her. The bride's only obligation to her husband is at the time of his death: The bride and all her children (by whatever father) must observe a death ritual for the husband. Bridegrooms have no formal obligations to their brides after the ritual marriage, although they can have sexual inter-

of the newborn. Nurturant socialization is the giving of emotional support and response to the child, predominantly by the mother and father, during the early years of life. Stated this way, Reiss argues that this function is provided by kinship-structured families in all societies, even those cited as exceptions to Murdock's four universal functions.

A second question that arises in the study of the family over time and across cultures is whether there are other universals associated with family life and the family as a social institution. The question of universal family functions is more theoretically relevant than the one about whether the family is universal because it deals with the question about social order and how the existence of the family relates to the existence and persistence of society (Lee 1982).

The matter of family universals is far from settled. Some social scientists still attempt to point to exceptions to the postulated universals, others debate the issue in theoretical or conceptual terms. The question about family universals no longer provokes the same heated debate as it did in the 1950s and 1960s, in part because of the decline in usage of the structural-functional theoretical framework and the increase in the use of other frameworks such as conflict theory, exchange theory, and the feminist perspective (see Chapter 2), which was the theoretical underpinning of the question about family universals. However, the question is still useful heuristically, if only to provoke thought about families in other times and other places.

course when their "wives" reach puberty. However, husbands who want sexual access to their brides have no priority over other men in the group.

Nayar women are allowed to have one or more husbands in addition to their "ritual" husband. Some Nayar women have six or seven husbands. If she becomes pregnant, a Nayar woman designates one husband to be the parent of the child. There was no limit on the number of wives a Nayar man might visit. Husbands visit their wives after supper at night and leave before breakfast the next day. The visiting husband leaves his weapons at the door of his wife's room. If other husbands arrive, they are free to sleep on the veranda of the woman's house.

Men often provide their wives with gifts of loincloths or skirts, but in no way are husbands responsible for providing their wives and children with food and support. Women receive food and support from their matrilineal group.

The union between a man and a woman can be terminated at any time without the need of a formal ritual or divorce decree.

The Nayar marriage system seems to have evolved as a result of the fact that Nayar men are often employed as mercenary troops and often absent from their villages. Their absences mean that they cannot be depended on for continued support and protection. The land the Nayar women work is passed from mothers to female children.

VARIATIONS IN FAMILY ORGANIZATION

Although marriage, family, and kinship appear to exist as social arrangements in most, if not all, known human societies, the exact nature of the arrangement varies over time and across societies. Societies have different ideal types regarding the best, or most appropriate, marital arrangement that should exist. This section examines the variations in family organizations along the following dimensions: (1) forms of marriage (number of spouses), (2) types of household structures, (3) rules of descent and inheritance, (4) rules of residence, and (5) authority patterns.

Forms of Marriage

Marriage, for Americans, means one wife or one husband at a time, or **monogamy.** We often think that this is the normal and most widespread form of marriage in the world. According to anthropologists, monogamy is the ideal or preferred form of marriage in only 17% to 25% of the world's societies (Murdock 1949, 1957). Some monogamous societies are modern, technological societies like our own, but monogamy is also the preferred form of marriage in other societies as well. The !Kung San of Africa and the Eskimos are hunting and gathering societies that have a norm of monogamous marriage.

In 75% to 80% of the world's societies (Murdock 1949, 1957), the preferred form of marriage is **polygyny,** or marriage involving a man having more than one wife. Polygyny is a form of **polygamy,** the practice of a man or a woman having more than one spouse. Polygyny was practiced in ancient China. Having more than one wife was also part of the Judeo-Christian tradition. Such biblical figures as Jacob, David, and Solomon all had more than one wife. The Mormons of Utah practiced polygyny until 1890. Today, Islam, the second largest religion in the world, allows men to have up to four wives, although polygyny has been outlawed in some Islamic countries. Today, in societies where polygyny is permitted, most men have no more than one wife. Two factors play a role in this limitation: first, the sex ratio of men to women (unless war, disease, or infanticide has reduced the population of men), and second, most men cannot afford more than one wife. Thus polygyny is practiced by the more wealthy men in the society. When polygyny occurs, the typical form is for a man to marry sisters, or what anthropologists call **sororal polygyny.**

A rare form of marriage that has been found in world societies is **polyandry**—the marriage of one woman to two or more men. Anthropologists have found evidence of polyandry in only four societies: the Nayar of

Monogamy—one husband and one wife at a time—is the preferred form of marriage in the United States and most of the modern Western world.

South India, the Tibetans of the Himalayas, the Toda of South India, and the Marquesans of the eastern Polynesian islands. As with polygyny, when polyandry is practiced, the multiple spouses are typically siblings. The nature of the economy, or the subsistence pattern of the society, influences whether polyandry will occur and can be sustained. The four societies that practice polyandry are characterized by infertile soil and thus poor crop-growing conditions. Property is handed down intact from one generation to the next through the woman's relatives, or **matrilineally** (see below for definition and discussion). The poverty of such agriculturally poor societies probably explains why multiple husbands are required to support a single women and her children. Polyandry, like any form of polygamy, requires an unbalanced sex ratio if it is to be more than a limited form of marriage. As a means of controlling the size of the female population, female infanticide occurs among the Toda and the Tibetans.

The rarest form of marriage is **group marriage,** which involves two or more men married to two or more women at the same time. George Murdock (1949, 1957) reported that group marriage never appears as a cultural norm. There are, however, societies that practice group marriage, even if it is not the ideal form of marriage in the society. Examples are the Marquesans and the Toda, who view polyandrous marriage as a cultural ideal but also engage in group marriage. This seems to occur if the wife is infertile and a second wife joins the marriage so that there will be children from the marriage. There is some debate as to whether even this practice constitutes group marriage (Linton 1936); thus the general view among anthropologists is that group marriage exists rarely, if at all, in the world's societies.

A look at contemporary marriage patterns in the United States yields another possible form of marriage: **serial monogamy.** Anthropologist Margaret Mead (1970) defined serial monogamy as one exclusive, legally sanctioned, but relatively short-lived marriage after another. Although Americans consider monogamy the most appropriate form of marriage, the high divorce rate in the United States as well as the likelihood that those who divorce will remarry (Glick 1988; see also Chapter 13) means that, even though Americans have one spouse at a time, they may have more than one spouse over their lifetime.

| Household Structures | Once a marriage is formed, the next major structural variation are the household structures that are formed. The conventional view of the historical family is that the dominant household structure was the **extended family,** in which three or more generations live in a single residence. The extended family is the so-called classical family that preceded industrialization (see Chapter 4). Alternatively, the classical image of the modern family is the **nuclear family,** which consists of a husband, wife, and their dependent children living in a home or residence of their own. The nuclear family is the idealized "golden family" of the 1950s in the United States (see Chapter 4). These are only two of the possible structures that marriages have taken over time and across cultures. |

The Classical Extended Family

The extended family consists of at least three generations who live in a single household or compound. Typically, in *patriarchal,* or male-dominated societies (see the following section on authority patterns), the eldest male grandfather is considered the family head and is the family decision maker.

The Nuclear Family

Sociologist Meyer Nimkoff (1965) stated that the smallest family unit usually consists of a father, mother, and their offspring living in a single household. Thus the fact that this is considered the smallest form of family household led social scientists to label the form "nuclear." Some observers of the nuclear family, especially the modern form of the nuclear family, see it as isolated from

The smallest form of a nuclear family is a parent and a child—single-parent-father families are much less common than single-parent-mother families.

relatives and other family units (Parsons 1949). Sociologist William Goode (1963), believing that nuclear residence patterns do not mean that nuclear families are cut off from or isolated from their relatives and kin, chose to use the term *conjugal* family for the same residence pattern. Goode describes a number of characteristics of the conjugal family system:

1. Extended family pattern becomes rare.
2. A relatively free choice of a spouse is possible based on love, and an independent household is set up.
3. Dowry and bride price payments disappear and marriage becomes less of an economic arrangement between families.
4. Marriages between kin become less common.
5. Authority of the parent over the child and of the husband over the wife diminishes.
6. Equality between the sexes is greater.

Nimkoff's (1965) definition of a nuclear family clearly implies that it requires a father and a mother and is irreducible. If the nuclear family must include both parents and is irreducible, what about single-parent families? Single-parent families make up one fourth of all households in the United States today (see Figure 3-1; U.S. Bureau of the Census 1992). In earlier times and in other cultures, death of a spouse also lead to single-parent households. According to Nimkoff's definition, these would be considered households but not families. However, it might be best to broaden Nimkoff's definition, as we did in Chapter 1, and state that the smallest form of nuclear family is a couple or a parent and their offspring. Couples without children and single parents are indeed families and not merely households.

Modified Extended Family

The term **modified extended family** was developed by Eugene Litwak (1960) to define those families that have a nuclear structure, may live in geographically dispersed locations, but still maintain close ties and are united by an ongoing network of interaction and aid and assistance. Litwak developed this term as a reaction against the characterization of the modern family as isolated-nuclear. Modern families, he found, may live miles apart but maintain a close bond through frequent contact, telephone calls, visits, and providing aid and support across families and generations.

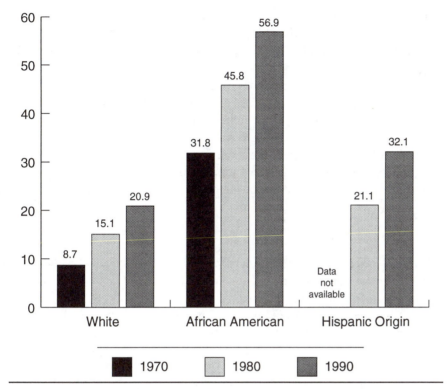

Figure 3-1
Percentage of
Children Under 18
Years of Age Living
in a Single-Parent
Household, 1970,
1980, 1992

SOURCE: U.S. Bureau of the Census. 1992. Current Population Reports, Series P-20, No. 468, *Marital Status and Living Arrangements: March, 1992,* page xii, table G. Government Printing Office, Washington, DC.

The Joint Family

The **joint family** is a form of extended family arrangement that has occurred in traditional Indian families as well as in other societies (Nimkoff 1965). The joint family is usually limited to three generations and consists of two or more brothers and their wives, with their children and unmarried sisters, living in one household, usually a compound of buildings. The oldest son assumes the leadership and decision-making position in the family when the father either dies or becomes disabled. Joint families pool their economic resources and have meals together in a common eating room.

The Stem Family

Stem families are a type of extended family that has been found in Japan and in rural Ireland. The stem family consists of at least two generations living in a single residence. For example, a mother and father live in the same household with a married son, his wife, and children. The stem family differs from a classical extended family in that the mother and father choose to live with only one son. In the classic extended family, all the children of the mother and father would live together, as would all the grandchildren. Stem families do not pool or share all economic resources. The economic resources, typically the family land, belong to only one son. The stem family system arises as a result of the combination of limited family land holdings and many sons. Because the family land cannot support all the sons, the father selects one son to inherit the family land and that son starts a "stem" of the family tree. Other sons may move to cities and start a "stem" of the family in another location.

Rules of Descent and Inheritance

All human societies provide individual members with a set of guidelines as to where he or she stands in terms of relatives, and all societies provide rules for the handling of family assets, resources, and property. Inheritance systems both define kinship and set rules for how the ownership and control of property will be managed in the society.

BOX 3-2: THE FAMILY OVER TIME

Two Views of Family Change

The conventional view of social change and modernization postulates that the nuclear family is the consequence of thousands of years of social change and development. Sociologist William Goode (1963) analyzed the development of family forms in his book *World Revolution and Family Patterns*. Goode proposed that as world societies moved toward modernization, industrialization, and urbanization the diverse family forms and patterns in traditional societies (polygyny, polyandry, matrilineal descent, patrilineal descent, extended family, stem family, joint family, etc.) all move toward a convergence in what Goode called the *conjugal family*. The conjugal family is one end of the continuum of family types, and the large extended family is at the opposite end.

An alternative view of family change is offered by Robert Winch and Rae Blumberg (1953), who proposed a curvilinear model of family change (see Figure 3-2) in place of Goode's linear convergence model. Winch and Blumberg's examination of the evidence on family change indicated that independent families, consisting of the husband-father, wife-mother, and child-sibling occur not only in times of urbanization and industrialization but among simple subsistence conditions as well.

Extended families are found mainly in the middle of the scale of technological development—mostly among agricultural societies where there is a reliable food supply, little geographic mobility, and a demand for the family as a unit of labor.

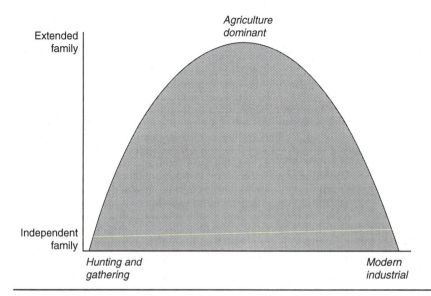

Extended
family

Agriculture
dominant

Independent
family

Hunting and
gathering

Modern
industrial

Figure 3-2 Winch
and Blumberg's
Model of Family
Change

SOURCE: "Societal Complexity and Familial Organizations" by Robert F. Winch and Rae
Lesser Blumberg in *Selected Studies in Marriage and Family,* edited by Robert F. Winch and
Louis Wolfe Goodman, 1953, New York: Holt, Rinehart & Winston. Copyright © 1953
by Holt, Rinehart & Winston. Adapted by permission.

Each individual descends from two separate bloodlines—the mother's and
the father's. Individuals can trace their lineage through either parent or
through both. Some societies have **unilineal** lineage systems. In unilineal
systems, names, authority, and property are traced through one line, usually
that of the father. Such a system of lineage and inheritance is called **patrilineal.**
Patrilineal systems are the most common across societies. In these systems, a
women who marries would take her husband's name. The relationship of
the couple's children to the wife's family is either downplayed or ignored.
George Murdock's (1949) examination of 250 societies found patrilineal
decent and inheritance in 42% of the world's societies. Most of the societies
in India, Asia, and Africa are patrilineal.

Matrilineal descent is a unilineal system in which lineage and inheritance
is traced through the mother's family. Because a child's status and descent is
a function of the mother in matrilineal societies, who the father is is relatively
unimportant in these societies. Thus marriage is of lesser consequence because
there need not be a formal determination of the role of husband/father-to-be.
Male children tend to be tied to their mother's brother (their uncle) as opposed to their genetic father. Less than 10% of the 250 societies surveyed by

Murdock were matrilineal. The Nayar are a matrilineal society as are the Fanti of West Africa.

Bilateral descent is the second most common form of descent and inheritance, making up 30% of the societies studied by Murdock. In bilateral descent societies, children trace their lineage through both genetic parents. This is the form of inheritance and descent found in the United States. The only deviation from complete bilateral descent is that women in the United States typically take their husband's name when they marry and the children also take the father's name. However, in the past two decades, and especially among well-educated women who delay marriage until after they have begun their careers, women are increasingly retaining their own names when they marry. In many cases, wives or both the husband and the wife use both names and hyphenate their last names. Children in these marriages receive hyphenated last names representing the last names of both mother and father.

The least common descent pattern found is **double descent**. Double descent means that at birth a child is assigned two lines of descent: the mother's matrilineal group and the father's patrilineal group. The other two lineages—mother's patrilineal and father's matrilineal—are disregarded for purposes of inheritance and family lineage. The pattern of double descent is found in 7% of the societies surveyed by Murdock.

Rules of Residence	All human societies have developed rules regarding where a newly formed family will live. Because husbands and wives come from different families and are typically expected to share a residence when they marry, societies develop norms regarding where the newlyweds will live. Not surprisingly, rules about where the newly married couple will live are closely tied to the rules of descent and inheritance in a society.

Historically, the most common residence pattern is **patrilocal**. Patrilocal societies require the newly married bride to live with her groom and his parents. **Matrilocal** societies require the groom to live with his bride and her parents. **Bilocal** residence rules allow the couple to choose which set of parents with whom to live. In **neolocal** societies, such as the United States, the married couple establishes a home of their own, apart from both sets of parents.

Because male children in matrilineal societies often establish close relationships with their mother's brother, some of these societies have an **avuncolocal** residence rule, whereby a boy returns to his mother's brother's village (the village in which his mother was born) either at puberty or at the time of his marriage.

Theoretically, there are three types of authority patterns found in the world's societies: **patriarchy,** in which the male has the greatest power; **matriarchy,** in which the female has the greatest power; and **egalitarian,** in which men and women share power. There has been considerable debate as to whether matriarchal societies exist or have ever existed (Rosaldo and Lamphere 1974). For example, research carried out by Margaret Mead (1935) on several tribes in New Guinea seems to suggest that women are the decision makers and leaders in some societies. On the other hand, Kathleen Gough (1971) states that, although there are matrilineal societies, there are no true matriarchal societies in current existence or known about in the literature.

Authority
Patterns

THE HUNTING AND GATHERING FAMILY

As noted earlier in this chapter, 90% to 99% of human history has been spent entirely in hunting and gathering societies. Compared to this, the 200 years in which industrial societies have existed is a relatively short period of time (Rossi 1978). Alice Rossi (1978), who uses a biosocial perspective (see Box 3-3) to examine the family, comments that Western human beings living in a technological world are still genetically equipped with ancient mammalian primate heritage that evolved through adaptations to the conditions of hunter and gatherer societies. Thus, although we now live in a modern, industrial, technological, and urban world, our genetic heritage adapted to fit into a hunter-gatherer society.

In hunting and gathering societies, men primarily hunted game and fish, and women primarily gathered food supplies from wild plants and roots. Hunters used bows, arrows, spears, knives, poisons, nets, axes, and clubs to kill their prey. Gatherers used sticks, knives, and axes to dig and created containers to carry the plants and roots home.

Hunting and gathering societies lived on all continents. The Bushman of southern Africa, the Eskimos, the Apache Indians of the Southeast United States, Pygmies, Australian Aborigines, Siberian hunters, and Amazonian hunters are recent examples of hunting and gathering societies (Murdock 1968) (see Figure 3-3).

Hunters and gatherers generally lived in small bands of between 20 and 200, with the majority of the bands having about 50 members (Gough 1971). Historically, hunters and gatherers lived in simple shelters, had simple clothing, and lived on a subsistence diet. Food was gathered to eat, not to be traded or sold. Food was generally shared with all those in the band or camp. Because

Figure 3-3
Distribution of
Recent Hunters
and Gatherers

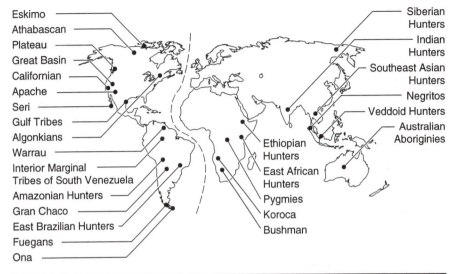

Eskimo
Athabascan
Plateau
Great Basin
Californian
Apache
Seri
Gulf Tribes
Algonkians
Warrau
Interior Marginal
Tribes of South Venezuela
Amazonian Hunters
Gran Chaco
East Brazilian Hunters
Fuegans
Ona

Siberian
Hunters
Indian
Hunters
Southeast Asian
Hunters
Negritos
Veddoid Hunters
Australian
Aboriginies
Ethiopian
Hunters
East African
Hunters
Pygmies
Koroca
Bushman

SOURCE: *Man the Hunter* (p. 14) edited by Richard B. Lee and Irven De Vore, 1968, Chicago: Aldine. Copyright © 1968 by the Wenner-Gren Foundation for Anthropological Research, Inc. Adapted by permission.

weather and climate changes influenced both game and plant supplies, hunters and gatherers had to be flexible and able to move to find new sources of plant and animal foods. Hunter and gatherer societies are generally classified as having no social classes and little inequality. There is no organized government or state in hunter-gatherer societies (Gough 1971).

BOX 3-3: THINKING ABOUT FAMILIES

A Biosocial Perspective on Families and Parents

Sociologist Alice Rossi (1978) is one of the most articulate spokespersons for a new theoretical model of family life and parent-offspring behavior. The model is called a "biosocial perspective." Rossi comments that Western human beings living in a technological world are still genetically equipped with ancient mammalian primate heritage that evolved through adaptations to the conditions of hunter-gatherer societies. Thus, although we now live in a modern, industrial, technological, and urban world, our genetic heritage adapted to fit into a hunter-gatherer society. Rossi criticizes the older sociological, structural functional approach to families that accepted as innate attributes and constant features of all family systems a particular division of labor between men and women. Rossi also criticizes the newer, feminist, Marxist approach that emphasizes an egalitarian ideology, denies any innate sex differences,

Families are extremely important to hunters and gatherers because collective work is required for obtaining sufficient food to support individuals and the band (O'Kelly and Carney 1986). Nearly everyone in hunter-gatherer societies marries, and marriages are arranged rather than formed by love, affection, or attraction. In addition, hunters and gatherers tend to be monogamous or serially monogamous. As Winch and Blumberg (1953) observed (see Box 3-2), hunter and gatherer families were generally nuclear families and were small. The number of children was regulated both by taboos that prohibited sexual intercourse after childbirth and by long lactation, or nursing, which lasted until the children were four or five years old. Lactation tends to inhibit ovulation, which enabled hunters and gatherers to space their children without the aid of birth control technology.

Marriage Patterns

Descent was often bilateral. Bilateral descent created a wide kinship system that was functional for sharing food. Residence was bilocal, which enhanced the society's flexibility.

Gender relationships in hunting and gathering societies tend to be egalitarian. However, there is a distinctive division of labor. There are female activities and male activities—females gather and males hunt. Among the !Kung, young girls learn to gather by accompanying their mothers when their mothers forage for food. Boys learn about hunting by listening to their fathers talk about hunting for game and animals. Although girls begin to gather with their mothers at relatively young ages, boys are older when they join hunting parties.

Gender and the Division of Labor

and assumes that a "unisex" socialization pattern will produce men and women who are free of traditional, culturally induced sex differences.

The older, traditional model and the newer egalitarian model ignore the central biological fact of human continuity through reproduction and child rearing. Rossi argues that much sociological research on the family ignores some fundamental human characteristics that are rooted in our biological heritage. A biosocial perspective does not argue that there is genetic determination of what men do compared to women; rather, it suggests that biological contributions shape what is learned and that there are differences in the ease with which the sexes can learn different things.

The overwhelming majority of women, Rossi notes, cradle their infants in their left arms, regardless of whether they are right- or left-handed. Infants held in the left arm can hear and be soothed by the maternal heartbeat. Women also tend to be better than men at hearing high-pitched sounds. Rossi also explains that films and videos of women and babies reveal common sequences of approaches and interactions across cultures.

Thus the biosocial perspective brings biology and human evolution into the study of families, parent and offspring behavior, and examinations of family development over time.

The Amazon Indians are a modern example of a hunting and gathering society.
SOURCE: Copyright © 1983 by Stock, Boston, Inc. Used by permission.

Anthropologist Marjorie Shostak (1981) provides a detailed description of the life of the !Kung women in her book *Nisa: The Life and Words of a !Kung Woman.* Nisa is a member of one of the last remaining traditional hunter-gatherer societies—the *Zhun/twasi,* or "the real people," who live in isolated areas of Botswana, Angola, and Namibia. !Kung women, like Nisa, contribute the majority (from 60% to 80% in actual weight) of the food consumed by the band. !Kung women spend an average of two days a week in the search for plant foods. They gather from among 105 species of wild plant foods, including nuts, beans, bulbs and roots, leafy greens, tree resin, berries, and an assortment of wild fruits and vegetables. They collect honey from beehives and occasionally catch small game, tortoises, snakes, caterpillars, insects, and birds' eggs. The main subsistence of the !Kung is a nut, the mongongo, which makes up about half the weight of vegetables consumed.

Groups of three to five women usually leave early in the morning and head for an agreed-on area. They gather food in a leisurely pace and return to their camps in mid to late afternoon. Most of the food collected is eaten in the next two days.

Men's principal contribution to the band is meat. Meat is highly valued, not because it makes up a substantial portion of the band's food but because it is so unpredictable. When meat is brought to the village it is the cause of great celebration.

Men hunt about three days each week. They too leave early in the morning, either alone or in pairs. They may return at sunset or stay away overnight, as hunting requires travel over distances of some miles.

Child Rearing

Parent-child relationships in hunter-gatherer societies are relaxed, and children are raised to be cooperative, generous, and peaceful. Emphasis is also placed on children becoming self-reliant and independent. Children are socialized for their later adult roles through play. Boys and girls play "house" as well as playing at hunting. The boys may practice catching animals with nets while the girls chase small game and beat at leaves and bushes with small sticks (Turnbull 1961).

Males as well as females are involved in child rearing, although women are generally more responsible for the children than are men. Unlike modern societies where women tend to raise children in relative isolation, hunter-gatherer women raise their children in the company of other women and members of the band. In addition, older children assume responsibility for the care of the younger children.

As noted in the beginning of this chapter, !Kung mothers have much more physical contact with their children than do modern mothers in industrialized countries. Children are nursed on demand, are rarely allowed to cry, and are held more than modern children (Konner 1976).

FROM HUNTERS AND GATHERERS TO INDUSTRIAL SOCIETIES

Horticultural, pastoral, and agrarian societies developed between the times of the hunters and gatherers and the modern, industrial society. **Horticultural societies** evolved beyond simple foraging for wild plant life and developed simple forms of plant cultivation, such as **slash and burn cultivation.** Slash and burn cultivation felled trees, cut underbrush, and burned the plant growth. The ashes from the burning provided fertilizer for the gardens that were planted. Gardens were relatively simple and were cultivated using simple digging sticks.

Pastoral societies rely on the herding of livestock, such as cattle, camels, and sheep. Pastoral societies are somewhat nomadic and move to obtain water and food for their animals.

Agrarian societies obtain most of their food supplies by farming and agriculture. Agriculture meant a commitment to a single area of land and cultivation using animals to pull ploughs or cultivators. More sophisticated methods of fertilization than simple burning were also developed. Agriculture is still the major form of subsistence for the majority of world societies.

Each subsistence form influenced the social organization of the society and the family. Horticultural societies were technologically more advanced than hunters and gatherers, and their societies were larger, more permanent, and more complex. Agricultural societies became more complex and cities developed. The need for labor to cultivate land, to plant, and to gather crops enhanced the development of the extended family. A sharper division of labor between the sexes developed in the more complex subsistence societies. Females became more involved in child rearing and males more responsible for food production.

SUMMING UP

We tend to think of the modern American family as the most advanced form of family organization in the world. Industrialization, urbanization, and modernization were forces that influenced the development of the form and function of the modern American family. The nuclear, monogamous, patriarchal family can also be found in most other modern industrialized and urbanized societies of the world.

An examination of family structure and form across cultures and over time indicates that there is, and has been, great variety in the social organization of families. For most of human history, individuals hunted and gathered for their main sources of food. They lived in small bands and in small, nuclear, monogamous families. Changes in subsistence patterns were associated with changes in family organization. Social scientists often debate which came first, the change in subsistence or the change in family organization. One side argues that families adapted to the society's subsistence needs. The other side argues that changes in family organizations created a fertile environment for changes in subsistence. Irrespective of which side of the argument has the most support—and neither side has totally conclusive evidence to support its theory—it is clear that family organization is closely tied to how a society produces and obtains its food.

Families appear to be a cultural universal—all known societies appear to have had some form of family. The family existed among the first human groups because of the need for prolonged child care and the need for hunting with weapons over large terrains.

Family scholars have long debated whether there are family universals that exist in all societies. Social scientists postulate that there are some universal functions of the family that regulate sex, reproduction, education, and the economy. Others propose that there are exceptions to each of these universals.

The preferred family organization and structure are polygynous marriage and extended family households, although monogamous marriages and nuclear household structures are the most common forms of family organization. No doubt the preference for polygamous marriage and extended families is because the most common form of subsistence pattern in the past 200 years has been agricultural. Agricultural societies require large families to produce sufficient food supplies to support the society. However, it is important to keep in mind that there are big differences in terms of the type of agricultural societies and these differences influence family organization and structure. The modified extended family structure characterizes contemporary family life, although again there are significant variations in family form in our own society.

Families also vary in terms of rules of descent and inheritance, rules of residence, and patterns of authority. One common feature that has existed across societies and over time is patriarchal family power. Irrespective of the social organization of the family, men tend to have the greatest amount of family power and the work that men do is accorded greater prestige than the work done by women. The extent of male authority and domination does vary both across societies and over time. Patriarchy is neither "natural" nor "inevitable."

Humans have spent 90% to 99% of human history in hunting and gathering societies. Marriages were arranged rather than formed by love, affection, or attraction. In addition, hunters and gatherers tended to be monogamous or serially monogamous. Gender relationships in hunting and gathering societies tended to be egalitarian. Both men and women were involved in child rearing.

Each subsistence form influenced the social organization of the society and the family. Family forms changed as subsistence patterns changed from hunting and gathering to horticulture to pastoral societies and finally to agricultural societies.

NOTE

1. Gough's (1959) analysis of the origins of the family drew on the work of Hockett and Ascher (1964).

REFERENCES

Bachofen, J. J. 1861. *Das Mutter-recht.* Basil: Benno Schwabe.

Briffault, Robert. 1931. *The Mothers.* New York: Macmillan.

Engels, Friedrich. 1884, 1962. "On the Origin of the Family, Private Property, and the State." In *Selected Works,* Vol. 3, by Karl Marx and Friedrich Engels. Moscow: Foreign Languages Publishing House.

Glick, Paul C. 1988. "The Role of Divorce in the Changing Family Structure: Trends and Variations." Pp. 3-34 in *Children of Divorce: Empirical Perspectives on Adjustment,* edited by Sharlene A. Wolchik and Paul Karoly. New York: Gardner Press.

Goode, William J. 1963. *World Revolution and Family Patterns.* New York: Free Press.

Gough, Kathleen E. 1959. "The Nayars and the Definition of Marriage." *Journal of the Royal Anthropological Institute* 89(1): 23-34.

———. 1971. "The Origin of the Family." *Journal of Marriage and the Family* 33(November):760-70.

Haviland, William A. 1990. *Cultural Anthropology.* 6th ed. New York: Holt, Rinehart & Winston.

Hill, Andrew, Steven Ward, Alan Deino, Garniss Curtis, and Robert Drake. 1992. "Earliest *Homo.*" *Nature* 355(February 20):719-22.

Hockett, Charles F. and Robert Ascher. 1964. "The Human Revolution." *Current Anthropology* 5(June):135-47.

Konner, Melvin. 1976. "Maternal Care, Infant Behavior, and Development Among the !Kung." Pp. 218-245 in *Kalahari Hunter-Gatherers: Studies of the !Kung San and Their Neighbors,* edited by Richard B. Lee and Irven Devore. Cambridge, MA: Harvard University Press.

Lang, Andrew. 1903. *Social Origins.* London: Longmans, Green.

Lee, Gary R. 1982. *Family Structure and Interaction: A Comparative Analysis.* 2nd ed. Minneapolis: University of Minnesota Press.

Lee, Richard B. and Irven Devore, eds. 1968. *Man the Hunter.* Chicago: Aldine.

Linton, Ralph. 1936. *The Study of Man.* New York: Appleton-Century-Crofts.

Litwak, Eugene. 1960. "Geographic Mobility and Extended Family Cohesion." *American Sociological Review* 25(June): 385-94.

Maine, Henry Summer. 1885. *Ancient Law.* 3rd ed. New York: Henry Holt.

McLennan, J. F. 1896. *Studies in Ancient History.* New York: Macmillan.

Mead, Margaret. 1935. *Sex and Temperament in Three Primitive Societies.* New York: Morrow.

———. 1970. *Culture and Commitment.* New York: Doubleday.

Morgan, Lewis Henry. 1878. *Ancient Society.* New York: Henry Holt.

Murdock, George P. 1949. *Social Structure.* New York: Free Press.

———. 1957. "World Ethnographic Sample." *American Anthropologist* 59(August):664-87.

———. 1968. "The Current Status of Hunting and Gathering Peoples." Pp. 13-20 in *Man the Hunter,* edited by Richard B. Lee and Irven Devore. Chicago: Aldine.

Nimkoff, Meyer F. 1965. *Comparative Family Systems.* Boston: Houghton Mifflin.

O'Kelly, Charlotte G. and Larry S. Carney. 1986. *Women and*

Men in Society. 2nd ed. Belmont, CA: Wadsworth.

Parsons, Talcott. 1949. "The Social Structure of the Family." Pp. 173-201 in *The Family: Its Function and Destiny,* edited by Ruth Nanda Anshen. New York: Harper.

Reiss, Ira L. 1965. "The Universality of the Family: A Conceptual Analysis." *Journal of Marriage and the Family* 27 (November):443-53.

Rosaldo, Michelle Zimbalist and Louise Lamphere. 1974. *Women, Culture and Society.*

Stanford, CA: Stanford University Press.

Rossi, Alice S. 1978. "A Biosocial Perspective on Parenting." Pp. 1-31 in *The Family,* edited by Alice S. Rossi, Jerome Kagan, and Tamara K. Hareven. New York: Norton.

Shostak, Marjorie. 1981. *Nisa: The Life and Words of a !Kung Woman.* New York: Random House.

Toffler, Alvin. 1970. *Future Shock.* New York: Random House.

Turnbull, Colin. 1961. *The Forest People.* New York: Simon & Schuster.

U.S. Bureau of the Census. 1992. *Statistical Abstracts of the United States.* Washington, DC: Government Printing Office.

Westermarck, Edward. 1921. *The History of Human Marriage.* 5th ed. London: Macmillan.

Winch, Robert F. and Rae Lesser Blumberg. 1953. "Societal Complexity and Familial Organization." Pp. 70-92 in *Selected Studies in Marriage and Family,* edited by Robert F. Winch and Louis Wolfe Goodman. New York: Holt, Rinehart & Winston.

CHAPTER 4

■■ Changing Family Organization in the United States

T he enduring image of the typical American family of old is described by William J. Goode (1963) as

a pretty picture of life down on grandma's farm. There are lots of happy children, and many kinfolk live together in a large rambling house. Everyone works hard. Most of the food to be eaten during the winter is grown, preserved, and stored on the farm. The family members repair their own equipment, and in general the household is economically self-sufficient. The family has many functions; it is the source of economic stability and religious, educational, and vocational training. Father is stern and reserved, and has the final decision on all important matters. Life is difficult, but harmonious because everyone knows his task and carries it out. All boys and girls marry, and marry young. Young people, especially the girls, are likely to be virginal at marriage and faithful afterward. Though the parents do not arrange their children's marriages, the elders do have the right to reject a suitor and have a strong hand in the final decision. After marriage, the couple lives harmoniously, either near the boy's parents or with them, for the couple is slated to inherit the farm. No one divorces. (p. 6).

This image of the American family from colonial times through the beginnings of the Industrial Revolution of the late 19th century is the historical benchmark against which many modern commentators measure change in the family and decry the decline and decay of the modern family. The image, however, is a stereotype, a myth. Goode calls it the "classical family of Western nostalgia."

The main components of the mythic historical family are that they were extended families, with three generations living under a single roof and maintaining the family farm. Families were thought to be more stable, better adjusted, and happier than modern families. This myth is perpetuated in many novels, movies, and television shows.

The reality of the historical family is quite different from the image of the "classical family of Western nostalgia." Goode (1963) explains that when we penetrate the mists of recent history we find few examples of the "classical" family. Few farms were self-sufficient, and few families lived together as large extended families under a single roof. The main reason was that people simply did not live long enough to survive their children's adulthood by many years. Families were extended, but they had boarders or lodgers in the home, not grandparents. Few families were three-generational extended families.

Historical records indicate that husbands deserted their wives, there were illegitimate children, and husbands abused their wives and parents abused their children (Gordon 1988). Historian John Demos (1974) debunks the myth of the "classical" family and says, pointedly, that there is no golden age of the family gleaming at us from far back in the historical past.

This chapter examines the changing organization of the family in the United States. The chapter provides a historical overview of American family structure and family life from the colonial family, through industrialization, to the modern, post-World War II family. Part of this analysis is a look at the major organizational changes in American families, including changes in the marriage rate, age at first marriage, birth rate, family size, divorce rate, employed women, and the implications of these changes for modern family life. The final section of the chapter looks at modern family organization.

A HISTORICAL PERSPECTIVE ON FAMILIES IN THE UNITED STATES

The most important correction that needs to be made regarding the vision of the family of the past is that there is no one monolithic family type (Cott 1979). Not only was there no "classical family of Western nostalgia," there was no one type of family in colonial America or thereafter. The geographic and ethnic diversity of the country led to a diversity of family structures and styles. Social change and social conditions in society had a profound influence on the family and social change in the family. Family form and family function was influenced by the nature of the economy, by disease and illness, and by the nature of religious beliefs in the community and region.

European Traditions That Shaped the Colonial Family

Family life in colonial America was shaped by the traditions of European family life and the ethnic and social makeup of the first colonists who arrived in America. The European family of the early Middle Ages (from about 400 to 1000 A.D.) was a nuclear family in residence. However, because the nuclear family was highly involved with its other kin in the community, functionally the family was more modified-extended than purely nuclear (Parish and Schwartz 1972). Stem family arrangements were also common in the early Middle Ages. Marriages were arranged and children began to work when they were as young as 7 years old (Beitscher 1976; Zaretsky 1976). The household of the early Middle Ages rarely had distinct rooms, such as a bedroom or living room. At bedtime, bedrolls or mattresses were laid out in the main room. There was no office to go to as we know it today, and so judges, merchants, bankers, and businessmen conducted their work in the same room of the house where everyone lived (Aries 1962; Laslett 1973). The early Middle Ages household had minimal privacy and a constant flow of family, kin, and community in and out of the home.

The later Middle Ages (1000 to 1500 A.D.) saw changes in household organization and family structure that would eventually have a strong influence on colonial families. The later Middle Ages family became more private and more separate from kin and community. The husband's dominance over the family and family life grew. The concept of romantic love also grew, and there was a decline in arranged marriages.

Colonial Families

The earliest settlers of the American colonies were from Great Britain and Holland. These colonists, who were from the lower social classes of Europe, brought with them their norms and values. For example, choice of a marital partner, not arranged marriage (as among the upper class), was the norm of the lower classes in Europe and was brought to the colonies (Smith 1976). Choice was accentuated because there was a shortage of women in the colonies and the emotional and practical needs for a spouse outweighed parental influence.

The colonial family was the basic economic unit of production in society. Family life and economic life were not separate. Families built their own homes, raised their own food, and made their own clothes (Demos 1974).

Families were the basic unit of production, but the form and structure that families took in colonial America depended on the type of economy and the region of the colony. Even in each colony there were periodic changes in the age of first marriage and the average number of children born in each family. The variation in family form and function in the colonies was strongly influenced by factors such as the regional economy and the rates of disease and death. The southern colonies developed a tobacco economy that required bringing in many indentured servants from Europe to raise and pick tobacco. Thus there were many more males in the southern colonies than in the north. Typhoid, malaria, and other diseases took a major toll on the southern colonists, thus greatly influencing the size and form of southern families.

Plymouth Colony and Massachusetts

Historians Philip Greven (1970), Kenneth Lockridge (1966, 1970), and John Demos (1970) provide a detailed look into the structure of family life in Plymouth Colony and the towns of Andover and Dedham, Massachusetts. These three historians used town records and reconstructed the makeup of the families in the three communities. The historical record reveals that the nuclear family was the main form of family structure. Extended families were uncommon. The average family had between four and six residents, larger than today's families but smaller than the stereotype of the large colonial family.

Marriages		Births			
Years	_Number_	_Years_	_Number_	_Births Per Marriage_
1650–1659	13	1655–1664	75	5.8
1660–1669	23	1665–1674	122	5.3
1670–1679	38	1675–1684	215	5.7

Table 4-1 Births per Marriage, 1650–1684

SOURCE: _Four Generations: Population, Land, and Family in Colonial Andover, Massachusetts_ (p. 23) by Philip J. Greven, Jr., 1972, Ithaca, NY: Cornell University Press. Copyright © 1972 by Cornell University Press. Adapted by permission.

Philip Greven (1972) estimated that between the years 1650 and 1684 there were between 5.3 and 5.8 births per marriage (see Table 4-1) compared to less than two per marriage today.

Households often included servants, boarders, and apprentices (Demos 1970). Greven (1972) describes the colonial family of Andover, Massachusetts as a "modified extended" form of family. Aging parents did not live in the same house as their adult son or sons but lived in the vicinity. Sons who expected to inherit the family land remained in the family residence, but the nuclear household was the norm in all other respects.

The average woman in the communities in the Northeast married in her late teens or early 20s. She had her first child within a year of marriage (Smith and Hindus 1975).

Greven (1972) found evidence of strong patriarchal control over family life—a vestige of latter Middle Age families in Europe. Greven noted that there was an unusually long life expectancy in Andover, probably because of the absence of malaria, typhoid, or other deadly diseases. Given the powerful value attached to family and community, fathers could wield considerable power. For example, a father who disapproved of his son's choice of a wife could delay turning his land over to his son and thus influence the mate selection.

Chesapeake Bay and Virginia

Three demographic factors molded family life in the Chesapeake Bay and Virginia colonies. First, these southern colonies were death traps for immigrants. Dangerous levels of typhoid fever, dysentery, and malaria produced high mortality rates in these colonies—malaria continued to be a risk until the end of the 1600s. Second, the population continued to be dominated by immigrants (due to the high mortality rates), and third, there was a severely imbalanced sex ratio, with many more men than women (Smith 1982). Parents died young, orphans and stepchildren abounded, and the society was dominated by young, single men who arrived in the colonies as indentured servants to help sustain the tobacco economy (Hawes and Hiner, 1985; Smith 1982). In 1625, in Virginia more than 60% of the couples had no surviving children (Hawes and Hiner 1985). Unstable family units were held together by widows. Sons, due to the early deaths of their fathers, gained autonomy and independence much earlier than their counterparts in New England. Kin networks in Maryland and Virginia remained small and undeveloped (Smith 1982).

Divorce

The popular image of the "classical family of Western nostalgia" is one of lifelong marriage ending with the death of one partner. Indeed, divorce was

---

BOX 4-1: THE FAMILY OVER TIME

Colonial Children and Child Rearing

Historian Philippe Aries (1962) examined children and child rearing in the Middle Ages. Aries asserted that parents in the Middle Ages had no awareness of the particular and distinct nature of childhood. Children were viewed as miniature adults and portrayed that way in their portraits (see also Chapter 8). Because childhood was not viewed as a distinctive stage, parents did not develop strategies for rearing their children.

John Demos (1970) claims that colonial society "barely recognized childhood as we know it today." Philip Greven (1970) however, finds the roots of current child-rearing practices, especially the use of corporal punishment, in the behavior of Puritan parents in the Massachusetts Bay Colony. Puritan parents viewed parental power as absolute and focused their energy on conquering their children's will. The means of conquest was strict physical punishment.

Regional differences introduced variations in family patterns. The high mortality rate in the Chesapeake colonies may have placed considerable emotional distance between parents and their children (Smith 1982). Parents did not devote themselves to their children and their children's welfare because so many children died in infancy.

Those children who survived infancy were viewed as economic resources by their families. Because colonial America was an agrarian society, many children worked at their parents' side, working on a farm. "Putting out" was the practice of sending children aged 10 or 11 away from home to learn a trade. There were two basic types of apprentice systems: (1) voluntary arrangements between parents and masters, and (2) compulsory arrangements where the town entered into a relationship with a master for orphaned or indigent children (Gordon 1978).

In the case of voluntary apprenticeships, parents often gave preference to their children's wishes about what type of work to do as well as their children's happiness. Apprenticeships often began for children as young as 7, although the typical age was between 10 and 14. The apprenticeship lasted until age 21 for a boy and 18 for a girl (Gordon 1978).

uncommon but not altogether absent from the life of colonial Americans. Attitudes toward divorce and the frequency of divorce varied in the colonies. The Puritans of the Massachusetts Bay Colony allowed divorce and administered divorce through civil councils, legislative bodies, or even the colonial governor. Arthur Calhoun (1945) reports on the slim available data on divorce in Massachusetts. There were 25 divorces granted between 1639 and 1692. Calhoun found no data for the years from 1692 to 1739. There were but three divorces between 1739 and 1760. The middle and southern colonies did not import the rebellion against the Church of England or a lenient view of divorce. Thus divorce was less common in the middle and southern colonies. Neither the church nor colonial councils or legislatures heard divorce petitions.

The Industrial Revolution, Immigration, and American Families

The Industrial Revolution and immigration were the two major social factors that influenced American families in the 19th and early 20th century. The Industrial Revolution began shortly after 1800 and was characterized by a shift from craft shops to a factory system of production. This change was made possible by harnessing new sources of energy—steam, coal, oil, and so on. Cities grew up around factories, and the United States became more urbanized. As a result of the shift from a craft shop economy to a factory economy, families were no longer the principal unit for production in the society. At the same time, as the country was becoming more industrialized and more urbanized, the nature of the population also began to change.

Prior to the Civil War, most of the immigrants to the United States were black slaves. After 1800, and especially after the Civil War, 38 million immigrants came from Europe. Immigration not only increased the population of the United States but also increased the ethnic and cultural diversity of the country. There were two waves of immigration. The first wave, from 1830 to 1890, consisted of immigrants who came mainly from western and northern Europe and arrived in the northern port cities of Boston and New York. The immigrants came from Ireland, Germany, the Scandinavian countries, and England. At the same time, Chinese immigrants were arriving in San Francisco. From 1890 to 1914—when World War I broke out in Europe—immigrants came mainly from eastern and southern Europe—Italy, Russia, Austria Hungary, Greece, and Poland. Japanese immigrants arrived in San Francisco and Hawaii. Immigrants brought with them family structures, values, and cultures, and added another dimension to family structural and functional diversity in the United States (Dyer 1979).

Immigration was one of the major social factors that influenced American families in the 19th and early 20th centuries. Immigrant families were often large and multigenerational.

Industrialization

Industrialization did not replace the extended family form with a nuclear family form—the nuclear family was already well established prior to 1800. Families remained as a unit of production (although not the primary unit), but instead of working at home or producing goods in the home, families, including children, were increasingly likely to work together in factories.

Families, however, did change and adapt to the industrialized society. The home was no longer the locale of work. More and more men left their homes to "go to work," as did women and children. The growth of factories as places of employment had a profound effect on parents', especially fathers', authority over their adolescent children. Factory jobs freed young adults from dependence on their families, as their ability to earn a living and support themselves was not dependent on working on or inheriting the family land or on serving as an apprentice and learning a craft. Cities also developed an infrastructure of housing and services—diners, restaurants, boarding houses, and so on—that allowed young adults to live apart from their families. Younger children were no longer economic assets after 1916, when child labor laws limited how much and where children could work.

As a consequence of industrialization and urbanization, households became smaller and more private. There were fewer strangers (boarders, servants, and apprentices) in households and fewer extended family members. The design of the home began to change as separate rooms for separate functions (e.g., dining rooms, living rooms, and bathrooms—with the advent of indoor plumbing) were incorporated in the typical household design (Hareven 1976; Laslett 1973). Affection became a significant part of the relationship between husbands and wives. At the same time, husbands and wives began to develop separate spheres of activities. Men were the primary wage earners, and women were the guardians, protectors, and nurturers of families and children. Although women, especially single women, had significant involvement in the industrial economy, the Industrial Revolution helped establish the sacred nature of the housewife role and the "good provider role."

Fertility declined and childhood became sentimentalized in the early decades of the 20th century (Hareven 1976). Childhood was now viewed as a separate stage of life, a stage that was worth recognizing, cherishing, extending, and protecting (Degler 1980; Zelizer 1985).

The trends described thus far that characterized the changing nature of families after industrialization were not monolithic. Not every family changed as a result of the Industrial Revolution. A great many families still were involved in craft enterprises. Nine in 10 families lived on farms and in small towns in 1800, and they did not all suddenly abandon these farms and towns for cities and factories. Some households continued to have lodgers, some had extended kin, and many moved from one type of family structure to another over the life course (Modell and Hareven 1973). Irrespective of the household structure, families generally continued to keep in close contact with their relatives and extended family (Hareven and Vinovskis 1978).

Family functions, such as education and job training, were gradually taken on by other institutions. The institution of the family began to become a specialist in procreation of children, child rearing, and consumption of material and economic goods and services (Hareven 1976).

THE EMERGENCE OF THE MODERN FAMILY: 1900 TO 1965

The turn of the century brought with it changes that led to the emergence of the modern American family. Modern families were smaller, older, and more

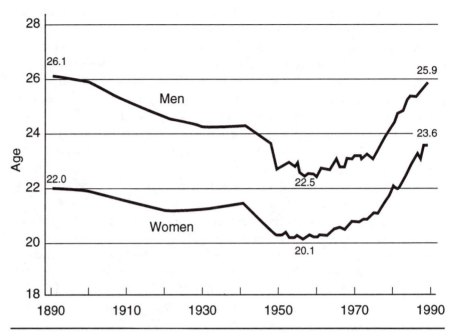

Figure 4-1
Median Age at
First Marriage, by
Sex, 1890–1988

SOURCE: Saluter (1989, p. 5), U.S. Bureau of the Census (1989 and earlier reports).

likely to end in divorce than were earlier families. The age at which men and women first entered into marriage began a steady decline in 1900, a decline that lasted for the first half of the century. When the century began, a man's median age when he first married was almost 26 (25.9 years) and for a woman nearly 22 (21.9 years—see Figure 4-1). By 1950, the median age for a man was about 23 (22.8 years) and for a woman about 20 (20.3 years). However, the trend reversed itself during the 1950s, and the median age at the time of first marriage began to increase, no doubt as a result of increased educational opportunities for both men and women and increased work opportunities for women (Cherlin 1990).

Families became smaller during the 20th century, continuing a trend that had begun during industrialization. The average woman born between 1901 and 1905 had 3.13 children in her lifetime, compared to 5.71 children for women born between 1846 and 1855 (Bane 1976). Women who were born between 1936 and 1940 had an even smaller number of children, an average of 3.06. Families became smaller not only because women had fewer children but because boarders and lodgers all but disappeared from the American household.

A third trend that marked the emergence of the modern family is the increase in marital disruption due to divorce. All marriages end, but the vast

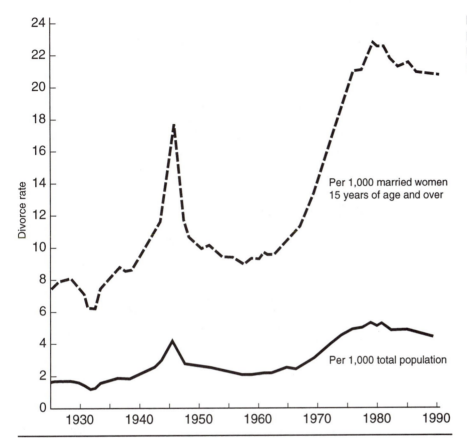

Figure 4-2
Divorce Rates:
United States,
1925–1988

Per 1,000 married women
15 years of age and over

Per 1,000 total population

SOURCE: National Center for Health Statistics (1989, p. 4, Table 1).

majority of marriages that ended in 1900 were due to the death of a spouse. Between 1900 and 1904, about 12% of marriages ended as a result of divorce (Glick and Norton 1979). During the first half of the century, two trends changed the normal way marriages ended. First, life expectancy increased, thus reducing the chances that a marriage would end early as the result of the death of a spouse. Second, the rate of divorce began to increase (see Figure 4-2 and Chapter 13).

As noted in the previous section, industrialization was the first major event in American history to have a profound and enduring impact on the shape of the American family. The second major event was World War II. The war made it necessary for hundreds of thousands of women to enter the labor force for both military and domestic production (Blumstein and Schwartz 1983). After the war ended in 1945, there was a brief attempt to defeminize the workplace, but many women remained on the job (see Chapter 11).

Figure 4-3 Total Fertility Rate and Number of Births, 1920–1989

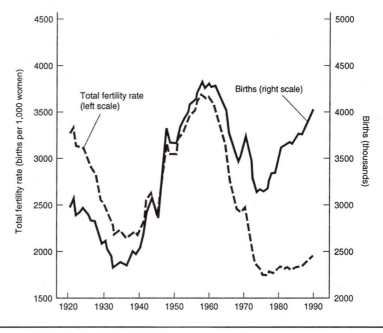

SOURCE: Saluter (1989), U.S. Bureau of the Census (1992, p. 65, Table 82).

The Fifties: The "Golden Age of the Family"

The 1950s are sentimentally thought of as the "Golden Age" of the American family. The form, structure, and supposed virtues of the '50s family were portrayed in television programs like *Father Knows Best, Leave It to Beaver, The Dick Van Dyke Show,* and *The Donna Reed Show.* As testimony to the enduring image of the 1950s family, each of these shows can still be viewed on television almost around the clock. In the 1950s, couples entered into marriage at the youngest age in this century. The baby boom, which began post-World War II, peaked in 1957 and concluded at the end of the decade. Figure 4-3 shows both the fertility rate, that is, the average number of children born to women of childbearing age, and the total number of births. Both the fertility rate and the number of births peaked in the mid 1950s. Fertility then fell precipitously during the 1960s and 1970s as the average woman had fewer than two children. However, because there were so many more women of childbearing age in the 1980s and 1990s (due to the baby boom) the total number of births remains high.

Even more important than the youth of the family and the baby boom, traditional gender roles were the hallmarks of the 1950s family. Beaver's mother and all the other television mothers were the family child rearers and nurturers. They were always home when school ended, dressed in an apron and ready to serve milk and cookies to their children. Fathers were the family breadwinners (although trivia experts still debate exactly what job Ozzie Nelson held on *The Adventures of Ozzie and Harriet*). Fidelity, chastity, and conventional family roles were the central values of the '50s families. Sociologist Andrew Cherlin (1990) notes that, although reliable information is limited, it appears that for the majority of women, and for many men, their first experience with sexual intercourse occurred with their future spouses, often only after the marriage began (see also May 1988). If a pregnancy occurred when a woman was single, the pregnancy likely led to what was referred to as a "shotgun" wedding. In the 1950s, more than 7 of 10 premaritally conceived pregnancies resulted in a wedding before the child was born (O'Connell and Moore 1980). Only 4% or 5% of babies were born out of wedlock in the 1950s.

The decade of the 1950s, however, was an exception or an aberration in the long-term trends and changes in the American family. At the end of the decade, the divorce rate began a rapid climb. The birth rate continued to decline, as it had for the entire century. Educational and occupational opportunities continued to liberate wives and mothers from their aprons, milk, and cookies, and the median age at first marriage began to increase. Gender roles became an issue rather than a taken-for-granted assumption.

The 1950s were an economic aberration as well. The decade was characterized by significant increases in real income. Inexpensive fuel prices made the American dream of a home, car, and family accessible to a substantial portion of the middle class.

THE MODERN FAMILY: 1965 TO PRESENT

If industrialization and the Second World War were the two benchmark events that influenced families during the first half of this century, the development and dissemination of the birth control pill is probably the defining event of the second half of the century. The birth control pill allowed women to have sexual relations without linking them to reproduction. This resulted in what has been called the "sexual revolution," but more important, it resulted in the ability to actually plan marriage and childbearing to a greater extent than was possible at any other time in history.

Sociologists Philip Blumstein and Pepper Schwartz (1983) state that the American family has changed more in the past 30 years than it had in the previous 250 years. Some of the changes were extensions of the structural and demographic changes discussed in the previous sections. The age at first

One of the techno-
logical innovations
that had a major im-
pact on the modern
family was the birth
control pill.

marriage continued to increase (Table 4-2), and fertility rates declined and then stabilized. However, because the baby boom children were now having children of their own (even though they had a smaller average number of children than their parents) the absolute number of children born increased (Figure 4-3). The divorce rate increased dramatically in the 1960s and 1970s and then leveled off in the 1980s and 1990s (see Figure 4-1).

Diversity is the best way to characterize the modern family that emerged after the 1950s. The classic image of the 1950s family—a husband, wife, and children—made up 40% of all households in 1970 and now makes up only 26% of all households (see Chapter 1, Figure 1-1). Francis Goldscheider and Linda Waite (1991) explain that the changes that have occurred since 1950 have created two new options that confront the family—"new families," in which men and women increasingly share the economic and domestic respon-sibilities, and "no families," in which men and women forgo marriage and children altogether. Finally, there has been a dramatic increase in single-parent families, especially single-parent homes that include a never-married mother and her children.

The proportion of "no family" households has increased, so that today more than one in four households is a "no family" household. Individu-als have increasingly postponed marriage. In 1960, only 28% of American women aged 20 to 24 had not yet married; today, nearly two thirds (64.1%)

Year	Men	Women	Year	Men	Women
1990	26.1	23.9	1965	22.8	20.6
1989	26.2	23.8	1964	23.1	20.5
1988	25.9	23.6	1963	22.8	20.5
1987	25.8	23.6	1962	22.7	20.3
1986	25.7	23.1	1961	22.8	20.3
1985	25.5	23.3	1960	22.8	20.3
1984	25.4	23.0	1959	22.5	20.2
1983	25.4	22.8	1958	22.6	20.2
1982	25.2	22.5	1957	22.6	20.3
1981	24.8	22.3	1956	22.5	20.1
1980	24.7	22.0	1955	22.6	20.2
1979	24.4	22.1	1954	23.0	20.3
1978	24.2	21.8	1953	22.8	20.2
1977	24.0	21.6	1952	23.0	20.2
1976	23.8	21.3	1951	22.9	20.4
1975	23.5	21.1	1950	22.8	20.3
1974	23.1	21.1	1949	22.7	20.3
1973	23.2	21.0	1948	23.3	20.4
1972	23.3	20.9	1947	23.7	20.5
1971	23.1	20.9	1940	24.3	21.5
1970	23.2	20.8	1930	24.3	21.3
1969	23.2	20.8	1920	24.6	21.2
1968	23.1	20.8	1910	25.1	21.6
1967	23.1	20.6	1900	25.9	21.9
1966	22.8	20.5	1890	26.1	22.0

Table 4-2 Median Age at First Marriage, by Sex, for the United States, 1890–1990

SOURCE: U.S. Bureau of the Census (1991, p. 1).
NOTE: Figures for 1947 to 1990 are based on the Census Bureau's Current Population Survey data, whereas those for earlier dates are from decennial censuses. A standard error of 0.1 years is appropriate to measure sampling variability for any of the above median ages at first marriage, based on Current Population Survey data.

of women in this age group are single (Cherlin 1990; U.S. Bureau of the Census 1992).

The single-parent family and the blended family have become more common as a result of the increase in the divorce rate and the increase in teenage childbearing. The number of single-parent households has tripled in the past two decades alone, reaching 14.2 million in 1991 (U.S. Bureau of the Census 1992). This figure is only a snapshot at a point in time. Estimates are that 60% of the children born during the 1980s will spend a year or more in a single-parent home before their 18th birthday (Norton and Glick 1986).

Family diversity is also evidenced throughout our society. Child care has become a significant family, social, and political issue in the past two decades. Thirty years ago the U.S. Census Bureau did not even tabulate the number of couples who cohabitated. In 1970, the Census Bureau estimated that a half-million couples lived together, and today the number exceeds 3 million (U.S. Bureau of the Census 1992). Gay and lesbian marriages also constitute

Mother-child families are common in Sweden, where 45% of children are born to women who are not married.

a form of family structure that has emerged in the 1980s and 1990s (although the emergence has more to do with social recognition and less to do with increases in this form of intimate relationship).

THE FAMILY TODAY

There are approximately 252 million residents in the United States population, of which 123 million are males and 129 million are females (U.S. Bureau of the Census 1992). The U.S. Census Bureau classifies the population into three major racial groups—white, black, and "other," which includes American Indians, Eskimos, Aleuts, Japanese, Chinese, Filipinos, Hawaiians, Samoans, Asian Indians, Koreans, Vietnamese, and Guamians, among others. Nearly

84% of the population is white, 12% is black, and 3.8% is "other." Latinos (who may be white, black, or "other") comprise 9% of the population.

There were 94 million households in the United States in 1991. A **household** is defined by the Census Bureau as a housing unit—a house, an apartment or other group of rooms, or a single room. Households can include related family members or unrelated persons. There were 66.3 million families in the United States in 1991. The Census Bureau defines a family as a group of two or more persons related by birth, marriage, or adoption and residing together in a household (see Chapter 1).

Of the 66.3 million families, 52.1 million were married couples—a husband and wife family; 2.9 million were male-headed families with no wife present, and 11.2 million were female-headed families with no husband present.

It is virtually impossible to define the "modern family," because the one attribute that characterizes families of the 1990s is diversity. However, there have been a number of general trends that characterize and define the modern family as a social institution. These include increases in the average age at the time of first marriage, cohabitation, individuals living alone, divorce, the number of single-parent families, the proportion of women who are employed, and premarital births. In addition, there have been decreases in the rates of marriage, fertility, and family size (see Table 4-3 for a summary).

	1965	1980	1985	1990
Employed women (percentage of all women, aged 16 and over)	36.7	61.5	65.2	65.1****
Fertility rate (number of children the average woman will have at the end of her childbearing years)	2.9	1.8	1.8	2.01***
Marriage rate (number of marriages per 1,000 population)	9.3	10.6	10.2	9.7**
Median age at first marriage				
Men	22.8	24.7	25.5	26.1
Women	20.6	22.0	23.3	23.9
Divorce rate (number of couples divorcing per 1,000 population)	2.5	5.2	5.0	4.7**
Single-parent families (percentage of all families with children under 18 years of age)	10.1	19.5	22.2	25.0***
Premarital births (percentage of all births)	7.7	18.4	21.5	27.0***
Living alone (percentage of all households occupied by single person)	15.0	22.6	23.7	25.0****

Table 4-3
The Changed
American Family

SOURCE: U.S. Bureau of the Census (1992 and earlier editions), National Center for Health Statistics; U.S. Department of Labor. **1988; ***1989; ****1991.

Marriage	Marriage is still a popular institution. The vast majority of men and women eventually marry, and estimates are that 95% of all men and women marry. Today, however, men and women are postponing marriage longer than in the past, and a growing number of individuals appear likely never to marry. The delay in marriage, as we have noted earlier in this chapter, is likely due to the fact that a larger portion of the population is attending college and thus postponing marriage until they complete their education and begin their careers. Another explanation for the increase in age at first marriage is a "birth cohort" explanation. Richard Easterlin (1980) argues that the size of the birth cohort one is born into influences one's life chances. Persons born into small birth cohorts (during World War II or in the mid-1970s—see Figure 4-2) find themselves in greater demand by employers who must fill jobs from a smaller pool of potential workers. Baby boom cohort children faced more competition in the labor force, job opportunities were poorer, and the young adults delayed marriage. Easterlin projects that as children of the baby boomers enter adulthood, the trend will reverse and marriage and birth rates will increase again. Irrespective of which theory is accurate, delay in first marriage also delays childbearing and, as a result, reduces the number of children born to each family.

Cohabitation and Singles	Delays in entering marriage, changing attitudes about sexuality, and the increasing divorce rate have doubtlessly combined to increase the number of unmarried couples. About 3 million unmarried couples lived together in 1991, more than five times more cohabitators than there were in 1970. Not all nonmarried cohabitators are young people who have never married. Demographer Larry Bumpass and his colleagues James Sweet and Andrew Cherlin (1991) estimate that 40% of cohabitating couples have children present. A number of cohabitators are also divorced individuals or widows and widowers. Ten years ago, social scientists expressed their doubts that the rate of cohabitation would continue to increase (see, e.g., Blumstein and Schwartz 1983), but the rate continues to rise, and it is certainly possible that the rate of cohabitation in the United States could begin to approach the rate in Sweden (see Box 4-2).

Cohabitation is not the only adaptation to delays in entering marriage, nor is it the only adaptation to life after a divorce. Living alone is another alternative. In 1991, there were 23.5 million individuals who lived alone—an increase of more than 100% since 1970 (12.7 million). This number includes people who live alone by choice, people who would like to be married but have not yet married, and widows and widowers.

One overriding characteristic of the family in the 1990s is that it is small. Today, families are smaller than they have ever been (see Figure 4-4). The average size of all families in 1990 was 3.17 persons. In homes where both husband and wife are present, the average size is 3.24 persons. Today, less than half of all married couples have at least one child 18 years old or younger living with them, compared to 56% of all married couples in 1970.

Family Size

A man and a women who marry in 1990, each for the first time, have between a 50% and 65% chance of having that marriage end in divorce (see Chapter 13). Although the divorce rate has stabilized, divorce is still a prominent facet

Divorce

BOX 4-2: THE GLOBAL VIEW

Changes in the Swedish Family

Profound changes in family organization and structure have occurred in Sweden in the past 25 years. No other element of Swedish society has changed more rapidly or in a more dramatic way than the Swedish family (Popenoe 1988). Sociologist David Popenoe (1988) sees the changes in the Swedish family as a foreshadowing of the future changes in store for the structure of families and family life in the United States.

The most dramatic and significant changes in the Swedish family are in the marriage rate, in the rate of nonmarital cohabitation, and in the rate of family dissolution, or divorce.

Beginning in the 1960s, the marriage rate (the percentage of individuals aged 20 to 44 who marry) dropped sharply in Sweden. During the eight years after 1966, the rate dropped 40%, a decrease that had not, and has not, occurred anywhere else or at any other time in world history. The decline in the marriage rate reflected a trend in increased age at first marriage—a trend that has also occurred in the United States. But in addition, a growing proportion of Swedes are not marrying at all. More than one third of Swedish women born in 1955 will not have married by the time they are 50 years of age.

Marriage in Sweden is being replaced by nonmarital cohabitation. Popenoe estimates that one quarter of all couples in Sweden are nonmarital cohabitants. This compares to perhaps 4% in the United States.

The proportion of couples who are not married is even greater among the young. More than half of men under age 30 are living in a nonmarital relationship, and 35% of women under 30 cohabitate. Even couples who have children are no longer rushing to get married. Forty-five percent of children born in Sweden are born to women who are not married.

The divorce rate in Sweden was high at the end of World War II. Beginning in 1963, the rate of divorce in Sweden climbed faster than in most countries, and the current rate of divorce is generally considered the highest in Europe. The rate is just a bit lower than that of the United States, which is the world leader in divorce. However, because so many Swedes no longer marry, using the divorce rate as a measure of family dissolution is no longer useful. If one considers the breakup of nonmarital relationships together with formal divorce, Sweden may now have the highest rate of marital dissolution in the world.

Figure 4-4
Number of
Persons per
Household,
1790–1991

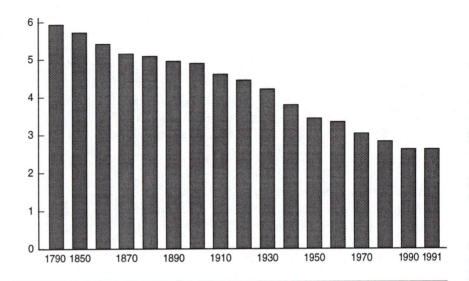

SOURCE: U.S. Bureau of the Census (1992 and computations from 1980 census).

of American family life. Many factors can account for the high divorce rate. Blumstein and Schwartz (1983) note that women who marry older, who have more education and stable careers, and who have few children have fewer impediments to divorce. Better educated women with careers and few or no children are more flexible and independent and thus are able to remove themselves from unsatisfactory marriages. Of course, Blumstein and Schwartz note that the same is true for men who also have the advantages of education, occupation, and smaller numbers of children.

Single-Parent Households

A direct consequence of the increased divorce rate is the increase in single-parent households. However, this phenomenon is not new, as Box 4-3 shows. Today, one in four households with children under 18 years of age is a single-parent home. Female-headed single-parent homes are often characterized by poverty and stress.

Employed Women

One of the most significant changes in the modern family and a change that has had a profound effect on the labor force is the increase in women's labor force participation, especially participation by mothers of school-aged children. Few married women worked outside the home in 1890. Prior to World

War II, less than 3 in 10 women (27.9%) were in the labor force. By 1991, more than half of all married women (58.5%) were employed (U.S. Bureau of the Census 1992). The greatest increase has been among mothers, especially mothers of babies and preschoolers (Hoffman 1989; Menaghan and Parcel 1990). In 1991, nearly two thirds all married women with children were employed (U.S. Bureau of the Census 1992). More important, 59.9% of mothers with children under 6 years of age were employed in 1991 (see Chapter 11).

It is impossible to discuss the changing family without discussing changing gender roles. Changing gender roles have both influenced the family as a social institution and been influenced by changes in the family. Women have moved from being the primary producers of family goods during colonial times to being primarily responsible for home and hearth during the Industrial Revolution to being central participants in the post-World War II labor market. Modern women are less economically dependent on men than ever before. Women and men, however, are still examining their roles in the workplace and the home, and many women find that they have not been liberated by changing gender roles but simply have assumed more and more responsibilities (see also Chapters 8 and 11).

Changing
Gender Roles

BOX 4-3: THE FAMILY OVER TIME

Single Parenthood in 1900

Precise figures concerning the extent of single parenthood have only been available since 1940. Thus some social observers assume that the single-parent family is either a relatively recent family form or one that has grown rapidly in modern times. Historian Linda Gordon and sociologist Sara McLanahan (1991) examined the Public Use Sample from the 1900 U.S. Census. This is a sample of 27,069 households. They found that the overwhelming number of children—about 86%—lived with two parents, 8.6% lived with one parent, and 3.2% lived with another relative. Of those children who lived in a single-parent home, 7 of 10 lived with their mothers. The vast majority of the

children living with single mothers or fathers were in single-parent homes as a result of the death of a parent, not divorce. Only 2% of all the children in single-parent homes were children with a divorced parent. Contrary to popular assumption, children of migrant and immigrant parents were actually more likely to live with two parents.

Gordon and McLanahan note that the most striking aspect of these numbers is that the same proportion of children lived in single-parent homes in 1900 as lived with single parents in 1960. Clearly, single motherhood is not a new phenomenon.

Perhaps the most significant change in the modern family is the increase in the percentage of married women—especially married women with children—who work.

SUMMING UP   The image of the large, extended, self-sufficient family of the past clashes with the historical realities of the American family. So, too, the so-called Golden Age of the American family of the 1950s stands in marked contrast to the trends and changes that have occurred in the modern family.

There are a few general statements that can be made about families in the United States. First, the most common form of family organization, from colonial times until the present, is the nuclear family. Although a portion of families have always been multigenerational extended families, and while the majority of families keep in regular contact with extended family members, the typical American household has been a nuclear household with husband, wife, and children present. We should point out, however, that there has been considerable variation. Boarders and apprentices were members of colonial households, and in the past 20 years there has been a great increase in single-parent households, cohabitation, and individuals living alone.

Over time, and especially since the beginning of this century, the American family has grown smaller. This is due in part to the general decline in the birth rate and also to the disappearance of boarders, apprentices, and relatives from the home. The family has also become smaller due to the increase in single-parent households. The divorce rate has risen twice during this century—rising sharply after World War II and then beginning a sharp increase again in the mid-1960s.

Many of the changes that have occurred in family organization have been the result of technological changes, such as industrialization and the development of the birth control pill; social events, such as immigration from Europe and world wars; or economic events, such as the depression of the 1930s or the affluence of the 1950s. Marriage rates, divorce rates, and birth rates fluctuated as a result of social and economic events and changes.

The recent developments in the American family include the increasing importance of cohabitation as a stage in the family life course, the continuing postponement of marriage, an increase in births to women in their 30s, an increase in the proportion of women, especially mothers, who are employed, and changes in gender roles and gender role expectations.

Stability in the nuclear family form and changes in the birth rate and divorce rate are not the only ways to describe the American family. One enduring feature of family organization in the United States has been diversity. The geographic and ethnic diversity of the colonies led to a diversity of family structure and style in the families of the first colonists. Immigration and industrialization also led to further diversification in family form and structure. Today, diversity is also a major characteristic of families. The traditional nuclear family organization remains as a cultural ideal, but an increasing number of individuals—adults and children—spend time in single-parent households. Cohabitation and individuals living alone are also important lifestyles. Even the bedrock nuclear family has changed. The two-paycheck household of today is a far different type of family from the agricultural nuclear family of colonial times or the industrial family at the turn of the century.

Racial and ethnic variation as well as variation due to social and economic status also are elements of family diversity in the United States that we examine in the following chapter.

REFERENCES

Aries, Philippe. 1962. "From the Medieval to the Modern Family." Pp. 375-404 in *Centuries of Childhood,* edited by Philippe Aries. New York: Random House.

Bane, Mary Jo. 1976. *Here to Stay: American Families in the Twentieth Century.* New York: Basic Books.

Beitscher, Jane K. 1976. " 'As the Twig Is Bent' . . . : Children and Their Parents in Aristocratic Society." *Journal of Medieval History* 2:181-90.

Blumstein, Philip and Pepper Schwartz. 1983. *American Couples: Money, Work, Sex.* New York: William Morrow.

Bumpass, Larry L., James A. Sweet, and Andrew Cherlin. 1991. "The Role of Cohabitation in Declining Rates of Marriage." *Journal of Marriage and the Family* 53(November):913-27.

Calhoun, Arthur W. 1945. *A Social History of the American Family From Colonial Times to the Present,* Vol. 2. New York: Barnes & Noble.

Cherlin, Andrew. 1990. "Recent Changes in American Fertility, Marriage, and Divorce." *Annals of the American Association of Political and Social Science* 510 (July):145-54.

Cott, Nancy. 1979. "Eighteenth Century Family and Social Life Revealed in Massachusetts Divorce Records." Pp. 107-35 in *A Heritage of Her Own,* edited by Nancy F. Cott and Elizabeth Pleck. New York: Simon & Schuster.

Degler, Carl. 1980. *At Odds: Women and the Family in America From the Revolution to the Present.* New York: Oxford University Press.

Demos, John. 1970. *A Little Commonwealth: Family Life in Plymouth Colony.* New York: Oxford University Press.

———. 1974. "The American Family of Past Time." *American Scholar* 43(Summer):422-46.

Dyer, Everett D. 1979. *The American Family: Variety and Change.* New York: McGraw-Hill.

Easterlin, Richard A. 1980. *Birth and Fortune: The Impact of Numbers on Personal Welfare.* New York: Basic Books.

Glick, Paul and Arthur Norton. 1979. "Marrying, Divorcing, and Living Together in the U.S. Today." *Population Bulletin* 32(October):2-39.

Goldscheider, Frances K. and Linda J. Waite. 1991. *New Families, No Families? The Transformation of the American Home.* Berkeley: University of California Press.

Goode, William J. 1963. *World Revolution and Family Patterns.* New York: Free Press.

Gordon, Linda. 1988. *Heroes of Their Own Lives: The Politics and History of Family Violence.* New York: Viking.

Gordon, Linda and Sara McLanahan. 1991. "Single Parenthood in 1900." *Journal of Family History* 16(2):97-116.

Gordon, Michael. 1978. *The American Family: Past, Present, and Future.* New York: Random House.

Greven, Philip J., Jr. 1970. *Four Generations: Population, Land, and Family in Colonial Andover, Massachusetts.* Ithaca, NY: Cornell University Press.

Hareven, Tamara K. 1976. "Modernization and Family History: Perspectives on Social Change." *Signs: Journal of Women in Culture and Society* 2(1):190-206.

Hareven, Tamara K. and Maris A. Vinovskis, eds. 1978. *Family and Population in Nineteenth-*

Century America. Princeton: Princeton University Press.

Hawes, Joseph M. and N. Ray Hiner, eds. 1985. *American Childhood: A Research Guide and Historical Handbook.* Westport, CT: Greenwood.

Hoffman, Lois W. 1989. "Effects of Maternal Employment in the Two-Parent Family." *American Psychologist* 44(2):283-92.

Laslett, Barbara. 1973. "The Family as a Public and Private Institution: An Historical Perspective." *Journal of Marriage and the Family* 35(August): 480-92.

Lockridge, Kenneth. 1966 "The Population of Dedham, Massachusetts, 1636–1746." *Economic History Review,* 2nd Ser., 19(August):318-44.

———. 1970. *A New England Town, The First Hundred Years: Dedham, Massachusetts, 1636–1736.* New York: Norton.

May, Elaine Tyler. 1988. *Homeward Bound: American Families in the Cold War Era.* New York: Basic Books.

Menaghan, Elizabeth C. and Toby L. Parcel. 1990. "Parental Employment and Family Life: Research in the 1980's" *Journal of Marriage and the Family* 52(November):1079-98.

Modell, John and Tamara K. Hareven. 1973. "Urbanization and the Malleable Household: An Examination of Boarding and Lodging in American Families." *Journal of Marriage and the Family* 35(August):467-79.

National Center for Health Statistics. 1989. "Advance Report of Divorce Statistics, 1986." *Monthly Vital Statistics Reports* 38(2). Hyattesville, MD: Public Health Service.

Norton, Arthur J. and Paul C. Glick. 1986. "One Parent Families: A Social and Economic Profile." *Family Relations* 35 (January):9-17.

O'Connell, Martin and Maurice J. Moore. 1980. "The Legitimacy Status of First Births to U.S. Women Aged 15-24, 1939-1978." *Family Planning Perspectives* 12(February): 16-25.

Parish, William L., Jr. and Moshe Schwartz. 1972. "Household Complexity in Nineteenth Century France." *American Sociological Review* 37(April):154-73.

Popenoe, David. 1988. *Disturbing The Nest: Family Change and Decline in Modern Societies.* New York: Aldine de Gruyter.

Saluter, Arlene F. 1989. "Changes in American Family Life." *Current Population Reports: Special Studies,* Series P-23, No. 163. Washington, DC: U.S. Government Printing Office.

Smith, Daniel Blake. 1982. "The Study of the Family in Early America: Trends, Problems, and Prospects." *The William and Mary Quarterly* 39(1):3-28.

Smith, Daniel Scott. 1976. "Parental Power and Marriage Patterns: An Analysis of Historical Trends in Hingham, Massachusetts." *Journal of Marriage and the Family* 35(August):419-28.

Smith, Daniel Scott and Michael S. Hindus. 1975 "Premarital Pregnancy in America, 1640–1971: An Overview." *Journal of Interdisciplinary History* 5 (Spring):537-70.

U.S. Bureau of the Census. 1989. *Marital Status and Living Arrangements: March 1988.* Current Population Reports: Population Characteristics, Series P-20, No. 433. Washington, DC: Government Printing Office.

———. 1991. *Marital Status and Living Arrangements: March 1990.* Current Population Reports: Population Characteristics, Series P-20, No. 450. Washington, DC: Government Printing Office.

———. 1992. *Statistical Abstracts of the United States.* Washington, DC: Government Printing Office.

Zaretsky, Eli. 1976. *Capitalism, The Family, and Personal Life.* New York: Harper & Row.

Zelizer, Viviana A. 1985. *Pricing the Priceless Child: The Changing Social Value of Children.* New York: Basic Books.

CHAPTER **5**

◨ Variations in Family Organization in the United States

Jimmy is a second grader. He pays attention in school, and he enjoys it. School records show that he is reading slightly above grade level and has a slightly better than average IQ. Bobby is a second grader in a school across town. He also pays attention in class and enjoys school, and his test scores are quite similar to Jimmy's. Bobby is a safe bet to enter college (more than four times as likely as Jimmy) and a good bet to complete it—at least twelve times as likely as Jimmy. Bobby will probably have at least four years more schooling than Jimmy. He is twenty-seven times as likely as Jimmy to land a job which by his late forties will pay him an income in the top tenth of all incomes. Jimmy has about one chance in eight of earning the median income. These odds are the arithmetic of inequality in America. They can be calculated with a few more facts about Bobby and Jimmy. Bobby is the son of a successful lawyer whose annual salary . . . puts him well within the top 10 percent of the income distribution. . . . Jimmy's father, who did not complete high school, works from time to time as a messenger or custodial assistant. His earnings . . . put him in the bottom 10 percent. (de Lone 1979, pp. 3-4)

Richard de Lone's comparison of the lives and life chances of Bobby and Jimmy graphically illustrates the impact of income, occupation, and education on the life chances of children whose intelligence and abilities appear to be equal but whose lives will be distinctly different. Social class not only influences the life chances of these two second graders, it has a direct impact on their families and life within their families. Bobby and Jimmy will grow up in homes with different values about gender roles, household responsibilities, and child rearing. They will differ in terms of when they have their first sexual relationship, when they marry, and the social class of the women they marry. The chances that their marriage will be stressful, have conflict, and will involve violence also vary. Finally, Bobby and Jimmy have different odds that their marriages will end in divorce.

In the previous chapter we saw how geographic and ethnic diversity shaped colonial families. In contemporary families, social class, race, and ethnicity are the major social structural forces that influence families and family life in the United States. This chapter examines variations in family organization in the United States by focusing on the influence of social structure on family structure. The first section looks at the determinants of social class and the consequences of social class on family structure and family life. The second section focuses on race and ethnicity. Blacks, Latinos, and Asian Americans are the major racial and ethnic minorities in the United States; thus we examine black, Latino, and Asian American families in the United States.

130

SOCIAL CLASS AND FAMILY STRUCTURE

The term **social stratification** refers to the division of society into layers or strata. Individuals and families who occupy a particular strata or layer have different access to the society's opportunities and rewards. Similarly, membership in a particular strata places the occupants at greater or lesser risk of experiencing the dangers, costs, and penalties of a society. People who occupy the same layer in the social stratification are known as a **social class.**

A society can be stratified along a number of dimensions, including wealth, occupation, education, prestige, power, celebrity, or any other attribute, social or otherwise, that is distributed unequally. Some social scientists identify three key factors as influencing an individual's position in the social strata: occupation, education, and income (Hodge and Treiman 1968; Jackman and Jackman 1983). Other social scientists, especially those who use the Conflict Theoretical perspective, see class membership as shaped by control and authority in the workplace (Robinson and Kelley 1979; Vanneman and Pampel 1977; Wright 1978): Those in the upper classes give the orders, those in the lower classes take the orders.

Social scientists often use objective measures of occupation, education, and income as well as residence to place individuals into the social structure. A second method is to study subjective factors, such as occupational prestige. Finally, some researchers arrive at a measure of social class by asking respondents to classify themselves and others into a position in the social stratification system. There are advantages and disadvantages to each approach. The method of asking individuals to place themselves into a social class typically yields an overwhelming membership in the "middle class."

In addition to variation in measuring social class, social scientists have different conceptualizations of how many social classes there are and what the key characteristics are of each social class. Most Americans view the United States as having three social classes: upper, middle, and lower. Social scientists have classified the American social class system into five, six, or even nine social classes. For our purposes, we use Dennis Gilbert and Joseph Kahl's (1993) conceptualization of six social classes (see Figure 5-1).[1]

The *wealthy class,* or the upper upper class, constitutes 1% of households. This small, exclusive class is made up of individuals and families who have accumulated wealth, prestige, and social influence over the years. The parents and children are educated at prestigious or elite universities. Wealth is not based on wages but on inherited assets, such as property, stocks, and bonds, that have been accumulated and passed along for generations. Family income exceeds $750,000 per year. Some members of the wealthy class

Figure 5-1 Model of the American Class Structure: Classes, by Typical Situations

Proportion of Households	Class	Education	Occupation of Family Head	Family Income, 1990
1%	Capitalist	Prestige university	Investors, heirs, executives	Over $750,000, mostly from assets
14%	Upper middle	College, often with postgraduate study	Upper managers and professionals; medium business owners	$70,000 or more
	Middle	At least high school; often some college or apprenticeship	Lower managers; semiprofessionals; nonretail sales; craftspeople; foremen	About $40,000
60%	Working	High school	Operatives; low-paid craftspeople; clerical workers; retail sales workers	About $25,000
	Working poor	Some high school	Service workers; laborers; low-paid operatives and clericals	Below $20,000
25%	Underclass	Some high school	Unemployed or part-time; many welfare recipients	Below $13,000

SOURCE: *The American Class Structure: A New Synthesis* (4th ed., p. 311, Table 11-1) by Dennis Gilbert and Joseph A. Kahl, 1993, Belmont, CA: Wadsworth. Copyright © 1993 by Wadsworth Publishing Company. Adapted by permission.

work, and others serve as members of the boards of directors of major corporations.

The *upper middle class* makes up 14% of households and is composed of top-level executives and highly paid professionals who have "made it" by most people's standards. Virtually all have college degrees, and most have postgraduate education as well. With household incomes in excess of $70,000 (in 1990), they can afford comfortable suburban homes, travel, new cars, and other symbols of success. They expect their children to do as well as they have. They are often active in local political and cultural affairs.

The *middle class* constitutes 30% to 35% of households. Middle-class occupations include small business operators, semiprofessionals—police, clergy, and social workers—and white-collar middle managers. Many members of the middle class have college educations, and increasingly, entrance into middle-class occupations requires a college degree. Income is about $40,000 per year and is based on wages, mostly salaries (although some middle-class workers are paid hourly wages). Many middle-class occupations involve authority and supervisory responsibility.

The *working class,* or what was traditionally called the blue-collar class, makes up about 30% of households. Working-class occupations include skilled and semiskilled factory and manufacturing workers, farm hands, "pink collar" clerical workers, salespeople, and a variety of service occupations. Blue-collar, pink-collar, and working-class occupations tend to be routine, mechanized, and with little opportunity for creativity, innovation, or occupational advancement. Working-class workers are closely supervised. They tend to have high school educations, although some have gone on for vocational education beyond high school. Wages tend to be paid on an hourly basis. Annual income is about $25,000 per year. Job security, especially in the past few decades, is a problem, as working-class occupations tend to be subject to the upward and downward swings of the economy.

The *working poor* make up between 20% and 25% of all households. They are likely to have dropped out of high school or earlier. Although the stereotype of the poor is that they are unemployed, a substantial portion work. Occupations tend to be semiskilled or unskilled service workers, laborers, operatives, and lower-paid clerical workers. Wages are paid hourly, and many occupations fail to provide fringe benefits, such as health insurance or contributions to retirement funds. With incomes typically less than $20,000 per year, the poor have little savings, little opportunity to save for a home or a college education for their children, and live a relatively precarious economic existence.

At the bottom of the social class ladder are the *underclass,* about 1% of all households. They typically have not gone beyond elementary school and live in a chronic state of poverty. Few work, many are on welfare, and a growing portion are without any permanent home. Although the stereotype of the underclass is that they are primarily black or minority men who have substance abuse problems or who are mentally ill, a substantial portion of the underclass are white, women, and children.

Women and Social Class Membership

Traditionally, class determination has been based on the occupation, income, and education of the family breadwinner—the man. Social scientists would measure the husband's education, occupation and occupational prestige score, and his total annual income and place the rest of the nuclear family—wife and children—into his social class. Such a model may be appropriate if a wife does not work. However, the fact that more than half of all married women work, and with the increasing numbers of women in upper-middle-class professions and occupations, the traditional form of class membership measurement has become outdated. Yet some have argued that even when women work, their husband's occupation, education, and income influence the wife's class status. Indeed, some social scientists have even argued that, within families, husbands are the principal source of status and this is unaffected by the wife's labor force participation (Jackman and Jackman 1983). Ida Simpson and her colleagues David Stark and Robert Jackson (1988) disagree, noting that working wives do not simply borrow their class identification from their husbands. When women are asked to identify which social class they belong to, their class identification is based on their own work experiences, as is true when men are asked to state what social class they belong to (Simpson et al. 1988).

Thus classifying a family into the class system requires taking into account women's as well as men's work, education, and income.

| Sources of Income and Family Life | Rayna Rapp (1982), in reviewing social structure and family structure, explains that households are shaped differently by poverty, wage earning, salaries, and inherited wealth. The structure of family relations depends on how stable and plentiful the sources of family income are. The socialization of children, their education and occupational aspirations, the health of family members, the life expectancy of each family member, and the risk of divorce and marital instability are all related to the source and size of family income. Social class membership influences how old people are when they first marry, their sexual behavior, family size, sleeping arrangements, how children are disciplined, and the likelihood of child abuse and wife abuse. Many of these differences will be expanded on in later chapters. |

The following is a brief snapshot of major structural features of families within each social class. Of course, it is important to realize that although there is variation between social classes there is also considerable variation within a social class. Thus not every family within a social class group behaves in the same manner. Although middle-class parents are generally less likely to use physical punishment on their children, some are more likely to use physical punishment than are parents in blue-collar homes. Although single-parent homes are much more likely to be found among the working poor and underclass, there are single-parent homes among the wealthy as well.

Wealthy Families

Wealthy families occupy the top position in the social structure. These families tend to be quite conscious of their top position and take careful note of the differences between themselves and what they might see as pretenders to the upper class. Wealth is accumulated and transmitted within wealthy families.

Women play a key role in wealthy families and are the guardians of the social rituals and institutions of the wealthy class. Wealthy women may serve on boards of schools and organizations, belong to numerous social and charitable organizations, and organize fund-raisers for "worthy" charities. Wealthy women rarely do housework or child care. They do not need paid employment. The oldest female member of a wealthy family is often viewed

A luxury car, such as a Bentley, is a sign of the kind of accumulated wealth possessed by wealthy families.

as the family "matriarch" and is seen as having considerable power over the activities and organization of the family across the generations. However, despite the title of matriarch, women in wealthy families actually hold a distinctly subordinate position to their husbands. There is considerable gender segregation in wealthy families (Ostrander 1984). Women's function is to support their husbands and their husbands' social position. Wealthy women often have an unequal voice in family decision making.

Upper-class children are raised in relative isolation from children from other social classes. Preschool children are cared for by nannies, nurses, or other in-home caretakers. Children tend to be enrolled in exclusive private schools from kindergarten through college. Relations with other family members are often formal and ritualistic. Correct dress and correct behavior, especially adultlike behavior, are stressed (Baltzell 1958; Ostrander 1984).

Wealthy-class children marry later than the average for the society (Warner and Lunt 1942; Whyte 1990). There is considerable pressure to date, court, and marry within one's social class, and this pressure is aided by the education and social segregation that characterize the lives of upper-class children and adolescents.

As noted above, marriages are patriarchal, with the eldest male wielding the most family power. Because the source of income for upper-class children is family wealth, children remain financially dependent on their parents for a considerable period of time.

Upper-Middle-Class Families

Upper-middle-class families are the families of professionals and executives. Income tends to be stable and is based on salaries or company profits. The home life of the upper middle class revolves around and is often subordinated to the husband's company or occupation. Social activities, moving, and family schedules tend to accommodate the demands of the husband's profession.

Upper-middle-class men and women marry earlier than those in the wealthy class but later than working-class individuals. They have their children later than working-class families and have fewer children. Upper-middle-class individuals tend to be less family and relative oriented than working-class families (Collins 1975, 1979; Gans 1962). The lower level of family and relative orientation in the upper middle class is not a result of these families ignoring their relatives but of the fact that they have wide social networks. They spend time with family, relatives, and a wide range of other people; thus their lives are less oriented to their family and relatives than are other class members. The large network of nonfamily friends and acquaintances is the result of the upper-middle-class orientation toward work and career.

Parents are much more involved in the daily routines of child rearing than are parents in wealthy families. One of the significant features of upper-middle-class child rearing is the push and pull of children and career. Time invested in a career is time taken away from children, whereas time invested in children is time taken away from career advancement.

The past few decades have seen the emergence of the two-career upper-middle-class family (Hertz 1986). Rosanne Hertz (1986) notes, somewhat sardonically, that the two-career family should be characterized as having two husbands and no wife. Today, some families revolve around the demands of the wife's occupation as much or more than around the husband's. It is less common, but not altogether impossible, that a family will move because of a change in the wife's work.

Middle-Class Families

The difference between upper middle class and middle class is one of degree and not kind. In other words, the dividing line between these two class groups is neither clear nor distinct. Middle-class families have somewhat lower incomes, less secure sources of income, and a lower level of commitment to a career that has distinctive upward paths than do upper-middle-class families. Thus middle-class family structures, patterns, and relations differ in only small ways from those found among the upper middle class.

On the other hand, the dividing line between middle-class and working-class families is much more distinct. Middle-class wage earners receive salaries, not an hourly wage. Thus the middle-class family tends to have more stable and secure economic resources than do working-class or lower-class families (Rapp 1982). Another feature that distinguishes middle class from working class is that the middle-class occupations tend to be the order givers in the workplace (Collins 1988).

As in the upper middle class, there is a much stronger belief in the ideal of equality between husband and wife in the middle class as compared to either wealthy or working-class families. Middle-class family values stress a belief that housekeeping and child rearing should be shared. Although research tends to find that women still do more of the housekeeping and child rearing than men in middle-class families (see Chapter 11), it is the belief in the ideal that distinguishes this social class. There is greater flexibility in the division of labor within middle-class homes than is found in homes at the higher or lower end of the social structure.

Melvin Kohn's (1963; Kohn and Schooler 1983) classic comparison of middle- and working-class parent-child relations found that middle-class parents tended to use reasoning, verbal threats, rewards, or withdrawal to dis-

Table 5-1 Mothers' Choices of "Most Desirable" Characteristics in Child, by Class (in percentages)

| | | Class | | | |
Characteristic	Upper	Upper Middle	Lower Middle	Upper Lower	Lower Lower
Obedience	14	19	25	35	27
Neatness, cleanliness	6	7	16	18	27
Consideration	41	37	39	25	32
Curiosity	37	12	9	7	3
Self-control	24	30	18	13	14
Happiness	61	40	40	38	30
Honesty	37	49	46	50	65

SOURCE: *Class and Conformity: A Study in Values* (p. 30) by Melvin L. Kohn, 1969, Homewood, IL: Dorsey Press. Copyright © 1969 by Wadsworth Publishing Company. Adapted by permission.

cipline their children and were less likely to use physical punishment than were working-class parents. Kohn pointed out in his study that this is probably due to the value system that men and women encounter at work. Upper-middle-class and middle-class occupations require workers to be able to manipulate symbols, ideas, and interpersonal relations, to be flexible in their thinking patterns, and to exhibit initiative and creativity. Middle-class occupational values of self-direction, freedom, independence, initiative, creativity, and self-actualization are translated into child-rearing practices that encourage children to develop internal standards such as consideration, curiosity, and self-control. Table 5-1 illustrates the differences across five class groups of mothers' choices of the most desirable characteristics in children. The upper-class mothers placed a higher value on curiosity, consideration, and happiness than did the lower-class mothers (Kohn 1969).

Middle-class families value ties with extended kin and relatives. Much of their social life revolves around visiting with relatives (Axlerod 1956; Bell and Boat 1957; Greer 1956). Here the pulls of work are less than in upper-middle-class families and thus there is not the wide work-related circle of friends and acquaintances. In addition to socializing with relatives, there is considerable "mutual aid" among middle-class families (Kulis 1992; Sussman 1953). Parents provide social and economic support to their children's families.

Working-Class Families

Working-class families have attracted the attention of social scientists over the years. Some of the classic social science investigations of marriage and families have been studies of working-class families, such as Mirra Komarovsky's

(1962) *Blue Collar Marriage,* Lillian Rubin's (1976) *Worlds of Pain: Life in the Working Class Family,* and Herbert Gans's (1962) *The Urban Villagers.*

As we noted earlier, working-class families are characterized as the order takers in the workplace who tend to work for hourly wages. Thus economic resources are not always stable or plentiful. Working-class families are often tossed and turned by economic upswings and downturns. An upswing may offer more income at the cost of more overtime hourly work, whereas a downturn may cut overtime hours or result in layoffs or even plant closings and unemployment. The gradual change from a manufacturing economy to a service/information economy has eroded the traditional working-class source of income—manufacturing jobs.

A notable feature of working-class families is that men and women marry young. Working-class boys and girls have their first sexual experiences earlier than do middle- and upper-class boys and girls. Working-class individuals often have a high school education or less. They are not looking forward to a long-term profession or career, and frequently they marry because of a desire to leave home and become independent.

The early stages of working-class family life are characterized by significant economic pressure. Both men and women need to work to maintain their standard of living. Earnings are dependent on hourly work. Working-class families tend to have their children earlier than middle-class families, and the birth of a child adds economic stress to the family. Often, the first child is conceived before the couple gets married. There are the costs associated with the newborn plus the loss of wages from the mother for the period of time just before the birth until she can return to work.

Working-class families are the most traditional social class in conforming to gender roles of husband and wife (Komarovsky 1962; Rubin 1976). There is considerable gender separation of social activities (Gans 1962), and the husband is considered the breadwinner and the wife the homemaker/child rearer. Working-class families hold strong values about the nature of man's work and woman's work. The high degree of gender segregation contributes to one of the central problems of working-class families—lack of communication between husband and wife. Lillian Rubin (1976) found this to be a common complaint of women who could not get their husbands to communicate with them and of husbands who were in a constant state of frustration about what their wives "wanted from them."

Melvin Kohn (1963; Kohn and Schooler 1983) found that working-class parents were more likely to use physical punishment to discipline their children than were middle-class parents. Again, the values associated with the nature of work were highly influential in the child-rearing practices used at home. Members of the working class receive orders, and the key to occupational success is discipline and following instructions. Thus working-class parents

Table 5-2 Poverty Thresholds in 1992, by Size of Family and Number of Related Children Under Age 18

Size of Family Unit	Weighted Average Threshold (in dollars)	Related Children Under Age 18								
		None	One	Two	Three	Four	Five	Six	Seven	Eight or More
One (unrelated individual)	7,143									
Under age 65	7,299	7,299								
Age 65 years and over	6,729	6,729								
Two	9,137									
Householder under age 65	9,443	9,395	9,670							
Householder age 65 and over	8,487	8,480	9,634							
Three	11,186	10,974	11,293	11,304						
Four	14,335	14,471	14,708	14,228	14,277					
Five	16,592	17,451	17,705	17,163	16,743	16,487				
Six	19,137	20,072	20,152	19,737	19,339	18,747	18,396			
Seven	21,594	23,096	23,240	22,743	22,396	21,751	20,998	20,171		
Eight	24,053	25,831	26,059	25,590	25,179	24,596	23,855	23,085	22,889	
Nine or more	28,745	31,073	31,223	30,808	30,459	29,887	29,099	28,387	28,211	27,124

SOURCE: U.S. Bureau of the Census (1993, p. A-8, Table A-3).

expect their children to follow orders and emphasize external control when raising the children.

Relationships with parents, siblings, and other relatives are the heart of the social life of working-class families (Gans 1962; Komarovsky 1962; Rubin 1976).

The Working Poor

The official definition of poverty in the United States is established by the federal government and is based on calculations that estimate the minimum level of income necessary to meet basic subsistence needs for differing family sizes and types. What is called the official "poverty line" is adjusted each year to reflect changes in the cost of living, or what the federal government calls the Consumer Price Index. In 1992, the poverty threshold for a family of four was $14,335. Table 5-2 presents the poverty line for families of varying sizes and composition. Looking at Table 5-2, the threshold or poverty line that defines who is poor depends on family size, age, and number of related children under the age of 18 in the household. For example, a single person under 65 years of age living alone would have to earn less than $7,299 to be considered "poor" by the federal government. A family of nine or more persons, with eight related children under the age of 18 living in the home would be considered poor if the family income was less than $27,124 in 1992. Because the federal government formula assumes that it takes more income

Table 5-3 Number of Families Below the Poverty Level and Poverty Rate, 1959–1992 (in thousands)

Year	Number of Poor Families	Poverty Rate for Families	Number of Poor Families With Female (NSP) Householder	Poverty Rate for Families With Female Householder	Families With Female Householder as a Percentage of All Families	Poor Families With Female Householder as a Percentage of All Poor Families	Nonpoor Families With Female Householder as a Percentage of All Nonpoor Families
1992	7,960	11.7	4,171	34.9	17.5	52.4	12.9
1991	7,712	11.5	4,161	35.6	17.4	54.0	12.7
1990	7,098	10.7	3,768	33.4	17.0	53.1	12.7
1989	6,784	10.3	3,504	32.2	16.5	51.7	12.5
1988	6,874	10.4	3,642	33.4	16.5	53.0	12.3
1987	7,005	10.7	3,654	34.2	16.4	52.2	12.1
1986	7,023	10.9	3,613	34.6	16.2	51.4	11.9
1985	7,223	11.4	3,474	34.0	16.1	48.1	12.0
1984	7,277	11.6	3,498	34.5	16.2	48.1	12.0
1983[a]	7,647	12.3	3,564	36.0	16.0	46.6	11.6
1982	7,512	12.2	3,434	36.3	15.4	45.7	11.2
1981	6,851	11.2	3,252	34.6	15.4	47.5	11.4
1980	6,217	10.3	2,972	32.7	15.1	47.8	11.3
1979	5,461	9.2	2,645	30.4	14.6	48.4	11.2
1978	5,280	9.1	2,654	31.4	14.6	50.3	11.1
1977	5,311	9.3	2,610	31.7	14.4	49.1	10.8
1976	5,311	9.4	2,543	33.0	13.6	47.9	10.1
1975	5,450	9.7	2,430	32.5	13.3	44.6	9.9
1974	4,922	8.8	2,324	32.1	13.0	47.2	9.7
1973	4,828	8.8	2,193	32.2	12.4	45.4	9.2
1972	5,075	9.3	2,158	32.7	12.2	42.5	9.0
1971	5,303	10.0	2,100	33.9	11.6	39.6	8.5
1970	5,260	10.1	1,951	32.5	11.5	37.1	8.6
1969	5,008	9.7	1,827	32.7	10.8	36.5	8.2
1968	5,047	10.0	1,755	32.3	10.7	34.8	8.0
1967	5,667	11.4	1,774	33.3	10.6	31.3	8.0
1966	5,784	11.8	1,721	33.1	10.5	29.8	7.9
1965	6,721	13.9	1,916	38.4	10.3	28.5	7.3
1964	7,160	15.0	1,822	36.4	10.4	25.4	7.8
1963	7,554	15.9	1,972	40.4	10.2	26.1	7.2
1962	8,077	17.2	2,034	42.9	10.0	25.2	6.8
1961	8,391	18.1	1,954	42.1	9.9	23.3	7.0
1960	8,243	18.1	1,955	42.4	10.1	23.7	7.0
1959	8,320	18.5	1,916	42.6	9.8	23.0	6.8

SOURCE: U.S. Bureau of the Census (1993, p. xvi, Table D).
a. Revised to reflect changes in weighting and imputation procedures.

to support an adult than a child and more income to support someone younger than 65 than someone older, the formula is adjusted depending on family size and family membership.

Using the official poverty line and the formula in Table 5-2, 7.9 million families, or 11.7% of all families, lived in poverty in 1992.

One of the distinctive features of poor families is that single-parent families headed by women make up more than half of the families below the poverty line and are the fastest growing category of the poor (see Table 5-3). The proportion of female-headed houses that live at or below the poverty line has led social critics to label this trend the "feminization of poverty." Never-married, deserted, or divorced mothers and their children are five times more likely to be poor than are two-parent households.

A second distinctive feature of poor families is that children are disproportionately likely to live in poverty. In fact, in this country, one in five children
under the age of 18 lives in poverty. In terms of absolute numbers, the majority
of children who live in poverty are white because about 86% of the population
is white. However, in terms of the risk or rate of being poor, minority children
are much more likely to live in poverty than are white children—38% of Latino
children and 46% of black children live in homes whose incomes fall below
the poverty line, compared to 16% of white children (U.S. Bureau of the
Census 1993).

Survival in poor families is dependent on social and family networks and
the pooling of resources. Anthropologist Carol Stack (1974) illustrated how
poor families in a black community shared child rearing, clothing, furniture,
food, and appliances. A national study of 2,533 black respondents who were
part of the Panel Study of Income Dynamics also found family and friends to
be important sources of emergency support for poor families (Taylor, Chatters,
and Mays 1988).

For many families, poverty is a persistent condition. However, although
the proportion of individuals and families who are poor at any given time is

---

BOX 5-1: WHAT THE RESEARCH SHOWS

Child Abuse in Single-Parent Families: Family Structure or Poverty?

One consistent finding in the research on
child abuse is that children in single-parent families are at much higher risk of being abused
than are children who live with two parents (Gil
1970; Sack, Mason, and Higgins 1985). Some
researchers and clinicians suspected that the
cause of the abuse was that single parents are
overloaded with the stresses and strains of child
rearing. Single parents not only have to raise
their children on their own, but they often are
forced to meet the demands of raising children
with far fewer economic resources than two-
parent homes have.

Richard Gelles (1989) examined the risk of
abuse in single-parent families by analyzing data
from the Second National Family Violence Survey. Not all the single parents in the survey were
raising their children on their own. About 16%
of the single parents lived with other adults,
most frequently their parents or other relatives.
When single parents who raised their children
on their own were compared to those who lived
with other adults, there was no difference in the
rate of child abuse. The demands and stresses of
raising children alone did not explain the high
rate of abuse.

Gelles then compared single parents who
lived below the poverty line to those whose incomes were above the poverty line. He found
that single mothers whose incomes exceeded
the poverty line were no more likely to abuse
their children than were mothers in two-parent
households. He concluded that poverty, not the
structure of the single-parent household, is
the reason for the high risk of abuse in single-
parent homes.

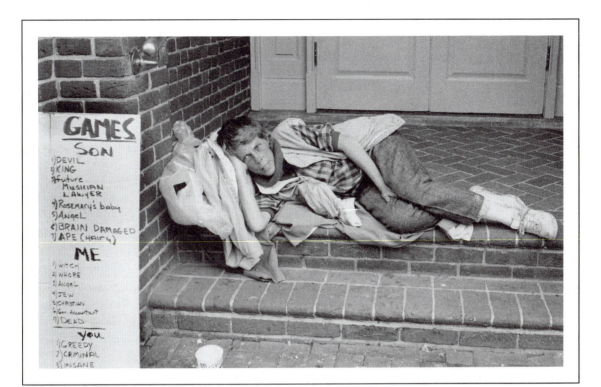

Although the stereotypical image of the homeless is one of men with substance abuse or mental health problems, women make up an increasing portion of the homeless population.

somewhat stable, the majority of poor people and families move in and out of poverty (Duncan et al. 1984). Most poor families stay on the welfare roles for a period of time and then move off.

The Underclass

Journalist Ken Auletta coined the term "the underclass" in his 1982 book of the same name. Auletta defined the underclass as a small minority of poor people made up of long-term welfare recipients, drifters, hustlers, drug addicts, and street criminals. Dennis Gilbert and Joseph Kahl (1993) describe the underclass as those who are seldomly employed and who are poor most of the time.

Underclass families are geographically concentrated in the ghettos of middle-size and large cities. Underclass males are isolated from the formal labor market, while underclass women with dependent children derive support from federal transfer payments, such as Aid to Families With Dependent Children (Kelly 1985). Stress, crime, and violence are persistent facets of underclass family life.

Perhaps the most graphic illustration of the insecurity and danger that pervades the lives of underclass families is a quote from a 10-year-old boy whose life was described in Alex Kotlowitz's (1991) book *There Are No Children Here: The Story of Two Boys Growing Up in the Other America.* Kotlowitz was describing the life of 10-year-old Lafayette in the Henry Horner Homes project in Chicago. Lafayette lived with his mother, younger brother, and three older siblings. His father, who had a serious substance abuse problem and was unable to hold a job, sometimes slept on the couch but often was out of the home. Lafayette's grandmother stayed with the family for a while, but the frequent violence in the project and the crowding in the apartment caused her to move out and live with another daughter. The family's AFDC support check was cut off for a period of time because the city welfare authorities were aware that the father sometimes stayed with the family. When Kotlowitz asked Lafayette what he wanted to be when he grew up, the boy replied, "If I grow up, I'd like to be a bus driver" (p. x). *If,* not *when.* At age 10, this child was not even sure he would survive to grow up and have a family.

There has been little detailed empirical research on the lives of underclass families and children, although there are extraordinary journalistic accounts such as those provided by Kotlowitz. Violence, despair, insecurity, poverty, illness, single-parent homes, and teenage pregnancy are all common characteristics in the lives of the underclass family. However, as Kotlowitz captured in the portrait of the life of Lafayette, his brother, mother, and family, there is also the daily struggle to raise children, make ends meet, find work, and get an education.

RACIAL VARIATIONS: BLACK FAMILIES

African Americans, or blacks,[2] are the largest racial minority in the United States. In 1991, there were 30.8 million blacks—12.1% of the population of the United States (U.S. Bureau of the Census 1992). The Census Bureau estimated that in 1991 there were nearly 7.5 million black family households (Table 5-4).

A number of features distinguish black families. First, they are young— 32% are under age 18 (U.S. Bureau of the Census 1992). Second, compared to the other major ethnic and racial groups, black families are much more likely

Table 5-4 Family and Nonfamily Households, 1970–1991

Race, Hispanic Origin, and Type	Number (per 1,000)					Percentage Distribution				
	1970	1980	1985	1990	1991	1970	1980	1985	1990	1991
FAMILY HOUSEHOLDS										
White, total	46,166	52,243	54,400	56,590	56,803	100	100	100	100	100
Married couple	41,029	44,751	45,643	46,981	47,014	89	86	84	83	83
Male householder[a]	1,038	1,441	1,816	2,303	2,276	2	3	3	4	4
Female householder[a]	4,099	6,052	6,941	7,306	7,512	9	12	13	13	13
Black, total	4,856	6,184	6,778	7,470	7,471	100	100	100	100	100
Married couple	3,317	3,433	3,469	3,750	3,569	68	56	51	50	48
Male householder[a]	181	256	344	446	472	4	4	5	6	6
Female householder[a]	1,358	2,495	2,964	3,275	3,430	28	40	44	44	46
Asian or Pacific Islander, total[b]	NA	818	NA	1,531	1,536	NA	100	NA	100	100
Married couple	NA	691	NA	1,256	1,230	NA	84	NA	82	80
Male householder[a]	NA	39	NA	86	112	NA	5	NA	6	7
Female householder[a]	NA	88	NA	188	194	NA	11	NA	12	13
Hispanic, total[c]	2,004	3,029	3,939	4,840	4,981	100	100	100	100	100
Married couple	1,615	2,282	2,824	3,395	3,454	81	75	72	70	69
Male householder[a]	82	138	210	329	342	4	5	5	7	7
Female householder[a]	307	610	905	1,116	1,186	15	20	23	23	24
NONFAMILY HOUSEHOLDS										
White, total	10,436	18,522	20,928	23,573	24,166	100	100	100	100	100
Male householder	3,406	7,499	8,608	9,951	10,312	33	40	41	42	43
Female householder	7,030	11,023	12,320	13,622	13,853	67	60	59	58	57
Black, total	1,367	2,402	2,703	3,015	3,200	100	100	100	100	100
Male householder	564	1,146	1,244	1,313	1,531	41	48	46	44	48
Female householder	803	1,256	1,459	1,702	1,670	59	52	54	56	52
Hispanic, total[c]	299	654	944	1,093	1,238	100	100	100	100	100
Male householder	150	365	509	587	669	50	56	54	54	54
Female householder	148	289	435	506	569	49	44	46	46	46

SOURCE: U.S. Bureau of the Census (1992, p. 47, Table 57).
NOTE: NA = not available.
a. No spouse present.
b. 1980 data as of April of that year.
c. Hispanic persons may be of any race. 1970 data as of April of that year.

to be female-headed households with no adult male present. Nearly 46% of the black family households were headed by females with no spouse in 1990 (see Table 5-4). Third, black families are more likely to be found in the southern states and in urban areas (cities larger than 5,000 population).

Three defining structural forces have influenced the form and function of African American families: (1) the historical legacy of slavery; (2) the impact of racism, both personal and institutional; and (3) economic disadvantage. Although there is some agreement that these structural forces have influenced the black family, there is not uniform agreement as to the strength or consequences of that influence. Thus the study of African American families has, in recent years, been marked by considerable debate and controversy.

The Historical Legacy of Slavery

The defining feature of African American minority group status in the United States is that African Americans are the only minority racial or ethnic group to enter the United States as slaves. Blacks were first brought to the Virginia colonies in 1619 as indentured servants who could work back their purchase price and be released from service (Frazier 1957; Pettigrew 1976). The first slave code was enacted in Virginia in 1661. The code singled out blacks for "perpetual servitude." By the early 1770s, most other states had followed suit. The *Dred Scott v. Sanford* U.S. Supreme Court ruling decreed that African slaves and their descendants had "no rights a white man need respect."

Most of the sociologists who first examined African American families portrayed slavery as having a devastating effect on families and family ties. Under slavery, individual slaves could be bought and sold, and adult black men were sold most often. This, according to E. Franklin Frazier (1957), Stanley Elkins (1959), and W.E.B. Du Bois (1899), disrupted husband-wife bonds and kinship networks. The resulting family form, according to these social scientists, was that mothers became the most important individuals in families, and the structure of the black family that developed during slavery and emerged from slavery at the end of the Civil War was at least **matrifocal** (family life is focused around the woman, even if she does not have dominance or power over the husband or family), if not **matriarchal** (a family in which the woman rules or has dominance over the man or family). Frazier (1948, 1957) and others traced the problems of the 20th-century black family to the impact of slavery, which created weak male-female bonds and a matriarchal family structure without a strong male role model present.

The vision of the pre- and postslavery black family as disrupted and matriarchal was challenged by historians and social scientists in the 1970s. Warren D. Ten Houten (1970) explained that Frazier's use of census data, social work case histories, and public records was, at best, marginal in meeting standards of evidence in present-day (1970s) social science. Historian Herbert Gutman (1976) examined birth records, marriage records, and other historical documentation and reconstructed the household structure for black families in a variety of southern and northern cities and communities. His data indicate that the majority of black households (70% to 90%) had a husband or a father present. When young black women had children out of wedlock, they tended to live with their parents, not in female-headed households. Sociologist Barbara Finlay Agresti (1978) supports Gutman's findings. She did find some evidence that in the rural farming areas of the South in 1870, a high percentage of blacks lived in nontraditional family groups—that is, non-nuclear or non-extended families—such as with other nonrelated black families or with white families. Thirty-one percent of the black families in the county examined by Agresti were one-parent households. However, by 1885, the percentage of one-parent families in that county was down to 13.6% and the two-parent family was the norm for the African American family.

Frank Furstenberg and his colleagues J. Brooks-Gunn, and S. Philip Morgan (1975) also caution against concluding that slavery destroyed the nuclear black family and produced a matrifocal or matriarchal family structure. Although the historical data are not entirely consistent, the evidence does not support the claim that slavery destroyed the black family, and the 20th-century black family structure is a direct linear descendent from the slavery experience.

A survey conducted by the National Research Council in 1989 was the first comprehensive study of the position of African Americans in the United States since Swedish social scientist Gunnar Myrdal's (1944) *An American Dilemma*. The survey examined blacks from the end of World War II until the late 1980s.

Racism: Individual and Institutional

BOX 5-2: THE FAMILY OVER TIME

The Moynihan Report and the Myth of the "Tangle of Pathology" of the Black Family

The structure and function of the black family was the focal point of a government report written in 1965 by now United States Senator Daniel Patrick Moynihan when he was an official with the U.S. Department of Labor. The report drew heavily on historical accounts of the black family, especially the work of E. Franklin Frazier. The black family, or what Moynihan then referred to as the Negro family, was at the heart of the deterioration of the fabric of black (Negro) society. The Negro family, according to Moynihan, constituted a "tangle of pathology." The tangle was caused by the high proportion of female-headed households, which constituted a matriarchy. In addition, Moynihan noted that blacks had high illegitimacy rates. But it was the female-headed family that was at the core of the pathology. The emasculation and family disorganization caused by female-headed households was the roadblock that prevented blacks from attaining equality in society.

The so-called "Moynihan Report" was a watershed in the study of black families. First, the report galvanized a wide range of social scientists who examined the data that Moynihan used and criticized both his data and his conclusions. Andrew Billingsley (1968) argued that the black family is an absorbing, adaptive, and resilient institution, not a tangle of pathology. Warren D. Ten Houten (1970) examined Moynihan's data and found it inaccurate and incomplete. He too noted the resilient and adaptive function of black families.

A basic flaw in Moynihan's report was that it failed to consider the impact on blacks and black families of individual and institutional racism and the resulting economic disadvantage. The positive feature of his report is that it raised the issue of the form and function of the black family from obscurity to a focal point for research and study. A proliferation of research on black families followed the publication of the "Moynihan Report," and, as a result, current analyses and discussions of the black family are much better informed than were the earlier, more stereotypic examinations of black families.

In almost every measure, such as education, income, health, and political participation, blacks are better off than they were 50 years ago. Yet in every measure there is stark evidence that blacks still have not achieved full equality. Sociologist William Julius Wilson (1980) argues that social class and economic disadvantage are more important in determining the life chances of African Americans than is race. Other sociologists, such as Charles Willie (1988), argue that the persistent inequality that blacks experience is the result of **individual** and **institutional racism,** the second structural feature that has affected the form and function of African American families. **Individual racism** is the act of individual discrimination that blocks the opportunities of minorities—for example, a personnel officer who does not hire a qualified candidate for a position because the candidate is black. **Institutionalized racism** is established social patterns and norms that have the unintended consequences of limiting opportunities of certain racial groups. For example, banks that will not grant mortgages for homes in what the banks consider high-risk neighborhoods may, unintentionally, discriminate against blacks.

Racism interferes with educational advancement and blocks blacks from entering the primary labor market where there are high-paying jobs, opportunities for career advancement, and fringe benefits, such as health care insurance and retirement fund contributions. Racism may drive black men out of their homes because the men are unable to be adequate providers. Willie (1988) states that racial discrimination and its negative effects on the economic status of blacks makes a substantial contribution to the high rate of divorce and desertion in black families.

Economic Disadvantage

The third structural feature that affects African American families is economic disadvantage. Whether the disadvantage is a product of individual or institutional racism or primarily a reflection of social class, blacks disproportionately experience economic disadvantage. African Americans have consistently had higher rates of unemployment than whites. Blacks who do find employment often take jobs in the secondary labor market. Positions are largely hourly work with limited opportunities for career advancement. Secondary labor market jobs, such as assembly line work, day labor, and domestic or service work, rarely have a full range of fringe benefits, such as health insurance, and are also subject to changes in the economy. Day labor jobs may be eliminated by automation; manufacturing jobs may be eliminated when a company elects to move production to Third World nations with lower labor costs and fewer government regulations regarding the workplace. Over the years, black families have consistently earned less than white families. The average (median) annual income of an African American family in 1991 was $21,423, compared to $36,915 for a white family (U.S. Bureau of the Census 1992). The difference between blacks and whites in 1991 is actually greater than the difference in 1960—before the passage of major civil rights legislation that was designed to eliminate discrimination in the workplace. Last, although the percentage of black men and women who have completed high school has increased by more than 100% since 1960 (U.S. Bureau of the Census 1992), blacks are still less likely than whites to complete high school.

The persistent pattern of educational, occupational, and income inequality has greatly influenced the form and functions that black families have taken in the United States. The following section examines the patterns of African American family life.

The persistent stereotype of the black family, from the early works of E. Franklin Frazier through Daniel Moynihan's mid-1960s report until the present, is that of a deviant, pathological institution, characterized by broken homes and young women with out-of-wedlock babies. As we explained earlier, part of the stereotype is the view that the current situation of black families is the product of 300 years of slavery.

Patterns of African American Family Life

The reality of the African American family is much more positive and much more diverse than the stereotype of the pathological deteriorating black family. Slightly less than half (48%—U.S. Bureau of the Census 1992) of all African American families have two parents present and more than 7 of 10 adult black men are working to support their households (Willie 1988).

Robert Taylor and his colleagues (1990) provide a profile of the patterns of black families in the past decade. These patterns include a declining rate of marriage, later ages of first marriage, higher divorce rates, an increase in female-headed households, higher proportions of births to unmarried mothers, and a larger percentage of children living in female-headed families. Whites have experienced these changes as well, but as Taylor and his colleagues note, black families have disproportionately suffered their impact.

Most notable among the patterns is the dramatic increase in female-headed households as well as the proportion of children born out of wedlock. In 1965, when Daniel Moynihan's report was published, nearly one in four black households was female headed. This percentage rose to 28% in 1970, 40% in 1980, and 45.9% in 1991 (U.S. Bureau of the Census 1992). Robert Staples (1985) stated that the prolific growth of the female-headed household is the most significant change in the black family in the past 30 years.

In 1940, less than 20% of black children were born out of wedlock; today, more than half are, as are nearly all children born to black teenage mothers (Furstenberg et al. 1987; Thornton and Freedman 1983). Both trends are important because they are associated with the likelihood of children living in poverty (Eggebeen and Lichter 1991).

Although they receive less attention than the issue of female-headed households and out-of-wedlock births, two other forces affect African American family life. As mentioned earlier, blacks have a higher risk of divorce than whites. The rate of divorce among black women in 1991 was 370 per 1,000 married couples, compared to a rate of 117 per 1,000 for white women (U.S. Bureau of the Census 1992). The higher rate is partly a function of the economic inequality we discussed in the previous section. A second feature of African American families is the shortage of men relative to the number of marriageable women. Among blacks between the ages of 14 and 24, there are only 98 men for every 100 women. This compares to 103 white men for every 100 white woman. Among blacks aged 25 to 44, there are only 88 men for every 100 women (U.S. Bureau of the Census 1992). The exceptionally high rate of homicide experienced by black teenagers is one contributor to the imbalanced sex ratio. Premature death due to illness is a second factor. The unbalanced sex ratio is another factor that increases the rate of female-headed households.

The focus on the problems experienced by African American families tends to obscure the positive features of black family life in the United States. Charles Willie (1988) points out that the middle-class, two-parent family is still a prominent family structure among African Americans. Willie (1988) describes three types of black families: the affluent or middle class, the working class, and the poor. Affluent families are typically two-parent families. Both spouses are likely to have college or graduate degrees and one or both spouses holds a professional job. The more wealthy the families, the more likely they are to isolate themselves from families of lower social status. Affluent families are likely to be patriarchal in that the man is typically the more powerful person in the family system. Working-class black families are also patriarchal. The problems of working-class families are the problems of stability and adequacy of economic resources. Poor black families receive a disproportionate amount of media and professional attention.

One of the most profound positive features of black families are strong family ties. Although the majority of African American families live in nuclear families, blacks are more likely than whites to live in three-generation or the "classical" extended family households (Angel and Tienda 1982; Beck and Beck 1989; Farley and Allen 1987; Hoffreth 1984; Tienda and Angel 1982; Wilkinson 1987). Even when blacks do not live in extended families, there is considerable sharing of resources and assistance. Anthropologist Carol Stack documented the sharing and "child keeping" in her 1974 book *All Our Kin,* an anthropological study of "The Flats," the poorest section of a black com-

Although a substantial proportion of African American families are female-headed, single-parent families, nearly half of all African American families are two-parent families.

munity in a midwestern city. Kin and friends were important to the people living there, as they provided a model for an urbanized lifestyle, were contacts for the exchange of goods, and reduced the sense of isolation that blacks felt by being a repressed minority in a small city. The "pooling" or sharing of economic resources was also found in statistical studies of black families. Research on sources of household income suggests that among blacks the relative contribution of a wife, adult children, and relatives constitutes a greater portion of the total household income than is the case among whites (Angel and Tienda 1982).

In addition to economic sharing, there is also interpersonal and social support from friends and relatives. Andrew Cherlin and Frank Furstenberg (1986) found that black grandparents take a more active part in the parenting of grandchildren than is the case in white families. The greater role for grandparents is partially due to high rates of divorce and separation in black families, the greater probability of blacks living in three-generation extended family households, and cultural norms that support extended family relations (Beck and Beck 1989; Cherlin and Furstenberg 1986; Sudarkasa 1981).

RACIAL VARIATIONS: ASIAN AMERICANS AND PACIFIC ISLANDERS

Asians and Pacific Islanders are the fastest growing racial and ethnic group in the United States. Their numbers increased by more than 100% between 1980 and 1990 (O'Hare 1993). Almost all of this increase has been due to a flood of immigrants and refugees. Nearly two thirds of today's Asian Americans and Pacific Islanders are foreign born (Bennett 1992; Hsia and Hirano-Nakanishi 1989).

The category "Asian American and Pacific Islander" includes anyone whose ancestors were among the original peoples of the Far East, Southeast Asia, the Indian subcontinent, or the Pacific Islands. This vast territory embraces people from dozens of different cultures with religious affiliations ranging from Buddhist to Zoroastrian. An Asian American might be a fourth-generation Japanese American who is fluent in English, is assimilated into the American mainstream, and has only a token knowledge of the Japanese language and culture; a recent immigrant from India, whose advanced degree, fluency in English and several other languages, and income allows him or her to fit smoothly into the upper middle class; or a rural Laotian who spent years in a refugee camp, speaks no English, and finds "life in the U.S. almost as alien as Alice found Wonderland" (Hsia and Hirano-Nakanishi 1989, p. 24). Chinese, Filipino, Japanese, Asian Indian, Korean, and Vietnamese each number a half million or more and account for 84% of today's Asian Americans; Hawaiians and other Pacific Islanders account for only 5%—see Table 5-5 (O'Hare 1993).

The diversity within Asian ethnic groups is almost as great. Chinese Americans distinguish between "ABCs," or American-born Chinese, a substantial percentage of whom are highly educated managers and professionals who are well integrated into society at large and realized the American dream, and "FOBs," or "fresh off the boat" immigrants, who are crowded into the nation's Chinatowns where rates of tuberculosis, mental illness, drug abuse, alcoholism, and crime run high (Brown and Pannell 1985; Feagin and Feagin 1993).

	Population		Change, 1980–1990	
	1980	*1990*	*n*	*%*
Chinese	806	1,645	839	104
Filipino	775	1,407	632	82
Japanese	701	848	147	21
Asian Indian	362	815	454	126
Korean	355	799	444	125
Vietnamese	262	615	353	135
Hawaiian	167	211	44	27
Cambodian[a]	16	147	131	819
Laotian[a]	48	149	101	210
Thai[a]	45	91	46	102
Hmong[a]	5	90	85	1,700
Pakistani[a]	16	81	65	406
Samoan	42	63	21	50
Guamanian	32	49	17	53
Indonesian[a]	10	29	19	190
Other Asian/Pacific Islander	86	233	147	171
Total[a]	3,726	7,274	3,548	95

Table 5-5 Growth of Asian and Pacific Islander Populations, 1980–1990

SOURCE: U.S. Bureau of the Census, Press Release CB91-215, June 12, 1991.
a. The 1980 data for these groups are from sample tabulations and are subject to sampling variability. All other 1980 data and the 1990 data in this table are based on 100% tabulations.

Asian American family structure and life varies, depending on the family's origin, when the immigrants arrived, the circumstances of the immigration— whether the individual and/or families fled a war-ravaged country or left for better educational or occupational opportunities—and the socioeconomic status of the family.

Patterns of Asian American Family Life

The variability of the family structure and family life of Asian American families can be seen in the case of Chinese Americans and Vietnamese families. As we saw in the previous section, Chinese Americans often classify themselves into two groups: ABCs and FOBs. The FOBs, or what Morrison Wong (1988) calls the "ghetto" or Chinatown Chinese, are newly immigrant families who live in or near urban Chinatowns. Half of these families are working class. The ABCs are middle-class families who hold white-collar jobs and have moved away from urban Chinatowns into other urban areas or to the suburbs.

There are at least four different types of Vietnamese family patterns in the United States (Tran 1988): (1) *nuclear,* made up of husband, wife, and children; (2) *incomplete extended,* consisting of the nuclear family, grandparents, and other relatives who live together; (3) *broken,* in which either the mother or the father and some children are in the United States while other nuclear

Cooperation, obedience, responsibility, and obligation to family are major socialization values in Asian American families.

family members are still in Vietnam or have died; and (4) *one-person,* which consists of the single person who left Vietnam, leaving behind either living relatives or a family that perished during or after the war.

Overall, the Census Bureau reports that Asian Americans have very high marriages rates—more than 80% of Asian Americans and 75% of Pacific Islanders over the age of 18 are married, compared to about 65% for whites, 47% for blacks, and 61% for Latinos (U.S. Bureau of the Census 1992).

In general, Asian American families are rigidly patriarchal. Men are the wage earners, decision makers, and disciplinarians. Women are expected to stay at home and care for the children. Even when women work, and many

Asian American women do work, they are still expected to carry out the housekeeping and child-rearing tasks (Kitano and Daniels 1988).

Asian American families appear to have generally similar values for socializing their children. Cooperation, obedience, responsibility, and obligation to the family are stressed (Kitano 1988; Oh and McAdoo 1993). Children are supposed to be loyal to their families and to defer to both parents' wishes (Kitano and Daniels 1988).

Given the patriarchal nature of Asian American families, it is not surprising that the gender role socialization is also traditional, with girls socialized to be caretakers and keepers of the home, while boys are not expected to do the dishes or laundry (Min 1988).

ETHNIC VARIATIONS: LATINO FAMILIES

After blacks, Latinos[3] are the second largest minority group in the United States. Latinos are also one of the fastest growing segments of the American population.

Before we examine Latino families, there are two conceptual issues we need to examine. The first is whether Latinos constitute a racial group or an ethnic group. Second, and related to the first, is to define what constitutes a Latino. **Racial groups** are made up of individuals who are related by a common heredity or ancestry and who are perceived and responded to in terms of external features or traits. Blacks and Asians are recognized and responded to in terms of external features and traits. Latinos, however, because of the diversity of the individuals who make up the group, are not uniformly perceived and responded to in terms of external features or traits. An **ethnic group** is made up of individuals who typically are of the same nationality or ancestry and who share a common heritage, culture, and lifestyle.

Latinos do not fall neatly into the category of a racial group or an ethnic group. The term **Latino** is applied to an ever changing group of residents of the United States. The terms "Hispanic" or "Latino" generally refer to individuals whose cultural heritage traces back to a Spanish-speaking country in Latin America. The group also includes individuals with links to Spain or from the southwestern region of the United States once under Spanish or Mexican control. Latinos include individuals with a Mexican heritage, Puerto Ricans, Cubans, and those with heritages that trace back to Central or South America (Valdivieso and Davis 1988). Thus the term Latino actually covers a range of ethnic groups having some link with a Spanish-speaking culture.

There were 22.3 million Latinos, as defined by the U.S. Census Bureau, in the United States in 1991. There were 4.9 million Latino family households. Mexican Americans tend to live in the Southwest, from Texas to California; Puerto Ricans tend to live in New York and other northeastern urban areas; and Cubans generally live in southern Florida.

The distinguishing feature of Latino families is that they are young. The median age of Latinos in the United States is 26.1, compared to 27.7 for blacks and 33.6 for whites (U.S. Bureau of the Census 1992). The youthfulness of Latinos is largely due to the high birth rate in Latino families—an average of 2.12 children, compared to 1.86 for blacks and 1.82 for whites (U.S. Bureau of the Census 1991). The high birth rate and large number of young children in Latino families has a built-in momentum factor for continued and increased population growth. When today's young children marry, if they have the same birth rate as their parents, the Latino population will continue to grow at greater rates than other racial or ethnic groups.

Latino families, like African American families, experience higher rates of poverty and are more likely to be female headed than are white families. Twenty-four percent of Latino families are female headed—nearly double the percentage for whites, almost double the rate for Asian Americans or Pacific Islanders, but nearly half the rate for African Americans (U.S. Bureau of the Census 1991).

As with our discussion of black families and Asian American families, it is not appropriate to make sweeping generalizations about the shape, form, function, and problems of Latino families. The difficulty is exacerbated because, as noted above, "Latino" is actually an umbrella term for a variety of ethnic groups. There is variation in family organization among Cubans, Puerto Ricans, Mexican Americans, and those with ties to Central and South America. Some researchers try to examine all Latino families, while others focus only on a single Latino ethnic group. As with black families, low income and poverty has a significant impact on Latino families. Because Latinos have lower educational attainment, higher unemployment, and higher rates of poverty compared to whites, poverty shapes the form and lives of many Latino families more than culture or ethnicity. Some Latino groups, such as Puerto Ricans, have higher rates of poverty than others—Cubans have the lowest rate of poverty of Latinos (Valdivieso and Davis 1988).

La familia: Familism and the Latino Family

One of the defining characteristics of Latino family life has been termed *la familia* or familism. Familism is the constellation of values that give overriding importance to the family and the needs of the collective as opposed to individual or personal needs (Bean, Curtis, and Marcum 1977; Queen, Habenstein, and Quadagno 1988). "La familia" is also a norm that families should live near their extended kin and have strong kinship ties, especially in times of need (Ramirez and Acre 1981).

Charles Mindel (1980) reports that Mexican Americans have higher levels of extended familism compared to either blacks or whites. The high levels of familism have been found to enhance mental health (Ramirez and Acre 1981) and has been found to reduce unemployment for Latinos, compared to blacks with similar education (Wilson 1991).

Some analysts of familism in Latino families, especially Mexican American families, have proposed that the importance of the family unit and the family as the focus of individual obligation has its roots in the Mexican cultural system and the agrarian way of life of Mexican families. Recent research, however, finds the roots of Latino familism in the United States in the racial and economic conditions in the United States (Alvirez and Bean 1976). Maxine Baca Zinn (1979) states that the current extended family relations in the United States may be due to residential and occupational concentration and insufficient external resources. Thus, just as the current situation of black families, such as the sharing described by Carol Stack (1974), is due to current economic conditions and not slavery, the current focus on the family in Latino families is the result of minority group status and economic disadvantage, not a cultural heritage of "la familia."

A second characteristic that has also been attributed to Latino families, and especially Mexican American families, is "machismo," or a patriarchal family structure (Clark 1959; Heller 1966; Rubel 1966). Machismo is a special type

Machismo and Patriarchy

BOX 5-3: DIVERSE FAMILIES

Religion and Families: The American Jewish Family

Religion has traditionally influenced families and family life. Jews are considered both an ethnic group and a religious group. Like Latinos and other minority groups, the family is a central focus of Jewish life (Brodbar-Nemzer 1988). Jews are more likely to marry than the general population (Brodbar-Nemzer 1988), and they have the highest rate of intrareligious marriage—the highest of all the major religious groups—about 80% of Jews marry other Jews.

Jews marry at older ages than other ethnic or religious groups and have fewer children (Brodbar-Nemzer 1988). These two trends likely reflect the higher educational attainment of Jews, especially Jewish women. Jews tend to have lower divorce rates than other religious or ethnic groups, although the rate of divorce has risen in recent years along with the general increase in divorce in our society.

of patriarchy that has been described as part of Latino culture and family life. Machismo is the ideal of male dominance over wives and daughters.

Current students of Latino family life have reacted against the characterization of machismo as typical of Latino family structure. They note that machismo is a stereotypic way of viewing the Latino family, and it is a way of "pathologizing" Latino family life. Recent research finds at least as much egalitarianism between men and women in Latino families as in white families with regard to caring for children, decision making, and sharing household tasks (Ybarra 1982).

Patterns of Latino Family Life

William Vega (1990) has reviewed changes in Hispanic or Latino families in the past decade. He notes that much of the population increase in Latino families in the past 10 years has been fueled by immigration from Mexico. Although Latinos have higher birth rates than whites, the average size of Latino families has declined in the past two decades. At the same time, the divorce rate in Latino families, which has been lower than the rate among blacks, has increased. Latino families still present the signs of "la familia" with considerable **geographic propinquity** (living near one another). The geographic propinquity facilitates visiting and exchange of financial resources as well as baby-sitting and other supportive activities. Sharing and cooperation are key values in Latino families (Markides, Boldt, and Ray 1986). Extended families play an important role in both migration and securing employment. Extended family assist family members in immigrating to the United States and finding housing and employment. Families pool their resources to buy food, pay for housing, buy a car, and pay for higher education. Family closeness and sharing enhance employment opportunities as Latinos refer friends and relatives for jobs (Wilson 1991).

SUMMING UP

In contemporary families, social class, race, and ethnicity are the major social structural forces that influence families and family life in the United States.

The structure of family relations depends on how stable and plentiful the sources of family income are. The socialization of children, their education and occupational aspirations, the health of family members, the life expectancy of each family member, and the risk of divorce and marital instability are all related to the source and size of family income. Social class influences values about gender roles, household responsibilities, and child rearing. Social class influences when individuals have their first sexual relationship, when they marry, and the social class of the women they marry. Class affects the chances that marriages will be stressful, have conflict, and involve violence. There is also considerable variation within a social class. Thus not every family within a social class group behaves in the same manner.

A number of features distinguish black families. First, they are young. Second, compared to the other major ethnic and racial groups, black families are much more likely to be female-headed households with no adult male present. Third, black families are more likely to be found in the southern states and in urban areas. Three defining structural forces have influenced the form and function of African American families: (1) the historical legacy of slavery; (2) the impact of racism, both personal and institutional; and (3) economic disadvantage.

The major patterns found in the African American family in the past decade include a declining rate of marriage, later ages of first marriage, higher divorce rates, an increase in female-headed households, higher proportions of births to unmarried mothers, and a larger percentage of children living in female-headed families.

The focus on the problems experienced by African American families tends to obscure the positive features of black family life in the United States. The two-parent family is still a prominent family structure among African Americans. One of the most profound positive features of black families are strong family ties.

Asians and Pacific Islanders are the fastest growing racial and ethnic group in the United States. Asian American family structure and life varies, depending on the family's origin, when the immigrants arrived, the circumstances of the immigration—whether the individual and/or families fled a war-ravaged country or left for better educational or occupational opportunities—and the socioeconomic status of the family. In general, Asian Americans have very high marriages rates and are rigidly patriarchal. Women are expected to stay at home and care for the children. Even when women work, which many do, they are still expected to carry out the housekeeping and child-rearing tasks. Cooperation, obedience, responsibility, and obligation to the family are stressed. Children are supposed to be loyal to their families and to defer to both parents' wishes. Gender role socialization is also traditional, with girls socialized to be caretakers and keepers of the home, while boys are not expected to do the dishes or laundry.

After blacks, Latinos are the second largest minority group in the United States. The distinguishing feature of Latino families is that they are young. The youthfulness of Latinos is largely due to the high birth rate in Latino families. Latino families, like African American families, experience higher rates of poverty and are more likely to be female headed than are white families. One of the defining characteristics of Latino family life has been termed "la familia," or familism. A second characteristic that has also been attributed to Latino families, and especially Mexican American families, is "machismo," or a patriarchal family structure. The average size of Latino families has declined in the past two decades. At the same time, the divorce rate in Latino families has increased.

NOTES

1. I use the term wealthy or upper class in place of Gilbert and Kahl's (1993) term "capitalist."

2. This chapter uses the terms blacks and African Americans interchangeably.

3. The U.S. Bureau of the Census uses the term "Hispanic" to refer to this group, and many individuals and scholars are comfortable with this term. However, many younger people reject this term as demeaning because it recalls Spanish and Portuguese conquest of their lands. The preferred term is Latino, which reflects the ethnic group's origins in Latin America (Gonzales 1992). Many Latinos use neither term but refer to themselves in terms of their country of origin—Mexican Americans, Cuban Americans, Puerto Ricans, or Nicaraguans. I have chosen to use the more modern term Latino.

REFERENCES

Agresti, Barbara Finlay. 1978. "The First Decades of Freedom: Black Families in a Southern County, 1970 and 1885." *Journal of Marriage and the Family* 40(November):697-706.

Alvirez, David and Frank D. Bean. 1976. "The Mexican-American Family." Pp. 271-92 in *Ethnic Families in America*, edited by Charles H. Mindel and Robert W. Habenstein. New York: Elsevier.

Angel, Ronald and Marta Tienda. 1982. "Determinants of Extended Household Structure: Cultural Patterns or Economic Model?" *American Journal of Sociology* 87(May): 1360-83.

Auletta, Ken. 1982. *The Underclass.* New York: Random House.

Axelrod, Morris. 1956. "Urban Structure and Social Participation." *American Sociological Review* 21(February):13-18.

Baltzell, E. Digby. 1958. *Philadelphia Gentlemen: The Makings of a National Upper Class.* Glencoe, IL: Free Press.

Bean, Frank D., Russell L. Curtis, and John P. Marcum. 1977. "Familism and Marital Satisfaction Among Mexican-Americans: The Effects of Family Size, Wife's Labor Force Participation, and Conjugal Power." *Journal of Marriage and the Family* 39(November):759-67.

Beck, Ruby W. and Scott H. Beck. 1989. "The Incidence of Extended Households Among Middle-Aged Black and White Women: Estimates From a 5-Year Panel Study." *Journal of Family Issues* 10(June):147-68.

Bell, Wendell and Marion Boat. 1957. "Urban Neighborhood and Informal Social Relationships." *American Journal of Sociology* 62(January):391-98.

Bennett, Claudia. 1992. *The Asian and Pacific Island Population in the U.S., March 1991 and 1990.* Washington, DC: U.S. Bureau of the Census.

Billingsley, Andrew. 1968. *Black Families in White America.* Englewood Cliffs, NJ: Prentice Hall.

Brodbar-Nemzer, J. Y. 1988. "The Contemporary American Jewish Family." Pp. 67-87 in *The Religion and Family Connection: Social Science Perspectives,* edited by Darwin L. Thomas. Salt Lake City, UT: Bookcraft.

Brown, C. L. and C. W. Pannell. 1985. "The Chinese in America." Pp. 195-216 in *Ethnicity in Contemporary America: A Geographical Appraisal,* edited by J. O. McKee. Dubuque, IA: Kendall/Hunt.

Cherlin, Andrew and Frank E Furstenberg, Jr. 1986. *The New American Grandparent: A Place in the Family, a Life Apart.* New York: Basic Books.

Clark, M. 1959. *Health in the Mexican-American Culture.* Berkeley: University of California Press.

Collins, Randall. 1975. *Conflict Sociology: Toward an Explanatory Science.* New York: Academic Press.

———. 1979. *The Credential Society: An Historical Sociology of Education and Stratification.* New York: Academic Press.

———. 1988. "Women and Men in the Class Structure." *Journal of Family Issues* 9(March):27-50.

de Lone, Richard H. 1979. *Small Futures: Children, Inequality, and the Limits of Liberal Reform.* New York: Harcourt Brace Jovanovich.

Du Bois, W.E.B. 1899. *The Philadelphia Negro.* Philadelphia: University of Pennsylvania Press.

Duncan, Greg J., with Richard D. Cox, Mary E. Corcoran, Martha S. Hill, Sal D. Hoffman, and James N. Morgan. 1984. *Years of Poverty, Years of Plenty: The Changing Economic Fortunes of American Workers and Families.* Ann Arbor, MI: Social Research Center, Institute for Social Research.

Eggebeen, David J. and Daniel T. Lichter. 1991. "Race, Family Structure, and Changing Poverty Among American Children." *American Sociological Review* 56(December):801-18.

Elkins, Stanley M. 1959. *Slavery: The Problem in American Institutional and Intellectual Life.* Chicago: University of Chicago Press.

Farley, Reynolds and Walter R. Allen. 1987. *The Color Line and the Quality of Life in America.* New York: Russell Sage.

Feagin, Joe R. and Clairece Booher Feagin. 1993. *Racial and Ethnic Relations.* 4th ed. Englewood Cliffs, NJ: Prentice Hall.

Frazier, E. Franklin. 1948. *The Negro Family in the United States.* New York: Dryden.

———. 1957. *The Negro in the United States.* New York: Macmillan.

Furstenberg, Frank E., Jr., J. Brooks-Gunn, and S. Philip Morgan. 1987. *Adolescent Mothers in Later Life.* New York: Cambridge University Press.

Gans, Herbert. 1962. *The Urban Villagers.* New York: Free Press.

Gelles, Richard J. 1989. "Child Abuse and Violence in Single-Parent Families: Parent Absence and Economic Deprivation." *American Journal of Orthopsychiatry* 59(October):492-501.

Gil, David. 1970. *Violence Against Children: Physical Child Abuse in the United States.* Cambridge, MA: Harvard University Press.

Gilbert, Dennis and Joseph A. Kahl. 1993. *The American Class Structure: A New Synthesis.* 4th ed. Belmont, CA: Wadsworth.

Gonzales, David. 1992. "What's the Problem With 'Hispanic'? Just Ask a Latino." *New York Times,* November 15, p. E-6.

Greer, Scott. 1956. "Urbanism Reconsidered: A Comparative Study of Local Areas in a Metropolis." *American Sociological Review* 21(February):19-25.

Gutman, Herbert. 1976. *The Black Family in Slavery and Freedom, 1750–1925.* New York: Pantheon.

Heller, Celia. 1966. *Mexican American Youth: Forgotten Youth at the Crossroads.* New York: Random House.

Hertz, Rosanna. 1986. *More Equal Than Others: Women and Men in Dual-Career Marriages.* Berkeley: University of California Press.

Hodge, Robert W. and Donald J. Treiman. 1968. "Class Identification in the United States." *American Journal of Sociology* 73 (March):535-47.

Hoffreth, Sandra L. 1984. "Kin Networks, Race, and Family Structure." *Journal of Marriage and the Family* 46(November): 791-806.

Hsia, J. and M. Hirano-Nakanishi. 1989. "The Demographics of Diversity: Asian Americans in Higher Education." *Change,* November-December, pp. 20-27.

Jackman, Mary R. and Robert W. Jackman. 1983. "An Interpretation of the Relationship Between Objective and Subjective Social Status." *American Sociological Review* 38(October): 569-82.

Kalmijn, Matthijs. 1991. "Shifting Boundaries: Trends in Religious and Educational Homogamy." *American Sociological Review* 6(December): 786-800.

Kelly, Robert E 1985. "The Family and the Urban Underclass." *Journal of Family Issues* 6(June):159-84.

Kitano, Harry H. L. 1988. "The Japanese-American Family." Pp. 258-75 in *Ethnic Families in America: Patterns and Variations,* 3rd ed., edited by Charles H. Mindel, Robert W. Habenstein, and Roosevelt Wright, Jr. New York: Elsevier.

Kitano, Harry H. L. and Roger Daniels. 1988. *Asian Americans: Emerging Minorities.* Englewood Cliffs, NJ: Prentice Hall.

Kohn, Melvin. 1963. "Social Class and Parent-Child Relationships: An Interpretation." *American Journal of Sociology* 68(January):471-80.

———. 1969. *Class and Conformity: A Study in Values.* Homewood, IL: Dorsey Press.

Kohn, Melvin and Carmi Schooler. 1983. *Work and Personality: An Inquiry Into the Impact of Social Stratification.* Norwood, NJ: Ablex.

Komarovsky, Mirra. 1962. *Blue Collar Marriage.* New York: Vintage.

Kotlowitz, Alex. 1991. *There Are No Children Here: The Story of Two Boys Growing Up in the Other America.* New York: Anchor Books.

Kulis, Stephen S. 1992. "Social Class and Locus of Responsibility in Relationships With Adult Children." *Journal of Family Issues* 13(December):482-504.

Markides, Kyriakos S., Joanne S. Boldt, and Laura A. Ray. 1986. "Sources of Helping and Intergenerational Solidarity: A Three Generation Study of Mexican Americans." *Journal of Gerontology* 41(July):506-11.

Min, Pyong Gap. 1988. "The Korean American Family." Pp. 199-

229 in *Ethnic Families in America: Patterns and Variations,* 3rd ed., edited by Charles H. Mindel, Robert W. Habenstein, and Roosevelt Wright, Jr. New York: Elsevier.

Mindel, Charles H. 1980. "Extended Familism Among Urban Mexican-Americans, Anglos, and Blacks." *Hispanic Journal of Behavioral Sciences* 2:21-34.

Moynihan, Daniel Patrick. 1965. *The Negro Family: The Case for National Action.* Washington, DC: Government Printing Office.

Myrdal, Gunnar. 1944. *An American Dilemma.* New York: Harper & Row.

National Research Council. 1989. *A Common Destiny: Blacks and American Society,* edited by Gerald D. Jaynes and Robin M. Williams. Washington, DC: National Academy Press.

Oh, Younh-Shi and Harriett Pipes McAdoo. 1993. "Socialization of Chinese American Children." Pp. 245-70 in *Family Ethnicity: Strength in Diversity,* edited by Harriet Pipes McAdoo. Newbury Park, CA: Sage.

O'Hare, William P. 1993. "America's Minorities—The Demographics of Diversity." *Population Bulletin* 47(4):1-45.

Ostrander, Susan A. 1984. *Women of the Upper Class.* Philadelphia: Temple University Press.

Pettigrew, T. F. 1976. "Race and Intergroup Relations." Pp. 461-508 in *Contemporary Social Problems,* 4th ed., edited by Robert K. Merton and Robert Nisbet. New York: Harcourt Brace Jovanovich.

Queen, Stuart A., Robert W. Habenstein, and Jill S. Quadagno. 1988. *The Family in Various Cultures.* New York: Harper & Row.

Ramirez, Oscar and Carlos H. Acre. 1981. "The Contemporary Chicano Family: An Empirically Based Review." Pp. 3-28 in *Explorations in Chicano Psychology,* edited by Augustine Baron, Jr. New York: Praeger.

Rapp, Rayna. 1982. "Family and Class in Contemporary America: Notes Toward an Understanding of Ideology." Pp. 168-87 in *Rethinking the Family: Some Feminist Questions,* edited by Barrie Thorne and Marilyn Yalom. New York: Longman.

Robinson, Robert V. and Jonathan Kelley. 1979. "Class as Conceived by Marx and Dahrendorf: Effects on Income Inequality and Politics in the United States and Great Britain." *American Sociological Review* 44(February):38-54.

Rubel, A. 1966. *Across the Tracks: Mexican-Americans in a Texas City.* Austin: University of Texas Press.

Rubin, Lillian B. 1976. *Worlds of Pain: Life in the Working Class Family.* New York: Basic Books.

Sack, William H., Robert Mason, and James E. Higgins. 1985. "The Single-Parent Family and Abusive Child Punishment." *American Journal of Orthopsychiatry* 55(April):252-59.

Simpson, Ida Harper, David Stark, and Robert A. Jackson. 1988. "Class Identification Processes of Married, Working Men and Women." *American*

Sociological Review 53(April): 284-93.

Stack, Carol B. 1974. *All Our Kin: Strategies for Survival in a Black Community.* New York: Harper & Row.

Staples, Robert. 1985. "Changes in Black Family Structure: The Conflict Between Family Ideology and Structural Conditions." *Journal of Marriage and the Family* 47(November):1005-14.

Sudarkasa, Niara. 1981. "Interpreting the African Heritage in Afro-American Family Organization." Pp. 37-53 in *Black Families,* edited by Harriet P. McAdoo. Newbury Park, CA: Sage.

Sussman, Marvin B. 1953. "The Help Pattern in the Middle Class Family." *American Sociological Review* 18(February): 22-28.

Taylor, Robert J., Linda M. Chatters, and Vickie M. Mays. 1988. "Parents, Children, Siblings, In-Laws, and Non-Kin as Sources of Emergency Assistance to Black Americans." *Family Relations* 37(July):298-304.

Taylor, Robert J., Linda M. Chatters, M. Belinda Tucker, and Edith Lewis. 1990. "Developments in Research on Black Families: A Decade Review." *Journal of Marriage and the Family* 52(November):993-1014.

Ten Houten, Warren D. 1970. "The Black Family: Myth and Reality." *Psychiatry* 33(2):145-55.

Thornton, Arland and Deborah Freedman. 1983. "The Chang-

ing American Family." *Population Bulletin* 38(4):1-43.

Tienda, Marta and Ronald Angel. 1982. "Headship and Household Composition Among Blacks, Hispanics, and Other Whites." *Social Forces* 61(December):508-31.

Tran, Than Van. 1988. "The Vietnamese Family." Pp. 276-302 in *Ethnic Families in America: Patterns and Variations,* 3rd ed., edited by Charles H. Mindel, Robert W. Habenstein, and Roosevelt Wright, Jr. New York: Elsevier.

U.S. Bureau of the Census. 1991. *Household and Family Characteristics: March 1990 and 1989.* Current Population Reports: Population Characteristics, Series P-20, No. 447. Washington, DC: Government Printing Office.

———. 1992. *Statistical Abstracts of the United States.* Washington, DC: Government Printing Office.

———. 1993. *Poverty in the United States: 1992.* Current Population Reports, Series P-60, No. 185. Washington, DC: Government Printing Office.

Valdivieso, Rafael and Cary Davis. 1988. *U.S. Hispanics: Challenging Issues for the 1990s.* Washington, DC: Population Reference Bureau.

Vanneman, Reeve and Fred C. Pampel. 1977. "The American Perception of Class and Status." *American Sociological Review* 42(June):422-37.

Vega, William A. 1990. "Hispanic Families." *Journal of Marriage and the Family* 52(November): 1015-24.

Warner, W. Lloyd and Paul S. Lunt. 1942. *Social Life of a Modern Community.* New Haven, CT: Yale University Press.

Whyte, Martin K. 1990. *Dating, Mating, and Marriage.* New York: Aldine de Gruyter.

Willie, Charles V. 1988. *A New Look at Black Families.* 3rd ed. Dix Hills, NY: General Hall.

Wilkinson, Doris. 1987. "Ethnicity." Pp. 183-210 in *Handbook of Marriage and the Family,* edited by Marvin B. Sussman and Suzanne K. Steinmetz. New York: Plenum.

Wilson, William Julius. 1980. *The Declining Significance of Race: Blacks and American Institutions.* 2nd ed. Chicago: University of Chicago Press.

———. 1991. "Plenary Address." Presented at the annual meeting of the National Council on Family Relations, Denver.

Wong, Morrison G. 1988. "The Chinese American Family." Pp. 230-57 in *Ethnic Families in America: Patterns and Variations,* 3rd ed., edited by Charles H. Mindel, Robert W. Habenstein, and Roosevelt Wright, Jr. New York: Elsevier.

Wright, Erik Olin. 1978. *Class, Crisis, and the State.* New York: New Left Books.

Ybarra, Lee. 1982. "When Wives Work: The Impact on the Chicano Family." *Journal of Marriage and the Family* 44 (February):169-78.

Zinn, Maxine Baca. 1979. "Chicano Family Research: Conceptual Distortions and Alternative Directions." *Journal of Ethnic Studies* 7(3):59-71.

CHAPTER 6

■■ Love, Courtship, and Mate Selection

THEORIES OF MATE SELECTION
Individualistic Theories
Sociological Theories

SUMMING UP

REFERENCES

When asked if they plan to marry, the majority of college students as well as the majority of the population say "yes." When asked if they have a list of the desired qualities in a potential mate, again the majority of college students and others surveyed can provide such a list—for some, the list may be as small as two or three items, for others as many as 10 or 20. When asked for another list of qualities sought in a potential date, students still produce a list, but some of the items have a different priority order when compared to the list of items for a potential mate. Physical attractiveness, which often is listed second, third, or lower for a mate, rises to the top of the list for both males and females contemplating a date. Given this seemingly clear and calculated approach to marriage as well as dating, it is often ironic and paradoxical that when asked "What determines who you will marry?" a substantial number of students answer "Fate" or "I don't know." Emotions and "fate" are often the central concerns of people involved in the process of dating, courtship, and mate selection. Social scientists, however, see much more of the rational and structural aspects to the complex and winding path to marriage.

Each year in the United States approximately 2.5 million marriages take place (U.S. Bureau of the Census 1992b). More than 95% of the population marries at least once, and for those whose first marriages end in divorce, nearly all will remarry within a few years (Cherlin 1992). Why do people get married? Most Americans think that love is the overarching reason. One study reported that 76% of those individuals surveyed cited love as the reason for marrying, with the desire for children a distant second at 24% (Brown 1966). Other studies also find that love is the main reason for marriage (Pietropinto and Simenauer 1979). For many but not all individuals, love is the essential prerequisite for marriage—marriage without love is almost unthinkable.

In other societies, past and present, love is a somewhat less important justification and motivation for marriage. As social anthropologist Ralph Linton noted in 1936, all societies recognize that a man and a woman may develop a violent emotional attachment to each other—what we call love—but few societies consider this attachment desirable, let alone a basis for marriage.

Throughout history, the preferred means of forming a marriage was for the union to be arranged by older relatives. If love followed the arranged union, so much the better.

Today, the ideas of love, free choice, and affection as the primary bases of selecting a marriage partner are spreading to non-Western societies. Marrying for love, however, is still not universally accepted (Murstein 1980).

Although this chapter provides a historical and cross-cultural glimpse at love, courtship, and mate selection, its primary focus is on examining the "paths to marriage" in contemporary American society. We begin by examining the concept of love. Next we look at the pathway to marriage—courtship and dating. Also discussed are premarital sexual relations. The chapter concludes with an examination of the process of mate selection in terms of the broad social factors that influence selection and the sociological and psychological theories of mate selection.

LOVE

"How do I love thee—let me count the ways!" So said the poet Elizabeth Barrett Browning (1977). For social scientists, the quote would read better if it said, "How do we define love? Let us count the ways"—because there is no concept that is as elusive and difficult to define, explain, and describe as is love. Poets, novelists, songwriters, screenwriters, psychiatrists, social scientists, and even politicians have attempted to define (or not define) the concept of love. On page 102 of his book *Paths to Marriage,* Bernard Murstein (1986) provides a partial listing of some of the attempts:

> Love is the delightful interval between meeting a beautiful girl and discovering that she looks like a haddock. —John Barrymore

> Aim inhibited sex. —Sigmund Freud

> Love is a game exaggerating the differences between one person and everyone else. —George Bernard Shaw

There are, of course, literally thousands of other definitions of love. *Bartlett's Familiar Quotations* lists more than 700 quotations on the word "love." Beyond the definitions and the quotations, there are poems, novels, movies, songs, and sonnets that attempt to capture the real and true meaning of love. Even the U.S. Senate became embroiled in the issue of defining "love" when, in 1975, then Senator William Proxmire bestowed what he called "The olden Fleece Award" on social psychologists Elaine Walster and Ellen Berscheid. Walster and Berscheid had received an $84,000 grant from the National Science Foundation to continue their research on passionate and companionate love (discussed below). Senator Proxmire cited this research as "fleecing" the taxpayers, since, in his opinion, money could not answer the question of "why" love, and besides, "I'm also against it [the grant] because I don't want the answer." Proxmire went on to claim that he believed that 200 million taxpayers didn't want the answer either because some things in life should remain a mystery (Walster and Walster 1978).

Social scientists, including Walster and Berscheid whose funding was eliminated after the Proxmire attack, cannot afford to indulge the so-called mystery of love. A concept that is considered the basis of forming a marriage by more than three quarters of the population needs to be both defined and understood by those concerned with contemporary families. The social scientists' struggle is not simply to capture the meaning and pain of love but to understand it as a concept and a social process fundamental to forming and maintaining a relationship and a marriage.

Defining Love
and the Types
of Love

Family social scientists have developed a variety of definitions of love. Sociologist Ira Reiss (1971) defines **courtship love** as a "type of intense emotional feeling developing from a primary relationship involving a single male and female consisting of rights and duties similar to those of husband and wife" (p. 125). Psychologist Harry Stack Sullivan (1947) said that a state of love exists "when the satisfaction of the security of another person becomes significant to one as is one's own security" (p. 292). Psychologist Bernard Murstein (1986) defines love as a decision on the part of an individual to regard another person as a love object, the conditions for defining love varying from individual to individual. Finally, William Kephart (1972) avoids a definition of love and simply identifies three characteristics shared by most definitions of love: "(1) a strong emotional attachment toward a person, (2) the tendency to think of this person in an idealized matter, and (3) a marked physical attraction, the fulfillment of which is reckoned in terms of touch."

Elaine and G. William Walster's program of research on love provides an alternative approach to coming to grips with "what is this thing called love?" The Walsters (1978) explain that there is no single type of love and thus no single definition. Rather, there is a variety of types of love and thus more than one definition.

The Walsters have identified two different forms of love: passionate love and companionate love. **Passionate love** is a wildly emotional state, a confusion of feelings: tenderness and sexuality, elation and pain, anxiety and relief, altruism and jealousy. Passionate love is a state of intense absorption in the other person. **Companionate love,** on the other hand, is a lower-key emotion—friendly affection and deep attachment to someone.

While it would seem that these two types of love are the opposite, they are better seen as complementary to one another. Passionate love, the more emotional form, provides the initial attraction between individuals and is the bond that keeps the relationship together; companionate love grows over time. When the fires of passionate love begin to die down, it is the deeper, less emotional companionate love that becomes the basis for the more enduring permanent relationship. If companionate love has not developed, the death of passion can signal the end of the relationship.

If love is a wonderful mystery that is difficult to define, then the process of falling in love may be an even deeper and more complex mystery. Ira Reiss (1980), however, notes that love is no more mysterious than digestion—a process we remain unaware of until we have a problem. Reiss developed the concept of the "Wheel of Love" as a means of analyzing how people fall in and out of love (see Figure 6-1).

The Development of Love: Reiss's Wheel of Love

According to Reiss's model, individuals "fall in love" by going through four stages: (1) rapport, (2) self-revelation, (3) mutual dependency, and (4) personality need fulfillment.

Rapport. When two individuals meet, they go through a process of assessing one another and determining whether there is a feeling of mutual rapport. Are they comfortable with one another? Do they communicate and understand each other? If they feel at ease, communicate, and feel they understand each other, the relationship begins to grow. The process of developing rapport is strongly influenced by social and cultural factors. Although rapport can develop between individuals from widely different backgrounds, Reiss and other social scientists who study love and marriage note that similarity of upbringing, religion, and education can ease and enhance the process of developing rapport.

Self-Revelation. As rapport builds and interaction increases, the relationship moves to the second stage on the wheel, self-revelation. At this stage, the two individuals begin to reveal intimate facts and feeling about themselves. Habits develop, cooperation increases, and the couple gets used to one another.

Mutual Dependency. The third stage on the wheel is mutual dependency where the two individuals become interdependent. They are a union, a couple. One

Figure 6-1 Reiss's
Wheel of Love

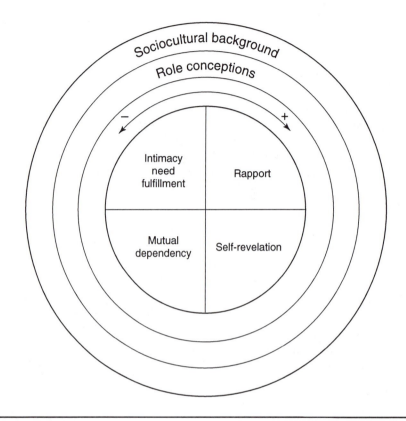

Figure 6-1 Reiss's Wheel of Love

SOURCE: Figure from *Family System in America,* Third Edition by Ira L. Reiss, copyright © 1980 by Holt, Rinehart and Winston, Inc.. Reprinted by permission of the publisher.

tells a joke, the other listens and laughs. They share rewarding activities and experiences, and they fulfill each other's sexual needs.

Personality Need Fulfillment. The fourth and last stage on the wheel is personality need fulfillment. Here the basic personality needs of each individual—the need to love and be loved, the need for someone to confide in, the need for understanding and support, the need to feel worthwhile—are fulfilled through the relationship.

The outer two rings of the wheel, "sociocultural background" and "role conceptions," are the contexts for the interpersonal processes described by the inner spokes of the wheel. All four stages or spokes are influenced by role conceptions because role conceptions define what is expected of a person in a love relationship. The sociocultural context consists of education, religion, social class, and race and ethnicity. As we saw in Chapter 5, all of these factors can shape role expectations and role conceptions.

The elegance of Reiss's "Wheel of Love" is not simply the four stages that individuals move through. The wheel is more than stages, it is a dynamic model. The wheel can spiral more and more as individuals increase their rapport and deepen their self-revelation, dependency, and fulfillment. The wheel can also unwind. Fights and arguments can lead to unmet needs, lessened dependency, decreased sharing, and finally a diminished sense of rapport. This unwinding of the wheel is what we call "falling out of love."

COURTSHIP

Traditional societies that arranged marriages had no need for courtship and dating—mate selection was a formal process that was the right of parents or family elders. Modern societies that allow choice of a mate have developed patterns of courtship, including dating, that are a significant part of the mate selection process. During colonial times, courtship went on under the watchful eyes and the imposed rules of parents (see Box 6-1). Improvements in transportation, lengthening of formal education, and the development of the stage of adolescence between childhood and adulthood introduced a new stage in the courtship process—dating.

Dating

Dating is a relatively new and rapidly changing pattern of courtship. Today in the United States, dating is an important but changing path that individuals travel when they move from being single to married. Sociologist Michael Gordon (1981) notes that dating among college students is believed to have begun after World War I and became widespread during the 1920s and 1930s. Dating among high school students and teenagers seems to have emerged in the late 1930s and became commonplace in the 1940s and 1950s. Industrialization, urbanization, and technology influenced the growth and the pattern of dating. The invention of the bicycle, automobile, and, to a lesser extent, the telephone, combined with the increase in mass education, especially higher education, to provide the key ingredients—mobility and privacy—to foster the growth of dating as a courtship practice.

Changing gender roles have brought about changes in dating patterns in the 1970s, 1980s, and 1990s. Between the 1940s and the 1970s dating was a highly structured, almost ritual-like behavior that involved the girl waiting to be asked out and the boy wrestling with whether or not he should call or ask and then contemplating the likelihood that his invitation would be accepted or rejected. If the request was accepted, the boy would arrive at the girl's home and chat with the parents while he waited for his date to make a grand entrance. A preexisting curfew for the girl's return would be stated, and the couple would leave on their date. They might go off together or with another couple on a "double date." Boys were expected to pay for the date and girls were expected to allow some form of physical intimacy: a good-night kiss, petting, or intercourse.

The women's movement and the development of more equitable gender roles eliminated the more formal and ritualistic aspects of dating, especially among the middle class and among college students. Since the 1970s it has become more acceptable for a girl to ask out a boy, and single and double dates have given way to group activities, such that dates occur without even a forma request. In the 1990s, some dating is arranged using computers and "e-mail." Sociologist David Hansen (personal communication) reports on the "BITNET Interchat Relay Network" that exists on college campuses. Individuals communicate on the network and use symbols for smiles, laughs, frowns, and winks.

Waller's Rating and Dating Complex

The first scholarly article on dating was published by Willard Waller in 1937. Waller had examined the patterns of dating among students at Pennsylvania

---

BOX 6-1: THE FAMILY OVER TIME

Courtship and "Bundling" in Colonial America

There are some scattered historical accounts of courtship patterns in colonial times. One reason for the scarcity of information on courtship practices in colonial America is that the process lacked the formality and ceremony that is so much the part of courtship today. There was no formal dating. There were no dances or parties (Demos 1970). The lack of privacy and mobility in the colonies meant that courtship often went on under the watchful eyes of family, relatives, and the community, although there was some leeway and freedom.

One courtship practice in colonial America that has been much discussed is "bundling." Courtship in colonial America could not be pursued in the daylight during the week, as this was reserved for farming and work. Evenings were short (and without electric light) and travel was perilous after dark. The colonial family often lived in a home without separate rooms (parlor, den, guest room) that we take for granted today. Thus the time and space opportunities for a young man and woman to spend time together were quite limited. However, a couple could

State University during the late 1920s and early 1930s. From these observations Waller developed his theory of the **rating and dating complex.** His portrait of dating is one of social status and stratification and less one of recreation and amusement. Dating at Penn State, a school at which half of the men belonged to fraternities, was a competition. The fraternities were ranked in a status system—the most prestigious fraternities were those with the highest-status members—football players, honor society members, "Big Men on Campus," and so on. The symbols of status and desirability—how they were rated—were fraternity membership, clothes, good looks, money to spend, a car, and dancing ability. The most desirable men competed to date the most desirable women. The goal of dating was thrills or psychological stimulation. Dancing, drinking, attending movies, necking, petting, and sometimes "going all the way" (sexual intercourse) were the shared activities. Waller saw men as seeking sexual gratification while women sought status by dating the more desirable men.

Exchange and bargaining were the core processes of the rating and dating complex. Waller found a general tendency for individuals with equal campus status to pair off. When the couples were of equal status, the relationship was equitable. However, when the match was not of equal status, the relationship was inequitable and led to exploitation. Waller called this exploitation the **principle of least interest.** From Waller's perspective, the individual who had the least interest in the relationship had the greatest amount of power in the bargaining and exchange. For example, a higher-status male dating a lower-status female could exploit the woman's desire to date a high-status man

spend the evening together if they were "bundled." Bundling was a custom that was imported to the New England colonies and New Amsterdam (New York) from Europe. An unmarried couple could go to bed at night, fully clothed or almost so, and continue their courtship under the covers, although without physical intimacy (see Stiles 1934). Sometimes, a wooden board or "bundling board" might be placed in the middle of the bed, or the young woman would be wrapped (bundled) in such a way as to prevent physical contact. The young women's parents often slept in the same room as the bundled couple. Bundling was somewhat more common among the lower social classes and was an adaptation to the conditions of colonial life. Bundling allowed courtship without requiring the male to return home after dark and without using precious fuel to light and heat the home.

Given the rather harsh view of premarital sex in northern colonial America and the apparent close supervision of couples who were courting, one might assume that premarital sex was either impossible or rare. In fact, close supervision, bundling, and harsh punishments for "fornication" did not eliminate premarital sex. Couples did engage in premarital sex, and historians estimate that between one fifth and one third of all colonial women were pregnant when they married (Demos 1970; Hawke 1988). Obviously, some couples did find times and places for physical intimacy.

Modern dating patterns are more casual and no longer involve the formal and ritualistic aspects common from the 1940s through the 1970s.

by demanding sexual gratification in exchange for continuing the relationship. In reality, because there was a 6 to 1 ratio of men to women at Penn State in the 1930s, men made fewer exploitive demands on lower-status females because of the scarcity of women. This meant that lower-status women could date higher-status men (and gain upward mobility) without granting too much physical accessibility.

Family scholars today have critiqued Waller's research on scientific grounds. Waller, scholars claim, placed too much emphasis on thrill seeking and gratification and too little on more idealistic and humanistic aspects of dating. Waller also failed to take into account that dating is an important path to marriage. Finally, Waller failed to place what he called "rating and dating" into the more general process of class homogamy (the tendency to date and marry those from the same social class) in dating and mate selection (Blood 1955; Reiss 1965; Rogers and Havens 1960; Smith 1952). More significantly, scholars were not generally able to replicate Waller's findings in studies of dating on other campuses.

Clearly, what Waller observed at Penn State may have been a brief episode in American courtship patterns and unique to the time and place. However, his observations about bargaining and exchange, similarity of social status of dating partners, and the principle of least interest were important observations about the social processes of dating.

James Skipper and Gilbert Nass (1966) focused on the purposes of dating. They suggest that the purposes of dating are courtship (mate selection), recreation (entertainment and enjoyment), socialization (learning how to interact and behave with members of the opposite sex) and, as Waller noted, status seeking.

Rebecca Vreeland's (1972) research documented the changes that occurred in dating in the 1960s and 1970s. Vreeland studied students at Harvard University where she noted that dating had became less formal, less exploitive, and somewhat less heterosexual. Students seemed to see dates more as friends and less as competitors or candidates for marriage.

Research on dating on college campuses in the 1980s revealed less structured and formal patterns. David Knox and Kenneth Wilson (1981) examined how men and women met at a southeastern college. They found that there were a large number of ways that people meet—through friends, at parties, at work, in class, and on the age-old blind date. Today, cars, clothes, and "a good line" have become less important than they were when Waller studied dating. Researchers report that friendship, intimacy, being able to listen, and having one's self-esteem raised are important (Knox and Wilson 1981; Laner 1989; Whyte 1990).

Bruce Roscoe and his colleagues Mark Diana and Richard Brooks II (1987) studied dating patterns of adolescents ranging from sixth graders (about 11 years old) to college-aged adolescents (18-21 years old). They found that early adolescents (6th graders) and middle adolescents (11th graders) were more interested in recreation, intimacy, and status as the most important purposes for dating. Late adolescents were more interested in intimacy, companionship, and socialization.

Newer, more recent research finds that changing gender roles and feminism have changed the structure of dating (Laner 1989; Roscoe et al. 1987; Whyte 1990). Sociologist Sheila Korman (1983) found that young women who hold egalitarian gender role preferences were more likely than women holding traditional views of gender roles to initiate dates and share date expenses; however, she did find that even traditional women were becoming more open to sharing expenses.

For a phenomenon that seems to be so central in the path to marriage, there is surprisingly little current research on dating. Family scholars focused on dating from the 1930s, when Waller wrote about the rating and dating complex, until the 1970s. The vast majority of dating research since then studied dating patterns among college students. This could have occurred because college students are more accessible to family scholars (it is rather easy to hand out questionnaires to students in class), because the dating patterns of college students were more familiar to the patterns experienced by middle-class professional family scholars, or because dating was primarily a phenomenon found among college students. The falloff in interest on dating research since the 1960s and early 1970s appears to be a function of the decline in dating as a formal pattern as well as of the changing interest of researchers.

Cohabitation

Cohabitation is the pattern of two unmarried persons of the opposite sex with a romantic interest in each other sharing a residence. It is an increasingly common phenomenon. Cohabitation itself is not new—people cohabitated during the Middle Ages (Murstein 1986). In colonial times, cohabitating was sometimes practiced by the lower classes or as a matter of practical convenience. Traveling preachers did not visit a community for months at a time, thus forcing couples who wished to be legally married to either wait for the preacher or to cohabitate. Thirty years ago, cohabitation as a form of courtship was frowned upon, and participants were subjected to negative social sanctions. Eleanor Macklin, writing about cohabitation in 1972, noted that in 1962 a graduate student at Cornell University was suspended for having a woman living in his apartment. The Cornell University Faculty Council on Student Conduct considered "overnight unchaperoned mixed company" a violation of sexual morality.

Eight years after Cornell's reprimand to students for cohabitation, there were about 450,000 couples living together in the United States (U.S. Bureau of the Census 1970). The number nearly doubled by 1975 and more than doubled again between 1980 and 1992 (U.S. Bureau of the Census 1983, 1985, 1992a). In 1992, there were 3.3 million unmarried-couple households, two thirds of which have no children under 15 years of age living in the home.

There are a number of reasons why cohabitation has become a more popular and socially acceptable form of relationship in the past 30 years. First, evidence from the Scandinavian countries, such as Denmark and Sweden, where cohabitation is much more common suggests that cohabitation does not undermine or destroy the family, although some sociologists, such as

Cohabitation has become so common and socially acceptable that couples who live together no longer feel they have to hide their relationship.

David Popenoe (1988) disagree (see Chapter 16). Second, modern advances in contraception make it possible for couples to cohabitate without the complications of pregnancy. Changing gender roles and the status of women have somewhat freed women from the double standard whereby women who cohabitated were seen as immoral and not suitable marriage partners. Colleges, like Cornell, have changed their views, values, and rules regarding student behavior. The concept of *in loco parentis* (in place of the parents) that dominated college rules and regulations in the 1950s and 1960s and that led to curfews, sign-ins, and other regulations has been eliminated. Campuses now have coeducational residence halls, classes on sex education, and dispense birth control pills and condoms (the latter may be more a concession to the threat of AIDS than a change in attitude about premarital sex).

Off college campuses, the increase in the divorce rate has produced a large pool of single individuals of all ages who seek heterosexual relations without immediately committing to a marriage (Murstein 1986). About one third of those who cohabitate are divorced individuals (Thornton 1988).

With the increase in cohabitation, there has been some discussion of whether cohabiting improves the chances of a successful marriage. There are four hypotheses regarding the impact of cohabitation on subsequent marriage:

1. Cohabitation serves as a training period for marriage and mate selection and improves the quality of subsequent marriages (Ridley, Peterman, and Avery 1978; Trost 1975).

2. Individuals who live together before marriage are less committed to marriage and are likely to have lower-quality marriages than individuals who do not live together (DeMaris and Leslie 1984).

3. Cohabitating couples begin their marriages earlier than noncohabitating couples and thus the chances are that marital satisfaction will decline rapidly among these couples (Booth and Johnson 1988).

4. Cohabitation might have a negative impact on marriage by pressuring individuals into getting married when they have doubts about marriage (Booth and Johnson 1988).

Alan Booth and David Johnson (1988) tested these four hypotheses on a national sample of 2,033 married individuals. Based on their data, they conclude that the first hypothesis is incorrect—cohabitation *does not* improve marital quality. Instead, cohabitation contributed to more disagreements and a greater chance of divorce. Thus the investigators did find support for the second hypothesis—that individuals who live together before marriage have somewhat lower-quality marriages than individuals who do not cohabitate. The researchers did not find specific support for the hypothesis that marital satisfaction declines because cohabitators begin their marriages earlier than noncohabitating couples, nor was there support for the hypothesis that cohabitators are pressured into getting married when they have doubts about marriage. Booth and Johnson did find that lower marital satisfaction seemed to be the result of the fact that those who cohabitate seem to be poor marriage risks before they marry. These poor risks include drug problems, inability to handle money, being in trouble with the law, unemployment, and personality problems. Thus cohabitation decreases marital satisfaction because a significant portion, but certainly not all, of cohabitators are poor marriage material.

PREMARITAL SEX

Fifty or 100 years ago it was assumed that sex had no place in the courtship process. Ira Reiss (1972) comments that "one of our most prevalent myths is that in past centuries the typical form of courtship was that of two virgins meeting, falling in love, and doing very little with each other sexually. They then married, learned about sex together in the marital bed, and remained faithful to each other until death separated them" (p. 167). Today, the

University of Rhode Island students joke that the next time a virgin graduates from the university this cannon will fire spontaneously.

prevailing assumption is that sex is a common part of courtship and premarital relations.

The reality of premarital sexuality, both historically and today, falls somewhere between these two mythical assumptions. Men and women have been entering marriage nonvirginally for centuries. Historical data from colonial New England indicate that as many as one third of all brides were pregnant at the time of marriage (Calhoun 1945; Smith and Hindus 1975). And it would not be a surprise to learn that brides who were *not* pregnant were also not virgins when they went to their wedding bed. Alfred Kinsey and his associates' (1948, 1953) study of sexual attitudes and behavior found that at least 50% of women born between 1900 and 1910 entered marriage nonvirginally. Other researchers also report that about half of the women born in this century were nonvirgins by the time they married (Burgess and Wallin 1953; Reiss 1960; Terman 1938).

The incidence of premarital sex remained stable from the beginning of the century until the late 1960s (Reiss 1960). While there may have been changes in attitudes toward sex, including people becoming more free in talking about sex and a reduction in feelings of regret or guilt about premarital sex, actual behavior did not change much (Reiss 1960).

Rapid changes in sexual behavior began to occur in the late 1960s. The incidence of premarital sex began to increase while the age at which individuals first had sexual intercourse declined (Bell and Chaskes 1970; Christensen and Gregg 1970; Clayton and Bokemeier 1980; Kantner and Zelnick 1972). Ira Robinson and his colleagues Ken Ziss, Bill Ganza, and Stuart Katz (1991) report that the percentage of college students who have premarital intercourse increased from 65.0% in 1965 to 79.3% in 1985 for men and from 28.7% in 1965 to 63.0% in 1985 for women (see Table 6-1).

Clearly, not everyone who married in 1900 was a virgin, and while we have gone through two decades of considerable change in both attitudes and behavior, not everyone who marries in 1995 has had sexual intercourse.

| Explaining the Changes in Attitudes and Behavior | Attitudes about sexuality and premarital sex began to change in the 1920s. As noted earlier, the greatest change in behavior occurred in the late 1960s and throughout the 1970s. Sociologists note that although there were changes among men (including changes in the percentage of men who engage in premarital sex, a decrease in age at the time of first sexual intercourse, and a decline in the proportion of men whose first sexual experience is with a prostitute), the greatest changes have been in the attitudes and behavior of women.

A number of factors appear to explain changing attitudes and behaviors among women. The most noteworthy change is in sexual standards, or a move

Date	Males		Females		% Difference
	%	n	%	n	
1965	65.1	129	28.7	115	36.4
1970	65.0	136	37.3	158	27.7
1975	73.9	115	57.1	275	16.8
1980	77.4	168	63.5	230	13.9
1985	79.3	208	63.0	257	16.3

Table 6-1
Percentage of College Students in 1965, 1970, 1975, 1980, and 1985 Samples Having Premarital Intercourse

SOURCE: "Twenty Years of the Sexual Revolution, 1965–1985: An Update" by Ira Robinson, Ken Ziss, Bill Ganza, and Stuart Katz, 1991, *Journal of Marriage and the Family* 53(February), p. 217. Copyright © 1991 by the National Council on Family Relations, 3989 Central Ave. NE, Suite 550, Minneapolis, MN. Adapted by permission.

away from the old "double standard" of sexual morality. Ira Reiss (1960, 1967) has identified four different premarital sexual standards: (1) *abstinence* (the belief that there should be no sexual activity before marriage), (2) *the double standard*, (3) *permissiveness with affection*, and (4) *permissiveness without affection*. The traditional double standard held that men engage in sex for erotic release while women engage in sexual intercourse for love and romance. While men sought sexual release by reducing the number of virgins, they also wanted to marry a virgin.

The feminist movement of the 1920s and the women's movement of the 1960s to the present raised consciousness both about women's status and about sexual attitudes and standards. The old double standard was assailed because it denied women both equality and autonomy. Although attitudes have changed and the double standard has been challenged as chauvinistic, we have not yet achieved a new "single standard" of sexuality. The old double standard appears to have been replaced by one that supports greater restraints on sexual behavior of others than on oneself (Reiss 1967). Researchers report that men still seem to prefer virgins as dating and mating partners (Jacoby and Williams 1985).

In addition to attitude changes and changing sexual standards playing a role in changing patterns of premarital sex, increased opportunities for contraception have enabled women to prevent pregnancy and explore and expand their own sexuality. However, although the opportunities to prevent pregnancy exist, contraception is not used by all those who engage in premarital sexual intercourse. Although the level of contraceptive use at the time of first sexual intercourse among teenage women has increased from a little less than half (48%) in 1985 to about two thirds (65%) in 1988, nearly one third of teenage women do not use contraceptives the first time they have intercourse (Forrest and Singh 1990). The younger the woman, the less likely she is to use contraception the first time she has intercourse.

Future Trends   Ira Reiss, writing in 1980, contended that the change in attitudes and behavior that some have called the "sexual revolution" is over. He noted that divorce rates have stabilized, the marriage rate has gone down, and the birth rate has stabilized. He predicts that we shall now see a period of consolidation during which attitudes and behavior come closer together. Reiss saw this period of consolidation lasting until the 1990s.

When Reiss made his prediction, the HIV/AIDS virus had not yet been identified as a sexually transmitted disease. Today we know that AIDS is a deadly disease, for which a cure has not yet been found. Nor is there reason to think the cure will be found in the near future. We know that AIDS is transmitted by bodily fluids and can be transmitted through sexual acts and by shared hypodermic needles. AIDS can be transmitted through sexual activity, especially through anal intercourse. Nonetheless, public awareness campaigns stressing safe sex and the use of condoms proliferated in the mid to late 1980s and early 1990s. It is not yet clear whether the threat of AIDS will change attitudes about premarital sex or behavior. Nor is it clear whether the threat of AIDS will promote the use of contraception among men and women

---

BOX 6-2: THE GLOBAL VIEW

Premarital Sex and Pregnancy: A Cross-Cultural Perspective

All societies control sexual behavior. Premarital sex has, however, received the most widespread acceptance and the least control. Anthropologist George Murdock (1949) examined the records of societies across cultures and over time and found that premarital sex was permitted in 70% of societies. Proscriptions against premarital sex were typically aimed at females as a means of guarding against bearing children out of wedlock. Where there are no proscriptions against premarital sex, children born out of wedlock are treated as equally as those born in a marriage.

Teenage fertility is considerably higher in the United States than in the great majority of the other developed nations of the world (Jones et al. 1985). The gap between the United States and other countries is greatest for younger adolescents than for older teenagers.

Why are the rates of pregnancy (and abortion) higher in the United States than other nations? American teenagers are not more sexually active than young people in other countries (Jones et al. 1985), yet they are more likely to get pregnant, give birth, and have abortions. The answer seems to be in the use of contraception. American teenagers are *less likely* to use the birth control pill and other contraceptives than are young adolescents in other developed nations (Jones et al. 1985). In addition, the United States has not committed itself to an unambiguous social policy, including advocacy and sex education, that aims at reducing teenage pregnancy.

who engage in premarital sex. The data that are available indicate that, at the moment, young men and women are aware of AIDS and its danger but have yet to actually practice "safe sex," use condoms, or avoid premarital sexual intercourse (Carroll 1988).

MATE SELECTION

We assume that because love is the reason for forming a marriage and there are no arranged marriages in our society, the basis for choosing a mate is unconstrained free choice. James Loewen (1979) has devised an exercise he calls the "Marriage Machine" that illustrates how, even in a culture where free choice and love are the guiding principles of mate selection, the actual choice is as tightly constrained for elite college students as for filling station attendants.

Loewen begins the exercise (illustrated in Figure 6-2) by choosing a hypothetical student named Suzie. Suzie is a single white Catholic student of average height. Assuming that Suzie says she will marry, Loewen takes her through the steps that guide her choice. From the available population (now about 250 million), Loewen and Suzie make the following assumptions and choices:

1. First, we assume that Suzie will want to marry a male. This roughly reduces the pool of eligibles by half.

2. The next assumption is that Suzie will, as do most individuals, choose to marry someone roughly in her same age group. Assuming a generous age range of seven years (18-25), and given that 14% of the population is between the ages of 18 and 25, this further reduces the number of eligible males.

3. If Suzie is like most women, she will choose to marry someone who is the same race as she is. Because Suzie is white and 86% of the population is white, this narrows the pool only slightly.

4. The next assumption is that Suzie, like many individuals, prefers to marry someone who is of the same religion as she is. She is Catholic and roughly 23% of the population is Catholic, so this reduces the pool again.

5. Other factors that Loewen and Suzie load into the marriage machine include assumptions that Suzie will marry someone who has a similar level of education and intelligence as she has. In terms of physical attributes, Suzie will likely chose to marry a man taller than she is. Loewen and Suzie also factor in the fact that Suzie will want to marry someone she likes and has interests and abilities that she finds attractive. And, of course, she can only marry someone who is eligible to marry (single or divorced) or wants to get married.

Figure 6-2
The "Marriage Machine" Table of Multipliers

Population of the United States	250,000,000
Multiplier for sex (males only)	.5
	125,000,000
Multiplier for age (18-25)	.14
	17,500,000
Multiplier for race (Caucasian)	.86
	15,050,000
Multiplier for religion (Catholic)	.23
	3,461,500
Multiplier for height (males 5'6" or taller)	.9
	3,115,350
Multiplier for education (B.A. or more)	.26
	809,991
Multiplier for marital status (single)	.5
	404,995
Multiplier for eligibility (will marry)	.95
	384,745
Multiplier for interests (congruent)	.5
	192,372
Multiplier for IQ (above 100)	.5
	96,186
Multiplier for fraction of the U.S. population whom Suzie knows (2,500/250,000,000)	.00001
Total population whom Suzie could marry	.9

SOURCE: "Introductory Sociology: Four Classroom Exercises" by James Loewen, 1979, *Teaching Sociology* 6(3), p. 231. Copyright © 1979 by the American Sociological Association. Adapted by permission.

6. During the course of the exercise the point is almost always made that "You have to *know* whom you will marry." To get at this point, Loewen asks Suzie to guess how many people she actually knows. With this number in hand (in the exercise it was a generous guess of about 2,500) Loewen factors in the final multiplier—that is, .00001% of the U.S. population (2,500/250,000,000).

When the final multiplier is applied to Suzie's preferences, the pool of 250 million eligible mates is reduced to .9! The final number, Loewen points out, is not independent of the other numbers since the people Suzie knows are likely to be white, Catholic, college educated, and her same age group and interest group. Thus .9 is a bit of an understatement.

Loewen's exercise with Suzie is not meant to be a statistical sleight of hand or hyperbole. The central goal of the "Marriage Machine" is to illustrate the social forces associated with marital choice.

Analysis of marriage patterns shows that Cupid, rather than exercising total free choice, is highly selective. The governing principal of marital choice appears to be **homogamy,** the tendency to marry someone who is like us in

Year	Men	Women
1992	26.5	24.4
1985	25.5	23.3
1980	24.7	22.0
1975	23.5	21.1
1970	23.2	20.8
1965	22.8	20.6
1960	22.8	20.3
1955	22.6	20.2
1950	22.8	20.3
1940	24.3	21.5
1930	24.3	21.3
1920	24.6	21.2
1910	25.1	21.6
1900	25.9	21.9
1890	26.1	22.0

Table 6-2 Median Age at First Marriage, by Sex, 1980–1992

SOURCE: U.S. Bureau of the Census (1992a, p. vii, Table B).
NOTE: A standard error of 0.1 years is appropriate to measure sampling variability for any of the above median ages at first marriage, based on Census Bureau Current Population Survey data.

the social attributes that our society considers important, such as age, education, race, religion, and ethnic background.

Age and Marital Choice

The data that have been recorded on the age at marriage show that from 1890 until 1956 men and women married at increasingly younger ages (Table 6-2). Since the mid-1950s the average age at first marriage has risen to an all-time high in 1992. The median age at first marriage for a man in 1992 was 26.5 and for a woman 24.4 (U.S. Bureau of the Census 1992a).

The same data reveal that couples tend to be highly similar in age at first marriage and the gap is narrowing. In the past, men tended to be older than women at first marriage. The traditional explanations for why men are older when they marry is that they physically mature at a slower rate than women, that men are expected to be the principal source of economic support for the family, and that more men than women pursue higher education (Murstein 1986). As more women are seeking higher education and securing economically secure careers, however, the age gap has narrowed, and some think it will soon disappear (Murstein 1986).

The tendency of females to marry males who are somewhat older produces a phenomenon that demographers have called the "marriage squeeze." The marriage squeeze occurs during periods of change in the birth rate. For example, the post-World War II baby boom resulted in a significant increase in the birth rate from 1946 to about 1957. Women born in the late 1940s who wanted to marry men two or three years older found fewer eligible men, and like a game of musical chairs, some women would get left out. Thus, in the 1970s, marriage-aged women faced a shortage of eligible men. At the other extreme of the baby boom, there is a surplus of eligible men (those born in 1957) for women born in the late 1950s or early 1960s. In the 1980s, men found a shortage of eligible women.

Education

Education, like age, plays a dual role in marital choice. First, education and plans for extended education result in delays in entering a first marriage. For women, education not only delays marriage, but extensive education frequently reduces the likelihood that a woman will marry at all. This could be the result of extensive education leading to so much economic security that women do not need to be married, or it could be a function of the fact that men tend to marry women with less education. Thus the highly educated woman may be perceived as a less desirable mate because men wish to be equal to or superior to women in terms of achieved social status.

The second role of education is that men and women tend to marry partners with similar levels of education. Alan Kerckhoff (1964) found that similarity of education increased from dating to engagement to marriage, with the least similarity of education between first daters and the most between marriage partners.

The trend in educational homogamy has strengthened over the past 70 years. Sociologist Matthijs Kalmijn (1991) reports that, although there is increasing intermarriage between religious groups, intermarriage between individuals with different levels of educational attainment has declined. The social boundaries between educational groups seem to have strengthened as the boundaries between religious groups have fallen.

Race

One of the strongest forms of homogamy is the tendency of individuals to marry partners of the same race. Until the late 1960s, a number of states had laws on the books that forbade **miscegenation,** marriage between people of different races. These laws were struck down by the U.S. Supreme Court in 1967. Census data show that only about 2% to 3% of marriages are mixed marriages (see Table 6-3; also see Box 6-3 on intermarriage) (U.S. Bureau of the Census 1992a). About one fourth of all mixed racial marriages are between blacks and whites (Murstein 1986).

Table 6-3 Married Couples of Same and Mixed Races and Origins, 1992, 1980, and 1970 (in thousands)

Race and Origin of Spouses	1992	1980	1980 Census	1970 Census	Percentage Distribution			
					1992	1980	1980 Census	1970 Census
Race								
Same-race couples	50,873	48,264	46,986	43,922	95.1	90.2	87.8	82.1
White/white	47,358	44,910	43,568	40,578	88.5	90.3	88.0	91.0
Black/black	3,515	3,354	3,418	3,344	6.6	6.7	6.9	7.5
Interracial couples	1,161	651	953	310	2.2	1.2	1.8	0.6
Black/white	246	167	121	65	0.5	0.3	0.2	0.1
Black husband/white wife	163	122	94	41	0.3	0.2	0.2	0.1
White husband/black wife	83	45	27	24	0.2	0.1	0.1	0.1
White/other race (excluding white and black)	883	450	785	233	1.7	0.9	1.6	0.5
Black/other (excluding white and black)	32	34	47	12	0.1	0.1	0.1	—
All other couples (excluding white and black)	1,478	799	1,574	366	2.8	1.6	3.2	0.8
Origin								
Hispanic/Hispanic	3,297	1,906	2,087	1,368	6.2	3.8	4.2	3.1
Hispanic/other origin (not Hispanic)	1,155	891	931	584	2.2	1.8	1.9	1.3
All other couples (not of Hispanic origin)	49,060	46,917	48,496	42,645	91.7	94.4	93.9	95.6
All married couples	53,512	49,714	49,514	44,598	100.0	100.0	100.0	100.0

SOURCE: U.S. Bureau of the Census (1980, Table 11; 1992a, p. xi, Table F).
NOTE: Persons of Hispanic origin may be of any race.

BOX 6-3: DIVERSE FAMILIES

Interracial Marriages

The majority of marriages in the United States each year are of couples in which both partners are members of the same racial group (U.S. Bureau of the Census 1992b). Although in excess of 95% of all marriages are between partners of the same race, the number and percentage of interracial marriages is increasing. Since 1970, the number of interracial marriages has nearly tripled—from 310,000 in 1970 to 1.1 million in 1992. Interracial marriages as a proportion of all marriages has increased from 0.6% in 1970 to 2.2% in 1992.

There are distinct patterns of interracial marriage. Nearly two thirds of the marriages between blacks and whites are between black men and white women. When Japanese or Filipino individuals marry whites, the situation is reversed, with white men marrying Japanese or Filipino women.

When whites marry Chinese persons or Native Americans, the ratio is about even, with as many white men marrying Chinese or Native American women as there are white women marrying Chinese or Native American men (U.S. Bureau of the Census 1992b).

Explanations for the differing patterns of intermarriage that are supported by empirical data are difficult to find. The pattern of white men marrying Asian women may be the result of the increased contact between white men and Japanese and Filipino women due to the stationing of the American military in the Philippines and Japan. Perhaps American men see Japanese and Filipino women as more submissive and passive than white or black women and thus appropriate marriage partners for men who want to dominate their marriages.

Overall, interracial marriages have higher divorce rates than marriages between individuals of the same race. David Heer's (1974) research found that white husband/black wife couples were least likely to be married 10 years after their wedding. The rate of marital dissolution was lower for black husband/white wife couples.

Religion   Traditionally, religion has been a strong cultural force in mate selection, although, as we noted above, the boundaries are shifting and the rate of intermarriage is increasing. Over the past 70 years, close to 90% of those who marry select a mate who is of the same religion. Table 6-4 provides data from the National Opinion Research Corporation's annual General Social Survey that illustrate the pattern of inter- and intrafaith marriage. Protestants, because they are the largest religious group, have the highest rate of religious homogamy. Given this, random selection would result in 68% of Protestants marrying Protestants (Murstein 1986). There is a strong tradition of homogamy among Jews, such that 80% of Jews marry other Jews (random selection would predict a 2.3% rate). The rate of intermarriage for Jews, however, has risen and continues to rise (Murstein 1986). Part of the reason for the rise in

The typical pattern of interracial relationships is a black male and a white female.

Religion in Which Respondent Was Raised	Religion in Which Respondent's Spouse Was Raised						
	Protestant	Catholic	Jewish	No Religion	Other	Total	n
Protestant	83.7	13.4	0.3	2.4	0.2	100.0	4,050
Catholic	34.9	62.0	0.5	2.1	0.5	100.0	1,568
Jewish	10.3	7.5	80.1	1.4	0.7	100.0	146
No religion	59.7	17.5	1.3	18.8	2.6	100.0	154
Other	31.3	25.0	0.0	1.6	42.2	100.0	64
Total	68.0	26.2	2.3	2.7	0.8	100.0	5,982

Table 6-4 Religion in Which Spouse Was Raised (percentage), by Religion in Which Respondent's Spouse Was Raised: Pooled Data From Six U.S. National Surveys

SOURCE: Copyrighted (1986) by the National Council on Family Relations, 3989 Central Ave. NE, Suite 550, Minneapolis, MN 55421. Reprinted by permission.

Jewish intermarriage is the continuing assimilation of Jews into the mainstream American culture. In addition, this is part of an overall trend in decreasing religious homogamy and increasing educational homogamy.

Social Class

Great love stories, songs, and sonnets often tell the story of the well-to-do young man who desperately wants to marry the girl from the "wrong side of the tracks" or of the well-born young woman who finds true love with a blue-collar man. Movies such as *Pretty Woman* and *Aladdin* have as a theme the story of love that crosses class boundaries.

Songs, sonnets, and movies tend to be the exception to the actual patterns of mate selection. Men and women generally select partners from the same social class. Because social class has a strong influence on individual attitudes, values, beliefs, behaviors, and lifestyles, it is not surprising that people who come from similar social classes tend to marry one another. Moreover, social class has a strong influence on the range and type of people you meet and with whom you interact. The choice of which college to attend is partially a function of one's abilities and achievements and partially a function of what one can afford. Thus who you meet and date in college may be partly determined by your social class.

There are, however, selective departures from class homogamy. Some social scientists have speculated that women who marry outside their social class would "marry up," that is, marry someone from a higher social class. The explanation for this hypothesis was that because a woman's social status is generally tied to the social status of her husband, woman marry up rather than lose social status by marrying down. Bernard Murstein (1986) reports that, although there was some initial support for this hypothesis from research carried out in the 1940s and 1950s, recent research finds little support for the "woman marrying up" hypothesis.

Propinquity

Social researcher James Bossard (1932) examined 5,000 marriage licenses in Philadelphia in 1931 and reported that more than one third of all applicants lived within five blocks of one another. Bossard noted that as distance between applicants increased, the percentages of marriages decreased. Later researchers refined Bossard's findings and noted that the probability of marriage varies directly with the probability of interaction (Stouffer 1940). Other researchers have found the same pattern as Bossard (Catton and Smircich 1964). Most people, the researchers concluded, marry someone who lives within a mile of their residence.

There have been few additional studies that test the theory of **propinquity** (nearness). Changes in the patterns of dating and courtship, as well as the increase in the proportion of young people who go on for higher education, would affect contemporary tests. First, given the increase in cohabitation preceding marriage, it is likely that a substantial number of applicants for marriage licenses are living at the same address. Thus address at time of application for a marriage licence is not a good indicator of whether the couple lived near each other when they began their relationship. Increased enrollments in higher education would also influence traditional measures of propinquity. If the college-aged applicants for marriage licenses used their "home addresses," this might suppress the percentage of applicants who live near one another. If, however, the applicants used a current address, this might support the thesis of propinquity.

THEORIES OF MATE SELECTION

Social factors generally define the likelihood of social interaction and the field of eligibles for marriage. Personality, physical attractiveness, and other factors influence who is attracted to one another. Love and the process of falling in or out of love is the emotional bond of a relationship that can push a couple toward marriage or pull them apart. Given these pushes and pulls, how do we explain why, within a field of eligibles and attractive possibilities, two individuals choose to marry each other?

Students of family relations have developed numerous theories of mate selection. There are two levels of theories that have been developed, discussed, and tested (to one degree or another): individualistic and sociological.

Individualistic theories of mate selection propose that the choice of marital partner is determined by a range of emotional experiences, subconscious drives, and needs of the individual making the choice.

Individualistic Theories

Psychoanalyst Sigmund Freud developed a theory of mate selection that has been called the **parent image theory** (Ecklund 1968). Freud's theory is based on his conceptualization of the Oedipus complex. Oedipus, the main character is Sophocles' tragedy, unknowingly both kills his father and marries his mother. Freud's theory of mate selection proposes that a boy seeks to marry someone like his mother and a girl seeks someone like her father.

Some scholars have attempted to conduct research on whether men are drawn to women who physically resemble their mothers and whether women are drawn to men who resemble their fathers. Bernard Murstein (1986), in reviewing these research studies, notes that researchers have either failed in their attempts to show a resemblance between marital partner and parent or that the results are equivocal.

The second and the best-developed individualistic theory of mate selection is Robert Winch's (1967) theory of complementary needs, which proposes that each individual seeks that person who will provide him or her with maximum personality need gratification. Winch proposed that complementary personality traits are the most significant determinant of romantic attraction and marital choice. Winch's theory refines the idea of "opposites attract." Thus a person who is dominant will be attracted to someone who is submissive, a nurturant person will want to select a partner who needs to be nurtured, and so on. Winch's own research found support for three types of complementary needs: (1) nurturance-receptiveness, (2) dominance-submissiveness, and (3) achievement-vicariousness. While other researchers have also found some evidence to support the theory of complementary needs, there has been little overall support of Winch's theory. On the contrary, much research actually finds that people are attracted to those who have similar personality traits (Whyte 1990).

Sociological theories of mate selection are based on the assumption that social factors, rather than individual needs, personalities, and drives, have the

Sociological Theories

strongest influence on marital choice. One of the first sociological theories of mate selection integrated Winch's ideas about complementary needs with the evidence of homogamy from social research on patterns of mate selection. From this integration, Alan Kerckhoff and Keith Davis (1962) developed a *filter theory of mate selection.* Kerckhoff and Davis proposed a two-step theory of marital choice. The first stage of the filter is an initial screening for homogamous cultural variables—race, age, and social class. Then a second screening occurs on the basis of values. The final filter is a screening for need compatibility. The screening process goes on during dating and courtship. Those relationships that do not share the same social factors or values will break up early on. Those who do share social factors and values move to the next level of screening. Although the filter theory of mate selection is an elegant attempt to link social and personality factors into a theory of mate selection, research has not generally supported this sociological theory (Murstein 1986).

Psychologist Bernard Murstein elaborated on Kerckhoff and Davis's filter theory and developed a three-stage exchange theory of mate selection that he calls the *stimulus-value-role* theory (SVR). Murstein (1970, 1971, 1980, 1986) bases his theory on the conceptual framework of social exchange theory (see Chapter 2). He proposes that interpersonal attraction depends on an exchange of assets and liabilities that each person brings to a relationship. Three types of variables influence the relationship: stimulus, values, and roles. In the *stimulus stage,* factors such as physical attractiveness, social skills, temperament, reputation, and mental abilities influence whether individuals are attracted to each other. During the next stage, the *value stage,* attitudes and values regarding marriage, sex, and life determine if the couple is compatible. The third and final stage is the *role stage,* in which couples assess role compatibility. They learn to examine how they will fulfill the various marital roles—provider, housekeeper, sexual partner, and parent.

The SVR theory of marital choice has been carefully tested and supported. Murstein's (1986) own program of research has supported most of the hypotheses that were developed based on SVR theory.

A third sociological theory of mate selection is Robert Lewis's (1972) *premarital dyadic formation* theory. The theory is also organized into stages. The first stage, *perceived stimulation,* is necessary for the development of the relationship. The key assumption in this stage is that when a couple sees themselves as similar they tend to feel positive about each other and become more involved. The second stage is the process of *pair rapport.* This stage involves attempts to communicate with one another. If one or both individuals feel they cannot communicate with one another, the relationship will likely dissolve. Next, the couple goes through the stage of *self-disclosure*. As the couple communicates, they tend to reveal more about one another. Self-revelation tends to be reciprocal—the more one reveals, the more the other partner self-discloses. From self-disclosure the couple then moves to the stage of *role-taking* accuracy. Role taking involves empathizing and understanding the position of the other person. The fifth stage is *interpersonal role fit*. This stage involves the process of fitting the two personalities together into a relationship. During this stage the couple identifies personality similarities and differences. They learn how they will function together. Role fit also involves learning whether the social roles each enacts fit together. The final stage is when the couple achieves *dyadic crystallization*. When they reach this stage the two individuals form an identity as a couple. They establish boundaries between themselves and the outside world and increase commitment to each other.

Lewis's six stages are sequential, much like Reiss's Wheel of Love that I described in the first part of this chapter. Lewis and others have carried out research that generally supports this six-stage theory of mate selection.

SUMMING UP

Love is considered the basis of forming a marriage by more than three quarters of the population. There are two different forms of love: passionate love and companionate love. **Passionate love** is a wildly emotional state, a confusion of feelings: tenderness and sexuality, elation and pain, anxiety and relief, altruism and jealousy. Passionate love is a state of intense absorption in the other person. **Companionate love,** on the other hand, is a lower-key emotion—friendly affection and deep attachment to someone. In Reiss's "Wheel of Love," individuals "fall in love" by going through four stages: (1) rapport, (2) self-revelation, (3) mutual dependency, and (4) personality need fulfillment.

Dating is a relatively new and rapidly changing pattern of courtship. Today in the United States, dating is an important but changing path that individuals travel when they move from being single to married. Exchange and bargaining are the core processes of modern dating patterns.

Cohabitation has become a more popular and socially acceptable form of relationship in the past 30 years. Researchers find that cohabitation *does not* improve marital quality. Instead, cohabitation contributed to more disagreements and a greater chance of divorce. Lower marital satisfaction seemed to be the result of the fact that those who cohabitate seem to be poor marriage risks before they marry.

Many people assume that the sexual revolution of the 1960s brought an end to a long era when both men and women stayed virginal until marriage. However, historical evidence indicates that both men and women did engage in sex before marriage. The rates of premarital sex remained stable until the 1960s. Since then there has been a steady increase in the proportion of both men and women who engage in premarital sex and a decrease in the age at which they first have sexual intercourse.

As Suzie found in James Loewen's "Marriage Machine," there are guiding forces that influence love, dating and courtship, and the choice of a marriage partner. Our choice of who we date, fall in love with, and marry is not completely open and free, nor is it as constrained as Loewen's marital calculations. The pool is defined by social factors such as age, education, race, religion, social class, and the likelihood of social interaction. Other factors such as intellectual ability, physical attractiveness, height, weight, eye color, and personality are important as well. The principle of social exchange is a major underlying force that influences dating, courtship, and, ultimately, mate selection.

REFERENCES

Bell, Robert R. and Jay B. Chaskes. 1970. "Premarital Sexual Experience Among Coeds, 1958–1968." *Journal of Marriage and the Family* 32 (February):81-84.

Blood, Robert O., Jr. 1955. "A Retest of Waller's Rating Complex." *Marriage and the Family* 17(February):41-47.

Booth, Alan and David Johnson. 1988. "Premarital Cohabitation and Marital Success." *Journal of Family Issues* 9(June):255-72.

Bossard, James. 1932. "Residential Propinquity as a Factor in Mate Selection." *American Journal of Sociology* 38(July): 219-24.

Brown, Sandford. 1966. "May I Ask a Few Questions About Love?" *Saturday Evening Post* (December 31-January 7): 24-27.

Browning, Elizabeth Barrett. 1977. *Sonnets From the Portuguese*. Edited with an introduction by William S. Peterson. Barre, MA: Barre Publishing.

Burgess, Ernest W. and Paul Wallin. 1953. *Engagement and Marriage*. Philadelphia: J. B. Lippincott.

Calhoun, Arthur W. 1945. *A Social History of the American Family*. New York: Barnes & Noble.

Carroll, Leo. 1988. "AIDS and the Sexual Behavior of College Students." *Journal of Marriage and the Family* 50(May):405-11.

Catton, William R., Jr. and R. J. Smircich. 1964. "A Comparison of Mathematical Models of the Effect of Residential Propinquity on Mate Selection." *American Sociological Review* 29(August): 522-29.

Cherlin, Andrew J. 1992. *Marriage, Divorce, Remarriage*. Rev. ed. Cambridge, MA: Harvard University Press.

Christensen, Harold and Christina Gregg. 1970. "Changing Sex Norms in American and Scandinavia." *Journal of Marriage and the Family* 32 (November):616-27.

Clayton, Richard and Janet L. Bokemeier. 1980. "Premarital Sex in the Seventies." *Journal of*

Marriage and the Family 42 (November):34-50.

DeMaris, Alfred and Gerald R. Leslie. 1984. "Cohabitation With Future Spouses: Its Influence on Marital Satisfaction and Communication." *Journal of Marriage and the Family* 46 (February):77-84.

Demos, John. 1970. *A Little Commonwealth.* New York: Oxford University Press.

Ecklund, Bruce. 1968. "Theories of Mate Selection." *Eugenics Quarterly* 15(June):71-84.

Forrest, Jacqueline and Sushecla Singh. 1990. "The Sexual and Reproductive Behavior of American Women." *Family Planning Perspectives* 22(September/October):206-14.

Gordon, Michael. 1981. *The American Family.* New York: Random House.

Hawke, David F. 1988. *Everyday Life in Early America.* New York: Harper & Row.

Heer, David. 1974. "The Prevalence of Black-White Marriages in the United States: 1960–1970." *Journal of Marriage and the Family* 36(May):246-58.

Jacoby, Arthur P. and John D. Williams. 1985. "Effects of Premarital Sexual Standards and Behavior on Dating and Marriage Desirability." *Journal of Marriage and the Family* 47 (November):1059-65.

Jones, Elise F., Jacqueline Darroch Forrest, Noreen Goldman, Stanley K. Henshaw, Richard Lincoln, Jeannie I. Rosoff, Charles F.

Westoff, and Deirdre Wulf. 1985. "Teenage Pregnancy in Developed Countries: Determinants and Policy Implications." *Family Planning Perspectives* 17 (March/April):53-63.

Kalmijn, Matthijs. 1991. "Shifting Boundaries: Trends in Religious and Educational Homogamy." *American Sociological Review* 56(December):786-800.

Kantner, John F. and Melvin Zelnick. 1972. "Sexual Experience of Young Unmarried Women." *Family Planning Perspectives* 5(Winter):21-35.

Kephart, William M. 1972. *The Family, Society, and the Individual.* Boston: Houghton Mifflin.

Kerckhoff, Alan C. 1964. "Patterns of Homogamy and the Field of Eligibles." *Social Forces* 42(March):289-97.

Kerckhoff, Alan C. and Keith E. Davis. 1962. "Value Consensus and Need Complementarity in Mate Selection." *American Sociological Review* 27(June):295-303.

Kinsey, Alfred C., Wardell B. Pomeroy, and Clyde E. Martin. 1948. *Sexual Behavior in the Human Male.* Philadelphia: W. B. Saunders.

Kinsey, Alfred C., Wardell B. Pomeroy, Clyde E. Martin, and Paul Gebhard. 1953. *Sexual Behavior in the Human Female.* Philadelphia: W. B. Saunders.

Knox, David and Kenneth Wilson. 1981. "Dating Behaviors of University Students."

Family Relations 30(April):255-58.

Korman, Sheila. 1983. "Nontraditional Dating Behavior: Dating Initiation and Date Expense-Sharing Among Feminists and Non-Feminists." *Family Relations* 32(October):575-81.

Laner, Mary Reige. 1989. *Dating: Delights, Discontents, and Dilemmas.* Salem, WI: Sheffield.

Lewis, Robert A. 1972. "A Developmental Framework for the Analysis of Premarital Dyads." *Family Process* 11(1):17-48.

Loewen, James W. 1979 "Introductory Sociology: Four Classroom Exercises." *Teaching Sociology* 6(April):221-44.

Linton, Ralph. 1936. *The Study of Man.* New York: Appleton-Century-Crofts.

Macklin, Eleanor D. 1972. "Heterosexual Cohabitation Among Unmarried College Students." *Family Relations* 21(October):95-104.

Murdock, George P. 1949. *Social Structure.* New York: Macmillan.

Murstein, Bernard. 1970. "Stimulus-Value-Role: A Theory of Marital Choice." *Journal of Marriage and the Family* 32 (August):465-81.

———. 1971. "A Theory of Marital Choice and Its Applicability to Marriage Adjustment." Pp. 100-51 in *Theories of Attraction and Love,* edited by Bernard Murstein. New York: Springer.

———. 1980. "Mate Selection in the 1970's" *Journal of Marriage and the Family* 42(November):777-92.

———. 1986. *Paths to Marriage.* Beverly Hills, CA: Sage.

Pietropinto, Anthony and Jacqueline Simenauer. 1979. *Husbands and Wives.* New York: Times Books.

Popenoe, David. 1988. *Disturbing the Nest: Family Change and Decline in Modern Societies.* New York: Aldine de Gruyter.

Reiss, Ira L. 1960. *Premarital Sexual Standards in America.* New York: Free Press.

———. 1965. "Social Class and Campus Dating." *Social Problems* 13(Fall):193-205.

———. 1967. *The Social Context of Premarital Sexual Permissiveness.* New York: Holt.

———. 1971. *The Family System in America.* New York: Holt.

———. 1972. "Premarital Sexuality: Past, Present, and Future." Pp. 167-89 in *Readings on the Family System,* edited by Ira L. Reiss. New York: Holt.

———. 1980. *The Family System in America.* 3rd ed. New York: Holt.

Ridley, Carl, Dan J. Peterman, and Arthur A. Avery. 1978. "Cohabitation: Does It Make for a Better Marriage?" *Family Coordinator* 27(April):129-36.

Robinson, Ira, Ken Ziss, Bill Ganza, and Stuart Katz. 1991. "Twenty Years of the Sexual Revolution, 1965–1985: An Update." *Journal of Marriage and the Family* 53(February): 216-20.

Rogers, Everett and A. Eugene Havens. 1960. "Prestige Rating and Mate Selection on a College Campus." *Marriage and Family Living* 22(February):55-59.

Roscoe, Bruce, Mark S. Diana, and Richard H. Brooks II. 1987. "Early, Middle, and Late Adolescents' Views on Dating and Factors Influencing Partner Selection." *Adolescence* 85 (Spring):59-68.

Skipper, James and Gilbert Nass. 1966. "Dating Behavior: A Framework for Analysis and Illustration." *Journal of Marriage and the Family* 28 (November):412-20.

Smith, Daniel S. and Michael S. Hindus. 1975. "Premarital Pregnancy in America, 1640–1971: An Overview and Interpretation." *Journal of Interdisciplinary History* 4(Spring): 537-70.

Smith, William M. 1952. "Rating and Dating: A Restudy." *Marriage and Family Living* 14 (November):312-16.

Stiles, Henry R. 1934. *Bundling: Its Origin and Decline in America.* New York: Book Collectors Association.

Stouffer, Samuel. 1940. "Intervening Opportunities: A Theory Relating Inability to Divorce." *American Sociological Review* 5 (December):845-67.

Sullivan, Harry S. 1947. *Conceptions of Modern Psychiatry.* Washington, DC: William Alanson White Psychiatric Foundation.

Terman, Lewis. 1938. *Psychological Factors in Marital Happiness.* New York: McGraw-Hill.

Thornton, Arland. 1988. "Cohabitation and Marriage in the 1980s." *Demography* 25 (November):497-508.

Trost, Jan. 1975. "Married and Unmarried Cohabitation: The Case of Sweden, With Some Comparisons." *Journal of Marriage and the Family* 37 (August):677-82.

U.S. Bureau of the Census. 1970. *U.S. Census of Population, 1970: Subject Reports, Marital Status, Final Report.* No. PC(2)-4E. Washington, DC: Government Printing Office.

———. 1980. *U.S. Census of Population, 1980: Marital Characteristics.* No. PC80-2-4C. Washington, DC: Government Printing Office.

———. 1983. *Marital Status and Living Arrangements, March 1983.* Current Population Reports: Population Characteristics, Series P-20, No. 389. Washington, DC: Government Printing Office.

———. 1985. *Statistical Abstracts of the United States.* Washington, DC: Government Printing Office.

———. 1992a. *Marital Status and Living Arrangements: March 1992.* Current Population Reports: Population Characteristics, Series P-20, No. 468. Washington, DC: Government Printing Office.

———. 1992b. *Statistical Abstracts of the United States.* Washington, DC: Government Printing Office.

Vreeland, Rebecca. 1972. "Is It True What They Say About Harvard Boys?" *Psychology Today* 5(8):65-68.

Waller, Willard. 1937. "The Rating and Dating Complex." *American Sociological Review* 2(October):727-34.

Walster, Elaine and G. William Walster. 1978. *A New Look at Love*. Reading, MA: Addison-Wesley.

Whyte, Martin King. 1990. *Dating, Mating, and the Marriage*. New York: Aldine de Gruyter.

Winch, Robert. 1967. "Another Look at the Theory of Complementary Needs in Mate Selection." *Journal of Marriage and the Family* 29(November): 756-62.

CHAPTER 7

■■ The Marital Dyad

"And so, they married and lived happily ever after."

So end many fairy tales. The theme of such fairy tales, like Snow White, Cinderella, Beauty and the Beast, and others, is that a man and a woman fall in love, struggle to overcome obstacles that stand in the way of their love, and, having overcome these obstacles, marry, ride off into the sunset on a white horse, and live happily ever after.

The reality of marriage is quite different from fairy tales and romance novels. Obstacles and problems that occur during courtship do not suddenly dissolve with the exchange of marriage vows. The newly married couple may ride off into the sunset on a horse or in a carriage or limousine, but the next morning they must begin the process of constructing a marriage and working out their marital relations.

The family is an intimate environment in which the couple or marital dyad fashions its own unique relationship. The family is also a **social institution**. A social institution is an established pattern of social relationships and behavior that structures a particular area of social life. More specifically, it is a system of statuses and roles, norms, and values that develops around a social goal or social function. Thus **marriage** is an institutionalized arrangement. This means that the marital dyad fashions its own marriage within the context of a social institution that defines statuses (husband, wife, mother, father, son, daughter, brother, sister), expectations for those who occupy the statuses, norms of behavior for those in the institution, and values and goals. Because the statuses, role, norms, and values are institutionalized, there is a certain predictable pattern of behavior in families across societies. Thus, as we will see in the first section of this chapter, although the marital dyad can construct its own marital reality and pattern of behavior within its own intimate environment, the fact that marriage and family are institutionalized in society means that there is an existing blueprint to guide each dyad in fashioning its individual marital reality.

This chapter examines marital relations by first discussing the process of making the transition from singlehood to married. Next we examine marital sexuality. Many discussions of sex and sexuality make the implicit assumption that only premarital or extramarital sexuality merits examination. Sexuality in marriage and sexual difficulties are fundamentally important in understanding marital relations. The chapter concludes by looking at the issues of decision making, power, and equity in contemporary families.

THE CONSTRUCTION OF MARRIAGE

Peter Berger and Hansfried Kellner (1964) describe marriage as a dramatic act in which two strangers come together and redefine themselves. Berger and Kellner draw on the symbolic interaction framework (Chapter 2) to describe the process of constructing a marriage. Long before the two strangers meet, they have begun to anticipate and learn about the roles and parts that they will play in a marriage. Early socialization includes the chance to observe marital roles and to enact the roles. "Playing house" is one way that children begin the process of learning about marital roles. Marriage and family is portrayed in a wide range of cultural media. Television programs, such as *The Cosby Show, Leave It to Beaver, Roseanne, Married With Children,* or even "soap operas," such as *All My Children,* present one set of norms, values, and scripts. Books, poems, and other media present other views of family life and family roles. Individuals also draw on their personal experiences, from growing up in a family to observing the family life of friends and relatives. There are also courses in high school and college that focus on family life education and that present discussions of marital relations and marital roles. Thus the two strangers draw on a range of models and scripts as they develop their images and expectations of the drama of marriage. The courtship process that we described in Chapter 6, as well as cohabitation, are the dress rehearsals for the drama of marital relations.

Of course, the two individuals are not exactly strangers. The data on homogamous marital choice reviewed in Chapter 6 indicate that the partners who enter a marriage are likely to come from similar social backgrounds and share social values. They are strangers in the eyes of Berger and Kellner because they typically come from different interactional settings. They do not share a past, they have not yet fully worked out their roles, nor have they completely participated in role taking with one another. With the exchange of marital vows, the two strangers from similar social backgrounds begin to exchange conversations and dialogues that focus exclusively on their marital relationship.

There are few institutions or social groups in the social structure where the individual has the chance to actually construct the reality of his or her social existence. The workplace, politics, religion, school, and other social institutions and groupings force an existing social structure on the individual. When you enter or re-enter school, become a first-year student in college, take your first job, or move to a new city or town, there is the apparent opportunity to redefine your identify and social roles. Yet this must be done within an ongoing tableau of norms, values, and structures. Political, educational, religious, and work organizations have an interest and desire in controlling all members, new and old, so that the goals of the organization can be realized. These organizations and institutions have no stake in controlling individuals in a private sector, unless the individual actors have a detrimental impact on social order, as in the case of child abuse or marital violence. Thus, although individual marriages exist within the institutional structure of the family, the family is one setting where the individual has the apparent power to fashion his or her own world, however small. Berger and Kellner point out that it is only in the private sphere of the family that individuals can take a slice of reality and produce for themselves a world in which they can feel at home. The fashioning, however, is an interactive process carried out with the marital partner.

The two actors come to the drama with their accumulated biographies and experiences. Because they often come from the same social structure, they have both internalized and share the same general expectations and definitions of marriage and family roles. Despite the fact that the actors often share the same social and cultural heritage, marital relations must still be created, negotiated, and constructed. Each partner must check and correlate his or her definitions of reality with the other partner. The identity that each partner brings to the marriage is also modified and changed through the process of interaction. No longer is it as important how others see them or how they see themselves. The reality of the individual marriage and individual identity depends on how the partner sees them.

Berger and Kellner point out that one of the more obvious examples of the construction of marriage and the modification of individual identities is the impact of marriage on men's relations with their friends. They note that it is nearly axiomatic that a man's relations with his single male friends rarely survive marriage. This typically has to do with the slow process of a man's image of his single male friends being transformed during conversations with his wife. Even if there is no pressure from his wife, a man will see his friends differently simply because he is talking about them with his wife. Old friends tend to slowly fade away, to be replaced by new ones formed by the couple together. If the man or his wife notice this process at all, they may comment that people change, or assume that the change is not theirs but their former friends'. The reality is that the change is a consequence of the conversations that form the substance of marital relations and the social construction of marriage. The conversations, Berger and Kellner explain, tend to be one-sided. The man talks to his wife about his friends but not to his friends about his wife. Of course, if the conversations go the other way—not talking to his wife but talking instead to his friends—the marriage itself may be jeopardized. Without marital conversations, partners cannot check their perceptions and

The marital conversation forms the core of marital relations and serves as the mechanism through which the marital reality is constructed.

definitions of identity and reality. Thus the core of marital relations and the process of social constructing and maintaining the reality of marriage are the conversations between the partners. As Berger and Kellner note, "In the marital conversation a world is not only built, but it is also kept in a state of repair and ongoingly refurbished" (p. 13).

The conversations that build the marital reality include the sharing of present thoughts as well as past histories. The couple begins with two distinct biographies and together constructs a new marital biography of roles and expectations. Life as a single person is altered to become a dyadic relationship. The past is modified, the present constructed, and the future projected given the present marital identities. Future plans are modified based on the constraints imposed by the structure and institutional demands of marriage.

The process described by Berger and Kellner goes on in all marital relations, but it typically is not understood or recognized by the participants. Men and women do not plan or even realize that they are creating the world they live in. Rather, they simply take for granted the roles and interactions in which they participate.

MARITAL SEXUALITY

One of the most important aspects of marital relations is intimacy and sexual relations. One of our expectations when we marry is that we will have a partner who we will love and with whom we can be intimate, both emotionally and physically. The marriage license legitimizes sexual relations—those sexual relations that occur outside of marriage are stigmatized to one degree or another.

Despite the centrality of sexual relations and physical intimacy to marital relations, there has been relatively little detailed research on marital sexuality. Of course, the abundance of research on premarital sexuality may be a consequence of the large populations of subjects who are available to family researchers and who engage in premarital sex—college students. Or, perhaps this is because of the assumption we began the chapter with—that once people marry, everyone lives happily ever after, both emotionally and sexually. A third possibility is that sex is a "taboo topic" (Farberow 1966). Some researchers may be embarrassed to ask questions about sex, or, if not embarrassed, they may assume that marital partners are reluctant to talk about or report on intimate sexual practices.

Sources of Data on Marital Sexuality

The earliest and, to this date, most widely referenced studies of sexual behavior are the Kinsey studies of male and female sexuality. Alfred Kinsey and his associates (Kinsey, Pomeroy, Martin, and Gebhard 1953) interviewed 5,300 men and 5,940 women in the late 1940s and early 1950s. The subjects were not a representative sample but, rather, were selected using "group sampling." The researchers approached existing groups (e.g., 4-H clubs, church groups, and community groups) to recruit subjects. Kinsey and his colleagues were concerned about whether respondents would provide truthful answers to questions about intimate sexual relations. To increase the validity of the responses, the Kinsey team used the "direct approach interview." The Kinsey researchers assumed that the burden of denial should be on the respondent and that the interviewer should not ask questions that made it easy to deny certain behaviors. Thus the Kinsey group began each interview assuming that every type of sexual practice had been engaged in by each respondent. Rather than asking "Do you masturbate?" the interviewers phrased the question as "When did you last masturbate?"

The next large-scale survey of sexual behavior was conducted in 1972. The Playboy Foundation survey of sexual behavior was reported by Morton Hunt (1974) in a series of articles in *Playboy*. The study was based on data collected in a telephone survey of 1,044 men and 982 women. This was not a true representative survey. First, the technology of generating representative telephone samples had not been perfected in the early 1970s. Second, the study had an exceptionally high refusal rate of 80%.

There have been additional smaller studies of marital sexuality as well as the much publicized examination of human sexual response carried out by William H. Masters and Virginia F. Johnson (1966, 1970).

Robert and Amy Levin (1975) conducted a survey of sexuality for *Redbook*, in which 100,000 women completed a questionnaire published in the magazine. Although the sample size is large, it again is not a representative sample of American women. *Cosmopolitan* conducted a similar survey of its readers in 1981 and received 106,000 responses.

Shere Hite (1976, 1981) carried out two surveys of sexuality. She collected data from 3,000 women for her 1976 book on female sexuality and conducted more than 7,000 interviews for her 1981 report on male sexuality. Although Hite makes allusions to her "scientific methodology," most social scientists cast a wary eye at her claims of scientific objectivity. Her samples are not representative and her findings are more a string of anecdotes and quotes than rigorously analyzed data.

One of the best examinations of marital sexuality is Philip Blumstein and Pepper Schwartz's (1983) survey of American couples. Blumstein and Schwartz collected 12,000 questionnaires that were completed by both partners who were either married, cohabiting, gay, or lesbian. As with other large surveys of marital sexuality, Blumstein and Schwartz did not collect data from a representative sample of couples but from a diverse sample using media advertisements and the "group sampling" method used by Kinsey and his colleagues. Blumstein and Schwartz then selected 300 couples for more intensive

---

BOX 7-1: THE GLOBAL VIEW

A Cross-Cultural Look at Sex

Marital and sexual scripts vary from group to group within a society and across cultures. In many cultures, sexual pleasure is defined by men as a man's right but not a woman's. In some societies, such as the Keraki of New Guinea, male homosexual relations are expected prior to marriage; in other societies, male homosexuality prior to marriage is strictly forbidden (Ford and Beach 1951).

Even the right to sexual pleasure varies from society to society. In some societies, such as the United States today, sexual pleasure is pursued as moral and correct. In other societies, such as Victorian England, it was condemned, while in others, such as the Lepchas of India, sexual pleasure is morally and emotionally neutral (Stephens 1963).

personal interviews. They examined frequency of sex, quality of sex life, initiating and refusing sex, and extramarital sex (or nonmonogamous sex).

The most recent examinations of sexuality in America were conducted by sociologist Andrew Greeley (1991). Greeley examined data from two national representative surveys on love and marriage commissioned by *Psychology Today* and carried out by the Gallop Organization between 1989 and 1990. In addition, Greeley analyzed questions that were part of the National Opinion Research Center's annual General Social Survey. The General Social Survey has interviewed 1,250 respondents each year since 1972.

The National Survey of Families and Households (Sweet, Bumpass, and Call 1988), conducted during 1987 and 1988 (see Chapter 2), also included questions about marital sex, but few articles that focus on marital sex have been published so far.

The Frequency of Sexual Relations

There is an old joke told that if a couple puts a nickel into a jar each time they have sex during the first year they are married and then takes a nickel out of the jar every time they have sex in the subsequent years of marriage, they will never take all the nickels out of the jar. Of course, one of the foundations of the joke is the assumption that couples do not begin having sex until they are

The frequency of sexual intercourse declines over the course of a marriage.

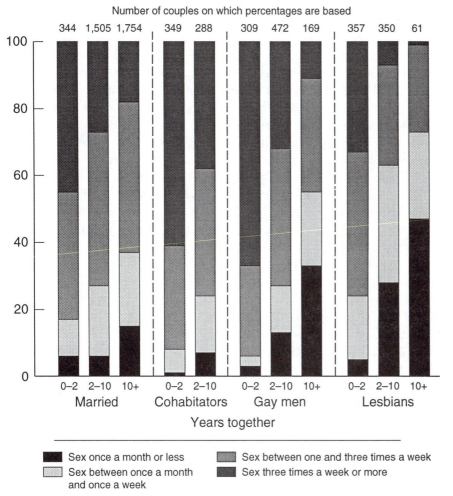

Figure 7-1
Sexual Frequency

Number of couples on which percentages are based

Sex once a month or less

Sex between once a month and once a week

Sex between one and three times a week

Sex three times a week or more

SOURCE: *American Couples: Money, Work, and Sex* by Philip Blumstein and Pepper W. Schwartz. Copyright © 1983 by Philip Blumstein and Pepper W. Schwartz. Reprinted by permission of William Morrow & Company., Inc.

married. We noted in Chapter 6, when we discussed premarital sexuality, that most couples begin sexual relations before they are married.

Nevertheless, research on marital sexuality indicates there is a grain of truth in the old joke about nickels in the jar. Cathy Greenblat (1983) asked a random sample of people married 5 years or less to report how often they had sexual intercourse with their partner during the first year of marriage. Subjects reported a range from once each month to 45 times each month. Research on marital sexuality consistently finds that the frequency of sexual intercourse drops as individuals grow older (Edwards and Booth 1992; McKinlay and Feldman 1992). Alfred Kinsey and his colleagues (1953) reported that the frequency of intercourse was about three times per week for married teens. This drops to under two times per week for those over 30 years of age and less than once per week for those 46 and older. More recently, researchers have found the same general trends of decreasing frequency with increasing age (McKinlay and Feldman 1992; Westoff 1974). Blumstein and Schwartz (1983) found that 45% of couples married less than 2 years had sexual intercourse three or more times each week. Only 27% of those married 2 to 10 years and only 18% of those married more than 10 years had intercourse three or more times per week (see Figure 7-1).

The decline in frequency in sexual intercourse is not entirely a function of aging. Length of marriage is also a factor. Men and women who enter new marriages later in life have higher frequencies of sexual intercourse than do men and women of the same age but who are in a marriage of longer duration (McKinlay and Feldman 1992).

Although the frequency of sexual intercourse declines over the life course, it does not stop. Sexual activity continues for most couples well into later life. Couples who have a regular and satisfactory sex life and are sexually active in their middle years continue to engage in genital sexual relations into old age (Ade-Ridder 1990; Allgeier and Allgeier 1988; Ripportella-Muller 1989; Weg 1990).

One of the interesting findings that emerges from surveys that report frequency of sexual intercourse is the reporting difference between men and women. Men tend to report a lower frequency of intercourse than do women. Some researchers conclude that this difference means that men want more sex than do women and that men who want more sexual intercourse underestimate the frequency of their intercourse while women who want less may overestimate the frequency. This assumption is supported by research on sexual desire. F. Ivan Nye (1976) interviewed 210 Washington State couples, who, when asked about desired frequency of intercourse, reported the following: About 80% of both husbands and wives said that the husband desired sex more frequently, 13% of husbands and 20% of wives reported their sexual desires as equal, and 8.3% of husbands and 7.3% of wives said that the wife desired more sex than her husband did.

Not surprisingly, given the data on husbands' sexual desire, husbands tend to initiate sex more than wives do. About half of the men interviewed by John Carlson (1976) felt that husbands and wives should have equal responsibility for initiating sex, and 44% said the husband should have the primary responsibility for initiating sex. Women were more likely to state that the man should initiate sex. In practice, men do initiate sexual intercourse more often than

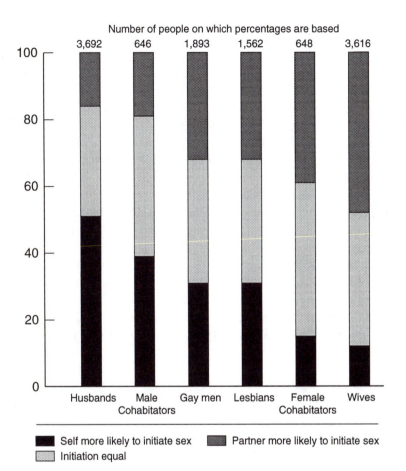

Number of people on which percentages are based

Figure 7-2 Who Initiates Sexual Intercourse

Self more likely to initiate sex   Partner more likely to initiate sex
Initiation equal

SOURCE: *American Couples: Money, Work, and Sex* by Philip Blumstein and Pepper W. Schwartz. Copyright © 1983 by Philip Blumstein and Pepper W. Schwartz. Reprinted by permission of William Morrow & Company, Inc.

women do. And, in practice, marital sexual relations tend to follow a script established by men. Eighty percent of both spouses interviewed by Carlson said that the husband initiates sex more often than the wife does.

Blumstein and Schwartz (1983) provide more recent data from a much larger sample on initiating and refusing sex. They state that, even though men and women try to share sexual responsibilities, initiation is still the husband's prerogative. Men in general, and husbands in particular, are more likely to report that they initiate sex (see Figure 7-2). Wives, on the other hand, are much less likely to report that they initiate sex.

Sexual
Satisfaction

When we began this chapter we noted that one of the pervasive cultural myths of marriage is that when a couple marries they live happily ever after. An important indicator is the level of sexual problems and difficulties reported by couples.

Constantina Safilios-Rothschild (1977) discovered that partners report sexual problems or difficulties in half of all marriages. About 80% of the husbands interviewed for the Playboy Foundation survey (Hunt 1974) stated that intercourse was too infrequent, as did 33% of wives polled for the same study.

Sexual satisfaction is not only related to the frequency of intercourse. The quality of sexual relations plays an important role in an individual's and a couple's level of sexual satisfaction. One important factor that seems to influence sexual satisfaction is orgasm. Paul Gebhard (1966) reanalyzed Kinsey's data and found that those marriages that were reported as "very happy" had higher proportions of orgasm. The same relationship was not found between the rate of orgasm and lower levels of happiness; thus orgasm seems to make a difference only for the highest levels of marital satisfaction. Other studies also find that the level of marital satisfaction is related to the proportion of female orgasm (Clark and Wallin 1965; Levinger 1966; Wallin and Clark

---

BOX 7-2: DIVERSE FAMILIES

African American Male Sexuality

In 1947, novelist Ralph Ellison provided an incisive and honest look into the hearts and minds of African American men and women. Ellison described his main character as an "invisible man." Benjamin Bowser (1992) explains that what was not apparent in Ellison's metaphor about African American men is that the sexuality of black men is nearly invisible. Although there are historical assumptions and cultural stereotypes about the sexuality of black men, there is precious little quality empirical research.

Research studies suggest that black males begin having sex earlier than whites, have sex more often, are less likely to use condoms, and practice the double standard with reference to their female partners. Yet, as Bowser points out, such conclusions rarely examine the causes of these differences. More important, such conclu-

sions are based on fragmentary data. Bowser points to the fact that since 1964 there have been no studies of black male sexual behavior that collected data from a representative sample of black males from any social class.

Bowser explains that African American men do indeed have their first sexual experience earlier, have sex more often and with more partners, and use condoms less frequently than white men. However, underneath these general conclusions is a variability of African American male sexual behavior across and within age cohorts. Bowser argues that the stereotype of the unidimensional sexual behavior of African American men needs to be replaced with a look at the impact of social and economic factors on black male sexuality as well as the variation in sexual behavior across groups and over the life span.

1958). Alexander Clark and Paul Wallin's (1965) examination of sexual satisfaction revealed that the first five years of a marriage are crucial for determining sexual satisfaction. This is a period when couples construct both their marriage and their sexual relationship. They must adjust to each other's past experiences and feelings about sex, sexual and erotic needs and tempos, and sexual desires. From Clark and Wallin's perspective, sexual satisfaction does not determine marital satisfaction. Rather, the quality of the marriage predicts whether the couple will achieve a satisfactory sexual relationship. As Berger and Kellner (1964) might suggest, the marital conversation is the key to sexual adjustment. If marital conversations lead to an overall feeling that the marriage is positive, the sexual component of the marriage tends to improve. If the adjustment is negative, the sexual relationship is not likely to improve after the first five years of marriage.

EXTRAMARITAL SEX

There are strong cultural norms against extramarital sexual intercourse, both within our society and across cultures. Anthropologist George Murdock (1949) reports that less than 20% of cultures surveyed for the Human Relations Area Files allowed or do not negatively sanction extramarital sexual relations. Surveys of the U.S. population reveal widespread opposition to extramarital sex. More than three quarters (77%) of those surveyed by the National Opinion Research Center stated that they believe extramarital sex is wrong (Smith 1992). In fact, there is more disapproval of extramarital sexual relations today than was present 20 years ago.

Despite the existence of strong norms against extramarital sex, many married individuals participate in extramarital sexual relationships at some point in their marriages. Empirical studies vary widely in their estimates of the incidence of extramarital sex. The most conservative estimates are that 10% of married men and women have engaged in extramarital sex, with the highest estimates being between 50% and 67% (Bell, Turner, and Rosen 1975; Blumstein and Schwartz 1983; Buunk 1980; Hunt 1974; Kinsey et al. 1948, 1953; Patterson and Kim 1991; Pietropinto and Simenauer 1977; Thompson 1983). The variation in the rates is the result of varying sampling methods in the different studies.

The double standard that applies to premarital sexual relations (see Chapter 6) also applies to extramarital sex. Men are less severely censured for extramarital sex than are women (Reiss 1973), and men are slightly more likely than women to be involved in extramarital sex.

There has been a good deal of discussion and speculation about why, given the strong norms against extramarital sex, it is so widely practiced. A number of factors have been found related to why individuals become involved in extramarital sexual relations: opportunity; reciprocity; higher-order beliefs; novelty, variety, and excitement; dissatisfaction in marriage; and love and friendship.

Opportunity. Opportunity, such as temporary or prolonged separation from a spouse, is one factor that is related to extramarital sex. A large number of those who have had extramarital sexual relations attribute the cause to opportunity (Buunk 1984). Physical separation from a spouse, however, does not cause affairs in and of itself.

Reciprocity. A number of couples refrain from extramarital affairs as part of a marital exchange that reasons "I won't if you won't." On the other hand, the same norm of reciprocity may serve as a motivator to engage in extramarital sex—"You did, so I will." Finally, some couples turn the norm of reciprocity to mean "I did, so you can" (Buunk and van Driel 1989).

Higher-Order Beliefs. One motivator behind involvement in extramarital sex is the belief in an obligation to live a full life. Many people see a sexually open marriage as one means of living a full life and being open to a range of experiences (Buunk and van Driel 1989).

Novelty, Variety, and Excitement. Another motivator behind extramarital sex is a desire for novelty, variation, and excitement. Gerald Neubeck (1969) suggested that some individuals and some marriages develop a certain satiation as a result of what Neubeck calls an "overexposure" to the same partner. A new sexual partner adds zest and excitement to one's sex life. The secretive aspects of extramarital affairs can also raise the excitement of sex.

Dissatisfaction With Marriage. An unsatisfactory marriage can be a major motivator for those who become involved in extramarital sexual relations. For some involved in extramarital affairs, however, an unsatisfactory marriage may be merely a rationalization for a relationship that was motivated by other factors.

Love and Friendship. Love and friendship can be important pulls into an extramarital affair. Many individuals who have extramarital affairs say that they have been in love with their partner for at least a year before beginning the sexual relationship (Buunk and van Driel 1989). Affairs can be the culmination of a friendship.

DECISION MAKING, POWER, AND EQUITY

Marital relations and interactions are made up of patterns of choices and decisions. A marriage begins with the choice or desire to be married and proceeds to choosing the wedding day, the color of the bridesmaids' dresses, and where to go on a honeymoon. Unless the couple is living together when they marry, they must choose where to establish their home, what furniture to purchase, the color and type of window shades, carpets, shower curtains, and so on. Other choices and decisions involve work and careers. If the wife is offered a promotion that requires a move to another city, the couple must choose whether to accept the promotion and relocation. Although the majority of married women work, many couples still discuss, debate, and ultimately decide whether the wife should work, at what kind of a job, and how many hours (see Chapter 11). Couples decide about children—when to have them, how many to have, and the spacing between them. Once children are born, other decisions arise—how and when to discipline a child and whether the child should take piano lessons or play Pop Warner football.

Clearly, one key aspect of marital relations are the decisions made, from the mundane ones to the major ones, from the sublime to the ridiculous. It is not uncommon for more energy and conflict to be invested in a decision such as what television program to watch than in the major decision of what house to purchase. Although the individual decisions are intrinsically important to the couple, the pattern of the decisions actually defines the structure of their marriage. Students of family relations have focused on decision making as a window into understanding the power structure of families, the sources of power, and the consequences.

Defining Power

Power and decision making are concepts that are often used interchangeably by students of the family (Safilios-Rothschild 1970). One commonly used definition of power is the ability of one person to modify or influence the behavior of another (Cromwell and Olson 1975). Sociologist Max Weber (1947) added that power is the ability to get what you want "despite resistance." Power is not a trait held by an individual but, rather, an outcome of two individuals engaging in social interaction. Power is related to the perception others have of you (French and Raven 1959; Raven, Centers, and Rodrigues 1975).

Sociologist Constantina Safilios-Rothschild (1976) proposes eight basic types of power that are exercised in marital relations:

1. *Authority or legitimate power,* which is entrusted to one's spouse by prevailing cultural or social norms

2. *Dominance power,* which is based on force or the threat of force and punishment

3. *Resource power,* which derives from the fact that one spouse has resources, such as money or prestige, that are considered desirable

4. *Expert power,* which is based on special knowledge, skill, or expertise

5. *Influence power,* which derives from the ability to successfully exert pressure on the other person

6. *Affective power,* in which one partner manipulates the other by granting or withholding affection, warmth, and sexual access

7. *Tension management power,* in which one spouse controls the other by managing existing tensions or conflicts

8. *Moral power,* in which one spouse supports a claim for power and control by appeals to religious, moral, or legal norms

---

Measuring Power in Families

The first and most widely referenced examination of marital power was the classic study conducted by Robert Blood and Donald Wolfe in 1960. They collected data from 731 urban and 178 farm wives living in the greater Detroit area. Blood and Wolfe measured power by asking their respondents who had the final say in each of eight areas (see Figure 7-3).

Blood and Wolfe developed two scoring methods to analyze their data. The first score is the "shared authority score," which ranges from zero through 8. The score is computed by simply adding the number of times the respondent answered "Husband and Wife Exactly the Same." The higher the score, the greater the shared decision making and thus, according to Blood and Wolfe, the more equal the family power.

The second scoring procedure produces a "relative authority score" by simply adding the total values of the respondents' answers. This score ranges from 8 to 40. The lower the score, the greater the wife's authority. Higher scores indicate that the husband has greater power.

Finally, Blood and Wolfe combined the two scoring methods to create four categories of family power:

1. *Wife Dominant.* A relative authority score less than 19 indicates that the wife has the greater authority in decision making.

2. *Syncratic.* A relative authority score between 20 and 28 and a shared authority score greater than 4 indicate syncratic power, which is characterized by a high degree of shared decision making and relatively equal relative authority.

3. *Autonomic.* A relative authority score between 20 and 28 and a shared authority score of 3 or less indicate autonomic power, which is characterized by little shared

Husband Always	Husband More Than Wife	Husband and Wife Exactly the Same	Wife More Than Husband	Wife Always
A. Who usually makes the *final* decision about what car to get?				
[5]	[4]	[3]	[2]	[1]
B. Who usually makes the *final* decision about whether or not to buy some life insurance?				
[5]	[4]	[3]	[2]	[1]
C. Who usually makes the *final* decision about what house or apartment to take?				
[5]	[4]	[3]	[2]	[1]
D. Who usually makes the *final* decision about what job the husband should take?				
[5]	[4]	[3]	[2]	[1]
E. Who usually makes the *final* decision about whether or not the wife should go to work or quit work?				
[5]	[4]	[3]	[2]	[1]
F. Who usually makes the *final* decision about how much money your family can afford to spend per week on food?				
[5]	[4]	[3]	[2]	[1]
G. Who usually makes the *final* decision about what doctor to have when someone is sick?				
[5]	[4]	[3]	[2]	[1]
H. Who usually makes the *final* decision about where to go on a vacation?				
[5]	[4]	[3]	[2]	[1]

Figure 7-3 Decision-Making Scale of Marital Power

SOURCE: Reprinted with permission of The Free Press, Macmillan Publishing from *Husbands and Wives: The Dynamics of Married Living* by Robert O. Blood, Jr. and Donald M. Wolfe. Copyright © 1960 by The Free Press.

authority and a roughly equitable division of labor between husbands and wives over who has the final say across the various types of decisions.

4. *Husband Dominant.* A relative authority score of 29 or more indicates that the husband has the greater authority in decision making.

Alternate means of measuring family power include the use of observational techniques or experimental designs. Some investigators have designed laboratory situations during which couples make decisions or settle disagreements (see, e.g., the ball and pusher experiment in Chapter 2). Observers either watch the sessions or record them on videotape. The tape can later be evaluated by judges and the interactions coded.

Although various methods have been used to measure and assess family power, none are considered totally adequate or acceptable and the debate over how to measure power continues. One major concern raised by critics of the measures of family power is the reliance on one partner's—most likely the

Choosing which car to buy is a key decision that indicates the balance of marital power.

wife's—reports of decision making and power. Research on power and decision making indicates that when husbands and wives are both interviewed there are substantial differences in their reports (Scanzoni 1965; Safilios-Rothschild 1969; Cromwell and Cromwell 1978). A second problem with most measures of power is the limited range of decisions included in the list of questions (Gillespie 1971; Olson, Cromwell, and Klein 1971; Szinovacz 1987). The measure used by Blood and Wolfe (1960) contains only eight items. Some of the decisions are more important than others and are made less often, such as when and which car to buy, while others are made frequently, such as what food to buy. Self-report measures of power, like the one used by Blood and Wolfe, neglect the different stages of decision making and do not consider or account for the differences in frequency and importance of the decisions that are made (Szinovacz 1987). Yet another concern is the exclusive focus on husbands and wives and the exclusion of other family members, especially children, from the measures of power.

Alternative methods of examining power have not escaped the same criticisms leveled at self-report measures. Critics of observational studies conducted in experimental settings point out that experiments like the ball and pusher task (see Chapter 2) or Strodbeck's (1951) revealed differences technique do not capture the essence of everyday marital relations. Simply stated, spouses behave differently when observed.

Rae Lesser Blumberg and Marion Tolbert Coleman (1989) propose that further research on marital power should involve interviews with both partners. They also suggest that the investigations be theory based. Researchers should give more attention to the relationships between factors such as employment, earnings, and ideology about male prerogatives and decision-making power. Blumberg and Coleman also suggest that power be conceptualized as a dynamic, multidimensional phenomenon rather than a static property of a marriage. Last, they point out that if information is collected from only husbands and wives, then researchers should generalize about marital power, not family power.

Methodological and conceptual problems and debates notwithstanding, a substantial body of knowledge exists on the factors that influence decision making and the balance of power in the marital dyad. Researchers have examined the relationship between occupation, income, education, social participation, children and marital power.

Marital Decision Making and Power

Occupation. Some observers of the family believe that lower-class husbands are more likely to dominate their wives than are middle- or upper-class men, many of whom profess to be egalitarian in their marital relations. Research, however, finds that the more prestigious the husband's occupation, the more likely he is to dominate decision making at home (Blood and Wolfe 1960; Gillespie 1971). The only exception to this is that unskilled and semiskilled blue-collar men have more power than blue-collar skilled workers (Blood and Wolfe 1960; Komarovsky 1962).

Income. Income is an even better predictor of decision-making power. Husbands who earn high incomes are more likely to dominate at home compared to men who earn smaller incomes. Blumstein and Schwartz (1983) asked the couples they interviewed, "In general, who has more say about important decisions affecting your relationship, you or your partner?" They report that money and income establishes the balance of power in relationships. Among married couples, the higher the wife's income, the freer she becomes to spend money as she sees fit. When women earn money, they gain clout. Blumstein and Schwartz also note that, for men, money represents identity and power. For women, money means security and autonomy.

Education. The spouse with the most education generally tends to dominate marital relations (Gillespie 1971; Komarovsky 1962).

Social Participation. The degree to which an individual becomes involved in activities and groups outside the home also plays a role in determining the relative level of decision-making power in the home. The more groups and organizations an individual belongs to, the greater his or her power at home (Blood and Wolfe 1960; Gillespie 1971).

Children. Another source of power is children. Although it has been proposed that having children increases power for women, the fact is that the arrival of the first child actually lowers a woman's power in the home (Blood and Wolfe 1960). No doubt, this is a result of the new mother having to leave, temporarily or permanently, the workforce and forgo the resources that work provides—prestige, income, and social contacts. Women with the youngest children report the least power, probably because they are more likely to be at home with child-care responsibilities, than do women with older children.

| A Resource Theory of Power | The research results that we have just summarized have been used to develop a *resource theory* of marital power. The earliest proponents of a resource theory of power were Blood and Wolfe (1960). They noted that, historically, husbands' economic and social roles have provided them the prerogative to be dominant, if not completely autocratic, in the home. Blood and Wolfe argue that since colonial times, American culture has gradually evolved from the system of male-centered authority to one of shared power. Consequently, the relative power between husbands and wives results from their relative resources as individuals—education, occupation, and income—rather than from the tradition gender-based source of authority, or what Safilios-Rothschild (1976) called *authority or legitimate power.* Of course, few social scientists believe that modern families exhibit real shared power. |

The resource theory of marital power has been modified by others. David Heer (1963) developed a theory of exchange that takes into account husbands' and wives' assessment of the alternatives to resources that are available in a marriage. Heer notes that, in addition to assessing the relative resources each partner has in a marriage, an individual compares the value of the resources provided by the spouse to the resources that might be available outside the marriage. Suppose a woman is married to a man who is better educated, makes a substantial income, and has a prestigious job. Blood and Wolfe's (1960) theory of power predicts that she would yield power to her husband because of his greater resources. According to Heer (1963), she might also consider her options outside the marriage. She might assume that she would be better off ending the marriage than yielding power to her husband. Her unwillingness to defer to her husband because of her assessment of her other options would result in diminishing his relative power.

Hyman Rodman (1967, 1972) places the resource theory of power in a cultural context. After examining cross-cultural studies of decision making and power—many of which produce contradictory findings from the studies of families in the United States—Rodman proposes that the distribution of power in marriage is the result of two forces: the comparative resources of husbands and wives as proposed by Blood and Wolfe (1960), and the prevailing social norms about power in a culture or subculture. Rodman examined the results of research on occupational prestige and power in the United States, France, Greece, and the former Yugoslavia and found that the United States and France have the most male dominance in the upper social classes, whereas upper-class husbands in Greece and Yugoslavia have the lowest power. Rodman resolves this apparent contradiction by explaining that in egalitarian countries, such as the United States and France, power must be earned—it is not taken for granted. Thus husbands earn power in egalitarian societies by accumulating resources. In more traditional patriarchal societies, such as Greece and Yugoslavia, power is normative. The upper classes in traditional societies are more likely to adopt more egalitarian customs. Husbands in these societies who are more educated and earn more income are more willing than lower-class men to grant their wives more power.

Critiques of the Resource Theory of Power

There have been strong criticisms of the resource theory of power, particularly from feminist scholars. Sociologist Dair Gillespie (1971) has criticized the work of Blood and Wolfe both on methodological and conceptual grounds. She takes exception to the claim that under modern conditions husbands and wives are potential equals. The balance of power in marriage, Gillespie states, remains tipped the same way it always has been—in the direction of the husband. Gillespie explains that the resource theory of power errs when it assumes that the control of competence and resources occurs in individual couples by chance rather than being structurally predetermined. Differential socialization of men and women, the normative structure of the marriage contract, and the economic sources of power all support a system in which the husband will accrue the greatest amount of power. Marion Kranichfeld (1987) has criticized the resource theory of power, saying that power has been masculinized. Power tends to be defined as whatever rights men have that women generally do not. Women, according to Kranichfeld, are by definition thought to be powerless. Kranichfeld views power from the perspective that it can be the ability to determine the outcome of each new generation. This kind of power, which is internal to the family, has received very little attention.

A General Model of Marital Power

Sociologists Rae Lesser Blumberg and Marion Tolbert Coleman (1989) have assessed the 30-year tradition of studying and theorizing about marital power. From three studies (Blumstein and Schwartz 1983; Hood 1983; Huber and Spitze 1983) and from Blumberg's own work on gender stratification in contemporary American society, they have developed a new model of marital power.

The central assumption derived from Blumberg's research on gender stratification is that economic power is the most important, although not the sole, contributing factor to women's relative position. Blumberg and Coleman's model for prediction of gender balance of power within contemporary mar-

---

BOX 7-3: THINKING ABOUT FAMILIES

The Marriage Contract and Marital Power

When two people marry and form a marital dyad, they enter into a formal marriage contract. The marriage contract is unwritten, yet it is legally binding and forms the basis of family law. Many of the legal rights and obligations of the marital dyad are based exclusively on gender. According to Lenore Weitzman (1981), there are four basic and traditional components of the marriage contract: (1) The husband is recognized as the head of the family; (2) the husband is responsible for providing support; (3) the wife is responsible for domestic activities, including household and domestic labor; and (4) the wife is responsible for care of the children.

The marriage contract is ideally a "free contract between equals." Dair Gillespie (1971), citing the work of Sheila Cronan (1969), finds that this supposed contract between equals actually stacks the cards against women. The implicit terms of the marriage contract provide the husband with the right to insist on sexual intercourse with his wife and the wife is duty bound to acquiesce as part of her "domestic responsibilities." Until the 1970s, women could not charge their husbands with rape, and today, in nearly two dozen states, laws still prohibit women from bringing rape charges against their husbands. Courts have also held that husbands are legally entitled to their wives' household services and that wives do not have to be paid for their work. Custom still requires that women change their names when they marry, and during the 1970s women had to go to court to get permission to retain their maiden names. Courts often denied these requests. The law of support provides that the husband's primary obligation under the marriage contract is to provide financial support for his family.

There have been notable changes in marriage laws over the past few decades and there continue to be challenges to the traditional components of the marriage contract. Women do not have to change their names when they marry. States are removing the marital rape exemption that prohibited wives from charging their husbands with rape. In addition, couples, especially middle- and upper-class couples, are increasingly entering into prenuptial contracts that specify the nature of their marital relationship and the division of property should the marriage end in divorce.

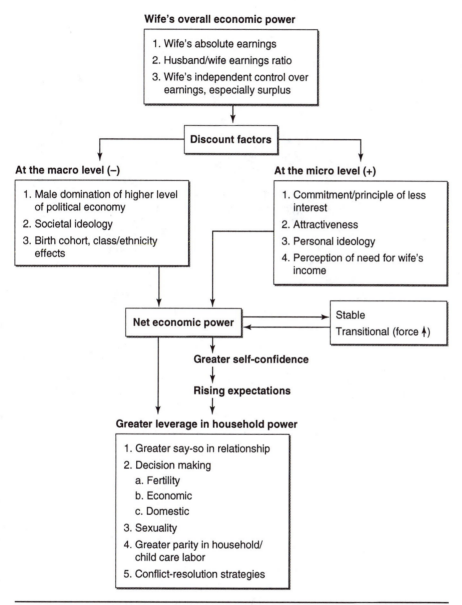

Figure 7-4
A Model for Prediction of Gender Balance of Power Within Contemporary Families

Wife's overall economic power

1. Wife's absolute earnings
2. Husband/wife earnings ratio
3. Wife's independent control over earnings, especially surplus

Discount factors

At the macro level (–)

1. Male domination of higher level of political economy
2. Societal ideology
3. Birth cohort, class/ethnicity effects

At the micro level (+)

1. Commitment/principle of less interest
2. Attractiveness
3. Personal ideology
4. Perception of need for wife's income

Net economic power

Stable
Transitional (force ↑)

Greater self-confidence

Rising expectations

Greater leverage in household power

1. Greater say-so in relationship
2. Decision making
   a. Fertility
   b. Economic
   c. Domestic
3. Sexuality
4. Greater parity in household/ child care labor
5. Conflict-resolution strategies

SOURCE: "A Theoretical Look at the Gender Balance of Power in the American Couple" by Rae L. Blumberg and Marion T. Coleman, 1989, *Journal of Family Issues* 10(June), p. 232. Copyright © 1989 by Sage Publications, Inc. Adapted by permission.

riages in the United States is presented in Figure 7-4. The authors begin by stating that there are three factors that make up a wife's overall economic power: her absolute earnings, the ratio of earnings between her and her husband, and her independent control over earnings, especially surplus earnings.

Women who work have higher self-confidence and more power in marital relations.

The impact of a wife's overall economic power on household power and decision making is mediated by a number of factors, some operating at the macrosocial level, some at the microsocial level, and some a product of the dynamic and changing nature of marital relations.

There are two sets of what Blumberg and Coleman refer to as "discount factors" that have a direct bearing on how a woman's economic power affects her power in a family. These discount factors can function to reduce the effect of economic power on family power. At the macro level, the extent to which the upper reaches of the political and economic pyramid are dominated by men, the extent to which prevailing ideological beliefs emphasize male upward mobility to the upper reaches of political and economic power, and a woman's place in a birth cohort can all act to reduce the influence of a woman's economic power on family power. The more that males control the political and economic system, the more they can limit females' attempts to gain economic power. An ideology such as "a woman's place is in the home" can further limit women's opportunities and claims to economic and family power. Finally, a woman's place in a birth cohort can also exert an influence. Blumberg and Coleman contend that women who were the suburban mothers of the 1950s, who were at home with two children, a washer and dryer, and a bridge club, were shaped by gender ideologies and structural arrangements that were different from the ideologies and arrangements in place when the feminist movement of the late 1960s and early 1970s emerged. Specifically, Blumberg and

Coleman expect that younger woman get more mileage out of the earning power and control over economic resources than their mothers or older sisters did.

There are four microsocial discount factors that also mediate the relationship between economic power and decision-making power: commitment, physical attractiveness, personal ideology, and perception of the need for the wife's income. We presented Waller's (1937) theory about the principle of least interest in our discussion of dating in Chapter 6. Briefly stated, the *principle of least interest* means that the partner who is less committed to the relationship has more leverage and power than the more committed partner. Thus, even if a woman has an abundance of economic power, if she is the most committed partner in the marriage, her actual power will be diminished, or as Blumberg and Coleman conceptualize it, the value of her overall economic power will be discounted. Similarly, physical attractiveness can discount economic power. An unattractive person who believes that she or he cannot find other or better options may sacrifice the benefits of economic power and cede authority in a relationship for the sake of remaining in the relationship.

Gender-role ideology can also discount economic power. A woman with considerable economic resources will cede power if she believes that it is normal and proper for a man to be the primary decision maker in a family. The deciding factor is the husband's perception of his wife's income. If a husband believes that his wife's income is not necessary to maintain the family standard of living, his wife will get less leverage out of the economic resources she brings into the family.

The result of the influence of macro- and microdiscount factors is the wife's net economic power. Net economic power is also influenced by stable and dynamic factors in a society. Relationships are dynamic, and as they change so too do the negotiations of power and decision making. Changes in either the husband's or the wife's occupational status or income will affect the net economic power of the wife.

Blumberg and Coleman propose that net economic power does not have a direct effect on decision making and power. Rather, net economic power operates through two social psychological variables: self-concept and rising expectations. Jane Hood's (1983) research finds that woman who begin earning or increasing their incomes report heightened feelings of self-esteem. Blumberg and Coleman (1989) believe that increased self-esteem will lead to increased sense of control over one's life and expectations of having greater bargaining power in the family.

The final stage of the Blumberg-Coleman model is household power. They conceptualize household power as multifaceted, including the normally conceptualized decision-making process and the lesser recognized overall say in the relationship, sexuality, parity in household/child-care labor, and conflict-resolution strategies.

The Blumberg-Coleman model is firmly grounded in the empirical research on the sources of marital power and is a logical extension of the resource theory of power. At the core of the model is the proposal that economic power is the main source of power in the marital dyad. Economic resources are modified by a number of cultural and individual variables.

SUMMING UP

The family is an intimate environment and a social institution. Each marital dyad fashions its own marriage within the context of a social institution that defines statuses, role expectations, values, and goals. Thus there is a certain predictable pattern of behavior in families across societies.

Marital relations are made up of a complex set of conversations, interactions, exchanges, and negotiations, the sum total of which constitute the construction of a marriage. Berger and Kellner (1964) draw on the symbolic interaction framework and describe marriage as a dramatic act in which two strangers come together and redefine themselves. The nature of the marriages that are constructed then constitute the structure of the family as a social institution. Thus the conversations that Berger and Kellner discuss when they illustrate the phenomenonological process of constructing a marriage are inextricably tied to the structure of the family in society. The structure influences the construction of individual marriages. The structure itself is influenced by the marriages that are the final products of marital conversations.

One of the most important aspects of marital relations is intimacy and sexual relations. Research on marital sexuality consistently finds that the frequency of sexual intercourse drops as the marriage progresses. Although the frequency of sexual intercourse declines over the life course, it does not stop. Sexual activity continues for most couples well into later life. Husbands tend to initiate sex more often than wives do and so marital sexual relations tend to follow a script established by men.

The first five years of a marriage are crucial for determining sexual satisfaction. Sexual satisfaction is directly related to the frequency of intercourse. The quality of sexual relations plays an important role in an individual's and a couple's level of sexual satisfaction.

There are strong cultural norms against extramarital sexual intercourse both within our society and across cultures. However, many married individuals participate in extramarital sexual relationships at some point in their marriages. Men are less severely censured for extramarital sex than are women. A number of factors have been found related to why individuals become involved in extramarital sexual relations: opportunity; reciprocity; higher order beliefs; novelty, variety, and excitement; dissatisfaction in marriage; and love and friendship.

Marital relations and interactions are made up of patterns of choices and decisions. The pattern of the decisions defines the structure of the marriage. Examining decision making is a window into understanding the power structure of families, the sources of power, and the consequences. Researchers have examined the relationship between occupation, income, education, social participation, children and marital power. The more prestigious the husband's occupation, the more likely he is to dominate decision making at home. Husbands who earn high incomes are more likely to dominate at home compared to men who earn smaller incomes. Similarly, the higher the wife's income, the more power she has in the dyad. The spouse with the most education generally tends to dominate marital relations. The more groups and organizations an individual belongs to, the greater power he or she has at home. Finally, the arrival of the first child lowers a woman's power in the home.

The *resource theory of marital power* proposes that the relative power between husbands and wives results from their relative resources as individuals—education, occupation, and income. Blumberg and Coleman have developed a newer model of marital power that proposes that economic resources are at the core of marital power.

Given the research on both marital sexuality and marital decision making, it is clear that men continue to dominate the domains of sexual relations and decision making. Women have made clear progress toward equity in the home, but real equity does not yet exist in modern American families.

REFERENCES

Ade-Ridder, Linda. 1990. "Sexuality and Marital Quality Among Older Married Couples." Pp. 48-67 in *Family Relationships in Later Life,* edited by Timothy H. Brubaker. Newbury Park, CA: Sage.

Allgeier, Albert R. and **Elizabeth Allgeier.** 1988. *Sexual Interactions.* 2nd ed. Lexington, MA: Lexington Books.

Bell, Robert R., Stanley Turner, and **Lawrence Rosen.** 1975. "A Multivariate Analysis of Female Extramarital Coitus." *Journal of Marriage and the Family* 37 (May):375-84.

Berger, Peter and **Hansfried Kellner.** 1964. "Marriage and the Construction of Reality." *Diogenes* 46:1-25.

Blood, Robert O., Jr. and **Donald M. Wolfe.** 1960. *Husbands and Wives: The Dynamics of Marital Living.* Glencoe, IL: Free Press.

Blumberg, Rae L. and **Marion T. Coleman.** 1989. "A Theoretical Look at the Gender Balance of Power in the American Couple." *Journal of Family Issues* 10(June):225-50.

Blumstein, Philip and **Pepper Schwartz.** 1983. *American Couples: Money, Work, and Sex.* New York: William Morrow.

Bowser, Benjamin. 1992. African-American Male Sexuality Through the Early Life Course." Paper presented at the MacArthur Foundation Research Network Conference on Successful Mid-Life Development.

Buunk, Bram. 1980. "Extramarital Sex in the Netherlands: Motivation in Social and Marital Context." *Alternative Lifestyles* 3(1):11-39.

———. 1984. "Jealousy as Related to Attribution for the Partner's Behavior." *Social Psychological Quarterly* 47(1):107-12.

Buunk, Bram and Barry van Driel. 1989. *Variant Lifestyles and Relationships.* Newbury Park, CA: Sage.

Carlson, John. 1976. "The Sexual Role." Pp. 101-10 in *Role Structure and Analysis of the Family,* edited by F. Ivan Nye. Beverly Hills, CA: Sage.

Clark, Alexander L. and Paul Wallin. 1965. "Women's Sexual Responsiveness and the Duration and Quality of Their Marriages." *American Journal of Sociology* 21(September):187-96.

Cromwell, Ronald E. and David Olson, eds. 1975. *Power in Families.* New York: Halsted Press.

Cromwell, Vicky L. and Ronald E. Cromwell. 1978. "Perceived Dominance in Decision-Making and Conflict-Resolution Among Anglo, Black and Chicano Couples." *Journal of Marriage and the Family* 40(November):749-59.

Cronan, Sheila. 1969. "Marriage." *The Feminist.* New York.

Edwards, John N. and Alan Booth. 1992. "Sexuality, Marriage, and Well-Being: The Middle Years." Paper presented at the MacArthur Foundation Research Network Conference on Successful Mid-Life Development.

Ellison, Ralph. 1947. *The Invisible Man.* New York: Signet Books.

Farberow, Norman, ed. 1966. *Taboo Topics.* New York: Atherton Press.

Ford, Clellan S. and Frank A. Beach. 1951. *Patterns of Sexual Behavior.* New York: Harper.

French, J.R.P. and Bertram H. Raven. 1959. "The Bases of Social Power." Pp. 607-23 in *Studies in Social Power,* edited by D. Cartwright. Ann Arbor: University of Michigan Press.

Gebhard, Paul. 1966. "Factors in Marital Orgasm." *Journal of Social Issues* 22(April):88-95.

Gillespie, Dair L. 1971. "Who Has the Power? The Marital Struggle." *Journal of Marriage and the Family* 33:(August) 445-58.

Greeley, Andrew. 1991. *Faithful Attraction.* New York: Tom Doherty Associates.

Greenblat, Cathy Stein. 1983. "The Salience of Sexuality in the Early Years of Marriage." *Journal of Marriage and the Family* 45(May):289-99.

Heer, David. 1963. "The Measurement and Bases of Family Power: An Overview." *Journal of Marriage and the Family* 25(May):133-39.

Hite, Shere. 1976. *The Hite Report.* New York: Macmillan.

———. 1981. *The Hite Report on Male Sexuality.* New York: Alfred A. Knopf.

Hood, Jane. 1983. *Becoming a Two-Job Family.* New York: Praeger.

Huber, Joan and Glenna Spitze. 1983. *Sex Stratification: Children, Housework, and Jobs.* New York: Academic Press.

Hunt, Morton. 1974. *Sexual Behavior in the 1970's.* Chicago: Playboy Press.

Kinsey, Alfred C., Wardell B. Pomeroy, Clyde E. Martin, and Paul Gebhard. 1953. *Sexual Behavior in the Human Female.* Philadelphia: W. B. Saunders.

Kinsey, Alfred C., Wardell Pomeroy, and Clyde Martin. 1948. *Sexual Behavior in the Human Male.* Philadelphia: W. B. Saunders.

Komarovsky, Mirra. 1962. *Blue-Collar Marriage.* New York: Vintage.

Kranichfeld, Marion. 1987. "Rethinking Family Power." *Journal of Family Issues* 8(March):42-56.

Levin, Robert and Amy Levin. 1975. "Sexual Pleasure: The Surprising Preferences of 100,000 Women." *Redbook* 145(September):51-58.

Levinger, George. 1966. "Systematic Distortion in Spouses' Reports of Preferred and Actual Sexual Behavior." *Sociometry* 29(September):291-99.

Masters, William H. and Virginia F. Johnson. 1966. *Human Sexual Response.* Boston: Little, Brown.

———. 1970. *Human Sexual Inadequacy.* Boston: Little, Brown.

McKinlay, John B. and Henry A. Feldman. 1992. "Changes in Sexual Activity and Interest in the Normally Aging Male: Results From the Massachusetts Male Aging Study." Paper presented at the MacArthur Foundation Research Network Conference on Successful Mid-Life Development.

Murdock, George P. 1949. *Social Structure.* New York: Macmillan.

Neubeck, Gerald. 1969. *Extra-marital Relations.* Englewood Cliffs, NJ: Prentice Hall.

Nye, F. Ivan, ed. 1976. *Role Structure and Analysis of the Family.* Beverly Hills, CA: Sage.

Olson, David, Ronald E. Cromwell, and David M. Klein. 1971. "Beyond Family Power." Pp. 235-40 in *Power in Families,* edited by Ronald E. Cromwell and David Olson. New York: Halsted Press.

Patterson, James and Peter Kim. (1991). *The Day America Told the Truth: What People Really Believe About Everything That Really Matters.* Englewood Cliffs, NJ: Prentice Hall.

Pietropinto, Anthony and Jacqueline Simenauer. 1977. *Beyond the Male Myth.* New York: Times Books.

Raven, Bertram H., Richard Centers, and Aroldo Rodrigues. 1975. "The Bases of Conjugal Power." Pp. 217-32 in *Power in Families,* edited by Ronald E. Cromwell and David Olson. New York: Halsted Press.

Reiss, Ira L. 1973. *Heterosexual Relationships Inside and Outside of Marriage.* University Programs Modular Series. Morristown, NJ: General Learning Press.

Ripportella-Muller, Roberta. 1989. "Sexuality in the Elderly." Pp. 210-35 in *Human Sexuality,* edited by Kathleen McKinney and Susan Sprecher. Norwood, NJ: Ablex.

Rodman, Hyman. 1967. "Marital Power in France, Greece, and Yugoslavia: A Cross-National Discussion." *Journal of Marriage and the Family* 29(May):320-24.

———. 1972. "Marital Power and the Theory of Resources in Cultural Context." *Journal of Comparative Family Studies* 3(May): 50-67.

Safilios-Rothschild, Constantina. 1969. "Family Sociology or Wives' Sociology: A Cross-Cultural Examination of Decision Making." *Journal of Marriage and the Family* 30 (May):290-301.

———. 1970. "The Study of Family Power Structure: A Review." *Journal of Marriage and the Family* 32(November):539-52.

———. 1976. "The Dimensions of Power Distribution in the Family." Pp. 275-292 in *Contemporary Marriage: Structure, Dynamics, and Therapy,* edited by Henry Grunebaum and Jacob Christ. Boston: Little, Brown.

———. 1977. *Love, Sex, and Sex Roles.* Englewood Cliffs, NJ: Prentice Hall.

Scanzoni, John. 1965. "A Note on the Sufficiency of Wife Responses in Family Research." *Pacific Sociological Review* 8 (Fall):109-15.

Smith, Tom W. 1992. "Attitudes Toward Sexual Permissiveness: Trends, Correlates, and Behavioral Connections." Paper presented at the MacArthur Foundation Research Network Conference on Successful Mid-Life Development.

Stephens, William N. 1963. *The Family in Cross-Cultural Perspective.* New York: Holt.

Strodbeck, Fred L. 1951. "Husband-Wife Interaction Over Revealed Differences." *American Sociological Review* 16 (August):468-73.

Sweet, James A., Larry L. Bumpass, and Vaughan R. A. Call. 1988. *The Design and Content of the National Survey of Families and Households* (NSFH Working Paper No. 1). Madison: University of Wisconsin, Center for Demography & Ecology.

Szinovacz, Maximiliane E. 1987. "Family Power." Pp. 651-93 in *Handbook of Marriage and the Family,* edited by Marvin B. Sussman and Suzanne K. Steinmetz. New York: Plenum.

Thompson, A. P. 1983. "Extramarital Sex: A Review of Research Literature." *Journal of Sex Research* 19(February):1-22.

Waller, Willard. 1937. "The Rating and Dating Complex." *American Sociological Review* 2(October):727-34.

Wallin, Paul and Alexander L. Clark. 1958. "Cultural Norms and Husbands' and Wives' Reports of Their Marital Partner's Preferred Frequency of Coitus Relative to Their Own." *Sociometry* 21(September):247-54.

Weber, Max. 1947. *The Theory of Social and Economic Organization.* Translated by A. M. Henderson and Talcott Parsons. Glencoe, IL: Free Press.

Weg, Ruth. 1990. "Sensuality-Sexuality of the Middle Years." Pp. 31-50 in *Midlife Myths,* edited by Ski Hunter and Martin Sundel. Newbury Park, CA: Sage.

Weitzman, Lenore J. 1981. *The Marriage Contract.* New York: Free Press.

Westoff, Charles F. 1974. "Coital Frequency and Contraception." *Family Planning Perspectives* 3(Summer):136-41.

CHAPTER **8**

■■ Marital Quality: Adjustment and Satisfaction

W hat makes a good marriage? For that matter, what *is* a good marriage? We know that at least one in two marriages will end in divorce (see Chapter 13). Are the 50% that end in divorce all poor-quality, unsatisfying marriages? Common sense would argue yes. Should we then assume that the 50% that do not end in divorce are high-quality, satisfying, and adjusted marriages? The answer is not so clear. We all know of marriages that do not end in divorce that nonetheless are not high quality, satisfying, or fulfilling. Thus divorce is not a totally accurate indicator of what constitutes a "good" marriage.

One comparison that is not always made is to look at the effect of marriage on the quality of life of both marriage partners. Perhaps this comparison is not made because marriage is taken for granted, and indeed, 95% of all individuals do marry at some time. However, because of divorce or death, a substantial group exists of nonmarried individuals—those who have never married, have divorced, or have had their marriage end by the death of a spouse—that can be used to compare whether marriage enhances or detracts from the overall quality of life. The first section of this chapter examines marital quality by comparing the life situation and status of married individuals to that of unmarried individuals. The unmarried comparison group includes both never-married and formerly married individuals.

Simple questions, like "Do I have a good marriage?", almost always lead to complicated answers. For researchers who study families, the first task in determining what is a "good marriage" is to define what they mean by "good" and then to develop a means of measuring "good" or of categorizing families in terms of their level of "goodness"—what most family researchers refer to as "marital quality." The second section of this chapter examines the quality of marriage by reviewing the components of marital quality and the different approaches researchers use to measure quality. Next, factors that are important contributors to marital quality are considered. The final section of the chapter examines how the quality of marriages changes over the life course.

THE QUALITY OF LIFE: MARRIED VERSUS SINGLE

Surveys that compare married with unmarried individuals find that married people in the U.S. report being happier, healthier, and less prone to premature death (Glenn and Weaver 1988; Gove 1972; Haring-Hidore et al. 1985; Veenhoven 1983). In fact, marital status is a better predictor of overall mental and physical health than education, income, age, race, or childhood background (Gove, Hughes, and Style 1983). This is true for men as well as women. Research in other cultures supports the contention that married individuals are happier and healthier than unmarried persons (Goldman 1993; Markides and Farrell 1985; Veenhoven 1983; Verbrugge and Madans 1985).

Of course, not everyone believes that the correlation between being married and higher rates of mental and physical health proves that marriage is *the cause* of a better-quality life. It is plausible that happier and healthier individuals are more likely to marry and stay married and that marriage itself is unrelated to quality of life. But research tends to support the notion that the institution of marriage causes healthier and happier individual lives. Leonard Pearlin and Joyce Johnson (1977) investigated the origins of personal stress by interviewing a representative sample of 2,300 people in the greater metropolitan Chicago area (see also Chapter 14). Pearlin and Johnson found that married persons were less depressed than either formerly married or never-married individuals. Moreover, married respondents were exposed to stress and strain as frequently as never-marrieds but still showed less depression. Pearlin and Johnson conclude that marriage does not prevent economic and social problems from invading life, but it does function as a protective barrier against the distressful consequences of external threats.

Marital status alone, however, is not a sufficient insulator against stress and strain. Walter Gove and his colleagues (1983) report that the *quality of a marriage* serves as a key factor that prevents stress. They found that people in unhappy marriages had poorer mental health than individuals who were not married. Thus a "good marriage" is an important contributor to personal, emotional, and physical health and happiness.

Norval Glenn and Charles Weaver (1988) have examined survey data collected by the National Opinion Research Center from 1972 to 1988. Although the analysis confirms earlier research that married individuals report being happier than never-married, separated or divorced, or widowed individuals (see Table 8-1), there has been a rather steady decline over the years in the relationship between being married and being happy. This change is the result of an increase in reported happiness of never-married males and a decrease in the happiness of married females.

THE COMPONENTS OF MARITAL QUALITY

Researchers who have explored the question of marital quality or "what is a good marriage?" tend to use the concept **marital quality.** Although there is apparent consensus in the use of "marital quality" as an umbrella term, it is by no means easily defined. The term is made up of a number of components,

Table 8-1 General Social Survey Respondents, Aged 18–31, Who Said They Were Very Happy, by Sex and Marital Status, 1972 and 1986

Marital Status	1972		1986		% Change
	%	n	%	n	
Both sexes					
Never married	14.7	156	27.2	184	+12.5
Married	37.9	290	30.6	184	−7.3
Difference	−23.2***		−3.4		+19.8**
Males					
Never married	11.1	99	31.3	99	+20.2**
Married	32.4	148	25.6	78	−6.8
Difference	−21.3**		+5.7		+27.0**
Females					
Never married	21.1	57	22.4	85	+1.3
Married	43.7	142	34.7	95	−9.0
Difference	−22.6*		−12.3		−10.3

SOURCE: "The Changing Relationship of Marital Status to Reported Happiness" by Norval D. Glenn and Charles N. Weaver, 1988, *Journal of Marriage and the Family* 50(May), p. 320. Copyright © 1988 by the National Council on Family Relations, 3989 Central Ave. NE, Suite 550, Minneapolis, MN. Adapted by permission. *Significant at the .05 level; **significant at the .01 level; ***significant at the .001 level, all on two-tailed tests.

and, as we shall see in the following section, there seem to be as many ways of measuring it as there are investigators (Johnson et al. 1986).

Happiness

One of the most frequently measured components of marital quality is **marital happiness.** This concept refers to the level of personal happiness *an individual* feels about his or her marriage. Happiness, however, is an elusive concept. Fifty years ago, one of the first scholars to investigate marital quality said that "There are so many kinds of happiness and unhappiness incident to marriage that no weighing in the balance one kind against another can do justice to the complex emotional facts in question" (Terman and Buttenwieser 1935, p. 153).

Satisfaction

A second component of quality is **marital satisfaction,** which is an individual's *subjective evaluation* of the overall nature of the marriage. Stephen Bahr (1989) explains that satisfaction is the degree to which *an individual's* needs, expectations, and desires are met in marriage.

Adjustment

Marital adjustment is a concept that taps the global sense of a marriage. It is more than an individual's subjective view of the marriage; it taps how individuals view their relationships with their partners. Graham Spanier (1976) states that marital adjustment can be viewed in two distinct ways: first, as a process, and second, as an evaluation of the state of the marriage. The assessment is a continuum, ranging from maladjusted at one end to well-adjusted at the other. Thus each family can be placed at some point on the continuum at a given point in time. Adjustment, as Spanier and others note, changes from time to time and over the course of a marriage.

One final conceptualization of marital quality is **marital instability,** defined as the propensity to divorce. This concept has two components: cognitive and behavioral. The cognitive element includes thinking the marriage is in trouble and contemplating getting a divorce. The behavioral component includes action, such as talking to friends about divorce; seeking help and advise from clergy, counselors, or attorneys; separating; or filing for a divorce (Johnson et al. 1986).

Instability

In 1986, David Johnson and his colleagues at the University of Nebraska examined all the above dimensions of marital quality and determined that there are two significant components of marital quality: (1) marital happiness and interaction and (2) marital disagreements, problems, and instability. Johnson and his colleagues warn that assuming that marital quality or adjustment are unidimensional qualities and simply summing the scores of a single measure will result in a misleading and inaccurate measure of marital quality. Marital rewards and satisfactions and marital tensions and problems are two distinct elements of a marriage. Johnson and his colleagues conclude that marital happiness, interaction, problems, disagreements, and instability appear to be distinct concepts and should be measured separately to assess marital quality. They are quite skeptical that "marital quality" exists as a measurable grand concept.

Components of Marital Quality: A Summary

MEASURING MARITAL QUALITY

Given that marital quality is central to understanding families and is one of the most frequently studied variables in the field, there is a long and rich tradition of developing ways to assess and measure marital quality, happiness, satisfaction, and adjustment. Some measures of marital quality are as simple as asking, "Taken all together, how would you describe your marriage? Would

Marital quality is most frequently measured by using a survey—often an interview—and asking couples about their perceptions of their marriage.

you say your marriage is very happy, pretty happy, or not too happy?" (Glenn and Weaver 1977). Researchers have long sought to develop more comprehensive, reliable, and valid measures of marital quality and its component properties. Although researchers have been successful in developing reliable measures—that is, ones that produce consistent results—the validity of the many measures is often criticized. The central concern is how well the measure actually does measure what is meant by marital quality.

The study of marital quality dates back to George Hamilton's (1929) classic study of marital adjustment in couples in the 1920s. The first comprehensive study of marital adjustment was conducted by pioneer University of Chicago sociologists Ernest Burgess and Leonard Cottrell, Jr. (1939). They developed a scale to predict marital quality that was distributed to nearly 7,000 couples in Illinois, of which 526 completed and returned the questionnaire. This is considered a low response rate by current standards, but it did provide the researchers with a large sample of couples. Burgess and Cottrell used 130 items to measure factors such as whether couples agree on critical issues in their relationship, share common interests and joint activities, demonstrate affection and mutual confidences, have few complaints about their marriage,

Most persons have disagreements in their relationships. Please indicate below the approximate extent of agreement or disagreement between you and your partner for each item on the following list.

Figure 8-1 Dyadic Adjustment Scale

	Always Agree	Almost Always Agree	Occa-sionally Disagree	Fre-quently Disagree	Almost Always Disagree	Always Disagree
8. Philosophy of life	5	4	3	2	1	0
10. Aims, goals, and things believed important	5	4	3	2	1	0
11. Amount of time spent together	5	4	3	2	1	0

How often would you say the following events occur between you and your mate?

	Never	Less Than Once a Month	Once or Twice a Month	Once or Twice a Week	Once a Day	More Often
25. Have a stimulating exchange of ideas	0	1	2	3	4	5
27. Calmly discuss something	0	1	2	3	4	5
28. Work together on a project	0	1	2	3	4	5

SOURCE: "Measuring Dyadic Adjustment: New Scales for Assessing the Quality of Marriage and Similar Dyads" by Graham B. Spanier, 1976. Reproduced by permission of Multi-Health Systems, Inc., 908 Niagara Falls Blvd., N. Tomawanda, NY, 14120-2060, 800-456-3003.

affection and mutual confidences, have few complaints about their marriage, and are not bothered by feelings of loneliness, irritability, and miserableness. The Burgess and Cottrell scale was used in numerous research studies and applied in clinical work as well.

Harvey Locke and Karl Wallace (1959) developed the 15-item Marital Adjustment Scale, which classifies individuals into high or low marital adjustment categories. This scale, too, has been widely used. The scale focuses on the degree of consensus between marital partners in such areas as money handling, in-law relationships, sexual relationships, and mutual friends.

One of the most widely used recent measures of marital adjustment is Graham Spanier's (1976; Spanier and Thompson 1982) Dyadic Adjustment Scale. This 32-item scale focuses on four components of marital adjustment: satisfaction, cohesion, consensus, and affectional expression.C. F. Sharpley and D. G. Cross (1982) report that one can use only 6 of Spanier's 32 items (see Figure 8-1, Items 8, 10, 11, 25, 27, and 28) as valid measures of marital adjustment because the remaining items measure other dimensions of the dyadic relationship. They also note that for a quick screening of marital adjustment, the global self-rating item (Item 31) is sufficient.

Which of these scales and measures is used depends on the purpose of the research and the time budgeted for data collection. Thus longer and more complicated measures, such as Gerald Patterson's (1976) 400-item Spouse

Observational Checklist, are used infrequently by survey researchers. In fact, as we will see in the discussions in the following sections, despite the major investment in developing measures of marital adjustment, many investigators still rely on simple, single-item measures. Again, although such single-item measures are reliable, many researchers question whether a single item can fully and accurately measure something as complex as marital quality. An alternative way of assessing marital quality—the use of qualitative classifications—is demonstrated in Box 8-1.

GLOBAL ASSESSMENTS OF MARITAL QUALITY

Researchers continually find that most people are happy with their marriages, no matter what instrument or what component of marital quality is examined.

BOX 8-1: WHAT THE RESEARCH SHOWS

Assessing Quality by Looking at Types of Marriages

Quality, satisfaction, and adjustment of marriages are often measured by asking individuals or couples to respond to a series of items in a questionnaire or interview survey. The researchers then score the items and place the couple at a point on a continuum from maladjusted to adjusted, unhappy to happy, or low quality to high quality.

A different approach to examining marital quality is to develop a typology of marriages. John Cuber and Peggy Harroff (1968) studied 437 married men and women who were between the ages of 35 and 50. Subjects were from the middle to upper end of the income distribution. From this large sample, Cuber and Harroff selected 107 men and 104 women who said they had never contemplated divorce. After analyzing the interviews with these 211 seemingly normal, stable marriages, Cuber and Harroff developed five categories of adjusted marriages:

Conflict-Habituated. Conflict-habituated couples are those who fight about everything.

Some couples note that this pattern emerged after the marriage, whereas others explain that the pattern of conflict and fights traces back to dating and engagement. Conflict and tension are so much part of the marriage that attempts to conceal fights and conflict from friends and children almost always fail. The conflict is controlled by the fact that the partners know that conflict is at the core of their relationship and each knows "how the game is played." The conflict and tension that pervade the marriage are also the glue that binds the marriage together.

Devitalized. One of the more common marital types is the devitalized marriage. Devitalized marriages had vitality and excitement at one point, but the spark is now gone. Sex has become less important in the relationship, little time is spent on mutual activities, and the partners have grown apart and now invest themselves in individual interests and activities. Although this marriage has little tension and conflict, it also has no zest. Devitalized mar-

Lewis Terman's (1938) survey of marital adjustment found that 85% of those studied said that their marriages were very happy. Ernest Burgess and Leonard Cottrell, Jr. (1939) found that 63% of those surveyed reported very happy marriages. Thirty years later, Susan Orden and Norman Bradburn (1968) reported that 60% of couples said their marriages were very happy. Norval Glenn and Charles Weaver (1978) found that 68% of couples rate their marriage as very happy. Data from the National Opinion Research Center's (1988) General Social Survey indicate that the percentage of individuals reporting that their marriage was very happy fluctuated between 68% and 56% between 1973 and 1988 (Glenn 1991). As revealed in Figure 8-2, there was a substantial temporary decline in 1985 in the percentage of men who reported being very happy. In addition, the overall trend of men reporting being very happy in their marriages shows a decline. The trend for women is about the same, with a substantial drop in 1985 and an overall decline in the percentage of women who report being very happy in their marriages.

riages continue in a perpetual state of emotional numbness.

Passive-Congenial. There is also no spark or excitement in the passive-congenial relationship, but unlike the devitalized marriage, there never was any. The marriage lacks vitality, and there is little that individuals care about deeply in their partners. The passivity of the relationship means that the couple probably just drifted into this way of life, perhaps by default. Passive-congenial couples are realistic about their relationships and accept the lack of excitement. They point to the similarity between their relationship and their friends' relationships.

A passive-congenial relationship provides the partners with independence and the opportunity to devote their energies to activities outside the relationship. Men talked about devoting themselves to their careers and women (this was in the 1960s) talked about investing their energies in their children. They did not, however, devote much energy or emotion to their marital relationship.

Vital. Participants in vital marriages enjoy each other's company. Vital couples argue, fight, disagree, and experience conflict. But such conflicts and tensions are exceptions and the partners work to forgive and forget as quickly as possible. Vital couples spend time together and enjoy this time, but they do not do everything together and do not monopolize each other's time. Vital marriages are few in number, according to Cuber and Harroff's study.

Total. The total marriage is a vital one in which the partners are totally enmeshed. They spend all their time together and are totally involved in each other's activities. If one partner takes a business trip, the other always goes along. The two individuals have become one.

When people read Cuber and Harroff's book or read or hear about the types, they almost always select the total marriage as their ideal or goal. It is unlikely that many marriages actually ever achieve this goal. Those that do are obvious in their state of marital bliss. Cuber and Harroff, however, do not consider their typology a continuum, with the total marriage as the highest point on the scale. All five types were well-adjusted marriages, and none of the respondents evidenced a desire to seek a divorce or even think about divorce. It is also worth noting that couples may move from one type of marriage to another over the life course and that one partner may see him- or herself in one type of marriage while the other sees him- or herself in another type.

A marriage that once had vitality and excitement but now has little zest is called a "de-vitalized marriage."

Clearly, a great majority of married individuals rate their marriage as very happy at any given time and have done so for over half a century. It is ironic, however, that a reasonably large portion of those who are rating their marriages as very happy will ultimately be divorced (as we will discuss in Chapter 13). It is also worth noting that the subjective experience of being very happy varies from husband to wife within a marriage and from marriage to marriage. Types of adjusted marriages also vary enormously (see Box 8-1).

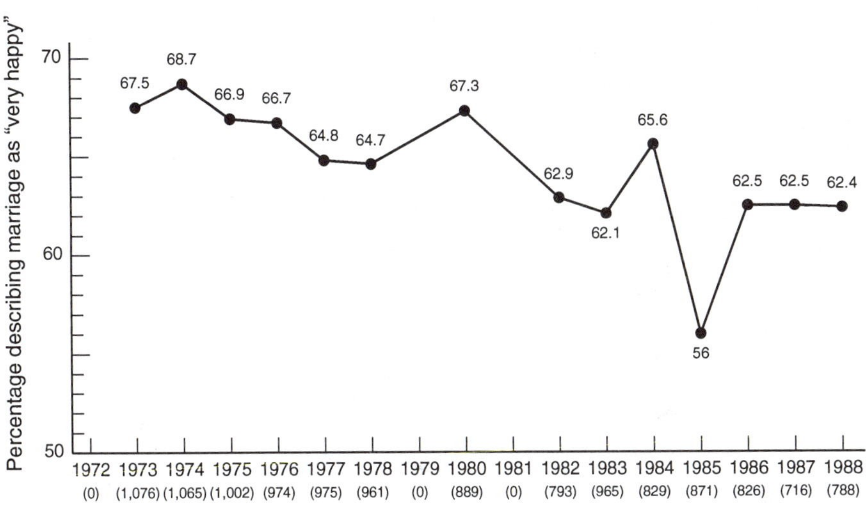

Figure 8-2 Percentage of Individuals Describing Their Marriage as Very Happy for Each Year of the National Opinion Research Center General Social Survey, 1972–1988

SOURCE: Data are from the 1972 through 1988 General Social Survey, conducted by the National Opinion Research Center, and are distributed by the Roper Center for Public Opinion Research.

INDIVIDUAL AND MARITAL ATTRIBUTES ASSOCIATED WITH MARITAL QUALITY

There are many different factors that influence marital quality and satisfaction. In addition, the way in which factors affect marital quality is often complex. As we noted earlier, economic hardship, while not having a direct negative impact on marital quality, does have an indirect impact by changing the nature of marital hostility and warmth.

Robert Lewis and Graham Spanier (1979) reviewed the literature on marital quality, developed nearly 100 propositions regarding factors related to marital quality, and then summarized these propositions in a theory of marital quality and marital stability (Figure 8-3). They theorized that marital quality is influenced by three sets of factors:

1. *Premarital.* These factors include homogamy, resources, role models, and support from significant others.

2. *Marital and relationship.* These factors include economic resources, satisfaction with wife's working, household composition, involvement in the community, role fit, emotional gratification, and effective communications.

3. *Social and personal.* These factors include satisfaction with lifestyle and rewards gained from spousal interaction.

Figure 8-3
A Theory of
Marital Quality and
Marital Stability

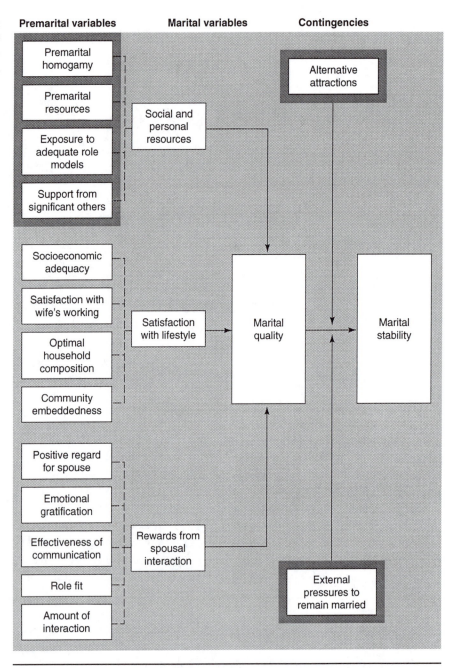

SOURCE: "Theorizing About the Quality and Stability of Marriage" by Robert A. Lewis and Graham B. Spanier in *Contemporary Theories About the Family,* Vol. 1, edited by Wesley R. Burr, Reuben Hill, F. Ivan Nye, and Ira L. Reiss, 1979, New York: Free Press. Copyright © 1979 by The Free Press. Adapted by permission.

Lewis and Spanier go on to explain that the level of marital quality, the availability of alternatives to marriage and one's spouse, and social pressure to remain married all influence the chances of a couple seeking a separation or a divorce.

A great deal of the research on marital quality has sought to identify and illuminate the factors and attributes that are associated with marital quality, satisfaction, and adjustment. Not surprising, there is a range of personal, social, and interpersonal factors that have been found to be related to marital quality.

Two cautions need to be introduced before we turn to the factors related to marital quality. The first is that there are hundreds of studies of marital quality, and findings often vary from study to study. The reason is that different studies define the components of marital quality differently or use different attributes and factors, thus leading to contradictory results. To sort out the differing findings, the following section draws from a variety of sources but mainly from the careful and thorough review of marital quality carried out by Lewis and Spanier (1979).

The second caution is that marriage is a complex institution and marital quality a complex concept. Thus our review of factors associated with marital quality should not be used as a guide to assure that one has a satisfactory marriage. Some marriages are quite satisfying, despite the fact that they have none of the qualities that researchers tend to find related to high marital quality. Other marriages are not satisfying, yet they tend to include many of the factors that we list.

Premarital Factors: Homogamy

Homogamy is the tendency to marry someone who is like us in the social attributes that our society considers important, such as age, education, race, religion, and ethnic background (see Chapter 6). Because homogamy is normal in mate selection, it is not surprising to find that when this norm is violated, there is an increased chance of lower marital quality and satisfaction (Lewis and Spanier 1979).

Suzanne Ortega, Hugh Whitt, and J. Allen Williams, Jr. (1988) analyzed a representative sample of 1,070 married Protestants and Catholics and assessed the relationship between religious homogamy and marital happiness. Marital happiness was measured by asking subjects, "Taking all things together, how would you describe your marriage? Would you say it was very happy, pretty happy, or not too happy?" Overall, homogamous couples (Protestants who married Protestants and Catholics who married Catholics) had no greater marital happiness than heterogamous (individuals with different religious preferences) couples. However, when the investigators assessed homogamy more finely by looking at marriage within denominations (i.e., Lutherans married to Lutherans, Methodists to Methodists, fundamentalists to fundamentalists, etc.) homogamous marriages were happier than marriages across denominations. The researchers concluded that differences in religious doctrine and ritual can affect marital happiness.

Marital and Relationship Factors

The properties of the marriage, marital relationship, and family structure all have an influence on marital quality. Lewis and Spanier list a number of marital and relationship factors in their model (Figure 8-3). Researchers have also examined additional marital and relationship factors and how these influence marital quality.

Linda Robinson and Priscilla Blanton (1993) examined marital quality by interviewing 15 couples who had been married at least 30 years. The couples were asked to give their perceptions on the qualities that had sustained their relationships in times of both closeness and marital strain. The key characteristics that contributed to marital quality for long-term married couples were physical and emotional intimacy balanced with autonomy, commitment, communication, congruence, and religious faith. Intimacy meant sharing interests, activities, thoughts, feelings, values, joys, and pains and grew out of involvement with one another in both good and bad times. The couples also reported that they needed and enjoyed time alone. Commitment was a second factor important for an enduring marriage. Many couples reported that they did not consider divorce an option, no matter what happened in their marriages. Communication, as we will see in the following section, was another important contributor to marital quality. Positive communications involved sharing thoughts and feelings, discussing important problems, and listening to the other person's point of view. Congruence, or similar perceptions about the strengths of the relationship, was cited by most couples as another feature of marital strength and quality. Finally, the majority of the couples cited religious faith as an important aspect of their marriage. This included shared involvement in church and religious activities. Even though the level of religious involvement differed, the shared involvement was thought to be an important ingredient of a quality marriage.

Effectiveness of Communication

It is common sense that good communication is a prerequisite for marital satisfaction and quality. Positive communication skills have been shown to be directly related to the quality and satisfaction of a marriage by many researchers (Fowers and Olson 1986; Levenson and Gottman 1983; Margolin and Wampold 1981; Olson, McCubbin, and Associates 1983; Olson, Russell, and Sprenkle 1983; Rusbult, Johnson, and Morrow 1986; Ting-Toomey 1983). Good communication during family/joint/marital activities is especially important (Barnett and Nietzel 1979; Fowers and Olson 1986; Jacobson, Waldron, and Moore 1980; Orthner 1975).

More detailed examinations of marital communication reveal that self-disclosure is a key element of effective marital communications and enhanced marital quality. Self-disclosure is a necessary part of developing intimacy and love (see Chapter 6). Individuals who are able to reveal personal information about themselves, including needs, attitudes, and feelings, tend to have more positive communications and more satisfying marriages.

Role Fit

Consensus and fit in marital roles are important aspects of effective and satisfying marriages. Stephen Bahr and his colleagues Bradford Chappell and Geoffrey Leigh (1983) have identified eight marital roles: provider, housekeeper, child care, child socialization, therapeutic, sexual, recreational, and kinship. The greater the degree of consensus that partners have about the nature of these roles, how they are to be filled, and by which partner, the greater the degree of marital satisfaction. Also, the better individuals are at fulfilling their spouse's expectations of their roles and at enacting specific roles in family relations, the better the marital quality (Bahr, Chappell, and Leigh 1983; Burr, Leigh, Day, and Constantine 1979).

Socioeconomic Adequacy/Economic Hardship

It would seem obvious that economic hardship adversely affects a marriage and the level of marital satisfaction, but research is divided about whether money and social status are related to marital quality. Some investigators report no relationship between income, social status, and marital quality (Bahr et al. 1983; Brinkeroff and White 1978; Jorgensen, 1979; Nye and McLaughlin 1982). Others do find a relationship, although it tends to be modest (Lewis and Spanier 1979; Piotrokowski, Rapoport, and Rapoport 1987).

A recent study by Rand Conger and his colleagues (1990) of 76 white, middle-class couples from a rural midwestern city found that economic hardship had no direct effect on couples' marital quality. Hardship did, however, tend to promote a husband's (and only the husband's) hostility in marital

Marital quality is higher when couples agree about their marital roles—especially about expectations regarding child care and child socialization.

relations and curtail his warmth and supportive interactions. These in turn led to a decline in marital quality.

Optimal Household Composition/Number of Children

It is ironic that the family has traditionally been the main societal mechanism for nurturing and caring for children; yet research on marital satisfaction generally finds that couples with children report lower levels of marital quality and satisfaction (Figley 1973; Glenn and McLanahan 1982; Lupri and Frideres 1981; Renne 1970; Rollins and Cannon 1974; Rollins and Feldman 1970; Ryder 1973). In the following section on marital quality over the life span, we will see that this finding has been interpreted to mean that couples have higher levels of marital satisfaction before their children are born and after their children leave home. The addition of children adds new roles for the partners (mother/father), new economic stresses, more crowding, new schedules, and less intimacy and free time. Parents of children of all ages report stresses and strains of child rearing as well as gratification and fulfillment.

Sharon Houseknecht (1979) compared 50 married women who had voluntarily chosen not to have children (there were no medical reasons for them not to have children) with 50 married mothers. Houseknecht carefully matched the two groups on three variables: education, religion, and participation in the labor force. All the women were between the ages of 25 and 40. The findings revealed that the women who were childless by choice had higher overall marital adjustment scores (as measured by Spanier's Dyadic Adjustment Scale—see Figure 8-1). The childless women had especially high scores for what Houseknecht called "marital cohesion." Married childless women said they were more likely to engage in outside interests, work on projects with their husbands, have more frequent exchanges of stimulating ideas, and have more quiet discussions with their husbands.

In 1980, Lynn White and Alan Booth conducted 2,033 telephone interviews with a national sample of married individuals under the age of 55. Interviews were conducted again in 1983 with 1,578 of the original respondents. Marital quality was assessed using an 11-item marital happiness scale. Marital quality did indeed deteriorate over the 3-year period. However, the transition to parenthood had little impact on the change. White and Booth (1985) concluded that having a first child did not contribute to declining marital happiness. On the other hand, having a child had no impact on marital instability either, as couples with and without children were as likely to get divorced or enter into a permanent separation. We will refer back to this study in the section on marital quality over the life span.

Personal and Social Characteristics

Personal characteristics, such as good physical and mental health and having a positive self-concept, have been found to be related to marital quality (Lewis and Spanier 1979). Studies of social factors—such as higher education, older at the time of marriage, higher social class, and degree of acquaintance with the future spouse—show themselves to be related to higher-quality marriages (Lewis and Spanier 1979). However, this is not always the case. For example, Norval Glenn and Charles Weaver (1978) report weak or nonexistent relationships between age at marriage, socioeconomic status, and marital happiness. It is important to note that Glenn and Weaver were studying marital happiness (see Figure 8-2 for the question used to measure marital happiness), which is only one component of marital quality. Factors that are not strongly related to happiness may still be associated with other aspects of marital quality, such as adjustment and satisfaction.

An important personal characteristic related to marital quality is the exposure that individuals have to role models for sound marital functioning. Individuals who grew up in families with high marital quality and whose parents were good role models for communications and marital relations are more likely to have higher-quality marriages (Lewis and Spanier 1979).

MARITAL QUALITY OVER THE LIFE SPAN

Marital quality and satisfaction are dynamic qualities that change across situations and over time. A number of family researchers have focused on changes in marital quality over the life span. One of the earliest and best-known examinations was conducted by Boyd Rollins and Harold Feldman (1970), who used an eight-stage family life cycle model (see Chapter 2) to assess the pattern of general and specific aspects of marital satisfaction. Rollins and Feldman obtained separate questionnaires from husbands and wives in

---

BOX 8-2: DIVERSE FAMILIES

Determinants of
Marital Happiness in Black Couples

The majority of research on marital quality is based on studies of white, middle-class couples. Large-scale surveys of marital happiness (see Glenn and Weaver 1978) include nonminority couples but often do not assess minority couples separately from the majority couples in the survey. Studies that either do not include minority couples or overlook them ignore the distinctive experience of minority couples and the impact these experiences have on life and marital satisfaction. Black families in particular have been characterized as having strong kinship bonds, strong work orientation, and strong achievement and religious orientations (Hill 1972). In addition, black family functioning has been demonstrated to be qualitatively different from that of white families (Thomas 1990).

Veronica Thomas (1990) surveyed 41 dual-career black couples in a northeastern metropolitan area. Subjects were recruited by announcements placed in a variety of black professional association and civic newspapers. Respondents were relatively young and were married an average of eight years.

Thomas looked at life happiness and family environment. She found that marital happiness was the strongest determinant of global life happiness. The strongest determinant of marital happiness for husbands was marital cohesion and for wives quality communications. Thus there were no major differences in the contributors to marital happiness among black couples compared to research on white couples.

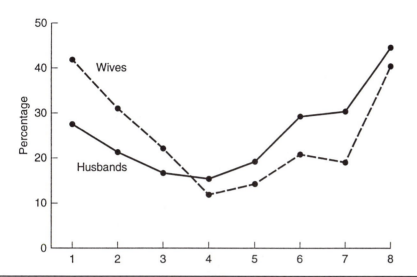

Figure 8-4 Percentage of Individuals Reporting That Their Marriage Was Going Well "All the Time," by Stage of Family Life Cycle

SOURCE: "Marital Satisfaction Over the Family Life Cycle" by Boyd C. Rollins and Harold Feldman, 1970, *Journal of Marriage and the Family* 32(February), p. 25. Copyright © 1970 by the National Council on Family Relations, 3989 Central Ave. NE, Suite 550, Minneapolis, MN. Adapted by permission.
KEY: Stage 1: Beginning families; Stage 2: Childbearing families; Stage 3: Families with preschool children; Stage 4: Families with school-aged children; Stage 5: Families with teenagers; Stage 6: Families as launching centers; Stage 7: Families in the middle years;

799 middle-class families. Overall, the percentage of individuals who reported that their marriage was "going well all the time" declined with the birth of the first child, bottomed out among families with school-aged children, rose when children began leaving home, and regained the earlier peak in the final stages of the family life cycle (see Figure 8-4).

The study also revealed that husbands and wives are influenced in different ways in different stages of the family life cycle. In general, family life-cycle experiences had a greater influence on the marital satisfaction of wives than of husbands. The decline in marital satisfaction of wives with children in the school-age stage was more pronounced than the decline for husbands, and thereafter, wives' scores for marital satisfaction never were as high as husbands'. Apparently, because wives tend to carry the greater responsibilities for child care compared to husbands, these excess responsibilities lower the level of marital satisfaction for wives.

Boyd Rollins and Kenneth Cannon (1974) reviewed other major studies of marital satisfaction over the family life cycle that had been conducted up to the 1970s. Three patterns were found. Rollins's own research and that of other investigators, such as Terman (1938) and Burr (1970), found that there was a U-shaped pattern, as in Figure 8-4. Other studies found a general overall decline in marital satisfaction (e.g., Blood and Wolfe 1960). Finally, one study found no statistical trends in the pattern of satisfaction over the life cycle (Bossard and Boll 1955). Rollins and Cannon's review of research concluded that the U-shaped pattern was the best representation of the data and that other studies were limited by measurement and analysis problems.

The U-shaped pattern of marital satisfaction over the life course was a consistent pattern found in the data on marital quality in the studies carried out in the 1960s and 1970s. However, some important cautions need to be introduced. As we noted earlier, researchers who have assessed marital quality over the life span have tended to use cross-sectional data—that is, they study families at only one point in time; they do not follow families over time. Samples are drawn at one point in time, categorized by stage of the family life cycle, and examined in terms of measures of marital adjustment or quality. This design may not account for factors that would bias the results. For example, a number of studies of marital satisfaction over the family life cycle were conducted in the 1960s and 1970s. Parents with children at home in the 1960s and early 1970s were the parents of the baby boom generation. Perhaps their low level of marital satisfaction was a result of the stresses of raising more children per family, overcrowded schools, or financial stress, and not the result of the stage of having children at home. A second caution needed when interpreting these results is that parents with children at home may believe it is more socially acceptable to report high stress and low satisfaction, whereas newly married couples may feel that they are expected to report high levels of happiness and satisfaction.

One solution to the problem of using cross-sectional data would be to follow a cohort of couples over the stages of the family life cycle and assess changes in marital satisfaction. As we discussed earlier, this is exactly what Lynn White and Alan Booth (1985) did. Although their study was limited to a 3-year period and to only the transition from childless to the birth of the first child, White and Booth did not find evidence that the decline in marital satisfaction was attributable to the birth of the first child, as is assumed by those who interpret the cross-sectional data on marital quality across the life cycle.

White and Booth's study suggests that the birth of children does not necessarily reduce the level of marital satisfaction. Caroline and George Vaillant (1993) report on a study that followed 268 college men and their wives (less 12 subjects who dropped out of the study) for 40 years, beginning in 1938 through 1942 when the men were college sophomores. Of the original 268, there were 169 long-term married couples who were analyzed. The researchers examined marital satisfaction both prospectively—that is, measuring it over the course of the 40 years—and retrospectively—that is, asking respondents to look back on their marriages and discuss marital satisfaction. The prospective analysis, which measured marital satisfaction about every 10 years, found no U-shaped curve of marital satisfaction. Marital satisfaction in this sample was relatively stable over the course of the marriages. Looking back over the 40 years, there was a slight decline in marital satisfaction at the 20-year mark of the marriages. Thus Vaillant and Vaillant believe that the U-curve of marital satisfaction is largely an illusion.

Rollins and Cannon (1974) add some additional caveats of their own about the U-curve. They note that the practical importance of the changes on marital satisfaction is minimal. The mean satisfaction scores of the persons with the *lowest* marital satisfaction are still relatively high. Moreover, stage of the marital life cycle plays only a minor role in explaining the changes in the scores that do occur.

Marital Quality Over the Life Cycle: A Cross-Cultural Comparison

Studies of marital satisfaction in the United States and other Western societies show that marital happiness seems to decline slightly over the course of a marriage (Pineo 1961; Renne 1970; Hicks and Platt 1970). Western "love" marriages are thought to start out "hot" and grow "cold" as the idealizations about marriage and wedded bliss fade into the routine of domestic chores, child care, and domestic responsibilities.

The trajectory of arranged marriages, such as occur in China, is thought to be different. These marriages are believed to start "cold" and grow "hot" over the life span (Xiaohe and Whyte 1990). Couples in arranged marriages start out without emotional involvement, romance, or expectations and have nowhere to go but up in terms of marital happiness and satisfaction.

Robert Blood (1967) put the notion of arranged marriages starting cold and growing hot to the test with a study of 444 married couples who lived in predominantly nuclear households in three white-collar housing projects in Tokyo, Japan. Blood found no evidence of arranged marriages starting cold and heating up. Both arranged and love marriages evidenced a long-term downward trajectory of marital happiness.

Xu Xiaohe and Martin King Whyte (1990) partially replicated Blood's research and studied a probability sample of 586 ever-married women between the ages of 22 and 70 in China. Xiaohe and Whyte found that wives in love marriages were more satisfied than their counterparts in arranged marriages. There appeared to be no decline in marital satisfaction among Chinese women in love marriages. In fact, for both arranged and love marriages, marital satisfaction was highest among women married for 20-24 years (see Figure 8-5), although there is an inexplicable decline in satisfaction among women married longer than 25 years.

Thus it appears that no matter how a marriage begins—through love or arrangement—marital satisfaction seems to gently decline over the length of the marriage.

Figure 8-5 Marriage Quality, by Mode of Mate Choice in Chengdu

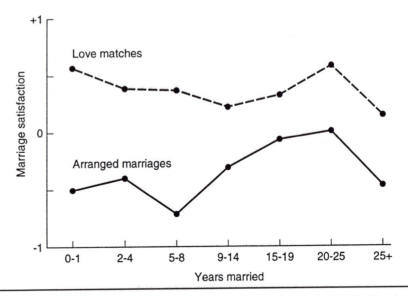

SOURCE: "Love Matches and Arranged Marriages: A Chinese Replication" by Xu Xiaoche and Martin King Whyte, 1990, *Journal of Marriage and the Family* 52(August), p. 718. Copyright © 1990 by the National Council on Family Relations, 3989 Central Ave. NE, Suite 550, Minneapolis, MN. Adapted by permission.

SUMMING UP

Contemporary American marriages appear to have considerable strength and quality, despite high divorce rates and the changes that the institution of the family has undergone in the past few decades. Married men and women are healthier and happier than unmarried persons and a sizable majority of married individuals report high levels of marital happiness and satisfaction.

The quality of a marriage is a major determinant of married individuals' health, happiness, and well-being. Economic hardship and stress and social isolation have less of an impact on married persons than on single individuals. Married men have lower mortality rates than same-aged single, divorced, or widowed men.

Marriages high in marital quality tend to be those where the partners come into the marriage with similar backgrounds, have consistent expectations for filling marital roles, and have solid role models for effective marital functioning. High-quality marriages are those with intimacy, good communication, and agreement about marital roles and role enactments.

There are some thorns in the rose garden of marital happiness. Although the level of personal happiness of married individuals is high, researchers have

Longitudinal studies over the life course find only a slight decline in marital satisfaction.

found a gradual decline in the personal happiness of married individuals. This is due to declines in married women's happiness and increases in happiness among never-married men.

Overall, the level of marital satisfaction and happiness has not changed greatly in the past 50 years. However, within marriages, there are some predictable trends. Marital happiness among American couples tends to gradually decline over the course of the marriage. Some family researchers have attributed this decline to the transition to parenthood and the stresses and strains of child rearing. However, more comprehensive research indicates that the decline is a general one and is not a function of the transition to parenthood. Although the U-curve of marital satisfaction seems to make sense, it appears to be mostly an illusion. Children do, however, have an impact on marital quality. Couples who are voluntarily childless report higher marital quality than do couples with children.

REFERENCES

Bahr, Stephen J. 1989. *Family Interaction*. New York: McGraw-Hill.

Bahr, Stephen J., C. Bradford Chappell, and Geoffrey K. Leigh. 1983. "Age at Marriage, Role Enactment, Role Consensus, and Marital Satisfaction." *Journal of Marriage and the Family* 45(November):795-803.

Barnett, Linda R. and Michael T. Nietzel. 1979. "Relationship of Instrumental and Affectional Behaviors and Self-Esteem to Marital Satisfaction in Distressed and Nondistressed Couples." *Journal of Consulting and Clinical Psychology* 47(October): 946-58.

Blood, Robert O., Jr. 1967. *Love Match and Arranged Marriage*. New York: Free Press.

Blood, Robert O., Jr. and Donald M. Wolfe. 1960. *Husbands and Wives: The Dynamics of Marital Living*. Glencoe, IL: Free Press.

Bossard, James H. S. and Eleanore S. Boll. 1955. "Marital Unhappiness in the Life Cycle of Marriage." *Marriage and Family Living* 17(February):10-14.

Brinkeroff, David B. and Lynn K. White. 1978. "Marital Satisfaction in an Economically Marginal Population." *Journal of Marriage and the Family* 40(May):259-67.

Burgess, Ernest W. and Leonard Cottrell, Jr. 1939. *Predicting Success or Failure in Marriage*. New York: Prentice Hall.

Burr, Wesley R. 1970. "Satisfaction With Various Aspects of Marriage Over the Life Cycle: A Random Middle Class Sample." *Journal of Marriage and the Family* 26(February): 29-37.

Burr, Wesley R., Geoffrey K. Leigh, Randall D. Day, and John Constantine. 1979. "Symbolic Interaction and the Family." Pp. 42-111 in *Contemporary Theories About the Family*, edited by Wesley R. Burr, Reuben Hill, F. Ivan Nye, and Ira R. Reiss. New York: Free Press.

Conger, Rand, Glen H. Elder, Jr., Frederick O. Lorenz, Katherine J. Conger, Ronald L. Simons, Les B. Whitbeck, Shirley Huck, and Janet N. Melby. 1990. "Linking Economic Hardship to Marital Quality and Instability." *Journal of Marriage and the Family* 52 (August):643-56.

Cuber, John and Peggy Harroff. 1968. *Sex and the Significant Americans: A Study of Sexual Behavior Among the Affluent*. New York: Penguin Books.

Figley, Charles R. 1973. "Child Density and the Marital Relationship." *Journal of Marriage and the Family* 35(May): 272-82.

Fowers, Blaine J. and David H. Olson. 1986. "Predicting Marital Success With PREPARE: A Predictive Validity Study." *Journal of Marital and Family Therapy* 12(October):403-13.

Glenn, Norval D. 1991. "The Recent Trend in Marital Success in the United States." *Journal of Marriage and the Family* 53 (May):261-70.

Glenn, Norval D. and Sara McLanahan. 1982. "Children

and Marital Happiness: A Further Specification of the Relationship." *Journal of Marriage and the Family* 44(February): 63-72.

Glenn, Norval D. and **Charles N. Weaver.** 1977. "The Marital Happiness of Remarried Divorced Persons." *Journal of Marriage and the Family* 39(May): 331-37.

———. 1978. "A Multivariate Multi-Survey of Marital Happiness." *Journal of Marriage and the Family* 40(May):269-82.

———. 1988. "The Changing Relationship of Marital Status to Reported Happiness." *Journal of Marriage and the Family* 50 (May):317-24.

Goldman, Noreen. 1993. "The Perils of Single Life in Japan." *Journal of Marriage and the Family* 55(February):191-204.

Gove, Walter. 1972. "The Relationship Between Sex Roles, Marital Status, and Mental Illness." *Social Forces* 51(1): 34-44.

Gove, Walter, Michael Hughes, and **Carolyn B. Style.** 1983. "Does Marriage Have Positive Effects on the Psychological Well-Being of the Individual?" *Journal of Health and Social Behavior* 24(2):122-31.

Hamilton, George. 1929. *A Research in Marriage.* New York: Boni.

Haring-Hidore, Marilyn, William A. Stock, Morris A. Okun, and **Robert A. Witter.** 1985. "Marital Status and Subjective Well-Being: A Research

Synthesis." *Journal of Marriage and the Family* 47(November): 947-53.

Hicks, Mary and **Marilyn Platt.** 1970. "Marital Happiness and Stability: A Review of Research in the Sixties." *Journal of Marriage and the Family* 32(November):553-74.

Hill, R. 1972. *The Strengths of Black Families.* New York: Emerson-Hall.

Houseknecht, Sharon K. 1979. "Childlessness and Marital Adjustment." *Journal of Marriage and the Family* 41(May): 259-65.

Jacobson, Neil S., Holly Waldron, and **Danny Moore.** 1980. "Toward a Behavioral Profile of Marital Distress." *Journal of Consulting and Clinical Psychology* 48(December): 696-703.

Johnson, David R., Lynn K. White, John N. Edwards, and **Alan Booth.** 1986. "Dimensions of Marital Quality: Toward Methodological and Conceptual Redefinition." *Journal of Family Issues* 7(March): 31-49.

Jorgensen, Stephen R. 1979. "Socioeconomic Rewards and Perceived Marital Quality." *Journal of Marriage and the Family* 41(November):825-35.

Levenson, Robert W. and **John M. Gottman.** 1983. "Marital Interaction: Physiological Linkage and Affective Exchange." *Journal of Personality and Social Psychology* 45(September):587-97.

Lewis, Robert A. and **Graham B. Spanier.** 1979. "Theorizing About the Quality and Stability of Marriage." Pp. 268-94 in *Contemporary Theories About the Family,* Vol. 1, edited by Wesley R. Burr, Reuben Hill, F. Ivan Nye, and Ira L. Reiss. New York: Free Press.

Locke, Harvey and **Karl Wallace.** 1959. "Short Marital Adjustment and Predictions Tests: Their Reliability and Validity." *Marriage and Family Living* 21 (August):251-55.

Lupri, Eugen and **James Frideres.** 1981. "The Quality of Marriage and the Passage of Time: Marital Satisfaction Over the Family Life Cycle." *Canadian Journal of Sociology* 6(3): 283-305.

Margolin, Gayla and **Bruce E. Wampold.** 1981. "Sequential Analysis of Conflict and Accord in Distressed and Nondistressed Marital Partners." *Journal of Consulting and Clinical Psychology* 49(August):554-67.

Markides, Kyriakos S. and **Janice Farrell.** 1985. "Marital Status and Depression Among Mexican Americans." *Social Psychiatry* 20(2):86-91.

National Opinion Research Center. 1988. *General Social Surveys, 1972–1988: Cumulative Data Set.* Distributed by the Roper Center for Public Opinion Research, Storrs, CT.

Nye, F. Ivan and **Steven D. McLaughlin.** 1982. "Role Competence and Marital Satisfaction." Pp. 67-79 in *Family Relationships: Rewards and Costs,* edited by F. Ivan Nye. Beverly Hills, CA: Sage.

Olson, David H., Hamilton I. McCubbin, and Associates. 1983. *Families: What Makes Them Work.* Beverly Hills, CA: Sage.

Olson, David H., Candyce S. Russell, and Douglas H. Sprenkle. 1983. "Circumplex Model of Marital and Family Systems: VI. Theoretical Update." *Family Process* 22(1): 69-83.

Orden, Susan R. and Norman M. Bradburn. 1968. "Dimensions of Marital Happiness." *American Journal of Sociology* 73(May):715-31.

Ortega, Suzanne T., Hugh P. Whitt, and J. Allen Williams, Jr. 1988. "Religious Homogamy and Marital Happiness." *Journal of Family Issues* 9(June): 224-39.

Orthner, Dennis K. 1975. "Leisure Activity Patterns and Marital Satisfaction Over the Marital Career." *Journal of Marriage and the Family* 37(February):91-101.

Patterson, Gerald R. 1976. "Some Procedures for Assessing Changes in Marital Interaction Patterns." *Oregon Research Bulletin* 16(7).

Pearlin, Leonard I. and Joyce S. Johnson. 1977. "Marital Status, Life Strains, and Depression." *American Sociological Review* 42(October):704-15.

Pineo, Peter C. 1961. "Disenchantment in the Later Years of Marriage." *Marriage and Family Living* 23(February):3-11.

Piotrokowski, Chaya S., R. N. Rapoport, and R. Rapoport. 1987. "Families and Work." Pp. 251-284 in *Handbook of Marriage and the Family,* edited by Marvin B. Sussman and Suzanne K. Steinmetz. New York: Plenum.

Renne, Karen S. 1970. "Correlates of Dissatisfaction in Marriage." *Journal of Marriage and the Family* 32(February): 54-66.

Robinson, Linda C. and Priscilla W. Blanton. 1993. "Marital Strength in Enduring Marriages." *Family Relations* 42 (January):38-45.

Rollins, Boyd C. and Kenneth L. Cannon. 1974. "Marital Satisfaction Over the Family Life Cycle: A Reevaluation." *Journal of Marriage and the Family* 36 (May):271-72.

Rollins, Boyd C. and Harold Feldman. 1970. "Marital Satisfaction Over the Family Life Cycle." *Journal of Marriage and the Family* 32(February): 20-28.

Rusbult, Carolyn E., Dennis J. Johnson, and Gregory D. Morrow. 1986. "Impact of Couple Patterns of Problem Solving on Distress and Nondistress in Dating Relationships." *Journal of Personality and Social Psychology* 50(4):744-53.

Ryder, Robert G. 1973. "Longitudinal Data Relating Marital Satisfaction and Having a Child." *Journal of Marriage and the Family* 35(November):604-6.

Sharpley, C. F. and D. G. Cross. 1982. "A Psychometric Evalu-

ation of the Spanier Dyadic Adjustment Scale." *Journal of Marriage and the Family* 44 (August):739-41.

Spanier, Graham B. 1976. "Measuring Dyadic Adjustment: New Scales for Assessing the Quality of Marriage and Similar Dyads." *Journal of Marriage and the Family* 38(February): 15-28.

Spanier, Graham B. and Linda Thompson. 1982. "A Confirmatory Analysis of the Dyadic Adjustment Scale." *Journal of Marriage and the Family* 44 (August):731-38.

Terman, Lewis and Paul Buttenwieser. 1935. "Personality Factors in Marital Compatibility." *Journal of Social Psychology* 6(May):143-71.

———. 1938. *Psychological Factors in Marital Happiness.* New York: McGraw-Hill.

Thomas, Veronica G. 1990. "Determinants of Global Happiness and Marital Happiness in Dual-Career Black Couples." *Family Relations* 39(April): 174-78.

Ting-Toomey, Stella. 1983. "An Analysis of Verbal Communication Patterns in High and Low Marital Adjustment Groups." *Human Communication Research* 9(4):306-19.

Vaillant, Caroline O. and George E, Vaillant. 1993. "Is the U-Curve of Marital Satisfaction an Illusion? A 40-Year Study of Marriage." *Journal of Marriage and the Family* 55 (February):230-39.

Veenhoven, Ruut. 1983. "The Growing Impact of Marriage." *Social Indicators Research* 12 (January):49-63.

Verbrugge, Lois M. and J. H. Madans. 1985. "Social Roles and Health Trends of American Women." *Health and Society* 63(4):691-735.

White, Lynn K. and Alan Booth. 1985. "The Transition to Parenthood and Marital Quality." *Journal of Family Issues* 6 (December): 435-49.

Xiaohe, Xu and Martin King Whyte. 1990. "Love Matches and Arranged Marriages: A Chinese Replication." *Journal of Marriage and the Family* 52 (August):709-72.

CHAPTER 9

■■ Parents and Parenthood

T o many people, a family is not a family unless there are children. The pitter-patter of little feet, a child's first words, first steps, and the pride taken in children's accomplishments are all considered part of life's greatest pleasures. Not only are married couples expected to have children but having them is thought to be natural. Many people still think it is unnatural and selfish for people not to want children, although this view has changed in the past few decades.

That most couples will bring a child into the world is born out in the statistics on marriage. A little less than 90% of all married women will eventually have a child (U.S. Bureau of the Census 1992). In fact, for many couples, the decision of whether to have a child never arises. When, and how many, are the most important questions these couples have to answer. For other couples, whether to have children is a continued subject of debate and discussion. Unless there are medical reasons that preclude having children or unless one or both members take irreversible steps to prevent conception, the decision about having a child can be discussed and postponed for many years.

The decision to become a parent and subsequent parenthood fundamentally change the nature of marital relationships. A baby alters time, space, relationships, and sense of self and self-worth. Actually, the changes begin with pregnancy, as couples anticipate the change from being a couple to becoming parents.

Although parenthood is a significant stage in the marital relationship, parents received surprisingly little attention (but most of the blame) from social scientists until the 1970s. Typically, discussions of parenthood focused almost exclusively on the child and child development (Rossi 1968).

This chapter focuses on parents and parenthood. The following chapter looks at children and child development. Our concern here is with the decision to have children, pregnancy, the impact of the first child on family relationships, and the impact of the next child on families. Next we look at mothers and fathers and the considerable debate over parent roles. Is there a maternal instinct? Are mothers biologically different from fathers? What about fathers and fatherhood? We also provide a developmental perspective and examine parenthood, not just when children are young but also parenthood in the later years.

TRANSITION TO PARENTHOOD

The Decision to Have Children

For most of human history, becoming a parent was not a matter of choice. Societies without birth control pills or devices offered no opportunity for deep discourse on whether or not to have a baby. More important, for most of human history, becoming a parent was the major criterion for defining when someone became an adult (Rossi 1983). Those who were childless were social failures and outcasts.

Today, families, and especially women, have choices. In one national survey, 4% of respondents said they did not have children, did not want them, and were glad they did not have any (Gallup and Newport 1990). Childlessness appears to be an increasingly attractive option for families, although it is not entirely clear or predictable how many of the women who claim a preference for childlessness will remain childless for life.

Theoretically, the decision about having children can be made by only one partner, but considerable marital discussion and some conflict surround decisions about having children. For some couples, the choice of whether or not to become parents may hinge on the career plans of the wife; for others, it is the career plans of the husband. Writer Gail Sheehy (1976) analyzed the passages that people make as they move through various stages of their adult lives. One crucial passage is the decision to have children. One couple Sheehy interviewed encountered conflict over the choice between work and child. The couple, Ginny and Rick, discover that Ginny is pregnant. Although Rick is delighted, Ginny is not and tells Rick so:

> I'm not ready to have a baby. You did this. You're forcing me to choose. . . . You made me pregnant to eliminate any possibility of my going to law school. (p. 155)

Although the couple considered an abortion, they chose to have the child and Rick became a lawyer while Ginny is a mother and, according to Sheehy's description, a "clipper of part-time want ads."

For many other couples, the decision is not so full of conflict. Sociologist Ralph LaRossa (1977) was one of the first behavioral scientists to systematically study pregnancy as part of the transition to parenthood. One of the couples he interviewed explained their decision to have the first child:

> It is probably because so many of our friends have adorable babies. . . . That had something to do with it I'm sure. Plus our relationship had something to do with it. When you're 22 or 23 and you're very independent and someone says, "Well don't you want to get married, settle down, and have kids," your first reaction is to tell them what they can do with it—"Go take a flying leap out the next highest window!" But I think after settling down and getting married, it just seemed like the logical thing to do! (p. 35)

Social pressure, the desire to settle down, and the feeling of wanting to be a family are all important pulls that influence choosing to have a child. The pushes include the belief that childless couples are lonely in their old age and that childless couples lead empty lives. Irrespective of the truth (childless couples are often happy and do not see themselves as living empty lives—see Chapter 8), the beliefs are powerful enough to influence the final decision, which the majority of couples make, to have a first child.

Pregnancy　The transition to parenthood begins with pregnancy. Husband and wife experience similar emotions on learning that she is pregnant for the first time. On the one hand, they are proud of this clear sign of fertility, but on the other, they worry about how the baby will change their lives. Expectant mothers find themselves the object of constant attention, both wanted and unwanted. Their husbands, friends, and relatives tend to fuss over them; strangers tend to stare and offer unsolicited advice. Many pregnant women worry that their husbands will find them fat and unattractive. Expectant fathers sometimes find they are the butt of jokes, or worse, ignored. Most parents-to-be report that they have sex less often, even though there is no medical reason not to have sex during pregnancy. Expectant parents also report that they feel closer because the pregnancy gives them a common focus (LaRossa 1986).

BOX 9-1: WHAT THE RESEARCH SHOWS

The Numbers of Parenthood: Birth Rates and Fertility

The "numbers" of parenthood are studied, analyzed, and debated by planners, policymakers, and the public. Colleges and universities need to know about births so they can plan for the future—faculty hiring and firing and whether or not to build more dormitories or convert dorm space into study or classroom space. Gerber needs to know about births so it can plan for the economic future of its baby food company. The federal government's entire social security system depends on knowing how many births there are now so it can plan for how many workers there will be to support those who have retired.

There are two key terms one must know when assessing the numbers of parenthood. The first is the **birth rate,** which is the given number of births per 1,000 people in the population in a given year. This is also known as the **crude birth rate.** One can also calculate the **refined birth rate** that measures the number of births per year per 1,000 women. The second important term is the **fertility rate,** defined as the number of live births per 1,000 women of childbearing age (15 to 44) in a population in a given year. The birth rate tells you about the total number of children born, and the fertility rate speaks to the average size of families in the society.

In 1850, there were more than 40 children born for every 1,000 people in the population. This was a period of time when the infant and

In late pregnancy, the division of labor in the household—who does the laundry, dishes, shopping, and so on—may be more equal than at any other time in the marriage, as the husband pitches in (Goldberg, Michaels, and Lamb 1985). But, although the balance of attention may shift to the wife, the balance of power tends to shift to the husband because some couples believe that a pregnant woman is in a "delicate condition" and/or because the wife might be giving up her job or going on maternity leave and depending more on her husband financially.

One of the major social issues faced today is teenage parenting. The United States has the highest rate of births to teenage mothers of any industrialized Western nation (see Table 9-1).

Teenage Pregnancy and Parenthood

The number of pregnancies to teenage women (aged 15 to 19) increased during the 1970s and leveled off in the 1980s. There were 839,000 teenage pregnancies in 1970, and by 1980, this figure had risen by more than a million to 1,151,800. The number stabilized at about 1 million thereafter (Henshaw and Van Vort 1989; Moore et al. 1987).

Two thirds of the pregnant teenagers are between 18 and 19 years of age, and of this group, 40% are married. The majority of the younger pregnant

child mortality rates were high and many children failed to survive until adulthood (see Chapter 4).

Today, there are fewer than 17 (16.4 in 1991) children born for every 1,000 people. Nearly all of the children born today can expect to survive until adulthood. The major exception in this trend toward a declining birth rate was the rather dramatic rise in the birth rate that followed World War II and lasted until 1960. This "bulge" in the birth rate (see Figure 9-1) has been labeled the "baby boom" and produced the special generation of baby boomers who were crowded into schools, competed for openings in college and universities, competed for entry-level jobs, competed for promotions in industry, and even have their own version of the board game Trivial Pursuit.®

Since 1960, the birth rate has continued to fall, with a rather dramatic fall in the 1970s.

There was a slight upward trend beginning in the late 1970s and early 1980s, which has continued to the present. Demographers attribute some of this to a rather subdued "baby boomlet"—the baby boomers having their own children.

Fertility rates have also fluctuated. During World War II, the average woman of child-bearing age had 2.5 children. Due to the baby boom, this figure edged up to over 3.3 children per woman in the first half of the 1950s and then peaked at 3.6 children in the decade's last half. Fifteen years later, the fertility rate had dropped to the point where the average woman had 1.7 children (see Figure 9-2).

The trend has reversed in the past 10 years, with fertility increasing to 2.0 children per woman of childbearing age in 1989. Again, this apparent baby boomlet may be the result of baby-boom women having children.

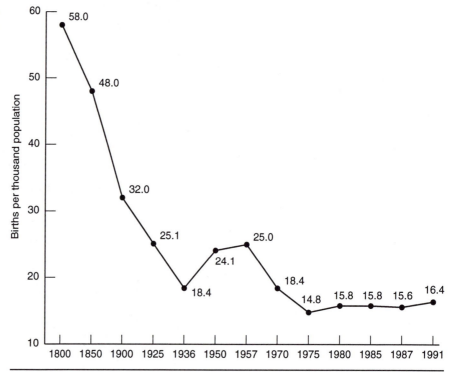

Figure 9-1 Birth Rate, 1800–1991

SOURCE: U.S. Center for Health Statistics (1992) and U.S. Bureau of the Census (1993).

teenagers (under age 18) are not married. The most important aspect of the issue of teen pregnancy is the latter group. The rate of out-of-wedlock birth to teenagers has risen consistently since 1960.

As Table 9-2 shows, the rate of pregnancy was higher among nonwhites than among whites.

All pregnancies do not culminate in the birth of a child. The number of births to teenagers rose during the 1960s and has declined since the 1970s. There were 650,000 births to teenagers in 1970 and 322,000 births in 1988 (National Center for Health Statistics 1990).

There are significant differences in the birth rates by age and by race. First, birth rates are higher for 18- and 19-year-old women compared to those aged 15 to 17. Again, it is important to point out that 40% of the pregnant 18- and 19-year-olds are married. However, the birth rates for the older teens have fallen more in recent decades, whereas the rates for the 15- to 17-year-olds have risen. Second, the birth rate for black teenagers is higher than the rate for white teenagers—although the birth rate has declined more among blacks than among whites.

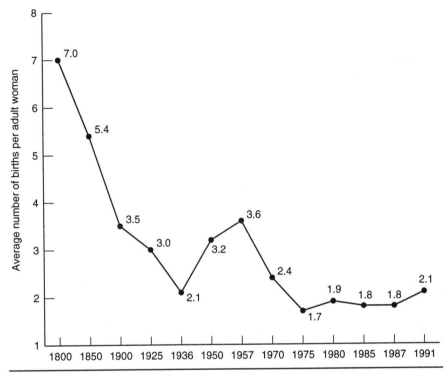

Figure 9-2 Fertility Rate, 1800–1991

SOURCE: U.S. Center for Health Statistics (1992) and U.S. Bureau of the Census (1993).

Given that the actual rate and numbers of pregnancies and births for teenage women has stabilized or declined, why is there so much concern about teenage pregnancy? The answer is that the rate of out-of-wedlock births has increased and that those teenagers who are having children out of wedlock tend to be unskilled, untrained, have low educational levels, and have minimal abilities to support themselves and their children (Blackwell 1991; Voydanoff and Donnelly 1990). Teenage mothers often live with their parents and are supported by their parents and relatives.

The First Child

The transition to parenthood is perhaps the most important and unique experience a couple will have. Some of the earliest research on the transition to parenthood characterized the change as one of "crisis." E. E. LeMasters (1957) interviewed 46 couples and discovered that more than 8 in 10 experienced severe or extensive crisis in adjusting to the birth of their first child.

Table 9-1 Birth Rates to Teens, Aged 15-19, for Selected Countries, 1970–1989

Country	1970	1980	1985	1989
United States	68.3	53.0	51.3	58.1
Denmark	32.4	16.8	9.1	9.2
France	27.0	17.8	11.6	9.2
West Germany	35.8	15.2	8.6	11.1
Japan	5.0	7.6	9.0	9.8
The Netherlands	17.0	6.8	5.0	5.9
United Kingdom	49.1	30.5	39.6	31.7

SOURCE: Eurostat, *Demographic Statistics, 1991;* Japan Ministry of Health and Welfare; and U.S. National Center for Health Statistics, *Final Natality Statistics, 1989.*
NOTE: Rates are per 1,000 teenagers, aged 15-l9.

In the later stage of pregnancy, the division of labor for household tasks, such as laundry, cooking, and child care, may become more equal—although pregnant wives still carry out the majority of the family domestic work.

Measure	Total	White	Nonwhite
Pregnancies, 1985			
< 15	1.7	0.9	5.1
15-19	11.0	9.3	18.6
15-17	7.1	5.7	13.4
18-19	16.6	14.5	26.1
Births, 1986			
< 15	0.1	0.1	0.5
15-19	5.1	4.2	9.8
15-17	3.1	2.3	7.0
18-19	8.1	7.0	14.1
Abortions, 1985			
< 15	0.9	0.5	2.7
15-19	4.4	3.8	7.1
15-17	3.1	2.6	5.3
18-19	6.3	5.5	9.7
Abortion ratio, 1985			
< 15	45.6	46.0	45.5
15-19	42.1	42.3	41.7
15-17	43.2	44.5	40.6
18-19	41.0	40.6	42.1

Table 9-2 Adolescent Pregnancies, Births, and Abortions (in percentages) and the Abortion Ratio, by Age and Race

SOURCE: Reproduced with the permission of The Alan Guttmacher Institute from Stanley K. Henshaw and Jennifer Van Vort, "Teenage Abortion, Birth and Pregnancy Statistics: An Update," *Family Planning Perspectives,* Vol. 21, No. 2, March/April 1989. And adapted with permission from Child Trends from Kristin A. Moore, *Facts at a Glance,* November 1988, p. 1.

For mothers, the crisis included chronic tiredness, extensive confinement in the home, curtailment of social contacts, and giving up the rewards of work outside the home. Fathers commented on their wife's reduced sexual responsiveness, the costs of having a child, the costs of the wife giving up her work, and general unhappiness with being a parent (LeMasters 1957).

The parents who experienced crisis were not those who had unplanned children or who did not want the child. Even when the marriage was happy and the child gleefully anticipated, the crisis occurred. The crisis was most severe for the mothers who held professional positions prior to the birth of the first child (LeMasters 1957). Although LeMasters' observation was made almost 40 years ago, the conclusion still appears to be valid.

Subsequent research uncovered other problems associated with the birth of the first child (Dyer 1963; Hobbs 1965, 1968; Hobbs and Cole 1976; Hobbs and Wimbush 1977; McLanahan and Adams 1989; Russell 1974; Voydanoff 1989). One of the conclusions of the series of studies on parenthood as crisis was that middle-class couples actually had more difficulties than did working-class couples. The studies concluded that middle-class families experience more difficult transitions because they have higher standards, are more career-oriented than family-oriented, have less experience caring for children, and the husband-wife bond may be stronger (Jacoby 1969). Also, middle-class couples generally wait a longer period of time between marriage and the birth of the first child than do working-class couples. Lillian Rubin (1976) found that a substantial majority of the working-class couples she interviewed had their first children within nine months of getting married. When children are born this soon after a marriage, there is almost no honeymoon period in the marriage and little time for the newlyweds to develop their relationship before becoming parents. On the other hand, the lack of a honeymoon period may be compensated in part by the husband and wife developing a close bond, which with the birth of the first child, perhaps lessens some of the crisis associated in response to impending parenthood.

The Uniqueness of the Transition to Parenthood

The transformation from couple to parents is perhaps the most unique transition in a marriage, if not human development. Sociologist Alice Rossi (1968) suggests that there are at least four unique aspects of becoming a parent:

1. *Cultural Pressure to Assume the Role.* As we noted at the beginning of this chapter, there is considerable pressure on couples to assume the parental role. Throughout history, the sign of adult status for a woman has been to be a mother. Today, even though couples have considerable control over reproduction, what with the availability of sex education information, contraceptive devices, and legal abortion, the pressure is still great. Abortion, while legal, is still a difficult decision, and a substantial majority of Americans reject abortion as a means of birth control (National Opinion Research Center 1991). Frequently, couples (and single mothers) will choose to have a child they neither want nor are ready for rather than suffer the social stigma of an abortion or violate moral principles.

There has been a century-long decline in the birth rate (the number of children born per 1,000 people in the population—see Figure 9-1) and a 20-year increase in the number of abortions (see Table 9-3); however, the decline in the number of babies born *does not* mean that parenthood is going out of fashion or that there is less pressure to have children. Rather, women still are pressured to have children, but they are frequently postponing when they have them and are choosing to have fewer children than their mothers had (Cherlin 1990, 1992; Goldscheider and Waite 1991). The concern and debate about women's participation in the workforce has not led to fewer women having children but, rather, to more women returning to (or staying at) work rather than conceiving a third or fourth child (Rossi 1968).

Table 9-3 Number and Rate of Abortions Among Women 15 to 44 Years Old at Time of Abortion, 1972–1988

	All Races				White				Black and Other			
		Abortions				Abortions				Abortions		
Year	Women 15-44 (1,000)	Number (1,000)	Rate per 1,000 Women	Ratio per 1,000 Live Births	Women 15-44 (1,000)	Number (1,000)	Rate per 1,000 Women	Ratio per 1,000 Live Births	Women 15-44 (1,000)	Number (1,000)	Rate per 1,000 Women	Ratio per 1,000 Live Births
1972	44,588	586.8	13.2	184	38,532	455.3	11.8	175	6,056	131.5	21.7	223
1975	47,606	1,034.2	21.7	331	40,857	701.2	17.2	276	6,749	333.0	49.3	565
1976	48,721	1,179.3	24.2	361	41,721	784.9	18.8	296	7,000	394.4	56.3	638
1977	49,814	1,316.7	26.4	400	42,567	888.8	20.9	333	7,247	427.9	59.0	679
1978	50,920	1,409.6	27.7	413	43,427	969.4	22.3	356	7,493	440.2	58.7	665
1979	52,016	1,497.7	28.8	420	44,266	1,062.4	24.0	373	7,750	435.3	56.2	625
1980	53,048	1,553.9	29.3	428	44,942	1,093.6	24.3	376	8,106	460.3	56.5	642
1981	53,901	1,577.3	29.3	430	45,494	1,107.8	24.3	377	8,407	469.6	55.9	645
1982	54,679	1,573.9	28.8	428	46,049	1,095.2	23.8	373	8,630	478.7	55.5	646
1983	55,340	1,575.0	28.5	436	46,506	1084.4	23.3	376	8,834	490.6	55.5	670
1984	56,061	1,577.2	28.1	423	47,023	1,086.6	23.1	366	9,038	490.6	54.3	646
1985	56,754	1,588.6	28.0	422	47,512	1,075.6	22.6	360	9,242	512.9	55.5	659
1986	57,483	1,574.0	27.4	416	48,010	1,044.7	21.8	350	9,473	529.3	55.9	661
1987	57,964	1,559.1	27.1	405	48,288	1,017.3	21.1	338	9,676	541.8	56.0	648
1988	58,192	1,590.8	27.3	401	48,325	1,025.7	21.2	333	9,867	565.1	57.3	738

SOURCE: U.S. Bureau of the Census (1992, p. 74, Table 100).

2. *The Parental Role.* Couples voluntarily choose to become engaged, get married, and even get divorced. Parenthood may be, and often is, the unintended consequence of a sexual act that was intended for recreation and pleasure, not for procreation (Rossi 1968). Birth control devices are not always 100% effective, nor are they always used (or used properly) by couples. Although legal, abortion is, as we stated just before, not socially accepted as a birth-control technique. The number of unwanted pregnancies may still far outnumber the number of unwanted marriages. The existence and effective use of contraceptives in the past few decades has had another impact on the inception of parenthood. In the past, without effective contraception and when abortion was illegal, parenthood typically commenced at about the same time as marriage. Thus, as noted earlier, marriage and parenthood was the major (and simultaneous) transition of a couple's life. First-time parents today, especially the middle and upper class, tend to be older and more established occupationally and socially than were their parents and grandparents.

3. *Irrevocability.* If your engagement is unhappy and you fight with your fiancée, you can break off the relationship. If your marriage does not work out, you can separate or seek a divorce as a solution to conflict and unhappiness. If you dislike your job, you can quit. If you hate your house or neighborhood, you can move. But once your child is born, there is little you can do but continue in the role of parent. Conflict, unhappiness, lack of commitment or preparation, need to grow, or need for a time-out are unacceptable grounds for seeking to get out of the parental role. For example, parents cannot leave young children home alone while they go off for a Caribbean vacation. Leaving young children alone for even a few hours is considered by many to be child maltreatment (National Committee For Prevention of Child Abuse 1993).

One can have former fiancées and ex-spouses, but it is nearly impossible to become an ex-parent. There are some instances when parents do surrender legal custody of their children, and there have been a few cases, most notably the case of Gregory K. in Florida in 1992, when children have actually sued abusive or neglectful parents for "divorce" (actually, these suits seek to terminate the biological parents' legal rights to custody, visitation, and contact).

4. *Preparation for Parenthood.* Dating and engagement provide couples with a training ground for marriage. Many couples also choose to live together in trial marriages before they "take the plunge" into matrimony. Such training does not occur with the transition to parenthood. In fact, Rossi (1968) notes the almost complete absence of training for the parental role. Schools teach, and sometimes require, sexual education and driver's education. Many high schools and some colleges offer programs of study in home economics and home management. Science, math, English, speech, computers, and a foreign language are typically part of the core curriculum you will take in your college studies. But, within 10 years, the majority of those reading this chapter will have a child, without benefit of a single formal course to prepare for that occasion, challenge, and difficulty. How would you like to be treated by a dentist who had the same level of preparation for her job that you will have when your first child is born? One could argue that baby-sitting or growing up in a large family and caring for one's younger siblings is adequate preparation. Of course, such responsibilities are typically of limited time duration (baby-sitters are responsible for an hour, two hours, a few days, or even a week or two at most). Moreover, such responsibilities cover only a fraction of the total development of a child. You are parents of children 24 hours a day from birth until either you or your child dies.

Although couples have nine months to get ready for the parent role, pregnancy provides only a limited period of learning and no on-the-job training. Since 1968 when Alice Rossi wrote her article about the transition to parenthood, there has been a tremendous increase in the availability of "preparation for childbirth classes," also known as natural childbirth or

Lamaze classes. Such courses—which run from 4 to 10 weeks—teach parents about the process of childbearing. Breathing techniques, lectures on medications, and a tour of the delivery room are all components of a course that demystifies childbirth and provides parents-to-be with an idea of what to anticipate. Such courses rarely include anything about child rearing after the baby goes home. When the baby arrives, it arrives *abruptly*. Becoming a parent is not a gradual process (just as there is no such thing as being a little bit pregnant). Upon release from the hospital, parents go on duty 24 hours a day. Few, if any, other social roles involve such a total and abrupt change of responsibilities and demands.

The goal of parenthood is to raise children to become the kind of competent adults valued by the society in which we live (Rossi 1968). How is this to be accomplished? A major stress of the transition to parenthood is that, while there is indeed a culturally recognized goal of parenthood, few or no guidelines exist for how this goal is to be reached. There are numerous "how to parent" books available. Pediatricians also stand ready to answer new parents' questions about the medical needs and physical development of children. Although it may be relatively easy to adequately feed, clothe, and medicate a child, the goal of raising that child to be a competent adult remains elusive, and there are few experts who can prove that the advice they give will help a parent reach the desired outcome. Thus it is within this maze of ambiguity that parents embark on the long, never-ending role of parenthood with their firstborn.

Guidelines for Successful Parenting

Not only is there social pressure to have a child, but there is considerable pressure to have more than one. For most of this century, the average family has had more than two children. Today, the average is still about two. One of our general cultural beliefs is that an only child is a deprived child. Parents who refuse to provide a brother or sister for their firstborn are thought to be selfish or neurotic. Of course, there is no proof for either of these statements. Research indicates that there are significant advantages to being an only child (see Chapter 10; also see Falbo 1976; Rosenberg 1965; Zajonc and Markus 1975).

The Second Child

The pressure to have a second child begins almost as soon as the firstborn returns home from the hospital and escalates until the child begins to take his or her first steps. Parents are told that the second will be easier, that raising two is as easy as raising one.

The truth of the claims used to motivate parents to have second children is that there are indeed rewards and advantages but also significant drawbacks and costs. A survey of parents having their second child revealed the two sides of this experience (Knox and Wilson 1978).

Half of the women polled said they had the second child because they enjoyed the first, and one fourth because they wanted the first child to have company. Most of those interviewed said that having two children involved more work, more time, and especially more noise than one child had. "Everything I do is interrupted by one or the other," said one mother.

Very few women actually regretted the decision to have a second child (less than 7%). While one in ten (10.8%) noted that the second child improved their marriage, the majority of the women interviewed (71.9%) said the marriage was unchanged, and 17 percent said the marriage got worse instead of better.

In general, the parents of second children heartily recommended having a second child. Of interest was that most parents of second children never even considered stopping after one child. Advice would not have influenced them— they had planned the second child even before they had given birth to the first!

BOX 9-2: THE GLOBAL VIEW

Childbearing in China

The population of China reached 1.1 billion people in 1989. Of this number, there are 318.9 million women of childbearing age (15 to 49). With such a large childbearing population (more than 25% greater than the entire population of the United States), China could conceivably be a "parenting and childbearing machine" that could increase its population for the foreseeable future. The number of women of childbearing age is expected to grow to nearly 340 million by the year 2000 (Kalish 1993). However, when the number peaks in 2000, the rate of population growth will stabilize, assuming that the fertility rate remains the same.

Although the birth rate was already declining in China in the late 1970s, China adopted a "one child" policy in 1979. The one-child ideal proved to be controversial and provoked strong resistance. There is a saying in China that "one

[child] is not wanting, two are good, three are excessive" (Kalish 1993, p. 5).

Today, Chinese women average about 2 children each, lower than in the past. Chinese women had an average of 5.8 children in 1970, which declined to 2.2 by 1980. Yet fertility is still lower than the one-child policy called for, largely because of an increase in the age at first marriage and not directly because of the one-child policy.

Given the decline in fertility, the number of young people in China has begun to decline— there were 112 million children under 5 years of age in China in 1990, and this number is expected to fall below 90 million by 2010, although there will be an increase to 95 million by 2025 (Kalish 1993). This increase is not due to an increase in fertility but is the result of the increases in the number of women of childbearing age.

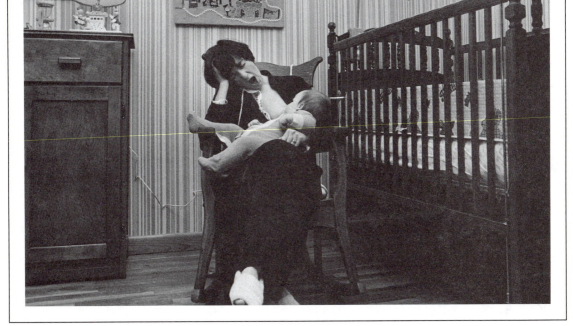

Parents who have a second child say that having two children involves more work and more fatigue.

MOTHERS AND FATHERS

Up to this point we have discussed parents and parenthood without differentiating between mothers and fathers. Most scholarly and public attention has examined mothers. Everyone concedes that mothers are biologically and socially necessary for children to be born and raised. Fathers, however, have either been ignored completely or shunted off to the side after they fulfill their necessary biological function. As one famous anthropologist has said, fathers are a biological necessity but a social accident (Parke 1981).

Recently, both mothers and fathers have begun to receive more attention. This is probably a result of the developing women's movement and the questioning of the supposed biological basis of the roles of mothers and fathers.

Traditionally, we have institutionalized motherhood in our society (Bernard 1974). The sole responsibility for child care was vested in the mother. Because mothers were held responsible for the care and development of children and because we live in an industrial society that separates homes from places of work (see Chapter 11; Oakley 1974) mothers were cut off from help and support. The 24-hour-a-day mother has been isolated in her household, providing round-the-clock care and nurturance. Motherhood continues to be an often exclusive activity.

In the 1970s, Jesse Bernard (1974) noted that young mothers began to question their roles. Mothers explained that while they found joy in their children they did not particularly like motherhood. As women began to question their institutionalized motherhood role and look for personal gratification outside the home, the institutionalized fatherhood role of "good provider" and disciplinarian was also questioned. Fatherhood was no longer seen as just a biological necessity and social accident but as a role that involved child rearing and receiving some of the rewards (and frustrations) of child care.

Rethinking the responsibilities of mothers and fathers begins with questioning the biological basis of parenthood. Is there a "maternal instinct"? Is there something in biology that makes mothers uniquely and specially qualified to care for children? Then we need to examine the social qualities of the mother's and father's status and roles—the institutionalized statuses and roles as well as the different experience of being a mother and being a father.

Biology, Gender, and Parenthood

For most of human existence, work and child rearing were centered in the home (see Chapters 4, 5, and 11). Both parents, as well as other family members, played significant roles in the raising of and caring for children. Industrialization separated work from the home. As fathers left the home to work, they left behind mothers to care for the children. This separation of function led to the ideology that women were the "best" or natural parents and caretakers. An ideology grew up that justified women being delegated the exclusive parenthood status. Having babies was seen as something women naturally do. Women were thought to instinctively want, need, and enjoy having children (Rollin 1971). The baby boom, which followed World War II, further enhanced the notion that women were instinctively driven to bear and care for children.

There are other supports for the ideology that women are instinctively motivated to be mothers. Biological explanations of sex differences date back to at least Plato, who claimed that men's actions are governed by their brain and women's by their womb. "The womb is an animal which longs to generate children," Plato argued. "When it remains barren too long after puberty, it is distressed and sorely disturbed" (in Tavris and Offir 1984, p. 12).

"Biology is destiny," declared psychologist Sigmund Freud (1865–1939). Freudian psychology and psychoanalysis are largely based on Freud's notion that little girls are psychologically wounded by the discovery that boys have something they lack (a penis), and this scar never quite heals. As a consequence, little girls feel inferior. Rather than emulate their mothers, little girls work at being adored by men. Freud ([1953] 1974) claims that only by giving birth to a child do women recover some of their lost self-esteem.

Some interpretations of Freudian psychology place a considerable emphasis on the mother-child relationship. A child who has a poor relationship with his or her mother is believed to suffer and fail to develop normally.

The women's movement that began in the 19th century and reemerged in the early 1960s challenged the proposition that "biology is destiny" and the terms "maternal instinct" and "maternal deprivation." Feminist author Betty Friedan (1963) claimed that the prosperity of the late 1940s and 1950s and the isolation of mothers in the home turned motherhood into a cult. Psychologist Karen Horney (1967) challenged the principles of Freudian psychology and said that women's envy often is not based on anatomical difference but on a realistic assessment of men's superior social power and status. Journalist Betty Rollin wrote a stinging critique of the "motherhood myth" for *Look* magazine in 1971. She cited numerous social scientists and psychiatrists who debunked the biological basis of motherhood. One psychiatrist noted that women don't need to be mothers any more than they need spaghetti (Rollin 1971). Family sociologist William Goode said that "there are no instincts. There are reflexes, like eye blinking, and drives like sex. There is no innate drive for children" (Rollin 1971, p. 15).

Feminist theorists have also challenged notions about maternal instinct and the fantasy of the perfect mother (Chodorow and Contratto 1992). Feminist theorists argued in the 1970s and 1980s that women's lives should not be totally determined and constrained by child care and childbearing. Nor should those women who choose to have children be held to the standard of the "perfect mother" and blamed for everything that goes wrong in their children. A feminist perspective on mothers and parenting recognizes the influence of mothers on their children but also incorporates the significant pressures on mothers and children from a male-dominated culture (Chodorow and Contratto 1992).

Research studies supporting the biological perspective were challenged on methodological as well as theoretical grounds. Social scientists argued that advocates of the biological point of view have transformed a cultural phenomenon into a biological one (Wortis 1977). Cross-cultural evidence was cited to demonstrate that parental roles vary by culture. Fathers play important parental roles, but so do other members of kin groups (Mead 1954).

The biological perspective declined in popularity—replaced with a more cultural explanation of parenthood that emphasized learned behavior and power differences in society and in the home. But perspectives and theories are always being reexamined and challenged. A newer challenge has come from those who feel that parenthood and motherhood is neither completely governed by biology nor by culture. Sociologist Alice Rossi (1978) has proposed a *biosocial perspective* on parenting (see also Chapter 3).

Rossi proposes that the older view on parenthood (that biology is destiny) and the newer view (behavior is entirely learned) distort and neglect the central biological fact that the core function of any family system is human continuity through reproduction and child rearing. Rossi argues that some of our fundamental human characteristics are indeed rooted in our biological heritage. Wheres many students of parenting use cross-cultural studies to inform their ideas and theories, Rossi explains our contemporary patterns by examining the historical record as well. History is not merely an examination of family life back to the 19th or even 18th century. Rossi, citing anthropologist S. L. Washburn, notes that we have spent 90% of human existence as hunters and gatherers. Men and women in industrial society are still genetically equipped with the ancient mammalian primate heritage that evolved as adaptations to the environments that hunters and gatherers encountered—not the deskbound sedentary environment we live in today.

Rossi goes on to note the genetic predispositions in maternal behavior (see also Chapter 3). Without apparently thinking about it, mothers in all cultures exaggerate their facial expressions and speech with babies. The sound of an infant crying stimulates the secretion of oxytocin in the mother's body, making her nipples erect for nursing. Rossi does not mean to suggest that men cannot care for infants. She does, however, point out that what women do seems to come naturally, whereas the same tasks require some learning by men. Rossi concludes by noting that a biosocial perspective does not imply a theory of genetic determination of what men can do compared to what women can do. Nor does it suggest that the outcome for children will be better if they are cared for by one sex as opposed to another. But a biosocial perspective does hold that there are real differences between men and women in terms of the ease with which the sexes can learn certain things. There is a difference, Rossi (1984) concludes, between men and women and mothers and fathers.

Mothers   Irrespective of the debate over the biological basis of motherhood and the historical legacy of our genetic heritage, the behavior expected of mothers—or the motherhood role—has undergone significant changes in the past 50 years. Simply put, the role of motherhood has expanded to one characterized by overcommitment.

Motherhood has always been centered in the home. When the Industrial Revolution removed men and their work from the home, women were left to care for the children. Transportation was limited, so mothers were forced to spend all of their time at home as full-time caretakers of their children. Later, industrialization produced many so-called labor-saving devices that were supposed to lighten the burden of homeworking—washing machines, dryers, vacuum cleaners, dishwashers, trash compactors, and microwave ovens were all designed to create free time for women at home. Of course, as one woman said, "That machine does not take the diapers off the baby and rinse them out. Nor does it put the diapers away or put them back on the baby" (LeMasters 1974, p. 115). Better roads and means of transportation freed women from the home but entrapped them in the role of full-time chauffeur for their children. In the end, the labor-saving devices saved little labor because cultural standards were raised higher because of the many resources women could draw on to be superior housekeepers.

Educational opportunities for women and better (although not equal) occupational opportunities for women also are thought to have liberated women from the home and child care. Here too, though, these opportunities only expand the mother role, raise the expectations for women, and serve to make mothers even more overcommitted.

One of the major social changes that has occurred in the past 20 years is the rapid increase in the number of mothers who work. In 1940, the Census Bureau did not even calculate the percentage of mothers with preschool children who worked. Today, more than half of mothers of preschoolers work outside the home, and the majority of all mothers work (see Chapter 11).

When women work outside the home, the expectations on them at home regarding housework and child care *do not decrease*. Estimates are that housework today consumes between 40 and 70 hours a week—even with all of the modern conveniences listed above (see Chapter 11; Hochschild and Machung 1989). All the available evidence indicates that working wives continue to bear the traditional responsibility for domestic chores. Husbands of working wives do contribute more to housework and child care, but both remain largely women's work. Some working wives adapt to the role overload of work, home, and children by lowering their standards—perhaps reducing housework to less than 30 hours a week. But the average working women today still works outside the home for paid wages and then comes home to unpaid work, or what Arlie Hochschild and Anne Machung (1989) call the "second shift."

In summary, today's mother faces demands from five different and expanding roles (LeMasters and DeFrain 1989):

1. The role of wife

2. The role of mother

3. Expansion of the home management role

4. Expansion of the community role

5. Expansion of the breadwinner role

Fathers

Fathers have, until recently, been the "missing persons" of parenting. Even those fathers who may have been interested in parenting their children found little sympathy and precious little information to draw on. A review of publications over the past 25 years finds that fathers are more or less absent from the titles and discussion of books and magazines for parents. T. Berry Brazelton's (1969) best-selling guide to parenting is titled *Infants and Mothers*. *Parents* magazine rarely contains an article that pertains to fathers, and nearly all the advertisements in the magazine are aimed at female readers. Social scientists have been no better to fathers. Many studies and articles on parenthood either ignore fathers altogether or pay them little more than lip service. The classic book, *Patterns of Child Rearing* (Sears, Maccoby, and Levin 1957), was based on interviews with 379 mothers but no fathers. William Goode (1956), quoted earlier in this chapter as saying there are no instincts and thus no inherent ability of women to parent, based a study of divorce on interviews with 425 mothers. No divorced fathers were interviewed. A noted handbook on child socialization ran more than 1,000 pages and contained only five specific references to fathers (LeMasters and DeFrain 1989).

Only recently, in the late 1980s and early 1990s, has there been a surge of interest in fathers and fathering. Beginning with Bill Cosby's best-selling *Fatherhood* (1986), there has been a growth in books that focus on fathers, including *The Father's Book, The Nurturant Father,* and *The Wonderful Father.* Social scientists as well (see Griswold 1993; Lamb 1987a, 1987b; LaRossa 1988; LaRossa and Reitzes 1993) have focused their attention on fathers.

The neglect of the father in both popular and scientific literature is not due to oversight. Two assumptions and the legacy of the Freudian theory of parenthood and child development are the basis of the neglect of fathers. The first assumption is that mothers are able to report on the thoughts and beliefs of fathers. Thus, if more mothers can be interviewed more easily and provide accurate insight into the feelings and behaviors of fathers, it is not necessary to interview fathers. The second assumption is that fathers are not important in the child-rearing process (LeMasters and DeFrain 1989). Freudian psychology was influential in generating the assumption that fathers are not important in child rearing. As we noted earlier, Freud believed that mothers are the crucial agents in infant development, although fathers are important in later stages of child development (Parke 1981).

British ethologist John Bowlby (1951) was also influential in keeping fathers behind the scenes in the assessment of the development of children. Bowlby examined infants who were housed in institutions and orphanages in England during the 1940s. The infants generally performed below average standards and failed to develop adequate social and emotional behaviors. Bowlby laid the blame for these deficits on "maternal deprivation." Again, mothers were seen as playing the central role in child development (and, of course, were then candidates for most of the blame for the developmental problems of their children). Bowlby believed that the adequate development of children was dependent on what he called an *attachment bond*. An attachment bond is the process by which infants come to prefer specific adults over others. For Bowlby, the preferred adult is the mother. Bowlby applied a bio-social perspective to this process and argued that attachment is an instinctual response required for the protection and survival of the species. Because the mother is typically the first adult an infant sees, the attachment bond is made with the mother. The bond, then, is biologically programmed (Bowlby 1951; Parke 1981).

An emerging body of literature has challenged traditional assumptions about the biological role of fathers and the impact of fathers on infant development and the notion of a maternal attachment bond (Eyer 1993). Recent examinations of animal behaviors find that fathers do play a role in infant development (Parke 1981). Males in certain nonhuman primate groups, such as marmosets and tamarins (monkeys that live in Central and South America), are intensively involved in infant care. They carry the infants and even chew the food for very young infants (Parke 1981). Males of other species of monkeys carry, groom, and protect their young. Psychologist Michael Lamb has reviewed the scattered literature on fatherhood and has conducted his own research. He finds that fathers are extremely salient individuals in the lives of their children, particularly their sons. Fathers may play an important role in the adoption of cultural rules and sex-typed behavior (Lamb and Lamb 1976).

Today, more and more fathers are making and seeking time to be involved in the raising of their children. Most industrial societies allow maternity leaves for mothers after the baby is delivered. Today, the idea of a parental leave, which allows fathers leave as well as mothers, is being recognized and accepted. Sweden now allows men a paid leave of absence from their work after their infant is born. The Parental Leave Act, enacted in the United States in 1993, allows both fathers and mothers unpaid leave for child care as well as caring for other family members.

Flexible work hours, or flextime (see Chapter 11) is another technique that allows both parents to gain more time with their children. The results of

Fathers have become more involved in child rearing and child care in the past two decades.

flextime seem to be mixed. Research in the United States tends to find that more time with children is not a product of flexible work schedules. However, households that have flextime work schedules report less conflict between work and home responsibilities (Voydanoff 1987).

There are other innovations that allow fathers greater participation in raising their children. Although rare, and probably confined to a few work settings, some husbands and wives share their jobs. A few colleges and universities have experimented with allowing a couple to share a single faculty position.

The increase in numbers of working wives has also been influential in moving fathers closer to center stage at home and with their children. We noted earlier that when mothers work they still are responsible for the majority of housework and child care. Fathers do, however, increase their effort at home when their wives work. Thus, by taking more responsibility, fathers can directly and indirectly enhance the development of their children.

In some households, fathers go so far as to actually reverse roles with their wives. Although such role reversals are rare, and are sometimes of rather short duration, they can inform us about the potential that males have for fatherhood and parenting. Studies of fathers who take equal or full-time responsibility for child rearing find that children rarely suffer—giving lie to the theory of *maternal* deprivation (Parke 1981). There are some advantages. Children whose fathers are the primary caretakers show a greater belief in their own ability (Radin 1978). Boys tend to profit more from their fathers in combatting sexist influences of the larger society (Radin 1978).

There is, however, a darker side of the modern father. Frank Furstenberg, Jr. (1988) points out that while television, magazines, and movies herald the coming of the modern father—the nurturant, caring, and emotionally attuned parent personified by Bill Cosby on *The Cosby Show*—a growing portion of men fathering children are denying paternity and shirking their financial obligations to their children. There has been, in Furstenberg's terms, the simultaneous appearance of both the good and the bad father, and this he attributes to the declining division of labor in families. Ironically, as women took on more responsibilities outside the home and shared responsibilities in the home, some men took on more family responsibilities while other men took the

---

BOX 9-3: WHAT THE RESEARCH SHOWS

Homosexual Parents/Homosexual Children

Approximately one in five gay men and one in three lesbian women have been married and have children (Bozett, 1987). Some lesbians have children with male partners; others have children through artificial insemination or adoption.

There is tremendous ambivalence in the society about homosexual parents. In September 1993, a judge in Virginia ruled that a mother's lesbian relationship with her lover makes her (the mother) an unfit parent and granted custody of the woman's 2-year-old son to the boy's grandmother (*U.S.A. Today* September 8, 1993). A week later, a judge in Massachusetts allowed the lesbian partner of a lesbian mother to legally adopt the child the two women had raised together (*The Providence Journal-Bulletin* September 15, 1953).

Inside the family, one of the major parenting issues for gay and lesbian parents is whether or not to reveal their sexual preference to their children. Many gay and lesbian parents refrain from directly discussing their sexual preferences with their children because of their concern about homophobia or vindictive reactions from former spouses (Bozett 1987).

Research suggests that children are generally accepting of a parent's homosexuality and rarely reject a homosexual parent. Furthermore, research has found no negative consequences for children who live with homosexual parents.

The other side of the coin is not so optimistic. Case studies and anecdotal data indicate that parents have a difficult time accepting their children's homosexuality (LeMasters and DeFrain 1989). Parents do reject homosexual children. Thus homosexual children are often reluctant to reveal their sexual preferences to their parents.

increase in women's social and economic standing as reason to abandon their own family responsibilities.

PARENTHOOD: A LIFE-SPAN PERSPECTIVE

The majority of research and "how to" books on parenting and parenthood tend to focus on the earliest years of the experience. The number of studies on the transition to parenthood has been increasing. Advice books and articles in popular magazines concentrate more on the early years of child rearing than on the later years, especially middle childhood. There is an implicit assumption that if parents can get through the trying first years and then get their children off to school, everything will be fine and go smoothly.

The concentration on the earliest years of parenting is undoubtedly another by-product of Freudian psychology, which, to oversimplify, assumed that a human being's personality was more or less fixed after the first five years of life. Thus the emphasis was clearly on what parents did during these years, as these were considered the crucial time that molded children for the rest of their lives. As we will see in the next chapter, studies of child and human development are clustered around the early years of life, with fewer popular and scientific analyses of human development after the age of 20.

The idea that humans continue to develop after they turn 20 has received increased attention in the past several decades. George Vaillant's (1977) *Adaptation to Life* reports the results of a 30-year follow-up of Harvard sophomores who were in their late forties and early fifties when the results were analyzed. The Oakland Growth Study and Berkeley Guidance Study have followed samples of people into their forties and fifties (Elder 1978). Yale psychologist Daniel Levinson and his colleagues' (1978) *The Seasons of a Man's Life* was an in-depth study of 40 American men between the ages of 35 and 45. Lillian Rubin's (1979) book, *Women of a Certain Age,* studies middle-aged women. Finally, Gail Sheehy's (1976) best-seller, *Passages,* laid out a series of adult life stages that people move through from their twenties to their fifties.

Parenthood, however, has been relegated to the backstage of all these examinations of the aging process, middle age, and supposed "midlife crises." What literature does exist tends to deal mostly with men's jobs and careers and with ideas such as midlife crisis. For women, the focus has been on the so-called empty nest period after their last child leaves home (see Chapter 12). Little attention is given to family roles, family role development, or parenthood (Rossi 1980). When parenthood is mentioned, it tends to be only in the context of a more general discussion of aging (e.g., Neugarten 1968).

One perspective used to study human development is the life span perspective. A life-span development perspective draws on the assumptions and concepts of the developmental conceptual framework reviewed in Chapter 2. The life-span perspective grows out of an integration of sociology, psychology, history, and demography. A life-span perspective focuses on the pathways through the age-differentiated life span (Rossi 1980). Aging, timing, spacing, and the ordering of events along a lifeline are the critical concepts used by those who apply a life-span perspective to human development and behavior (Baltes and Brim 1979; Elder 1978; Lerner, Belsky, and Lerner 1983; Rossi 1980). A life-span perspective allows us to break out of the narrow confines of viewing parenthood as the battle to diaper babies and cope with children until they are ready for school. A life span perspective also means that we will not make the mistake of assuming that when the oldest leaves home the parents move into a "postparental" stage of life (Hill 1964). Rather than seeing the last child leaving home as the end of the parental role, a life-span perspective informs us that this event is a transition into a new phase of the parental role (Rossi 1980).

Richard Lerner, Jay Belsky, and Jacqueline Lerner (1983) provide a framework for a life span perspective on parenting and parent development. They explain that parenthood must be examined as part of the adult development sequence and that it is closely tied to the other roles of adulthood. There are a number of specific influences on persons that affect their own parent behavior and their relationships with their children:

1. *The Timing of Parenthood.* People become parents at different ages. The experience of becoming a first-time parent when you are 15 is quite different from having your first child when you are 40. Moreover, there are times when you are expected to have children (twenties to early thirties), and times when you are not (early teens and over 40). Of note is that the age you are "supposed" to have children has increased in recent years along with the increase in the average age at the time of first marriage. Today, more and more women in their forties are having children, in part due to changes in cultural expectations and in part due to technological advancements, such as "ultrasound," that reduce the risks and problems associated with childbearing among older women. The skills one brings to parenting and the meaning of parenting will vary according to how old you are when you have a child and whether you are having a child "on time" versus "off time" (Neugarten 1969).

2. *Personality.* By personality, Lerner and his colleagues (1983) mean psychological individuality and overall psychological well-being of the parents. Students of parenthood assume that the experience of parenthood has a strong influence on the psychological functioning of a parent. Sound psychological functioning can enhance parenting, whereas psychological problems can lead

A Framework
for a Life-Span
Perspective

The graduation of a child from college marks a new stage of parenting.

to problems and even maltreatment. Evidence from studies of child abuse and other parenting problems support the claim that an individual's personality can either support or undermine parenting ability (Straus, Gelles, and Steinmetz 1980).

3. *Developmental History.* Because personality appears to be linked to parenthood and parenting, the developmental history of a parent must also be consequential for their parenting experience across the life span. There is rather compelling evidence from research on child abuse (see Chapter 15) that if one is mistreated when growing up there is a greater likelihood of that person mistreating his or her children than will someone who was not mistreated as a child. Similarly, experiencing depression in early life is related to later experiences with depression and thus is related to parental functioning.

Developmental history is most important for understanding the role of fathers. Research has found that a father's involvement in parenting is positively related to the involvement exhibited by his own father (Reuter and Biller 1973).

4. *The Context of Parenting.* A life-span perspective not only focuses on the parent but on the context of parenting. The most important facets of the context of parenting are the stresses and supports that parents experience. Support can be provided by physical health and social, economic, and psychological well being. Stress can also be caused by health, economic problems, social isolation, and lack of a social network (see Chapter 14). Central to the context of the parenting experience is the marital relationship. The higher the quality of the marital relationship, the more effectively parents can meet the expectations of the parent role.

With the increase in public as well as scholarly attention being focused on the role of fathers, it is imperative to examine the marital relationship when considering the sources of support and stress on parents.

Work and career are sources of both stress and support. One of the more obvious relationships between work and parenthood is the finding that child abuse is more common in homes where the father is unemployed (Straus et al. 1980). In addition, there is considerable research and debate on the impact of maternal employment on the parent-child relationship.

Parenthood in the Middle Years

A few studies have examined parenthood at stages other than the first few years. The pathfinding sociologist Alice Rossi (1980) broke new ground in the study of parenthood by focusing on parents in their middle years. In a preliminary study of this issue, Rossi collected questionnaire data from 68 women who lived in intact families, who had children at home, and who were in their middle years. Women ranged in age from 33 to over 55. The sample actually consisted of two groups—young middle-aged mothers, whose average age was 37, and older middle-aged mothers, whose average age was 47.5.

Among Rossi's questions were items that sought the best and worst aspects of age and aging. Family roles and parent roles were central to the women's answers, and they frequently described family-related matters rather than personal ones. For example, one woman noted that the worst thing about her present age was the fights between her teenagers and their father. Another reported that the worst thing was that her children were not old enough to be independent. Parent issues took precedence over such things as energy level, personal health, and physical or psychological matters.

Another portion of Rossi's questionnaire asked about pleasure and worry. Here, too, parenting came to center stage. Mothers, especially the older mothers, said that most of the pleasure in their lives came from their children. Less gratification came from marriage or personal accomplishments. Those women who had adult children who were settled in both family and work roles reported substantial levels of personal gratification. Comments such as "I am delighted with the girls my sons have married and happy to welcome each grandchild" marked the responses of middle-aged mothers (Rossi 1980).

SUMMING UP Married couples are expected to have children; having children is considered to be natural. Most couples will bring a child into the world—a little less than 90% of all married women will eventually have a child. Few roles in society have such high expectations, so few opportunities for training, and such ambiguous standards for evaluation and success as the parent role. Cultural pressures and normative standards motivate us to become parents and often set rather unrealistic goals and standards for our performance. Becoming a parent for the first time may or may not be a crisis, but it is clear that it involves major transitions, adjustments, and reorganizations. Both the decision to become a parent and parenthood fundamentally change the nature of marital relationships. A baby alters time, space, relationships, and sense of self and self-worth. The changes begin with pregnancy, as couples anticipate the change from being a couple to becoming parents.

One of the major social issues today is the issue of teenage parenting. The United States has the highest rate of births to teenage mothers of any industrialized Western nation. Two thirds of pregnant teenagers are between 18 and 19 years of age, and only 40% are married. The vast majority of younger pregnant teenagers (under age 18) also are not married.

The transition to parenthood is perhaps the most important and unique experience a couple will have. It is perhaps the most unique transition in a marriage, if not in human development. Sociologist Alice Rossi (1968) suggests that there are at least four unique aspects of becoming a parent: cultural pressure to assume the role, the involuntary nature of the role, the irrevocability of the role, and the lack of preparation for the role. Not only is there social pressure to have a child, but there is considerable pressure to have more than one.

Opportunities for preparation, expectations, and standards differ for men and for women. Mothers are allocated the primary responsibility for child rearing and receive much of the blame for whatever happens to their children. Modern research has generally refuted the notion that there is a maternal instinct or that the children whose mothers work suffer from maternal deprivation. Modern fathers have been gradually moving back into parenting roles, having once been the "missing persons" of parenthood. Yet moving back into a parenthood role is not without major problems. We have not yet worked out cultural standards for fathers and fatherhood. Fathers (and mothers) must constantly balance work roles and parent roles, adjusting to the demands of both, while trying to fulfill cultural and social standards that are often unrealistic.

Contrary to popular belief, parenthood problems do not end when children enter school. As Alice Rossi pointed out 30 years ago, one never really becomes an ex-parent. Thus we are just beginning to realize that each stage of parenting involves different and unique challenges and transitions. A life-span perspective is a useful approach to understanding these differing demands and changes, allowing us to examine parent behavior over a complete life span of parent and child.

The next chapter looks at the other half of parent-child relations—socialization and child development.

REFERENCES

Baltes, Paul B. and Orville G. Brim. 1979. *Life Span Development and Behavior,* Vol. 2. New York: Academic Press.

Bernard, Jesse. 1974. *The Future of Motherhood.* New York: Dial Press.

Blackwell, James E. 1991. *The Black Community: Diversity and Unity.* 3rd ed. New York: Harper Collins

Bowlby, John. 1951. *Maternal Care and Maternal Health.* Geneva: World Health Organization.

Bozett, Fred W. 1987. *Gay and Lesbian Parents.* New York: Praeger.

Brazelton, T. Berry. 1969. *Infants and Mothers.* New York: Delacourt.

Cherlin, Andrew. 1990. "Recent Changes in American Fertility, Marriage, and Divorce." *Annals of the American Association of Political and Social Science* 510 (July):145-54.

———. 1992. *Marriage, Divorce, Remarriage.* Rev. ed. Cambridge, MA: Harvard University Press.

Chodorow, Nancy and Susan Contratto. 1992. "The Fantasy of the Perfect Mother." Pp. 191-214 in *The Family: Some Feminist Questions,* rev. ed., edited by Barrie Thorne and Marilyn Yalom. Boston: Northeastern University Press.

Cosby, Bill. 1986. *Fatherhood.* New York: Doubleday.

Dyer, Everett D. 1963. "Parenthood as Crisis: A Restudy." *Marriage and Family Living* 25(May):196-201.

Elder, Glen. 1978. "Family History and the Life Course." Pp. 17-64 in *Transitions: The Family and the Life Course in Historical Perspective,* edited by Tamara Kitareuem. New York: Academic Press.

Eyer, Diane E. 1993. *Mother-Infant Bonding: A Scientific Fiction.* New Haven, CT: Yale University Press.

Falbo, Toni. 1976. "Does the Only Child Grow Up Miserable?" *Psychology Today* 9(May): 60ff.

Friedan, Betty. 1963. *The Feminine Mystique.* New York: Dell.

Freud, Sigmund. [1953] 1974. *The Standard Edition of the Complete Psychological Works of Sigmund Freud.* Rev. ed. Translated from German by J. Strachly in collaboration with Anna Freud, assisted by Alex Strachly and Alan Tyson. London: Hogarth Press and Institute of Psychoanalysis.

Furstenberg, Frank F., Jr. 1988. "Good Dads-Bad Dads: Two Faces of Fatherhood." Pp. 193-218 in *The Changing American Family and Public Policy,* edited by Andrew J. Cherlin. Washington, DC: Urban Institute Press.

Gallop, George, Jr. and F. Newport. 1990. "Virtually All Adults Want Children, But Many of the Reasons Are Intangible." *Gallop Poll Monthly,* June, 8:9-22.

Goldberg, Wendy A., Gerald Y. Michaels, and Michael E. Lamb. 1985. "Husbands' and Wives' Adjustment to Pregnancy and First Parenthood." *Journal of Family Issues* 6 (December):483-503.

Goldscheider, Frances K. and Linda J. Waite. 1991. *New Families, No Families: The Transformation of the American Home.* Berkeley: University of California Press.

Goode, William J. 1956. *After Divorce.* Glencoe, IL: Free Press.

Griswold, Robert L. 1993. *Fatherhood in America: A History.* New York: Basic Books.

Henshaw, Stanley K. and J. Van Vort. 1989. "Teenage Abortion, Birth, and Pregnancy Statistics: An Update." *Family Planning Perspectives* 21(March/April):85-88.

Hill, Reuben. 1964. "Methodological Issues in Family Development Research." *Family Process* 3(March):186-206.

Hobbs, Daniel F., Jr. 1965. "Parenthood as Crisis: A Third Study." *Journal of Marriage and the Family* 27(August):367-72.

———. 1968. "Transition to Parenthood: A Replication and Extension." *Journal of Marriage and the Family* 30(August): 413-18.

Hobbs, Daniel F., Jr. and Sue P. Cole. 1976. "Transition to Parenthood: A Decade Replication." *Journal of Marriage and the Family* 38(November): 723-31.

Hobbs, Daniel F., Jr. and Jane M. Wimbush. 1977. "Transition to Parenthood by Black Couples." *Journal of Marriage*

and the Family 39(November):677-89.

Hochschild, Arlie and Anne Machung. 1989. *The Second Shift.* New York: Viking.

Horney, Karen. 1967. *Feminine Psychology.* New York: Norton.

Jacoby, Arthur P. 1969. "Transition to Parenthood: A Reassessment." *Journal of Marriage and the Family* 31(November): 720-27.

Kalish, Susan. 1993. "In China, the Peak Childbearing Years Have Peaked." *Population Today* 21(January):5.

Knox, David and Kenneth Wilson. 1978. "The Difference Between Having One and Two Children." *The Family Coordinator* 27(January):23-25.

Lamb, Michael E., ed. 1987a. *The Father's Role: Applied Perspectives.* New York: John Wiley.

———. 1987b. *The Father's Role: Cross-Cultural Perspectives.* Hillsdale, NJ: Lawrence Erlbaum.

Lamb, Michael E. and Jamie E. Lamb. 1976. "The Nature and Importance of the Father-Infant Relationship." *Family Coordinator* 25(October):379-85.

LaRossa, Ralph. 1977. *Conflict and Power in Marriage: Expecting the First Child.* Beverly Hills, CA: Sage.

———. 1986. *Becoming a Parent.* Beverly Hills, CA: Sage.

———. 1988. "Fatherhood and Social Change." *Family Relations* 37(October):451-57.

LaRossa, Ralph and Donald C. Reitzes. 1993. "Continuity and Change in Middle Class Fatherhood, 1925–1939: The Culture-

Conduct Connection." *Journal of Marriage and the Family* 55(May):455-68.

LeMasters, E. E. 1957. "Parenthood as Crisis." *Marriage and Family Living* 19(November):352-55.

———. 1974. *Parents in Modern America.* Rev. ed. Homewood, IL: Dorsey Press.

LeMasters, E. E. and John DeFrain. 1989. *Parents in Contemporary America: A Sympathetic View.* 5th ed. Belmont, CA: Wadsworth.

Lerner, Richard, Jay Belsky, and Jacqueline Lerner. 1983. "Child and Parent Development: A Life Span Perspective." Paper presented at the Social Science Research Council Conference on Biosocial Life-Span Approaches to Parental and Offspring Behavior, Elkridge, Maryland.

Levinson, Daniel, with Charlotte N. Darrow, Edward B. Klein, Maria H. Levinson, and Braxton McKee. 1978. *The Seasons of a Man's Life.* New York: Alfred A. Knopf.

McLanahan, Sara S. and Julia Adams. 1989. "The Effects of Children on Adults' Psychological Well-Being: 1957–1976." *Social Forces* 68(September):79-91.

Mead, Margaret. 1954. "Some Theoretical Considerations on the Problems of Mother-Child Separation." *American Journal of Orthopsychiatry* 24(July):471-83.

Moore, Kristen A., Dee Ann Wenk, Sandra L. Hofferth, and Cheryl D. Hayes. 1987. "Trends in Adolescent Sexual and Fertility Behavior." Pp. 353-520 in *Risking the Future: Adolescent Sexuality, Pregnancy, and*

Childbearing, Vol. 2, edited by Sandra L. Hofferth and Cheryl D. Hayes. Washington, DC: National Academy Press.

National Center for Health Statistics. 1990. "Advance Report of Final Natality Statistics, 1989." *Monthly Vital Statistics* 9(4), Supplement. Hyattsville, MD: Public Health Service.

National Committee for Prevention of Child Abuse. 1993. *Public Attitudes and Actions Regarding Child Abuse and Its Prevention, 1993.* Chicago: Author.

National Opinion Research Center. 1991. *General Social Surveys, 1972–1991.* Storrs, CT: Roper Center for Public Opinion Research.

Neugarten, Bernice L., ed. 1968. *Middle Age and Aging.* Chicago: University of Chicago Press.

———. 1969. "Continuities and Discontinuities of Psychological Issues Into Adult Life." *Human Development* 12(2):121-30.

Oakley, Ann. 1974. *Women's Work: The Housewife, Past and Present.* New York: Vintage.

Parke, Ross D. 1981. *Fathers.* Cambridge, MA: Harvard University Press.

Radin, N. 1978. "Childrearing Fathers in Intact Families With Preschoolers." Paper presented at the annual meeting of the American Psychological Association, Toronto, August.

Reuter, Mark W. and Henry Biller. 1973. "Perceived Parental Nurturance-Availability and Personality Adjustment Among College Males." *Journal of Consulting and Clinical Psychology* 40(April/May):339-42.

Rollin, Betty. 1971. "The Motherhood Myth." *Look,* September 22, 15-17.

Rosenberg, Morris. 1965. *Society and Adolescent Self Image.* Princeton, NJ: Princeton University Press.

Rossi, Alice. 1968. "Transition to Parenthood." *Journal of Marriage and the Family* 30(February):26-39.

———. 1978. "A Biosocial Perspective on Parenting." Pp. 1-31 in *The Family,* edited by Alice Rossi, Jerome Kagan, and Tamara Hareven. New York: Norton.

———. 1980. "Aging and Parenthood in the Middle Years." Pp. 137-205 in *Life Span Development and Behavior,* Vol. 3, edited by Paul Baltes and Orville G. Brim, Jr. New York: Academic Press.

———. 1983. "Parenthood in Transition: Demographic and Social Pressures for Change in Human Parenting in Post-Industrial Society." Paper presented at the Social Science Research Council Conference on Parenting and Offspring Development in Life Span Perspective, Belmont, MD.

———. 1984. "Gender and Parenthood." *American Sociological Review* 49(February):1-19.

Rubin, Lillian B. 1976. *Worlds of Pain: Life in the Working Class Family..* New York: Basic Books.

———. 1979. *Women of a Certain Age.* New York: Basic Books.

Russell, Candyse S. 1974. "Transition to Parenthood: Problems and Gratifications." *Journal of Marriage and the Family* 36 (May):294-302.

Sears, Robert, Eleanor Maccoby, and H. Levin. 1957. *Patterns of Child Rearing.* Evanston, IL: Row, Peterson.

Sheehy, Gail. 1976. *Passages.* New York: Dutton.

Straus, Murray A., Richard J. Gelles, and Suzanne K. Steinmetz. 1980. *Behind Closed Doors: Violence in the American Family.* New York: Anchor/ Doubleday.

Tavris, Carol and Carol Offir. 1984. *The Longest War: Sex Differences in Perspective.* 2nd ed. New York: Harcourt Brace Jovanovich.

U.S. Bureau of the Census. 1992. *Statistical Abstracts of the United States.* Washington, DC: Government Printing Office

Vaillant, George. 1977. *Adaptation to Life.* Boston: Little, Brown.

Voydanoff, Patricia. 1987. *Work and Family Life.* Newbury Park, CA: Sage.

———. 1989. "Work and Family: A Review and Expanded Conceptualization." Pp. 1-22 in *Work and Family,* edited by Elizabeth B. Goldsmith. Newbury Park, CA: Sage.

Voydanoff, Patricia and Brenda W. Donnelly. 1990. *Adolescent Sexuality and Pregnancy.* Newbury Park, CA: Sage.

Wortis, Rochelle P. 1977. "The Acceptance of the Concept of Marital Role by Behavioral Scientists: The Effects on Women." *American Journal of Orthopsychiatry* 41(October): 733-46.

Zajonc, Robert B. and Gregory B. Markus. 1975. "Birth Order and Intellectual Development." *Psychological Review* 82(January):75-88.

CHAPTER 10

■■ Child Socialization

The previous chapter examined parents and parenthood. This chapter looks at child rearing and socialization. Human infants come into the world uniquely helpless. Human mothers stand upright on two feet and have narrow hips, and consequently, human offspring cannot develop in the uterus nearly as much as do offspring of other species (Washburn and De Vore 1961). Human infants come into the world with lesser developed brains than other animal offspring, and as a result, human infants are unable to feed themselves, care for themselves, walk, move, or do very much to protect themselves. Most first-time parents are struck, and frequently overwhelmed, by just how helpless their newborns are.

The process of moving from a state of complete helplessness to being able to communicate, eat, find shelter, and provide care is part of the process of **socialization.** Socialization is defined as education in the broadest sense. It is the process whereby one acquires a sense of personal identity and learns what people in the surrounding culture believe and how they expect one to behave (Musgrave 1988). Through socialization, a helpless infant is gradually transformed into a more or less knowledgeable, more or less cooperative member of society. Through socialization, individuals not only learn the values, norms, and skills of their culture but also acquire a sense of who they are and where they belong. Socialization involves both explicit instruction and unconscious modeling; it influences both personality development and social behavior. Although the foundations of personality are established and basic skills acquired in early childhood, socialization continues throughout life.

Parents are the primary **agents of socialization,** and the family is the major setting for socialization. There are other agents (peers, teachers, the mass media), and other settings (schools, playgrounds, the movies), but in this chapter we focus exclusively on socialization in families.

Socialization of young children has been described as perhaps the single universal function of the family (Reiss, 1965; see also Chapter 3). For thousands of years the family exercised a virtual monopoly over child socialization. Prior to industrialization, small children spent most of their time with parents, siblings, grandparents, aunts, uncles, and cousins. Since industrialization, child rearing has been the primary function of the immediate or nuclear family—parents and siblings. In the past few decades, time with the immediate family has given way to more time spent with peers in day care centers, with babysitters, and in schools. Yet, even with these changes, parents and family remain the central agents and settings where socialization takes place.

This chapter begins by examining one of the classic debates in the study of child rearing and socialization—the debate over the contributions of biology and environment to human nature. How much of human behavior is determined by heredity? How much by environment? In the following section, theories of socialization are reviewed. This section also reviews the stages of child and human development in terms of personal and social growth. Gender socialization is the topic of the next section. The previous chapter (Chapter 9) looked at gender in terms of parent roles and parenting. This chapter considers gender from the point of view of the child and child development. The final section discusses one of the most vexing problems parents face in raising children—discipline.

THEORIES OF SOCIALIZATION

All human beings are alike in some ways but different in others. Explaining the similarities and differences among people is a major goal of those who study children, the family, and socialization.

Fundamentally important to any discussion of parents, offspring, and child rearing is the long-standing debate about human nature. This debate has occupied scientists for centuries. On one side are those who have argued that human behavior is the product of heredity, or "nature." Those who take this position claim that our personality and behavior are predetermined by our genetic inheritance. The alternative argument is that human behavior is a product of human experience and learning, or "nurture," and that the person we become is dependent on the way we were raised and our learned experiences.

Nature and Nurture

The publication of Charles Darwin's *On the Origins of Species* in 1859 ([1859] 1958) pushed the "nature" perspective into the forefront of 19th-century thinking. Darwin held that human beings are the product of the same natural processes that produced snails, elephants, mice, and monkeys. Darwin proposed that genetic mutations (mistakes or accidents in genetic copying) produce variations in every generation of living organisms. In most cases, these changes are either insignificant, such as a third nipple or a webbed toe, or are harmful, such as Down's syndrome. In some cases, however, a mutation gives an individual an advantage over others of its kind. The individual organism is better adapted to its environment and therefore survives longer and produces more offspring. Those offspring may inherit the traits that give them the adaptive advantage. Over time, the adaptive trait spreads, producing changes in the species or even leading to new species. Thus evolution is the result of **natural selection**—nature acting on genetic diversity, selecting the most adaptive traits.

The cornerstone of the "nature" viewpoint is the idea that most individual and social behavior is genetically predetermined. Obviously, those who pro-

Children's interests and abilities—such as music or arts—are a product of a combination of nature *and* nurture.

pose a nature theory of human behavior have less interest in the role of parents and the process of child rearing than in genetic or biological factors.

The cornerstone of the "nurture" position is the belief that human infants come into the world "tabula rasa" (Latin for "blank slate"). The nurture position places considerable emphasis on learning and social interaction. Human behavior is seen as malleable or plastic. The work of Russian physiologist Ivan Pavlov (1927) and American psychologists B. F. Skinner (1938) and John B. Watson (1938) led to social scientists focusing on learning and the impact of learning on human behavior. Most school children learn about Pavlov's experiments where he trained dogs to salivate at the sound of a metronome. Skinner and Watson expanded on Pavlov's work and conducted learning experiments with pigeons who learned to play Ping-Pong and rats who learned to run mazes.

The nurture position emphasizes the impact of parents on child rearing. The most extreme statement of the nurture position is that any healthy infant can be trained to become anything—doctor, lawyer, artist, or mechanic—regardless of talent, interests, abilities, or ancestors (Watson 1924). In other words, people are dependent upon and molded by the environment in which they exist.

The debate over nature versus nurture raged for much of the past century. Today, the debate has cooled somewhat. David Reiss (1992) suggests that the Cold War in the nature versus nurture debate is over. Developmental psychologists and others who study individual differences have begun to understand how genes and environments *interact*—that is, how genetic factors influence environmental variables and vice versa. Because of his or her unique genetic characteristics, each child elicits special responses from the environment—including his or her parents. Easy babies may evoke warm, playful parenting, for example, whereas whiny, difficult babies may evoke harsh treatment or neglect, with many variations in between. Thus children in the same family can grow up quite differently because they may be treated quite differently within the family and so their social interaction experiences will be quite different. As a result of unique individual environments, some genetic predispositions will be expressed fully and others masked or repressed. No wonder there is an almost infinite variety among human beings.

Although the so-called Cold War between the nature and nurture views may be over, "nature" and "nurture" are issues for parents who struggle with the trials, tribulations, and anticipated outcomes of child rearing. Parents often take a nurture approach to raising their children and anguish about whether their parenting style will harm or help their children. Of course, no matter which style parents choose, they still anguish because they assume that nurture influences their children's development.

There are two main sources of evidence about the impact of socialization, especially environmental factors: studies of children kept in isolation and studies of cross-cultural variations in behavior.

The Impact of Socialization

Isolated Children

History provides dozens of stories of children who were supposedly abandoned and raised by animals. When discovered, these so-called **feral children** usually resist attempts to civilize them, suggesting that what we call "human nature" depends on normal, human upbringing. Such stories are largely speculative, and there are few scientifically documented cases of children raised by animals. However, there are documented cases of socially isolated children that do provide strong evidence for the impact of socialization (Davis 1940, 1947).

"Genie" (not her real name) is a recent example of a socially isolated child (Curtiss 1977; Ruch and Shurley 1985; Rymer 1993). Genie first came to public attention when she limped into a Los Angeles County welfare office with her battered and nearly blind mother in fall 1970. The welfare worker who interviewed them estimated that Genie was 6 or 7 years old and suspected that Genie was autistic. In fact, although she weighed only 59 pounds, Genie was a teenager. Her emotionally disturbed father had confined her to an empty room, where she was either strapped onto an infant's potty chair or enclosed in a straitjacketlike sleeping bag day after day, year after year. Genie's mother was allowed to feed her only milk, cereal, and an occasional egg and was never allowed to play with the child. If Genie attempted to attract attention by making noises, her father beat her with a wooden bat. Somehow, she survived this silent, isolated, and abusive childhood. Finally, when Genie was 13½, her mother summoned the courage to escape with her daughter (Genie's father committed suicide shortly thereafter).

A medical examination of Genie revealed that she could not chew solid food, control her bowels, walk normally, or talk beyond a few utterances ("stopit" and "nomore"). She did not react to heat or cold. She did not cry. She treated people as if they were objects, inspecting them with her eyes and hands but not responding to social overtures. Observers who saw her at this time often commented that there was something almost "ghostlike" about her (Rymer 1993).

With care and attention, Genie began to recover in some ways but not others. She became attached to her caretakers but sometimes was attracted to complete strangers as well. She began to talk but never progressed beyond the level of a 2-year-old child. She learned to bathe and dress herself but continued to have toilet problems.

Whether Genie's limited, uneven recovery was the result of early and prolonged social isolation, emotional trauma, and/or physical neglect and abuse is difficult to say. One interesting finding was that the left hemisphere of Genie's brain did not function normally. In most people, the left hemisphere controls language and logic. Genie's extreme asymmetry suggests that the physiological structures of the brain that enable us to communicate symbolically depend on exposure to language at an appropriate age—a clear example of the interaction of nature and nurture. Perhaps because Genie was deprived of normal social contact, her brain failed to develop normally.

Genie's case illustrates that most of basic human characteristics depend on socialization. The abilities to walk and talk do not develop spontaneously, according to nature's plan. Neither do emotions, personality, or intelligence. All depend to some degree on social interaction. Studies of children who have been raised in large impersonal orphanages where human contact and physical stimulation are minimal confirm this view (Rutter 1988; Spitz 1945). Although physically healthy, these babies are much slower to develop than babies raised at home. They do not walk, talk, or begin to play with other children "on schedule." Whether they ever achieve their full potential as human beings and as individuals is doubtful (Provence 1989; Rutter 1988).

Cross-Cultural Variations

A second source of evidence on the impact of socialization on human behavior are cross-cultural studies. Margaret Mead's (1935) *Sex and Temperament in Three Primitive Societies* is a classic in this field. Mead set out to test the belief that men and women are emotionally and psychologically different by looking at three New Guinea tribes. She asked whether women are "by nature" nurturant and men "by nature" aggressive.

Among the Arapesh, Mead found that men were as mild-mannered and nurturant as the women. Little boys treated the infant girls they hoped to marry like dolls, dressing them in bead and feather jewelry. Men could not stand to hear a baby cry. Members of both sexes behaved in ways that we would call "feminine."

In the second tribe that Mead visited, the Mundugumor, the pattern was reversed. The women were as hot-tempered, combative, and uncaring as the men. A woman who tried to rescue an infant who had been abandoned or abused was subjected to intense ridicule. In different ways then, neither the Arapesh nor the Mundugumor recognized differences in temperament or personality between the sexes.

The Tchambuli, the third tribe in Mead's study, did make a distinction, but their gender stereotypes were the opposite of our own. The plainspoken, practical Tchambuli women took care of business matters while the men primped and gossiped in their clubhouses. No self-respecting Tchambuli woman pined for love, but the men and boys were in constant romantic turmoil.

Although Mead's work has been questioned (Freeman 1983; Harris 1968), the anthropological literature provides abundant examples of human plasticity.

Are women, by nature, nurturant and men, by nature, aggressive? Cross-cultural variations in differences between the sexes, in sexual behavior, and in many other areas show that human behavior is, in large part, learned behavior. Specific behavioral patterns are not the only cultural variable; the sense of self—the way people define themselves in relation to others and to nature—also varies cross-culturally (Hsu 1985). Western cultures, for example, treat each person as a unique, independent individual. In some cultures, however, the individual is second only to the group, be it a family group, school group or political or religious group. The needs of the group come first.

In summary, biology sets the stage, but socialization writes the script. Socialization strongly influences what kind of individuals we become, how we feel about such things as being males or females, indeed, whether we become "human" at all.

Three Theories of Socialization	We come into the world helpless and dependent. By the end of adolescence we take for granted the acquisition of the skills and abilities that allow us to function as adults. How do we acquire these skills and abilities? How does the process of socialization work?

This section reviews three theories of the socialization process. Sigmund Freud's examination of the psychodynamics of socialization has been widely discussed and analyzed. Jean Piaget's concern was with the process of cognitive, or intellectual, development. Sociologists Charles Horton Cooley (1902) and George Herbert Mead (1934) developed the symbolic interactionist perspective (see Chapter 2) and analyzed the process by which a self-concept emerged as a result of human interaction.

Each theorist and each theory focuses on a different aspect of the socialization process. Each theory is based on different assumptions and applies different concepts to analyzing the process of human development. Each theory also makes different assumptions about the roles of nature and nurture in child socialization.

The Psychoanalytic Perspective

Sigmund Freud (1865–1939) developed a theory of the stages of child development that has had a profound impact on our thinking about children and the impact of parents on child development.

Freud ([1953] 1974) portrayed socialization as a constant struggle between the child and the child's parents. On one side of the battle is the child—driven by powerful, inborn sexual and aggressive urges, or **instincts.** On the other side are parents who try to curb the natural instincts and mold the child into a productive and conforming citizen of society. According to Freud, socialization is the confrontation between the child's biological urges and society's (parents) attempts to "civilize" the child.

Freud based his theory of socialization on the assumption that all children go through *fixed stages of psychosexual development*. At each stage the pleasure-

According to Freud, children discover their genitals during the phallic stage—between ages 3 and 6—although their curiosity about their bodies begins earlier.

eeking urges of the child are focused on a specific body area. These stages begin at birth and culminate at the end of adolescence.

During the first year of life, the child goes through the **oral stage.** Pleasure is derived from sucking, and children typically will put anything in their mouths to satisfy their oral urges. During the second year of life, attention shifts to the **anal stage.** Children gain satisfaction and pleasure in learning to release and control their bowels. Children aged 3 to 6 discover their genitals in the **phallic stage.** Children become aware of the differences between the sexes. It is during this stage that the **oedipal conflicts** occur. Freud believed that children want to possess (have sexual intercourse with or marry) the parent of the opposite sex, and this creates an intense rivalry between the child and the same-sex parent. The **latency stage** occurs at age 6 or 7. At this point, sexual urges are latent while the child's attention turns to developing skills to cope with the environment. Adolescence brings on the **genital stage.** Sexual desire emerges and adolescents begin to seek mature love.

Each stage involves a battle between urges and control. Parents' actions are designed to interfere and interrupt the child's quest for pleasure. Weaning, toilet training, and sexual norms are introduced by parents and society. Freud believed that the child's personality development was dependent on how the child resolved the conflicts between internal urges and external controls. If the conflict was not resolved satisfactorily, the child could become fixated at a stage—oral fixations, anal compulsive fixations, and so on.

Freud's primary concern was **personality.** His theory proposed that adult personality is the product of the early battles and conflicts between the child and the parents (see Box 10-1).

Freud believed that personality was composed of three interrelated parts: the id, the ego, and the superego. Primitive, asocial sexual urges and aggressive urges are located in the **id.** The id operates on a pleasure principle, seeking immediate gratification of sexual and aggressive urges. The **superego** is the internalized understanding of society's rules and values. Children learn about these rules and values from their parents as part of the process of socialization. The superego is what we would commonly call a conscience. Guilt is the primary operating principle of the superego. Freud believed that children internalize their parents' attitudes and values. Then, throughout their lives children "hear" their parents' voice in their minds, telling them what to do and what will happen if they do the wrong thing—"Wear your boots or you will catch cold," "Don't do that or you will regret it," and so on. The final component

---

BOX 10-1: WHAT THE RESEARCH SHOWS

The Impact of Socialization: The Case of Infant Training Procedures

A central theme of Freud's theory of socialization and personality development was that infant training procedures play a crucial role in personality development. Parents' actions or lack of actions determined whether infants successfully passed through the various stages of development or became fixated at one stage. Too-early toilet training, for instance, may fixate the child at the anal stage of development and result in the child growing up to be extremely fastidious (or what we call "anal compulsive").

William Sewell's (1952) study of 162 children, ages 5 and 6, is now more than 40 years old, but it remains a classic test of Freud's theory of socialization. Sewell administered a number of personality tests to the children and also collected data from each child's mother and teacher. He asked about infant training procedures that were thought central to the development of personality: whether the child was nursed or bottle-fed; if the child was fed on a set schedule or whenever he or she was hungry

of personality, the **ego,** is the rational part of the personality that deals with the external world. The ego serves to channel impulses from the id into socially acceptable behavior. Freud saw the ego as a mediator between the urges of the id and the literal demands of the superego.

Freud emphasized biological drives or instincts. He believed that the stages of psychosexual development are biologically determined. The driving force of all human behavior is sexual energy, or **libido.** At the same time, Freud also recognized the central role of the family and social interaction in the development of human beings. How parents react to and deal with their children's sexual and aggressive urges makes a crucial difference in determining the nature of the personality the child develops.

Freud has been widely read and widely criticized. Critics note that Freud's assumptions and theories grew out of his treatment of emotionally troubled individuals—not "normal" or "happy" people. Other critics argue that Freud's theories are not scientifically testable, and are thus merely intuitive or speculative. Finally, critics argue that his theories are limited to the European Victorian era in which he lived and practiced. His notions of sexual and aggressive urges may not fit other times and other cultures.

The Cognitive View: Jean Piaget

Swiss psychologist Jean Piaget (1896–1980) focused on the cognitive development of young children. At the core of Piaget's theory of cognitive

(a demand schedule); when and how the child was weaned from either the breast or the bottle; when the child was toilet trained and whether he or she was punished for toilet accidents; and whether the child slept alone or with his or her parents.

After collecting all the data from the children, parents, and teachers and then assessing whether there was a relationship between specific infant training procedures and later personality, Sewell found few statistically significant relationships. Having tested Freud's theory, Sewell was forced to conclude that infant training procedures per se do not play a crucial role in personality development and adjustment.

Social scientists continued to subject Freud's notions and theories to empirical test. The evidence collected is, at best, contradictory (Caldwell 1964). Some investigators do find some relationships between infant training techniques and personality; others do not.

One crucial factor that may explain the contradictory results is that few investigators attempt to assess the attitudes behind the procedures. Why parents select a procedure (breast vs. bottle feeding; early vs. late toilet training) may be more consequential to personality development than the actual procedure used. Also, researchers tend to ignore the role and behavior of the child. The child's temperament, sex, and birth order may be related both to the child's personality development and to the parents' behavior.

development is the principle that children move through fixed stages. The age that children are when they move from one stage to the next might vary a bit, but the sequence is universal and invariable. A stage cannot be skipped.

Piaget spent most of his career observing children and inventing games to serve as experiments that focused on understanding the process of the development of intellectual abilities. Piaget, like Freud, saw development as a process of moving through fixed stages, each stage qualitatively different from the last. The way children think and process information actually changes as they move from one stage to the next (Piaget and Inhelder 1969).

The first stage is the **sensorimotor stage** that begins at birth and lasts until about 2 years of age. During the first two years of life, children explore the relationship between movements and their sensations. Piaget believed that, at first, children cannot distinguish themselves from their environment. They do not realize that their movements cause noise (e.g., shaking a rattle). They do not realize that objects have permanence. That is, if their toy rolls away or gets lost under a blanket, they lose interest, believing that the object no longer exists. During the sensorimotor stage, children develop a sense of their being a separate object and an object of permanence. They may realize that their mother is there, even if they do not see her, but children do not "think" in the ordinary sense of the word. For example, now if their toy rolls under a blanket, they know that the toy is not gone—that if they lift up the blanket the toy will be there.

From age 2 to 7, children are in the **preoperational stage.** These are the years during which children learn to speak, use words, and represent objects and images symbolically. Thinking is largely intuitive. At this stage of their cognitive development, children cannot perform simple mental operations. Piaget demonstrated this in his now famous experiment with two glasses of water. Piaget poured water from a tall thin glass into a short wide glass. Although the amount of water remained the same (the law of conservation), and although children could see that the amount of water remained the same, they stated that there was more water in the tall thin glass than in the short wide one. In another demonstration, a researcher asked a 4-year-old boy if the boy had a brother. The child said, "Yes—Jim." The researcher then asked if Jim had a brother. The child responded with an emphatic "No!" (Phillips 1975).

Children begin to perform logical operations in the **concrete operational stage** (about age 7 to 12). They learn to consider more than one dimension at a time. They can look at objects or persons from different points of view. They can retrace their own thoughts and correct them. Although they develop the ability to use concepts and categories in more sophisticated ways, they still remain concrete in their thinking. Ask a child in the concrete operational stage about death and the child will recite individual cases but be unable to conceptualize death.

Abstract thinking is developed in the **formal operational stage** (beginning around age 12). Trial-and-error approaches to problem solving are abandoned, and children seek out general rules for problem solving. Hypothetical situations are considered as well as concrete instances. At this stage, children think about what might be in addition to what is.

Because cognitive development is based on maturation, biology has a direct impact on cognitive development. Thus children are genetically predetermined to go through specific stages of learning. Piaget also believed that environment plays a role in cognitive development. Culture and social settings influence the content of children's cognitive development and the level of development that children reach.

The Symbolic-Interactionist Approach

The first sociological model of socialization was articulated by American sociologists Charles Horton Cooley (1984–1929) and George Herbert Mead (1863–1931). The **self**—the individual's sense of identity—was the core concern of both Cooley and Mead.

In Cooley's (1902) view, social interaction is the mechanism that both defines and develops the self. Cooley believed that our image of ourselves is largely a reflection of how other people react to us—or what Cooley referred to as a **looking-glass self.** There are three parts to the looking-glass self: (1) how we imagine others see us, (2) how we imagine they judge what they see, and (3) how we feel about those reactions. As we consider our looking-glass self, we decide whether we are attractive or unattractive, smart or dumb, considerate or selfish.

Cooley's theory of the development of self placed a major emphasis on family. It is through intimate face-to-face associations and mutual identification that we develop a solid sense of who we are and where we fit into the social world.

George Herbert Mead (1934) saw the self as a product of **symbolic interaction**—the symbolic communications contained in a smile or frown, hug or slap, and, most important, indirectly through the symbols of language. Symbols or language play a key role in the emergence of self. It is largely through the use of symbols or language that children come to think of themselves as separate and unique objects in the social world. They use language as means of describing themselves—for example, "I am a good girl" or "I am smart."

According to Mead, the *play stage* is an important stage in the socialization process during which children learn to acquire different perspectives on social roles and social behavior.

Mead also used the idea of "stages" to express his theory of socialization. He identified two stages in the emergence of self: the play stage and the game stage. He also developed the concept of the generalized other.

During the **play stage,** children play at being different people—Mommy, Daddy, a fireman, teacher, rock singer, or president. They dress up, imitate speech, deliver imaginary letters, have parties for imaginary people, and so on. Adults view all this as make-believe, but for children, it is serious business. Mead theorized that when children pretend to be other people, they are acquiring vicarious experience of different perspectives. Later, they actually begin to act out social interactions and relationships ("You be the mommy, I'll be the daddy"). They also change roles. One minute they are the misbehaving child, the next the scolding parent. According to Mead, what the child is doing is *taking the role of the other*—putting him- or herself in another person's shoes. By taking the role of the other, children learn to see themselves as other people see them. By age 7 or 8, children can take the role of the other in their imaginations. They can see themselves as objects; they acquire a sense of themselves as distinct people.

The next stage of development is the **game stage.** Here children do not merely play at roles but actually engage in social interaction with others. In these social interactions, children come to recognize the "rules of the game"—that there are other players, what is expected of other players, and that the game involves an organized structure with rules and expectations of people who occupy certain positions. Mead believed that once children became aware of external structures, this gave structure to their own internal lives. The process by which external structures are translated into the internal lives of children was called the **generalized other** by Mead. The generalized other is the child's image of the norms (rules), values, and structure of society as a whole. Like Freud's superego, the generalized other guides behavior in a socially acceptable direction. Unlike the superego, the generalized other is acquired through a process of social interaction—what Mead saw as the game stage.

Social interaction does not produce social robots—children who mindlessly follow the rules and regulations of society. Mead's concept of the socialized self included two components: the *me*—the socialized self, which is composed of internalized norms and values—and the *I*—the impulsive, creative, self-centered self.

Mead's concept of "I" and "me" appears similar to Freud's notions about id, ego, and superego. The id and the "I" resemble one another, while the "me" and the ego and superego are similar. But Freud saw the id and the superego as locked in a continuing struggle, whereas Mead believed that the "I" and the "me" were collaborators. Freud's vision of socialization was discontent caused by the blocking of the impulses of the id. Mead saw the relationship between the self and society as cooperation. Socialization does not frustrate and beat down inner urges, as it does in Freud's view of the world; rather, socialization gives direction to life. Whereas Freud saw personality as being fixed by the time an individual reaches adolescence, Mead's and Cooley's theory of social development saw the self as constantly changing in response to life's experiences and continuing social interaction. Figure 10-1 summarizes the stages of the three theories of socialization.

GENDER SOCIALIZATION

Are boys and girls different? Are men and women different? If so, what accounts for these differences. Gender socialization is another area where the nature and nurture debate has raged.

Approximate Age	Psychosexual Stage (according to Freud)	Cognitive Stage (according to Piaget)	Social Stage (according to Mead)
1–2	**Oral stage:** Preoccupation with getting and sucking	**Sensorimotor stage:** Child explores relationship between self and environment	**Preverbal:**
2–3	**Anal stage:** Child is interested in releasing or controlling bowels	**Preoperational stage:** Child learns to speak and use symbols, but thinking is intuitive and egocentric	**Play stage:** Imitative play; child learns to take the role of the other
3–6	**Phallic stage:** Child discovers sexual sensations; competition with parent of same sex leads to oedipal conflict		
6–12	**Latency stage:** Sexual feelings are dormant; child focuses on mastery of skills	**Concrete operations stage:** Child learns to perform logical operations, but thinking is concrete	**Game stage:** Participation in organized games and reciprocal relationships; development of generalized other
13 . . .	**Genital stage:** Young person begins to search for adult, sexual love	**Formal operations stage:** Young person begins to think in abstract, hypothetical terms	

Figure 10-1 Stages of Psychosexual, Cognitive, and Social Development

Biological explanations of sex differences date back at least as far as Plato (see Chapter 9). There are indeed biological differences between men and women. To what degree these explain differences in behavior has been questioned over the years. A number of studies have shown that injections of the male hormone testosterone will make normally mild-mannered male and female laboratory animals become aggressive. Studies of human behavior find that men at all ages are more aggressive than women (Jacklin 1977). However, there is considerable debate as to whether the differences noted in humans are a result of hormonal differences or are due to the different ways boys and girls are socialized, and those who advocate a nurture explanation emphasize socialization patterns (Fausto-Sterling 1985; Maccoby 1980; Tavris 1992).

Gender socialization begins at the moment of birth. The obstetrician announces whether the child is a boy or girl; hospital staff often wrap boys in blue blankets and girls in pink blankets, and the processes of differential socialization begins.

Researchers have taken advantage of the fact that it is often difficult to tell if a newborn is a boy or a girl. Investigators will often dress an infant in neutral-colored clothing (e.g., yellow) and randomly tell subjects that the child is a boy (John) or a girl (Jane). Adult behavior is observed and the subjects are also questioned about their experiences. "Girls" are offered dolls and are described as sweet and soft. "Boys" are given trains and are played with more physically (Walum 1977).

Although parents may claim that they do not treat boys differently from girls, the evidence suggests that they do. Parents describe growing boys as messy and noisy. Girls are described as neater and better behaved. The perceived "natural" differences between boys and girls then result in differential parental responses to behavior (Maccoby and Jacklin 1974).

Evidence to support the impact of socialization comes from two different sources: studies of children born with "mixed sex" identities and cross-cultural research.

In rare cases, genetic abnormalities or hormonal imbalances result in the sex of a newborn child being ambiguous. The child may have the genetic structure of one sex but the genitals of the other. Other times, unfortunate accidents may occur—such as the case of a male twin whose penis was accidentally burned beyond repair during a circumcision. In the former instance, parents may simply "assign" a gender to the child; in the latter case, the parents reluctantly agreed to surgery that changed the penis into a vagina.

Evidence suggests that children accept the gender identity that is assigned to them (Money and Ehrhardt 1972). The twin who had the sex-change operation exhibited characteristics we would call "feminine"—she fussed over her appearance, liked to cook, and clearly thought of herself as a girl.

These types of cases suggest that parental socialization can override the effects of genes and biology. But there are three important caveats that need to be added to these cases. First, the number of children studied has been relatively small. Second, the children are treated with "sex appropriate" hormones. And third, the parents of such children may have devoted special attention and energy to establishing and reinforcing their child's gender identity.

Mixed-Sex Newborns

If gender identities and gender-linked behavior are the sole product of biology, than we would expect to find that gender behavior is identical in all societies. It is not. All societies differentiate between sexes and attach meaning and status to the differences (Rosaldo and Lamphere 1974). In most societies, boys are

Cross-Cultural Studies

taught different games than girls are. Men and women dress differently and follow different rules of behavior. All preindustrial societies have a division of labor based on sex.

Cross-cultural studies of gender behavior result in two important conclusions. First, what is considered masculine or feminine behavior varies from culture to culture. Our society believes that men are better suited for hard labor. Societies in sub-Saharan Africa expect the women to haul firewood and construct houses. Men in ancient Greece shopped for food and household items. The Toda of India thought women were incapable of properly doing household work—that was left for men.

While sex-appropriate behavior and tasks may vary from society to society, gender stratification does not (Rosaldo and Lamphere 1974). In virtually all societies, the tasks assigned to men are considered more important and more prestigious than those assigned to women. In virtually every known society, women are considered somewhat inferior to men (Ortner 1974).

BOX 10-2: THE FAMILY OVER TIME

Images of Children: A Historical View

We take for granted, as did Freud, Piaget, Cooley, and G. H. Mead, that childhood is a distinct stage of life. This view of children is a rather modern one. Childhood as a distinct stage of life did not exist in medieval societies (Aries 1962). During the Middle Ages, children were not seen as being fundamentally different from adults. No one recognized that children may think differently than adults or move through different stages of cognitive development. The image of children as being the same as adults is best viewed in the art of the Middle Ages. Children were portrayed as miniature adults—with adult clothing, expressions, and behaviors. Children worked in the home and the fields and served as apprentices to craftsmen, merchants, and lawyers. Children lived and slept in the same world as adults. They were exposed to the adult realities of life, such as birth, sexuality, illness, and death.

During the advent of Calvinism in Europe, the child as miniature adult gave way to the image of child as demon. Puritan parents saw their children as possessing a corrupt and evil nature

that called for extreme discipline (Greven 1991). "Beat the devil out of the child" and "spare the rod and spoil the child" became the major mandates for raising children during this era—traditions that continue into our present-day attitudes about discipline (Greven 1991).

The invention of childhood—the notion that children are different from adults and are not ready for adult responsibility—emerged in the Romantic Era of the 19th century (Aries 1962). Children were separated from the world of adults. They had separate rooms and separate functions. But children could also be the recipients of neglect and abuse. Children were exploited in mines and sweatshops, and Victorian families also were prone to be cruel or neglectful (Johansson 1987).

In the 19th and 20th centuries, Freud's concept of the id recreated the Puritan image of the child as evil. But the demon could be controlled by the superego and the ego. The late 19th and early 20th centuries ushered in the era of viewing children as moving through developmental stages.

In most societies, boys are taught different games than girls, and even at an early age, boys and girls play in separate groups and in different activities.

In summary, gender behavior is the result of both hormones and socialization. Although there is some research that shows that certain differences between men and women are directly the result of biological differences, men and women are more alike in their brains and abilities then they are different (Tavris 1992). It would be as incorrect to say that we are creatures of our genes as it would be to claim that all gender differences are the result of differential socialization. Biology and environment combine to produce gender differences (Marini 1990).

DISCIPLINE

One of the most significant dilemmas for parents is the issue of discipline. Irrespective of which theory of child and personality development one believes in, a central issue that each parent must face is how much freedom to allow a growing child or how much control to exert. A great deal of the anguish of parenting involves trying to assess how to discipline a growing child and what the consequences of a particular form of discipline might be for the child's development. Advice is common; sound scientific evidence is somewhat rare and sometimes contradictory.

Permissiveness Versus Restriction

In theory, there are two schools of thought about discipline. On the one hand is the **permissive school;** on the other is the **restrictive school.** In the real world, parents' behavior tends to fall somewhere between the two extremes.

The Permissive School

Parents who advocate the permissive school of child rearing see children as having certain developmental needs, or rights. Growing children are believed to need considerable freedom to express themselves. Excessive control and interference are thought to impede a child's ability to reach his or her developmental potential.

Some parents believe that those who advocate permissive child rearing are against *any* form of discipline. They tend to think that permissiveness automatically produces wild, undisciplined children. In most cases, permissive child rearing does not mean that there is no discipline; rather, discipline is less of a focus of the child rearing than is understanding the child's basic needs.

The Restrictive School

"Spare the rod and spoil the child" might be the motto for those who believe in the restrictive model of child rearing (Greven 1991). Proponents of the restrictive school believe that children would run amok if they did not receive proper training and rigid discipline. Parents who believe in restriction argue that if children are left to their own devices they would stick their fingers in sockets, run randomly into the streets, eat junk food until they are sick, and so on. Moreover, advocates of the restrictive school claim that not enough discipline produces children who are disrespectful to other children and to adults. "Children need the proper respect for authority, the rights of others, and property," argue restrictionists. Those who adopt a restrictive approach to child rearing believe that discipline, and typically physical punishment, is the best means of teaching children proper respect.

Neither permissive parents nor restrictive parents love their children more. Rather, they choose different philosophies of child rearing to express their love.

Permissiveness and restrictiveness are actually two ends of a continuum of approaches to disciplining children. Parents do not actually choose to be *either* restrictive or permissive. Social psychologist Diana Baumrind (1967, 1968, 1971, 1972, 1980, 1989) identified three broad types of parents and their styles of child rearing and discipline: (1) **the authoritarian,** (2) **the permissive,** and (3) **the authoritative.**

Types of Parents

The Authoritarian Parent. Authoritarians try to shape, mold, and control the behavior of their children according to absolute standards of behavior. Obedience is the most important quality the child of an authoritarian parent can display. Authoritarian parents stress respect for authority. Talking out problems is not the solution to problems between authoritarian parents and their children. Problems are solved when children obey their parents.

The Permissive Parent. The common perception of permissive parents is that they do not provide any discipline and let their children "run wild." Baumrind describes permissive parents as people who deal with their children in a non-punishing, accepting, and affirming manner. Children are not told what to do by permissive parents; rather, they are consulted and made part of the family decision process. Baumrind states that permissive parents present themselves as "resources" for their growing children instead of active, demanding authority figures who try to mold their children's behavior.

The Authoritative Parent. Authoritative parents are considered the most nurturant of all parents that Baumrind surveyed. Authoritative parents' style is characterized by a use of positive reinforcement and minimal use of punishment. They are also quite responsive to their children's demands for attention. The image of authoritative parents seems to imply that they are overly indulgent of their children. Baumrind found that authoritative parents are ready and willing to control their children's behavior. Control, however, is applied within the context of considering what is best for the children's developmental needs.

Differences in
Child Rearing
and Discipline

What explains the differences in the way parents choose to raise and discipline their children? Sociologist Melvin Kohn (1963; Kohn and Schooler 1983; see also Chapter 5) found that social class had a profound effect on the way parents viewed and reared their children. Kohn discovered a number of differences between socialization in blue-collar and white-collar families. Blue-collar parents (those who had manual labor occupations) wanted their children to be neat, clean, and obedient. These parents tended to use physical punishment as the primary form of discipline. White-collar parents (those who had non-manual-labor occupations) wanted their children to be communicative, eager to learn, ready to share and cooperate, and be healthy and well. White-collar parents tended to use love-withdrawal and reasoning more than physical punishment as a means of disciplining their children. Although there are differences in the ways parents discipline their children, the differences are not so large that we could categorically say that blue-collar parents "typically" use physical punishment while other parents "typically" use other means (Erlanger 1974).

What explains the class differences that do exist? Kohn suggests that the differences are a consequence of the parents' value systems, which are a product of parents' experiences at work. Success at white-collar jobs is based on self-direction, creativity, and skill at interpersonal relationships. Success at blue-collar jobs is based on the ability to work effectively in a routine and standardized environment and to manipulate things (as in work on an assembly line). Getting ahead on a blue-collar job depends on collective efforts. Opportunities for self-direction and creativity are limited—creativity is not typically valued in assembly line or routinized work settings.

Parents, then, socialize their children for success in the world the parents themselves know. Parents "know" what it takes to succeed in the world they work in, and they choose socialization techniques and discipline forms that they feel will best prepare their child to succeed in the world.

The differences in discipline patterns are not entirely a function of occupation or social class. Factors such as race, ethnicity, and religion also influence how parents discipline their children. Blacks and Latinos and those who belong to fundamentalist religious groups are more likely to use physical punishment compared to whites or those who do not belong to fundamentalist churches (Straus, Gelles, and Steinmetz 1980). Fundamentalists often justify their use of physical punishment as called for by biblical scripture (Greven 1991). Blacks' and Latinos' use of physical punishment may be partially the function of social and economic factors and partially a cultural adaptation to living in dangerous environments. Black and Latino parents will often justify the use of physical punishment as the only resource they have to protect their children from violence outside the home (see, e.g., Kotlowitz 1991).

A second example of how parents' perceptions of the traits their children will need to succeed in the world influences discipline techniques is research that finds that boys are more likely than girls to be physically punished (Straus, 1993; Wolfner and Gelles 1993). Most studies of physical punishment and discipline find that parents are more likely to use physical punishment on their sons than their daughters. The rate of physical punishment of boys is sometimes double that for girls (Straus 1994). Parents report that they believe that the life conditions for adult males involve much more violence than do those for adult females. Thus parents tend to use more physical punishment with their sons to prepare the boys for the harsh, violent world they must cope with as adults (Straus 1971).

The findings that social class and sex of the child influence socialization techniques and the use of physical punishment underscore a larger theory of socialization that has been referred to as the "linkage theory" (Inkeles 1960;

BOX 10-3: THE GLOBAL VIEW

Sweden's Law Prohibiting Physical Punishment of Children

Most Americans take for granted that spanking children is a necessary, normal, and useful means of disciplining children (Gelles and Straus 1988; also see Chapter 15). Few Americans think that spanking can or will lead to the abuse of children. In Sweden, parents are required to think twice before hitting their children, because in 1979 the Swedish Parliament enacted legislation that made it illegal for parents to strike or spank their children.

The Swedish Children's Rights Commission argued that the primary purpose of an anti-spanking law would be to prevent *aga*, the beating of children. The Commission believed that by sanctioning any form of physical punishment a society was also sanctioning severe and abusive discipline.

How is the law working? Even though more than 10 years have passed since the law was enacted, it is probably still too early to say. A study that compared American parents' use of physical punishment and violence with Swedish parents' found that Swedes were less likely to

use physical punishment but equally likely to use severe forms of violence toward their children—see Table 10-1 (Gelles and Edfeldt 1986).

However, that study was carried out only three years after the anti-corporal-punishment law was passed. A law that is designed to force parents to think twice before spanking is likely to take some time filtering down into everyday behavior. Moreover, there is no penalty for violating the law—the Swedish Parliament did not provide for a punishment. That there is no punishment may strike Americans as odd, but it is quite consistent with the anti-spanking law. The law was designed to change a pattern of thought that required punishment for misdeeds—and thus justified spanking children.

Today, it appears that the major consequence of the law is that Swedish parents have begun to think twice about the utility and acceptability of physical punishment. Swedes, unlike Americans, see physical punishment linked to the abuse of children (Gelles and Edfeldt 1986).

Table 10-1
Violence Toward
Children in the
United States and
Sweden (in
percentages)

Table 10-1 Violence Toward Children in the United States and Sweden (in percentages)

Type of Violence	United States		Sweden	
	1975	Ever	1980	Ever
1. Threw things at	5.4	9.0	3.6	13.2
2. Pushed, grabbed, or shoved	40.5	46.0	49.4	63.3
3. Hit (spanked or slapped)	58.2	71.0	27.5	51.2
4. Kicked, bit, or hit with a fist	3.2	8.0	2.2	8.4
5. Hit with an object[a]	13.4	20.0	2.4	7.7
6. Beat up	1.3	4.0	3.0	8.0
7. Threatened with a weapon	0.1	2.8	0.4	1.5
8. Used a weapon	0.1	2.9	0.4	1.3
All forms of violence (3-8)	63.0	73.0	29.8	66.0
Severe violence (Index A: 4-8)	14.2	—	4.6	—
Severe violence (Index B: 4, 6-8)	3.6	—	4.1	—

SOURCE: "Violence Towards Children in the United States and Sweden" by Richard J. Gelles and Ake W. Edfeldt, 1986, *Child Abuse and Neglect: The International Journal* 10(4), p. 506. Copyright © 1986 by Elsevier Science Ltd. Adapted by permission.
a. In the United States, this item referred to attempted or completed hits. In Sweden, the item referred only to completed hits.

Kohn 1963; Straus 1971). The linkage theory proposes that socialization patterns and choice of discipline technique are not simply a function of the individual and idiosyncratic choices made by parents. Instead, socialization techniques tend to result from the social structure in which the parents and family are embedded. The economic and occupational world the parents and family are enmeshed in exert a significant influence over how they go about raising their children.

The Consequences of Discipline

Students of child socialization have devoted extensive research to assessing the impact and consequences of varying forms of discipline. Baumrind (1967, 1968, 1971, 1972, 1980, 1989) assessed the consequences of the three types of parents she had identified (authoritarian, permissive, and authoritative).

Children of authoritative parents were found to be the most socially competent. These children were characterized by Baumrind as being energetic,

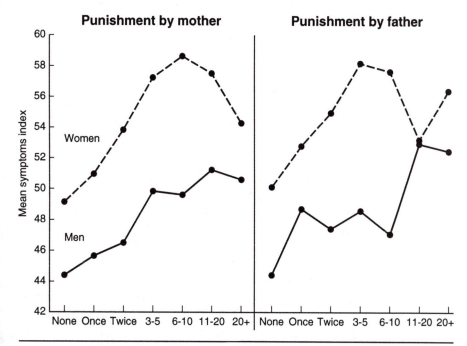

Figure 10-2 Teenage Depressive Symptoms Caused by Parental Corporal Punishment

SOURCE: "Corporal Punishment of Children and Depression and Suicide in Adulthood" by Murray A. Straus, in *Coercion and Punishment in Long Term Perspective,* edited by Joan McCord, 1994, New York: Cambridge University Press. Copyright © 1994 by Cambridge University Press. Adapted with the permission of Cambridge University Press.

friendly, curious, self-reliant, and cheerful. Children of authoritarian parents were less cheerful, moody, apprehensive, unhappy, easily annoyed, and vulnerable to stress (Belsky, Lerner, and Spanier 1984). Children with permissive parents were found to be somewhat impulsive-aggressive (the stereotypical uncontrolled child of a permissive parent). These children had low levels of self-reliance, were frequently out of control, and had difficulty controlling their impulses (Baumrind 1967; Belsky et al. 1984). Children with permissive parents were more cheerful than those who had authoritarian parents.

Not surprising, children who experienced physical punishment are more likely to be aggressive than children whose parents used psychological forms of discipline (Feshbach and Feshbach 1972; Hoffman 1970; Straus 1993). More surprising is the finding that the more children experience corporal punishment, the more likely they are as adults to be depressed and think about suicide—see Figure 10-2 (Straus 1993). Finally, researchers find that the consistent use of discipline is more effective than inconsistency in controlling behavior (Hetherington, Cox, and Cox 1978; Patterson 1976).

SUMMING UP

Our identities, understandings, and behavior are shaped by the lifelong process of socialization. Families are a major agent of socialization and are especially significant agents of child socialization. For many years, social scientists were divided into two camps: those who believed that behavior is the product of nature (genes) and those who saw behavior as determined by nurture (child socialization). Today, most social scientists agree that nature and nurture interact.

There are three major schools or theories of child socialization. Freud saw socialization as the struggle between a willful, pleasure-seeking child and parents intent on proper behavior. Freud believed that personality developed in stages and consisted of three parts: the **id,** the **ego,** and the **superego.**

Piaget also examined personality development in terms of stages. He divided development into four stages: **sensorimotor, preoperational, concrete operational,** and **formal operational.**

Both Cooley and G. H. Mead stressed the role of symbolic interaction in the development of the self. Cooley introduced the concept of the **looking-glass self,** whereas Mead held that children learn to take the role of the other in the play stage and developed a **generalized other** in the game stage. The socialized "me" continues to provide direction for the spontaneous "I."

Although the general debate between nurture and nature may have cooled, there is still significant debate concerning the issue of nature and nurture on the development and behavior of males and females. Here the debate about biological determinants of behavior versus differential socialization still rages. Clearly, there are biological differences between males and females, but just as clearly, boys and girls are treated differently by all the agents of socialization. While nature and nurture still may combine, the impact of socialization is a strong influence in male and female behavior.

How children should be disciplined is a final issue in child socialization. Here the debate centers on whether children need to be punished, and if so, how much and what type of punishment. The accumulated evidence strongly suggests that, although children need discipline, physical and emotional punishments are generally detrimental for children.

REFERENCES

Aries, Philippe. 1962. *Centuries of Childhood: A Social History of Family Life.*

Translated by Robert Baldick. New York: Alfred A. Knopf.

Baumrind, Diana. 1967. "Child Care Practices Anteceding Three Patterns of Preschool

Behavior." *Genetic Psychology Monographs* 75(February): 43-83.

————. 1968. "Authoritarian Versus Authoritative Parental Control." *Adolescence* 3(Fall):255-72.

————. 1971. "Current Patterns of Parental Authority." *Developmental Psychology Monographs* 4(1, Part 2).

————. 1972. "Socialization and Instrumental Competence in Young Children." Pp. 202-24 in *The Young Child: Reviews of Research,* Vol. 2, edited by Willard W. Hartup. Washington, DC: National Association for the Education of Young Children.

————. 1980. "New Directions in Socialization Research." *American Psychologist* 35(July):639-52.

————. 1989. "Rearing Competent Children." Pp. 349-78 in *Child Development Today and Tomorrow,* edited by William Damon. San Francisco: Jossey-Bass.

Belsky, Jay, Richard M. Lerner, and Graham B. Spanier. 1984. *The Child in the Family.* Reading, MA: Addison-Wesley.

Caldwell, Bettye. 1964. "The Effects of Infant Care." Pp. 9-87 in *Review of Child Development Research,* Vol. 1, edited by Martin L. Hoffman and Lois W. Hoffman. New York: Russell Sage.

Cooley, Charles Horton. 1902. *Human Nature and Social Order.* New York: Scribner.

Curtiss, Susan. 1977. *Genie: Psycholinguistic Study of a Modern Day Wild Child.* New York: Academic Press.

Darwin, Charles. 1859/1958. *The Origin of Spcies.* New York: Mentor.

Davis, Kingsley. 1940. "Extreme Social Isolation of a Child." *American Journal of Sociology* 45(January):554-64.

————. 1947. "Final Note on a Case of Extreme Isolation." *American Journal of Sociology* 50(March):432-37.

Erlanger, Howard. 1974. "Social Class and Corporal Punishment in Child Rearing: A Reassessment." *American Sociological Review* 39(February):68-85.

Fausto-Sterling, Ann. 1985. *Myths of Gender: Biological Theories About Women and Men.* New York: Basic Books.

Feshbach, Norma D. and Seymore Feshbach. 1972. "Children's Aggression." Pp. 248-302 in *The Young Child: Reviews of Research,* Vol. 2, edited by Willard W. Hartup. Washington, DC: National Association for the Education of Young Children.

Freeman, D. 1983. *Margaret Mead and Samoa: The Making and Unmaking of an Anthropological Myth.* Cambridge, MA: Harvard University Press.

Freud, Sigmund. [1953] 1974. *The Standard Edition of the Complete Psychological Works of Sigmund Freud.* Rev. ed. Translated from German by J. Strachly in collaboration with Anna Freud, assisted by Alex Strachly and Alan Tyson. London: Hogarth Press and the Institute of Psychoanalysis.

Gelles, Richard J. and Ake Edfeldt. 1986. "Violence Towards Children in the United States and Sweden." *Child Abuse and Neglect: The International Journal* 10(4):501-10.

Gelles, Richard J. and Murray A. Straus. 1988. *Intimate Violence.* New York: Simon & Schuster.

Greven, Philip. 1991. *Spare the Child: The Religious Roots of Punishment and the Psychological Impact of Physical Abuse.* New York: Alfred A. Knopf.

Harris, Marvin. 1968. *The Rise of Anthropological Theory.* New York: Crowell.

Hetherington, E. Mavis, Martha Cox, and Roger Cox. 1978. "The Development of Children in Mother-Headed Families." Pp. 117-46 in *The American Family: Dying or Developing,* edited by Harvard Hoffman and David Reiss. New York: Plenum.

Hoffman, Martin L. 1970. "Moral Development." Pp. 261-359 in *Carmichael's Manual of Child Psychology,* Vol. 2, edited by Paul H. Mussen. New York: John Wiley.

Hsu, Francis L. K. 1985. "The Self in Cross-Cultural Perspective." Pp. 24-55 in *Culture and Self-Esteem: Asian and Western Perspectives,* edited by Anthony J. Marsella, George DeVos, and Francis L. K. Hsu. New York: Tavistock.

Inkeles, Alex. 1960. "Industrial Man: The Relation of Status to Experience, Perception, and Value." *American Journal of Sociology* 66(July):1-31.

Jacklin, Carol N. 1977. "Sex Differences and Their Relationship to Sex Equity in Learning and

Teaching." Paper presented at the National Institute of Education, Washington, DC.

Johansson, Sheila R. 1987. "Neglect, Abuse, and Avoidable Death: Parental Investment and the Mortality of Infants and Children in the European Tradition." Pp. 57-93 in *Child Abuse and Neglect: Biosocial Dimensions,* edited by Richard J. Gelles and Jane B. Lancaster. New York: Aldine de Gruyter.

Kohn, Melvin. 1963. "Social Class and Parent-Child Relationships: An Interpretation." *American Journal of Sociology* 68(January):471-80.

Kohn, Melvin and **Carmi Schooler.** 1983. *Work and Personality: An Inquiry Into the Impact of Social Stratification.* Norwood, NJ: Ablex.

Kotlowitz, Alex. 1991. *There Are No Children Here: The Story of Two Boys Growing Up in the Other America.* New York: Anchor Books.

Maccoby, Eleanor E. 1980. *Social Development: Psychological Growth and the Parent-Child Relationship.* New York: Harcourt Brace Jovanovich.

Maccoby, Eleanor E. and **Carol N. Jacklin.** 1974. *The Psychology of Sex Differences.* Stanford, CA: Stanford University Press.

Marini, Margaret Mooney. 1990. "Sex and Gender: What Do We Know?" *Sociological Forum* 5(1): 95-120.

Mead, George Herbert. 1934. *Mind, Self, and Society.* Chicago: University of Chicago Press.

Mead, Margaret. 1935. *Sex and Temperament in Three Primitive Societies.* New York: William Morrow.

Money, John and **Anke Ehrhardt.** 1972. *Man and Woman, Boy and Girl.* Baltimore: Johns Hopkins University Press.

Musgrave, Peter W. 1988. *Socialising Contexts.* Sydney: Allen & Unwin.

Ortner, Sherry B. 1974. "Is Female to Male as Nature Is to Culture?" Pp. 67-68 in *Women, Culture, and Society,* edited by Michelle Z. Rosaldo and Louise Lamphere. Stanford, CA: Stanford University Press.

Patterson, Gerald R. 1976. *Living With Children: New Methods for Parents and Teachers.* Champaign, IL: Research Press.

Pavlov, Ivan P. 1927. *Conditioned Reflexes.* Trans. G. V. Anrep. London, UK: Oxford University Press.

Phillips, John L., Jr. 1975. *The Origins of Intellect: Piaget's Theory.* 2nd ed. San Francisco: Freeman.

Piaget, Jean and **Baerbel Inhelder.** 1969. *The Psychology of the Child.* New York: Basic Books.

Provence, Sally. 1989. "Infants in Institutions Revisited." *Zero to Three* 9(February):1-4.

Reiss, David. 1992. "The Cold War Is Over in the Nature vs. Nurture Debate." *Child and Adolescent Behavior Letter* 7(July):1ff.

Reiss, Ira L. 1965. "The Universality of the Family: A Conceptual Analysis." *Journal of Marriage and the Family* 27 (November):443-53.

Rosaldo, Michelle Z. and **Louise Lamphere,** eds. 1974. *Women, Culture, and Society.* Stanford, CA: Stanford University Press.

Ruch, Jean and **Jay Shurley.** 1985. "Genie as an Adult." Paper presented at the Center for Advanced Study in Behavioral Sciences, Stanford, CA, March.

Rutter, Michael. 1988. "Functions and Consequences of Relationships: Some Psychopathological Considerations." Pp. 332-353 in *Relationships Within Families: Mutual Influences,* edited by Robert Hinde and Joan Stephenson Hinde. Oxford, UK: Oxford University Press.

Rymer, Russ. 1993. *Genie: An Abused Child's Flight From Silence.* New York: Harper Collins.

Sewell, William. 1952. "Infant Training and the Personality of the Child." *American Journal of Sociology* 58(September):150-59.

Skinner, B. F. 1938. *The Behavior of Organisms: An Experimental Approach.* New York: Appleton-Century.

Spitz, Rene A. 1945. "Hospitality: An Inquiry Into the Genesis of Psychiatric Conditions in Early Childhood." In *The Psychoanalytic Study of the Child,* edited by Anna Freud. New York: International Universities Press.

Straus, Murray A. 1971. "Some Social Antecedents of Physical Punishment: A Linkage Theory Interpretation." *Journal of Marriage and the Family* 33(November):658-63.

———. 1994. "Corporal Punishment of Children and Depression and Suicide in Adulthood." In *Coercion and Punishment in Long-Term Perspective,* edited by Joan McCord. New York: Cambridge University Press.

Straus, Murray A., Richard J. Gelles, and Suzanne K. Steinmetz. 1980. *Behind Closed Doors: Violence in the American Family.* New York: Anchor/Doubleday.

Tavris, Carol. 1992. *The Mismeasure of Women: Why Women Are Not the Better Sex, the Inferior Sex, or the Opposite Sex.* New York: Touchstone.

Walum, Laurel Richardson. 1977. *The Dynamics of Sex and Gender: A Sociological Perspective.* Chicago: Rand McNally.

Washburn, Sheldon L. and Irven DeVore. 1961. "The Social Behavior of Baboons and Early Man." Pp. 96-100 in *Social Life of Early Man,* edited by Sheldon L. Washburn. Chicago: Aldine.

Watson, John B. 1924. *Behavior.* New York: Norton.

Wolfner, Glenn and Richard J. Gelles. 1993. "A Profile of Violence Toward Children: A National Study." *Child Abuse and Neglect: The International Journal* 17(2):197-212.

CHAPTER 11

■ Work and Family

Mornings at the Alberts' home are hectic. Alan, a marketing director for a bank, is up at 5:30 a.m. He scans the morning paper, gulps a cup of coffee, and then wakes his 4-year-old son, Cal. His 11-month-old daughter, Alex, is already awake and playing (or crying) in her crib. Alan puts in a load of laundry and hopes that the cycle will end before his wife Catherine is ready to take her morning shower. Catherine Albert, an Assistant Professor of Psychology at the local university, rises at 6:15 a.m. She showers, dresses quickly, and prepares breakfast for her son and daughter, all the while mentally reviewing her lecture notes for her 8 a.m. class. Alan is ready to leave home at 7 a.m. He grabs his briefcase, kisses Catherine and his daughter, and takes Cal with him. Cal is dropped off at the university child care center, and Alan then drives an hour to work. If he is lucky and the traffic isn't bad, he is at his desk by 8:30 a.m. Catherine dresses Alex and hurries off with her to a local day care provider who watches four young children in her home. This morning Alex is cranky and doesn't want her mother to leave. Catherine stays with Alex for a few minutes but then leaves for the university, which is 10 minutes away. Catherine parks in the last spot in the faculty lot closest to her office, rushes to her office to pick up the papers she is returning to her students, and arrives in class at 8:05 a.m. She launches into her lecture amidst titters from her 50 or so students. When she realizes the titters are aimed at her, she glances down to notice a large glob of dried oatmeal stuck to the front of her blouse.

At 5 p.m. the process is reversed. Alan and Catherine leave work, rush to the child care center and day care provider, pick up Alex and Cal, and return home. Catherine prepares dinner while thumbing through the first set of exams she needs to correct that night. Alan glances at the mail, changes Alex's diaper, and sets out the paperwork he wants to do that evening. After dinner, while the children play, both Alan and Catherine fall asleep in front of the evening news.

Next to our family roles, work roles are the most significant and demanding roles we enact. The juggling of both work and family roles now defines the relationship between work and families.

Scheduling of work, hours at work, work responsibilities, and the possibility of geographic mobility all influence workers, their work roles, their family roles, and their families. Alan, for instance, works at a firm where it is expected that you will be at your desk at 8:30 a.m. and stay there until 4:45 p.m. If one of the children is sick during the day, Catherine is expected to be available, as Alan does not believe he can leave work.

Family structures and organizations influence the workplace and the organization of work. For example, more than half of all married women who have children are in the workforce. Catherine, for instance, has only recently returned to work after being home with Alex for eight months. While she was on leave, her department hired a temporary faculty member to teach her courses. This caused the department to exceed its personnel budget, which resulted in the Dean asking its faculty and staff to cut back in other areas. Catherine stills worries that her colleagues will blame her for having their travel budget cut. More important, Catherine worries that she may have more difficulty gaining tenure, being promoted, or receiving merit raises, compared to her male colleagues or her female colleagues who do not have children.

This chapter examines the interface between work and the family. The chapter begins by looking at recent trends in the work/family relationship, including changes in the structure of work and the workplace, the increase in the number of women in the workplace, and changes in family structures and how these changes affect the workplace. The second section considers the relationship between work roles and family roles. Next, we consider the influence of work on family roles and family life. The final section looks at how family life affects work and the workplace.

RECENT TRENDS IN WORK AND FAMILY PATTERNS

Prior to the Industrial Revolution, the family was the primary unit of economic production in the United States and England (see Chapter 4). Peasant and laboring-class families produced food and clothing for themselves and to sell for cash or to barter for goods and services. Before the 1900s, pre-Industrial Revolution society was agrarian and family members worked on farms. Well into the 19th century most of the goods produced in the United States were produced by artisans. All family members—wives, husbands, children, and other relatives—participated in the family economic activity (Piotrokowski, Rapoport, and Rapoport 1987). Crafts were learned during years of apprenticeship. Most artisans, such as carpenters, silversmiths, coopers, and others either worked for themselves or worked at home at piece rates (they were paid for each product they produced), not hourly rates. Many artisans worked in their own homes. Even those who worked outside the home rarely worked under the direct supervision of the person who paid them. Products and goods were produced by the artisan and sold to the consumer; products were not produced for a company, with the work directed by a foreman or supervisor.

The Social Organization of Work and Production

Industrialization began the process of separating the location of production activities from the family home. Legislation that regulated the work and work hours of children and women resulted in women staying home to care for their children. The workplace became a place for men, unmarried women, or married women who did not have children. Women with children were mainly out of the workplace and were assigned the role of homemaker. The measure of a good provider in the age of industrialization was whether a man's wife worked. If she did, he was not considered an adequate breadwinner.

In the early years of industrialization the trend was toward longer hours and more days worked each year. Craftsmen worked from 14 to 18 hours per day, and the number of days off declined from the 15th century on. By 1850, the average workweek in French cities was 70 hours. Daily and weekly hours also climbed in England (Wilensky 1961).

The Industrial Revolution that began in the early 19th century changed the social organization of work and had profound effects on workers, work roles, families, and, ultimately, family life. Mechanized farm equipment reduced the need for farm laborers. Goods that had been produced by artisans were now produced in factories. Work moved from the home to factories and was carried out under the direct supervision of employers. Manufacturing jobs could be learned in a matter of weeks, not years. Workers were more easily replaced. Earnings were based on hours worked and were set by owners or managers, not workers. High-skilled jobs were replaced with low-skilled jobs. Creativity and craftsmanship were replaced by manufacturing and the assembly line.

Some early industrial mills did employ family members together and sometimes compensated families as a unit. Boardinghouses established by the Lowell, Massachusetts textile mills for young girls were modeled on the family (Piotrokowski et al. 1987). Eventually, these paternal factory organizations gave way to more bureaucratic and impersonal models, and factories replaced workshops and households as centers of economic production.

The burden of labor declined after 1850. From 1900 to 1950, the hourly workweek was reduced by 4.2 hours per week per decade in the United States (see Table 11-1). Similar declines occurred in Great Britain, Canada, and Germany. The reduction in the workweek varied by occupation, with the greatest decreases in manufacturing, mining, and agriculture. Professionals, executives, and civil servants benefited little (Wilensky 1961).

Today, the postindustrial economy has replaced industrialization. We are now in the midst of a social revolution as profound as the agrarian and industrial revolutions. Sociologist Daniel Bell (1973) argues that new information technologies are changing the basis of social organization and producing a new "postindustrial" or "information society."

Year	Average Hours Worked
1901	58.4
1948	40.8
1960	38.6
1965	38.8
1970	37.1
1975	36.1
1980	35.3
1985	34.9
1990	34.5
1991	34.3

Table 11-1 Average Workweek of Non-agricultural Workers

SOURCE: U.S. Bureau of the Census (1992, p. 403).

Computers are the most visible sign of the new postindustrial society. Information and services have gradually replaced manufacturing as the focus of work. The continuing decline in manufacturing jobs is the result of more and more goods, such as automobiles, being produced by means of high technology. In addition, jobs are lost in the United States as manufacturing plants are established in Third World countries that offer an abundance of cheap labor and minimal government control over manufacturing. In the postindustrial society, the United States has gradually ceased to be a nation that manufactures or makes goods and products and has increasingly become a nation that consumes goods made in other countries. The nature of work is changing, and this has profound implications for families.

Economic and Occupational Changes

There are a number of significant trends that have occurred in the American economy and the workplace in the past 30 years that relate to the work-family interrelationship. The major trends have been a decline in the real earnings (the buying power of wages earned) of American workers, a decline in the rate of growth of production of American workers, and a change in the nature of available employment (Cyert and Mowery 1987). Manufacturing jobs are being replaced by jobs in four industry groups: wholesale and retail trade; transportation and utilities; finance, insurance, and real estate; and services (Cyert and Mowery 1987).

Unemployment occurred as a result of recessions that occurred in the years 1974–1975, 1981–1982, and 1990–1992. More important, certain types of

The greatest growth in jobs is in occupations that require the use of computers for information processing and services.

jobs simply ceased to exist, such as manufacturing, mining, and construction jobs. Moreover, there was a growth in structural unemployment, unemployment caused by changes in the nature of the economy, automation, and technological change. Structural unemployment was the result of mismatches between worker skills, work locations, and types of jobs that were available (Cyert and Mowery 1987). An unemployed steelworker in the Northeast found little comfort in the expansion of high-tech employment in Palo Alto, California. As white-collar jobs continued to expand, blue-collar employment opportunities declined. The greatest impact of the decline of blue-collar jobs has been felt in the inner-city and minority communities, especially in the "rust belt" cities in the Midwest and the Northeast.

During the past 30 years, men's rate of labor force participation has declined while women's has increased. In 1991, 70.2% of all males aged 16 and older were employed, a decline from 72% in 1980 and 76.2% in 1970 (U.S. Bureau of the Census 1992b). There was a greater decline in workforce participation among black men compared to white men. Latino men, however, had greater rates of workforce participation than either blacks or whites. Declines in white male participation in the labor force were primarily the result of white males retiring at younger ages. Black men, on the other hand, suffered from the effects of unemployment and increasingly dropped out of the labor force after failing to find work (Blau and Ferber 1986). The number of displaced or discouraged male workers also increased in rural areas due to the decrease in farm product prices and the continued consolidation of farms.

The most profound change in the labor force, and the one that has had the most significant impact on contemporary families, is the increase in women's labor force participation, especially participation by mothers of pre-school children. From 1890 until World War II, less than 3 in 10 married women were in the labor force (see Figure 11-1). By 1984, more than half of

Changing
Employment
Patterns of Men
and Women

BOX 11-1: DIVERSE FAMILIES

African American Families and Female Employment

Race has a significant effect on work opportunities, work, and the impact of work on families. In recent years, African American women have come to make up the majority of the black workforce. Black women make up more than half of the total employment of blacks, whereas white women make up about 44.7% of employed whites. The differences are even greater for certain types of employment. Black women make up more than 60% of black professionals compared to white women, who constitute 50% of white professional employment. Black women make up a greater proportion of managers and technical workers compared to white women.

One reason why African American women make up a larger proportion of the black workforce compared to white women in the white workforce is economic necessity. More black women must manage on their own, without a wage-earning housemate or partner (see Chapter 5). However, even black women who have employed partners are still more likely to work than their white counterparts. Again, the reason is partially economic—it takes two paychecks for a black family to match the paycheck that one white wage earner can bring in.

Employer attitudes, prejudice, and discrimination are a second explanation. If and when businesses, corporations, or organizations hire more black employees, they tend to hire females rather than males. Employers tend to believe that black women are less assertive, more accommodating, and show less resentment and hostility than black males. The desire not to have black men work with white women may also be a reason for hiring preferences.

SOURCE: Andrew Hacker (1992).

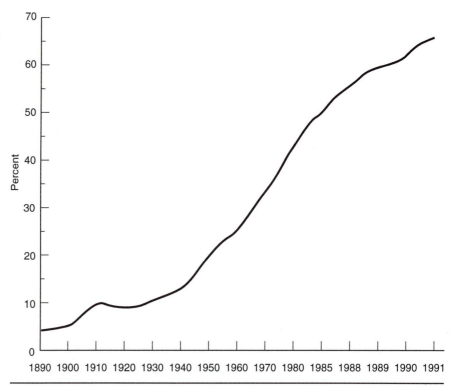

SOURCE: U.S. Bureau of the Census (1992b, p. 382).

all women (53.7%) were employed, and by 1991 the percentage had risen to 57.3 (U.S. Bureau of Census 1992b). The pre-World War II employed woman was typically young and single. During and after the war, there was an increase in older married women entering the labor force (Menaghan and Parcel 1990). Younger married women began to enter the labor force in increasing numbers after 1960.

The most striking change in women's labor force participation is the increase in employed mothers, especially mothers of babies and preschoolers (Hoffman 1989; Menaghan and Parcel 1990). Few married women worked outside the home in 1890 (see Figure 11-1). In 1991, two thirds (66.8%) of all married women with children were employed (U.S. Bureau of the Census 1992b). More important, 59.9% of mothers with children under 6 years of age were employed in 1991 (Table 11-2). Divorced mothers' participation in the labor force is even greater—nearly 8 in 10 divorced mothers work outside the home (Hayghe 1984).

The proportion of U.S. mothers who work outside the home is comparable to mothers in other developed countries (see Table 11-3). In Denmark,

Year	Total	No Children Under 18	With Children Under 18	Children Under 6	Children Under 1
1975	44.5	44.0	44.9	36.8	30.8
1980	50.2	46.0	54.3	45.3	39.0
1986	54.6	48.2	61.4	53.9	49.8
1988	56.7	49.1	65.2	57.4	51.9
1991	58.5	51.2	66.8	59.9	55.8

Table 11-2
Percentage of Married Women in the Labor Force, by Age of Youngest Child, 1975–1991

SOURCE: U.S. Bureau of the Census (1992b, p. 388, Tables 620, 621).

	Percentage of Mothers in the Labor Force With Children	
Country	Under Age 18	Under Age 3
United States	65	53
Canada	67[a]	58
Denmark	86	84
West Germany	48	40
France	66	60
Italy	44	45
Sweden	89[a]	86[b]
United Kingdom	59	37

Table 11-3 Mothers in the Labor Force for Selected Countries, 1988

SOURCE: "New Realities of the American Family" by Dennis A. Ahlburg and Carol J. De Vita, 1992, *Population Bulletin* 47(2), p. 26. Copyright © 1992 by Population Research Bureau, Inc. Adapted by permission.
NOTE: Data for United States, Canada, and Sweden are for 1988; data for other countries are for 1986.
a. Children under age 16.
b. Children under age 7.

more than 8 of 10 mothers with children under age 18 work, and nearly 90% of mothers in Sweden with children under age 16 work (Ahlburg and DeVita 1992).

The growth of female employment has increased the number of two-income families. Families with both a male and a female wage earner are called **dual-earner households.**

The nature of women's participation in the labor force is more diverse than that of men. Women are more likely to work part-time and part-year, and, as in the case of Catherine, described in the introduction of this chapter, women are more likely to interrupt work to care for ill children, aged parents, or young family members (Masnick and Bane 1980; Menaghan and Parcel 1990; Voydanoff 1987; U.S. Bureau of the Census 1987). Relatively few women work continuously over their entire adult lives. A study of the work history of 5,000 families indicated that about 1 in 5 married women, aged 18 to 47, was continuously employed for 7 of 10 years (Masnick and Bane 1980).

The most likely reason for leaving the labor force is that women cycle out for childbearing and child rearing.

The types of work that women do and the financial rewards are also different from men. Women are most likely to work in technical, administrative, and support occupations, holding positions such as technicians, retail sales workers, secretaries, and typists. The next most likely class of occupations includes managerial and professional jobs, such as teachers, writers, nurses, and managers. Women also are employed in service occupations, where they work as child care workers, waitresses, health aides, or hairdressers. About 8% (7.6%) of employed women are laborers and assembly line workers (U.S. Bureau of the Census 1992b).

The division of labor by gender is not strictly an American phenomenon; it exists across time and cultures. Table 11-4 presents results of anthropologist George Murdock's (1937) analysis of comparative data on the division of labor across cultures. The table shows that in most cultures, at all levels of social complexity, most tasks are assigned to *either* males *or* females.

Women still earn considerably less than men. Women have generally earned between 60% and 64% of what men earn (O'Neill 1985). By the mid-1980s, women earned between 72 and 75 cents for each $1.00 earned by a man (Nasar 1992; U.S. Bureau of Census 1992b). The earning gap ranges from women computer programmers who earn 81 cents for each $1.00 earned by a male programmer to female sales supervisors who earn 55 cents for each $1.00 earned by a male in a similar position (U.S. Bureau of the Census 1992b).

There are a number of theories for why the wage gap exists between men and women. One theory is that the persistent gap is a function of occupational sex segregation (Quarm 1984; Roos 1981). This theory explains that women are channeled into specific occupations, such as nurses, secretaries, teachers, and child care workers, that pay less than typical male jobs. A second explanation is that there exists segregation within jobs. Thus, within a specific occupation, women are placed into lower-status, lower-paying positions. For example, women entering medicine cluster into a small number of specialties, such as pediatrics and obstetrics, that pay less than specialties where males predominate, such as surgery (Reskin and Roos 1990). Another explanation is that women earn less than men in similar occupations because women are more likely to cycle out of the workforce for childbearing and child rearing, thus failing to accrue seniority and higher-status positions within occupations (Jacobs 1989). Last, the fact that males are still considered the "primary" breadwinner and "need" higher salaries to support their families influences the gender income gap.

One frequent question asked about employment is why do women, and particularly mothers of school-aged children, work? Of course, as feminist theorists point out, this seems to be a question directed only at women. No

	Number of Societies in Which Activity Is Performed by					Table 11-4
	Men Always	Men Usually	Either Equally	Women Equally	Women Always	Comparative Data on the Division of Labor, by Sex
Metalworking	78	0	0	0	0	
Weapon making	121	1	0	0	0	
Pursuit of sea mammals	34	1	0	0	0	
Hunting	166	13	0	0	0	
Manufacture of musical instruments	45	2	0	0	1	
Boatbuilding	91	4	4	0	1	
Mining and quarrying	35	1	1	0	1	
Work in wood and bark	113	9	5	1	1	
Work in stone	68	3	2	0	2	
Trapping or catching small animals	128	13	4	1	2	
Work in bone, horn, and shell	67	4	3	0	3	
Lumbering	104	4	3	1	6	
Fishing	98	34	19	3	4	
Manufacture of ceremonial objects	37	1	13	0	1	
Herding	38	8	4	0	5	
House building	86	32	25	3	14	
Clearing of land for agriculture	73	22	17	5	13	
Net making	44	6	4	2	11	
Trade	51	28	20	8	7	
Dairy operations	17	4	3	1	13	
Manufacture of ornaments	24	3	40	6	18	
Agriculture—soil preparation and planting	31	23	33	20	37	
Manufacture of leather products	29	3	9	3	32	
Body mutilation (e.g., tattooing)	16	14	44	22	20	
Erection and dismantling of shelter	14	2	5	6	22	
Hide preparation	31	2	4	4	49	
Tending of fowl and small animals	21	4	8	1	39	
Agriculture—crop tending and harvesting	10	15	35	39	44	
Gathering of shellfish	9	4	8	7	25	
Manufacture of nontextile fabrics	14	0	9	2	32	
Fire making and tending	18	6	25	22	62	
Burden bearing	12	6	33	20	57	
Preparation of drinks and narcotics	20	1	13	8	57	
Manufacture of thread and cordage	23	2	11	10	73	
Basket making	25	3	10	6	82	
Mat making	16	2	6	4	61	
Weaving	19	2	2	6	67	
Gathering fruits, berries, and nuts	12	3	15	13	63	
Fuel gathering	22	1	10	19	89	
Pottery making	13	2	6	8	77	
Preservation of meat and fish	8	2	10	14	74	
Manufacture and repair of clothing	12	3	8	9	95	
Gathering herbs, roots, and seeds	8	1	11	7	74	
Cooking	5	1	9	28	158	
Water carrying	7	0	5	7	119	
Grain grinding	2	4	5	13	114	

SOURCE: "Comparative Data on the Division of Labor by Sex" by George P. Murdock, 1937, *Social Forces* 15(May), p. 552. Copyright © 1937 by The University of North Carolina Press. Adapted by permission.

one asks why men, and men with children, work. The answer is that women and mothers work for the same reasons men and fathers do. Most women who work outside the home do so because they are members of dual-earner households needing additional income or are the sole source of support for themselves and their children (Voydanoff 1987). Two thirds of employed women are single, divorced, widowed, separated, or are married to men who earn less than $10,000 per year (Mortimer and Sorensen 1984; Voydanoff 1987). As we noted in the beginning of this section, there has been a decline in real earnings of the American worker in the past 30 years. Although the actual amount of money earned has increased, what the average worker can purchase with a week's pay has actually declined due to inflation. Combine this with an increase in both the divorce rate and the number of single-parent households, and there are real and significant economic pressures for women to work.

Other factors also pull women to work. The nonmonetary gains from work include increased independence, self-esteem, approval from others, and feelings of accomplishment (Cotton, Antill, and Cunningham 1989; Hoffman 1963).

Structural factors can influence the desire to work and the desirability of working. Availability of jobs, availability of part-time work, age of mother and

---

BOX 11-2: THE FAMILY OVER TIME

Child and Adolescent Employment

Children and adolescents were part of the labor force through the 19th century. Children and adolescent wage earners and laborers can be traced back to the colonial apprenticeship system. The rapid industrialization of the United States following the Civil War increased children's participation in the labor force (Dorne 1989). Census Bureau data indicate that, in 1870, one of every eight children under 18 years of age was employed. By 1890, it was one in six—mostly agricultural or industrial workers (Dorne 1989). Hours were long and wages low. Child labor laws were enacted in the early 20th century to regulate the age at which children could legally begin to work and the number of hours they could work.

Although laws still prevent children under 15 years of age from participating in the workforce (with the exception of tasks such as delivering newspapers) and limits the nature and amount of work they do, the rise of the postindustrial service economy at the end of the 20th century has produced a new demand for adolescent workers. Data from the U.S. Bureau of the Census indicate that between 1947 and 1980 the labor force participation of school-aged and school-attending 16 and 17-year-olds increased by 65% for boys and by 240% for girls (Greenberger 1987), although the percentage has actually declined between 1980 and 1990 (U.S. Bureau of the Census 1992b). White, middle-class suburban adolescents are the most likely workers to engage in part-time jobs that require little skill and can be engaged in at night or on weekends (Lewin-Epstein 1981). Earnings often are used for luxury clothing items, stereos, cars, and recreation and are not directly used for family or personal necessities.

child, number of children, and health and disabilities of the worker or spouse all influence choices about working (Aneshensel and Rosen 1980; Ferber 1982; Oppenheimer 1977).

Changes in family structures and family patterns also influence the relationship between work roles and family roles. Two significant trends in the past 30 years have been the increase in the divorce rate (see Chapter 13) and increases in out-of-wedlock births. Both trends have resulted in an increased number of single-parent families, typically headed by women. Today, more than 20% of households with children under the age of 18 are headed by a woman as compared to fewer than 1 in 10 (8%) in 1960. Most of these households are characterized by significant economic disadvantage. More than half of all single-mother families fall below the poverty line (U.S. Bureau of the Census 1993). One source of this disadvantage is the absence of a second wage earner, and another source, as noted above, is the persistent earnings gap between men and women.

Changes in Family Patterns

WORK ROLES AND FAMILY ROLES

The structure of work and work roles has direct effects on family roles and family life. Similarly, family roles and family structure influence work and work roles. There is a tremendous variation in the nature of work and work activities as well as in family structures and family roles. Thus the interrelationship between the spheres of work and family is quite complex.

Among the most significant aspects of work roles that influence family life and family roles are (1) the amount of time worked and the location of work, (2) the nature of the work schedule, (3) the geographic mobility associated with work, (4) work-related travel, and (5) the need for child care. An additional consideration is the kind of family work that men and women engage in. Last, the interrelationship between work and family is influenced by whether there is one or two adult workers in the family.

Time, how it is spent and how it is scheduled, has a direct effect on family life and work. Some jobs, like Alan Albert's described in the beginning of this chapter, require a rigid full-time schedule. Hourly work is even more rigid, requiring workers to clock in and clock out. Hours missed from the normal

Time, Schedule, and Geographic Mobility

work schedule lead to a loss of wages, and sometimes there are wage incentives to work longer than the scheduled day (time-and-a-half pay for work beyond the normal workday, double pay for holidays). While many jobs involve work schedules that are Monday through Friday during the daylight hours, others involve work on weekends, holidays, and evening or early morning schedules. Catherine Albert has a flexible workday that allows her some freedom in the scheduling of her classes. Her work year, as a college professor, is from September to May. But she often teaches in the evening to make extra money and has taught summer school as well. Time at work may be spent in one location, such as an office, or in many locations. Alan Albert is often called upon to make business trips that last from 3 to 7 days. His business trips place extra stress on Catherine, who has to juggle child care for both children as well as her own work responsibilities.

Number of Hours Worked

The number of hours worked influences the nature, rhythm, and quality of family life. Over the past century there has been a steady decrease in the average hourly workweek of individuals employed in nonagricultural jobs (see Table 11-1). The decline in the average workweek is a function of the changing nature of work (declines in manufacturing jobs and increases in service-related jobs) and changes in the workforce—increasing proportions of women and adolescent (student) workers who work part-time (Hedges and Taylor 1980; Owen 1976).

Although the average workweek is less than 40 hours, there is considerable variation in the work hours of different occupations. Managers, farm workers, sales workers, and transport workers tend to work more than 40 hours per week (Voydanoff 1987). Full-time male workers are more likely to work more than 40 hours than are full-time female workers (Voydanoff 1987).

Marital status is also related to work hours. Married men work longer hours than unmarried men, but the reverse is true for women, with unmarried women working longer hours than married women (Taylor and Sekscenski 1982; Voydanoff 1987). Last, fathers of young children work longer hours than those of older children, most likely because fathers with young children are younger and have lower earnings (Moen and Moorehouse 1983). Thus married men, and especially married men with young children, have less time with their families and children.

Research indicates that the number of hours worked is related to the quality of family life. Patricia Voydanoff (1987) reviewed various research studies that used diverse samples of workers and their families and found that those

Over the past century, there has been a consistent decline in the workweek; however, an increasing number of workers supplement their earnings with additional part-time work—in this case, selling jewelry at a flea market.

who work long hours are likely to have higher levels of work/family conflict and strain, greater probability of divorce, and more job tension.

Work Schedules

The normal work schedule is a 7- to 8-hour workday during the daylight hours Monday through Friday. The two most common deviations from this norm are shift work and flextime.

Shift work is common in manufacturing industries, such as automobile assembly, and continuous process operation industries, such as mining and petroleum refining. Close to one third of all families with children under the age of 14 have at least one spouse who works a nonstandard shift (Presser 1986; Presser and Cain 1983). Males are more likely to be shift workers than females. Among younger parents, fathers and mothers are equally likely to do shift work (Presser 1986). Nonregular shifts are afternoon/evening shifts that begin around 3 p.m. and end around 11 p.m. and the "graveyard shift" that begins around 11 p.m. and ends around 7 or 8 a.m. Some workers, like nurses, work "rotating shifts" that involve day work some weeks and evening or night work other weeks. Rosabeth Kanter (1984) found that each shift has its own characteristic family patterns. Afternoon/evening shift workers have more problems with the father role, whereas night or graveyard shift workers report more friction between husband and wife. Shift workers who work nonday shifts rely more on spouses for child care than do day shift workers (Presser 1986). Fathers are especially involved in child care—although still less than mothers—in families with non-overlapping-shift work schedules.

A newer form of variable work schedule is **flextime**. Flextime involves a flexible schedule around the traditional or normal core working hours of 9 a.m. to 5 p.m. Flextime employees may choose to arrive at work early and leave early, perhaps to be home when children arrive home from school. Others may report to work later and work later. Flextime is more common in government work, white-collar professional and managerial work, sales workers, and transportation operatives (Voydanoff 1987). Men are slightly more likely than women to work flexible hours, and married men and men with children have higher rates of flextime work than married women and women with children (Nollen 1982).

Flextime workers report more problems with the scheduling of work time than with how many hours they work (Voydanoff 1987). Problems include inconvenient or excessive work hours, irregular or unpredictable work hours, and lack of control over work hours. Although research on the impact of flextime schedules on family life is sparse, the available data indicate that flextime workers spend more time with their children and with their spouses and children together than do regular-hour workers. Flextime workers, however, spend less time alone with spouses (Winett and Neale 1980).

Work-Related Travel and Geographic Mobility

Geographic mobility is an additional component of work time and work schedules. As we mentioned earlier, one important aspect of work time and schedules is work-related travel. A second important aspect is job-related moves and transfers.

Work travel can be as short as the time it takes to commute to and from work and as long as months away from home for military service. Business trips can last a few days or a week. Some research on the effect of work-related travel has been conducted with men who are corporate managers, traveling salesmen, and members of the military. Male managers who engage in considerable work-related travel report problems fulfilling family-related roles, such as companionship with spouse and children, household responsibilities, and attending family and school functions (Kanter 1977; Renshaw 1976; Young and Willmott 1973). Not surprising, research studies of wives whose husbands are often away from home on work-related travel or who travel for long periods of time report high levels of strain and loneliness (Hollowell 1968; Hunter and Nice 1978; Renshaw 1976).

Job transfers and the resulting geographical mobility also affect work and family and life. The U.S. Bureau of Census (1992a) estimates than a little less than one fifth of all Americans move each year—17% of the U.S. population moved in the 12 months prior to March 1991. Perhaps half of these moves are job related (Gaylord 1979). Some moves are the results of transfers within the same company, other moves are for finding work, and still others are for the purpose of improving an individual's occupational and economic status and opportunities.

Family structures and situations directly influence the likelihood of job-related moves and the effects of such moves on the family. Older individuals and persons with strong extended family ties are less likely than others to initiate or accept an occupationally related move (Markham and Pleck 1986; Miller 1976). Families with children younger than 6 years of age are more likely to move than families with school-aged children (U.S. Bureau of the Census 1992a).

The effects of job-related moves on individuals and families are mixed. In general, the worker who moves has an easier time adjusting than his or her spouse and children (Foy 1975). Corporations expect that men who are dedicated to their jobs will accept moves, and they also expect that wives will follow and adjust (Margolis 1979).

Research on the effects of geographic mobility yields mixed results. Some researchers report high levels of family stress (Gaylord 1979; Packard 1972; Tiger 1974), while others find that spouses and children have little trouble adjusting (Brett 1982; Jones 1973; McAllister, Butler, and Kaiser 1973).

Child Care

One of the most important aspects of the relationship between work and family roles is the need for child care. The amount of child care assistance that is available has an important impact on a worker's (especially a mother's) children, work, their relationship with their partners, and themselves.

The 1990 National Child Care Survey (Hofferth et al. 1991) found that the most common primary child care arrangement for children under 13 years of age, whose mothers were employed, was for them to be cared for by a parent. Sixteen percent of children were cared for in day care centers, and 10% were cared for in family day care centers (see Table 11-5). Relatives, such as

Child-Care Arrangement	Total	Employed Mother	Nonemployed Mother	Father	No Parent
Center	13.1	16.6	8.6	14.4	5.3
Parent	44.9	34.9	60.9	21.5	8.1
Relative—child's home	7.0	8.5	4.8	10.6	8.0
Relative—other home	7.3	8.8	4.9	10.1	11.2
In-home provider	2.9	3.5	1.9	8.6	2.7
Family day care	6.9	10.8	1.6	8.3	5.0
Self-care	1.4	2.1	0.5	2.4	0.0
Lessons	13.8	12.8	15.6	7.7	9.9
Other	2.6	1.8	1.2	16.5	49.8
Total	100.0	100.0	100.0	100.0	100.0
Population estimate (in thousands)	47,718	26,675	19,487	795	761
Sample size	7,575	4,234	3,093	126	121

SOURCE: *National Child Care Survey, 1990* (p. 29) by Sandra B. Hofferth, April Brayfield, Sharon Deich, and Pamela Holcomb, 1991, Washington, DC: Urban Institute Press. Copyright © 1991 The Urban Intitute. Adapted by permission.

grandmothers, also provide child care. Among children under 5 years of age, 3 in 10 are cared for by a parent, more than 1 in 4 is in a day care center, and about 1 in 5 in a family day care setting (see Table 11-6).

Employed mothers are increasingly choosing day care center care as their primary form of child care. Only 6% of employed mothers used day care centers for child care in 1960, compared to 28% in 1990 (Hofferth et al. 1991).

Child-Care Arrangement	Total	Employed Mother	Nonemployed Mother	Father	No Parent
Center	20.5	26.5	14.7	17.5	3.3
Parent	46.3	29.9	65.2	13.3	5.5
Relative—child's home	5.9	6.3	5.2	0.0	17.3
Relative—other home	8.7	11.3	5.5	26.5	12.3
In-home provider	3.0	3.7	2.2	13.2	0.0
Family day care	10.7	18.6	2.6	6.1	10.4
Self-care	0.1	0.1	0.0	0.0	0.0
Lessons	2.0	1.2	2.9	4.7	0.0
Other	2.8	2.3	1.7	18.8	51.2
Total	100.0	100.0	100.0	100.0	100.0
Population estimate (in thousands)	18,579	9,319	8,881	151	228
Sample size	2,949	1,479	1,410	24	36

SOURCE: *National Child Care Survey, 1990* (p. 33) by Sandra B. Hofferth, April Brayfield, Sharon Deich, and Pamela Holcomb, 1991, Washington, DC: Urban Institute Press. Copyright © 1991. The Urban Intitute. Adapted by permission.

Parents seem to be relatively satisfied with their child care arrangements—96% of those surveyed by Hofferth and her colleagues said they were either satisfied or very satisfied with their child care arrangements. However, about one in four parents said they would prefer an alternative type of care arrangement or combination of care arrangement, such as day care for part of the day and a parent caring for the child the remainder of the day. For those who wanted a different type, the preferred type is a day care center or pre-school.

Although parents seem generally satisfied with their child care arrangements, the arrangements are not uniformly reliable. Child care failures caused 15% of employed mothers to lose some time from work and 7% to miss at least one day of work in the past month alone. Employed mothers miss 1.6 days of work each month because of breakdowns in their child care plans. Low-income mothers are especially hard hit by child care breakdowns and miss more work and lose more wages than do higher-income mothers.

Men's Family Work

The traditional role for men, beginning in the 19th century with the Industrial Revolution, was to be the "good provider." The good provider held a steady job, made a comfortable wage, owned a home, paid the bills, and provided for his family's economic and material needs. Any additional household and child rearing responsibilities were assigned to the wife or "homemaker."

Changes in the labor force and decreased job opportunities for men, increases in women's participation in the workforce, and changing attitudes about gender roles have altered the nature of men's work roles and of their family roles or "family work," including bill paying, yard work, home maintenance and repair, child care, cooking, and cleaning the inside of the home. As we noted earlier in this chapter, the percentage of men in the labor force has declined over the past 30 years. The decline is due to the fact that men are older when they enter the labor force (as a result of an increase in the time spent in school) and because men are retiring at younger ages (Spitze 1988).

As men's participation in the labor force has declined and women's has increased, what has been the effect on men's household responsibilities? There is considerable disagreement among researchers regarding changes in men's household work (Shelton 1990). Some studies have found that since the 1960s there has been a slight increase in the proportion of family work done by husbands whose wives are employed (Juster 1985; Maret and Finlay 1984; Pleck 1985; Pleck and Rustad 1981; Szinovacz 1984). Other researchers claim that there has been little significant increase in men's housework and child care (Coverman and Sheley 1986; Sanik 1981). Beth Anne Shelton's (1990) examination of the study of time use data collected by the Institute for Social

With more women in the labor force, men have become a little more involved in child care.

Research at the University of Michigan found that men's housework was not related to whether their wives were in the labor force.

In general, husbands, including husbands whose wives work, do proportionately less household work than their wives. Peter Kooreman and Arie Kapteyn (1987) collected detailed information on time use by asking respondents to complete daily diaries. They found that husbands generally allocated more of their time to employment-related work and less to family-related work. Even in homes where both husband and wife worked, the wife did more of the household work and child care. Similarly, Francis Goldscheider and

Task	Children	Husband	Wife	Nonfamily
Laundry	10	7	81	2
Shopping	3	19	78	0
Cooking	7	15	77	1
Cleaning	19	12	66	3
Dishwashing	26	13	60	1
Paperwork	1	29	70	0
Child care	4	32	63	2
Yard work	9	49	40	2

Table 11-7
Percentage Distribution of Household Tasks, by Family Member, Mid-1980s

SOURCE: *New Families, No Families? The Transformation of the American Home* (p. 176) by Francis K. Goldscheider and Linda J. Waite, 1991, Berkeley: University of California Press. Copyright © 1991 by The Regents of the University of California. Adapted by permission.

Linda Waite (1991) found that for every activity but yard work, wives do more of the family work than their husbands (see Table 11-7).

Cynthia Rexroat and Constance Sheehan (1987) looked at men's and women's performance of housework across the family life cycle. For all stages of the family life cycle, women put in more hours of paid employment, housework, and child care. The smallest gap between men and women was for young childless couples, and the largest gap was for couples whose oldest child was newborn to 3 years old (see Figure 11-2).

Women's Family Work

The traditional role for women since the age of industrialization has been that of housewife or homemaker (Degler 1980). Homemakers are expected to fulfill all the obligations of keeping house, purchasing food, preparing meals, doing laundry, and raising children. Today, a little less than half of all women are not in the labor force and are "keeping house" (Berk 1988). Much is said in praise of the housewife role and how important it is to be a good homemaker, caring wife, and nurturing mother. Indeed, without housework it is unlikely that the family could survive (Berk and Berk 1983). Yet the role of housewife is allocated little status and respect. The qualifications are few—female and being married—and the status low (Oakley 1985). The job title "homemaker" is almost never listed in scales of occupational prestige, and the assumption is that the prestige score is zero—although "housekeeper in a private home" does receive a prestige score of 34 out of a possible 100 (Nakao and Treas 1990). The work itself is often the same as one would expect a servant to perform (Oakley 1981). In addition, housework isolates women at home, is unstructured, monotonous, and repetitive, and involves long hours (Ferree 1976; Oakley 1985).

Figure 11-2 Mean Total Hours in Work Week for Husbands and Wives Who Are Employed Full-Time, by Life Cycle Stage

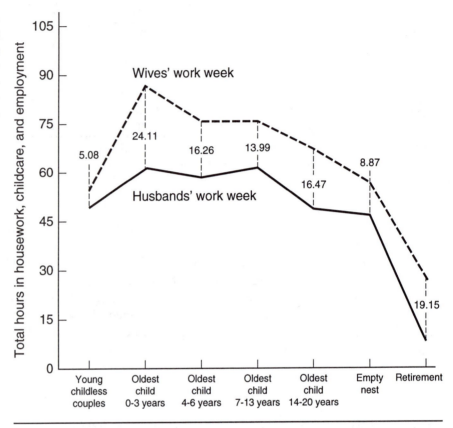

SOURCE: "The Family Life Cycle and Spouses' Time in Housework" by Cynthia Rexroat and Constance Sheehan, 1987, *Journal of Marriage and the Family* 49(November), p. 746. Copyright © 1987 by the National Council on Family Relations, 3989 Central Ave. NE, Suite 550, Minneapolis, MN. Adapted by permission.

Women spend considerably more time in housework than men (Ferree 1991). Donna Berardo, Constance Sheehan, and Gerald Leslie (1987) report that nearly 80% of all housework is done by women. Data collected by Kooreman and Kapteyn (1987) indicate that, overall, women spend about 30% of their time on household work and child care. Women who work spend 23% of their time on household duties, compared to women in one-earner homes who spend 35% of their time on such activities. To appreciate the full demands of work and family on an employed woman, add her 40-hour work-week to her 30 to 40 hours of housework. This 70- to 80-hour workweek exceeds those of workers in the early years of industrialization!

The hours are long, the pay low, and the status low, but what is the level of satisfaction with doing housework? Alfreda Iglehart (1980) cites surveys conducted by the Survey Research Center at the University of Michigan, which indicate that half of all housewives had a positive opinion of housework, while 44% had neutral or ambivalent views. Only 6% reported negative opinions. Those wives with the most education and who were younger were the most likely to report negative views of housework. Working-class homemakers are more likely than middle-class women to report satisfaction with the role (Rubin 1976).

One type of dual-earner family is the **dual-career household**. Dual career, as opposed to dual earner, implies that both husband and wife are committed to work that has developmental progress and that is intrinsically rewarding. Alan and Catherine Albert, who were described in the opening of this chapter, are an example of a dual-career couple. Both are committed to their work, expect to move up the hierarchy within their place of employment, and devote time and commitment to their work outside regular work hours. Alan describes himself as "in marketing," not as an employee of a bank; Catherine describes herself as a psychologist, not as an employee of a university.

Sociologist Arlie Hochschild and her colleague Anne Machung (1989) interviewed 50 dual-career couples over a 6-year period. They also interviewed 45 other people, including baby-sitters, day care workers, schoolteachers, traditional (non-dual-career) couples with small children, and divorcées who had been in dual-career households. Hochschild also conducted in-depth observations of 12 families selected from the 50 couples she had interviewed. Hochschild found three basic orientations to work and family roles in the families of dual-career couples. The wife in the *traditional household* who works outside the house bases her identity on her activities around the home. She sees herself as a wife and mother and her husband as the breadwinner who should be the head of the household. The husband in the traditional household holds the same views. The *egalitarian* husband and wife believe that husbands and wives should identify with the same spheres and share power within the family equally. Some egalitarian couples put their family first, some put their work first, and some strive to find a balance between the two. Egalitarian couples do not see the husband or the wife as the primary breadwinner. The third type of dual-career family is the *transitional couple*. The transitional wife wants to be seen as a worker *and* a wife/mother but expects her husband to focus on earning a living. Catherine Albert describes herself as having four jobs— psychologist, wife, mother, and maintainer of the house. Her husband, she says with a sigh, has one job, marketing director (even though he does "help" with the children and housework as seen in the opening vignette). The transitional husband is pleased that his wife works but expects her to

Dual-Earner/
Dual-Career
Families

assume primary responsibility for the home and the children. Although most of the couples Hochschild studied claimed egalitarian views on work and family, most were transitional couples.

Hochschild found that just as there is a wage gap in the workplace, there is a leisure gap in the home. Most women in both dual-earner and dual-career marriages work one shift at the office and a second shift at home. This second "shift" amounts to nearly an extra month of work per year. The burden of the second shift occurs even among dual-career couples who profess egalitarian ideals. One middle-class couple described their idea of sharing as the wife being responsible for the "upstairs" and the husband the "downstairs" parts of the house. The upstairs, however, included the kitchen and first-floor living areas as well as the second-floor bedrooms, whereas the downstairs comprised the basement where the husband kept his tools and an extra television (Hochschild and Machung 1989). The wife took care of the children; the husband took care of the dog. Hochschild called the gap between the egalitarian ideal and the second-shift responsibilities of the wife the "family myth" that rationalizes or covers up the actual unequal division of labor in the home.

One factor that distinguishes dual-career families from dual-earner households is the greater financial resources of dual-career couples. Rosanna Hertz

---

BOX 11-3: WHAT THE RESEARCH SHOWS

Commuter Marriages

A more complicated lifestyle than the dual-career marriage is the **commuter marriage.** Commuter marriages are common among certain professions—professional athletes, musicians, entertainers, politicians, members of the military, and salespersons who spend long periods of time away from their families.

A commuter marriage involves a decision to establish two separate residences and live in two separate locations. For instance, a couple who are both college professors may find it impossible to get academic positions on the same campus. They choose to take positions at different schools, establish separate residences, and be together on weekends and vacations. This decision is typically made because one partner, traditionally the wife, does not opt to give up her position and move to her husband's place of work. Rather than choose not to marry, to separate, to divorce, or to give up

one career, the couple establishes a commuter marriage.

Although commuter marriages allow each partner to fulfill work obligations and hold a rewarding position or advance in a career, such marriages have significant costs. One obvious cost is the financial burden of maintaining two residences. Commuter marriage couples also spend less time with one another, have fewer common social activities, have little social or cultural support for their lifestyles, and run the risks of extramarital relationships or simply growing apart.

Commuter marriages are the most successful when the two jobs are located relatively close to each other, when both partners are strongly career oriented, when at least one partner has an established career, and when the couples are older, married longer, and have no children at home (Gerstel and Gross 1984).

(1986) interviewed dual-career couples employed in corporate settings. The financial rewards that accompany high-level positions provide a buffer against some of the stresses inherent in the demands of two higher-level careers, a marriage, and possibly children. Nevertheless, despite the fact that dual-career couples may have the resources to afford good child care, help to clean and maintain their homes, and have the chance to take vacations, they still share some of the stresses and strains experienced by dual-earner families. These include negotiating roles, division of labor, and setting priorities for work and family. The result of these strains is that dual-career women often slow down their career advancement to accommodate the needs of their children.

Thus, irrespective of whether both workers are wager earners or see themselves in careers, the fundamental problem in dual-earner/dual-career marriages is finding time to meet both family and work obligations. **Role strain** is the concept that best describes this problem. Role strain can take the form of **overload,** which means that the demands of work and family roles are more than the person can handle (Voydanoff and Kelly 1984), or **interference,** where the demands of work call for one thing to be done while the demands of family call for another—such as when a parent has to decide whether to go to a late afternoon meeting or go to the school and see his or her child in a play.

THE EFFECTS OF WORK ON FAMILY LIFE

The previous discussion of work roles and family roles has alluded to the impact of work on family roles, responsibilities, and relationships. In this section, we take a more detailed look at some specific effects of work on family life. First we examine the question of the impact of women's employment on their relationships with their children and their marital relations. Clearly, as we have discussed earlier, men's work affects children and family relations in a variety of ways, even though men traditionally have less responsibility for child care than do women. Our focus is on employed women because, with the rapid increase in employment of women and mothers in the past 40 years, the question of how this has affected the family has been a major issue in the study of family relations. Finally, we look at how losing a job and being unemployed influences family relationships.

Do children suffer when their mothers work? Numerous studies have explored the possible effects of mothers' work roles on their children, beginning with the increase in the employment of mothers during World War II up to the

Employed
Women and
Their Children

present. The general conclusion of this line of research is that employment of mothers, in and of itself, has little effect on children (Hoffman 1989; Lerner 1994). Children whose mothers work do as well in school as those children whose mothers are at home. In fact, some research reports that children with employed mothers actually do better in school (Moore and Sawhill 1984). Daughters whose mothers work tend to develop less traditional gender role attitudes and value female achievement more (Hoffman 1984; Lamb 1984; Moore and Sawhill 1984). Some studies find that children with employed mothers are somewhat more responsible and independent than children with mothers at home (Hoffman 1984; Moore and Sawhill 1984).

Research has identified two important moderating factors that influence the effect of maternal employment: (1) the extent of the husband's participation in family tasks and (2) the match between the wife's employment status, her own preferences about working, and her husband's preferences about her work (Menaghan and Parcel 1990). Other important factors are social class, whether the mother works full-time or part-time, age of the children, the mother's attitudes toward unemployment, and the mother's social and psychological factors.

Employed Women and Marital Relations

Does working improve or undermine a woman's relationship with her husband? The impact of female employment varies, depending on many of the same factors that influence the impact of employed mothers on children—full-time versus part-time employment, whether there are preschool children at home, the ages of these children, age of the spouse, attitudes toward work and gender roles, and stage of the family life cycle.

One of the most important influences on the relationship between work and family life is the husband's and wife's preferences about the wife's work. Catherine Ross, John Mirowski, and Joan Huber (1983) found that men and women are less depressed when the wife's employment status is consistent with their preferences. Wives are also less depressed if their husbands help with the housework. Helping with housework does not increase the husband's own depression.

Working gives women more power and choice in their marital relations (Spitze 1988; also see Chapter 7). Income and increased independence provide women with greater resources in families and thus more decision-making power (although again, the power is rarely equal, despite what the partners may say or believe). Women who work tend to have more decision-making power in financial and economic matters but lose some power in household matters (Bahr 1974).

Working women are less depressed if their husbands help with the housework—such as mopping floors.

The impact of employed wives on marital satisfaction is variable and depends on a variety of factors associated with the nature of work and family. In general, when there are two workers in the home, if there is less time spent together there will be lower marital quality and satisfaction (Kingston and Nock 1987). Some data indicate that employed women are more likely to divorce than will women who do not work (Cherlin 1979; Mott and Moore 1979). The risk of divorce is especially great among women who hold non-traditional jobs (Philliber and Hiller 1983). Also, the more hours a wife works, the greater the probability of divorce (Booth et al. 1984; Spitze and South 1985). Working per se does not cause divorce. Rather, working and the wages received from work give women the option of leaving an unsatisfying marriage. The risk of divorce seems to be a function of low marital satisfaction than simply the effects of working. Employed women who are satisfied with their marriages do not have a greater risk of divorce (Booth et al. 1984).

The Effects of Unemployment	The traditional assumption in the study of the impact of work on family was that employed women and unemployed men both caused problems for their families (Mortimer and Sorensen 1984; Spitze 1988). Thus the study of the impact of men's work on the family tends to focus on unemployed men. Studies of married fathers' unemployment find powerful negative effects on the men's individual well-being and the quality of their participation in family life (Elder 1974; Elder, Liker, and Cross 1984; Elder, Van Nguyen, and Caspi 1985; Kessler, House, and Turner 1987; McLoyd 1989). Unemployment leads to a decrease in the quality of marital communications and satisfaction and an increase in marital conflict (Atkinson, Liem, and Liem 1986; Linn, Sandifer, and Stein 1985; Voydanoff 1987; also see Chapter 8).

As with the other factors considered in this section, the effects of unemployment on family relations are not uniform. Research on the effects of the Great Depression of the 1930s and on the effects of unemployment and economic distress on families find that several characteristics that affected families prior to unemployment and economic hardship influenced the consequences of unemployment. Families that operated with a high degree of unity and reciprocal functioning before the breadwinner became unemployed remained organized and functional during the period of unemployment. Families that were disorganized before the unemployment became more disorganized (Cavan and Ranck 1938). The effects of unemployment may be less negative when family support is high (Linn et al. 1985).

Unemployment also affects children. Research indicates that children of unemployed fathers have higher risk of illness, infant mortality, and child abuse (Margolis 1982; Straus, Gelles, and Steinmetz 1980). Glen Elder, Jr. (1974) conducted extensive research on the effects of the Great Depression. He found that girls assumed more household responsibilities and boys worked at paid jobs as an adaptation to unemployment and economic deprivation.

EFFECTS OF FAMILY LIFE ON WORK

In general, business firms in the United States have been laggards with respect to providing benefits that would ease conflicts between employees' work and family responsibilities (Aldous 1990). Among the reasons for the fact that other countries are more likely to have employer-sponsored programs to ease the strain between work and family is the absence of pronatalist concerns (a societal expectation that women are expected to and want to have children) and the presence of socialist political traditions. There is a strong conservative political tradition in the United States that refuses to accept the reality that women's employment is essential for the health of both the family and the economy (Aldous 1990).

Most of the focus on the relationship between work and family is on how work affects family roles and family life. But family roles and family life also have an impact on the workplace and the structure of work. Catherine Albert's decision to stay home with her newborn child (described in the opening of this chapter) had a direct fiscal impact on her department and university. If Catherine were offered a position at a better university in another state and her husband Alan decided to move with her, Alan's bank would have to find a replacement for him and would have to pay the cost of retraining the replacement.

As with the case of Catherine, one major impact that family life has on the workplace is the effect of parental responsibilities. New mothers sometimes choose to leave the workforce for varying periods of time to be home with their newborns. The more children a mother has and the higher her husband's income (and thus the less the family is dependent on her income), the less likely she is to stay at work after her child is born (Gordon and Kammeyer 1980; Perrucci and Targ 1982). Women with younger children are more likely to leave the workforce than are women with older children (Felmlee 1984). Mothers also can negotiate to reduce their work hours, change shifts, or "jobshare," that is, to share a full-time position with another worker—perhaps another mother.

The impact of motherhood on work is relatively brief, and most previously employed women choose to return to work (Waite, Haggstrom, and Kanouse 1986). However, once they return to work, many women find that their employers place them on the so-called **mommy track** that leads to fewer promotions and fewer career rewards. On the other hand, some mothers (a minority) place *themselves* on the "mommy track" and willingly trade some career growth and financial reward for freedom from the constant pressure to work long hours and weekends (Schwartz 1989).

Fatherhood also influences the workplace. Linda J. Waite and her colleagues (1986) found that parenthood alters men's occupational behaviors and expectations. Men's involvement in their work, their wages, and their occupational status decline after the birth of their first child. Alan Albert, for instance, devoted much less time doing office work at home after the birth of his children. As a result, he suspects that he did not get a promotion that he might otherwise have received. Perhaps a **daddy track** also exists at work.

Parenthood and Work

Employer/ Workplace Responses

In general, businesses and corporations in the United States do little to facilitate a smoother relationship between work and family. Few businesses offer on-site child care facilities, and few offer flextime or flexible work schedules. Most businesses pay little attention to the impact of job transfers of families. Worse, many businesses actually penalize workers, especially mothers, who devote time to family issues instead of work issues (the mommy and daddy tracks are one form of penalty).

The changes in the nature of the workforce have stimulated some in the business community to become increasingly sensitive to the nature of their workers and their workers' family roles and responsibilities. As a result, a handful of businesses and corporations have begun to experiment with policies and programs that respond to and support the needs of workers and families. These family support policies have been motivated primarily by business needs and concerns rather than concern for the personal lives and obligations of families (Axel 1985). Helen Axel's (1985) study of 73 major corporations found that family support policies were most likely to be developed and adopted by companies with high proportions of young, female, technically skilled, and nonunion workers as well as by businesses that had strong consumer orientations, a strong sense of social responsibility, or were family owned.

The family supportive programs that were developed included flextime, employer-sponsored child care, and flexible benefit programs. R. L. McNeely and Barbe A. Fogarty (1988) surveyed 276 companies that were members of the Wisconsin Association of Manufacturers and Commerce. They found that the most common programs and policies in place in the firms were part-time work, maternity leave, sick-child leave, and flextime. Employer-sponsored child care programs are still relatively rare, although they continue to increase. About 2% of the firms employing 10 or more persons sponsor child care for their employees' children. An additional 3% subsidize employees' child care (Hayghe 1988). Institutions of higher education and health-related industries tend to be the leaders in developing company-sponsored child care. Flexible benefit programs include maternity leave (and rarely, paternity leave) and paid leave programs to care for ill children or elderly relatives.

SUMMING UP

Family roles and work roles are the two most important roles that adults enact in contemporary society. There have been significant changes in how work and family have affected one another in the last 30 years, and there has also been a stark absence of change in some areas. The increase in paid employment of women, especially women with young children, has had a profound effect on both the family and the workplace. While there is some indication that this change has influenced men's family roles and the workplace, there is also evidence that the social structure of the home is not much different today from what it was 30 to 50 years ago. Working has relieved women of some household responsibilities, but women still carry the bulk of the housework and child care. Thus the major change we have seen is the addition of the "second shift" for women.

Research evidence indicates that the increase in paid employment of women has *not* resulted in negative outcomes for children and marriages. Maternal employment itself has not had major direct negative effects on children or marital relationships.

The workplace has been slow to react to the changing composition of the workforce, and although some family support policies have been enacted, widespread adoption of such policies has still not been achieved.

REFERENCES

Ahlburg, Dennis A. and Carol J. De Vita. 1992. "New Realities of the American Family." *Population Bulletin* 46(2):1-44.

Aldous, Joan. 1990. "Specification and Speculation Concerning the Politics of Workplace Family Policies." *Journal of Family Issues* 4 (December):355-67.

Aneshensel, Carol S. and Bernard C. Rosen. 1980. "Domestic Roles and Sex Differences in Occupational Expectations." *Journal of Marriage and the Family* 42(February): 121-31.

Atkinson, Thomas, Ramsay Liem, and Joan H. Liem. 1986. "The Social Costs of Unemployment: Implications for Social Support." *Journal of Health and Social Behavior* 27 (4):317-31.

Axel, Helen. 1985. *Corporations and Families: Changing Practices and Perspectives.* New York: The Conference Board.

Bahr, Steven J. 1974. "Effects of Power and Division of Labor in the Family." Pp. 180-81 in *Working Mothers,* edited by Lois W. Hoffman and F. Ivan Nye. San Francisco: Jossey-Bass.

Bell, Daniel. 1973. *The Coming of Post Industrial Society.* New York: Basic Books.

Berardo, Donna Hodgkins, Constance L. Sheehan, and Gerald R. Leslie. 1987. "A Residue of Tradition: Jobs, Careers, and Spouses' Time in Housework." *Journal of Marriage and the Family* 49(May): 381-90.

Berk, Sara Fenstermaker. 1988. "Women's Unpaid Labor:

Home and Community." Pp. 287-302 in *Women Working,* edited by Ann Helton Stromberg and Shirley Harkness. Mountain View, CA: Mayfield.

Berk, Richard A. and Sara Fenstermaker Berk. 1983. "Supply-Side Sociology of the Family: The Challenge of the New Home Economics." *Annual Review of Sociology* 9: 375-95.

Blau, Francine D. and Marianne A. Ferber. 1986. *The Economics of Women, Men, and Work.* Englewood Cliffs, NJ: Prentice Hall.

Booth, Alan, David R. Johnson, Lynn White, and John N. Edwards. 1984. "Women, Outside Employment, and Marital Instability." *American Journal of Sociology* 90(November):567-83.

Brett, J. M. 1982. "Job Transfer and Well-Being." *Journal of Applied Psychology* 67(4):450-63.

Cavan, Ruth S. and K. H. Ranck. 1938. *The Family and the Depression*. Chicago: University of Chicago Press.

Cherlin, Andrew. 1979 "Work Life and Marital Dissolution." Pp. 161-66 in *Divorce and Separation,* edited by George Levinger and O. C. Moles. New York: Basic Books.

Cotton, Sandra, John K. Antill, and John D. Cunningham. 1989. "The Work Motivations of Mothers With Preschool Children." *Journal of Family Issues* 10(June):189-210.

Coverman, Shelley and Joseph F. Sheley. 1986. "Men's Housework and Child-Care Time, 1965–1975." *Journal of Marriage and the Family* 48(May): 413-22.

Cyert, Richard M. and David C. Mowery, eds. 1987. *Technology and Employment: Innovation and Growth in the U.S. Economy.* Washington, DC: National Academy Press.

Degler, Carl. 1980. *At Odds.* New York: Oxford University Press.

Dorne, Clifford K. 1989. *Crimes Against Children.* New York: Harrow & Heston.

Elder, Glen H., Jr. 1974. *Children of the Great Depression.* Chicago: University of Chicago Press.

Elder, Glen H., Jr., Jeffery K. Liker, and Catherine E. Cross. 1984. "Parent-Child Behavior in the Great Depression: Life Course and Intergenerational Influences." Pp.

109-58 in *Life-Span Development and Behavior,* Vol. 6, edited by Paul B. Baltes and Orville G. Brim, Jr. New York: Academic Press.

Elder, Glen H., Jr., Tri Van Nguyen, and Avshalan Caspi. 1985. "Linking Family Hardship to Children's Lives." *Child Development* 56(2):361-85.

Felmlee, Diane H. 1984. "A Dynamic Analysis of Women's Employment Exits." *Demography* 21(2):171-83.

Ferber, Marianne A. 1982. "Labor Market Participation of Young Married Women: Causes and Effects." *Journal of Marriage and the Family* 44(May): 457-68.

Ferree, Myra. 1976. "The Confused American Housewife." *Psychology Today* 10(September): 76-80.

———. 1991. "The Gender Division of Labor in Two-Earner Marriages." *Journal of Family Issues* 12(June):158-80.

Foy, Nancy. 1975. *The Sun Never Sets on IBM.* New York: William Morrow.

Gaylord, Maxine. 1979. "Relocation and the Corporate Family: Unexplored Issues." *Social Work* 24(May):186-91.

Gerstel, Naomi and Harriet E. Gross. 1984. *Commuter Marriages.* New York: Guilford.

Goldscheider, Francis K. and Linda J. Waite. 1991. *New Families, No Families? The Transformation of the American Home.* Berkeley: University of California Press.

Gordon, Henry A. and Kenneth W. Kammeyer. 1980. "The

Gainful Employment of Women With Small Children." *Journal of Marriage and the Family* 42(May):327-36.

Greenberger, Ellen. 1987. "Children's Employment and Families." Pp. 396-406 in *Families and Work,* edited by Naomi Gerstel and Harriet Engle Gross. Philadelphia: Temple University Press.

Hacker, Andrew. 1992. *Two Nations: Black and White, Separate, Hostile, Unequal.* New York: Scribner.

Hayghe, Howard. 1984. "Working Mothers Reach Record Number in 1984." *Monthly Labor Review,* December, 31-34.

———. 1988. "Employers and Child Care: What Roles Do They Play?" *Monthly Labor Review,* September, 38-43.

Hedges, Janice N. and Daniel E. Taylor. 1980. "Recent Trends in Worktime: Hours Edge Downward." *Monthly Labor Review,* March, 3-11.

Hertz, Rosanna. 1986. *More Equal Than Others: Women and Men in Dual-Career Marriages.* Berkeley: University of California Press.

Hochschild, Arlie and Anne Machung. 1989. *The Second Shift.* New York: Viking.

Hofferth, Sandra B., April Brayfield, Sharon Deich, and Pamela Holcomb. 1991. *National Child Care Survey, 1990.* Washington, DC: Urban Institute Press.

Hoffman, Lois W. 1963. "The Decision to Work." Pp. 18-39 in *The Employed Mother in Amer-*

ica, edited by F. Ivan Nye and Lois W. Hoffman. Chicago: Rand McNally.

———. 1984. "Work, Family, and the Socialization of the Child." Pp. 223-82 in *Review of Child Development Research, Volume 7: The Family,* edited by Ross D. Parke, R. N. Emde, Harriet P. McAdoo, and G. P. Sackett. Chicago: University of Chicago Press.

———. 1989. "Effects of Maternal Employment in the Two-Parent Family." *American Psychologist* 44(2):283-92.

Hollowell, P. G. 1968. *The Lorry Driver.* London: Routledge & Kegan Paul.

Hunter, Edna J. and D. Stephen Nice, eds. 1978. *Military Families.* New York: Praeger.

Iglehart, Alfreda. 1980. "Wives, Work, and Social Change: What About the Housewives?" *Social Service Review* 54(September):317-30.

Jacobs, Jerry. 1989. *Revolving Doors: Sex Segregation and Women's Careers.* Stanford, CA: Stanford University Press.

Jones, Stella B. 1973. "Geographic Mobility as Seen by the Wife and Mother." *Journal of Marriage and the Family* 35(May):210-18.

Juster, F. Thomas 1985. "Investments of Time by Men and Women." Pp. 177-204 in *Time, Goods, and Well Being,* edited by F. Thomas Juster and Frank P. Stafford. Ann Arbor, MI: Survey Research Center, Institute for Social Research.

Kanter, Rosabeth Moss. 1977. *Men and Women of the Corporation.* New York: Basic Books.

———. 1984. "Jobs and Families: Impact of Working Roles on Family Life." Pp. 111-18 in *Work and Family,* edited by Patricia Voydanoff. Palo Alto, CA: Mayfield.

Kessler, Ronald C., James H. House, and J. Blake Turner. 1987. "Unemployment and Health in a Community Sample." *Journal of Health and Social Behavior* 28(1):51-59.

Kingston, Paul W. and Steven L. Nock. 1987. "Time Together Among Dual-Earner Couples." *American Sociological Review* 52 (June):391-400.

Kooreman, Peter and Arie Kapteyn. 1987. "A Disaggregated Analysis of the Allocation of Time Within the Household." *Journal of Political Economy* 95(21):223-49.

Lamb, Michael E. 1984. "Fathers, Mothers, and Child Care in the 1980s." Pp. 61-88 in *Women in the Workplace: Effects on Families,* edited by Kathryn M. Borman, Daisy Quarm, and Sarah Gideonse. Norwood, NJ: Ablex.

Lerner, Jacqueline V. 1994. *Working Women and Their Families.* Thousand Oaks, CA: Sage.

Lewin-Epstein, Noah. 1981. *Youth Employment During High School.* Washington, DC: National Center for Educational Statistics.

Linn, Margaret W., Richard Sandifer, and Shayna Stein. 1985. "Effects of Unemployment on Mental and Physical

Health." *American Journal of Public Health* 75(5):502-6.

Maret, Elizabeth and Barbara Finlay. 1984. "The Distribution of Household Labor Among Women in Dual-Earner Families." *Journal of Marriage and the Family* 46(May):357-64.

Margolis, Diane R. 1979. *Managers: The Corporate Life in America.* New York: William Morrow.

Margolis, Lewis H. 1982. *Helping the Families of Employed Workers.* Chapel Hill: University of North Carolina Press.

Markham, William T. and Joseph H. Pleck. 1986. "Sex and Willingness to Move for Occupational Advancement." *Sociological Quarterly* 27 (Spring):121-43.

Masnick, George and Mary Jo Bane. 1980. *The Nation's Families: 1960-1990.* Cambridge, MA: Joint Center for Urban Studies, MIT and Harvard University.

McAllister, Ronald J., Edgar W. Butler, and Edward J. Kaiser. 1973. "The Adaptation of Women to Residential Mobility." *Journal of Marriage and the Family* 35(May):197-204.

McLoyd, Vonnie C. 1989. "Socialization and Development in a Changing Economy: The Effects of Paternal Job and Income Loss on Children." *American Psychologist* 44(2): 293-302.

McNeely, R. L. and Barbe A. Fogarty. 1988. "Balancing Parenthood and Employment: Factors Affecting Company Receptiveness to Family-Related Innovations in the

Workplace." *Family Relations* 37(April):189-95.

Menaghan, Elizabeth C. and Toby L. Parcel. 1990. "Parental Employment and Family Life: Research in the 1980s." *Journal of Marriage and the Family* 52 (November):1079-98.

Miller, Sheila J. 1976. "Family Life Cycle, Extended Family Orientations, and Economic Aspirations as Factors in the Propensity to Migrate." *Sociological Quarterly* 17(Summer): 323-35.

Moen, Phyllis and M. Moorehouse. 1983. "Overtime Over the Life Cycle: A Test of the Life Cycle Squeeze Hypothesis." Pp. 201-18 in *Research in the Interweave of Social Roles: Family and Jobs,* Vol. 3, edited by Helen Z. Lopata and Joseph H. Pleck. Greenwich, CT: JAI.

Moore, Kristen A. and Isabell V. Sawhill. 1984. "Implication of Women's Employment for Home and Family Life." Pp. 153-71 in *Work and Family,* edited by Patricia Voydanoff. Palo Alto, CA: Mayfield.

Mott, Frank L. and Sylvia F. Moore. 1979. "The Causes of Marital Disruption Among Young Married American Women: An Interdisciplinary Perspective." *Journal of Marriage and the Family* 41(May): 355-65.

Mortimer, Jeylan T. and Glorian Sorensen. 1984. "Men, Women, Work, and the Family." Pp. 139-67 in *Women in the Workplace: Effects on Families,* edited by Kathryn M. Borman, Daisy Quarm, and Sarah Gideonse. Norwood, NJ: Ablex.

Murdock, George P. 1937. "Comparative Data on the Division of Labor by Sex." *Social Forces* 15 (May):551-53.

Nakao, Keiko and Judith Treas. 1990. "Revised Prestige Score for All Occupations." Unpublished manuscript, National Opinion Research Center, Chicago.

Nasar, Sylvia. 1992. "Women's Progress Stalled: Just Not So." *The New York Times,* October 18, sec. 3, 1ff.

Nollen, D. S. 1982. *New Work Schedules in Practice.* New York: Van Nostrand Reinhold.

Oakley, Ann. 1981. *Subject Women.* New York: Pantheon.

———. 1985. *Sociology of Housework.* New York: Pantheon.

O'Neill, June. 1985. "Role Differentiation and the Gender Gap in Wage Rates." Pp. 50-75 in *Women and Work: An Annual Review,* edited by Laurie Larwood, Ann H. Stromberg, and Barbara A. Gutek. Beverly Hills, CA: Sage.

Oppenheimer, Valerie Kincade. 1977. "The Sociology of Women's Economic Role in the Family." *American Sociological Review* 42(June):387-406.

Owen, John D. 1976. "Workweeks and Leisure: An Analysis of Trends." *Monthly Labor Review,* August, 3-8.

Packard, Vance. 1972. *A Nation of Strangers.* New York: David McKay.

Perrucci, Carolyn C. and Deng B. Targ. 1982. "The Influence of Family and Work Characteristics on Sustained Employ-

ment of College-Aged Wives." *Sociological Focus* 15(3):191-201.

Philliber, William W. and Dana V. Hiller. 1983. "Relative Occupational Attainments of Spouses and Later Changes in Marriage and Wife's Work Experience." *Journal of Marriage and the Family* 45(February):161-70.

Piotrokowski, Chaya S., Robert N. Rapoport, and Rhona Rapoport. 1987. "Families and Work." Pp. 251-84 in *Handbook of Marriage and the Family,* edited by Marvin B. Sussman and Suzanne K. Steinmetz. New York: Plenum.

Pleck, Joseph H. 1985. *Working Wives, Working Husbands.* Beverly Hills, CA: Sage.

Pleck, Joseph H. and M. Rustad. 1981. *Husbands' and Wives' Time in Family Work and Paid Work in the 1975–1976 Study of Time Use.* Wellesley, MA: Wellesley College Center for Research on Women.

Presser, Harriet B. 1986. "Shift Work Among American Women and Child Care." *Journal of Marriage and the Family* 48 (August):551-63.

Presser, Harriet B. and V. S. Cain. 1983. "Shift Work Among Dual-Earner Couples With Children." *Science* 219 (4586):876-79.

Quarm, Daisy. 1984. "Sexual Inequality: The High Cost of Leaving Parents to Women." Pp. 187-208 in *Women in the Workplace: Effects on Women,* edited by Kathryn M. Borman, Daisy Quarm, and Sarah Gideonse. Norwood, NJ: Ablex.

Renshaw, Jean R. 1976. "An Exploration of the Dynamics of the Overlapping Worlds of Work and Family." *Family Process* 15(1):143-65.

Reskin, Barbara and Patricia Roos. 1990. *Job Queues, Gender Queues: Explaining Women's Inroads Into Male Occupations.* Philadelphia: Temple University Press.

Rexroat, Cynthia and Constance Sheehan. 1987. "The Family Life Cycle and Spouses' Time in Housework." *Journal of Marriage and the Family* 49(November):737-50.

Roos, Patricia A. 1981. "Sex Stratification in the Workplace: Male-Female Differences in Economic Returns to Occupation." *Social Science Research* 10(3): 195-224.

Ross, Catherine E., John Mirowski, and Joan Huber. 1983. "Dividing Work, Sharing Work, and In-Between: Marriage Patterns and Depression." *American Sociological Review* 48 (December):809-23.

Rubin, Lillian. 1976. *Worlds of Pain.* New York: Basic Books.

Sanik, Margaret M. 1981. "Division of Household Work: A Decade Comparison, 1967–1977." *Home Economics Research Journal* 10(2):175-80.

Schwartz, Felice N. 1989. "Management, Women, and the New Facts of Life." *Harvard Business Review* 67(January-February): 65-76.

Shelton, Beth Anne. 1990. "The Distribution of Household Tasks: Does Wife's Employment Status Make a Differ-ence?" *Journal of Family Issues* 11(June):115-35.

Spitze, Glenna. 1988. "The Data on Women's Labor Force Participation." Pp. 42-60 in *Women Working,* edited by Ann Helton Stromberg and Shirley Harkness. Mountain View, CA: Mayfield.

Spitze, Glenna and Scott J. South. 1985. "Women's Employment, Time Expenditure, and Divorce." *Journal of Family Issues* 6(September):307-29.

Straus, Murray A., Richard J. Gelles, and Suzanne K. Steinmetz. 1980. *Behind Closed Doors: Violence in the American Family.* New York: Anchor Press.

Szinovacz, Maximiliane E. 1984. "Changing Family Roles and Interactions." *Marriage and Family Review* 7(Fall/Winter): 163-201.

Taylor, Daniel E. and Edward S. Sekscenski. 1982. "Workers on Long Schedules, Single and Monthly Jobholders." *Monthly Labor Review,* May, 47-53.

Tiger, Lionel. 1974. "Is This Trip Necessary? The Heavy Human Costs of Moving Executives Around." *Fortune,* September, 139-41.

U.S. Bureau of the Census. 1987. *Male-Female Differences in Work Experience, Occupation, and Earnings, 1984.* Current Population Reports, Series P-60, No. 163. Washington, DC: Government Printing Office.

———. 1992a. *Geographic Mobility, March 1990 to March 1991.* Current Population Reports, Series P-20, No. 463. Washing-ton, DC: Government Printing Office.

———. 1992b. *Statistical Abstracts of the United States.* Washington, DC: Government Printing Office.

———. 1993. *Poverty in the United States, 1992.* Current Population Reports, Series P-60, No. 185. Washington, DC: Government Printing Office.

Voydanoff, Patricia. 1987. *Work and Family Life.* Newbury Park, CA: Sage.

Voydanoff, Patricia and Robert F. Kelly. 1984. "Determinants of Work-Related Family Problems Among Employed Parents." *Journal of Marriage and the Family* 46(November): 881-92.

Waite, Linda, G. Haggstrom, and D. E. Kanouse. 1986. "The Effects of Parenthood on Career Orientation and Job Characteristics of Young Adults." *Social Forces* 65(1): 28-43.

Wilensky, Harold L. 1961. "The Uneven Distribution of Leisure: The Impact of Economic Growth on 'Free Time'." *Social Problems* 9(Summer): 32-54.

Winett, Richard A. and Michael S. Neale. 1980. "Modifying Settings as a Strategy for Permanent Preventive Behavior Change." Pp. 407-37 in *Improving the Long-Term Effects of Psychotherapy,* edited by Paul Karoly and John J. Steffan. New York: Gardner.

Young, M. and P. Willmott. 1973. *The Symmetrical Family.* New York: Penguin.

CHAPTER 12

■■ # Marriage, Family, and the Later Years

Three couples and a divorced woman sat around the dinner table. They were neighbors and friends ranging in age from their 40s to their early 60s. The conversation revealed that, aside from living in the same neighborhood and being about the same ages and social class, they had little in common. Jerry and Beatrice had been married for five years. Jerry was a successful trial lawyer and at 62 was the oldest at the table. He had been married twice before. Beatrice was 45 and had been married once before she married Jerry. Jerry's children from his first two marriages were grown, married, and had children. Beatrice had no children from her first marriage. Beatrice and Jerry's main concern this evening was their 4-year-old son, Damont. Damont had not been accepted into the elite private school in which his parents hoped to enroll him. Jerry and Beatrice were weighing the other school options they had and could not decide where to send Damont. Neil and Carol were both in their late 40s. They had been married 25 years. Their youngest daughter had just finished college and was about to leave home to attend graduate school in New York. Neil joked that he was hoping to recoup the cost of their daughter's college education by renting out her room. Carol saw no humor in Neil's remarks and was clearly mourning the loss of her youngest daughter. Sue, also in her 40s, comforted Carol and told her not to worry, that children always come home. Both of Sue's older daughters had returned home in the past 18 months. One daughter had finished college and moved home when she could not find a job. The oldest daughter had just divorced her husband and moved back home with an 18-month-old son. Frank, Sue's husband, was feeling overwhelmed by the return of his daughters and grandson. He had just sold his auto parts business and was hoping to retire and move to Florida so that he could play golf. There was no way, he moaned, that all five of them could live in the condo he had just bought, and he could not afford to pay for the condo if he had to keep the house as well. Alice left the conversation to go to the kitchen. Alice, 51, had been divorced for five years and was just about to tell her friends that she was going to remarry. Her husband-to-be was 15 years younger than her. Her only problem was what she was going to do about her 78-year-old mother, who lived with Alice.

STAGES OF MID- AND LATER-LIFE MARRIAGES

Students of family relations who use the developmental framework (see Chapter 2) see the middle stage of family life as beginning when the last child leaves home and the later stage as commencing with retirement (Duvall 1977). Others who examine the middle and later part of family life mark the stages by chronological age. Thus the middle stage is the period from 45 to 65 years of age, while later family life begins at age 65. Sociologist J. Ross Eshleman (1991) combines developmental stages with chronological age and conceptualizes four postparental stages: (1) families launching their children, age 45 to 54; (2) families of preretirement age, 55 to 64; (3) "young old" retired families, age 65 to 74; and finally, (4) "old old" families, age 75 and older.

There are problems with both the developmental conceptualization of stages and the chronological ordering of stages. The developmental notion of traditional middle- and later-life families is based on the stereotypical view that all or most families consist of individuals who marry in their late teens or early 20s, have children two to three years after marriage, have one or two children, launch their children 20 years later, and retire at age 65 or 70, with the marriage terminating in the death of one of the partners. The chronological notion assumes that both partners will be roughly the same age—following from the principle of homogamy discussed in Chapter 6. However, given the high rate of divorce and remarriage (see Chapter 13), marital partners are less likely to be of similar age. Thus both the developmental view and the chronological views of marriage and families apply only to a portion of American families. For example, while one 45-year-old woman and her 47-year-old husband may indeed be launching their last child, another 45-year-old woman may be in her second marriage with a young child about to go off to nursery school. Her ex-husband may have married a 34-year-old women, have an infant, and be contemplating retirement at age 55—when his youngest child is but 8 years old. Another couple, both of whom are 44 years old, may be in their first marriage and having their first child—as there has been a tendency for men and women from the "baby boom" to delay both marriage and having their first child.

Childless couples are overlooked by those who use the launching of the last child as a marker of the middle stage of family life. At what point does a childless couple become a middle-life marriage? Finally, what of the children who are launched and then return? Many a couple has bid farewell to a child who goes off to college or gets married, only to have the child return home for varying periods of time. Adult children return home for a number of reasons: to save money, because of divorce, or to have a place to stay while looking for a job.

Given the diversity of family forms and the lack of utility of chronological age as an indicator of a stage of family life, we will apply Timothy Brubaker's (1985) definition of middle- and later-life families as those who are beyond the childbearing stage *and* have begun to launch their children. For those who are childless, the age of 50 serves as a crude indicator of a later-life family.

The first section of this chapter examines the launching stage, the point at which children are going off to college or entering into marriage. Next we look at the major transitions of the launching stage. Much has been written on the so-called "midlife crisis" that men experience and the "empty nest" stresses and depressions experienced by women. Are these crises fact or fiction? And, if they occur, do all men and women experience these transitions, or are the experiences a function of social and occupational status? The final portion of this section looks at the growing number of individuals who take on the caretaker role for their own parents during the middle stage of family life.

The later years are characterized by the period leading up to retirement, followed by retirement and postretirement. Although these stages involve giving up the work role, many later-life families take on the role of grandparent.

The death of a spouse marks the final transition of a marriage, and the chapter concludes with a look at widows and widowers and how they cope with this transition.

AFTER CHILD REARING: THE MIDDLE YEARS

For some families, the middle years of marriage could last 25 or 30 years. Individuals who marry in their late teens or early 20s and have two children within the first five years of marriage could complete launching their children by age 45. Retirement may not occur until age 70. For those who marry late, or remarry and have children, the middle years may be but a few short years. For the former group, the middle (postparental) stage is likely to be the longest stage of the marriage.

A long postparental stage of marriage is a modern phenomenon. Individuals who married in 1900 were, on average, 26 years old. They had an average of four children, and thus their last child may have been born when they were in their mid-30s. Their last child would marry 20 or so years later. One spouse would likely die in his or her late 50s or early 60s. Thus the middle stage might last from 3 to 7 years, while child rearing would last nearly 20 years. Demographer Paul Glick (1977) estimated that the postparental stage increased from 2 years to 13 years during the 20th century (see Figure 12-1).

Launching Children
The **launching stage** is the period when children begin to leave home. Some children go off to college; others get married and move directly from their family of orientation to a family of procreation. Other children move out, establish their own residence, and may later go to college or get married. The launching stage is a gradual transition. College-aged children may return home

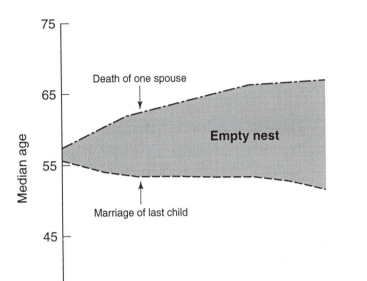

SOURCE: "Updating the Life Cycle of the Family" by Paul Glick, 1977, *Journal of Marriage and the Family* 39(February). Copyright © 1977 by the National Council on Family Relations, 3989 Central Ave. NE, Suite 550, Minneapolis, MN. Adapted by permission of the author.

Figure 12-1 Median Age of Mothers at Time of Marriage of Last Child and Death of Spouse: The Duration of the "Empty Nest"

for periods as short as a weekend or as long as a summer (or even a full year if they choose—or are chosen—to take time off from school). Marriage is considered the official launching of a child, but even that transition may be gradual. The extremely high cost of housing in some parts of the country causes many newly married couples to take up residence with one of their sets of parents. This resembles a pattern of family life last witnessed before the great housing boom that followed World War II.

We have experienced a gradual delay in the launching of children in the past 20 years. The number of adult children, especially males, who live with their parents increased during the 1970s and 1980s, although the proportion of adult men and women living with their parents is still much less than the proportion in 1940—see Table 12-1 (Ahlburg and De Vita 1992; Clemens and Axelson 1985; Glick and Lin 1986; Schnaiberg and Goldenberg 1989). Sociologists Allan Schnaiberg and Sheldon Goldenberg (1989) refer to young adults who have not yet left home or who have returned home as "incompletely launched young adults." They also note that the pattern of increase in the number of these young adults is more typical of the middle class.

Table 12-1 Young Adults Living With Their Parents, by Age: United States, 1940, 1970, 1984, and 1991

		Percentage Living With Their Parents			
Year	Total 18-29 Years of Age (in thousands)	18-19	20-24	25-29	Total 18-29
1940	11,983	75	49	23	43
1970	12,361	77	37	9	34
1984	18,436	80	45	14	37
1992	15,809	83	58	30	35

SOURCE: U.S. Bureau of the Census (1943, 1971, 1977, 1985, 1992).

The increase is a function of a number of factors, including an increase in the age at first marriage, reduced employment opportunities for young adults, and the fact that smaller families are more able to accommodate a young adult who chooses to live at home. Schnaiberg and Goldenberg (1989) also note that in recent years there has been an educational squeeze. The rapid increase in the cost of higher education has constricted the ability of many families to pay for their children's college education. This in turn means that young adults have fewer options for type of school and location, more pressure to work during school, and higher personal and family financial indebtedness when they complete school. Audra Clemens and Lee Axelson (1985) studied two samples made up of a total of 39 respondents and found that financial

BOX 12-1: THE GLOBAL VIEW

Launching Children: Cross-Cultural Comparisons

The patterns of children leaving home vary in different countries. Danish young people appear to leave home late in their teens, and the majority have moved out by age 21. The pace of leaving home is more gradual for British teenagers, with greater activity in their early 20s and most having left by age 25.

In contrast, the rate of leaving home in the United States first peaks the year or so after high school and then slows down, with the majority of young adults having left by age 25 (Kiernan 1989).

There are a number of factors that account for the different pace of leaving home, including the extent to which young adults go on to higher education. The rate of enrollment in higher education is higher in the United States than in either Great Britain or Denmark. The variations may also depend on the availability of affordable (cheap) rental accommodations for students and young workers. Denmark has an abundance of cheap rentals, but such accommodations are scarce in Great Britain (Kiernan 1989).

problems and the need to save money are compelling factors in the decision of a young adult to live at home.

Today, most parents expect to launch their children when the children become young adults. Clemens and Axelson (1983) report that about 80% of parents with children 22 years of age or older had not expected their child to be living at home. Most parents said they wanted their children to be "up, gone, and on their own." Parents with young adults still in the home were not entirely pleased by the situation and mentioned problems such as the hours of their children's coming and going and their children's failure to clean and maintain the house. Nearly half of the 39 respondents who were interviewed said they had significant conflicts with their adult children.

Transitions

The longer postparenting stage has been associated with two significant transitions that individuals and families experience. For men, it is the midlife crisis; for women, it is the empty nest.

The Midlife Crisis

Midlife for men has often been viewed as a time of crisis. Popular as well as serious psychology converged in the mid-1970s and focused attention on the so-called male midlife crisis. Author Gail Sheehy captured considerable attention with an examination of what she called the predicable crises of adulthood in *Passages,* her 1976 book. Sheehy follows these crises from the stage of pulling up roots and breaking away, through the "Trying Twenties," the passage through the "Thirties," and into the "Deadline Decade" of one's 40s. Sheehy explained that simply turning 40 in our society is a marker event in itself. This is the time when men are "sized up" by their superiors, colleagues, and friends and size up their own lives as well. For many men, the end result of this "sizing up" is the need to let go of their dreams.

A more serious and scientific evaluation of men at midlife is offered by Daniel Levinson (1978) in *The Seasons of a Man's Life.* Sheehy, by the way, based much of her popular discussion of passages on Levinson's scientific writings that were available before he published his book. Levinson conducted in-depth interviews with 45 American males from a variety of walks of life—executives, scientists, laborers, and novelists. Levinson found that male adult life was marked by crises brought on by changes in social expectations, social roles, and social definitions of achievement.

The adult developmental stages of a man's life begin in his 20s (see Figure 12-2). Here he cuts free from childhood and adolescence and begins to

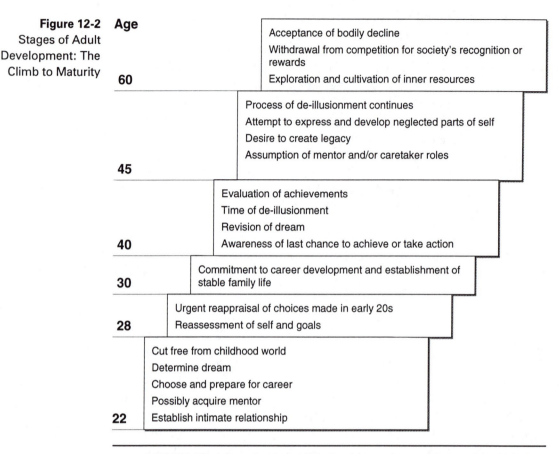

Figure 12-2
Stages of Adult
Development: The
Climb to Maturity

Age

Acceptance of bodily decline
Withdrawal from competition for society's recognition or rewards
60 Exploration and cultivation of inner resources

Process of de-illusionment continues
Attempt to express and develop neglected parts of self
Desire to create legacy
Assumption of mentor and/or caretaker roles
45

Evaluation of achievements
Time of de-illusionment
Revision of dream
40 Awareness of last chance to achieve or take action

Commitment to career development and establishment of stable family life
30

Urgent reappraisal of choices made in early 20s
28 Reassessment of self and goals

Cut free from childhood world
Determine dream
Choose and prepare for career
Possibly acquire mentor
22 Establish intimate relationship

SOURCE: *The Seasons of a Man's Life* by Daniel J. Levinson et al. Copyright © 1978 by Daniel J. Levinson. Reprinted by permission of Alfred A. Knopf, Inc.

formulate his life's dream. The dreams vary—from owning a successful business to winning a Pulitzer or Nobel prize. The dream may be specific or vague. Plans for achieving these dreams begin to be formulated. The 30s are a decade of discontent. Men who only dreamed about work and family begin the process of living these dreams on a day-by-day basis. The honeymoon stage of marriage is over, and the daily routines and constraints of family and work take on a numbing sameness. The choices men make in their 20s make are reevaluated in light of the reality of their 30s. Levinson notes that the mid-30s is the period during which men "settle down for real." The range of choices is narrowed, and men begin to settle for a few choices and invest themselves in these as fully as possible. Men at this stage become preoccupied with "making it" in their chosen field. They also focus on establishing a stable family and community life.

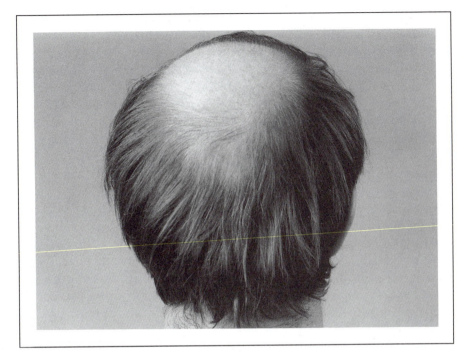

Thinning hair or becoming bald are two signs of the significant changes men go through in middle age.

The 40s are the period of evaluation. Men begin to experience significant physical changes, such as decreasing physical strength, thinning hair or balding, declining visual acuity, and hormonal changes. It should be noted that, with the exception of balding, women are experiencing the same physical changes in their 40s. With regard to work and career, men generally talk about this period as the "last chance" for realizing their dreams. Some men use this period to "run faster" and stay ahead of the younger men who are coming up the career ladder. Other men give up running and begin to believe that it is not possible to achieve their dreams or to outpace the competition. This may become a period of de-illusionment. De-illusionment continues into the 50s as men attempt to express and develop parts of the self that may have been neglected in earlier years. For example, men who have focused their energy on work and career may now concentrate on relationships. Men at midlife also begin to face death. Men (and women) tend to shift their perspectives from "time lived" to "time left" (Hagestad and Burton 1986; Tamir 1982).

Research on the Midlife Crisis

Research on midlife crisis has successfully delineated the stages of men's lives but has not successfully demonstrated that the midlife stage constitutes a genuine crisis for men. James Ciernia (1985) surveyed 227 businessmen between the ages of 25 and 60 and found that 69% acknowledged having a midlife crisis. However, the men noted that it was not a severe crisis but more of a period of assessment and readjustment. Michael Farrell and Stanley Rosenberg (1981) interviewed 300 men entering middle age. They found that only 12% evidenced classic signs of a midlife crisis. The symptoms of the crisis were depression, alienation, dissatisfaction with work, anxiety, and psychological distress, such as agitation and restlessness. Although the other men were not suffering from a diagnosable crisis with defined symptoms, they also were not completely happy and content. Farrell and Rosenberg's assessment of the psychological measures administered to these men indicated feelings of desperation, loss, and confusion. Similar findings are reported in a study by sociologist Robert Weiss (1990). Weiss interviewed 80 men between the ages of 35 and 55. These men were successful, upper-middle-class white men who were well established in their careers and settled into stable and secure marriages. Although these men were selected because they were stable and secure, they all reported stress and irritability. Half said they had trouble sleeping. The men reported few close personal friends, and over half reported having an affair.

Thus the research by Farrell, Rosenberg, and Weiss reveal men at midlife not in the throes of a full-blown crisis but settled into a life of chronic discontent. Because both studies used somewhat small and nongeneralizable samples, we should be cautious and note that these findings may not be representative of all midlife men. Much of the research on men at midlife is based on samples of middle- and upper-class men. Nevertheless, the studies do substantiate the notion that midlife is a definable stage for many men that involves significant changes and transitions.

Women at Midlife: The Empty Nest

The conventional wisdom and stereotypical view of women at midlife has been that they begin to experience the depression and dissatisfaction with the "empty nest" period. The stage at which all the children have left home and the husband is still deeply involved in his career has been considered a time of significant stress for midlife women (Harkins 1978). In both the popular literature, such as women's and "pop psychology" magazines, and the clinical literature, the empty nest has often been characterized as producing negative changes in women's psychological and physical condition. Elizabeth Harkins (1978) points out that medical journals have run full-page advertisements heralding the use of antidepressants to remedy the symptoms of the "empty nest syndrome."

Scientific evidence has been, at best, equivocal about the existence of an empty nest syndrome, and recent demographic evidence even questions the actual existence of the empty nest. Some research carried out and reported in the 1960s, a time during which few mothers worked and more children were launched as young adults, found that the quality of marital relationships was either unchanged or actually improved during the postparental period (Deutscher 1969). On the other hand, other studies report increased marital discord (Blood and Wolfe 1960) and feelings of maternal role loss (Bart 1971). A substantial percentage of mothers who reported maternal role loss said they were overprotective and overinvolved with their children. Many of these mothers reported being depressed.

Studies in the 1970s reported no apparent ill effects of the launching stage of family life and the resulting empty nest. Sociologist Norval Glenn's (1975) review of data from six national surveys found that middle-aged women whose children had left home reported somewhat greater happiness and enjoyment of life than did women of a similar age with a child or children still living at home.

Summarizing her own study of the empty nest transition, Elizabeth Harkins (1978) concludes that the transition has, at most, a rather slight and transitory effect on the psychological well-being of women and no effect on their physical well-being.

The existence of an empty nest period was questioned in the 1980s and is still being questioned in the 1990s. The increase in the percentage of working mothers has reduced considerably the number of women who would be left home alone, without work or a career, upon the launching of the last child. In addition, current changes in family structure indicate that many nests are not emptying; rather, they are getting more crowded. The delay in launching children, which we discussed in an earlier section of this chapter, and the increase in middle-aged women who are caring for older parents, which we discuss in the following section, have created a rather full nest and an overload of responsibilities for women in the 1990s.

Popular magazines and television talk shows notwithstanding, the notion of crises and depressions as marking the middle years of family life appear to be more myth than fact. Midlife constitutes a significant transition for men, women, and families. Some men do indeed have significant adjustment problems and crises in their 40s. Some women may also suffer physically and emotionally when their children leave home. But, in general, midlife is a period of transition, transitional tasks, and considerable personal and marital satisfaction.

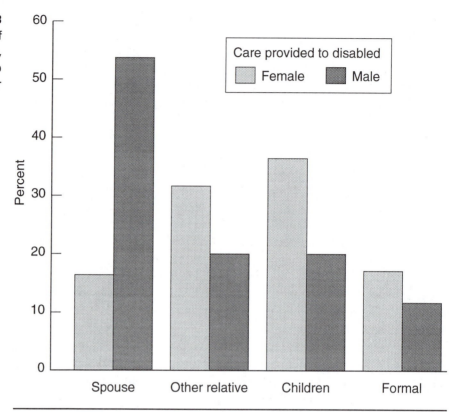

Figure 12-3 Percentage of Caregiving Days, by Relationship of the Caregiver

SOURCE: "Caregivers of the Frail Elderly: A National Profile" by Robyn Stone, Gail Lee Cafferata, and Judith Sangl, 1987, *The Gerontologist* 27(October) 616-626. Copyright © 1987 by the Gerontological Society of America. Adapted by permission.

Caregiving

Caregiving of older, frail, elderly relatives is one of the role responsibilities that those at midlife can expect to take on. Over 90% of older disabled people who are not in institutions depend, in whole or in part, on family and friends for care and help with household tasks, meal preparation, and personal hygiene (Soldo and Agree 1988).

Disabled elderly who are married are most likely to receive care from their spouses (Stone, Cafferata, and Sangl 1987). Because older men are more likely to have a living spouse, over half of the care received by elderly men is provided by their wives (see Figure 12-3). Older women, who are more likely to be widowed, receive the bulk of their care from adult children—most likely from daughters or daughters-in-law (Soldo and Agree 1988).

American children generally expect that they will be responsible for caring for their aging parents (Campbell and Brody 1985; Finley, Roberts, and Banahan III 1988; Schorr 1960). In fact, children often expect to provide more help and assistance than their elderly parents expect to receive (Martin, Ko, and Bengston 1987). Daughters feel more responsibility than do sons (Brubaker 1985). Most children in a family participate in caregiving in some fashion, including direct caregiving, providing backup for the main caregiver, and less direct and sporadic assistance (Mathews 1987).

The changes in structure of the American family and the age distribution of the population has highlighted the issue of caregiving and care-getting responsibility. The increase in working mothers has removed women from the home who 30 years ago would have been available to care for aging parents. More than 90% of adult men and 71% of adult women, aged 45 to 54, are in the labor force (U.S. Bureau of the Census 1992) At the same time, the proportion of the population that is aging and in need of care has increased. In 1900, fewer than 1 in 8 Americans was 55 older and only 1 in 25 was 65 or older. By 1991, 21% were 55 and older and 12% were at least 65 (U.S. Bureau of the Census 1992). The aging of the population has also increased the proportion of individuals who require long-term care. Of those between the ages of 65 and 72, 1 in 50 needs long-term care. Of those over 73 years of age, the chances are that 1 in 15 will need long-term care (Koch and Koch 1980).

A 1988 U.S. House of Representatives report, discussed in the July 16, 1990 issue of *Newsweek* ("Trading Places," 1990), noted that the average American woman will spend 17 years raising her children and 18 years helping her aging parents. *Newsweek* noted that just as women were departing the so-called mommy track of having to balance work, career, and raising children they moved into the "daughter track" of balancing work, career, and care for their aging parents.

Research on "filial responsibility" reports a somewhat more balanced view of the relationship between middle-aged children and their elderly parents than does the popular press. Research indicates that there is considerable and regular interaction between a substantial portion of children and their aging parents. Between 80% and 90% of older individuals report frequent contact with their children (Brubaker 1985). Three quarters of older parents have face-to-face contact with their children on a weekly or semiweekly basis (Troll, Miller, and Atchley 1980). When geographical distance precludes such regular contact, parents and children rely on the telephone or letters to stay in contact.

The nature of the contact between middle-aged children and their aging parents includes a wide range of reciprocal exchanges, including caring for someone during an illness, giving money, providing nonmonetary gifts, running errands, assistance with household repairs and upkeep, helping with transportation, and giving emotional support and affection (Lee and Ellithorpe 1982; Louis Harris and Associates 1975; Mancini and Blieszner 1989). Contrary to the current portrait of the dependent elderly, the general trend is for older persons to give more help to their children than they receive, although this is dependent on the age, health status, and economic status of the elderly parents (Riley and Foner 1968).

The crises of caregiving for elderly parents that led to the creation of the term the "daughter track" arise from the stresses and burdens of caring for ill or disabled parents (Brody 1985; Sheehan and Nuttall 1988). Providing such care has a profound impact on the primary caregiver and her family. Routines are disrupted, work plans are changed, and caregivers often experience physical or emotional strain, including depression, anxiety, frustration, helplessness, sleeplessness, lowered morale, and emotional exhaustion (Brody 1985; Chenoworth and Spencer 1986; Fengler and Goodrich 1979; George and Gwyther 1986; Mancini and Blieszner 1989; Robinson and Thurnher 1979; Snyder and Keefe 1985). Parent-child conflict may increase, and some researchers have attributed some instances of elder abuse to the demands on children of caring for elderly parents (Steinmetz 1988). The degree of stress

---

BOX 12-2: WHAT THE RESEARCH SHOWS

Elder Abuse

The darker side of later-life families is the occurrence of elder abuse. Abusive treatment toward the elderly can take many forms. Caregivers may tie an aged relative to a bed or chair while they go out shopping or finish their housework. They may overmedicate their parents to "ease" the older person's discomfort and to make them more manageable. Other caregivers resort to physical attacks to "make them mind" or to coerce their elderly relatives into changing a will or signing the house or social security checks over to them. Some caregivers have used such excessive physical violence or have neglected the needs of the older person to such an extent that death has resulted.

It is difficult to assess exactly how many elderly people are abused each year. Estimates of the proportion of those 65 years of age or older who are abused range from 4% to 10% (Pagelow 1989). The frequency of elder abuse could vary from 500,000 cases a year (for acts of physical violence only) to 2.5 million cases annually (U.S. Congress 1980).

People generally assume that the offenders in cases of elder abuse are the victims' children and the victims are disabled and dependent elderly. Sociologists Karl Pillemer and David Finkelhor (1988) conducted the first large-scale, random-sample survey of elder abuse and neglect. Interviews were conducted with 2,020 community-dwelling (noninstitutionalized) elderly persons in the Boston metropolitan area. Overall, 32 elderly persons per 1,000 reported experiencing physical violence, verbal aggression, and/or neglect in the past year. Although the conventional view of elder abuse is that of middle-aged children abusing and neglecting their elderly parents, Pillemer and Finkelhor found that spouses were the most frequent abusers of the elderly and that roughly equal numbers of men and women were victims. Women, however, suffered from the most serious forms of abuse.

and burden is a function of the nature of the parent's disability, the previous relationship between the parents and their children (Springer and Brubaker 1984), and the amount of interpersonal conflict in the relationship between the elder and the caregiver (Brody 1985; Sheehan and Nuttall 1988). Parents who suffer from cognitive disabilities, such as diverse dementias (e.g., Parkinson's disease or Alzheimer's disease), who cannot take care of routine daily tasks and bodily functions, and who engage in disruptive or destructive behavior are the most difficult to care for (Deimling and Bass 1986).

The caregiving relationship is not all stress and problems. Research on caregiving finds that many daughters report that there are gratifications derived from caregiving and that they felt appreciated by the care receiver (Lawton et al. 1989; Montenko 1989). Alexis Walker, Hwa-Yong Shin, and David Bird (1990) found that a majority of the caregivers they studied report that caregiving either had a positive impact on the relationship with their mothers or had no impact. Only 5.4% of the daughters reported a negative impact.

Researchers recognize that adults are now living longer and some will experience many years of poor health and become dependent on younger family members. The dimensions of this issue will likely change in the next few years. Today, and for the next few years, the ranks of the middle-aged will swell as the baby boomers born between 1946 and 1957 become middle-aged. Thereafter, we will see a continued increase in the proportion of the population that is elderly, but a decrease in the number of middle-aged and young adults who are available to care for their parents due to the fact that baby boomers had lower fertility than their parents (see Chapter 9). These trends seem to point toward increasing complexity and possibly stress in the relationships between the middle-aged and their aging parents.

THE LATER YEARS

The later years of family life have taken on greater significance for students of the family and family relations as more people live to old age and an increasing proportion of the total number of families in the United States are later-life families. Today, many families spend four or five times more years together as a couple in the later stages than in the earlier stages of the family life cycle (Brubaker 1985). In addition, later-life families today interact across a wider range of generations than did their counterparts in the past.

Later-life families are characterized by some distinct social and demographic characteristics. One unique feature is that they are multigenerational

Figure 12-4 Marital Status, by Sex and Age, 1991

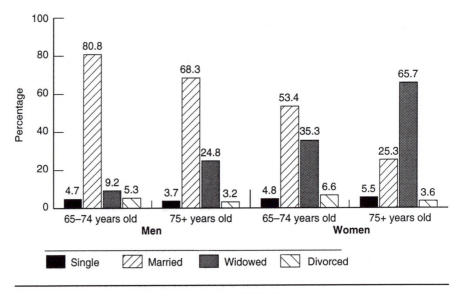

SOURCE: U.S. Bureau of the Census, 1992.

(Brubaker, 1985), Second, later life families have a lengthy family history (Brubaker 1985). They have lived together, gone through numerous family and personal transitions, coped with happiness and tragedy, made decisions, and developed affection and hostility.

Later-life families are also unique demographically. The later-life male (age 65 to 74) tends to be married and living with his spouse (79% in 1991). However, a little more than half (51%) of later-life women are married and live with their spouses (U.S. Bureau of the Census 1992). The difference is even more pronounced among men and women 75 and older. Nearly two thirds of men are married with a spouse present, compared to only 24% of women (Figure 12-4). These differences, of course, are due to women having a greater life expectancy than men and the fact that women tend to marry men two or three years older than themselves.

There is a misperception that the majority of later-life individuals are institutionalized in nursing homes. Only about 5% of the elderly population is institutionalized at any point in time (Soldo and Agree 1988). This figure rises to 21% for those over 85 (Soldo and Agree 1988). Estimates are that the chances of an elderly individual spending some time in an institution is about 4 in 10 (Cohen, Tell, and Wallack 1986; Liang and Jow-Ching Tu 1986). Thus the general pattern for later-life individuals is to be married and live with a spouse (especially for men), be widows and live alone, and have continued contact with their children and other relatives.

Grandparents have either been sentimentalized in the professional and popular literature or ignored. The sentimentalized image of grandparents is part of the mythology of the "classical family of Western nostalgia" (see Chapter 4). The sentimentalized grandparent was seen as the family patriarch or matriarch, watching over the three-generation extended family as they tended the family farm. Of course, this view of grandparents was largely a myth, as few families lived as extended families and few individuals lived long enough to be grandparents for more than a few years.

The increase in life span and demographic changes in families have allowed individuals to be grandparents for longer periods of time. Ironically, as this occurred, very little attention has been paid to the grandparent role. Three quarters of all individuals over 65 years of age have living grandchildren (Brubaker 1985; Shanas 1980). For many years, grandparents were the missing persons of the marriage and family literature. What little literature

Grandparents

Three quarters of all living individuals over 65 years of age have grandchildren.

there was considered grandparents as isolated and cut off from kin (Cherlin and Furstenberg 1986) The grandparent role was thought to be marginal at best and pathologically troubled at worst.

Grandparents were "rediscovered" in the 1980s (Hagestad and Lang 1986). This may have been a function of the new attention focused on the variety of family structures and roles. It also, no doubt, was the result of the increasing proportion of the population that is elderly, and thus grandparents, in society. New research on grandparents and the grandparent role indicates that there is no single type of grandparent. Sociologists Andrew Cherlin and Frank Furstenberg, Jr. (1986) surveyed a national sample of 510 grandparents and distinguished three types of grandparent styles: companionate, remote, and involved.

Companionate. Most of the grandparents surveyed (55%) viewed their relationships with their grandchildren as companionate. These relationships are characterized by closeness, affection, companionship, and play. Companionate grandparents tend to live close to their grandchildren and have regular contact with them. Companionate grandparents do not see themselves as responsible for setting rules or disciplining their grandchildren, and they rarely take on parent-type roles or responsibilities.

Remote. Remote grandparents, as the term implies, are not intimately or closely involved in the lives of their grandchildren. The remoteness is a function of geographical distance and not choice. About 3 in 10 grandparents surveyed fit into this category.

Involved. Involved grandparents, who made up 16% of those surveyed, are in regular contact with their grandchildren. Unlike companionate grandparents, involved grandparents assume parentlike roles and responsibilities. They set and enforce rules and discipline their grandchildren. Involved grandparents are more likely to be grandmothers than grandfathers. The involvement often emerges in times of crisis, such as when the mother is an unmarried teenager or a divorced mother who has to enter the workforce. Some involved grandparents can become overinvolved and blur the line between grandparent and parent. Cherlin and Furstenberg note that there are three factors that determine how much interaction grandparents have with their grandchildren: distance, distance, and distance! Most grandparents live close enough to their grandchildren to have regular interaction with them. One study found that three fourths of the grandparents surveyed see a grandchild at least once a week (Troll 1983).

Grandparents generally get a great deal of pleasure and satisfaction from their role. About 80% of a sample of 90 grandmothers said they valued this intergenerational relationship because it provided a continuation of themselves through another generation (Timberlake 1980). Similarly, in a sample of 125 grandmothers, 80% reported being happy with the grandparent-grandchild relationship (Robertson 1977). Most grandparents surveyed agreed that being a grandparent is easier than being a parent. Nearly three in five of those surveyed said that grandchildren filled a need of creativity, accomplishment, competence, and reconfirmation of their own identity. Grandmothers tend to derive greater satisfaction from the grandparent role than do grandfathers (Thomas 1986).

One difficulty that grandparents do encounter with their role results from the divorce of the grandchildren's parents. Grandparents report that they are not always informed about an impending divorce. In one survey of grandparents, only 22% said that they had been informed about the divorce before the final decision was made (Mathews and Sprey 1984). Forty percent of the grandparents said they were surprised by the divorce, whereas 30% said they had anticipated it.

The resulting custody assignment of the children greatly affects the grandparent-grandchild relationship. Generally, wives receive custody of dependent children after a divorce and so maternal grandparents are able to continue their relationship with their grandchildren. When the children of a divorce are younger, the relationship between the grandparent and grandchild may be more intense, as the divorced parent needs both financial and emotional support from the grandparents. The situation for the paternal grandparents may not be as satisfying and the quantity and quality of paternal grandparents' relations with their grandchildren tends to decline after a divorce (Cherlin and Furstenberg 1986). This is especially the case because grandparents' legal rights to visitation with children of divorce are ambiguous. Grandparents tend to have minimal legal standing or rights when parents divorce (Wilson and DeShane 1982). One state, Oregon, enacted legislation in 1979 that permitted visiting rights to grandparents. However, in 1990, a New York State Supreme Court Appellate Division said that grandparents do not have a legal right to visit a grandchild over the objection of the child's parents.

RETIREMENT

Retirement constitutes a significant marital and personal transition for individuals. Although many men and women look forward to retirement and both expect and experience many personal and marital benefits from it, there is also the view that retirement can have important negative consequences for individuals and their marriages. Retirement is often thought to be associated with increased physical and mental health problems, lowered standards of living, and conflictual marital relationships, as both the husband and the wife adjust to their new relationship. However, research indicates that retirement *does not* generally lead to increased physical, mental health, or marital problems (Szinovacz, Ekerdt, and Vinick 1992).

| Age of Retirement | The federal government enacted legislation in 1979 that outlawed compulsory retirement at age 65. Except for a few occupations, mandatory retirement ages have been totally eliminated. Thus nearly all workers can choose when, and if, they retire. The impact of eliminating mandatory retirement has not swelled the ranks of the workforce with older workers. In fact, an increasing number of workers are opting for early retirement before the age of 65. |

Marriage influences when men and women chose to retire, and the influence is especially strong for married women (Atchley and Miller 1983). Married women are generally more likely to retire before they reach 65, but unmarried women (mostly divorced or widowed women) tend to retire after the age of 65. This is likely due to the fact that older couples who both work try to coordinate their retirements and that women tend to marry men older than they are (Henrette and O'Rand 1980).

| The Impact of Retirement on Marriage | It is impossible to generalize about the impact of retirement on marriage for all later-life families. The impact depends on a number of factors, including the economic situation of the family, physical health of the individuals, and the type of retirement. |

One of the realities of retirement for most individuals and families is that income declines substantially. For many families, this decline puts them below the official poverty line. The Census Bureau found that 12.9% of those over 65 years of age live in households below the poverty line (U.S. Bureau of the Census 1993). Later-life minority families are even more likely to live in poverty. Nearly 34% of elderly blacks and 22% of elderly Latinos over 65 years of age live in poverty.

Health problems can also influence the impact of retirement. Although health problems generally increase with old age, there is no evidence that retirement per se causes health problems to increase (Atchley and Miller 1983). Some of the physical and mental health problems that appear associated with retirement may have had their onset before retirement and may indeed have been the motivating factors for retiring.

Retirement can have a variety of consequences for older couples— one positive consequence is more time to do things together or "play."

Finally, the type of retirement has some bearing on how the partners adjust to retirement. One later-life family structure, the "traditional" or "single" retirement (Brubaker 1985), occurs when only one partner, usually the husband, works and then retires. There are also two forms of dissynchronized retirements (Brubaker 1985). In the "dissynchronized husband initially" couple, the husband retires before the wife. This may occur because the husband started his career before the wife and can retire earlier, or it can be a function of the husband being older than his wife and thus eligible to retire earlier. In the "dissynchronized wife initially" retirement, the wife retires before the husband. This type of retirement pattern occurs infrequently. When it does, it may be because the wife is not satisfied with her work or because her husband urges her to retire. In some instances, the wife may retire because of health-related concerns. Finally, "synchronized retirement" or "dual retirement" occurs when both husband and wife are employed and elect to retire at the same time.

Research on the impact of retirement on marital satisfaction and marital quality finds variable outcomes (Atchley 1992). There are indeed women who complain about having their newly retired husbands underfoot 24 hours a day, but this reaction is more stereotype than reality. Robert Atchley and Sheila Miller (1983) examined a sample of 208 married, middle-class couples. The study found that retirement had no measurable effect on these couples' lives. Those who placed a high value on intimacy and family ties said that retirement gave them the freedom to enjoy a healthy and vital relationship. Sociologist Graham Spanier and his colleagues Robert Lewis and Charles Cole (1975) found that retired families experienced the same high degree of marital satisfaction that they had experienced early in the family life cycle when they had no children. Elizabeth Hill and Lorraine Dorfman (1982) interviewed 36 housewives whose husbands had recently retired. Among the positive aspects of retirement mentioned were time available to do what they wanted to do, increased companionship, flexibility of schedule, and the husband did more household chores. The negative aspects of retirement included financial problems, too much togetherness, and not enough for the husband to do.

In general, research does not find that retirement has a direct effect on marital satisfaction (Atchley 1992). Maximiliane Szinovacz (1980) assessed the effects of a wife's retirement on marital quality. When the husbands and the wives were asked how the wife's retirement affected the quality of the marriage, only 1 man in 24 said the marriage was "worse." About half of the husbands and wives said the marriage was the same. The remaining husbands and wives (46% of the husbands and 48% of the wives) said there had been at least a slight improvement in the marriage. The wives who said that the marriage had improved based this conclusion on the reduction of the levels of stress they were under due to pressures on their time and conflicting time schedules. On the other hand, retired wives reported that they did find it difficult to settle into full-time housework and that housework was not a satisfying substitute for outside employment.

Unhappiness and dissatisfaction with marriage following retirement are related to older age, low income, poor health, and a lack of satisfaction with life in general and marriage in particular (Heyman and Jeffers 1968). Clearly, marital adjustment of retirees and their spouses is related to the level of marital quality, adjustment, and satisfaction from earlier in the marriage (Medley 1977). Timothy Brubaker (1985) concludes that retirement amplifies both the positive and the negative qualities of a marriage.

DEATH AND WIDOWHOOD

Perhaps the most profound stage in the family life cycle is the transition from married to widowed. Widowhood is a stage of marriage and family life that is largely experienced by women—there are more than 8 million widows but only 1.8 million widowers (males) aged 65 or older in our society (U.S. Bureau of the Census 1992). Seventy percent of women outlive their husbands (Treas and Bengston 1987). The explanation for the great disparity between the number of widows and widowers is that women have a greater life expectancy than men and women also tend to marry men who are a few years older. The death of a spouse ends the marriage but not the family life cycle. The marriage continues in the mind of the survivor (Brubaker 1985) as the widow or widower goes through the process of bereavement and adjusts to life without her or his partner.

Although death is a common factor that ends many marriages, the process of becoming a widow differs. The least common path to widowhood is the sudden death of a spouse (Bowling and Cartwright 1982; Lopata 1973). A sudden massive heart attack, a stroke, or even a fatal accident may be the cause of death. The sudden death of her husband means that the wife had little warning and little time to plan for his death.

The more common path to widowhood is when death occurs after a long illness or series of health problems. The illness—heart disease, cancer, a disabling stroke, or some other chronic problem—may have become the focal point of the couple's interaction for some time (Brubaker 1985). One partner may have organized his or her life and routines around the demands of caring for the ill spouse. Helena Lopata (1973) found that half of all widows cared for their husbands shortly before death, while 40% had cared for their husbands for more than a year preceding death. This type of widowhood, while it can be planned for, still produces significant issues and stresses. On one hand, the widow is relieved of the caretaking responsibility that she has shouldered for some time. On the other hand, the entire routine of caregiving and planning has now been disrupted. Before her husband died, her life may have been organized around trips to the hospital or a caretaking routine in the home. Her network of friends, associates, and supporters may have included physicians, nurses, or hospice workers. Once her partner dies, she no longer organizes her day and routine around caretaking activities and her social and

The Process of Becoming a Widow

support network loses the health-care professionals who she interacted with on a regular basis.

A third path to widowhood is when a chronically ill husband dies unexpectedly. In some instances, the illness took a sudden turn for the worse and resulted in death; in other instances, the wife may not have been adequately informed about the seriousness of her husband's illness.

Grief and Bereavement
The first stage of widowhood is grief and bereavement. Grief, disbelief, a sense of loss or abandonment, and mourning characterize this initial stage. During the first few days and weeks, widows tend to be in a state of chaos and crisis.

BOX 12-3: WHAT THE RESEARCH SHOWS

The Legacy of Aging: Inheritance and Disinheritance

An often overlooked legacy of aging are the patterns of inheritance and disinheritance that occur in the relationships between aging family members, their kin, and their social networks of friends. Sociologist Jeffrey Rosenfeld (1979) has examined these patterns in a book, *The Legacy of Aging: Inheritance and Disinheritance in Social Perspective,* and in articles and essays (e.g., Rosenfeld 1990).

Rosenfeld notes that one of the legacies of aging in America today is that there are now more opportunities for involvements outside the family. Old age brings with it new social networks and thus, according to Rosenfeld's research, new patterns of inheritance and disinheritance. The new social networks, such as retirement communities, religious organizations, and close groups of elderly friends and neighbors, mean that children can no longer take for granted that they will inherit their parents' estate.

Although a substantial number of aging parents naturally assume that they will name their children as their heirs, others are not so certain. Some of the individuals that Rosenfeld interviewed live in retirement communities in Arizona or Florida and see their family only once or twice a year. Others, who may have divorced or been widowed earlier in life, have lost touch with their one or two children. In place of these contacts, they have established close ties with new friends or with church-related organizations. For these individuals, who to leave their estate to is neither simple nor clear.

Rosenfeld predicts that in 30 years 15% of all trust and estate plans could include bequests that are unconventional by today's standards. These include bequests to church groups, to neighbors and friends rather than children, and to heterosexual or homosexual lovers. Others may simply chose to follow the guidance of the bumper sticker that says "I'm Spending My Kid's Inheritance."

The stage of moving from having a partner to being alone involves considerable disorganization and the newly bereaved tend to have significantly more depression and psychic distress compared to longer-term widows (Farberow et al. 1987).

The second stage is a transitional period during which the surviving partner attempts to organize a new life. Feelings of grief begin to lessen. New relationships are established, old ones are reorganized, and the widow develops a new identity as a single person.

The final stage is the establishment and maintenance of the new lifestyle as a widow.

The bereavement process varies for each individual, and much depends on the nature of the marital relationship, the process by which the individual became a widow (sudden death or death after a long illness), and the personal and structural characteristics of the widow (friends, relatives, social networks). Lopata (1973) suggests that the intense feelings of grief begin to subside between six weeks and six months after the death of the partner. However, 20% of the widows Lopata studied said they never have gotten over the death of their husbands.

Widowhood as a Stage of Life

Immediately after the spouse's death, the widow or widower may have an abundance of help and social support. Friends and relatives call, visit, prepare meals, and invite the bereaved to dinner or to go out. As time goes on, this level of social support begins to decrease. It is expected that the widow will move beyond the crisis stage of death and bereavement and "get on with her life."

The major continuing support that widows receive is from their children. Daughters and daughters-in-law provide more help and assistance than do sons or sons-in-law (Lopata 1973, 1979).

Widowhood tends to be an enduring role for women. Estimates are that fewer than 5% of women widowed after the age of 55 will remarry (Hiltz 1978).

Widows, similar to those women who are separated or divorce, tend to be at higher risk than single or married persons for physical and mental illness, accidents, suicides, and death (Kitson et al. 1989). In many areas, the impact of the loss of a spouse is greater for men than for women. Men have higher rates of mental illness (Gove 1972) and suicide (Rico-Velasco and Mynko 1973).

Because men tend to die at a younger age than women, there are more elderly widows than elderly widowers.

SUMMING UP

We have examined two important stages in the family life cycle—the middle, postparental stage and the later stage. Because of demographic changes, both stages have lengthened and taken on considerable importance. Yet we have only begun to experience the beginnings of significant and profound changes in the nature and structure of middle- and later-life families. Increased life expectancy means that more and more people are living to older ages. Longer life expectancy means that the later stages of family life—the postparenting stage, retirement, and widowhood—are lasting longer for larger portions of the population. More middle-aged individuals have older parents than did their counterparts 30 or 50 years ago. Because of lower fertility rates, older parents have fewer children to count on for help, and the children have fewer siblings to share the burdens of caring and supporting older parents (Treas and Bengston 1987). Increasingly, the aging parent is older, female, and widowed. Middle-stage family life is experiencing significant changes as children delay leaving home and older relatives require help and assistance. The notion of the "empty nest" turns out to be more myth than reality, and the label for that stage of the family life cycle is more appropriately replaced by the term "postparental stage" (even though adult children may still be in the home).

The media have often portrayed the middle and later stages of family life as characterized by depression and crises—the male midlife crisis, the depression of the empty nest, the isolation and desperation of the elderly, the loneliness and despair of widowhood, and the entrapment of having to care for dependent parents and partners. In reality, the middle and later stages of life have a greater balance of positives and negatives than the popular conceptions of the family portray. Some roles and responsibilities are indeed stressful and problematic; others, like becoming a grandparent, contain far more joy than pain. Other roles are merely significant transitions in the family and personal life cycle that involve both positive and negative elements.

REFERENCES

Ahlburg, Dennis A. and Carol J. De Vita. 1992. "New Realities of the American Family." *Population Bulletin* 47(2):2-44.

Atchley, Robert C. 1992. "Retirement and Marital Satisfaction." Pp. 145-58 in *Families and Retirement,* edited by Maximilian E. Szinovacz, David J. Ekerdt, and Barbara H. Vinick. Newbury Park, CA: Sage.

Atchley, Robert C. and Sheila J. Miller. 1983. "Types of Elderly Couples." Pp. 77-90 in *Family Relationships in Later Life,* edited by Timothy H. Brubaker. Beverly Hills, CA: Sage.

Bart, Pauline. 1971. "Depression in Middle-Aged Women." Pp. 163-86 in *Women in Sexist Society,* edited by Vivian Gornick and Barbara K. Moran. New York: Basic Books.

Blood, Robert and Donald Wolfe. 1960. *Husbands and Wives: The Dynamics of Marital Living.* Glencoe, IL: Free Press.

Bowling, Ann and Ann Cartwright. 1982. *Life After Death: A Study of the Elderly Widowed.* New York: Tavistock.

Brody, Elaine M. 1985. "Parent Care as a Normative Family

Stress." *The Gerontologist* 25 (February):19-29.

Brubaker, Timothy H. 1985. *Later Life Families.* Beverly Hills, CA: Sage.

Campbell, Ruth and Elaine M. Brody. 1985. "Women's Changing Roles and Help to the Elderly." *The Gerontologist* 25(6):584-92.

Chenoworth, Barbara and Beth Spencer. 1986. "Dementia: The Experience of Family Caregivers." *The Gerontologist* 26 (June):267-72.

Cherlin, Andrew J. and Frank F. Furstenberg, Jr. 1986. *The New American Grandparent: A Place in the Family, a Life Apart.* New York: Basic Books.

Ciernia, James. 1985. "Myths About Male Midlife Crisis." *Psychological Reports* 56(June): 1003-7.

Clemens, Audra and Lee J. Axelson. 1985. "The Not-So-Empty-Nest: The Return of the Fledgling Adult." *Family Relations* 34(April):259-64.

Cohen, Marc, Eileen Tell, and Stanley Wallack. 1986. "The Lifetime Risks and Costs of Nursing Home Use Among the Elderly." *Medical Care* 24(12): 1161-72.

Deimling, Gary T. and David M. Bass. 1986. "Symptoms of Mental Impairment Among Elderly Adults and Their Effects on Family Caregivers." *Journal of Gerontology* 41(November): 778-84.

Deutscher, Irwin. 1969. "From Parental to Post-Parental Life." *Sociological Symposium* 3(Fall): 47-60.

Duvall, Eleanor M. 1977. *Marriage and Family Development.* Philadelphia: J. B. Lippincott.

Eshleman, J. Ross. 1991. *The Family: An Introduction.* 6th ed. Boston: Allyn & Bacon.

Farberow, Norman L., Dolores E. Gallagher, Michael J. Gilewski, and Larry W. Thompson. 1987. "An Examination of the Early Impact of Bereavement in Psychological Distress in Survivors of Suicide." *The Gerontologist* 27 (October):592-98.

Farrell, Michael and Stanley Rosenberg. 1981. *Men at Midlife.* Boston: Auburn House.

Fengler, Alfred and Nancy Goodrich. 1979. "Wives of Elderly Disabled Men: The Hidden Patients." *The Gerontologist* 19(April):175-83.

Finley, Nancy J., M. Diane Roberts, and Benjamin F. Banahan III. 1988. "Motivators and Inhibitors of Attitudes of Filial Obligation Toward Aging Parents." *The Gerontologist* 28(February): 73-78.

George, Linda K. and Lisa P. Gwyther. 1986. "Caregiver Well-Being: A Multidimensional Examination of Family Caregivers of Demented Adults." *The Gerontologist* 26 (June):253-59.

Glenn, Norval. 1975. "Psychological Well-Being in the Postparental Stage: Some Evidence From National Surveys." *Journal of Marriage and the Family* 37 (February):105-10.

Glick, Paul. 1977. "Updating the Life Cycle of the Family." *Journal of Marriage and the Family* 39(February):5-14.

Glick, Paul and Sung-Ling Lin. 1986. "More Young Adults Are Living With Their Parents: Who Are They?" *Journal of Marriage and the Family* 48 (February):107-12.

Gove, Walter R. 1972. "Sex, Marital Status and Suicide." *Journal of Health and Social Behavior* 13(June):204-13.

Hagestad, Gunhild O. and Linda M. Burton. 1986. "Grandparenthood, Life Context, and Family Development." *American Behavioral Scientist* 29(4):471-84.

Hagestad, Gunhild and Mary E. Lang. 1986. "The Transition to Grandparenthood: Unexplored Issues." *Journal of Family Issues* 7(June):115-30.

Harkins, Elizabeth. 1978. "Effects of Empty Nest Transition on Self-Report of Psychological and Physical Well-Being." *Journal of Marriage and the Family* 40(August):549-56.

Henrette, John C. and Angela M. O'Rand. 1980. "Labor Force Participation of Older Married Women." *Social Security Bulletin* 43(August) 10-16.

Heyman, Dorothy K. and Frances C. Jeffers. 1968. "Wives and Retirement: A Pilot Study." *Journal of Gerontology* 23(October):488-96.

Hill, Elizabeth A. and Lorraine T. Dorfman. 1982. "Reactions of Housewives to the Retirement of Their Husbands." *Family Relations* 31(2):195-200.

Hiltz, Roxanne. 1978. "Widowhood: A Roleless Role." *Marriage and Family Review* 1(6):1-10.

Kiernan, Kathleen. 1989. "The Departure of Children." Pp. 120-44 in *Later Phases of the Family Life Cycle,* edited by E. Grebenik, Charlotte Hohn, and Rainer Mackensen. Oxford, UK: Clarendon.

Kitson, Gay C., Karen Benson Babri, Mary Joan Roach, and Kathleen S. Placidi. 1989. "Adjustment to Widowhood and Divorce: A Review." *Journal of Family Issues* 10(1):5-32.

Koch, Lewis and Joanne Koch. 1980. "Parent Abuse—A New Plague." *Parade,* January 27, pp. 14-15.

Lawton, M. Powell, Morton H. Kleban, Miriam Moss, Michael Rovine, and Allen Glicksman. 1989. "Measuring Caregiver Appraisal." *Journal of Gerontology: Psychological Sciences* 44(May):P61-P71.

Lee, Gary R. and Eugene Ellithorpe. 1982. "Intergenerational Exchange and Subjective Well-Being." *Journal of Marriage and the Family* 44 (February):217-24.

Levinson, Daniel, with Charlotte N. Darrow, Edward B, Klein, Martha H. Levinson, and Braxton McKee. 1978. *The Seasons of a Man's Life.* New York: Alfred A. Knopf.

Liang, Jersey and Edward Jow-Ching Tu. 1986. "Estimating Lifetime Risk of Nursing Home Residency: A Further Note." *The Gerontologist* 26 (October):560-63.

Lopata, Helena Z. 1973. *Widowhood in an American City.* Cambridge, MA: Schenkman.

———. 1979. *Women as Widows.* New York: Elsevier.

Louis Harris and Associates. 1975. *The Myth and Reality of Aging in America.* Washington, DC: National Council on Aging.

Mancini, Jay A. and Rosemary Blieszner. 1989. "Aging Parents and Adult Children: Research Themes in Intergenerational Relations." *Journal of Marriage and the Family* 51(May):275-90.

Martin, M. E., C. Ko, and Vern L. Bengston. 1987. "Filial Responsibility and Patterns of Caregiving in Three Generational Families." Paper presented at the annual meeting of the Pacific Sociological Society, Eugene, OR.

Mathews, Sarah H. 1987. "Provision of Care to Old Parents: Division of Responsibility Among Adult Children." *Research on Aging* 9(March):45-60.

Mathews, Sarah H. and Jetse Sprey. 1984. "The Impact of Divorce on Grandparenthood: An Exploratory Study." *The Gerontologist* 24(1):41-47.

Medley, Morris L. 1977. "Marital Adjustment in the Post Retirement Years." *Family Coordinator* 26(January):5-11.

Montenko, Aluma K. 1989. "The Frustrations, Gratifications, and Well-Being of Dementia Caregivers." *The Gerontologist* 29:166-72.

Pagelow, Mildred. 1989. "The Incidence and Prevalence of Criminal Abuse of Other Family Members." Pp. 263-313 in *Family Violence,* edited by Lloyd Ohlin and Michael Tonry. Chicago: University of Chicago Press.

Pillemer, Karl and David Finkelhor. 1988. "The Prevalence of Elder Abuse: A Random Sample Survey." *The Gerontologist* 28(1): 51-57.

Rico-Velasco, Jesus and Lizbeth Mynko. 1973. "Suicide and Marital Status: A Changing Relationship?" *Journal of Marriage and the Family* 35(May):239-44.

Riley, Matilda W. and Anne Foner. 1968. "The Family in an Aging Society: A Matrix of Latent Relationships." *Journal of Family Issues* 4(September):439-54.

Robertson, Joan F. 1977. "Grandmotherhood: A Study of Role Conceptions." *Journal of Mar-*

riage and the Family 39(February):165-74.

Robinson, Betsy and Majda Thurnher. 1979. "Take Care of Parents: A Family-Cycle Transition." *The Gerontologist* 19 (December):586-93.

Rosenfeld, Jeffrey P. 1979. *The Legacy of Aging: Inheritance and Disinheritance in Social Perspective.* Norwood, NJ: Ablex.

———. 1990. "To Heir Is Human." *Probate and Property* 4(July/August):21-25.

Schnaiberg, Allan and Sheldon Goldenberg. 1989 "From Empty Nest to Crowded Nest: The Dynamics of Incompletely-Launched Young Adults." *Social Problems* 36(June):251-69.

Schorr, Alvin L. 1960. *Filial Responsibility in the Modern American Family.* Washington, DC: Government Printing Office.

Shanas, Ethel. 1980. "Older People and Their Families: The New Pioneers." *Journal of Marriage and the Family* 42 (February):9-15.

Sheehan, Nancy W. and Paul Nuttall. 1988. "Conflict, Emotional and Personal Strain Among Family Caregivers." *Family Relations* 37(January): 92-98.

Sheehy, Gail. 1976. *Passages.* New York: Dutton.

Snyder, Barbara and Kathy Keefe. 1985. "The Unmet Needs of Family Caregivers for Frail and Disabled Adults." *Social Work in Health Care* 10(Spring):1-14.

Soldo, Beth J. and Emily M. Agree. 1988. "America's Elderly." *Population Bulletin* 43(September):1-53.

Spanier, Graham B., Robert A. Lewis, and Charles L. Cole. 1975. "Marital Adjustment Over the Family Life Cycle: The Issue of Curvilinearity." *Journal of Marriage and the Family* 37(2):263-75.

Springer, Dianne and Timothy Brubaker. 1984. *Family Caregivers and Dependent Elderly: Minimizing Stress and Maximizing Independence.* Beverly Hills, CA: Sage.

Steinmetz, Suzanne K. 1988. *Duty Bound: Elder Abuse and Family Care.* Beverly Hills, CA: Sage.

Stone, Robyn, Gail Cafferata, and Judith Sangl. 1987. "Caregivers of the Frail Elderly: A National Profile." *The Gerontologist* 27(October):616-626.

Szinovacz, Maximiliane E. 1980. "Female Retirement: Effects on Spousal Roles and Marital Adjustment." *Journal of Family Issues* 1(September):423-40.

Szinovacz, Maximiliane E., David J. Ekerdt, and Barbara H. Vinick, eds. 1992. *Families and Retirement.* Newbury Park, CA: Sage.

Tamir, Lois M. 1982. "Men at Middle Age: Developmental Transitions." *Annals of the American Academy of Political and Social Sciences* 464(November):47-56.

Thomas, Jeanne L. 1986. "Age and Sex Differences in Perceptions of Grandparenting."

Journal of Gerontology 41(3): 417-23.

Timberlake, E. M. 1980. "The Value of Grandchildren to Grandparents." *Journal of Gerontological Social Work* 3 (Fall):63-76.

"Trading Places." 1990. *Newsweek,* July 16, pp. 48ff.

Treas, Judith and Vern L. Bengston. 1987. "The Family in Later Years." Pp. 625-48 in *Handbook of Marriage and the Family,* edited by Marvin B. Sussman and Suzanne K. Steinmetz. New York: Plenum.

Troll, Lillian E. 1983. "Grandparents: The Family Watchdogs." Pp. 63-76 in *Family Relationships in Older Life,* edited by Timothy H. Brubaker. Beverly Hills, CA: Sage.

Troll, Lillian E., Sheila J. Miller, and Robert J. Atchley. 1980. "The Family of Later Life: A Decade Review." *Journal of Marriage and the Family* 33 (November):187-241.

U.S. Bureau of the Census. 1943. *Sixteenth Census of the United States, 1940: Vol. 4, Characteristics by Age.* Washington, DC: Government Printing Office.

U.S. Bureau of the Census. 1971. *Marital Status and Family Status: March, 1970.* Current Population Reports, P-20, No. 212. Washington, DC: Government Printing Office.

U.S. Bureau of the Census. 1977. *Marriage, Divorce, Widowhood, and Remarriage by Family Characteristics: June, 1975.* Current Population Reports, P-20,

No. 312. Washington, DC: Government Printing Office.

U.S. Bureau of the Census. 1985. *Marital Status and Living Arrangements: March, 1984.* Current Population Reports, P-20, No. 399. Washington, DC: Government Printing Office.

U.S. Bureau of the Census. 1992. *Statistical Abstracts of the United States.* Washington, DC: Government Printing Office.

————. 1993. *Poverty in the United States, 1992.* Washington, DC: Government Printing Office.

U.S. Congress, House Select Committee on Aging, Subcommittee on Human Services. 1980. *Domestic Abuse of the Elderly.* Washington, DC: Government Printing Office.

Walker, Alexis, J., Hwa-Yong Shin, and **David N. Bird.** 1990. "Perceptions of Rela-tionship Change and Caregiver Satisfaction." *Family Relations* 39 (2):147-52.

Weiss, Robert S. 1990. *Staying the Course: The Emotional and Social Lives of Men Who Do Well at Work.* New York: Free Press.

Wilson, Keren B. and **Michael R. DeShane.** 1982. "The Legal Rights of Grandparents: A Preliminary Discussion." *The Gerontologist* 22(April): 67-71.

CHAPTER **13**

■■ Divorce and Remarriage

Wendy and Christopher are two corporate attorneys who were interviewed by Philip Blumstein and Pepper Schwartz (1983) as part of their study of American couples. Wendy and Christopher first met in college and then drifted apart until they met one summer as clerks working in the same law office. Their relationship blossomed and they were married. When they graduated from law school, they had to struggle over who would stay with the firm they had clerked for and who would move to another firm (the law firm had a rule that prohibited married couples working together). Wendy and Christopher set up an apartment in a high-rise luxury building and embarked on a fast-lane marriage and law careers. But strain and other problems caught up with Wendy and Christopher, and within a year of the time they were interviewed by Blumstein and Schwartz, the marriage was over and Christopher had moved to Chicago.

Pete and Nancy's marriage lasted considerably longer than Wendy and Christopher's. Pete was a graduate assistant and Nancy a sophomore in college when they met. They fell in love and were married. Nancy dropped out of school when Pete moved to California to finish his doctorate degree. Pete and Nancy had two children. Nancy stayed home to raise the children while Pete climbed the academic ladder—Instructor, Assistant Professor, Associate Professor, Professor. Money was tight, but Pete always managed to teach night school or summer school so that their economic problems were never really severe. They were married 21 years. Many people seeing Pete and Nancy in church, shopping together, or planning for a trip to Europe with the whole family thought they had the ideal marriage and the perfect family. But appearances can be deceiving. Nancy began to express her dissatisfactions about her life. She tried to get part-time work. Finally, Nancy and Pete went for marriage counseling. Four months after the counseling started, Nancy announced that she wanted a divorce. The ideal marriage was over.

Although the two marriages just described are quite different in terms of length, presence of children, and other details they shared some common features. In each case, the failure of the marriage caused significant personal problems for all involved. Divorce is among the most stressful events a person can experience (along with the death of a loved one). It is a personal tragedy for the husband and wife, their children, family, and friends.

At another level, many people look to the rate of divorce as a temperature reading on the health of the family as an institution. Increases in the divorce rate in the 1970s prompted some social observers to make dire forecasts about the future of the family (Etzioni 1977; Packard, 1972; Toffler 1972; see also Chapter 16). However, statistics also indicate that 65% to 70% of those who separate or divorce remarry (Bumpass, Sweet, and Martin 1990). Thus it would appear that people are dissatisfied with a marriage but are not dissatisfied with the institution of marriage (Berger and Kellner 1964).

This chapter examines the causes of divorce, the consequences of divorce, and remarriage. We begin by first assessing divorce, the various statistics on divorce, and the factors that are associated with higher or lower risk of divorce. We then turn to divorce as a process—the steps people go through in deciding they want to end a marriage and how the marriage ends. When a marriage ends, the world does not. People move on and "go it alone." The next section looks at the world of divorced individuals and the consequences of divorce for children. The final section focuses on the 65% to 70% of divorced individuals who remarry and the issues and concerns surrounding remarriage and "second," "reconstituted," or "blended" families.

THE RISK OF DIVORCE: CALCULATING THE RATES AND ASSESSING THE TRENDS

The current concern with the high divorce rate in the United States obscures the fact that some form of marital dissolution has existed across societies and over time. Divorce, or some provision for ending a marriage, exists in most societies. Settlers in the American colonies were devout Protestants and held deep beliefs about lifelong marriage, even if it meant unhappiness and suffering (Price and McKenry 1988). However, even in the colonies, lower courts would sanction some divorces (see Chapter 4). As the culture changed and individuals began to assert greater control over their personal lives in the 1800s, there was a substantial increase in the rate of divorce (Price and McKenry 1988). Today, in the 1990s, most people in the United States and many other Western nations assume that divorce is an appropriate means to ending an unhappy or unfulfilling marriage.

When a man and a woman walk down the aisle to be married, what are the chances that their marriage will end in divorce? A simple question. But answering it is not quite so simple. Judging by the quotes attributed to social commentators, advice columns in newspapers, and television talk shows, we might believe that more than half of all marriages will end in divorce. Rarely, however, are the sources or validity of such claims ever provided. Sociologist John Scanzoni (1972) suspects that "there is a circle of 'analysts' who quote each other on divorce statistics, and whose quotes are in turn disseminated to millions of people through the media, but no one (including the experts) bothers to check the validity of anyone else's sources" (p. 5).

What does the evidence say? Well, it depends on how one goes about measuring the chances for divorce. There are a number of methods by which the chances of a person getting divorced can be calculated.

The Marriage-to-Divorce Ratio

In 1990, almost 2.5 million marriages were performed (U.S. Bureau of Census 1992b). That same year, 1.175 million divorces were granted (U.S. Bureau of the Census 1992b). One suspects that the notion that half of all marriages end in divorce derives from the data on the marriage-to-divorce ratio in any given year. Of all the possible ways of measuring the risk of divorce, this one seems to be the most widely reported in the media and *the most inaccurate and least valid!* The problem with this statistic should be immediately obvious. The people getting married in 1995 are not the same as the people who are getting divorced. The pool of potential divorces comes from *all those who were married,* not just those who were married that year.

The Crude Divorce Rate

The drawback of the marriage/divorce ratio is that it does not assess the yearly divorce chances of all married people. A second means of measuring divorce is to use what social scientists and population experts call the "crude divorce rate." The crude divorce rate calculates the number of divorces per 1,000 people in the population. Thus, in 1867, when national divorce statistics were first collected and tabulated, there were about 0.5 divorces per 1,000 people in the population (Phillips 1988). By 1960, the rate was 2.2 per 1,000. In 1970, when some of your parents were married, the rate was 3.5. In 1980, the rate was 5.2 divorces per 1,000, and by 1990, the rate was down slightly to 4.7.

The crude divorce rate has a very important limitation. By calculating the rate per 1,000 people in the population, the statistic includes people who are not married, as well as children. These are obviously people who are not at risk of being divorced. In that respect, the crude rate drastically underestimates the yearly risk of divorce for a married person.

The "refined divorce rate" is designed to compensate for the major limitation of the crude rate by calculating the yearly number of divorces for every 1,000 married persons over 15 years of age. Thus, in 1960, there were 9.2 divorces for every 1,000 marriages. In 1970, the rate was 14.9, the 1980 rate was nearly 23, and the rate in 1989 was 20.7 (U.S. Bureau of the Census 1992b). Thus, even with the increase in the rates of divorce, each year 98% or so of all marriages *do not end in divorce*. The bad news is that each year a marriage has a new chance of ending in divorce, so we should not be so wildly optimistic about statistics that say that each year 98% of marriages do not end in divorce.

The Refined Divorce Rate

I have presented the three statistical procedures that can be used to measure the chances of a person getting divorced in one year. Unfortunately, this discussion probably still does not answer the question "What is the chance that any one marriage will end in divorce?" The most reliable and perhaps the best way to answer this question would be to follow a national sample of couples who get married in a given year until the marriages end in either divorce or the death of a spouse. No investigator has yet carried out this time-consuming and expensive study (Scanzoni 1972), nor would I image that it would be worthwhile for anyone to invest the time and money to do the research. First, by the time you got the answer to your question, you would either be divorced, a widow or widower, or dead. Second, and most important, the results of the long, expensive, and complex research would only be applicable to the cohort that was followed. One could not really generalize the results of the study to people who begin their marriage in another year. Changes in the laws pertaining to divorce, economic conditions, and social attitudes about divorce all change and all have an impact on the chances of divorce. Thus even the "perfect" study would not answer our question.

There is one more possible way to answer the question on chances of divorce. In November 1980, the National Center for Health Statistics released a study that reported on the chances for "marital dissolution and survivorship." The study examined marriages that began in three different years— 1952, 1962, and 1972—and then assessed how many marriages had ended

Life Chances of Being Divorced

Table 13-1
Life Chances of
Getting Divorced
(in percentages)

	Year of Marriage		
	1952	1962	1972
Already divorced by 1977	28.9	29.7	19.6
Likely post-1977 divorces	3.2	10.3	29.6
Total to be divorced	32.1	40.0	49.2

SOURCE: National Center for Health Statistics (1980).

in divorce by 1977 (National Center for Health Statistics 1980). In general, the study found that marriages that began in the 1960s compared to the 1950s had a greater likelihood of ending in divorce. Couples who married in 1952 were projected to end up with a 32.1% divorce rate. The rate for couples married in 1962 was about 4 in 10, whereas for couples married in 1972 the rate might be 1 in 2 (see Table 13-1).

The study went on to project the divorce rate for those couples who married in 1977. About 47% of those marriages were projected to end in divorce within 30 years (National Center for Health Statistics 1980). Add to this desertions and separations, and nearly half of all marriages beginning in 1977 would be dissolved by the beginning of the next century (of course, marriages also end as a result of the death of a spouse; however, these were not part of the study's calculations). The Population Reference Bureau has updated the National Center for Health Statistics report (Ahlburg and De Vita 1992). The report found that nearly 30% of the couples married in 1952 were divorced 25 years later, 30% of those married in 1957 were divorced by the time of their 20th anniversary, and 30% of the couples married in 1962 were divorced by the time of their 15th anniversary.

Demographers Arthur Norton and Jeanne Moorman (1987) estimate that 56% of the women aged 35 to 39 will end their first marriage in divorce. Teresa Castro Martin and Larry Bumpass (1989) estimate that the numbers are actually as high as two thirds.

Trends in the Divorce Rate

Many people believe that the divorce rate has risen dramatically *and consistently* in the past half-century. Sixty years ago, the refined divorce rate in the United States was between 6 and 8 per 1,000 married women per year. But the rate of divorce dropped sharply during the years of the Great Depression (1928–1933; see Figure 13.1). The cost of obtaining a divorce and the cost of maintaining two separate households seemed to keep people together during this and other periods of economic hardship. After World War II, the divorce rate

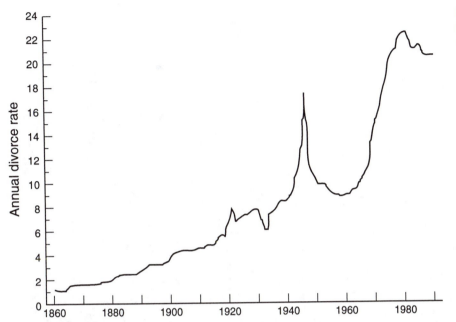

Figure 13-1 Divorce Rate Trends, 1860–1988

SOURCE: *Marriage, Divorce, Remarriage* (p. 21) by Andrew J. Cherlin, 1992, Cambridge, MA: Harvard University Press. Copyright © 1981, 1992 by the President and Fellows of Harvard College. Adapted by permission.
NOTE: For 1860–1920, divorces per 1,000 existing marriages; for 1920–1988, divorces per 1,000 married women, aged 15 and over.

jumped to 25 per 1,000 married women. Wartime marriages seem to be quite unstable. The rate then declined and remained relatively level until the mid-1960s when it began a dramatic and consistent climb. From 1965 to 1975, the divorce rate doubled. The peak of the divorce rate was 1979 (U.S. Bureau of the Census 1992b); in the past few years, the rate of divorce has leveled off and declined somewhat.

What caused the rapid rise in the rate of divorce from 1965 to 1979, and why does the rate of divorce remain so high? One factor is that many of the legal barriers to divorce have fallen. Prior to the 1960s, state laws limited the grounds for divorce to desertion, nonsupport, adultery, or physical or mental cruelty. North Carolina would not permit divorce on any grounds until 1949! Individuals, especially well-to-do individuals, could find a state with liberal divorce laws or find a country that would grant a divorce (for instance, Mexico). Other couples would agree to "fabricate" one of the legal reasons, but that often meant one spouse would have to accept the social stigma of being an abuser, deserter, or philanderer.

Although most states now allow couples to have a "no fault" divorce, attorneys are still significant participants in the divorce process.

In 1970, California instituted the nation's first "no fault" divorce law, which permitted couples to divorce on the basis of irreconcilable differences or of the marriage being irretrievably broken. Today, all states except South Dakota allow a couple to end a marriage due to irreconcilable differences, although the exact grounds vary from state to state (Price and McKenry 1988; White 1990). The waiting period between filing for divorce and the final decree has also been shortened in many states.

It is unclear whether the change to more liberal divorce laws is an adequate and complete explanation for the rise in the divorce rate. Roderick Phillips (1988) points out that divorce rates had begun to rise in the United States and European nations before divorce laws were changed.

There are other social changes that probably have had a significant impact on the change in divorce rates. The increase in the number of working wives has liberated many women from financial dependence on their husbands. Women who work may no longer face the choice of staying in a bad marriage or leaving their husbands and either moving back with their parents or living in poverty. Also, because their wives work, men who want a divorce may no longer be constrained by the financial burden of needing to pay alimony.

Women's fear of divorce may have lessened, and there is some evidence that the greater a woman's income, the greater are her chances of separating from her husband (Cherlin 1992; Phillips 1988; Ross and Sawhill 1975).

Attitudes toward divorce have also changed (Price and McKenry 1988; Weiss 1975; White 1990). In the 1950s, marriage was viewed by most Americans as a sacred institution, the foundation of Western civilization. Today, our view of marriage seems to have changed. Individual self-actualization and satisfaction are more important than the social responsibility of marriage (Bellah et al. 1985).

The change from our view of divorce as a scandal—an event that dashed political careers and that was seen as a sign of selfishness, irresponsibility, and immaturity—to our more liberal attitudes (Ronald Reagan was divorced; Edward Kennedy's divorce was not viewed as a problem for him politically) seems to be a function of a change from a commitment to marriage as an institution to the rise of the "ethic of self-realization." Sociologist Robert Weiss (1975) claims that industrial societies require mobile and adaptive persons whose first loyalty is to the development of their individual capabilities. Americans claim "the right to the unimpeded pursuit of happiness" (p. 8).

BOX 13-1: THE GLOBAL VIEW

Cross-Cultural Comparisons of Divorce

Are rising divorce rates unique to the United States? The United States has the highest rate of divorce among industrialized societies. Other societies with high divorce rates are the former Soviet Union, Hungary, and the former East Germany. Sweden has a high rate that does not show up in the formal divorce statistics because so many Swedish couples cohabitate. When these relationships end, they are not recorded as formal divorces (Popenoe 1988). Table 13-2 shows that the same trends in divorce rates in the United States have occurred in many other industrialized countries. The crude rate of divorce in 1935 in the United States was 1.71 per 1,000 people in the population. No other industrial nation had a crude rate that exceeded 0.8. World War II produced rising divorce rates in all countries, although the rise was delayed in some countries (e.g., England and Wales), most likely because it took most European countries longer than the United States to recover from the physical and economic impact of the war. Crude rates dropped in the 1950s but then increased between 1960 to 1979. Rates have generally stabilized or declined in many countries, although the rate in the former East Germany, Czechoslovakia, Hungary, and Scotland increased in the 1980s.

Table 13-2 does not include data on divorce in China. A survey conducted by the Jiangsu Provincial Academy of Social Sciences (*Associated Press*, November 8, 1992) indicates that the number of divorces in China has doubled in the 1980s. One reason for the increase in divorces is the change in attitudes toward divorce in China. Less than 12% of those surveyed by the Academy of Social Sciences thought that divorce was disgraceful. The report went on to note that one quarter of all divorces were the result of extramarital affairs.

Table 13-2 Crude Divorce Rates for Some Industrialized Countries, 1935–1987 (number of divorces per 1,000 Citizens)

Country	1935	1946	1950	1955	1960	1965	1970	1975	1979	1983	1984	1985	1986	1987
England and Wales	.10	.69	.69	.59	.51	.78	1.18	2.43	2.93[c]	2.95	2.89	3.20	—	—
Scotland	.10	.56	.42	.40	.35	.51	.88	1.59	1.63[c]	2.57	2.31	2.60	—	—
United States	1.71	4.35	2.55	2.29	2.18	2.47	3.46	4.82	5.30	4.93	4.93	4.97	4.80	—
Canada	.13	.63	.39	.38	.39	.46	1.37	2.22	2.38	2.75	2.59	2.44	—	—
Australia	.36	.96	.90	.73	.65	.75	.98	1.76	3.21[b]	2.83	2.77	2.53	2.49	—
New Zealand	.44	1.29	.86	.69	.69	.69	1.12	1.55	1.86[c]	—	—	—	—	—
Sweden	.44	1.04	1.14	1.21	1.20	1.24	1.61	3.14	2.41	2.47	2.44	2.37	2.28	2.14
Denmark	.81	1.83	1.61	1.53	1.42	1.37	1.93	2.62	2.56[c]	2.89	2.83	2.81	2.83	2.83
Finland	.42	1.36	.90	.84	.84	1.00	1.31	2.04	2.18[c]	2.01	1.97	1.85	1.98	2.10
Norway	.34	.66	.71	.58	.66	.69	.88	1.29	1.54[c]	1.86	1.92	1.95	1.89	1.65
Austria	.11	1.91	1.52	1.29	1.14	1.16	1.40	1.43	1.55[b]	1.94	1.97	2.04	1.94	1.88
Belgium	.31	.68	.59	.50	.50	.58	.66	1.12	1.37	1.74	1.89	1.87	1.85	—
France	.51	1.29	.84	.67	.66	.72	.79	1.16	1.39[c]	1.80	1.89	1.95	1.96	—
West Germany	—	—	—	—	.80	.99	1.26	1.73	1.30	1.97	2.14	2.10	2.00	—
Switzerland	.73	.96	.90	.89	.87	.85	1.04	1.39	1.66[c]	1.82	1.74	1.76	1.75	—
The Netherlands	.35	1.07	.64	.51	.49	.50	.79	1.47	1.60[c]	2.27	2.36	2.35	2.05	1.90
Poland	—	—	—	.49	.50	.75	1.06	1.21	1.02	1.25	1.43	1.32	1.34	1.33
Hungary	.63	—	—	1.63	1.66	2.00	2.21	2.46	2.62	2.47	2.69	2.75	2.78	2.89
Yugoslavia	.32	—	1.10	1.10	1.20	1.11	1.01	1.18	1.06	.97	.97	1.03	.95	.89
East Germany	—	—	—	—	1.40	1.56	1.61	2.47	2.67	2.97	3.02	3.08	3.14	3.04
Czechoslovakia	.50	.96	—	1.05	1.12	1.32	1.74	2.18	2.20[c]	2.35	2.42	2.47	2.51	—
Soviet Union	—	—	—	.80	1.27[a]	1.56	2.62	3.08	3.48[c]	3.47	3.39	3.36	3.35	3.36
Israel	—	—	2.13	1.32	1.05	.90	.80	.90	1.11	1.24	1.16	1.16	1.18	—
Japan	.70	—	1.01	.85	.74	.79	.93	1.08	1.17	1.50	1.49	1.38	1.37	—

SOURCE: Selected volumes of 1987 *Demographic Yearbook*.

a. 1961.
b. 1977.
c. 1978.

Industrialization and the ethic of self-realization set up a clash between self-fulfillment and family commitment. The cultural mandate for individual happiness makes Americans less willing to tolerate an unhappy, unsatisfying marriage.

FACTORS ASSOCIATED WITH DIVORCE

The chances of a marriage ending in divorce are not the same in all segments of society. Marital dissolution through divorce varies by social group, with some groups having a greater risk of divorce than others. An analysis of the different rates of divorce illustrates the pushes and pulls exerted by social factors on marriages.

Families with low income, where the husband and wife are not highly educated and where the head of the household holds a low status job, have always run the greatest risk of divorce (Kitson and Raschke 1981; Raschke 1987). Interestingly, until 1948, most people believed that just the opposite was true—that divorce was more common among the well to do (Kitson and Raschke 1981). Perhaps this was the result of media reports of divorces of movie stars and the very rich, as opposed to divorce among the lower class.

In the past 20 years, lower-class families have still run the highest risk of divorce, but the gap between the lower and the middle class has narrowed (Raschke 1987). As divorce rates rose in the 1960s and 1970s, the impact of social and economic resources seemed to decline. Today, socioeconomic differences in divorce rates are considerably smaller than they used to be.

What one does for a living influences the chances that a marriage will end in divorce. An examination of divorce records in California assessed the risk of divorce among 12 professional groups. Authors, social scientists, and architects had the highest rates of divorce, while dentists, physicians, and natural scientists had the lowest (Rosow and Rose 1972). So perhaps it is true that the media influence our perceptions of Hollywood divorces.

Another important factor that influences the chances of divorce is the employment status of the husband. Marriages in which men are periodically unemployed have higher rates of divorce than when men are steadily employed (Coombs and Zumeta 1970; Martin and Bumpass 1989; Raschke 1987). Divorce experts Gay Kitson and Helen Raschke (1981) note that unemployment itself probably does not account for a marriage ending in divorce, since national divorce rates fall during periods of high unemployment (see Figure 13-1, especially the Depression years 1928–1932). However, unemployment, the husband being around the house, and other stresses may highlight additional problems in the marriage (Kitson and Raschke 1981). John Scanzoni (1968) adds to this discussion by noting that whether a husband has a job or not, a critical factor in the decision to end a marriage is his wife's satisfaction with his occupational achievement. The more dissatisfied a wife is, the greater the chances that the marriage will end in divorce.

There have been numerous discussions about the effect of income on the risk of divorce. In general, the lower the family income, the higher the rate of divorce (Glick and Norton 1977; Raschke 1987). However, more refined analysis of the income-divorce relationship finds that *income instability,* not just low income, is the best predictor of divorce (Cherlin 1978; Ross and Sawhill 1975).

Generally, the more education one has, the lower the risk of divorce (Furstenberg 1990). This relationship holds up quite well when one examines the relationship between education and divorce for men. Men who have

Socioeconomic Status

graduated college or gone on to graduate school have the lowest divorce rates. But the relationship between education and chances of divorce among women is more complex. Women with less than high school educations have higher divorce rates than those who continue on to high school. High school graduating women have lower divorce rates than women who have not completed high school, and women who go on to college are less likely to divorce than women who are high school graduates. However, those women with the most education—college degrees and graduate school—have a rate of divorce as high as that for women who did not finish high school. This could be a function of the best-educated women having more options and thus not needing to remain in a bad marriage. It could also be because many of the best educated women marry men who have less education than they have, and this could lead to stress and strain due to the husband feeling that he does not have the educational status to be the dominant person in the marriage. Finally, it could be the result of the strains of dual-career or commuter marriages (see Chapter 11).

Race

It is difficult to separate race from socioeconomic factors such as education, income, occupational prestige, and unemployment. Because there are pronounced differences in socioeconomic status among racial groups, it is difficult to assess divorce rates among various racial groups without considering that each racial group also experiences differential economic advantages and disadvantages.

Most studies report that African Americans are more likely than whites to separate and divorce (see, e.g., Carter and Glick 1976; Martin and Bumpass 1989; Norton and Glick 1979; Sweet and Bumpass 1987; Udry 1966; White 1990). However, African Americans who own homes, have the same incomes as whites, and have the same family size as whites actually are found to have a divorce rate 6% lower than whites in the same economic situation (Hampton 1975; Raschke 1987). The divorce rate for Latinos is between that of whites and African Americans (U.S. Bureau of the Census 1992a).

Age at Time of First Marriage

Generally, the longer one delays entering marriage for the first time, the lower the chances of that person's marriage ending in divorce. Couples who marry when they are in their teens are twice as likely to have their marriages end in divorce as are couples who marry in their 20s (Norton and Glick 1979; Spanier and Glick 1981; White 1990). After age 26 for men and 23 for women, age at marriage seems to make little difference (Glenn and Supancic 1984). There is, however, a threshold. Couples who marry in their 30s or later have a higher rate of divorce than couples marrying in their 20s (Glick and Norton 1977).

High divorce rates among couples who enter marriage in their teens have been tied to teenagers' lack of emotional maturity and educational resources (Kitson and Raschke 1981). Another view is that teenagers who marry have not had an opportunity to separate from their parents and establish their own psychological identities. Waiting until you are 20 to marry allows a person to separate from parents, complete an education, and have experience living independently (Bumpass and Sweet 1972). Those who wait to marry until their 30s might have more emotional problems than people who marry at earlier ages. Of course, they might be *too* used to living independently, having done so for a longer time than people who marry earlier.

Religion

Divorce rates are higher for Protestants than for Catholics, although more Catholic marriages end in separation. Homogamous Jewish marriages are more stable than Jewish-Gentile and Protestant-Catholic marriages (Raschke 1987). People who do not attend church or synagogue regularly are more likely to divorce than regular churchgoers. Most people are interested in knowing whether interfaith marriages are less stable than marriages between individuals with the same religious affiliation. Early studies of religion and divorce confirm the commonsense notion that interfaith marriages are less stable (Bell 1983; Landis 1949). Researchers, however, have had a difficult time analyzing the impact of religion on divorce. One major problem is that only two states (Iowa and Indiana) ask applicants for a marriage license to state their religious preference. Thus there is not an abundance of data available to assess commonsense notions about mixed marriage and divorce. A second problem is that the social factors we have previously discussed (age at first marriage, income, education, and occupational status) are related to *both* divorce and interfaith marriage. Yet, even considering age and social factors, mixed-faith marriages still run a higher risk of divorce (Burchinal and Chancellor 1962; Christensen and Barber 1967; Glenn and Supancic 1984; Raschke 1987).

One of the misleading conclusions that people may come away with from a review of these studies is that mixed marriages *cause* divorce. Obviously, the research that has been carried out only finds associations, not causation. The reason why mixed-faith marriages have high rates of divorce may be the commonly held assumption that such marriages do not work, or it could be a variety of other factors. First, unconventional people may be the most likely to enter a mixed-faith marriage, and, because they are unconventional, they may also be more willing to terminate an unhappy marriage with a divorce.

Couples who marry within their religious faith tend to have lower divorce rates than those who have interfaith marriages.

Secondly, families of orientation may put the newly married couple under so much stress and strain that this may actually create the problems that lead to a divorce (a self-fulfilling prophesy in which the expectation that an interfaith marriage is likely to fail helps bring about the actual failure).

"Children hold marriages together" is yet another commonsense assumption. Again, some statistical data tend to support such a claim. Women without children are more likely to be separated or divorced, whereas women with three or more children are the least likely to encounter marital disruption (Spanier and Glick 1981). However, today close to 60% of all divorces involve children under the age of 18 (Ahlburg and De Vita 1992; Raschke 1987).

Lynn White (1990) found that the birth of the first child reduces the chance of divorce to almost nothing in the year following the birth; however, the insulating effect does not hold true for subsequent births.

Children and Divorce

Those who analyze divorce statistics have found other factors that are related to a couple's chances of a divorce. However, readers of this list should keep in mind that each one of these factors is also partially related to social status, age at first marriage, and the other factors we have chronicled.

1. Premarital childbearing is known to increase the chances that a marriage will end in divorce, although by itself premarital conception does not increase the risk of divorce (Billy, Landale, and McLaughlin 1986; Christensen and Meissner 1953; Furstenberg 1976; Hampton 1979; Martin and Bumpass 1989; Morgan and Rindfuss 1984; Teachman 1983; Wineberg 1988). Even when researchers take into consideration the age of first marriage (premarital pregnancy is more common among the young), divorce is still a greater risk when a pregnancy predates the marriage (Bumpass and Sweet 1972).

2. Where one lives also can affect chances of divorce. Urban couples have higher rates of divorce than rural couples (Glick and Norton 1977; Norton and Glick 1976). Divorce rates are also higher in the West and South Central, Mountain, and Pacific areas of the country (Glenn and Shelton 1985).

3. If you knew your spouse for more than two years before you married, your chances of divorce are less than if you knew your spouse for less than two years. Finally, if your friends and family approve of your marriage, share your attitudes about marriage, and view their marriage as stable, then you will be more likely to stay married than someone whose friends and family do not share the same constellation of attitudes about marriage and family (Goode 1956).

It is not likely that knowing that these factors are related to the chances of divorce will (a) help you select a mate that reduces your chances of divorce or (b) help you predict which of your friends will be divorced. Our inventory of factors merely helps us to understand that certain types of marriages are at greater risk of ending in divorce. Furthermore, we know that no one factor operates independently of the other possible forces that influence a marriage.

Other Factors Related to Divorce

Last, although these factors have been found to be related to divorce, they do not, in and of themselves, *explain* why people get divorced. In the next section we review some of the theories of divorce.

EXPLAINING DIVORCE

What causes divorce? Again, a simple question with not such a simple answer. One obvious explanation is that people get divorced because they become unhappy with their partner and their marriage. Sociologists who explain divorce can point to one or all of the correlates reviewed in the previous section. Observers of a marriage, with the benefit of hindsight, also can single out factors that may have led to the divorce of their friends and family members: "They married too young"; "Mixed marriages do not work"; "They had a lot of problems"; and "They are going through a midlife crisis" are all standard observations made by outsiders. Insiders—the married couples—are not nearly so consistent in their explanations. In fact, marital partners are often likely to quote different explanations for why their marriage dissolved (Weiss

---

BOX 13-2: THINKING ABOUT FAMILIES

The Process of Divorce

The case studies that introduced this chapter describe marriages that ended in divorce. The personal tragedy and trauma of divorce and the divorce process are not, and probably cannot be, captured in these brief snapshots of Wendy and Christopher's and Pete and Nancy's divorces.

Anthropologist Paul Bohannon (1970) explains that the complexity of divorce arises because at least *six different things* are happening at once to a couple moving toward and then through a divorce. He calls these six different experiences "The Six Stations of Divorce." Although they may come in different orders than he presents them and vary in intensity for the divorcing couple, they are experiences that nearly every divorcing couple shares.

1. *The Emotional Divorce.* The emotional divorce is the first sign of a crumbling mar-

riage. The couple may stay together and even keep up the appearance of a happily married couple, but they begin to withhold emotion from their relationship. Feelings of dislike, antagonism, hatred, and imprisonment arise during this stage.

2. *The Legal Divorce.* One can desert a spouse, but in the eyes of the law the marriage has not ended. The dissolution of a marriage in American society requires a formal legal decree. Such a decree requires that there be legally acceptable grounds for divorce, although most states now have some form of no-fault or "irreconcilable differences" grounds.

3. *Economic Divorce.* Western societies view a marriage as a single economic unit. Thus, when a marriage ends, that economic unit must be divided. Irrespective of who worked, whose savings went into the down payment for the

1975). "He hit me"; "She drank too much"; "He wasn't affectionate enough"; "I don't love her anymore"; "Her mother interfered too much"; and "Our sex life was awful" are all explanations offered for terminating a marriage (Levinger 1966).

Social exchange theory (see Chapter 2) has been used by students of divorce to help pull together the various pushes and pulls that lead to dissolving a marriage. Exchange theorists propose that divorce is likely when the rewards for maintaining relationships are low and the costs of continuing in the marriage are higher than the costs might be in another relationship or by living alone (Kitson and Raschke 1981). Many times there may be a third person who is part of a divorce (the husband or wife has an affair or another relationship). Although the partner who is being left may blame this third person for the end of the marriage, a social exchange theory explanation might propose that the availability of the third person changes the cost/reward calculus in an already fragile marriage. Another application of social exchange theory is when a couple decides to end their marriage at the point when their

Theories of the Causes of Divorce

house, or who purchased the television and the VCR, a dissolving marriage requires a division of the joint property. Income tax law, legal advice, and emotions are all part of the economic divorce.

4. *Coparental Divorce.* When a couple has children, a divorce involves the delicate and emotionally charged decisions surrounding the children. Where will they live? Who will take care of them? What and how much access to the children will the parent who does not live with them have? What are the financial responsibilities of each parent? All these questions must be answered in the process of ending a marriage.

5. *Community Divorce.* Not too long ago, a couple my wife and I were close with ended a long marriage. My wife and I were disappointed but not really surprised. *Our* problem was that my wife was quite close to the wife and I was very friendly with the husband. How would we maintain our relations? Would we maintain our relations? Should I stop being friendly with him if my wife stayed friends with her? While we grappled with our dilemmas, the couple strug-

gled with their own relationships with the community. No longer would they be invited out as a couple. They each had to construct and reconstruct relations with their own circle of friends and acquaintances (their community).

6. *The Psychic Divorce.* The final stage in the process is the most difficult. Each person in the marriage must turn from being part of a couple to being an autonomous individual. New friends, new residence, and new patterns of economics all take a backseat to the process of developing a completely new social identity.

Few people who have not gone through a divorce can fully appreciate how bewildering it must be to go through these six stations. Legal complications, changes in economics, changes in relations with one's entire social circle, all happening sometimes at once, leave divorcing individuals often confused, distraught, and at a loss for guidelines as to how they will or should behave. Bohannon notes one final aspect of the six stations—it seems that nothing in our socialization has actually taught us what to do or even how to feel in such situations.

last child leaves the home. Although divorces at this stage of a marriage are less common than divorces earlier on, one reason for divorce at this stage is that all the children have been "launched" and the partners believe that the costs of a divorce for themselves and their children have been significantly lowered.

Those who use the developmental theoretical framework focus on the likelihood of divorce at various stages in the family life cycle. Divorce is most likely to occur during the earliest stages of marriage. This is a function of the interpersonal and financial stresses that need to be worked out during the first stages of a marriage. When the developmental tasks are not accomplished, the risk of divorce is increased. Similarly, those who use the developmental framework would argue that the risk of divorce in later stages of family life is increased if the developmental tasks specific to those stages are not accomplished—such as the transition that partners need to make when their last child leaves home.

Whereas structural functionalist theorists view divorce as a failure or breakdown of the social system, conflict theorists and feminist theories often approach divorce as a solution to conflict and domination rather than simply the failure of a relationship. Divorce is one way that women can free themselves from male domination and control.

Crisis theory (see Chapter 14) has also been used to explain divorce. Crisis theory explains divorce as a function of stressor events and the family's and individuals' abilities to manage and cope with various personal, economic, and social stressors.

THE CONSEQUENCES OF DIVORCE

When Wendy and Christopher's marriage ended, Christopher moved to another city. He and Wendy picked up the pieces and moved ahead with their lives and careers. When contacted by Blumstein and Schwartz after her marriage had ended, Wendy reported some regrets. She missed the advantages of marriage. Being a single female corporate lawyer had some definite disadvantages. Wendy was afraid that some of her old-fashioned clients would be shocked that she was divorced. She also feared that, as a single woman, she would be more likely to be the target of sexual harassment in her law firm. The main impact of the divorce on Wendy is the vision of hindsight. She sees clearly the problems with her marriage and advises friends that if they have any doubts they should not marry. Wendy cautions her friends that they need to allocate time to work on their relationships. She explains that people need to work on relationships, not just to work on their jobs.

For Pete and Nancy, the dissolution of the marriage was not so simple. First, there was the fight over the property settlement and who would keep the house. Then there were disagreements over child custody and visitation. Lawyers' fees piled up and court visits were postponed and rescheduled, but finally, Nancy and her children moved to live with her parents, while Pete kept the house and began to think about what it would be like to date again after 20 years of marriage.

Most people who have thought about the consequences of divorce think first about the children and what happens to them. But before we look at the consequences of divorce for children, let us consider what happens when a couple splits up and has to "go it alone."

Sociologist Robert Weiss (1975) studied adults who came to a series of eight weekly discussion and counseling sessions that Weiss had organized for individuals in Boston who had been separated or divorced for less than a year. Obviously, separated or divorced people who enroll in an eight-week counseling course are not the same as separated or divorced individuals who would not enroll in such a course, but Weiss's study was one of the few investigations that tried to assess the impact of divorce on the partners or ex-partners.

Going It Alone

Weiss found that nearly all the separated or divorced men and women he observed went through a period of emotional and social upset (see Bohannon's "psychic divorce"). During the period prior to the divorce (Bohannon's "emotional divorce"), the couple's fondness for each other erodes. Trust evaporates, the couple becomes estranged and alienated from one another, and what was desire becomes anger. Faults are seen clearly and then magnified. With all these changes and problems, with love faded, the couple is still attached—there is still the feeling of being emotionally bound to the other person (Weiss 1975).

Because of this feeling of attachment that is part of a marriage, Weiss found that most of the people he interviewed suffered from "separation distress." For a time after the separation and divorce, all their attention was focused on the lost spouse. Inaccessibility to that person caused discomfort, anxiety, and sometimes even panic. Sleeping difficulties and problems concentrating at work were common. Some people experienced severe depression. Of course, the depression could have preceded and actually caused the divorce, or it could be a consequence.

Those individuals who did not experience "separation distress" often became euphoric. A great weight had been lifted off their backs. Life became

Many men and women go through a period of emotional and social upset, including depression, after they divorce.

an adventure. Anything was possible. Great plans were made. Money could be spent to decorate the new or old residence.

Over time, at least a year, both the separation distress and the euphoria begin to disappear. Loneliness replaces the depths of depression and the heights of euphoria. People become concerned that they might not meet anyone who they can care for and who will care for them.

The consequences of divorce for those who have to go it alone depends on whether the individuals see themselves as initiating the divorce or having it imposed on them (Weiss 1975). Those individuals (like Pete in the introduction to this chapter) who feel that everything in their marriage is fine and then wake up to have a spouse unexpectedly announce that the marriage is over suffer the most. Their feet are swept out from under them. Their very identity is challenged. Their ability to perceive reality seems threatened and precarious.

The economic divorce, coparental divorce, and community divorce take a toll on the former marriage partners. Friends, social standing, possessions, cars, houses, children, and identity may be lost in the divorce process. Nancy is no longer "the professor's wife." She may have lost some valuable possessions. Pete is no longer at home to watch the children when she wants to go out. Jobs that were shared now are done by one person. The free tuition that she had at the university where Pete worked is no longer available to her. For Pete, his identity as husband and father are shaken. Nancy's elaborate meals are replaced by take-out meals, TV dinners, or, at best, invitations to the homes of his remaining friends.

Adjustment to the various changes and losses of a divorce depends on social as well as emotional resources. Adequate financial resources, loyal and giving friends and relatives, the wife's education and job skills, and the husband's homemaking skills all influence the adjustment.

The Spouse With the Children

Although both partners are affected by divorce, it would appear that the greatest weight of divorce is felt by the single parent and children. Over 90% of the children living with one parent live with their mothers (U.S. Bureau of the Census 1992b). It is extremely difficult for single parents to function effectively. Weiss (1979) identifies three sources of strain: (1) responsibility overload—single parents make all the decisions and must provide for all the needs for themselves and their children; (2) task overload—there is frequently too much to do, what with working, housework, and parenting all competing for time and attention; and (3) emotional overload—single parents are always on call to meet the emotional demands of their children.

The primary and overwhelming disadvantage that single parents (women) experience is that their financial position deteriorates considerably. In general, after a divorce, wives are worse off economically than their husbands (Cherlin 1992; Duncan and Hoffman 1985; Espenshade 1979; Hoffman and Duncan 1988; Holden and Smock 1991; Peterson 1989; Weiss 1979; Weitzman 1985). Fathers are supposed to provide child support, but many do not (Cherlin 1992). Only about 6 in 10 single mothers with children under 21 years of age have a child support award, and only about half of those actually receive the full payments (U.S. Bureau of the Census 1989). Because most single mothers have to establish separate households after a divorce, their financial needs rise while their financial resources plunge.

The situation for the single parent is not totally bleak. After all, according to social exchange theorists, many women who seek a divorce have already

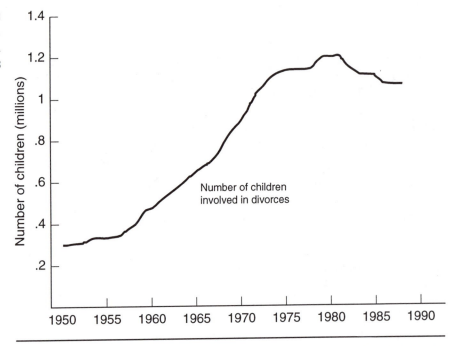

Figure 13-2 Annual Number of Children Involved in Divorce, 1950–1988

SOURCE: National Center for Health Statistics (1991, p. 2, Figure 1).

measured the costs against the rewards. Divorce brings an escape from the conflict and emotional toll inflicted by a bad marriage. Single parents often experience a gain in self-esteem as they succeed in meeting the demands of being a single parent. They have independence and develop closer relations with their children (Cherlin 1992)

The Impact on Children

The number of children involved in divorces each year nearly tripled between 1960 and 1980 but has declined somewhat since 1980 (see Figure 13-2). More than 1 million children under the age of 18 see their parents divorce each year (U.S. Bureau of the Census 1992b). Experts estimate that half of all children born today will see their parents separate or divorce before these children reach their 18th birthday (Bumpass 1984).

Traditionally, popular and professional belief was that divorce always brought with it negative consequences for the children who were involved. Parents were advised that they should try to keep their marriage together, at least for the sake of the children. Emotional problems, juvenile delinquency, and an assortment of social and individual problems were laid at the doorstep of the broken home. On the other side of the argument were those who protested that it might be better for children if their parents ended an unhappy marriage, rather than remaining in a home torn by conflict, arguing, and quarreling.

A study conducted by psychologists Judith Wallerstein and Joan Kelly sought to bring scientifically gathered evidence to bear on the question of what the consequences of divorce are for children. Wallerstein and Kelly (1980) launched their Children of Divorce Project in 1971 in Marin County, California (north of San Francisco and reputedly having a high divorce rate). The researchers studied 131 children from 60 recently divorced families and conducted in-depth interviews (along the same lines used by Lillian Rubin in her 1976 study of working-class families—see Chapter 2). Families were recontacted 18 months after the initial interviews and then were interviewed again 5 years later.

The families and children who participated in this 5-year study (Wallerstein and Kelly 1976, 1980) are not at all representative of all families and all divorces in the United States. The subjects were middle-class suburban families and their children were, by and large, happy and healthy. Although this sample cannot be generalized to all families, the sample selection was designed to rule out the effects of poverty and urban living on children as well as to eliminate emotionally disturbed children. By doing this, the investigators tried to assess the impact of divorce on children rather than poverty, urban living, or other extrafamilial factors.

The initial impact of the divorce was similar for most children. Divorce hit the children like a bolt of lightning (Kelly and Wallerstein 1976; Wallerstein and Kelly 1976, 1980). The children were totally unprepared for the divorce. Often, when the announcement came that their parents were ending the marriage, the children sat in stunned silence. Few children saw their own families as worse than others; few saw them as better. None of the children thought of the divorce as a solution to the problem of unhappiness.

The short-term reactions to divorce varied by the age of the children. The youngest children—preschoolers—simply pretended that their families were not breaking up. Elementary school children (7 to 10 years of age) reacted as if someone had died. One 7-year-old boy told an interviewer, "I have to hold it in 'cause I'd be crying all the time" (Wallerstein and Kelly 1980, p. 66). Children feared that they would be forgotten by the parent who left (typically the father). The older children reacted with shame and anger. They were embarrassed that their family was breaking up, ashamed of their parents' behavior, and ashamed of being rejected themselves. They saw their parents as selfish and juvenile. Few blamed themselves for the divorce (contrary to popular conventional wisdom), and most saw no justification for the divorce. They tended to blame one or the other parent for ending the marriage.

Five years after the breakup, the interviews revealed mixed reactions to and consequences of the divorce. Looking back, 28% of the children strongly approved of the divorce, 30% still strongly disapproved, and about half (48%) were in the middle. Most of the children still nurtured the hope that their parents would get back together.

Data collected from the children, their teachers, and their parents were used to assess the children's adjustment to divorce. About 3 in 10 (29%) were rated as doing reasonably well. Nearly 4 in 10 (39%) were moderately or severely depressed. Their most frequent complaint was loneliness. Between 3 and 4 in 10 (34%) seemed to be thriving. They had survived the divorce and this seemed to bolster their self-esteem.

The same children were followed up 10 years after the breakup (Wallerstein and Blakeslee 1989). The picture of children 10 years after divorce is even more pessimistic. The older males, who were between 19 and 29 at the time of the 10-year follow-up interviews, were found to be generally unhappy and lonely and had developed few lasting relationships with young women. Many of the older girls appeared to be adjusted at first but encountered problems later. At the 10-year follow-up, most of the 19- to 23-year-old women were said to be overcome by fear and anxiety at the prospect of making an emotional commitment to a man.

Although Wallerstein and her colleague's research is one of the most comprehensive studies of the consequences of divorce, it does have some limitations. The prevalence of long-term problems in the general population of those who experienced parental divorce is probably lower than found by Wallerstein and her associates. Wallerstein's subjects were referred to her clinic by lawyers, clergy, and the courts. Many of the parents who were divorced had mental health problems. Wallerstein employed no comparison or control group of children in families that were not so disrupted that they required a referral to a mental health clinic. Given the nature of her sample, it is surprising that so many children actually survived the divorce with little or no impairment (Cherlin 1992).

Overall, evidence from national surveys of children from divorce does find that experiencing divorce and growing up in a single-parent family diminishes an individual's chances for a successful adult life (McLanahan 1988).

REMARRIAGE

Nearly 70% of divorced men and 60% of divorced women remarry. Not only do people tend to remarry, but they do so somewhat quickly. Half of all remarriages in 1988 occurred within four years of the divorce (Wilson and Clarke 1992).

People prefer to be married. The importance of marriage as an institution is perhaps best demonstrated by the fact that remarriage has always been a facet of the kinship system in the United States as well as Western Europe (Cherlin 1992; Furstenberg 1990). Americans whose marriages have dissolved have always tended to remarry. From the time of the Puritans and Plymouth Colony through the 1920s, most of those who remarried had seen their first marriage end as the result of a spouse's death (Cherlin 1992). But in more recent times, with the rise in the rate of divorce in the 1960s and 1970s and the decline in mortality rates, those entering a second or third marriage have typically been divorced (Cherlin 1992).

Sex, age, the presence of children, and factors such as education and race all influence a divorced person's chances of getting remarried. Men appear to prefer being married to being single. Divorced men are more likely to remarry than are divorced women. The rate of marriage for divorced men is 80% greater than the marriage rate for men who have never married and are eligible to enter a first marriage (U.S. Bureau of the Census 1992b).

The younger a woman is when she is divorced, the greater are the chances of her remarrying (Ahlburg and De Vita 1992; Bumpass, Sweet, and Martin 1990). Age does not appear to be an important factor influencing the remarriage rates of men (Ahlburg and De Vita 1992).

The data on whether the presence of children exerts an important influence on whether or not a woman will remarry (remember that most children live with their mothers after the divorce) are mixed (Bumpass et al. 1990). Some investigators find that the presence of children reduces the likelihood that their mothers will remarry (Becker, Landis, and Michael 1977; Thornton 1977); others find either no effect (Grady 1980) or that the effect is dependent on how old the mother is (Koo and Suchindran 1980).

Other factors that influence the chances of remarriage are race and education. Better-educated women are less likely to remarry than are women with less education, whereas better-educated men are more likely to remarry than are less-educated men (Bumpass et al. 1990). Remarriage is less common among African Americans than whites, and the remarriage rates for blacks have been declining for the past two decades (Bumpass et al. 1990; Wilson and Clarke 1992). The rates of remarriage for Latinos is between the rate for African Americans and whites (Ahlburg and De Vita 1992).

Factors Influencing the Chances of Remarriage

Nearly 70% of divorced men and 60% of divorced women remarry.

The Second Time Around   As common as remarriages are, until quite recently all we have had to draw on in discussing remarriage were remarriage statistics. Few social scientists had ever examined remarriage, especially remarriages that included children, prior to the 1970s.

Research on the nature and process of remarriage indicate that, at least from the point of view of the participants, second marriages are really quite different from first marriages. Sociologists Frank Furstenberg, Jr. and Graham Spanier (1984) collected data on the transition from divorce to remarriage in Centre County, Pennsylvania. Furstenberg and Spanier used both structured interviews and qualitative data to gain insight into how the remarried view their world. The researchers report that their informants believe that life is indeed different the second time around. Remarried couples believe that they have a different conception of love than couples in their first marriages. Remarried couples tend to think that people who enter a second marriage are less likely to stay married if they are unhappy than will people in a first marriage. Most remarried people agree that there are different expectations of marriage the second time around.

Helen Weingarten (1980) analyzed interviews with 2,264 adults that were collected by the Survey Research Center at the University of Michigan. From these quantitative data, Weingarten concludes that people who have experienced an unsuccessful first marriage do change their standards for success when they enter into a second marriage. Because no one wants to be thought of as a "two-time loser," people seem to become more sensitive to their own and their partner's limitations. In the end, these modified adjustments may help, since Weingarten finds that remarried individuals report having no more difficulty getting along with their spouses than first-time married individuals.

Within the second marriage, there seem to be some important differences from first marriages. Furstenberg (1980) explains that the remarried couples in Pennsylvania report greater flexibility of household tasks, more shared decision making, and a greater degree of emotional exchange than in their first marriage. Are these differences real or just the result of a biased view of those who remarry? Actually, it does not really matter what the answer is—what is obvious is that people who remarry tend to see their second marriage as different from their first.

Our public view of **blended families**—families where there are children from a first marriage and perhaps children born to the second marriage—is mixed. The "wicked stepmother" is a staple of American culture and children's storybooks. Snow White was sent out into the forest by her stepmother to be beheaded by the woodsman. Cinderella suffered greatly from the taunts and tortures of her stepmother and her big-footed stepsisters. On the other hand, television programs like *The Brady Bunch* tend to paint an almost unbelievably rosy picture of family life in blended families. What is the reality of the blended family?

Children and
Remarriage

Complexity

The most striking element of blended families is complexity. A child in a blended family may have

- two biological parents
- two stepparents
- biological siblings
- stepsiblings
- half-siblings
- as many as eight grandparents (more if a grandparent had been divorced)
- innumerable uncles, aunts, and cousins

Moreover, children in blended families may shuttle between the two residences of their birth parents. It is not unusual for the visitation and custody decision to provide for a child to spend one Christmas with one parent and the next Christmas in the household of the other parent.

The complexity of these arrangements is increased because our culture has yet to develop even the most elementary institutionalized supports and solutions for the problems and complexities faced by parents and children in blended families. How should a child refer to his or her new stepfather—should he be called "Dad," or should he be referred to by his first name, or should another kinship term be used, perhaps "Uncle"? The solution favored by the stepfather, say he prefers to be called "Dad," could produce resentment from the genetic father who may feel that his identity and very status as father are being threatened.

A second element of the complexity is that there are many different types of blended families that can be formed, each of which may have its own unique structural character. Sociologists Kay Pasley and Marilyn Ihinger-Tallman (1982) have identified nine types of remarried families (Table 13-3). They note that each type of family has its own unique character and problems. The problems and stresses of blended families are discussed in the following section.

Stresses in Blended Families

A variety of stresses confront remarried families, and, to a large degree, these stresses stem from several factors: (a) presence or absence of children with prior family experience; (b) custody or visitation arrangements involving

Table 13-3
Nine Types of
Remarried Families

1. No children

2. Children of this marriage only

3. Custodial[a] children from a prior marriage only

4. Noncustodial[b] children from a prior marriage only

5. Adult children only

6. Custodial children from a prior marriage and children from this marriage

7. Noncustodial children from a prior marriage and children from this marriage

8. Noncustodial children and custodial children from a prior marriage

9. Noncustodial children and custodial children from a prior marriage and children from this marriage

SOURCE: "Stress in Remarried Families" by Kay Pasley and Marilyn Ihinger-Tallman, 1982, *Family Perspectives* 12(Fall). Copyright © 1982 by Brigham Young University. Adapted by permission.
a. A custodial child is a child who lives in the blended family.
b. A noncustodial child lives in the home of the spouse from the first marriage.

children from a prior marriage; (c) number of persons directly and indirectly involved in the new family (e.g., stepmother, mother, and children are directly involved; in-laws, ex-inlaws, ex-spouses, school officials, etc., are indirectly involved); and (d) lack of clarity regarding appropriate behavior between the current and prior families (Ihinger-Tallman and Pasley 1987; Pasley and Ihinger-Tallman 1982).

After families confront the problem of what names to use when referring to one another, they face a variety of other tensions and problems. One major problem is that of financial obligations. A father entering a new marriage and a blended family may already have financial obligations to his first wife (alimony) and his children from the first marriage (child support). Should he marry a woman with children, and should he and his second wife have children of their own, these financial obligations are increased since he now must face supporting two wives and two or even three sets of children (children from his first marriage, children from his second wife's first marriage, and children they have together). Child support is a two-edged sword, and a wife who remarries with children from a first marriage may find that the child support she receives (or perhaps does not receive) from her first husband is inadequate to raise her children. Thus she may begin her second marriage by facing the problem of having her new spouse provide some or all the support for children from her first marriage. I could go on enumerating all the logical possibilities here, but the general issue is that remarriage poses problems of financially supporting hers, his, and theirs. New wives may resent seeing family resources being sent to support another woman and her children. New husbands may resent supporting children who are not theirs. Both partners may find that they have to work longer and harder to meet obligations outside their new nuclear family.

A second major source of stress and problems is the appropriate child-rearing role in blended families. More specifically, the issue tends to concentrate on the appropriate discipline role of a parent with his or her stepchildren. What rights does a father have with regard to punishing children from his wife's first marriage? What rights does a stepmother have when her husband's children from a first marriage come to visit? Are the children from both marriages being treated fairly and equitably? Some stepparents may unconsciously take out their anger and resentment by being overly severe with their stepchildren. On the other hand, a parent may be more severe with his or her natural children to demonstrate that he or she is *not* favoring the natural children.

The Impact of Blended Families on Children

Given the complexity of blended families and the stresses and problems that they face, do children in blended homes suffer? There is really no clear-cut answer to this important question. Lucille Duberman's (1975) pioneering

---

BOX 13-3: WHAT THE RESEARCH SHOWS

The Darker Side of Divorce: Child Abduction

One of the darker aspects of the divorce process is the occurrence of parental kidnapping. Parental kidnapping (also referred to as child abduction, child snatching, and legal kidnapping) receives considerably less public and policy attention than is given cases of children abducted by strangers. Originally, parental kidnapping was not considered an illegal activity. Legal precedents, such as the 1932 federal kidnapping legislation, also called the "Lindbergh Law" (in reference to aviator Charles Lindbergh's infant son who was kidnapped and murdered), specifically *excluded* the taking of a child by one parent from another as a case of kidnapping requiring legal action. Researchers estimate that 354,000 children were abducted by their parents in 1988 (Finkelhor, Hotaling, and Sedlak 1991).

Child abduction takes various forms. In some instances, a child will leave his or her mother to spend time visiting the father. When the visitation period ends, the father will refuse to return the child to the mother. Some of these "abductions" are legalized when the fathers get legal custody of the child in a state other than the one that granted the original custody order. The Uniform Child Custody Jurisdiction Act was passed by Congress in an attempt to eliminate this kind of "child custody forum shopping."

In other instances, a parent will "snatch" a child from the playground, front yard, or school and flee with the child. In these cases, the child is hidden from the custodial parent. Child abductors sometimes change their name, their children's names, and move frequently

study of reconstituted families found that the adaptation of both children and parents depended on the age of the children, whether both sets of children lived in the same home, and whether or not the couple had their own children. The more interaction the parents had with the children and the more the children had a favorable attitude about the family, the better things were (Duberman 1975). However, James Peterson and Nicholas Zill (1986) reported that children of divorce and remarriage exhibit more stress and more disruptive behavior than children in the general population.

The contradictory findings produced by researchers studying the impact of stepparents on children and the rather tentative way in which these researchers put forth their findings underscores the fact that the whole situation of stepfamilies is rather new and thus underresearched. Historically, if a parent and a child moved into a second marriage it was because the other parent had died. Thus there was no biological parent around, no custody or visitation stresses, no financial obligations, no moving back and forth from one household to another. Today, most children enter a blended family because of divorce. As Andrew Cherlin (1992) so carefully points out, although remarriages follow most divorces, we still have not worked out the ground rules and guidelines for sharing parenthood. Without rules, guidelines, and social and institutional supports, blended families are often left to their own resources to work out and improvise rules and arrangements for dealing with

to keep the custodial parent from tracing them down.

In light of the fact that mothers are typically granted custody of their children, it is easy to understand that most kidnappings involve fathers snatching children from custodial mothers.

Why children are kidnapped by one parent from the other raises another series of interesting questions. In many instances, the children are simply pawns in a power struggle between the former partners. Embittered former spouses may battle to punish one another through the affections and custody of their children.

In other instances, parents may have some legitimate concerns for the well-being of their children, and when legal means fail, they might resort to kidnapping in an attempt to "rescue" the child from what they perceive to be an abusive or neglectful home environment.

Last, some kidnapping may arise from what we might refer to as the "Kramerization" of American fathering (from the film *Kramer vs. Kramer*). In the past two decades, fathers have been "brought into" parenting and have learned to experience the joys and frustrations of child rearing. However, courts still prefer to award custody to mothers (unless the mother is judged unfit or gives up claims to custody). Fathers who are bonded and attached to their children may not accept the court's traditional views of who is the "best" parent or what is in the "best interest" of their children and thus resort to kidnapping.

The problem of child abduction is likely to be with us for some time. First, divorce rates will remain relatively high. Second, mothers will continue to get preference in child custody decisions. And third, courts are still reluctant to view parental kidnapping as a crime—thus they may actually encourage embittered parents to resort to kidnapping since the punishment for such actions is relatively mild.

this rather new family form. Cherlin (1978) thus called remarried families an "incomplete institution." This situation inevitably leads to conflict and confusion among family members.

Marital Success the Second Time Around

A famous Frank Sinatra ballad claims that love is indeed lovelier the second time around. Perhaps people are more mature and aware when they have both feet on the ground. If one does not live happily ever after the first time, are that person's chances for a happy and successful marriage improved in a second marriage?

Looking at marriage from a purely statistical point of view, one finds that the rate of divorce among remarried couples is slightly higher than the divorce rate among those in their first marriage (Cherlin 1992; Furstenberg 1990). While it might be tempting to leap at an individual-level explanation for the greater divorce rate, such as "some people have divorce-prone personalities," it is advisable to remember the unique social and structural situations in which remarried families find themselves. Unique problems, self-doubt, financial difficulties, and special family structures all weigh heavily on the remarried couple. Also, remarried couples tend to be less integrated with their parents or in-laws (Booth and Edwards 1992).

Chance of divorce is not necessarily the best way to measure the satisfaction and success of a remarriage. Various studies conducted by those interested in comparing first marriages to remarriages produce somewhat more upbeat results. Sociologists Norval Glenn and Charles Weaver (1977) compared remarried couples to couples in their first marriage. As a whole, a remarriage that did not end in a quick divorce turned out to be about as successful as the intact first marriage. A later study by Glenn (1981) found that remarried women report lower levels of marital satisfaction than remarried men. The differences between remarried African American men and women were even larger than the differences for whites.

A different way of measuring comparative marital happiness and success would be to ask individuals in a second marriage to compare that marriage to their first. William Goode (1956) and Stan Albrecht (1979) both found that individuals rated their second marriage as better than their previous one.

In general, the differences in marital satisfaction between first-married and remarried couples are quite small (Vemer et al. 1989).

SUMMING UP

The discussion of divorce and remarriage is much like viewing the classic glass of water that is either half full or half empty. Doom-and-gloom forecasters tend to latch onto statistics like "half of all first marriages end in divorce" and "remarriages have a slightly higher rate of divorce than first marriages" and use these statistics to forecast the imminent collapse of the family system. On the other hand, those who wear rosier-colored glasses will comment on how divorce can solve problems and liberate people from oppressive and bad unions. In general, however, the discussion of divorce and remarriage tends to attract more negative comments than positive. We still refer to single-parent homes as "broken homes." Children from divorced families tend to have their acting out and emotional ups and downs attributed to the divorce, but the same behaviors among children in first marriages are written off as mood swings and developmental changes.

There is no getting away from the fact that, for most couples and children, divorce is a crisis. There is also the fact that our social support systems still have not worked out appropriate solutions for the complexities of remarried families. However, nothing is all black or all white. Divorce is a process. It involves many factors—financial, emotional, and legal—and it has many stages that people and families move through.

The current situation with divorce in our society seems to revolve around the conflict between commitment to the ideals of family and family life and the struggle for individual self-actualization. In first and subsequent marriages, this struggle plays an important role in determining marital success and happiness and the likelihood of marital dissolution.

There are four methods of measuring the chances of divorce: the marriage-to-divorce ratio, the crude divorce rate, the refined divorce rate, and the life chances of being divorced. The most accurate measure is the refined divorce rate, although most people are interested in the life chances data.

Over time, the divorce rate has fluctuated, but generally there has been a rise in the rate. The peak of the refined divorce rate was in 1979, and then the rate leveled off and declined somewhat in the 1980s and 1990s.

The chances of a marriage ending in divorce are not the same in all segments of society. Marital dissolution through divorce varies by social group, with some groups having a greater risk of divorce than others. The factors that are related to high risk of divorce are low or unstable income, low education (although highly educated women are as likely to be divorced as women with little education), and low occupational status. Most studies report that African Americans are more likely to separate and divorce than whites. The divorce rate for Latinos is between that of whites and African Americans. Generally, the longer one delays entering marriage for the first time, the lower the chances of that person's marriage ending in divorce. Divorce rates are higher for Protestants than for Catholics, although more Catholic marriages end in separation. Homogamous Jewish marriages are more stable than Jewish-Gentile and Protestant-Catholic marriages.

With regard to the consequences of divorce, separated or divorced men and women tend to go through a period of emotional and social upset. After the divorce, couples are often still attached—there is still the feeling of being emotionally bound to the other person. Many people who go through divorce suffer a period of "separation distress." Others experience euphoria. Over time, both the separation distress and the euphoria begin to disappear. Loneliness often replaces the depths of depression and the heights of euphoria.

Adjustment to the various changes and losses of a divorce depend on social as well as emotional resources. Adequate financial resources, loyal and giving friends and relatives, the wife's education and job skills, and the husband's homemaking skills all influence the adjustment.

Although both partners are affected by divorce, it would appear that the greatest weight of divorce is felt by the single parent (usually mothers) and children. More than 1 million children under the age of 18 see their parents divorce each year and experts estimate that half of all children born today will see their parents separate or divorce before the child's 18th birthday.

Nearly 70% of divorced men and 60% of divorced women remarry. Sex, age, the presence of children, and factors such as education and race all influence a divorced person's chances of getting remarried. Research on the nature and process of remarriage indicate that, at least from the point of view of the participants, second marriages are really quite different from first marriages. Sociologists have identified nine types of remarried families and note that each type of family has its own unique character and problems. Although remarriages follow most divorces, we still have not worked out the ground rules and guidelines for sharing parenthood. Without rules, guidelines, and social and institutional supports, blended families are often left to their own resources to work out and improvise rules and arrangements for dealing with this rather new family form.

REFERENCES

Ahlburg, Dennis A. and Carol J. De Vita. 1992. "New Realities of the American Family." *Population Bulletin* 46(2):1-44.

Albrecht, Stan L. 1979. "Correlates of Marital Happiness Among the Remarried." *Journal of Marriage and the Family* 41 (November):857-67.

Becker, Gary, Michael Landis, and Robert Michael. 1977. "An Economic Analysis of Marital Instability." *Journal of Political Economy* 85(December): 1141-87.

Bell, H. 1983. *Youth Tell Their Story.* Washington, DC: American Council on Education.

Bellah, Robert N., Richard Madsen, William Sullivan, Ann Swidler, and Steven Tipton. 1985. *Habits of the Heart: Individualism and Commitment in American Life.* Berkeley: University of California Press.

Berger, Peter and Hansfried Kellner. 1964. "Marriage and

the Social Construction of Reality." *Diogenes* 46:1-25.

Billy, John, Nancy Landale, and Steven McLaughlin. 1986. "The Effects of Marital Status at First Birth on Marital Dissolution Among Adolescent Mothers." *Demography* 23(3):329-49.

Blumstein, Philip and Pepper Schwartz. 1983. *American Couples: Money, Work, and Sex*. New York: William Morrow.

Bohannon, Paul. 1970. "The Six Stations of Divorce." Pp. 33-62 in *Divorce and After*, edited by Paul Bohannon. Garden City, NY: Doubleday.

Booth, Alan and John N. Edwards. 1992. "Starting Over: Why Remarriages Are More Unstable." *Journal of Family Issues* 2(June):179-94.

Bumpass, Larry. 1984. "Children and Marital Disruption: A Replication and Update." *Demography* 21(February):71-82.

Bumpass, Larry L. and James A. Sweet. 1972. "Differentials in Marital Instability: 1970." *American Sociological Review* 37(December):754-66.

Bumpass, Larry, James Sweet, and Teresa Castro Martin. 1990. "Changing Patterns of Remarriage." *Journal of Marriage and the Family* 52 (August):747-56.

Burchinal, Lee G. and Loren E. Chancellor. 1962. "Survival Rates Among Religiously Homogamous and Interreligious Marriages." *Iowa Agricultural and Home Economics Experimental Station Research Bulletin* 512 (December):743-70.

Carter, H. and Paul Glick. 1976. *Marriage and Divorce: A Social and Economic Study*. Cambridge, MA: Harvard University Press.

Cherlin, Andrew J. 1978. "Remarriage as an Incomplete Institution." *American Journal of Sociology* 84(November):634-50.

———. 1992. *Marriage, Divorce, Remarriage*. Cambridge, MA: Harvard University Press.

Christensen, Harold T. and Kenneth E. Barber. 1967. "Interfaith vs. Intrafaith Marriages in Indiana." *Journal of Marriage and the Family* 29 (August):461-69.

Christensen, Harold T. and Hanna H. Meissner. 1953. "Studies in Child Spacing: III—Premarital Pregnancy as a Factor in Divorce." *American Sociological Review* 18(December):641-44.

Coombs, Lolagene C. and Zena Zumeta. 1970. "Correlates of Marital Dissolution in a Prospective Fertility Study: A Research Note." *Social Problems* 18(Summer):92-102

Demographic Yearbook 1987. New York: Department of Economic and Social Affairs Statistical Office, United Nations.

Duberman, Lucille. 1975. *The Reconstituted Family: A Study of Remarried Couples and Their Children*. Chicago: Nelson-Hall.

Duncan, Greg J. and Saul D. Hoffman. 1985. "Economic Consequences of Marital Instability." Pp. 427-70 in *Horizontal Equity, Uncertainty, and Economic Well-Being*, edited by Martin David and Timothy Smeedings.

Chicago: University of Chicago Press.

Espenshade, Thomas J. 1979. "The Economic Consequences of Divorce." *Journal of Marriage and the Family* 41(August): 613-25.

Etzioni, Amitai. 1977. "The Family: Is It Obsolete?" *Journal of Current Social Issues* 14 (Winter):4-9.

Finkelhor, David, Gerald Hotaling, and Andrea Sedlak. 1991. "Abduction of Children by Family Members." *Journal of Marriage and the Family* 53 (August):805-17.

Furstenberg, Frank F., Jr. 1976. "Premarital Pregnancy and Marital Instability." *Journal of Social Issues* 32(Winter):67-86.

———. 1980. "Reflection on Remarriage: Introduction to *Journal of Family Issues* Special Issue on Remarriage." *Journal of Family Issues* 1(December):443-53.

———. 1990. "Divorce and the American Family." *Annual Review of Sociology* 16:379-403.

Furstenberg, Frank F., Jr. and Graham B. Spanier. 1984. *Recycling the Family: Remarriage After Divorce*. Beverly Hills, CA: Sage.

Glenn, Norval D. 1981. "The Well-Being of Persons Remarried After Divorce." *Journal of Family Issues* 2(March):61-75.

Glenn, Norval D. and Beth Ann Shelton. 1985. "Regional Differences in Divorce in the United States." *Journal of Marriage and the Family* 47 (August):641-52.

Glenn, Norval D. and Michael Supancic. 1984. "The Social and Demographic Correlates of Divorce and Separation in the United States: An Update and Reconsideration." *Journal of Marriage and the Family* 46 (August):563-75.

Glenn, Norval D. and Charles Weaver. 1977. "The Marital Happiness of Remarried Divorced Persons." *Journal of Marriage and the Family* 39(May):331-37.

Glick, Paul C. and Arthur J. Norton. 1977. "Marrying, Divorcing, and Living Together in the U.S. Today." *Population Bulletin* 32(5):1-39.

Goode, William J. 1956. *After Divorce.* New York: Free Press.

Grady, William R. 1980. "Remarriage of Women 13-44 Years of Age Whose First Marriage Ended in Divorce: United States, 1976." Advance Data No. 58, National Center for Health Statistics. Washington, DC: U.S. Department of Health and Human Services.

Hampton, Robert L. 1975. "Marital Disruption: Some Social and Economic Consequences." Pp. 163-87 in *Five Thousand Lives,* Vol. 3, edited by Greg J. Duncan and James N. Morgan. Ann Arbor, MI: Institute for Social Research.

———. 1979. "Husband's Characteristics and Marital Disruption in Black Families." *Sociological Quarterly* 20 (Spring):255-66.

Hoffman, Saul D. and Greg J. Duncan. 1988. "What *Are* the Economic Consequences of Divorce?" *Demography* 25 (November):641-45.

Holden, Karen C. and Pamela J. Smock. 1991. "The Economic Costs of Marital Dissolution: Why Do Women Bear a Disproportionate Cost?" *Annual Review of Sociology* 17:51-78.

Ihinger-Tallman, Marilyn and Kay Pasley. 1987. *Remarriage.* Newbury Park, CA: Sage.

Kelly, Joan B. and Judith S. Wallerstein. 1976 "The Effects of Parental Divorce: Experiences of the Child in Early Latency." *American Journal of Orthopsychiatry* 46(January):20-32.

Kitson, Gay C. and Helen J. Raschke. 1981. "Divorce Research: What We Know, What We Need to Know." *Journal of Divorce* 3(Spring):1-37.

Koo, Helen P. and C. M. Suchindran. 1980. "Effects of Children on Women's Remarriage Prospects." *Journal of Family Issues* 1(December):497-515.

Landis, Judson T. 1949. "Marriages of Mixed and Non-Mixed Religious Faith." *American Sociological Review* 14(August): 401-7.

Levinger, George. 1966. "Sources of Marital Dissatisfaction Among Applicants for Divorce." *American Journal of Orthopsychiatry* 36(October): 803-7.

Martin, Teresa Castro and Larry Bumpass. 1989. "Recent Trends in Marital Disruption." *Demography* 26(February):37-51.

McLanahan, Sara. 1988. "The Consequences of Single Parenthood for Subsequent Generations." *Focus* 11(Fall):16-21.

Morgan, S. Philip and Ronald Rindfuss. 1984. "Marital Disruption: Structural and Temporal Dimensions." *American Journal of Sociology* 90(March):1055-77.

National Center for Health Statistics. 1980. *National Estimates of Marriage Dissolution and Survivorship.* Health and Vital Statistics, Series 3, No. 19 (November). Washington, DC: Author.

———. 1991. "Advanced Report of Final Divorce Statistics, 1988." *Monthly Vital Statistics Report* 29(May 21):Suppl. 2. Washington, DC: Author.

Norton, Arthur J. and Paul C. Glick. 1976. "Marital Instability: Past, Present, and Future." *Journal of Social Issues* 32(1):5-19.

———. 1979. "Marital Instability in America: Past, Present, and Future." Pp. 6-19 in *Divorce and Separation: Context, Causes, and Consequences,* edited by George Levinger and Oliver C. Moles. New York: Basic Books.

Norton, Arthur J. and Jeanne H. Moorman. 1987. "Current Trends in Marriage and Divorce Among American Women." *Journal of Marriage and the Family* 49(February):3-14.

Packard, Vance. 1972. *A Nation of Strangers.* New York: David McKay.

Pasley, Kay and Marilyn Ihinger-Tallman. 1982. "Stress in Remarried Families." *Family Perspectives* 12(Fall):181-90.

Peterson, James L. and Nicholas Zill. 1986. "Marital Disruption, Parent-Child Behavior, and Behavior Problems in Children." *Journal of Marriage and the Family* 48(May):295-307.

Peterson, R. R. 1989. *Women, Work, and Divorce*. Albany: State University of New York Press.

Phillips, Roderick. 1988. *Putting Asunder: A History of Divorce in Western Society*. New York: Cambridge University Press.

Popenoe, David. 1988. *Disturbing the Nest: Family Change and Decline in Modern Societies*. New York: Aldine de Gruyter.

Price, Sharon J. and Patrick C. McKenry. 1988. *Divorce*. Newbury Park, CA: Sage.

Raschke, Helen J. 1987. "Divorce." Pp. 597-624 in *Handbook of Marriage and the Family*, edited by Marvin B. Sussman and Suzanne K. Steinmetz. New York: Plenum.

Rosow, Irving and K. Daniel Rose. 1972. "Divorce Among Doctors." *Journal of Marriage and the Family* 34(November):587-98.

Ross, Heather L. and Isabell Sawhill. 1975. *Time of Transition: The Growth of Families Headed by Women*. Washington, DC: Urban Institute.

Rubin, Lillian B. 1976. *Worlds of Pain: Life in the Working Class Family*. New York: Basic Books.

Scanzoni, John. 1968. "A Social System Analysis of Dissolved and Existing Marriages." *Journal of Marriage and the Family* 28(August):407-11.

———. 1972. *Sexual Bargaining*. Englewood Cliffs, NJ: Prentice Hall.

Spanier, Graham B. and Paul C. Glick. 1981. "Marital Instability in the United States:

Some Correlates and Recent Changes." *Family Relations* 30(July):329-38.

Sweet, James and Larry Bumpass. 1987. *American Families and Households*. New York: Russell Sage.

Teachman, Jay D. 1983. "Early Marriage, Premarital Fertility, and Marital Dissolution." *Journal of Family Issues* 4(March): 105-26.

Thornton, Arland. 1977. "Decomposing the Remarriage Process." *Populations Studies* 31 (July):383-92.

Toffler, Alvin. 1972. *Future Shock*. New York: Random House.

Udry, J. Richard. 1966. "Marital Instability by Race, Sex, Education, and Occupation Using 1960 Census Data." *American Journal of Sociology* 72(September):203-9.

U.S. Bureau of the Census. 1989. *Child Support and Alimony, 1985*. Current Population Reports, Series P-23, No. 154. Washington, DC: Government Printing Office.

———. 1992a. *Marital Status and Living Arrangements, March 1992*. Current Population Reports, Series P-20, No. 468. Washington, DC: Government Printing Office.

———. 1992b. *Statistical Abstracts of the United States*. Washington, DC: Government Printing Office.

Vemer, Elizabeth, Marilyn Coleman, Lawrence H. Ganong, and Harris Cooper. 1989. "Marital Satisfaction in Remarriage: A Meta-Analysis." *Journal of Marriage and the Family* 51(August):713-25.

Wallerstein, Judith S. and Sandra Blakeslee. 1989. *Second Chances: Men, Women, and Children a Decade After Divorce*. New York: Ticknor & Fields.

Wallerstein, Judith S. and Joan B. Kelly. 1976. "The Effects of Parental Divorce: The Experiences of the Child in Later Latency." *American Journal of Orthopsychiatry* 46(April): 256-69.

———. 1980. *Surviving the Breakup: How Children and Parents Cope With Divorce*. New York: Basic Books.

Weingarten, Helen. 1980. "Remarriage and Well-Being: National Survey Evidence of Social and Psychological Effects." *Journal of Family Issues* 1(December):533-59.

Weiss, Robert S. 1975. *Marital Separation*. New York: Basic Books.

———. 1979. *Going It Alone: The Family Life and Social Situation of the Single Parent*. New York: Basic Books.

Weitzman, Lenore. 1985. *The Divorce Revolution*. New York: Free Press.

White, Lynn. 1990. "Determinants of Divorce: A Review of Research in the Eighties." *Journal of Marriage and the Family* 52(November):904-12.

Wilson, Barbara Foley and Sally Cunningham Clarke. 1992. "Remarriages: A Demographic Profile." *Journal of Family Issues* 13(June):123-41.

Wineberg, Howard. 1988. "Duration Between Marriage and First Birth and Marital Stability." *Social Biology* 35(Spring-Summer):91-102.

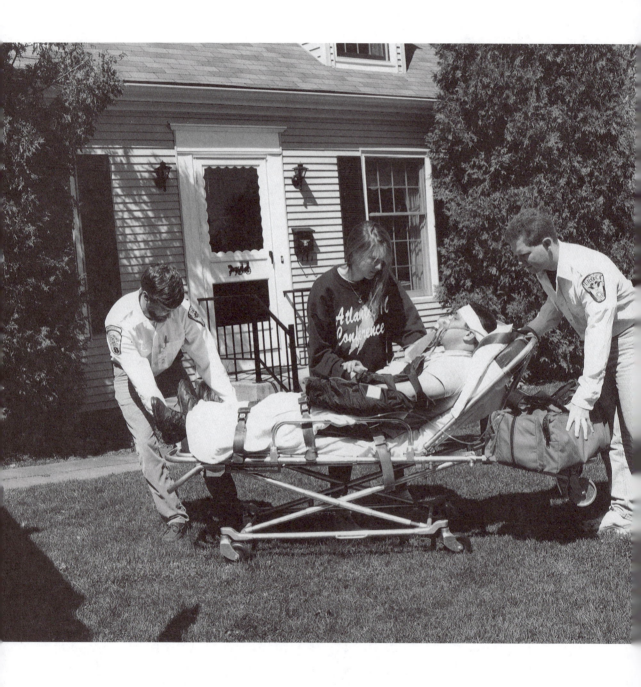

CHAPTER 14

■■ Stress and Coping in Families

Somehow I thought that if I made it by the first years of marriage, then everything would be much easier. After learning to live with my wife and adjust our needs and patterns, we went through the difficult years of having young kids. For at least 5 years, we never had a full night's sleep. Getting baby sitters, never having time to ourselves, the various crises of starting school, and childhood illnesses and accidents were behind us. I never expected that it could get worse. But then, 15 years after we were married and I was about 39 years old, our son became schoolphobic. He just refused to go to school. If this has never happened to you, it might not seem like a big deal, but it was terrible. One morning he got up at 6 a.m. and hid behind the house so that we couldn't find him. Another morning I had to chase him around the house, and I ended up carrying him kicking and screaming to the car. I had to get my wife to help hold him down in the back seat while we drove to school. Just when I thought that this was more than I could deal with, my father had a stroke that left him brain damaged—a vegetable. My sister, my mother, and I had to go through weeks of agony deciding whether to keep my dad on life support. At this point, I was sure things had piled up so high there was no way I could go on. My wife felt the same way.

Throughout this book we have contrasted the image of the peaceful and loving family that serves to reduce stress and support its members with the reality of families as stressful intimate environments. Both the external pressures of work and society and the internal demands of marital and parental roles place extraordinary demands on individuals as well as on family systems. Sometimes, external and internal pressures can lead to violence (see Chapter 15), divorce (see Chapter 13), or personal health problems and crises. Other times, families not only endure troubles and pressures, they seem to be strengthened and hardened by coping with stress.

This chapter focuses on stress and coping in families. We begin by briefly describing the history of family scholars' concern with stress and how it affects family systems. The key terms of **stressor, stress, crisis,** and **coping** are defined and placed in the frameworks that social scientists have used to conceptualize stress and coping in families. Next, we survey the key stressor events that influence families and family functioning. These include both "normal" stressor events as well as unexpected events. The chapter concludes with a discussion of how families manage and cope with stressful events and the impact of stress on families.

FAMILIES AND STRESS

Major economic and social events, such as the Great Depression of the 1930s, World War II, and the Vietnam War, were the wellspring of social science's concern for how stress is managed by families. Research on the effects of these events on individuals and families led to the development of models of stress and its impact on families. This section reviews the history of the study of stress and families as well as the major models of stress and its effect on family life.

Systematic concern with stress and how it affects families began at the University of Michigan and the University of Chicago in the 1930s (Boss 1987). Robert Angell (1936) and Ruth Cavan and Katherine Ranck (1938) examined the impact of the Great Depression on families in the 1930s. These researchers used case studies to investigate how families adapted to a sudden loss of income. Cavan and Ranck (1938) employed a longitudinal design to follow families from 1927 to 1935. They found that a family's previous methods of dealing with difficulty were related to how they met present problems. Well-organized families continued to function effectively, despite the Depression, while poorly organized families became further disorganized. Well-organized families tended to have a defined structure, including well-defined boundaries about who were and were not members of the family, agreed-on expectations regarding positions and roles in the family, and routines for how family members dealt with one another as well as with new or stressful events. Poorly organized families had ambiguous boundaries, poorly defined expectations about positions and roles, and no set pattern of interacting or dealing with events.

Earl Koos (1946) advanced the study of stress and coping in families. He too was concerned with economic stress, but he also focused on the impact that living in a high-stress urban environment had on families. Koos developed what he called a "profile of trouble," which traced the pattern of how economic difficulties affect families. Koos's research illustrated that the living conditions in an urban slum, such as the one he studied in New York City, created stressors more profound, and that had a greater impact, than simply low income.

The modern focus on family stress and coping was more fully developed and articulated by Reuben Hill (1949). Hill was the first scholar to look at a family difficulty other than loss of income or economic crisis. His concern was the impact on separated families as a result of World War II. Hill saw two dimensions of the family that were related to how well the family could manage stressful events: family integration or coherence and family adaptability

Much of the modern research on stress and families was carried out with families who had members who were prisoners of war or missing in action in Vietnam—those who were missing or killed in action have their names engraved on the "Wall"—the Vietnam War Memorial in Washington, DC.

or flexibility. Hill's research led to the development of the ABC-X model of family stress, which became the main guiding model for the study of family stress.

Hans Selye (1974, 1976, 1980, 1982) linked the experience of family and individual stress to general health and disease. Selye identified physiological changes that occur when individuals experience prolonged physical or emotional stress.

More recently, Charles Figley (1978), Hamilton McCubbin and his colleagues (McCubbin et al. 1976; McCubbin, Hunter, and Dahl 1975) and Pauline Boss (1980) examined how families coped with husbands and fathers being prisoners of war (POWs) or missing in action (MIAs) in the Vietnam War. The initial investigations of how families coped with family members who were POWs or MIAs applied Hill's ABC-X model of family stress. Later, McCubbin and his colleagues elaborated the ABC-X model into what they called the double ABC-X model. Both models are discussed in detail in the following section.

FAMILY STRESS: BASIC CONCEPTS AND MODELS

A few basic terms need to be defined in order to understand the nature of stress and coping in families. **Stressors** or **stressor events** are those life events or changes in life circumstances that are of a significant magnitude to provoke a change in the family system (Boss 1988). Stressors can be events that occur within the family, such as a child's school phobia or the death of a family member, or they can be external to the family, such as an economic recession or depression. Stressors can also include things like the birth of a baby, a promotion at work, or a significant increase in family income—perhaps winning a lottery. We will provide a more complete inventory of stressor events in a later section.

Stress is how a family responds to a stressor event. Hans Selye (1974) defined stress as "the state manifested by a specific syndrome which consists of all the nonspecifically-induced changes within a biologic system" (p. 14). Pauline Boss (1988) defined it as pressure or tension in the family system. Stress is a disturbance in the steady-state of the family. Boss notes that stress is inevitable, normal, and even desirable at times because people develop and change over time. Children are born, family members move in or out, family members die, and families change. Thus the dynamic nature of individual and family development means that stress is a normal part of individual and family life.

The next key concept is **crisis.** A family crisis occurs when family members face stressors that create stress that seems, for some period of time, insurmountable. Ordinary coping measures do not work, and the family needs to reorganize in order to manage the crisis.

Coping is defined as the management of a stressful event or situation by the family as a unit, with no detrimental effects on any individual in that family. Coping is the family's ability to manage, not eradicate or eliminate, the stressful event.

Models of
Family Stress

Hill's ABC-X Model of Family Stress

Reuben Hill's (1949) study of family separation during World War II led to his development of a model or theory of how stress affects families (Hill 1958). His ABC-X model of family stress became a basis for scientific inquiry into the effects of stress on family systems. Hill's model consists of four components, identified by the letters ABCX.

A: The Stressor Event. The first component of the model, the A factor, is the stressor event—the event or events that trigger change and disrupt individuals and families. As we noted earlier and will elaborate on later, these events can be internal or external to the family as well as normal or abrupt.

B: Resources. The B facet of the model represents the family's resources for dealing with the stressor event. Resources include financial, economic, social and organizational resources. The two key system resources are *integration* and *adaptability.* Integration refers to strengths such as affection, interests, and economic interdependence. Adaptability indicates how flexible a family is and the family's ability to develop and implement problem-solving strategies.

C: The Definition of the Stressor. The C factor is related to how a family interprets and defines the stressor event. It is a subjective factor—each family will bring a somewhat unique definition to a stressor event, depending on history, cultural factors, and resources. For example, some families may view the birth of a baby or a move to a new city as exciting new beginnings. Other families may view the same events as extremely disruptive and stressful.

X: The Crisis. The last feature of the model, the X factor, represents the total impact of the stressor, resources, and definition on the family—it is the amount of disequilibrium, instability, or disorganization that results from the combination of A, B, and C.

Figure 14-1 displays Hill's ABC-X model, and Figure 14-2 depicts the interplay of the stressor events, contributing hardships, and family resources as they are related to producing a family crisis. Figure 14-2 illustrates that a number of factors influence whether a stressful event becomes a crisis. These factors include family resources: whether the interpersonal relationships are adequate, whether family roles are harmonious or conflictual, the economic

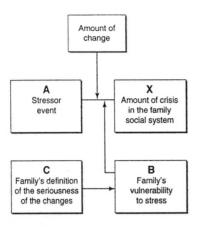

Figure 14-1
The ABC-X Model

SOURCE: Derived from Hill (1958).

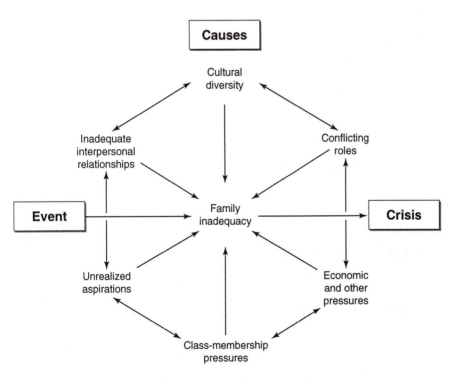

Figure 14-2
Schema for Depicting the Interplay of Stressor Event, Contributing Hardships, and Family Resources in Producing a Family Crisis

SOURCE: "Social Stresses on the Family: Generic Features of Families Under Stress" by Reuben Hill, 1958, *Social Casework* 39(February), p. 145. Copyright © 1958 by Families International, Inc. Adapted by permission.

Figure 14-3 Process of Adjustment

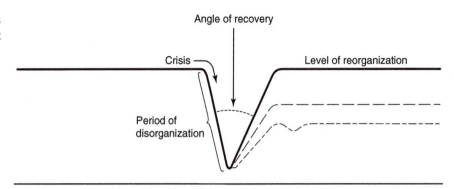

SOURCE: "Social Stresses on the Family: Generic Features of Families Under Stress" by Reuben Hill, 1958, *Social Casework* 39(February), p. 146. Copyright © 1958 by Families International, Inc. Adapted by permission.

pressures on the family, and family members' individual and collective goals and aspirations. In addition, cultural factors, such as class membership and cultural beliefs and values, influence how adequate a family will be in dealing with stressful events.

The Roller Coaster of Adjustment

If the combination of stressor events, family resources, and family definition of the event lead to a crisis, the family then moves through what Hill (1958) called the "roller-coaster" profile of adjustment. The roller coaster begins with the crisis, which in turn produces family disorganization. Disorganization is followed by a period of recovery, and finally, reorganization (see Figure 14-3).

The Double ABC-X Model

Hamilton McCubbin and his colleagues (e.g., McCubbin and Patterson 1982, 1983) built on Hill's ABC-X model and proposed a double ABC-X model of family stress that captures the dynamic and changing nature of stress, crisis, and adaptation (see Figure 14-4). McCubbin and his colleagues studied families of POWs from the Vietnam War, families coping with caring for chronically ill family members, and families coping with normal developmental changes in family life.

The A, or stressor event, element in the double ABC-X model becomes a double A, aA, called "family pileup." Pileup includes not only the stressor event (A) but other prior stressors and hardships that occur, irrespective of

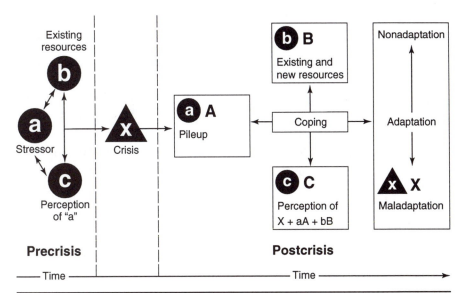

Figure 14-4 The Double ABC-X Model

SOURCE: "Family Adaptation to Crisis" by Hamilton I. McCubbin and Joan Patterson in *Family Stress, Coping, and Social Support* (p. 46) edited by A. Elizabeth McCubbin, 1982, Springfield, IL: Charles C Thomas. Copyright © 1982 by Charles C Thomas, Publisher. Adapted by permission.

the stressor that continue to affect family life (Olson and McCubbin 1983). For example, the father whose quote opened this chapter not only had to deal with his son's school phobia and the illness of his father, but his family life continued to be affected by the stressful job he held (attorney), and the fact that his wife was a full-time student during the time the phobia and illness were going on. These are the "a" stressors.

The B factor becomes a double B, bB, by differentiating the resources already available to the family from those coping resources developed or enhanced in response to the crisis. The father and his family we described sought family counseling to deal with the school phobia and used the counseling to help them deal with the crisis of the ill father and the decision regarding life-support systems. In addition, existing resources, such as friends, financial resources, and health insurance that paid for the counseling, were brought to bear during the crisis of the son's school phobia.

The perception of the event becomes a double C, cC, by distinguishing the perceptions prior to the stressor event about stress and stress levels from those perceptions that emerge as a result of the stressful event. Combining the pre- and postcrisis ABC elements produces the family's adaptation or lack of adaptation to the crisis.

TYPES OF STRESSOR EVENTS

At first glance it would seem easy to identify significant stressors that affect families. Death, serious illness, unemployment, and divorce are among the most noteworthy and are often perceived as crises. Other stressors can also be identified—a less serious illness, sexual difficulties, problems with children, a job transfer. Fewer people would immediately classify the birth of a child, children going off to school, children leaving home, or a promotion at work as significant stressors. Box 14-1 describes a classic and standard means of measuring stress, and Table 14-1 provides a list of the major stressor events that individuals and families experience.

Pauline Boss (1987) defines a stressor event as "an event that is capable of causing change and stress, but does not necessarily do so every time" (p. 698). Stressors are not only negative events but any events that have the potential to cause change.

Because stressful events are neither positive nor negative and only have the potential for causing change, there are varying and multiple types of stressors that can affect families. Pauline Boss (1988) developed a list of stressor events.

BOX 14-1: WHAT THE RESEARCH SHOWS

Measuring Stressors

Although we can identify the different types of stressors, the concept of stress has proved difficult to measure. Social scientists typically measure stress by assessing stressor events that individuals and families experience. The Social Readjustment Scale developed by Thomas Holmes and Richard Rahe (1967) is a widely used measure of stress.

The Social Readjustment Scale ranks 43 life events that can create stress. Holmes and Rahe interviewed more than 400 people and developed a weighting system, or ranking, of the stressors people experience. Each stressor is assigned a numerical value representing "life crisis units" (see Table 14-1). The most significant and stressful stressor is death of a spouse, which is assigned a value of 100. Vacations, Christmas, and minor violations of the law—for instance, a speeding ticket—are assigned the lowest values.

The Social Readjustment Scale asks individuals to indicate whether they experienced any of the 43 events in the previous year. The number of "life crisis units" are summed to produce a total score. Families that score 300 or more have experienced major life change, whereas those that score 149 or lower have experienced very little life change.

Rank	Life Event	Mean Value
1	Death of spouse	100
2	Divorce	73
3	Marital separation	65
4	Jail term	63
5	Death of close family member	63
6	Personal injury or illness	53
7	Marriage	50
8	Fired at work	47
9	Marital reconciliation	45
10	Retirement	45
11	Change in health of family member	44
12	Pregnancy	40
13	Sex difficulties	39
14	Gain of new family member	39
15	Business readjustment	39
16	Change in financial state	38
17	Death of close friend	37
18	Change to different line of work	36
19	Change in number of arguments with spouse	35
20	Mortgage over $10,000	31
21	Foreclosure of mortgage or loan	30
22	Change in responsibilities at work	29
23	Son or daughter leaving home	29
24	Trouble with in-laws	29
25	Outstanding personal achievement	28
26	Wife begins or stops work	26
27	Begin or end school	26
28	Change in living conditions	25
29	Revision of personal habits	24
30	Trouble with boss	23
31	Change in work hours or conditions	20
32	Change in residence	20
33	Change in schools	20
34	Change in recreation	19
35	Change in church activities	19
36	Change in social activities	18
37	Mortgage or loan less than $10,000	17
38	Change in sleeping habits	16
29	Change in number of family get-togethers	15
40	Change in eating habits	15
41	Vacation	13
42	Christmas	12
43	Minor violations of the law	11

Table 14-1 Social Readjustment Rating Scale

SOURCE: "The Social Readjustment Rating Scale" by Thomas H. Holmes and Richard H. Rahe, 1967, *Journal of Psychosomatic Research* 11, p. 216. Copyright © 1967 by Elsevier Science, Ltd., Pergamon imprint. Used by permission.

A child's first day of school can be an important stressor event for a family.

Normative
Developmental
Stressors

Normative developmental stressors are predictable changes and transitions that are part of everyday life. The first such normative change is marriage and the formation of the marital dyad. The birth of a child, the first day of school, children leaving home, and retirement are examples of normal development and changes that can affect families. Additional normative developmental stressors are graduation from high school or college and beginning a first job. Other transitions, such as becoming a parent, child development, and aging and retirement, are discussed in other chapters in this text.

Unexpected or
Disaster Events

Disasters or unexpected events are the types of stressors that originally attracted family scholars to the study of family stress. The Great Depression,

World War II, the Vietnam War, and natural disasters such as floods, earthquakes, and hurricanes are events that have general social impact and affect individual families. Unexpected stressors typically occur outside the family and either have their origins in nature, such as natural disasters, or are manmade, such as war. Unexpected stresses can be global; national, such as the Great Depression; or regional, such as the farm crisis in the Midwest in the 1980s (Elder et al. 1992).

One example of how natural disasters can affect families is the report that rates of child abuse and wife abuse increased in southern Florida in the wake of the devastation by Hurricane Andrew in late summer 1992.

The occurrence of a disaster is typically outside the control of individuals or family members. These nonvolitional events are those that are thrust upon a family and are not directly the result of actions by family members. Disasters and unexpected external events are examples of nonvolitional stressors. Being laid off from work or being the victim of a robbery, housebreaking, car theft, or mugging is also nonvolitional. An unwanted pregnancy can be considered a nonvolitional event that has its occurrence within the family.

Some types of stressor events are classified as volitional because they occur as the result of conscious individual or family decisions. A marriage, a divorce, and a planned pregnancy are examples of volitional events that can be stressors.

Volitional and Nonvolitional Events

A stressor event can arise from an inability to get facts about an event or anticipated event. Such stressors are called ambiguous stressor events. During periods of economic crisis, business and government agencies deal with budget deficits by laying off workers. Typically, rumors about how many people will be laid off and who will be affected circulate around the company or agency for weeks or months before the final layoff notices are sent. This period of uncertainty and ambiguity, while not a concrete event, is a stressor event nonetheless. So too may be the worry and uncertainty a parent has about a child going off to college for the first time or leaving home to start a first job. Families with members who have been treated for cancer but who are in remission are also in situations of ambiguity.

Nonambiguous stressors are those that are clear and predictable. When the layoff notice does arrive, the ambiguous stressor becomes nonambiguous. A hurricane or earthquake, a death, and a move to a new state are all nonambiguous stressors.

Ambiguous and Nonambigious Stressor Events

Acute and Chronic Stressor Events

Most of the examples of stressors we have described up to now are specific events. Acute stressor events happen suddenly and last only a short time. A chronic stressor is a situation that persists over a long period of time. Chronic illnesses, such as Alzheimer's disease, or an economic situation, such as a recession or depression or even a period of affluence, or a social condition, such as racism, sexism, and prejudice, are examples of chronic stressors. Other chronic stressors are linked to living situations—say, living near a potential disaster, such as a nuclear power plant, or an active volcano, such as Mount St. Helens in Washington State. Individuals who live near airports experience the dual chronic stressor condition of constant noise and potential accidents.

Pauline Boss (1988) explains that chronic stressors have special characteristics that influence the degree of impact the stressor will have on families. First, chronic stressors can be ambiguous or nonambiguous. Second, the context of the stressor is important. Stressors exist in large contexts, such as a widespread economic recession or the closing of a factory, or in small,

Traffic jams are a form of chronic stress for many families who have members who commute to work each day.

individual contexts, such as a lifetime of smoking or a persistent illness. Finally, the chronic stressor can be either visible or invisible. High blood pressure is a chronic illness that has few visible or noticeable symptoms. Other illnesses have more direct and debilitating manifestations.

There is some overlap between acute and chronic stressors. A natural disaster happens suddenly and although it lasts but a brief time, its impact may become a chronic stressor. An example of an acute stressor that became chronic is the Buffalo Creek dam collapse that occurred in February 1973 in the Appalachian Mountains of West Virginia. The Buffalo Creek disaster has been chronicled by sociologist Kai Erickson in his 1976 book, *Everything in Its Path: Destruction of Community in the Buffalo Creek Flood*. At 8 a.m. on the morning of February 25, 1973, the Buffalo Creek dam collapsed, sending 130 million gallons of water into a community of 5,000 people. By 10 a.m., the waters had subsided, leaving 125 townspeople dead and 4,000 homeless. Although the actual event was brief and acute, the consequences affected the lives of Buffalo Creek residents for years.

Each of the three characteristics mentioned can affect a family's perception of the event and determine the level of crisis and stress the family will experience.

BOX 14-2: DIVERSE FAMILIES

Chronic Societal Stress:
Prejudice, Discrimination, and the African American Family

Stress is usually conceptualized as an acute event that disrupts the family. When chronic distress is discussed, it is typically chronic illness of a family member or chronic environmental stress, such as an economic depression or recession. Another type of chronic environmental stressor is the experience of racial prejudice.

Black psychiatrist Chester Pierce (1975) compared the stress on African Americans in the United States with the harsh physical stress on those who live in extreme climates (see also McAdoo 1983). Just as the day-to-day demands of coping with severe cold and scarce food define the life of the Eskimo people in the Arctic, so racial prejudice defines life for African Americans.

African American families experience the same developmental and normative stressors as white families but are much more likely to experience economic and social stressors. As has been noted in earlier chapters, African American families are more likely to be poor and be headed by single parents, the unemployment rate for black men is considerably higher than that for white men, and African American teenagers have much higher rates of violent death compared to white teens.

The lower economic status of most African Americans results in poorer housing conditions in high-crime environments, which in turn results in high stress. Reduced income also limits access to quality health care. The prejudice and discrimination that blacks encounter intensify the impact of social and economic stressors.

Isolated Stressor Events	Isolated stressor events are single events that occur at a time when nothing else is disturbing the family. This single event can be accurately pinpointed as the event that causes family disturbance.

Accumulation of Stressor Events	Stressful events do not always occur one at a time or in isolation. Stressful events can occur at the same time or in quick sequence. One example is Rhode Island's banking crisis that closed nearly two dozen credit unions in early 1991. At the same time, the state was undergoing a severe economic downturn that caused taxes to be raised and state government to lay off 1,000 state workers and reduce the wages of all other workers by 10%. At exactly the same time, many families, battered by the economic recession and unable to access their money in the closed credit unions, were consumed with worry about relatives about to go to battle in the Persian Gulf War. These families experienced an unusual and severe pileup of stressor events.

COPING WITH STRESS AND CRISIS

The first few decades of research on family stress were devoted to defining the components of stress, developing conceptual models, inventorying the types of stressor events, and assessing the impact of stressors on personal health and family life. Thomas Holmes and Richard Rahe (1967), for example, examined the correlation between family stress scores and individual health and well-being.

There was a shift in emphasis in family stress research in the 1970s and 1980s that placed greater emphasis on coping, rather than crisis. The central question changed from "what are the events that create crises for families?" to "how do families cope with the crises they encounter?"

How Families Cope: The Stages of Coping	There are two stages to coping in families. The first is the acute stage, during which the family devotes its energy to minimizing the impact of the stress. For example, the parents whose child was schoolphobic devoted their immediate energy to forcing their child to go to school and to finding a family counselor to provide them immediate help and guidance about the problem. Similarly, when the father had a stroke, the family immediately mobilized its

resources to obtain proper medical attention and advice for the stricken family member.

The second stage is a reorganization phase in which a new reality is faced and accepted (McCubbin and Dahl 1985). The family recognizes and begins to adapt to the changes caused by the stressor event. For example, counseling may continue beyond the acute phase of school phobia to deal with the underlying issues that brought about the problem. When the family chose to cut off life support for a stricken parent, they had to deal with the loss of a family member and the consequences of their volitional act to terminate life support.

Hamilton McCubbin (1979) has identified a number of positive coping strategies employed by families:

Coping Strategies

■ *Maintaining Family Togetherness*. Families that take time to do things with their children, husbands and wives who spend time with one another, and families that do things together, such as taking family trips or outings, all enhance their abilities to cope with crisis and stress.

■ *Developing Self-Reliance and Self-Esteem*. Individual self-reliance and self-esteem aid families in learning and adopting new skills to help deal with family problems. Those families that have members who have high self-esteem or that collectively promote members' self-esteem tend to cope with stressor events better than families that either do not have members with sound

---

BOX 14-3: WHAT THE RESEARCH SHOWS

Stress and Coping Among Parents of Children With Cancer

Chronic illness is perhaps one of the most stressful events a family can encounter. When the ill family member is a child and the illness is cancer, the impact can be devastating. Oscar Barbarin, Diane Hughes, and Mark Chesler (1985) interviewed 32 married couples about their experiences and strategies for coping with their children's cancer. The effects of coping with childhood cancer were not necessarily debilitating for the families. Most of them reported that they actually became closer during their experiences with the illness. Spouses were the most important sources of social support. However, as the number of hospitalizations of the ill child increased and stressors began to "pile up," issues rose to the surface and families became more distressed. The more a husband was involved in the care of the child, the more his wife saw him as providing helpful support. Husbands, on the other hand, saw their wives as supportive if the wives were available to carry on household responsibilities in addition to providing help and support during the hospital care of the child.

self-esteem or engage in interactions that attack and undermine feeling of self-worth.

■ *Developing Social Support.* A crucial coping mechanism is social support (see the following section). Families that spend time with friends and relatives, participate in clubs and organizations, and who are willing to accept assistance can draw on existing networks to aid them in times of stress.

■ *Developing a Positive Outlook.* Optimism in the face of strain, crisis, and stress can help individuals and families cope.

■ *Learning About a Problem.* One effective means of coping with problems is to learn more about them. Families that encounter illness and disease can read books or articles about the disease or alternative treatments, family members can attend classes, and families can seek out professional advice or counseling.

■ *Reducing Tension.* Exercise, reading, watching television, hobbies, talking things out, or even crying can be important means of reducing tension and allowing families to clearly face crises and stress.

■ *Balancing Coping Efforts.* Families that cope successfully use a variety of coping strategies in a balanced manner to care for themselves and their family members during crises. It is important to point out that the coping strategies that work in some families do not necessarily work in other households and vice versa.

Social Support

One of the key factors that influences a family's ability to cope with and manage stress is the availability and accessibility of community and social supports (McCubbin and Patterson 1982). Social support may take the form of one person helping another, or the transfer of economic resources from one person to another, or more formal community and agency supports. Physician Sidney Cobb (1976) has identified three components of social support:

1. *Emotional.* Emotional support involves empathy and letting the other person know that he or she is cared for and loved.

2. *Esteem.* Esteem support is making the other person feel that he or she is valued, respected, and considered a good or worthwhile individual.

3. *Network.* Network support lets the other person know that he or she fits into a social network that involves regular communication and exchange of responsibilities and obligations.

Social support has been found to play a significant role in the health of individuals as well as mitigating stress that can lead to child abuse, wife abuse, and family violence (Garbarino 1977; Straus, Gelles, and Steinmetz 1980).

Marriage counseling is one way through which families cope with stress.

Social networks and social support form a significant insulator that helps families cope with unemployment or stressful occupations, such as being a police officer (Gore 1978; Maynard et al. 1980). Other stressors, such as raising a child with a chronic illness, recovering from a natural disaster such as the Buffalo Creek dam collapse, or adjusting to being married to a prisoner of war, are also managed through the use and availability of social support (de Araujo et al. 1973; Erickson 1976; McCubbin, Hunter, and Dahl 1975).

The earliest research on the factors most effective in helping individuals and families cope with crisis and stress examined psychological factors and personality traits. The results of these projects were not conclusive and it did not seem that an individual's personality or psychological state was predictive of whether he or she would effectively cope with stress (Boss 1987).

Factors Associated With Effective Coping

Recent research on coping has examined the behaviors of individuals and family members after the onset of a stressor event. For example, Hamilton McCubbin and his colleagues (McCubbin et al. 1975) developed the Coping With Separation Inventory (CSI) to measure coping behaviors of wives in military families who encountered the stressor of separation from their husbands. The findings from this investigation indicated that both individual and family factors influenced coping. Establishing independence and self-sufficiency (an individual factor) and maintaining family integrity and stability (the family factor) were the most effective coping strategies used by wives whose husbands were away on military duty (Boss 1987).

Pauline Boss (1987) explains that assessing effective coping strategies can be quite complex. Although some coping strategies may indeed reduce stress and help manage a crisis, other strategies may well increase vulnerability to stress. Sometimes, a radical change in behavior is more effective than simply trying to manage or cope. For example, a battered wife who flees her home and attempts to divorce her husband is coping more successfully than a battered wife who remains in the home, denying her husband's abusive behavior and trying to keep her marriage together. A family member who copes with a partner's alcoholism by throwing him- or herself into work or a hobby may produce exhaustion, anger, and isolation rather than an effective means of managing a problem.

The effectiveness of coping strategies must be measured by assessing the short- and long-term outcomes for each member of the family in terms of psychological, sociological, and physiological outcomes (Monat and Lazarus 1977).

A general summary of research on coping indicates that active rather than passive behaviors are better predictors of how effectively individuals and families cope with stress and crisis. In addition, a coping behavior may be more functional if it is used in the context of socializing with other people rather than isolating oneself from people—a further indication of the importance of social networks and social support. The family described in the introduction to this chapter was helped immeasurably by turning to friends for advice, counseling, or just to talk about the stress these family members were under.

Yoav Lavee and David Olson (1991) explain that different types of families respond to and cope with stress differently. The effects of both normative transitions and stressful events on families depend on the family's level of cohesion, or how connected the family members feel toward one another, as well as the family's level of adaptability, or how flexible it is. Those families that were flexible and connected were more affected by stressful events but were not affected by normative transitions. Nonadaptable and separated families were primarily affected by normative changes. The other two types of families (flexible-separated and nonadaptable-separated) were affected by both normative changes and stressful events.

Although love and nurturing are the ideals of family life, stressors, stress, and crises are often the norm of family living. Major economic and social events, such as the Great Depression of the 1930s, World War II, and the Vietnam War, were the source of social scientists' concern for how stress is managed by families. Systematic concern with stress and how it effects families began at the University of Michigan and the University of Chicago in the 1930s.

There are a number of key concepts used in the study of stress and coping in families. **Stressors** or **stressor events** are those life events or changes in life circumstances that are of a significant magnitude to provoke a change in the family system. Stressors can be events that occur within the family or they can be external to the family. **Stress** is how a family responds to a stressor event. A family **crisis** occurs when family members face stress that seems insurmountable. Finally, **coping** is defined as the management of a stressful event or situation by the family as a unit.

The typical framework for examining stressors and their impact on families looks at stressor events, family and individual resources, and definitions of the stressor. Reuben Hill's ABC-X model of family stress became a basis for scientific inquiry into the effects of stress on family systems. Hill's model consists of four components: (1) the stressor event, (2) resources, (3) the definition of the stressor, and (4) the crisis.

Hamilton McCubbin and his colleagues built on Hill's ABC-X model and proposed a double ABC-X model of family stress that captures the dynamic and changing nature of stress, crisis, and adaptation.

There are numerous types of stressors that affect and influence families. Some of the stressors are normal developmental changes in families or individual family members, and others are abrupt and disruptive events. Some stressors are isolated, while others occur at the same time or can accumulate in rapid succession. Stressors are not only negative events but any events that have the potential to cause change. Because stressful events are neither positive nor negative and only have the potential for causing change, there are varying and multiple types of stressors that can affect families.

Family coping with the crises caused by stressors or the pileup of stressors involves responding to the immediate and practical requirements of the situation and then dealing with the longer-term emotional consequences of the crisis. Some coping strategies alleviate the crisis; other strategies can exacerbate the problem. There are two stages to coping in families. The first is the acute stage, during which the family devotes its energy to minimizing the impact of the stress. The second stage is a reorganization phase in which a new reality is faced and accepted. Community and social supports are key factors that influence how well families cope with stressors and crises.

A general summary of research on coping indicates that active rather than passive behaviors are better predictors of how effectively individuals and families cope with stress and crisis. In addition, a coping behavior may be more functional if it is used in the context of socializing with other people rather than isolating oneself from people—a further indication of the importance of social networks and social support.

REFERENCES

Angell, Robert C. 1936. *The Family Encounters the Depression.*. New York: Scribner.

Barbarin, Oscar A., Diane Hughes, and **Mark A. Chesler.** 1985. "Stress, Coping, and Marital Functioning Among Parents of Children With Cancer." *Journal of Marriage and the Family* 47(May): 473-80.

Boss, Pauline G. 1980. "The Relationship of Psychological Father Presence, Wife's Personal Qualities, and Wife/Family Dysfunction in Families of Missing Fathers." *Journal of Marriage and the Family* 42(3):541-49.

———. 1987. "Family Stress." Pp. 695-723 in *Handbook of Marriage and the Family,* edited by Marvin B. Sussman and Suzanne K. Steinmetz. New York: Plenum.

———. 1988. *Family Stress Management.* Newbury Park, CA: Sage.

Cavan, Ruth S. and **Katherine H. Ranck.** 1938. *The Family and the Depression.* Chicago: University of Chicago Press.

Cobb, Sidney. 1976. "Social Support as a Moderator of Life Stress." *Psychosomatic Medicine* 38(September-October):300-14.

de Araujo, Gilberto, Paul P. Van Aresdale, Thomas H. Holmes, and **Donald L. Dudley.** 1973. "Life Change, Coping Ability and Chronic Intrinsic Asthma." *Journal of Psychosomatic Research* 17 (December):359-63.

Elder, Glen H., Jr., Rand D. Conger, E. Michael Foster, and **Monika Ardlt.** 1992. "Families Under Economic Pressure." *Journal of Family Issues* 13(March):5-37.

Erickson, Kai. 1976. *Everything in Its Path: Destruction of Community in the Buffalo Creek Flood.* New York: Simon & Schuster.

Figley, Charles R. 1978. *Stress Disorders Among Vietnam Veterans: Theory, Research, and Treatment.* New York: Brunner/Mazel.

Garbarino, James. 1977. "The Human Ecology of Child Maltreatment." *Journal of Marriage and the Family* 39(4):721-35.

Gore, Susan. 1978. "The Effect of Social Support in Moderating Health Consequences of Unemployment." *Journal of Health and Social Behavior* 19 (June):157-65.

Hill, Reuben. 1949. *Families Under Stress.* New York: Harper & Row.

———. 1958. "Generic Features of Families Under Stress." *Social Casework* 39(February):139-50.

Holmes, Thomas H. and - **Richard H. Rahe.** 1967. "The Social Readjustment Scale." *Journal of Psychosomatic Research* 11(September):213-18.

Koos, Earl L. 1946. *Families in Trouble.* New York: King's Crown Press.

Lavee, Yoav and **David H. Olson.** 1991. "Family Types and Response to Stress." *Journal of Marriage and the Family* 53(August):786-98.

Maynard, Peter, Nancy Maynard, Hamilton I. McCubbin, and **David Shao.** 1980. "Family Life and the Police Profession: Coping Patterns Wives Employ in Managing Job Stress and the Family Environment." *Family Relations* 29(October):495-501.

McAdoo, Harriet P. 1983. "Societal Stress: The Black Family." Pp. 178-87 in *Stress and the Family: Volume 1. Coping With Normative Stress,* edited by Hamilton I. McCubbin and

Charles R. Figley. New York: Brunner/Mazel.

McCubbin, Hamilton I. 1979. "Integrating Coping Behavior in Family Stress Theory." *Journal of Marriage and the Family* 41(May):237-44.

McCubbin, Hamilton I. and Barbara B. Dahl. 1985. *Marriage and Family: Individuals and Life Cycles.* New York: John Wiley.

McCubbin, Hamilton I., Barbara B. Dahl, Gary R. Lester, Dorothy Bensen, and Marilyn L. Robertson. 1976. "Coping Repertoires of Families Adapting to Prolonged War-Induced Separation." *Journal of Marriage and the Family* 38(3): 471-78.

McCubbin, Hamilton I., Barbara B. Dahl, Gary R. Lester, and Pauline G. Boss. 1975. *Coping With Separation Inventory (CSI).* San Diego: Naval Health Research Center.1

McCubbin, Hamilton I., Edna J. Hunter, and Barbara B. Dahl. 1975. "Residuals of War: Families of Prisoners of War and Servicemen Missing in Action." *Journal of Social Issues* 31(Fall): 95-109.

McCubbin, Hamilton I. and Joan Patterson. 1982. "Family Adaptation to Crisis." Pp. 26-47 in *Family Stress, Coping, and Social Support,* edited by Hamilton McCubbin, A. Elizabeth Cauble, and Joan Patterson. Springfield, IL: Charles C Thomas.

———. 1983. "The Family Stress Process: The Double ABCX Model of Adjustment and Adaptation." Pp. 7-37 in *Social Stress and the Family,* edited by Hamilton I. McCubbin, Marvin Sussman, and Joan Patterson. New York: Haworth.

Monat, Alan and Richard S. Lazarus, eds. 1977. *Stress and Coping.* New York: Columbia University Press.

Olson, David H. and Hamilton I. McCubbin. 1983. *Families: What Makes Them Work.* Beverly Hills, CA: Sage.

Pierce, Chester. 1975. "The Mundane Extreme Environment and Its Effects on Learning." Pp. 111-19 in *Learning Disabilities: Issues and Recommendations for Research,* edited by Suzanne C. Brainerd. Washington, DC: National Institute of Education.

Selye, Hans. 1974. *The Stress of Life.* Rev. ed. New York: McGraw-Hill.

———. 1976. "Stress." *The Rotarian,* October, 12-18.

———. 1980. "The Stress Concept Theory." Pp. 127-43 in *Handbook of Stress and Anxiety,* edited by Irwin L. Kutash and Louis B. Schlesinger. San Francisco: Jossey-Bass.

———. 1982. "History and Past Status of the Stress Concept." Pp. 7-17 in *Handbook of Stress,* edited by Leo Goldenberger and Sholomo Breznitz. New York: Free Press.

Straus, Murray A., Richard J. Gelles, and Suzanne K. Steinmetz. 1980. *Behind Closed Doors: Violence in the American Family..* New York: Anchor/Doubleday.

CHAPTER **15**

■■ Family Violence and Abuse

P eople are more likely to be killed, physically assaulted, sexually victim- ized, hit, beat up, slapped, or spanked in their own homes by other family members than anywhere else, or by anyone else, in our society. Family life is thought to be warm, intimate, and stress reducing. It is the place that people *flee to* for safety. Our desire to idealize family life is partly responsible for the tendency to either not see family violence or to condone it as being a necessary and important part of raising children, relating to spouses, and conducting other family transactions.

Although the issues of child abuse, sexual abuse, wife abuse, and the abuse of the elderly appear to be new phenomena, violence has been a part of American family life throughout its history. Not only are American families violent, but there is family violence in England, Western Europe, and many other countries and societies around the globe.

This chapter provides an overview of violence and sexual abuse in the family. We begin by reviewing the historical roots of family violence. The next section discusses the extent of the various forms of family violence. We then examine the factors associated with family violence and theories that have been developed to explain violence and abuse of family members. The final section examines current interventions and policies designed to treat and prevent violence in the home.

FAMILY VIOLENCE IN HISTORICAL AND CROSS-CULTURAL PERSPECTIVE

Violence and abuse of women and children date back to biblical times and extend across a wide range of cultures and societies. Anthropologist David Levinson (1981) examined data on 46 well-described, small-scale, and folk societies that represented all the major cultural regions of the world for which there were data on violence toward wives. He found that wife beating was common or frequent in more than 40% of the societies (see Table 15-1). When Levinson examined the data on physical punishment of children (there were no data on abuse) he found that punishment was common or frequent in 25% of the societies.

The Historical Legacy of Violence

The history of Western society is one in which women and children have been subjected to unspeakable cruelties. Historian Samuel Radbill (1980) reports that in ancient times infants had no rights until the right to live was bestowed upon them by their father, usually as part of a cultural ritual. If the right to live was withheld, infants were abandoned or left to die. Although we do not know how often children were killed or abandoned, we do know that infanticide was widely accepted among ancient and prehistoric cultures. Infants could be put to death because they cried too much, because they were sickly or deformed, or because they had some perceived imperfection (of course, this still occurs today). Girls, twins, and the children of unmarried women, for example, were the special targets of infanticide (Robin 1982). Infanticide continued worldwide throughout the 18th and 19th centuries. Illegitimate children continue to run the greatest risk of infanticide, even today.

Not only were children killed, but from prehistorical times right through colonial America, children were mutilated, beaten, and maltreated. Such treatment was not only condoned but was often mandated as the most appropriate child-rearing method. Children were hit with rods, canes, and switches. Some boys were castrated to produce eunuchs for harems in the Orient and, in the West, to preserve effeminate bodies and retain boys' good singing voices (Radbill 1980). Our forefathers in colonial America were implored to "beat the devil" out of their children (Greven 1991).

Table 15-1 Relationship Between Physical Punishment and Wife Beating

Wife Beating	Physical Punishment			
	Rare	Infrequent	Frequent	Common
Rare	Andamans Copper Eskimo Ifugao Iroquois Ona Thai	Rural Irish Hopi Trobrianders		
Infrequent	Kanuri Lapps Lau Mataco Tucano	Klamath Masai Ojibwa Pygmies Santal Taiwanese Tikopia Tzeltal	Ashanti Cagaba Garo Pawanee Wolof	
Frequent	Bororo Iban Tarahumara	Kapauku Koreans Kurds Toradja	Azande Dogon Somali	Amhara
Common	Chuckchee Tlingit Yanoama	Aymara Hausa	Ganda Truk	Serbs

SOURCE: "Physical Punishment of Children and Wifebeating in Cross-Cultural Perspective" by David Levinson, 1981, *Child Abuse and Neglect* 5(4). Copyright © 1981 by Elsevier Science Ltd. Adapted by permission.

The subordinate status of women in America and in most of the world's societies is well documented. Because physical force and violence are considered the ultimate means of keeping subordinate groups in their place, the history of women in European and American societies is one in which women have been victims of physical assault.

In ancient Rome, a husband could chastise, divorce, or kill his wife on grounds of adultery, public drunkenness, or attending public games—the very same behaviors that Roman men engaged in daily (Dobash and Dobash 1979)!

Blackstone's codification of English common law in 1768 asserted that husbands had the right to "physically chastise" an errant wife, provided that the stick was no thicker than his thumb—thus the "rule of thumb" was born. The legacy of British common law carried over into the United States well into the 19th century. Wife abuse, however, was effectively illegal in the United States by 1870 (Gordon 1988; Pleck 1987).

THE DISCOVERY OF FAMILY VIOLENCE

The treatment of children throughout history is not entirely bleak. Children's rights were recognized, but slowly. Six thousand years ago, children in Mesopotamia were protected by a patron goddess. The Greeks and Romans established orphan homes, and some historical accounts also mention the existence of foster care for children. Child protection laws were legislated as long ago as 450 B.C. (Radbill 1980). The Renaissance, a 300-year period spanning 1300–1600, was the beginning of a new morality regarding children. Children were seen as a dependent class in need of the protection of society (Robin 1982). The Enlightenment of the 18th century brought children increased attention and services. For example, the London Foundling Hospital founded during that time not only provided pediatric care but was also the center of the moral reform movement on behalf of children (Robin 1982).

The case of Mary Ellen Wilson, an illegitimate child born in 1866 in New York City, led to increased public concern about child maltreatment and the founding of the Society for the Prevention of Cruelty to Children (see Box 15-1). Interest in the issue of abused children decreased, however, after the turn of the century. Technology paved the way for a rediscovery of child abuse, but full recognition of the extent and scope of the problem was slow. In 1946, radiologist John Caffey reported on a number of cases of children who had multiple long bone fractures and subdural hematomas (Caffey 1946). Nearly 10 years later, Paul V. Woolley, Jr. and William A. Evans, Jr. (1955) speculated that the injuries might be inflicted by the children's parents. But child abuse was still thought to be a rare and an unusual event and not as relevant for physicians as a com- municable disease such as polio or small pox.

By 1962, physician C. Henry Kempe and his colleagues at the University of Colorado Medical Center were quite certain that many of the injuries they were seeing and the healed fractures that appeared on X rays were intentionally inflicted by parents. Their article, "The Battered Child Syndrome" (Kempe et al. 1962), which details their findings, became the benchmark of the modern public and professional discovery of child abuse.

Protecting Children

There was no Mary Ellen for battered women. No technological breakthroughs such as pediatric radiology to uncover years of broken jaws and broken bones. No medical champion would capture public and professional attention in the way that Henry Kempe had for battered children. Although

Battered Women

various efforts were made to define violence against women as a social problem throughout history (Pleck 1987), modern concern about wife abuse as a social problem became one issue of the feminist movement. A women's center in the Chiswick section of London, founded by Erin Pizzey in the early 1970s, became a refuge for victims of battering. Women's groups began to organize safe houses or battered wife shelters in the United States as early as 1972. In 1975, the National Organization for Women created a task force to examine wife battering.

Other Forms of Family Violence

The discovery of other forms of family violence followed, in part, from the public recognition of physical child abuse and wife abuse. Elder abuse was recognized as a problem in the late 1970s, partly as a result of increased attention to child abuse and wife abuse and partly as a result of the efforts of those concerned with the overall health and well-being of the elderly population. Child sexual abuse received increased attention in the 1970s and 1980s.

BOX 15-1: THE FAMILY OVER TIME

The Discovery of Child Abuse: The Case of Mary Ellen

In the United States, the case of Mary Ellen Wilson is almost always singled out as the turning point in concern for children's welfare. Mary Ellen Wilson was an illegitimate child born in 1866 in New York City. She was in the care of foster parents when she was discovered beaten and neglected. Etta Wheeler, the charity worker who discovered Mary Ellen, turned to the police and the New York City Department of Charities for help for the girl but was turned down—first by the police, who said there was no proof of a crime, and then by the charity agency, who said they did not have custody of Mary Ellen. The story goes on to note that Henry Berge, founder of the Society for the Prevention of Cruelty to Animals, intervened on behalf of Mary Ellen, and the courts accepted the case because Mary Ellen was a member of the animal kingdom. In reality, the court reviewed the case because the child needed protection. The case was argued not by Henry Berge but by his colleague, Elbridge Gerry.

The story of Mary Ellen Wilson, told in books and articles about child abuse, ends with her removal from her abusive foster home. Her story, however, continues and symbolizes some of the positive aspects of child protection efforts. After Mary Ellen was removed from the abusive foster home, she was sent to live with Etta Wheeler's mother in Rochester, New York and was later raised by Wheeler's youngest sister. Mary Ellen married at age 24 and had two daughters, one named after Etta Wheeler. Both daughters attended college and became teachers. A school in Rochester is named after Mary Ellen's second daughter, Florence Brasser. Mary Ellen died at the age of 92 in 1956 (Lazoritz 1990).

THE EXTENT OF FAMILY VIOLENCE

Until the early 1960s, violence between family members was considered rare and committed only by mentally ill or otherwise disturbed individuals. Only the most sensational and lurid cases received public attention, and there was a general belief that even though family violence was a significant problem, it was not widespread.

Various methods have been used in attempts to achieve an accurate estimate of child abuse in the United States. In 1967, David Gil (1970) conducted a nationwide inventory of reported cases of child abuse (before, however, all 50 states had enacted mandatory reporting laws). He found 6,000 confirmed cases of child abuse. Gil also used a self-report survey to estimate that between 2.53 and 4.07 million children were abused each year.

Child Maltreatment

The National Center on Child Abuse and Neglect (NCCAN) has conducted two surveys designed to measure the national incidence of reported and recognized child maltreatment (Burgdorf 1980; NCCAN 1988). Both surveys assessed how many cases were known to investigatory agencies, school professionals, hospitals, and other social service agencies. The 1988 study found that 1,025,900 maltreated children were known by the agencies surveyed (Table 15-2).

A second source of data on the extent of child abuse is the National Study of Child Neglect and Abuse reporting conducted each year by the American Association for Protecting Children (AAPC), a division of the American Humane Association. This annual study measured the number of families, alleged perpetrators, and children involved in official reports of child maltreatment (AAPC 1989). During 1987, the last year the survey was conducted, 2,178,384 children were reported to state agencies for suspected child abuse and neglect. Of these, it is estimated that 686,000 reports were substantiated, or considered valid reports, by state child protective service agencies.

There are problems with the AAPC studies of reported child maltreatment. First, definitions of maltreatment—including physical abuse—and reporting practices vary from state to state, from profession to profession, and from agency to agency. Second, individual, agency, and state participation in the surveys is variable. Some states provide complete data to the AAPC; other states do not even participate. The study of cases known to professionals also has problems, with some agencies fully cooperating but others failing to take part or providing only the most meager help.

Table 15-2 Number and Rate of Recognized Cases of Child Maltreatment: Estimated Number of Recognized Children (per 1,000 per year)[a]

Form of Maltreatment and Severity of Injury/Impairment	Number of Affected Children	Incidence Rate
Forms of maltreatment		
Total of all maltreated children	1,025,900	16.3
Total of all abused children[b]	580,400	9.2
Physical abuse	311,200	4.9
Sexual abuse	138,000	2.2
Emotional abuse	174,400	2.8
Total of all neglected children[b]	498,000	7.9
Physical neglect	182,100	2.9
Emotional neglect	52,200	0.8
Educational neglect	291,100	4.6
Severity of child's injury/impairment		
Fatal	1,100	0.02
Serious	157,100	2.5
Moderate	740,000	11.7
Probable	127,800	2.0

SOURCE: National Center on Child Abuse and Neglect (1988, Tables 3-2, 3-3, 3-4).
a. National incidence estimates by major form of maltreatment and by severity of maltreatment-related injury or impairments.
b. Totals may be lower than sum of categories because a child may have experienced more than one category of maltreatment.

A source of data not based only on official reports or official awareness are the National Family Violence Surveys carried out in 1976 and again in 1985 by Murray Straus and Richard Gelles (Gelles and Straus 1987, 1988; Straus and Gelles 1986; Straus, Gelles, and Steinmetz 1980). The National Family Violence Surveys interviewed two nationally representative samples of families—2,146 family members in 1976 and 6,002 family members in 1985. One part of the study focused on the homes in which children under 18 years of age lived. In each of the families studied, parents were asked to report on their own use of violence toward their children.

Milder forms of violence, violence that most people think of as physical punishment, as represented by the first three items in Table 15-3, were, of course, the most common. However, even with the severe forms of violence, the rates were surprisingly high. Abusive violence was defined as acts that had a high probability of injuring the child. These included kicking, biting, punching, hitting or trying to hit a child with an object, beating up a child, burning or scalding, and threatening to use or using a gun or a knife. Slightly

Table 15-3
Frequency of
Parental Violence
Toward Children
Under Age 18

Violent Behavior	Percentage of Occurrences in Past Year				Percentage of Occurrences Ever Reported
	Once	Twice	More Than Twice	Total	
Threw something at child	1.5	.7	.9	3.1	4.5
Pushed, grabbed, or shoved child	5.8	7.5	14.9	28.2	33.6
Slapped or spanked child	8.1	8.5	39.1	55.7	74.6
Kicked, bit, or hit with fist	.7	.5	.3	1.5	2.1
Hit or tried to hit child with something	2.4	2.0	5.3	9.7	14.4
Beat up child	.3	.1	.2	.6	1.0
Burned or scalded child	.2	.1	.1	.4	.6
Threatened child with knife or gun	.1	.1	0	.2	.3
Used a knife or gun	.1	.1	0	.2	.2

SOURCE: *Intimate Violence* by Richard J. Gelles and Murray A. Straus, 1988, New York: Simon & Schuster. Copyright © 1988 by Richard J. Gelles and Murray A. Straus. Used by permission.
NOTE: Percentages reflect responses to Second National Family Violence Survey.

more than 2 parents in 100 (2.3%) engaged in one act of abusive violence during the year prior to the survey. Seven children in 1,000 were hurt as the result of an act of violence directed at them by a parent in the previous year.

Projecting the rate of abusive violence to all children under the age of 18 who live in the home means that 1.5 million children experience acts of abusive physical violence each year. Likewise, projecting the rate of injury means that about 450,000 children are injured each year as a result of parental violence.

Acts of violence not only affect a large number of children but, on average, happen more than once a year. Straus and Gelles found that even the extreme forms of parental violence occur periodically and even regularly in some families. The median number of occurrences of acts of abusive violence was 4.5 times per year.

Straus and Gelles's surveys of violence toward children confirmed previous findings that violence does not end when the children grow up. More than 80% of 3 to 9 year olds were hit at least once a year (Wauchope and Straus 1990), as were two thirds of the preteens and young teenagers and more than one third of 15 to 17 year olds.

One of the important limitations of the surveys conducted by Straus and his associates is that they measured only self-reports of violence toward children. Thus the results indicate the rates of violence admitted to by parents, not the true level of violence toward children. In addition, the actual measure of violence and abuse was confined to a small number of violent acts. Sexual abuse and other forms of maltreatment were not measured in the study.

Sexual Abuse of Children

Among the most dramatic changes taking place over the past few decades has been the increased attention to child sexual abuse. Sexual abuse of younger persons by older persons involves a wide range of behaviors. Sexual abuse is defined as forced, tricked, or coerced sexual behavior between a young person and an older person. Many current definitions of sexual abuse include the element of an age difference of at least five years between victim and offender. Elements of force, manipulation, or coercion are also characteristics of sexual abuse. Sociologist David Finkelhor (1979, 1984) adds that children are assumed to be incapable of consenting to sex with an adult because they lack the power to decline involvement and often have not reached a stage of cognitive development so that they know to what they are consenting. The abusive sexual behaviors most often reported in the literature are direct contact by one body to another, as in fondling; penetration of the child's body by nonsexual objects or the offender's sexual organ; and noncontact behaviors, such as voyeurism or pornography.

In a comprehensive review of studies on the incidence and prevalence of child sexual abuse, Stephanie Peters, Gail Wyatt, and David Finkelhor (1986) report that estimates of the prevalence range from 6% to 62% for females and from 3% to 31% for males. They point out that this variation may be accounted for by a number of methodological factors, such as differences in definitions of abuse, sample characteristics, interview format (e.g., in-person vs. phone interview) and number of questions used to elicit information about abuse experiences.

Child Homicide

Homicide is one of the five leading causes of death for children between 1 and 18 years of age. More than 1,300 children are killed by their parents or caretakers each year (Daro 1992). Even with an estimate this high, researchers believe that homicide of infants is probably underreported in health statistics (Jason, Carpenter, and Tyler 1983). Homicides may be misrecorded as accidents either because the medical examiner is unable to verify the exact cause of death or because the medical examiner wants to protect the family as a result of their status and position in the community.

Infants (from 1 week to 1 year of age) are most likely to be killed by a parent. Parents and caretakers (including stepparents) are the most likely perpetrators of child homicide of children under 5 years of age. The cause of death is usually a beating, burns, or neglect, and the circumstances of the death are either discipline or neglect of the victim (Christoffel 1990).

Courtship violence is a newly recognized and quite extensive form of intimate violence and abuse.

Dating and Courtship Violence

The virtues of romantic love, a phenomenon considered synonymous with American dating patterns, have been extolled in poems, songs, romance novels, television soap operas, and folklore. Sadly, violence is very much a part of American dating patterns along with the moonlight cruises, the first kiss, and the flirtations and affection. Studies that examine the possibility of violence in dating and courtship find that between 10% and 67% of dating relationships involve violence (Sugarman and Hotaling 1989). Researchers have found that the rate of severe violence among dating couples ranged from about 1% each year to 27% (Arias, Samios, and O'Leary 1987; Lane and Gwartney-Gibbs 1985; Makepeace 1983). This violence also occurs among couples of high school age; 12% reported experiencing a form of dating violence (Henton et al. 1983). Perhaps the most disturbing finding from the research on dating violence is how the individuals perceive the violence. In a study conducted by sociologist June Henton and her colleagues (1983), more than one fourth of the victims and 3 of 10 offenders interpreted the violence as a sign of love.

The biggest surprise from the research on dating violence is that, rather than the violent episodes shattering the romantic images held by the participants, one gets the impression that violence serves to protect the romantic illusions of dating. Victims of dating violence were likely to take the blame for helping to start the violence and were reluctant to blame their partners for the abuse. In addition, victims of courtship violence were reluctant to tell others about their experiences. If they did talk about the violence, it was with peers and not parents or teachers.

It is quite clear from the studies of courtship violence that many of the patterns we find in martial violence emerge long before a person gets married. One study that interviewed battered women who had sought shelter found that 51% said that they had been physically abused in a dating relationship (Roscoe and Bernaske 1985).

Spouse Abuse

The National Family Violence Surveys examined violence between husbands and wives by interviewing a national sample of families (Gelles and Straus 1988; Straus and Gelles 1986). The surveys found the following:

- In 16% of the homes surveyed in 1985, some kind of violence between spouses had occurred in the year prior to the survey. More than one in four couples (28%) reported marital violence at some point in the marriage.

As with violence toward children, the milder forms of violence were the most common (see Table 15-4):

- In terms of those acts of violence that would be considered wife beating (that is, had the high potential of causing an injury), 3.4% of American women, or 1 in 22, was a victim of abusive violence during the 12-month period prior to the interview.

Wife beating is a pattern, not a single event, in most violent households. On average, a woman who is a victim of wife abuse is abused three times each year.

Spousal Homicide

Homicide is the one aspect of spousal violence on which official data are available. Researchers generally report that intrafamilial homicides account for between 20% and 40% of all murders (Curtis 1974). Each year, about 700 husbands and boyfriends are killed by their wives and girlfriends, and more than 1,400 wives and girlfriends are slain by their husbands and boyfriends (U.S. Department of Justice 1993).

Table 15-4
Frequency of Marital Violence: Comparison of Husband and Wife Violence Rates (in percentages)

	Frequency					
	Incidence Rate		*Mean*		*Median*	
Violent Behavior	*Husband*	*Wife*	*Husband*	*Wife*	*Husband*	*Wife*
1. Threw something at spouse	2.9	4.6	3.7	2.7	1.5	1.0
2. Pushed, grabbed, or shoved spouse	9.6	9.1	2.9	3.1	2.0	2.0
3. Slapped spouse	3.1	4.4	2.8	2.7	1.0	1.0
4. Kicked, bit, or hit with fist	1.5	2.5	3.9	2.9	1.5	1.0
5. Hit or tried to hit spouse with something	1.9	3.1	3.6	3.3	1.2	1.1
6. Beat up spouse	.8	.5	4.2	5.7	2.0	2.0
7. Choked spouse	.7	.4	1.9	2.9	1.0	1.0
8. Threatened spouse with knife or gun	.4	.6	4.3	2.0	1.8	1.1
9. Used a knife or gun	.2	.2	18.6	12.9	1.5	4.0
Overall violence (1–9)	21.3	12.4	5.4	6.1	1.5	2.5
Wife beating/husband beating (4–9)	3.4	4.8	5.2	5.4	1.5	1.5

SOURCE: *Intimate Violence* by Richard J. Gelles and Murray A. Straus, 1988, New York: Simon & Schuster. Copyright © 1988 by Simon & Schuster, Inc. Used by permission.
NOTE: Percentages reflect responses to Second National Family Violence Survey.

Elder Abuse

Sociologists Karl Pillemer and David Finkelhor (1988) interviewed 2,020 elderly persons who were not living in homes for the aged, hospitals, or other institutions in the Boston metropolitan area. Overall, 32 elderly persons per 1,000 reported experiencing physical violence, verbal aggression, and/or neglect in the past year. The rate of physical violence was 20 per 1,000. Although the conventional view of elder abuse is that of middle-aged children abusing and neglecting the elderly parents, Pillemer and Finkelhor found that spouses were the most frequent abusers of the elderly and that roughly equal numbers of men and women were victims. Women, however, suffered from the most serious forms of abuse (see also Chapter 12).

Hidden Violence

Sibling Violence. Although parent-to-child and marital violence have received the most public attention, physical fights between brothers and sisters are by far the most common form of family violence. It is, however, rare that someone considers siblings fighting as violence. Violence between siblings often goes far beyond so-called normal violence. The First National Family Violence Survey found that 42% of children had either kicked, bit, or punched a brother or sister, 40% had hit a sibling with an object, and 16% had beat up a sibling. Projecting to all children who live with a brother or sister, at least 109,000 children use guns or knives in fights with siblings each year (Straus et al. 1980).

Parent Victims. Child-to-parent violence is rarely mentioned in public discussions of family violence. Here the reason is less public acceptance for this type of violence and more the shame of the parent-victims who are reluctant to seek help or call attention to their plight for fear of being blamed for the violence. According to the First National Family Violence Survey, each year between 750,000 and 1 million parents have violent acts committed against them by their teenaged children (Cornell and Gelles 1982). Most violence toward parents is perpetrated by teenage males and the victims are most often their mothers.

BOX 15-2: WHAT THE RESEARCH SHOWS

Is Family Violence Increasing?

Since the early 1960s the widespread belief has been that the rates of family violence are increasing. Data collected by the American Association for Protecting Children (1989) support this belief. For all forms of maltreatment, there has been a 225% increase in reporting between 1976 and 1987.

The National Center on Child Abuse and Neglect reports that countable cases of child maltreatment increased by 51% between 1980 and 1986 (NCCAN 1988). There were significant increases in the incidence of physical and sexual abuse, with physical abuse increasing by 58% and sexual abuse more than tripling between 1980 and 1986.

On the other hand, Straus and Gelles (1986) found that parent self-reports of very severe violence toward children had *declined* 47% between 1976 and 1985. Noting the contradictory findings, the National Center on Child Abuse and Neglect (1988) stated that the decline in the rate of violence toward children

reported by Straus and Gelles could be a function of parents becoming less candid because of the difficulty of admitting to abusive behavior. Straus and Gelles (1986) recognized that changing attitudes about child abuse could be a plausible explanation for their findings. They also note, however, that the declining rate of child abuse is consistent with the changing character and structure of the American family, the improved economy between 1976 and 1985, increased publicity about child abuse, and the rapid expansion of treatment and prevention programs for child abuse. The change was also partly the result of the fact that the average age of the population increased between 1976 and 1985 and violent family members are more likely to be young (Egley 1991).

There are no national official report data on marital violence that can be used to examine changing rates. Straus and Gelles (1986) report that the self-reports of the rate of wife abuse declined 21.8% between 1976 and 1985.

VIOLENT AND ABUSIVE FAMILIES

Much of the early thinking and writing on family violence was dominated by a psychopathological model. Child abuse researchers discounted social factors as playing any causal role in violence toward children (Steele and Pollock 1968). Rather, the explanation was thought to lie in personality or character disorders (Galdston 1965). Wife abuse was also seen as a product of the mental illness of the husband, and even the wife's mental status was considered a possible cause of the abuse.

There are a number of problems with the psychopathological or mental illness model of family violence and abuse. First, most of the conclusions about the causes of family violence are based on post hoc studies of a limited number of cases (Spinetta and Rigler 1972). A second problem is the confusing of cause with consequence. We are told that people who abuse their children or spouses are mentally ill. How do we know they are mentally ill? Because they have committed such an outrageous act of violence or abuse. A third problem is that the psychopathological model ignores the fact that certain social factors are related to family violence. The remainder of this section examines those social factors.

Gender Differences in Violence

Outside the American family, violent men clearly outnumber violent women. In the home, women are frequently as, or even more, violent than men. Not surprising, research on child abuse often finds that mothers are slightly more likely than fathers to abuse children (Gil 1970; Parke and Collmer 1975; Straus et al. 1980; Wolfner and Gelles 1993). Of course, one obvious explanation for this is that mothers spend more time with their children than do fathers, so they have more opportunity to be violent and abusive. Moreover, irrespective of the amount of time fathers spend with children, mothers tend to be the ones who have the greatest responsibility for child rearing. Leslie Margolin (1992) found that when one controls for the amount of responsibility males and females have for child care, males were more likely to be abusive.

There is considerable debate about the comparative rates of violence against husbands and wives. While some investigators report that the rate of wife-to-husband violence is about the same as the rate of husband-to-wife violence (Straus and Gelles 1986), others explain that women are the disproportionate victims of family violence (Dobash and Dobash 1979; Dobash et al. 1992). If one goes by how much harm is done, who initiates the violence, and how easy it is for a victim to escape violence, women clearly are the disproportionate victims of domestic violence.

Boys are the more violent siblings and offspring. Mothers and sisters are the more frequent targets of the young or adolescent boys' family violence.

Social Characteristics and Family Violence	There are two persistent myths concerning the relationship between social class and family violence. The first is that violence is *confined* to lower-class families. Because the poor are more likely to go to emergency rooms or clinics, they are more likely to come to the attention of the authorities if their children are bruised or battered. Similarly, clinics or emergency rooms are the most likely source of medical aid for lower-class battered women.

The second myth, virtually the opposite of the first, is that family violence cuts evenly across the society. There is, of course, a grain of truth in this: Family violence does occur in virtually every social category. But the distribution is far from equal. Rates of family violence are highest in urban families, low-income families, and homes where the husband is unemployed; among members of racial minorities; people with no religious affiliation; and people with some high school education, blue-collar workers, and those under the age of 30.

Stress and Family Violence	The finding that homes where husbands are unemployed are the most likely to be violent suggests that stress is related to domestic assault. Figure 15-1 shows that as the number of stressful events experienced in a home increases, so does the likelihood of parent-to-child and husband-to-wife violence. Specific stressful situations also increase the chances that violence will erupt in the home. Financial problems, pregnancy, being a single parent, being a teenaged mother, and sexual difficulties all are risk factors (Gelles 1989; Gelles and Straus 1988; Parke and Collmer 1975; Straus et al. 1980; see Chapter 14 for a discussion of stressors and family stress).

Social Isolation	People who are socially isolated from neighbors and relatives are more likely to be violent toward spouses and children. One major source of stress reduction and an insulator to family violence is being able to call on friends and family for help, aid, and assistance. The more a family is integrated into the community, the more groups and associations they belong to, the less likely they are to be violent (Milner and Chilamkurti 1991; Straus et al. 1980).

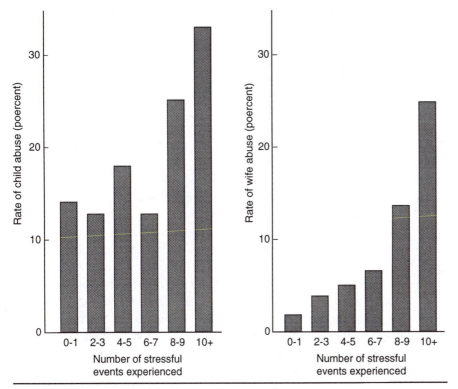

Figure 15-1 Rates of Child Abuse and Wife Abuse by Family Stress

SOURCE: *Behind Closed Doors: Violence in the American Family* (pp. 183, 185) by Murray A. Straus, Richard J. Gelles, and Suzanne K. Steinmetz, 1980, New York: Anchor/Doubleday. Copyright © 1980 by Murray A. Straus and Richard J. Gelles.

The Cycle of Violence

The notion that abused children grow up to be abusing parents and violent adults has been widely expressed in the child abuse and family violence literature (Gelles 1980). Joan Kaufman and Edward Zigler (1987) reviewed the literature that tested the hypothesis of the intergenerational transmission of violence and concluded that the best estimate of the rate of intergenerational transmission is 30% (plus or minus 5%). Although a rate of 30% intergenerational transmission is quite a bit less than the majority of abused children, the rate is considerably more than the 2% to 4% rate of abuse found in the general population (Straus and Gelles 1986).

Evidence from studies of parental and marital violence indicate that, while experiencing violence in one's family of origin is often correlated with later violent behavior, such experience is not the sole determining factor. When the cycle of violence occurs, it is likely the result of a complex set of social and psychological processes. The continuation of a pattern of violence is most likely among those individuals who do not receive emotional support from an adult during childhood, who have not participated in therapy during any period in their lives, and who live in abusive, unstable, and emotionally unsupportive and unsatisfying relationships (Egeland, Jacobvitz, and Sroufe 1988).

Factors Associated With Sexual Abuse of Children

There has been a great deal of research on the characteristics of sexual abusers of children, but current research has failed to isolate characteristics, especially demographic, social, or psychological characteristics, that discriminate between sexual abusers and nonabusers (Quinsey 1984).

One of the key questions raised in discussions about sexual abuse is whether all children are at risk for sexual abuse or whether some children, because of some specific characteristic (e.g., age or poverty status), are at greater risk than others. In their review of studies on prevention, David Finkelhor and Larry Baron (1986) conclude that it is currently not clear what factors increase children's risk for sexual abuse. It appears that girls are at greater risk, although boys are also victimized. Girls are more likely to be victimized if they have sometimes been separated from their mothers (e.g., ever lived away from mother, mother ill or disabled) or if they report poor relationships with their mothers. As the researchers note, these factors may be consequences of sexual abuse as much as risk factors.

EXPLAINING FAMILY VIOLENCE

A number of sociological and psychological theories have been used to explain the various forms of family violence. The following are the major theoretical explanations.

Social Learning

The family has been referred to as a "training ground for violence" (Steinmetz and Straus 1973). The family is the institution and social group where people learn the roles of husband and wife, father and mother. The home is also the prime location where people learn how to deal with various stresses, crises, and frustrations. In many instances, the home is also the site where a person first experiences violence. Learning to hit people you love is part of the growing-up experience in many homes. Not only do people learn violent

Learning theorists argue that children learn to use violence and aggression—playing with guns is only one form of this learning process.

behavior, but they learn how to justify being violent. It is not uncommon to hear parents who have just physically punished their children explain that they were punishing the child for the child's own good. Husbands who assault their wives may also use the same justification.

The learning theory explanation accounts for the intergenerational transmission of family violence, but it does not explain why violence is used in some situations and not others and by some of those who were exposed to violence and not others. A social-situational explanation of family violence proposes that abuse and violence arise out of two main factors. The first is stress. The

A Social-Situational Explanation

association between low income and family violence indicates that an important factor in violence is inadequate financial resources. Stressful events, such as unemployment, underemployment, illness, and sexual difficulties are another source of stress. The second factor is the cultural norm concerning the use of force and violence. In contemporary American society, as well as many other Western industrialized societies, violence in general, and violence toward children in particular, is normative (Straus et al. 1980).

When a society approves of violence and when certain groups encounter the stresses of low income, poor jobs, or even unemployment and high levels of other types of stressors (see Chapter 14), these families will be the most likely to resort to violence to deal with stress, frustration, and marital conflict.

Resource Theory

Another explanation of family violence that is supported by the available scientific data is resource theory (Goode 1971). This model assumes that all social systems (including the family) are based to some degree on force or the threat of force. The more resources—social, personal, and economic—a person can command, the more force he or she can muster. However, according to William Goode, the author of this theory, the more resources a person actually has, the less he or she will actually use force in an open manner. Thus a husband who wants to be the dominant person in the family but has little education, has a job low in prestige and income, and lacks interpersonal skills may choose to use violence to maintain the dominant position. In addition, family members (including children) may use violence to redress a grievance when they have few alternative resources available.

An Ecological Perspective

Psychologist James Garbarino (1977) has proposed an ecological model to explain the complex nature of child maltreatment. Garbarino applies what he refers to as the ecological, or human development, approach.

Briefly, the ecological model proposes that violence and abuse arise out of a mismatch of parent to child and family to neighborhood and community. The risk of abuse and violence is greatest when the functioning of the children and parents is limited and constrained by developmental problems. Children with learning disabilities and social or emotional handicaps are at increased risk for abuse. Parents under considerable stress or who have personality problems are at increased risk for abusing their children. These conditions are worsened when social interaction between the spouses or the parents and children heighten the stress or make the personal problems worse. Finally, if there are few institutions and agencies in the community to support troubled families, then the risk of abuse is further raised.

Social exchange theory (Gelles 1983) proposes that behavior is governed by the principle of costs and rewards. Violence is used when the rewards are higher than the costs. The private nature of the family, the reluctance of social institutions and agencies to intervene—in spite of mandatory child abuse reporting laws—and the low risk of other interventions reduce the costs of abuse and violence. The cultural approval of violence as both expressive and, in the case of disciplining children, instrumental behavior raises the potential rewards for violence.

Exchange/Social Control Theory

The previous models have been different only in degree. They tend to examine individuals and family relations in their search for the explanation for family violence. Sociologists Russell and Rebecca Dobash (1979) see wife abuse as a unique phenomenon that has been obscured and overshadowed by what they refer to as the "narrow" focus on domestic violence. The Dobashes' central thesis is that economic and social processes operate directly and indirectly to support a patriarchal (male-dominated) social order and family structure. Their central theoretical argument is that patriarchy leads to the subordination of women and causes the historical pattern of systematic violence directed against wives.

Patriarchy and Wife Abuse

David Finkelhor (1984) has reviewed research on the factors that have been proposed as contributing to sexual abuse of children and has developed what he calls the Four-Precondition Model of Sexual Abuse (see Figure 15-2). His review suggests that all the factors relating to sexual abuse can be grouped into one of four preconditions that need to be met before sexual abuse can occur:

A Model of Sexual Abuse

1. A potential offender needs to have some motivation to abuse a child sexually.
2. The potential offender has to overcome internal inhibitions against acting on that motivation.
3. The potential offender has to overcome external impediments to committing sexual abuse.
4. The potential offender or some other factor has to undermine or overcome a child's possible resistance to sexual abuse.

Figure 15-2 Four
Preconditions:
A Model of
Sexual Abuse

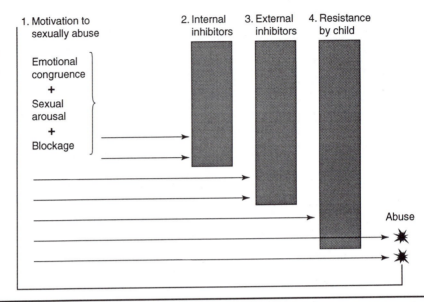

SOURCE: Adapted with permission of The Free Press, Macmillan Publishing, from *Child Sexual Abuse:
New Theories and Research* (p. 55) by David Finkelhor, 1984. Copyright © 1984 by David Finkelhor.

BOX 15-3: THE GLOBAL VIEW

Wife Abuse Among the Papua of New Guinea

Wife abuse is certainly not unique to modern societies, nor is it confined to Western societies. Some scholars assume that when wife abuse occurs in developing nations, it is the result of social disorganization caused by modernization. This notion assumes that the social, economic, and political complexity of modern societies are underlying causes of wife abuse. Thus, when wife abuse occurs in developing nations, it is because of the rapid social changes caused by modernization that break down traditional structures.

Rebecca Morley (1994) tested these assumptions in her study of wife beating among the Papua. Papua New Guinea is a Melanesian island of approximately 3.5 million people from an estimated 700 to 800 different language groups and associated cultures. Papua New Guinea gained its independence from Australia in 1975.

Morley's study refutes the claim that wife beating increases as a result of modernization, at least in the case of Papua New Guinea. Her findings support a patriarchical explanation for wife abuse. Morley found that men's right to control their wives through violence and beatings had a long history on Papua New Guinea. Men abused their wives before the islanders has contact with Westerners or began a process of modernization.

Modernization has had a contradictory impact on wife abuse among the Papua. In the urban areas, modernization has brought about a new sensitivity among women about their right not be abused. At the same time, however, traditional cultural constraints that controlled men's violence have eroded as a result of modernization, increasing the vulnerability of women. Increased independence among urban women has increased men's suspicions about sexual fidelity and increased their attempts to control their wives by physical force.

THE CONSEQUENCES OF FAMILY VIOLENCE

Physical harm is but one consequence of violence in the home. There are emotional consequences as well.

Impact on the Victims

Children

A number of people believe that untreated abused children frequently grow up to be delinquents, murderers, and batterers of the next generation of children (Schmitt and Kempe 1975). Criminologist Cathy Spatz Widom (1989) identified a large sample of validated cases of child abuse and neglect from approximately 20 years ago, established a control group of nonabused children, and assessed official arrest records to establish occurrences of delinquency, criminal behavior, and violent criminal behavior. She reports that abused and neglected children have a higher likelihood of arrest for delinquency, adult criminality, and violent criminal behavior than the matched controls.

Abused children have been frequently described as having a number of cognitive, emotional, and social difficulties (Starr 1988). Studies find various social and emotional deficits, including communication problems, poor performance in school, and learning disabilities (Starr 1988). Adults who were abused as children are also thought to have higher rates of drug and alcohol abuse, criminal behavior, and psychiatric disturbances (Smith, Hansen, and Nobel 1973).

Women

For female victims of domestic assault, the consequences also extend beyond physical injury. Research using clinical as well as survey data consistently reports a high incidence of depression and anxiety among samples of battered women as well as an increased risk of suicide attempts (Christopoulos et al. 1987; Gelles and Harrop 1989; Hilberman 1980; Schechter 1983).

One of the most pervasive myths in the field of family violence is that battered wives like being hit, otherwise they would leave. Considerable research has been conducted that refutes the notion of the masochistic battered wife. In general, the studies find that many factors—economic, relational, cultural, and social—constrain women from leaving a battering relationship.

Psychologist Lenore Walker (1979) has examined numerous cases of battered women and applied Martin Seligman's (1975) theory of "learned helplessness" to explain why so many women endure extreme violence for so long. Walker notes that women who experience repeated physical assaults at the hands of their husbands have much lower self-esteem than women whose marriages are free from violence.

Learned helplessness implies a rather passive nature for battered women. Most battered women, however, are far from passive. They call the police, they go to social workers or mental health agencies, they flee to shelters or the homes of friends or parents, and they fight back. But, in many ways, women are constrained by social forces from permanently leaving a violent relationship. Legal writer Elizabeth Truninger (1971) lists seven factors that help explain why women do not break off relationships with abusive husbands: (1) They (the women) have negative self-esteem, (2) they believe their husbands will reform, (3) there is economic hardship, (4) they have children who need a father's economic support, (5) they doubt they can get along alone, (6) they believe divorcées are stigmatized, and (7) it is difficult for women with children to get work.

In a 1976 study by Richard J. Gelles, certain factors distinguish women who stay in the violent relationship from women who sought help or left a violent husband. First, those women who leave seem to experience the most severe and frequent violence. Second, women who experienced more violence as children were more likely to remain in violent relationships. Third, women with limited educational attainment and occupational skills were more likely to stay with battering husbands. The fewer resources a woman had and the less power she had, the more she was entrapped in a marriage and the more she suffered at the hands of her husband (Gelles 1976).

Sociologists Michael Strube and Linda Barbour (1983) talked with 98 battered wives and confirmed that economically dependent women were more likely to remain with an abusive husband. They also found that wives who stayed with violent men reported they were more "committed" to the marital relationship.

PREVENTION AND TREATMENT

While most people believe that abusive acts of violence toward women, children, and the elderly are wrong and that something should be done to prevent these acts, the prevention and treatment of violence in the home presents society with a dilemma. On one hand, the sacred nature of the family has traditionally protected it from outside intervention. "A man's home is his castle" is more than a homily, it represents the cultural view of the sanctity of the family and the belief that family relations are special and should not be controlled or governed by the state. The castle metaphor includes the idea of sturdy walls, a moat, and a drawbridge that imply freedom from outside interference. But the castle might, and sometimes does, contain a torture chamber where untold harm can be committed against family members. This is the other side of the dilemma: Although we may think a man's home is his castle, society also believes that it has a basic responsibility to protect people from physical harm. This responsibility is heightened in cases where people are dependent, namely children and the elderly. Following the spirit of one cultural tradition (for instance, protecting people from harm) means violating the other (protecting the sacred and private nature of the family).

Abuse and abusers create a problem for society. A man may punch his child or his wife. Many people may find this act repulsive and want to do something to protect the victims or punish the man. Yet the man may retort, "This is my wife or child, and I have the right to treat them any way I want!" How do we respond? Often the dilemma is confounded by disagreements over what is and is not abuse. One way that people deal with the dilemma is to view their own behavior as "normal" and others' acts as wrong. One reason why people nurture the myth that people who abuse family members are mentally ill is both to protect themselves from the possible label "abuser" and to make it justifiable to intervene in the family life of the supposed "sick" person who needs help.

Protecting Children

All 50 states had enacted mandatory reporting laws for child abuse and neglect by the late 1960s. These laws require certain professionals (or in some states, all adults) to report cases of suspected abuse or neglect. When the report comes in, state protective service workers typically investigate the report to determine if it is accurate and if the family is in need of help or assistance. Although a wide array of options is available to public social workers, they typically have two options: either removal of the child from the parents and placement in a foster home or institution or provide the family with social support, such as counseling, food stamps, day care services, a homemaker, and so on.

Neither solution is ideal, and there are risks in both. Removing a child from the home involves two risks. First, the child may not understand why he or she is being removed. Children have little basis of comparison and might not realize they are being treated differently from other children. To them, the removal might be just another instance of them doing something wrong and being punished. Children who are removed from abusive homes may well be protected from physical damage but still suffer emotional harm. The second problem is finding a suitable placement for an abused child. Given that abused children may suffer physical and emotional damage, they frequently require special care. They could well become a burden for any foster parent or institution that has to care for them. The risk of abuse might actually be greater in a foster home or institution than in the home of the natural parents.

Leaving children in an abusive home and providing social services involves another type of risk. The typical situation in human service and protective service agencies is that protective service workers are overworked, under-trained, and underpaid. Family services are also limited. There are horror stories in every state about children who were reported as abused, investigated by state agencies, supervised by state agencies, and killed during the period the family was supposedly being monitored by a social worker.

Given the dilemma between control and compassion (Rosenfeld and Newberger 1977) and the imperfect functioning of social service systems and foster care programs, social service and protective service agencies are left to consider each case and choose the least detrimental course of intervention that appears to be in the best interests of the child.

There are only a handful of evaluations of prevention and treatment programs for child maltreatment. Pediatrician David Olds and his colleagues (1986) evaluated the effectiveness of a family support program, which included regular home visits by nurses during pregnancy and the first two years after a child's birth for low-income, unmarried, teenaged first-time mothers. They found that in contrast with comparison groups whose rate of chid abuse and neglect was 19%, only 4% of mothers in the program were later reported for abuse to the state protection agency.

Deborah Daro and Ann Cohn (1988) reviewed a number of evaluations of child maltreatment programs. They found that there was no noticeable correlation between a given set of services and positive client outcomes. In fact, the more services a family received, the worse the family got. Lay counseling, group counseling, and parent education classes resulted in more positive treatment outcomes. The optimal treatment period appeared to be between 7 and 18 months. Those projects that were successful in reducing abuse accomplished this by separating children from abusive parents, either by placing them in foster homes or requiring the maltreating adult to move out of the house.

Interest in designing programs to help children escape or prevent sexual abuse began early in the 1980s. By the end of the decade, prevention programs had been developed for every conceivable audio-visual technology (e.g., film, video, audiotape, filmstrip) and format (e.g., story books, coloring books, songs, plays, board games). These programs and materials are based on a set of core assumptions: that many children do not know what sexual abuse is, that sexual touch need not be tolerated, that adults want to know about sexual touching by older persons, and that it is possible to tell about sexual abuse in order to have it cease. Children can be taught knowledge (e.g., the difference between a safe and unsafe touch or whom to tell about abuse) and skills (e.g., how to assertively say "No" to unwanted touch) that will be useful in preventing or escaping their own abuse (Conte and Fogarty 1990; Kolko 1988).

Prevention programs often teach children to follow three strategies in a "dangerous" or sexually abusive situation. Children are taught to say "No," get away from the assailant or dangerous situation, and report the incident to a trusted adult.

Protecting Women

There are a number of options available to women who want to either escape the violence or force their husbands to cease hitting them. One option is to call the police. The best-known assessment of intervention in episodes of marital violence is the Minneapolis Police Experiment (Sherman and Berk 1984). This study called for the police to randomly assign incidents of misdemeanor family assaults to one of three experimental conditions: arrest, separation, or advice/mediation. Those households receiving the arrest intervention had the lowest rate of recidivism (10%), and those who were separated had the highest (24%). More recent research, however, does not support the results of the Minneapolis study. Replications of the Minneapolis experiment in Omaha, Milwaukee, and Charlotte, North Carolina (Dunford, Huizinga, and Elliott 1990; Hirschell, Hutchinson, and Dean 1990; Sherman 1992; Sherman et al. 1991) not only failed to find that arrest deterred abusive husbands but found that unemployed abusers actually increased their use of violence (Sherman 1992).

A second possibility is for the wife to go to a shelter or safe house. There were only 6 such shelters in the United States in 1976; today, there are perhaps more than 1,000. *If* a shelter is nearby a woman, *if* she knows how to get to it, and *if* there is room, shelters provide physical protection, social support, counseling, legal aid, and even occupational counseling. Shelters are clearly the most cost-efficient form of intervention in cases of wife battering. Researchers find that the effects of shelters seem to depend on the attributes of the victims. When a victim is actively engaged in taking control of her life, a shelter stay can dramatically reduce the likelihood of new violence. For other victims, a shelter stay may have no impact; for still others, it may actually lead to an escalation of violence when they return home (Berk, Newton, and Berk 1986). Sociologist Lee Bowker (1983) talked to women who had been beaten

Shelters for battered women provide safety and social support—but they are often filled to the point of overcrowding, with a number of women and their children sharing a single bedroom.

and who managed to get their husbands to stop being violent. Among the things these women did were to talk to friends and relatives, threaten their husbands, aggressively defend themselves from their husbands, go to shelters, call social service agencies, call the police, and various other actions. No one action worked best. Bowker concluded, that ultimately, the crucial factor was the woman taking a stand and showing her determination that the violence had to stop.

Researchers have also evaluated group programs developed for violent men. Donald Dutton (1986) reports that 50 men enrolled in a court-mandated program and followed for up to three years had recidivism rates as low as 4%. Edward Gondolf (1987) reports that two thirds to three quarters of the men who complete voluntary programs show improvement in their nonviolent behavior. Results of assessments of men's groups must be read cautiously because such groups tend to have low recruitment rates and high attrition rates (Pirog-Good and Stets 1986). The more optimistic findings typically apply only to those men who complete counseling programs.

Preventing Abuse and Violence

At present, the majority of programs aimed at dealing with family violence are implemented *after* the abusive incident. In many ways, these programs, no matter how effective, are little more than ambulance services at the bottom of a cliff. What is needed, what has not been attempted on any large scale, and what would prevent violence and abuse before they begin are services that fix the road at the top of the cliff. But such sweeping prevention programs require large-scale changes in both the society and the family. After the conclusion of their national survey of family violence, Straus, Gelles, and Steinmetz (1980) proposed the following steps for the *prevention of violence:*

1. Eliminate the norms that legitimize and glorify violence in the society and the family.
2. Reduce violence-provoking stress created by society.
3. Integrate families into a network of kin and community.
4. Change the sexist character of society.
5. Break the cycle of violence in the family.

Public awareness campaigns—such as this bumper sticker created by John Valusek—are one means of preventing family violence and abuse.

Such steps require long-term changes in the fabric of society. These proposals call for such fundamental changes in families and family life that many people resist them and argue that they could not work or would ruin the family. The alternative, of course, is that not making such changes continues the harmful and deadly tradition of family violence.

SUMMING UP

The dark side of family life is that the family is one of society's most violent social institutions. Women and children are especially at risk of physical and sexual abuse in their homes at the hands of loved ones. Family violence has occurred over time and across cultures. The history of Western society is one in which women and children have been subjected to unspeakable cruelties.

Violence between family members has been considered rare and committed only by mentally ill or otherwise disturbed individuals. Research, however, documents an extremely high rate of child maltreatment, sexual abuse of children, wife abuse, and elder abuse. Violence between siblings and violence by teenagers toward their parents remain largely hidden from public view or policy discussions, even today. The issue of violence toward men is quite controversial, and although some men are battered, the number of battered men is much smaller than the number of battered women.

Much of the early thinking and writing on family violence was dominated by a psychopathological model. However, social factors are related to family violence. Males tend to be the more violent family members, except in the case of violence toward children. Violence is most likely to occur in low-income families, among those who are unemployed, in homes that experience high levels of social stress, among those who are socially isolated, and among those who have experienced and witnessed violence as children.

Six theoretical models have been developed to explain the various forms of family violence: (1) social learning theory, (2) social situational/stress and coping theory, (3) resource theory, (4) an ecological perspective, (5) exchange/social control theory, and (6) patriarchy. In addition, Finkelhor proposed the Four-Precondition Model of Sexual Abuse.

Physical harm is but one consequence of violence in the home. There are emotional consequences as well. Abused and neglected children have a higher likelihood of arrest for delinquency, adult criminality, and violent criminal behavior compared to nonabused children. Abused children also tend to have a number of cognitive, emotional, and social difficulties. Research on battered women reports a high incidence of depression and anxiety as well as an increased risk of suicide attempts.

Prevention and treatment programs have been developed for child maltreatment, sexual abuse, and wife abuse. Some programs provide services and support, while other efforts seek to protect victims and punish offenders. No one intervention or prevention effort works for all families and individuals. The most effective strategies are those that are aimed at the structural causes of violence between family members.

REFERENCES

American Association for Protecting Children (AAPC). 1989. *Highlights of Official Child Neglect and Abuse Reporting, 1987.* Denver, CO: American Humane Association.

Arias, Ileana, Mary Samios, and K. Daniel O'Leary. 1987. "Prevalence and Correlates of Physical Aggression During Courtship." *Journal of Interpersonal Violence* 2(1): 82-90.

Berk, Richard A., Phyllis Newton, and Sara F. Berk. 1986. "What a Difference a Day Makes: An Empirical Study of the Impact of Shelters for Battered Women." *Journal of Marriage and the Family* 48 (August):481-90.

Bowker, Lee H. 1983. *Beating Wife Beating.* Lexington, MA: Lexington Books.

Burgdorf, Kenneth. 1980. *Recognition and Reporting of Child Maltreatment.* Rockville, MD: Westat.

Caffey, John. 1946. "Multiple Fractures in the Long Bones of Infants Suffering From Chronic Subdural Hematoma." *American Journal of Roentgenology,* *Radium Therapy, and Nuclear Medicine* 58(August):163-73.

Christoffel, Katherine K. 1990. "Violent Death and Injury in U.S. Children and Adolescents." *American Journal of Diseases of Children* 144(June):697-705.

Christopoulos, Chistrina, Deborah A. Cohn, Daniel S. Shaw, Susan Joyce, Jean Sullivan-Hanson, Sherry P. Kraft, and Robert Emery. 1987. "Children of Abused Women: Adjustment at Time of Shelter Residence." *Journal of Marriage and the Family* 49 (August): 611-19.

Conte, Jon R. and Linda Fogarty. 1990. "Sexual Abuse Prevention Programs for Children." *Education and Urban Society* 22(May):270-84.

Cornell, Claire P. and Richard J. Gelles. 1982. "Adolescent to Parent Violence." *Urban Social Change Review* 15(Winter): 8-14.

Curtis, Lynn. 1974. *Criminal Violence: National Patterns and Behavior.* Lexington, MA: Lexington Books.

Daro, Deborah. 1992. *Current Trends in Child Abuse Reporting and Fatalities: NCPCA's 1991 Annual Fifty State Survey.* Chicago: National Committee for the Prevention of Child Abuse.

Daro, Deborah and Anne H. Cohn. 1988. "Child Maltreatment Evaluation Efforts: What Have We Learned?" Pp. 275-87 in *Coping With Family Violence: Research and Policy Perspectives,* edited by Gerald T. Hotaling, David Finkelhor, John T. Kirkpatrick, and Murray A. Straus. Newbury Park, CA: Sage.

Dobash, Rebecca E. and Russell Dobash. 1979. *Violence Against Wives.* New York: Free Press.

Dobash, Russell P., Rebecca E. Dobash, Margo Wilson, and Martin Daly. 1992. "The Myth of Sexual Symmetry in Marital Violence." *Social Problems* 39 (February):71-91.

Dunford, Frank W., David Huizinga, and Delbert S. Elliott. 1990. "The Role of Arrest in Domestic Assault: The Omaha Police Experiment." *Criminology* 28(2):183-206.

Dutton, Donald G. 1986. "The Outcome of Court-Mandated Treatment for Wife Assault: A Quasi-Experimental Evaluation." *Violence and Victims* 1(3): 163-76.

Egeland, Byron, Deborah Jacobvitz, and L. Alan Sroufe. 1988. "Breaking the Cycle of Abuse." *Child Development* 59 (4):1080-88.

Egley, Lance C. 1991. "What Changes the Societal Prevalence of Domestic Violence?" *Journal of Marriage and the Family* 53 (November):885-97.

Finkelhor, David. 1979. *Sexually Victimized Children.* New York: Free Press.

———. 1984. *Child Sexual Abuse: New Theories and Research.* New York: Free Press.

Finkelhor, David and Larry Baron. 1986. "High Risk Children." Pp. 60-88 in *A Sourcebook on Child Sexual Abuse,* edited by David Finkelhor. Beverly Hills, CA: Sage.

Galdston, Richard. 1965. "Observations of Children Who Have Been Physically Abused by Their Parents." *American Journal of Psychiatry* 122(4): 440-43.

Garbarino, James. 1977. "The Human Ecology of Child Maltreatment." *Journal of Marriage and the Family* 39 (4):721-35.

Gelles, Richard J. 1976. "Abused Wives: Why Do They Stay?"

Journal of Marriage and the Family 38 (November):659-68.

———. 1980. "Violence in the Family: A Review of Research in the Seventies." *Journal of Marriage and the Family* 42 (November):873-85.

———. 1983. "An Exchange/Social Control Theory of Intrafamily Violence," Pp. 151-65 in *The Dark Side of Families: Current Family Violence Research,* edited by David Finkelhor, Richard J. Gelles, Gerald Hotaling, and Murray A. Straus. Beverly Hills, CA: Sage.

———. 1989. "Child Abuse and Violence in Single Parent Families: Parent-Absence and Economic Deprivation." *American Journal of Orthopsychiatry* 59 (October):492-501.

Gelles, Richard J. and John W. Harrop. 1989. "Violence, Battering, and Psychological Distress Among Women." *Journal of Interpersonal Violence* 4(December):400-20.

Gelles, Richard J. and Murray A. Straus. 1987. "Is Violence Toward Children Increasing? A Comparison of 1975 and 1985 National Survey Rates." *Journal of Interpersonal Violence* 2(June):212-22.

———. 1988. *Intimate Violence.* New York: Simon & Schuster.

Gil, David. 1970. *Violence Against Children: Physical Child Abuse in the United States.* Cambridge, MA: Harvard University Press.

Gondolf, Edward W. 1987. "Evaluating Progress for Men Who Batter: Problems and Prospects." *Journal of Family Violence* 2(1):95-108.

Goode, William J. 1971. "Force and Violence in the Family." *Journal of Marriage and the Family* 33(November):624-36.

Gordon, Linda. 1988. *Heroes of Their Own Lives: The Politics and History of Family Violence.* New York: Viking.

Greven, Philip. 1991. *Spare the Child: The Religious Roots of Punishment and the Psychological Impact of Physical Abuse.* New York: Alfred A. Knopf.

Henton, June, Rodney Cate, James E. Koval, Sally A. Lloyd, and Christopher F. Scott. 1983. "Romance and Violence in Dating Relationships." *Journal of Family Issues* 4 (September):467-82.

Hilberman, Elaine. 1980. "Overview: 'The Wife-Beater's Wife' Reconsidered." *American Journal of Psychiatry* 137(11): 1336-46.

Hirschell, J. David, Ira W. Hutchinson III, and Charles W. Dean. 1990. "The Failure of Arrest to Deter Spouse Abuse." *Journal of Research in Crime and Delinquency* 29 (February):7-33.

Jason, Janine, Mary M. Carpenter, and Carl W. Tyler, Jr. 1983. "Underrecording of Infant Homicide in the United States." *American Journal of Public Health* 73(February): 195-97.

Kaufman, Joan and Edward Zigler. 1987. "Do Abused Children Become Abusive Parents?" *American Journal of Orthopsychiatry* 57(2):186-92.

Kempe, C. H., Frederic N. Silverman, Brandt F. Steele, William Droegemueller, and Henry K. Silver. 1962. "The Battered Child Syndrome." *Journal of the American Medical Association* 181(July 7):107-12.

Kolko, David J. 1988. "Educational Programs to Promote Awareness and Prevention of Child Sexual Victimization: A Review and Methodological Critique." *Clinical Psychology Review* 8:195-209.

Lane, Katherine E. and Patricia A. Gwartney-Gibbs. 1985. "Violence in the Context of Dating and Sex." *Journal of Family Issues* 6(1):45-59.

Lazoritz, Stephan. 1990. "What Ever Happened to Mary Ellen?" *Child Abuse and Neglect* 14(2): 143-49.

Levinson, David. 1981. "Physical Punishment of Children and Wifebeating in Cross-Cultural Perspective." *Child Abuse and Neglect* 5(4):193-96.

Makepeace, James. 1983. "Life Events, Stress and Courtship Violence." *Family Relations* 32 (1):101-9.

Margolin, Leslie. 1992. "Beyond Maternal Blame: Physical Child Abuse as a Phenomenon of Gender." *Journal of Family Issues* 13 (September):410-23.

Milner, Joel S. and Chinni Chilamkurti. 1991. "Physical Child Abuse Perpetrator Characteristics: A Review of the Literature." *Journal of Interpersonal Violence* 6(September): 345-66.

Morley, Rebecca. 1994. "Wife Beating and Modernization: The Case of Papua New Guinea." *Journal of Comparative Family Studies* 25(Spring): 25-52.

National Center on Child Abuse and Neglect (NCCAN). 1988. *Study Findings: Study of National Incidence and Prevalence of Child Abuse and Neglect: 1988.* Washington, DC: U.S. Department of Health and Human Services.

Olds, David L., Charles R. Henderson, Jr., R. Tatelbaum, and R. Chamberlin. 1986. "Preventing Child Abuse and Neglect: A Randomized Trial of Nurse Home Visitation." *Pediatrics* 78(July):65-78.

Parke, Ross D. and Candace W. Collmer. 1975. "Child Abuse: An Interdisciplinary Analysis." Pp. 1-102 in *Review of Child Development Research,* Vol. 5, edited by Mavis Hetherington. Chicago: University of Chicago Press.

Peters, Stephanie D., Gail E. Wyatt, and David Finkelhor. 1986. "Prevalence." Pp. 15-59 in *A Sourcebook on Child Sexual Abuse,* edited by David Finkelhor. Beverly Hills, CA: Sage.

Pillemer, Karl A. and David Finkelhor. 1988. "The Prevalence of Elder Abuse: A Random Sample Survey." *The Gerontologist* 28(1):51-57.

Pirog-Good, Maureen A. and Jan Stets. 1986. "Programs for Abusers: Who Drops Out and What Can Be Done." *Response* 9(2):17-19.

Pleck, Elizabeth. 1987. *Domestic Tyranny: The Making of American Social Policy Against Family Violence From Colonial Times to the Present.* New York: Oxford University Press.

Quinsey, Vernon L. 1984. "Sexual Aggression: Studies of Offenders Against Women." Pp. 84-121 in *Law and Mental Health: International Perspectives,* Vol. 1, edited by David N. Weisstub. New York: Pergamon.

Radbill, Samuel X. 1980. "A History of Child Abuse and Infanticide." Pp. 3-20 in *The Battered Child,* rev. ed., edited by Ray Helfer and C. Henry Kempe. Chicago: University of Chicago Press.

Robin, Michael. 1982. "Historical Introduction: Sheltering Arms: The Roots of Child Protection." Pp. 1-41 in *Child Abuse,* edited by Eli H. Newberger. Boston: Little, Brown.

Roscoe, Bruce and Nancy Bernaske. 1985. "Courtship Violence Experienced by Abused Wives: Similarities in Patterns of Abuse." *Family Relations* 34(July):419-24.

Rosenfeld, Alvin and Eli H. Newberger. 1977. "Compassion vs. Control: Conceptual and Practical Pitfalls in the Broadened Definition of Child

Abuse." *Journal of the American Medical Association* 237 (May 2):2086-88.

Schechter, Susan. 1983. *Women and Male Violence.* Boston: South End Press.

Schmitt, Barton and C. Henry Kempe. 1975. "Neglect and Abuse of Children." Pp. 107-111 in *Nelson Textbook of Pediatrics,* edited by Victor Vaughan and R. James McKay. Philadelphia: W. B. Saunders.

Seligman, Martin E. P. 1975. *Helplessness: On Depression, Development, and Death.* San Francisco: Freeman.

Sherman, Lawrence W. 1992. *Policing Domestic Violence.* New York: Free Press.

Sherman, Lawrence W. and Richard A. Berk. 1984. "The Specific Deterrent Effects of Arrest for Domestic Assault." *American Sociological Review* 49 (April):261-72.

Sherman, Lawrence W., Janell D. Schmidt, Dennis R. Rogan, Patrick R. Gartin, Ellen G. Cohn, Dean J. Collins, and Anthony R. Bacich. 1991. "From Initial Deterrence to Long-Term Escalation: Short-Custody Arrest for Poverty Ghetto Domestic Violence." *Criminology* 29 (November):821-50.

Smith, Selwyn, Ruth Hansen, and Sheila Nobel. 1973. "Parents of Battered Babies: A Controlled Study." *British Medical Journal* 5(November 17): 388-91.

Spinetta, John J. and David Rigler. 1972. "The Child-Abusing Parent: A Psychological Review." *Psychological Bulletin* 77(April):296-304.

Starr, Raymond H., Jr. 1988. "Physical Abuse of Children." Pp. 119-55 in *Handbook of Family Violence,* edited by Vincent B. Van Hasselt, Randall L. Morrison, Alan S. Bellack, and Michel Hersen. New York: Plenum.

Steele, Brandt F. and Carl Pollock. 1968. "A Psychiatric Study of Parents Who Abuse Infants and Small Children." Pp. 103-47 in *The Battered Child,* edited by Ray Helfer and C. Henry Kempe. Chicago: University of Chicago Press.

Steinmetz, Suzanne K. and Murray A. Straus. 1973. "The Family as a Cradle of Violence." *Society* 10(6):50-56.

Straus, Murray A. and Richard J. Gelles. 1986. "Societal Change and Change in Family Violence From 1975 to 1985 as Revealed in Two National Surveys." *Journal of Marriage and the Family* 48(August): 465-79.

Straus, Murray A., Richard J. Gelles, and Suzanne K. Steinmetz. 1980. *Behind Closed Doors: Violence in the American Family.* New York: Anchor/Doubleday.

Strube, Michael J. and Linda S. Barbour. 1983. "The Decision to Leave an Abusive Relationship: Economic Dependence and Psychological Commitment." *Journal of Marriage and the Family* 45(November): 785-93.

Sugarman, David B. and Gerald T. Hotaling. 1989. "Dating Violence: Prevalence, Context, and Risk Markers." Pp. 3-32 in *Violence in Dating Relationships: Emerging Issues,* edited by Maureen A. Pirog-Good and Jan E. Stets. New York: Praeger.

Truninger, Elizabeth. 1971. "Marital Violence: The Legal Solutions." *Hastings Law Review* 23(November):259-76.

U.S. Department of Justice. 1993. *The Uniform Crime Reports for the United States.* Washington, DC: Government Printing Office.

Walker, Lenore. 1979. *The Battered Woman.* New York: Harper & Row.

Wauchope, Barbara A. and Murray A. Straus. 1990. "Physical Punishment and Physical Abuse of American Children: Incidence Rates by Age, Gender, and Occupational Class." Pp. 133-48 in *Physical Violence in American Families: Risk Factors and Adaptations in 8,145 Families,* edited by Murray A. Straus and Richard J. Gelles. New Brunswick, NJ: Transaction Books.

Widom, Cathy Spatz. 1989. "The Cycle of Violence." *Science* 244(April 14):160-66.

Wolfner, Glenn D. and Richard J. Gelles. 1993. "A Profile of

Violence Toward Children." *Child Abuse and Neglect: The International Journal* 17(2): 197-212.

Woolley, Paul V., Jr. and William A. Evans, Jr. 1955. "Significance of Skeletal Lesions Resembling Those of Traumatic Origin." *Journal of the American Medical Association* 158(June 18):539-43.

CHAPTER **16**

▉▉ Families in the Future

Television situation comedies of the 1950s and 1960s provide the cultural benchmark against which modern family life is often measured. The cultural image of the white, suburban father working, mother at home, two-children family, in the house with the picket fence is the standard of what we thought families used to be like in the past and ought to be like today. Writer David Halberstam (1993) noted that one reason why Americans as a people are nostalgic about the 1950s is not so much because life was better then but because the 1950s, and 1950s families, were, and continue to be, portrayed so idyllically on television.

Even today, one can sit down and watch reruns of 1950s situation comedies (sitcoms) each evening on countless television channels. *The Adventures of Ozzie and Harriet* remains the prototypical 1950s television family sitcom. On a typical episode, Ozzie and Harriet Nelson sit down to dinner with their sons David and Ricky and discuss what happened in school, girlfriends, or the antics of their next-door neighbor, Thorny. On another '50s sitcom, Theodore "Beaver" Cleaver is yet again getting into mischief that will end up with him being gently scolded by his father Ward and mother June. Other 1950s and 1960s family sitcoms gave us the Andersons on *Father Knows Best* and the Petries on *The Dick Van Dyke Show,* as well as the *Donna Reed Show* and *The Waltons.* A saccharine-sweet version of the blended family, *The Brady Bunch,* is still popular. These families, more than the real families of the 1950s, are the standard against which current family life and projections of the family of the future are compared.

A discussion of the "future of the family" often begins with the thesis of the "breakdown of the family." High divorce rates, dramatic increases in the number of single-parent homes, declines in the birth rate and in the marriage rate, increases in cohabitation and in teenage pregnancy, and gay and lesbian couples adopting children are seen by many as stark indicators of the decline and imminent death of the family. On the other hand, some observers take note of the changes that have occurred in the institution of the family and state that the family is not dying but, rather, is changing, evolving, and adapting.

In this concluding chapter of this text on families, we consider the future of families, first by reviewing past predictions about the future of the family and then turning to the current debate on the "crisis of the contemporary family." Finally, some tentative attempts are made to peer into my own crystal ball and examine the likely direction and future of families.

486

PAST PREDICTIONS:
THE DEATH OF THE FAMILY

Arguments that the crisis of the family will eventually lead to the collapse of the family as a social institution and the ultimate death of the family are not new. The history of predictions for the future of the family is long (Clayton 1979). Plato thought the Greek family system was too weak to be responsible for the education and socialization of its children. In his view, gifted children should be made wards of the state and receive their training and education from schools.

August Comte, the "father" of sociology, was concerned in the early 1800s that the social disorganization and anarchy created by the French Revolution would destroy the family as a social institution. Comte argued that the family must retain a monogamous and patriarchal structure if it was to protect itself from the anarchic pressures of the times (Clayton 1979).

Modern social scientists were even more pessimistic about the fate of the family. Behavioral psychologist John Watson (1928) predicted that marriage would no longer exist by 1977. Watson felt that family standards were on their way to a complete breakdown. According to Watson, it was the automobile that would be the implement of destruction of the family. Mobile, irresponsible youths with money to spend would bring the family to the point of extinction.

Two years later, in 1929, as the Great Depression was unfolding, the President's Research Committee on Social Trends, reporting to President Herbert Hoover on the state of American society, pointed to the rising divorce rate as a sign of strain in the family. In the Committee's report, published in 1933, sociologist William Ogburn explained that the family had lost many of its economic functions and thus was held together by rather tenuous bonds. Also in 1929, the eminent British philosopher Bertrand Russell (1929) commented that the family in the entire Western world had become a mere shadow of what it had been. Russell went on to explain that the decline of the family was the result of partly economic and partly social factors, but, overall, the family as a social institution was never really suitable either to urban populations or seafaring populations. Of course, the pessimism of Watson, Russell, Ogburn, and the members of the President's Research Committee must be considered in light of the rather dire economic circumstances of the worldwide depression and its impact on all social institutions, including the family.

Eight years later, with the Great Depression not yet over, sociologist Pitrim Sorokin (1937) observed that the family was becoming merely an overnight parking lot. Divorce and separation were becoming so pervasive, Sorokin noted, that soon there would be no difference between marital and nonmarital sex. The sacred union of husband and wife and parent and children had begun to degenerate so much that soon the main sociocultural function of the family would be to provide a parking space for people who would meet at night for sex. Unlike Watson, Sorokin chose (wisely) not to set a date for the total collapse of the family.

Twenty years later, another social scientist put the family on life support. As political scientist Barrington Moore, Jr. (1958) carefully explained it, conditions had arisen whereby the family would soon be unable to perform its most important social and psychological functions. The family, according to Moore, was unable to withstand the forces of social and technological change. Modern demands on the time and energy of individual family members would tear apart the family institution. Moore, however, proposed a cure for the family's ills. He explained that if parents would once again assert their authority over their children, this would insulate the family against the forces of social change.

Writing in 1977, the year in which James Watson had predicted the family would be extinct, psychologist Urie Bronfenbrenner spoke pessimistically about the modern family, although he did not go so far as to offer it an obituary. The problem with the family, according to Bronfenbrenner, was that nobody was home. He explained that the growing number of single parents and working mothers was creating problems for individuals and society. Too many children and adolescents were returning home each day and were being raised by television and their peers. Bronfenbrenner, like many current social critics, believed that a host of problems, such as reading difficulties, drug problems, and childhood depression were caused by children being left on their own. Worse, this situation had dire consequences for future families and future children, as children who are not cared for do not learn to care for others.

Other doomsayers included sociologist Amitai Etzioni (1977), who, like Watson, not only predicted the demise of the family but set a date. Etzioni claimed that not one family would be left by 1990. Historian Christopher Lasch, also writing in 1977, addressed what he saw as the erosion of family life in contemporary society. As was noted earlier in this text, Lasch envisioned the family as a haven for private life, personal relations, and the last refuge of love and decency. The family should be a haven in a heartless world. But, according to Lasch's view, the family has slowly been coming apart for more than 100 years and is becoming increasingly incapable of providing comfort. The signals that concerned Lasch were rising divorce rates, falling birth rates, the changing status of women, and what he called the "so called" revolution in morals.

Those who predict the demise of the family as a social institution often point to the increasing number of "latchkey" children as an indicator that the family is not meeting the needs of its members and of society.

THE CRISIS OF CONTEMPORARY FAMILIES

Casting aside the inaccuracy of predictions (there are still families as you read this chapter) and the excesses of hyperbole used by social critics, social scientists still voice their concern about the current state of the family. One of the more recent and careful examinations of the decline of the family is sociologist David Popenoe's (1988) *Disturbing the Nest: Family Change and Decline in Modern Societies.* In his book, Popenoe examines historical changes in the American family and compares the current direction of American families to those in Sweden. Popenoe concludes, as have others, that the institution of the family is growing weaker. The family as a social institution is losing its power and social functions, losing its influence over behavior and opinion, and generally becoming less important in life. Popenoe bases this dire assessment on his assumption that the family is primarily a social instrument for child rearing. Increased cohabitation, increases in births of children before a legal marriage has occurred, increased numbers of working mothers, and increased numbers of children being reared from early ages in day care and other child care centers are the trends that have weakened the family. Using data from Sweden (see Box 16-1), Popenoe argues that the family has declined further in Sweden than in any other society.

Sar Levitan, Richard Belous, and Frank Gallo (1988) are other social scientists who take a dim view of the current condition of the contemporary family. Examining statistical trends and evidence they argue that

> American families are besieged from all sides. The divorce rate is close to record heights; marriage is being postponed, if not rejected; fertility rates are below zero population growth; increasing numbers of children are being raised in poverty by their mothers only; and mothers are rushing out of the home and into the workplace in record numbers. The traditional Ozzie and Harriet family (a breadwinner, homemaker wife, and children) constitutes only a tenth of all households. (p. vii)

Interestingly, these trends were well under way when Levitan and Belous (1981) wrote the first edition of *What's Happening to the American Family?* However, they believed that the new American conservatism that swept Ronald

---

BOX 16-1: THE GLOBAL VIEW

The Family in Sweden:
Popenoe's Case Study of Family Decline

Sociologist David Popenoe (1988) sees events occurring in Sweden as foreshadowing the kinds of social changes that the American family will likely go through in the next few years. No other element of Swedish society has changed more rapidly or in a more dramatic way than has the Swedish family (p. 167). The changes in the Swedish family are an extension of those occurring in families around the world. The fundamental aspect of the changes is the release of young people at or before marriage from the authority of, and the need to contribute to, their families of orientation. At the core

of family systems around the world is the ideal of the traditional nuclear family. Although the traditional nuclear family began to decline in Western nations following World War II, the Swedish family, Popenoe asserts, has moved farther from that ideal than has the family in any other society.

The specific changes that Popenoe points to as "disturbing the nest" and indicating decline in the family as a social institution are that the marriage rate in Sweden is the lowest in the industrialized world and that the rates of non-

Reagan into the White House would also affect the stability of the American family. Alas, Ronald Reagan and the "Moral Majority" were far more successful in the ballot box than the bedroom, and the trends identified in the early 1980s continued and even increased over the next eight years. The divorce rate managed to stabilize, but out-of-wedlock births continued to rise, as did the percentage of children living in poverty and with single mothers.

Unlike earlier predictors of the family's decline and demise, Levitan and his colleagues (1988) do not offer an obituary for the family nor do they even put it on the endangered species list. Rather, they argue that more needs to be done by government to ensure that a stable family is maintained for the rearing of children and preserving the vitality of American society.

THE MYTH OF FAMILY DECLINE: THE ALTERNATIVE VIEW

Perhaps it is no coincidence that all of the prophets of doom who decry the decline and predict the demise of the family are men and that one of the focal points of their concern is the decline of the birth rate and the increase in working mothers. It is not Ozzie that concerns the prophets of doom, it is the

marital cohabitation and marital dissolution are perhaps the highest in the world.

In 1966, 194 of every 1,000 Swedish women, aged 20 to 24, married. The marriage rate began to drop in 1966 and has decreased some 40% since then, so that by 1980 only 53 in 1,000 married each year. The decline in the rate of marriage not only reflects an increased willingness to postpone marriage but an increased tendency to not marry at all. Marriage in Sweden is gradually being replaced by non-marital cohabitation. Popenoe estimates that today about one quarter of all couples in Sweden are not married. Nonmarital cohabitation is legally and culturally accepted as both a prelude to marriage and, more important, an alternative to marriage.

As a consequence of the increase in the acceptability of nonmarital cohabitation, nearly half of all children born in Sweden are born to unmarried parents.

Finally, the rate of marital dissolution in Sweden, including both legal divorce and the ending of nonmarital relationships, is estimated to be the highest in the world. However, unlike the United States and other Western nations, remarriage is not likely to follow a divorce—45% of Swedish divorces are followed by remarriage, compared to 85% in the United States (see Chapter 13).

Popenoe does not contend that the family as a social institution has collapsed in Sweden; rather, he argues that these trends indicate an institution that is in decline. The decline is because the family has lost social power and has become less important in present-day Sweden and is less relevant to other social institutions than in previous times.

thought of Harriet not having babies, entering the workforce, and having David and Ricky cared for in a day care center.

The other side of the claim that the family is dying, doomed, or declining is the contention that the changes we have seen in the family are signs of adaptation and development, not decay and death.

Mary Jo Bane (1976) examined the same data used by those who forecast the death of the family and suggests that the data indicate that the family is "here to stay." Much of the concern about the family relates to concern about whether the family is adequately meeting the socialization and nurturance needs of children. Most of the social critics reviewed earlier in this chapter believe that children are less well cared for today than in the past. Bane disagrees. The declining birth rate is frequently cited as evidence that Americans neither want nor value children as they once did. Bane points out that the birth rate is not falling because fewer people want children but because more people want fewer children. Overall, childlessness has declined since the 1930s, largely due to improvements in health and new treatments for infertility. Voluntary childlessness has indeed increased, but this is matched by a decline in involuntary childlessness.

Bane sees parent-child bonds as stronger today than in the past. In fact, she points out that more children live with at least one parent today than in the past. There are two reasons for this: (1) Fewer children lose a parent through death than in the past, and (2) social programs allow more widowed and divorced women to keep their children with them. Although evidence indicates that there are disadvantages to having only one parent as opposed to two, these disadvantages are largely the result of the poverty of single-parent families and not an inherent dysfunction.

Women working is often cited by the social critics as a sign that the family is failing. If mothers were not at work, children would not be coming home to empty houses, laying in front of the television, or getting into drugs or some other trouble. Although more women are working, the evidence suggests (see Chapter 11) that these mothers spend as much or more time in planned activities with their children as nonworking mothers do. And given that mothers are having fewer children today than 30 years ago, today's working mother with one or two children is probably spending as much, or more, time with each of her children than the nonworking mother who has five or six children at home. According to Bane (1976), there is little evidence that the family's role in caring for children has declined.

Bane also examined the rising (but now stable) divorce rate. Here too, she found evidence of stability in marriage. Although the divorce rate has increased, 80% to 85% of those who divorce remarry, most within three years of the divorce. As we noted in Chapter 13, these data indicate that individuals are unhappy with *a marriage* but not with the *institution of marriage*. Using a historical referent, even with the high divorce rate, today's families are at least as stable as families in the past, where death was the most likely end of a marriage.

A team of sociologists led by Theodore Caplow who examined individual and family life in Muncie, Indiana also pronounced the contemporary family as healthy. Muncie had been the focus of Robert and Helen Lynd's ([1929] 1956) book, *Middletown: A Study in American Culture.* Looking at Muncie 50 years after the Lynds' study in the 1920s and 1930s, Caplow and his colleagues (1982) found increased family solidarity, a smaller generation gap, closer marital communication, more religion, and less mobility. One aspect of their findings is shown in Table 16-1, which presents data comparing disagreements between teenagers and parents in 1924 compared to 1977. Overall, the pattern is quite similar, despite the difference of more than 50 years. There were some changes, however. Boys in 1977 had more disagreements with their parents about home duties and responsibilities, friends, dress and hairstyle, and going to unchaperoned parties compared to boys in 1924. Disagreements declined over Sabbath observance and church attendance. Girls in 1977 had more disagreements about friends and home duties and fewer disagreements about church attendance and Sabbath observance and the clubs and societies to which they belonged.

Sociologist Alice Rossi (1978) argues that the so-called decline and death of the family is an issue of semantics and language, not statistics. She explains that what we defined a decade ago as "deviant" is today labeled "variant." The changes that have occurred and continue to occur in the family are signs of a healthy, experimental quality in which the family is adapting to the conditions of modern society and other social institutions.

Sociologist Edward Kain (1990) states flatly that the notion of family decline is a myth. The myth of family decline is based on a desire to return to some idealized vision of the family in the past—either "the classical extended family" or the 1950s "Ozzie and Harriet"-type traditional nuclear family. Kain goes on to demythologize some notions that feed theories of family decline. First, he points out that the divorce rate was higher in the United States in 1945 after World War II than it was in 1965. Second, although there has been an increase in children living in single-parent families, children today are *not* more likely to live in single-parent homes than children in the past. As Bane (1976) explained, death of a parent was the most likely source of family breakup historically, which resulted in numerous orphans and single-parent families. Kain also explodes the myth of the classical three-generation extended family, an issue explored in Chapter 4 of this text. Kain reviews a number of other myths and concludes by explaining that our notions about family decline are based more on a romantic vision of past families than on hard scientific evidence of decline and decay. He makes the important point that because the

Table 16-1 Percentage of Middletown Adolescents Reporting Disagreement With Their Parents, by Subject and by Sex, 1924 and 1977

Source of Disagreement	Boys		Girls	
	1924	1977	1924	1977
The hours (1924: hour) you get in at night	45	46	43	42
The number of times you go out on school nights during the week	45	31	48	35
Your grades at school (1924: grades at school)	40	34	31	28
Your spending money	37	38	29	29
Use of the automobile	36	29	30	22
The people (1924: boys or girls) you choose as friends	25	33	27	36
Home duties (yard work, cooking, helping around the house, etc.) (1924: . . . [tending furnace, cooking, etc.]	19	45	26	46
Church and attendance at religious services (1924: . . . and Sunday School attendance)	19	11	19	13
The way you dress (including hairstyle, general grooming) (1924: the way you dress)	16	25	25	19
Going to unchaperoned parties	15	27	28	29
Sunday (or Sabbath) observance, aside from attendance at services (1924: Sunday observance, aside from just going to church and Sunday School)	14	6	14	3
Clubs or societies you belong to	6	6	10	5
Other causes of disagreement (please explain) (1924: state any other causes of disagreement)	10	16	8	28
Number of cases (*n*)	(348)	(442)	(382)	(488)

SOURCE: *Middletown Families: Fifty Years of Change and Continuity* (p. 373) by Theodore Caplow, Howard Bahr, Bruce Chadwick, Reuben Hill, and Margaret Holmes Williamson. Copyright 1982 by the University of Minnesota. Published by the University of Minnesota Press.

future is, to a substantial degree, an extension of the past, any predictions about the future of the family depends on an accurate understanding of what the family of the past was like. Unfortunately, the benchmark standard of families of the past is often the idyllic image of the 1950s families portrayed on television sitcoms or the "classical family of Western nostalgia" described in books and magazine articles (and occasional television programs).

Many people consider the 1950s as the "Golden Age" of the American family. Restoring 1950s cars and dressing in 1950s clothing—such as poodle skirts—are ways of keeping alive this vision of the family's golden age.

Finally, demographer Paul Glick (1988) believes that family life in the United States has actually become better, not worse, in recent years. The fact that American men and women are marrying at a later age increases the chances that they will make rational, mature choices of marriage partners. Early marriages, as we saw in Chapter 13, tend to be unstable. Delay in first marriage may lead to lower risk of divorce. Delay in getting married also means that a couple will be older when they have their first child. Delaying having a first child also leads to a decrease in the number of children a couple has. Having fewer children means that parents can devote more time to each child and to each other. Glick also believes that it is beneficial for families that women work. He concludes by stating his belief that, despite changes in marriage rates and divorce rates and the fact that divorce seems more "taken for granted" today than in the past, most young adults still prefer to enter into a permanent first marriage.

Despite the optimistic assessments of the data on families, positive views on the future of the family were few and far between by the end of the 1980s. Paul Glick and Edward Kain were two of a small handful of observers and scholars who saw any silver lining at all in the clouds that seemed to hang over the contemporary family.

EMBATTLED PARADISE: THE FAMILY IN THE AGE OF UNCERTAINTY

Sociologist Arlene Skolnick (1991) also invokes the image of the idealized media family when she begins her examination of the American family. She opens Chapter 1 of her book by commenting on a 1990 television documentary produced by the NBC affiliate in San Francisco entitled "Who Killed Ozzie and Harriet?" The documentary cuts between the cheerful black-and-white scenes from the '50s television family shows and the not so cheerful full-color scenes of contemporary family life. Skolnick refers to the modern family as an "embattled paradise," an expression that seems to be a contradiction in terms. She explains that the family can be a cherished value, a durable institution, and "in trouble" at the same time (p. xvi).

According to Skolnick, one problem with the examination of the state of the family is that the discourse suffers from some important flaws:

■ Discussions of the crisis of the family often lack a historical context. Those who wax nostalgic about the family in the past seem oblivious to the devastating impact of disease and mortality on children and family structure. The historical family (see Chapter 4) was not without change and variation.

■ Using the family of the 1950s as the cultural benchmark for what families should be like creates an unrealistic standard. The 1950s and its families were a social and economic aberration (see Chapter 4). In fact, Skolnick states that the upheavals of the 1960s and 1970s grew directly out of the contradictory demands and expectations on women and families in the '50s.

■ It is inappropriate to lump together all the changes and social problems into one big "crisis" of the family. Divorce, single parents, working mothers and wives, child abuse, teenage pregnancy, high rates of poverty, sex before and outside marriage, alcoholism, drug abuse, and gay couples are simply not one neat package with the same social and structural causes and consequences. Politicians and social commentators often seem able to connect any social issue or problem that affects women and men to the family. Often, however, decrying the crisis and collapse of the family is merely a convenient "smokescreen" to deflect attention away from the structural problems and defects in society. The economy and economic policies are often the causal agents that create problems for men, women, children, and families, and politicians often use political rhetoric about the decline of the family to deflect attention from their own economic policies.

Skolnick proposes that three related structural changes seem to have set the current cycle of family change in motion. The first is the shift into the "postindustrial" and service economy. The second is a demographic revolution that not only created mass longevity but reshaped the individual and family life course, creating life stages and circumstances unknown to earlier generations. The lengthening of the life span is arguably the single most important

Sources of Family Change

BOX 16-2: THINKING ABOUT FAMILIES

Psychological Gentrification and Family Change

One of the significant changes that has occurred in the United States that has both influenced family life *and* how we look at and perceive families, is what sociologist Arlene Skolnick (1991) calls "psychological gentrification." Psychological gentrification involves an introspective approach to experience, a greater sense of one's own individuality and subjectivity, and a concern with self-fulfillment and self-development.

As late as the 1920s, fewer than one in five young people earned a high school diploma. Few jobs required learning or personal development, and work hours were long—about 55 hours per week. For the majority of families—those without college degrees or servants in the home—there was little time for leisure, vacations, or concern with self-development or improvement.

The process of psychological gentrification began after World War II. The G.I. Bill of Rights, which funded the education, including college, of World War II veterans, was the main force in democratizing America. More and more

Americans were able to afford a college education. The number of people who obtained a college education doubled between 1950 and 1965.

Psychological gentrification was not tied only to education. Museums, theaters, symphony orchestras, and dance companies spread across the country. Quality paperbacks, cheap and affordable, became available and reading was democratized. Television, initially seen as destroying American culture, now spread culture to every corner of society. Better housing, shorter work weeks, and paid vacations increased leisure time for the working class.

Psychological gentrification created a larger public who were more introspective, more attentive to their inner experiences, and more willing to admit marital and personal problems than in the past and yet, at the same time, were more satisfied with their marriages. Psychological gentrification also placed new burdens on families and relationships. The self-examination of the individual, relationships, and families created discontents that did not exist prior to the psychological gentrification of America.

change in American society, having a profound impact on individuals and all aspects of family life. Last, we have gone through a process of "psychological gentrification," which involves an introspective approach to experience (see Box 16-2). Americans have become more introspective, more attentive to inner experience, and more willing to admit marital and personal problems.

Skolnick concludes her examination of family change from the 1950s to the 1990s by neither imposing a death sentence on the family nor arguing that the family is entirely secure and solid. Instead she finds a realistic, optimistic middle ground. "The optimists," she says, "are certainly correct and the pessimists wrong. For better or worse, family life and the idealized image of what the family should be, remain at the source of our greatest joys, our deepest worries, and our most painful hurts" (p. 220).

PRINCIPLES FOR PREDICTING THE FUTURE OF FAMILY LIFE

Current concern about the family focuses on two issues: "Is the family in trouble?" and "Where is the family going?" We are concerned about the family at two levels. At one level, we wonder how the institution of the family will change and adapt in the years to come. At another level, we wonder what our family life will be like. What will life be like for our children and our grandchildren? Will the divorce rate increase? Will we be divorced? Will our children be divorced? Will there be another baby boom? How many children will our children have? The questions alternate between the structural context we and our children live in and our own personal experiences.

Sociologist Edward Kain (1990) offers "Nine Principles for Predicting the Future of Family Life":

1. *Any predictions we make about the future must be probabilistic rather than deterministic.* A probabilistic prediction would state that change or a condition is likely or unlikely to occur, as opposed to a determinist statement, such as "there will be no families left by 1990."

2. *The near future is more easily predictable than the distant future.* We can be more confident about changes that may occur in the next decade than in the next century.

3. It is important to *check on the assumptions of any predictions that are made, including the definitions that are used by those making the predictions.* It is important to know how the predictor defines terms such as "family" when we assess the prediction.

4. *The future, to a substantial degree, is an extension of the past.* To make accurate predictions, we need to be accurate in our understanding about the nature of the past. Predictions based on nostalgic rather than accurate images of the past are doomed to fail.

5. *Extrapolation of trends in data are not enough, we need to understand what forces resist or encourage these trends.* Thus we cannot merely look at a graph or chart and use the trend in the chart to predict the future. We need to understand what the causes behind the trends are and to know whether the same causal forces will continue to operate.

6. *It is easier to predict demographic and technological trends than it is to predict ideological and political trends.* Social scientists tend to have a better understanding of the causes behind trends on birth rates, fertility, mortality, and divorce and less insight into ebbs and flows in political or ideological values.

7. *It is easier to predict future problems than it is to suggest adequate solutions to those difficulties.* We know, for example, that the population is aging and that the fertility rate has declined. These two trends will likely create a problem of supporting the needs of an aging population. While we can predict that medical issues will be a major concern of the aging population, we have no clear insight into what steps might reduce this problem.

8. *It is often easier to predict what will not happen than what will.* Social scientists are relatively confident in predicting that the divorce rate will neither decline nor increase substantially in the next decade. What will happen regarding marital relations other than divorce is much more difficult to predict.

9. *Some of the most useful predictions about the future are self-defeating.* The most important purpose of those who predict the demise and death of the family is to sensitize people to important family issues. Thus, for example, David Popenoe (1988) wrote on disturbing the family nest because he wanted to stimulate concern for rebuilding it.

SOME THOUGHTS ON THE FAMILY IN THE FUTURE

Where is the family going? What is the future of the family? The answer to these questions depends, to a large degree, on how one defines the family. If by family and the future of the family we mean an institution whose primary function is socioemotional gratification and consists of intimate relationships, our answer will take us in one direction. If, on the other hand, we see the family the same way as David Popenoe does, as primarily an institution that is a social instrument for child rearing, then our answer will take us in another direction.

The future of families seems to fall somewhere between the dire warning of Popenoe's "disturbed nest" and the cautious optimism of Skolnick's (1991) "embattled paradise." The family seems strongest as the source of socioemotional support for adults. The family is most problematic as an instrument of child rearing.

One way to provide a framework for forecasting the future is to consider some statistical trends and where they seem to be going with regard to families. The major trends that seem to capture the attention of those who sound dire warnings about the family are (1) divorce rates, (2) marriage rates, (3) birth rates, and (4) working women.

Divorce Rates

The loudest warning bell that sounded during the 1970s and early 1980s regarding the family was the rapidly increasing divorce rate. The rate peaked in the late 1970s and then fluctuated throughout the 1980s, with an overall general downward trend. There is very little reason to believe that we will see another dramatic upward turn in divorce in the next decade or so. The baby boom generation has already passed the prime years in which they would be ending a first marriage. Second, the general increase in age at first marriage that has occurred in the past few decades provides reason for optimism that, with marriage commencing later, there is a slightly lower risk of divorce.

On the other hand, there is no reason to believe that the divorce rate will decline a great deal. For example, the baby boomers whose first marriage ended in divorce can still contribute to the overall divorce rate because they have a high risk of divorce in their second and third marriages. The data on divorce rates in the early 1990s may well indicate a downward trend, but this is likely the result of the severe economic recession that affected a large portion of the country, especially the Northeast, Middle Atlantic states, and parts of the Midwest. Economic downturns tend to temporarily depress the divorce rate, and it is quite likely that this occurred in the early 1990s. On the other hand, because there has been no significant reversal in the trend of psychological gentrification, individuals will still demand a great deal from their intimate relationships. When those expectations are not met, individuals and couples will choose to end an unfulfilling relationship. For the foreseeable future, divorce will continue to be the typical way the majority of marriages end.

Marriage Rates

Marriage rates remain high in the United States and are among the highest of all developed nations in the world (Glick 1988). The rate of entering into a

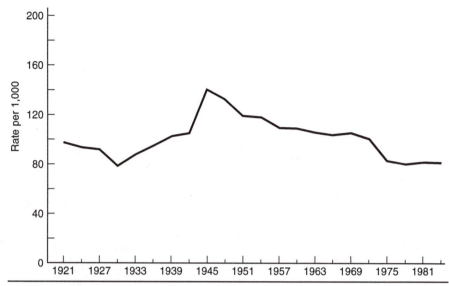

Figure 16-1 Rates of First Marriage per 1,000 Single Women, Aged 14–44, 1921–1981

SOURCE: Adapted from Saluter (1989, p. 7).

first marriage peaked in the United States following World War II. There was a decline in the rate of marriage after this peak that has continued to the present (see Figure 16-1).

The rate of marriage declined for a number of reasons. First, young men and women have delayed entering into their first marriage. These delays are the result of (1) postponing marriage to complete a college education or to establish one's working career and (2) the increase in the rate of cohabitation, which has become at least a new stage prior to marriage, if not an alternative to marriage.

Delaying the first marriage might actually result in men and women not marrying at all. One group of family demographers examined data on marriage rates and noted that a marriage postponed too long was a marriage forgone (Bennett, Bloom, and Craig 1986). The June 2, 1986 issue of *Newsweek* interpreted these findings to mean that 40-year-old women's probability of marrying was so low they were more likely to be killed by a terrorist! Of course, such a prediction violates Kain's (1990) second rule of predictions, for although 40-year-old women might not marry in the near future, it is impossible to predict that they will never marry. Moreover, as sociologist Andrew Cherlin (1990) stated when commenting on the prediction about marriage and being killed by a terrorist, "No demographic method can be used confidently to predict future behavior during a time of great social change" (p. 122).

Delays in beginning the first marriage and delays in having the first child mean that more women in their 30s and 40s are having their first child.

Thus it appears that, even with delays in first marriage and the increase in cohabitation, marriage remains the choice for the majority of Americans. Cohabitation, while more popular and more socially acceptable than decades ago, does not seem likely to replace marriage as a social institution. There seems to be little danger in the short run that the home will become an overnight parking lot used simply for sex.

Birth Rates   The baby boom was an aberration, a statistical and cultural fluke that occurred at the end of World War II. The baby boom interrupted a general decline in fertility and the birth rate that had begun at the turn of the century. Some demographers predicted that there would be a "baby boom echo" in the 1970s or 1980s as the baby boom generation began to form their own families and have their own children. However, although there was a slight upward "blip" in the rate and number of children born in the late 1960s, there has been no evidence of a significant baby boom echo. Children's overall share of the population has declined since 1970 and will continue to decline in the foreseeable future as fertility rates stay low and the baby boomers age (Figure 16-2).

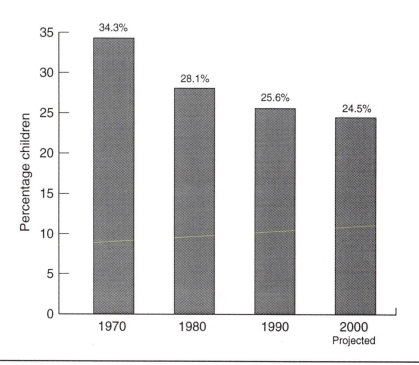

Figure 16-2 Children's Share of Total Population, 1970–2000

SOURCE: *Kids Count Data Book* by the Annie E. Casey Foundation, 1992, Greenwich, CT: Annie E. Casey Foundation. Copyright © 1992 by The Annie E. Casey Foundation. Adapted by permission.

Delays in first marriage often mean that couples will delay having their first child. Of course, having children does not always follow getting married. The birth rate among never-married women is rising and will likely continue to rise. Delays in having the first child tend to delay having subsequent children and a reduced likelihood of having a large number of children. Couples are having fewer children, and there is an increase in the proportion of families that have only one child. Thus there seems to be little evidence that we will ever return to the time when the average woman had 3.7 children. The fertility rate will likely stay below replacement (2.0) for the general population, although, as we saw in earlier chapters, there is significant variation in the fertility rate across socioeconomic, racial, and ethnic groups.

Working Women

The proportion of married women and women with children employed in the workforce has increased rapidly in the past 40 years, with the greatest growth among married women with preschool children. Obviously, the rate of growth in the near future cannot be as great as it was when the rate of maternal employment for women whose youngest child was under 6 years of age grew from less than 15% in 1950 to more than 60% in 1991 (U.S. Bureau of the Census 1992b). However, there is still room for growth, and the combined effects of the economy and the women's movement will continue the upward trend in maternal employment. Despite the concern of those who feel that increased employment of mothers with preschool children is at the core of family decline and dysfunction, there is no practical or theoretical reason to think that the trend will reverse itself and mothers will return to the stereotypical "Harriet" role of the 1950s. Working mothers are here to stay.

Areas of Concern: The Status of Children

Families will continue to get older and smaller, and mothers will work. Individuals will still seek to dissolve unsatisfactory marriages and find more fulfilling intimate relationships. One significant area of concern, however, is the future of children in general and children in families in particular. The status of children in families has changed in the past 50 years and the changes have not all been in their best interests. Although some have argued that the key change is the absence of fathers—take, for instance, former Vice President Dan Quayle's attack on television character "Murphy Brown's" decision to have a child out of wedlock—the major structural change is the poverty that affects children in single-parent homes.

The increase in divorce and the increase in out-of-wedlock births has resulted in a much greater proportion of children living in single-parent households, with other relatives, and outside the family (Figure 16-3). Since 1970, the number of children living in single-parent families has increased 64%, those living with other relatives has increased 34%, and the number living outside the family, while small, has increased 36% (U.S. Bureau of the Census 1992b).

In addition to the significant increase in children who are not living with one or both of their natural parents, there has been a significant increase in the percentage of children in the United States who live in poverty (Figure 16-4). Across all racial groups, more children today live in poverty than a decade ago.

This disturbing trend shows no sign of abating. If there is one significant problem that is undermining the American family it is that more and more children are growing up without both parents and in economic conditions that place them at significant risk of disease, violence, and other threats to their physical and mental health.

I do not share the opinion that socialization of children is the central and most important aspect of the family as a social institution, nor do I believe

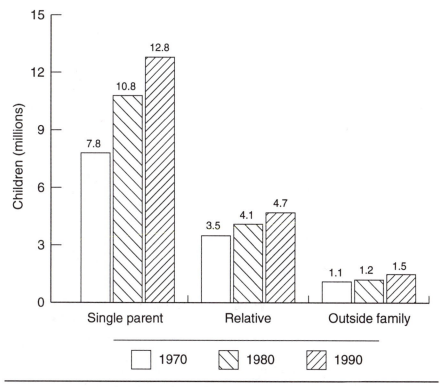

Figure 16-3
Children Living
Without Their Two
Parents, 1970–1990

SOURCE: *Kids Count Data Book* by the Annie E. Casey Foundation, 1992, Greenwich, CT: Annie E. Casey Foundation. Copyright © 1992 by The Annie E. Casey Foundation. Adapted by permission.

that the major problems children face come from cohabitation, day care, and the fact that more of their mothers work. However, it is quite clear to me that the economic policies of the 1980s and the significant concentration of wealth among the wealthy elite at the expense of minorities and lower-class families has created a situation of dire peril for an increasing proportion of American children. The family is not declining because of divorce, working mothers, and lower fertility. The family is declining because this society continues to ignore the needs of a substantial portion of its children. Many children are not immunized, are not adequately fed or clothed, are not provided with adequate and complete access to affordable health care, and live in dangerous and sometimes lethal environments. There is a desperate need for social policies that improve the quality of life and life chances for the nation's children, especially those who live in poor families and poor neighborhoods.

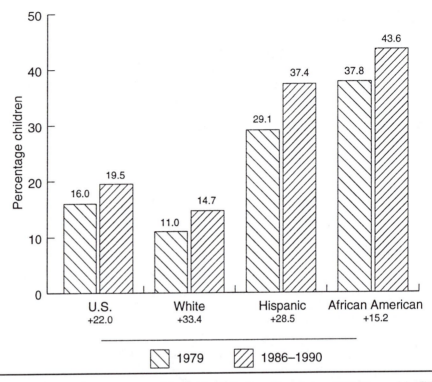

Figure 16-4
Percentage Children in Poverty, by Race and Ethnicity: 1979 to 1986–1990

SOURCE: *Kids Count Data Book* by the Annie E. Casey Foundation, 1992, Greenwich, CT: Annie E. Casey Foundation. Copyright © 1992 by The Annie E. Casey Foundation. Adapted by permission.

Changing Marital Forms

The future of families is one of diversity of family forms and structures. There is little evidence that any of the forces that influence the family as a social group or social institution will move the family back toward the so-called idyllic nuclear family of the 1950s. Nor is there reason to think that the family will ever become the idealized three-generation extended family or the "classical family of Western nostalgia." Families and intimate relations will continue to evolve. As noted in the previous section, one continued development is the growth of single-parent families. A second significant change is the growth of, and increased acceptance of, gay and lesbian relationships that are publicly displayed and more socially approved. As recently as 10 years ago, gay and lesbian couples faced significant social stigma and discrimination if they publicly announced or demonstrated their relationships. Today, although the majority of the public still disapproves of homosexuality (Davis and Smith 1989), gay and lesbian relationships have become part of publicly expressed intimate relationships. In addition, lesbian couples have succeeded in adopting children. Thus, even though about three quarters of the general public continues to disapprove of these relationships, they have become a social reality, and the overt discrimination that gay and lesbian couples experienced in the past has abated somewhat.

Diversity includes both cohabitation and living as a single. While neither household form is likely to replace marriage, both forms have become increasingly common and will certainly continue to increase.

A final form of diversity is the "new extended family." The economic recession of the 1990s fueled a rise in the new extended family—single parents who are choosing to live in multigenerational families. The Census Bureau (1992a) reported that the number of single parents who lived in households headed by other adults grew from 859,000 in 1980 to more than 2 million in 1991. Three quarters of the single parents are living with other relatives, usually their parents. The remainder are living with boyfriends or other nonrelatives. The "doubling up" of single parents is due to the flat incomes of young single parents and the high costs of housing, particularly in some urban areas.

Some students of the family continue to peer into their crystal balls and look for a time when marital roles will change and the family will become a truly androgynous institution. Twenty years ago, the rapid increase in working

Changing Marital Roles

BOX 16-3: DIVERSE FAMILIES

Minority Families and the Future

One major change that is occurring, and will continue to occur, is the increasing cultural diversity of the society. The minority population in the United States is large and growing. The growth is a function of increased immigration, especially from Southeast Asia and Central America, the young average age of minorities, and the higher fertility rates in minority families compared to nonminority families. Between 1960 and 1990, the minority population of the United States tripled in size, reaching 61 million (O'Hare 1992). Demographers predict that by the year 2050, if present trends continue, African Americans, Latinos, Asians, and Native Americans together will make up nearly half of the U.S. population (O'Hare 1992). By the year 2000, one in three schoolchildren will be from a minority population.

Racism, poverty, and discrimination affect the lives of minority families more than they do the lives of majority families (see Chapter 5). Thus the problems afflicting children in our society in general are more likely to be felt by minority children, especially African American, Latino, and Native American children.

Minority children are more likely to be poor, to grow up in a single-parent household, to be born out of wedlock, and to live in a poor and dangerous inner-city environment.

women and the pervasiveness of the women's movement caused many fore-casters to predict that household equality was quickly approaching. However, working women simply added a second "shift" to their lifestyles. Although some "househusbands" emerged in the 1970s and 1980s, the home and child care are still considered the province and responsibility of women. The women's movement waned in popular support, and worse, produced a "backlash" (Faludi 1991) against women, which was designed to "keep them in their place." Although more men are involved in housework and child care, more men have also abandoned their families and failed to provide court-ordered child support after a divorce. Thus an increase in "good dads" has been counterbalanced by an increase in what Frank Furstenberg (1988) calls "bad dads."

The crystal ball holds no magical transformation of the American household; however, there is reason to think that role options in families will continue to become more flexible. Although I have warned about deterministic and absolute predictions about future families, it seems that families will always have a gender-based division of labor. We can hope, however, that the division of labor will increasingly be based on interests and abilities and decreasingly based simply on sex and gender.

Threats and Unknowns

The cloud that hangs over the family and intimate relations is not divorce, cohabitation, working mothers, or alternative lifestyles. Today's cloud is AIDS (Acquired Immunodeficiency Syndrome). Ten years ago, the disease was barely recognized, and when it was, it was considered a problem confined to gay men in urban areas or a handful of hemophiliacs. AIDS spread quickly among the population of gay men and then turned up among intravenous drug users. Today, scientists believe that heterosexual adolescents are the group at highest risk for HIV (Human Immunodeficiency Virus) transmission and infection (Ehrhardt, Yingling, and Warne 1991). HIV can be transmitted through heterosexual intercourse and American adolescents are low in their consistent use of condoms. Although knowledge of AIDS and HIV transmission has increased rapidly, sexual practices, especially among heterosexuals, have not changed rapidly.

One population that has changed its sexual practices is gay men (Ehrhardt et al. 1991). There has been a dramatic change in the sexual behavior of gay men in the past 10 years, and this has resulted in a decline in the rate of HIV infection in this population, especially in the so-called "epicenters of risk"—the urban areas on both coasts—although some worry that safe sex practices are no longer as widespread in the gay community.

With regard to sexual behavior among heterosexuals, we can make two predictions with some confidence. First, assuming the evidence on heterosex-

The AIDS epidemic—memorialized in the AIDS quilt—is having a significant effect on intimate relations, families, and society.

ual HIV transmission is accurate, unless there is a significant change in sexual practices among adolescents and young adults, we may witness a tragedy of untold magnitude in the next 10 to 20 years. Although the diagnosis of HIV infection is presently low among heterosexuals, we may find an epidemic of diagnoses of HIV infection among young adults in the next decade, because of the lag time in diagnosis and detection. Unless a miraculous cure for AIDS is found in the next decade, death rates for young heterosexual adults will soar. This is especially true for those who live in poverty.

On the other hand, if adolescents and young adults change their sexual practices and attempt to prevent HIV infection, this will have a dramatic effect on premarital, marital, and extramarital sexual behavior. In either case, AIDS will almost certainly have a direct effect on intimacy and families in the years to come.

A second significant social issue looms over the family and intimate relations. American women have had the legal right to obtain an abortion during the first 20 weeks of a pregnancy for nearly 20 years—since the U.S. Supreme Court's ruling on *Roe v. Wade*. Although some social observers thought that the *Roe* decision would end public debate about abortion, just the opposite has happened (supporting Kain's 1990 idea about the difficulty in predicting ideological and political trends). In the late 1980s and early 1990s, the Supreme Court was poised to strike down *Roe*, although the election of Bill Clinton as president in 1992 seemed to quell concerns that the Court would soon overturn its original ruling. If the Supreme Court ever did overturn *Roe*, this would put the issue of abortion into the hands of each state legislature. It is impossible to predict what each of 50 state legislatures would do with regard to abortion rights, but one thing is clear: If *Roe* is struck down, abortion will no longer be a taken-for-granted woman's right. The impact on fertility, families, and women would be significant, especially for women who could not afford to pay for abortions even if legally available in some states or jurisdictions.

Government Policies	What role should government play in supporting or preserving the family? What role will the government play in the family as a social institution and a social group? These are difficult questions to answer. The first question is difficult because government at the local, state, and federal level is subjected to bids for attention and social action from often diametrically opposed interest groups. Conservatives pressure government to support traditional family values by restricting abortion, not recognizing homosexual marriages, and not providing support for sex education so as not to promote early sexual intercourse and out-of-wedlock births. Liberals press for increased government support for families, especially disadvantaged families and children. Pro-choice advocates lobby for a women's right to have an abortion. Child advocates (liberal, moderate, and conservative) demand that more attention be paid to children's issues, such as poverty, abuse, neglect, and sexual abuse. Women's advocates decry the continued inequality that women face in the workplace, the violent oppression of women at home, and the lack of a national child care system. Advocates for the elderly are concerned about problems of aging, medical care, and elder abuse.

Predicting future government policies violates Kain's (1990) sixth rule of predictions: that it is not easy to predict ideological or political trends. It is not clear which special interests will prevail, and if they prevail, for how long.

One thing we can be confident in is that families and family values will be at the center of government policies in the years to come. The population will continue to age, and the proportion of women in the workforce will stay high and perhaps rise higher. Thus the issues of child care, parental leave, and health care for families and especially the elderly will continue to hold center stage in all government policy discussions. The United States remains the last industrialized country in the world to have no national child care policy. Clearly, in the next decade or so, this policy issue will be addressed.

SUMMING UP

There is little doubt that families are now more diverse than ever. It is impossible to talk about one form of family that is typical across all social and ethnic groups. Perhaps the greatest strength of the family as a social institution is its ability to adapt and change in the face of social and cultural changes. The family as a social institution has passed through the hunter and gatherer stage, through pastoral and horticultural societies, through an agrarian period, and now through industrialization and the transition into a postindustrial society. The family has outlasted its most severe social critics and the dates for its demise. Although the optimists about the nature of the family and its future tend to be outnumbered by the pessimists, there is reason to heed the advice that families are here to stay. Changes in family structure and household composition have had the most profound impact on the lives of children, but even here the positive data outweigh the pronouncements of the doomsayers.

Modern families will continue to age and get smaller. Singles, cohabitation, and the new extended family will continue to be alternatives to the traditional nuclear form. Because women are in the workforce to stay, the issue of child care is a major concern for a society that must give up a sentimental attachment to a vision of the past that has women in the traditional homemaker role.

Perhaps the greatest strength of the family is that it inspires so much concern and debate. An institution that is on life support would not fuel the heated discussions that the family has generated and continues to generate. The family remains at the core of human existence—the source of comfort and the source of concern.

REFERENCES

Bane, Mary Jo. 1976. *Here to Stay: American Families in the Twentieth Century.* New York: Basic Books.

Bennett, Neil G., David E. Bloom, and Patricia H. Craig. 1986. "Black and White Marriage Patterns: Why So Different?" Discussion Paper No. 500. New Haven, CT: Yale University, Economic Growth Center.

Bronfenbrenner, Urie. 1977. "Nobody Home: The Erosion of the American Family." *Psychology Today* 10(May):41-47.

Caplow, Theodore, Howard Bahr, Bruce Chadwick, Reuben Hill, and Margaret Holmes Williamson. 1982. *Middletown Families: Fifty Years of Change and Continuity*. Minneapolis: University of Minnesota Press.

Annie E. Casey Foundation. 1992. *Kids Count Data Book: State Profiles of Child Well-Being*. Washington, DC: Center for the Study of Social Policy.

Cherlin, Andrew. 1990. "The Strange Career of the 'Harvard-Yale Study.' " *Public Opinion Quarterly* 54(Spring):117-24.

Clayton, Richard R. 1979. *The Family, Marriage, and Social Change*. 2nd ed. Lexington, MA: D. C. Heath.

Davis, James A. and Tom Smith. 1989. *General Social Surveys, 1972–1987*. Cumulative data. Storrs: University of Connecticut, Roper Center for Public Research.

Ehrdardt, Anke A., Sandra Yingling, and Patricia A. Warne. 1991. "Sexual Behavior in the Era of AIDS: What Has Changed in the United States?" *Annual Review of Sexual Research* 2:25-27.

Etzioni, Amitai. 1977. "The Family: Is It Obsolete?" *Journal of Current Social Issues* 14 (Winter):4-9.

Faludi, Susan. 1991. *Backlash: The Undeclared War Against American Women*. New York: Crown.

Furstenberg, Frank F., Jr. 1988. "Good Dads-Bad Dads: Two Faces of Fatherhood." Pp. 193-218 in *The Changing American Family*, edited by Andrew Cherlin. Washington, DC: Urban Institute Press.

Glick, Paul C. 1988. "Fifty Years of Family Demography: A Record of Social Change." *Journal of Marriage and the Family* 50(November):861-73.

Halberstam, David. 1993. *The Fifties*. New York: Villard Books.

Kain, Edward L. 1990. *The Myth of Family Decline: Understanding Families in a World of Rapid Social Change*. Lexington, MA: Lexington Books.

Lasch, Christopher. 1977. *Haven in a Heartless World: The Family Besieged*. New York: Basic Books.

Levitan, Sar A. and Richard S. Belous. 1981. *What's Happening to the American Family?* Baltimore: Johns Hopkins University Press.

Levitan, Sar A., Richard S. Belous, and Frank Gallo. 1988. *What's Happening to the American Family?* Rev. ed. Baltimore: Johns Hopkins University Press.

Lynd, Robert S. and Helen M. Lynd. [1929] 1956. *Middletown: A Study in American Culture*. New York: Harcourt Brace Jovanovich.

Moore, Barrington, Jr. 1958. *Political Power and Social Theory*. Cambridge, MA: Harvard University Press.

O'Hare, William P. 1992. "America's Minorities—The Demographics of Diversity." *Population Bulletin* 47(4):1-47.

Popenoe, David. 1988. *Disturbing the Nest: Family Change and Decline in Modern Societies*. New York: Aldine de Gruyter.

President's Research Committee on Social Trends. 1933. *Recent Social Trends in the United States*. New York: McGraw-Hill.

Rossi, Alice S. 1978. "A Biosocial Perspective on Parenting." Pp. 1-31 in *The Family*, edited by Alice S. Rossi, Jerome Kagan, and Tamara K. Hareven. New York: Norton.

Russell, Bertrand. 1929. *Marriage and Morals*. New York: Horace Liveright.

Saluter, Arlene F. 1989. *Changes in American Family Life*. Current Population Reports, Special Studies, Series P-23, No. 163. Washington, DC: Government Printing Office.

Sorokin, Pitrim. 1937. *Social and Cultural Dynamics*. Vol. 5. New York: E. P. Dutton.

Skolnick, Arlene. 1991. *Embattled Paradise*. New York: Harper Collins.

U.S. Bureau of the Census. 1992a. *Household and Family Characteristics, March 1991*. Current Population Reports: Population Characteristics, Series P-20, No. 458. Washington, DC: Government Printing Office.

———. 1992b. *Statistical Abstracts of the United States*. Washington, DC: Government Printing Office.

Watson, John. 1928. *Psychological Care of Infant and Child*. New York: Norton.

■■ Glossary

Agents of socialization
An individual, group, or organization that influences a person's behavior and sense of self.

Agrarian societies
Food is obtained by farming and agriculture.

Anal stage
According to Freud, during this stage children gain satisfaction and pleasure in learning to release and control their bowels.

Authoritarian parent
Baumrind's type of parent who tries to shape, mold, and control the behavior of his or her child according to absolute standards of behavior.

Authoritative parent
Baumrind's type of parent whose style is characterized by the use of positive reinforcement and minimal punishment.

Avuncolocal residence
A boy returns to his mother's brother's village (the village in which his mother was born) either at puberty or at the time of his marriage.

Bilateral descent
Children trace their lineage through both genetic parents.

Bilocal residence
Rules that allow the newly married couple to choose which set of parents with whom they will live.

Birth rate (or crude birth rate)

The given number of births per 1,000 people in the population in a given year.

Commuter marriage

A marriage that involves a decision to establish two separate residences and live in two separate locations.

Companionate love

A lower-key emotion—friendly affection and deep attachment to someone.

Conceptual frameworks

Clusters of interrelated but not as yet interdefined concepts for viewing the phenomenon of marriage and family behavior and classifying its parts.

Concrete operational stage

According to Piaget, the third stage of human development, from about age 7 to 12. During this stage, children learn to consider more than one dimension at a time.

Conflict theory

An approach to sociological analysis that stresses the differences in people's interests, their clashes over limited goods, and the extent to which society is held together by power.

Conjugal relationship

A nuclear family that always has a husband and wife and may or may not include children.

Consanguine relationships

A family, typically an extended family, based on blood relationships as the basis of descent from the same ancestors.

Control group

The group that is put through the experimental design but is *not* exposed to the experimental treatment.

Coping

The management of a stressful event or situation by the family as a unit, with no detrimental effects on any individual in that family.

Crisis

Stressors that create stress that seems, for some period of time, insurmountable.

Crude birth rate (see *Birth rate*)

Developmental framework

A perspective that emphasizes the life cycle, stages of the life cycle, and the specific tasks to be accomplished at each stage.

Developmental tasks

Tasks are those that arise at particular points in an individual's life. Successful achievement of these tasks leads to happiness and success in later tasks. Failure leads to unhappiness, later failure, and disapproval by society.

Discretionary kin

Individuals who are ordinarily distant in normal kinship terms, who may or may not be included in the family based on a member's inclination.

Double descent

At birth, a child is assigned two lines of descent—the mother's matrilineal group and the father's patrilineal group. The other two lineages—mother's patrilineal and father's matrilineal—are disregarded for purposes of inheritance and family lineage.

Dual-career households

Both husband and wife are committed to work that has the probability of career advancement and that is intrinsically rewarding.

Dual-earner households

Families with both a male and a female wage earner.

Ego

According to Freud, the rational part of the personality that deals with the outside world and mediates between the id and the superego.

Ethnic group

Group made up of individuals who typically are of the same nationality or ancestry and who share a common heritage, culture, and lifestyle.

Ethnocentrism

A tendency to evaluate other cultures in terms of one's own and to conclude that the other culture is inferior.

Experimental group

The group in an experiment that is exposed to the experimental treatment.

Extended family

Three or more generations related by blood or marriage living together in the same household.

Extramarital sex

Sexual intercourse between two people, at least one of whom is married to someone else.

Family

A social group and a social institution that possesses an identifiable structure made up of positions (e.g., breadwinner, child rearer, decision maker, nurturer), and interactions among those who occupy the positions. The structure typically carries out specialized functions (e.g., child rearing), is characterized by biologically and socially defined kinship, and typically involves sharing a residence.

Family career

The timing, sequence, and occurrence of family structural changes over time.

Family of orientation

The nuclear family into which one was born and reared.

Family of procreation

The nuclear family formed by a marriage.

Feral children

Children raised in isolation with little or any human contact.

Fertility rate

The number of live births per 1,000 women of childbearing age (15 to 44 years of age) in a population in a given year.

Fictive kin

Individuals referred to using kinship terms (e.g., uncle, aunt, cousin) but who are not related by blood.

Field study

A research method involving direct observation of social behavior in its natural setting.

Flextime

A flexible schedule around the traditional or normal core working hours of 9 a.m. to 5 p.m.

Formal operations stage

According to Piaget, this is the fourth stage of human development, beginning around age 12, during which abstract thinking is developed.

Function

A term used in the context of the structural functional perspective (or functional perspective) that refers to what an institution or system does or the consequences it has for a given form of structure or system.

Game stage

According to Mead, children engage in social interaction with others during this stage of socialization.

Genital stage

According to Freud, this stage occurs during adolescence. Sexual desire emerges and adolescents begin to seek mature love.

Generalized other

According to Mead, this is the internalized image people have of the structure and norms of society as a whole.

Geographic propinquity

Living near one another.

Group marriage

Two or more men married to two or more women at the same time.

Hominid

Member of the human family.

Homogamy

The tendency to marry someone who is like us in the social attributes that our society considers important, such as age, education, race, religion, and ethnic background.

Horticultural societies

Food is obtained through simple forms of plant cultivation, such as slash and burn cultivation.

Household

A housing unit—a house, an apartment or other group of rooms, or a single room.

Id

According to Freud, the part of the personality that serves as a reservoir of innate, primitive, asocial, sexual, and aggressive urges.

Individual racism

An act of individual discrimination that blocks the opportunities of minorities.

Instincts

According to Freud, powerful, inborn sexual and aggressive urges.

Institutional racism

Established social patterns and norms that have the unintended consequences of limiting opportunities of certain racial groups.

Joint family

Three generations that consist of two or more brothers and their wives, with their children and unmarried sisters, living in one household, usually a compound of buildings.

Kinship

Relationships based on birth and the birth cycle.

Latency stage

According to Freud, this stage occurs at age 6 or 7. At this point, sexual urges are latent while the child's attention turns to developing skills to cope with the environment.

Launching stage

The period in the family life cycle when children begin to leave home.

Libido

According to Freud, the sexual energy that is the driving force of all human behavior.

Linkage theory

Proposes that socialization patterns, and choice of discipline technique results from the social structure in which the parents and family are embedded. The economic and occupational world the parents and family are enmeshed in exerts a significant influence over how they go about raising their children.

Looking-glass self

According to Cooley, the image we have of ourselves that is a reflection of how other people react to us.

Macrosocial perspective

A perspective that examines the larger forms of social behavior—e.g., social system, social institutions, or the relationship between social institutions.

Marital adjustment

A concept that taps the global sense of a marriage, an individual's subjective view of the marriage that taps how individuals view their relationships with their partners.

Marital happiness

The level of personal happiness *an individual* feels about his or her marriage.

Marital instability

The propensity to divorce.

Marital satisfaction

An individual's *subjective evaluation* of the overall nature of the marriage.

Marriage

A socially approved and institutionalized union of some permanence between two or more persons.

Matrifocal

Family life is focused around the woman, even if she does not have dominance or power over the husband or family.

Matrilineal descent

A family system that traces lineage and inheritance through the mother's line or family.

Matrilocal residence

Societal rules that the newly married couple lives with the parents of the bride.

Microsocial perspective

A perspective that examines the smaller forms of social behavior—e.g., everyday individual social interaction.

Miscegenation

Marriage between people of different races.

Modified extended family

Families that have a nuclear structure, may live in geographically dispersed locations, but still maintain close ties and are united by an ongoing network of interaction and aid and assistance.

Monogamy

Marriage with one husband or one wife at one time.

Natural selection
Nature acting on genetic diversity, selecting the most adaptive traits.

Neolocal residence
The married couple establishes a home of their own, apart from both sets of parents.

Norms
Specific rules or sets of rules about what people should or should not do or say in a given situation.

Nuclear family
A husband, wife, and their dependent children living in a home or residence of their own.

Nurturant socialization
Socialization that involves a strong emotional attachment between the agent of socialization and the person who is being socialized (*see also Socialization*).

Observational research
A research method involving direct observation of social behavior in its natural setting (*see Field study*).

Oedipal conflicts
According to Freud, children want to possess (have sexual intercourse with or marry) the parent of the opposite sex, and this creates an intense rivalry between the child and the same-sex parent.

Oral stage
According to Freud, during this stage, pleasure is derived from sucking and children typically will put anything in their mouths to satisfy their oral urges.

Participant observation research
A research method involving direct observation of social behavior in its natural setting in which the researcher participates in the activity or group being studied (*see Field study*).

Passionate love
A wildly emotional state, a confusion of feelings: tenderness and sexuality, elation and pain, anxiety and relief, altruism and jealousy; a state of intense absorption in the other person.

Pastoral societies
Food is obtained by the herding of livestock, such as cattle, camels, and sheep.

Patrilineal descent
A family system that traces lineage and inheritance through the father's line or family.

Patrilocal residence
Societal rules that the newly married couple lives with the parents of the groom.

Permissive parent

Baumrind's type of parent who deals with his or her children in a nonpunishing, accepting, and affirming manner.

Personality

An individual's characteristic patterns of behavior and thought.

Phallic stage

According to Freud, during this stage children discover their genitals and become aware of the differences between the sexes.

Play stage

According to Mead, this is the stage of socialization during which children play at being different people.

Polyandry

Marriage of one woman to two or more men at one time.

Polygamy

The practice of a man or a woman having more than one spouse.

Polygyny

Marriage of one man to more than one woman at one time.

Position

The location an individual occupies in a social structure.

Postparental stage of marriage

Stage in the family life cycle when children have left home.

Preoperational stage

According to Piaget, the second stage of human development that occurs when children are ages 2 to 7. These are the years during which children learn to speak, use words, and represent objects and images symbolically.

Premarital sex

Sexual intercourse between two individuals who are not, and have never been, married.

Racial groups

Groups made up of individuals who are related by a common heredity or ancestry and who are perceived and responded to in terms of external features or traits.

Reference group

A group or social category that an individual uses as a guide in developing his or her values, attitudes, behavior, and self-image.

Refined birth rate

The number of births per year per 1,000 women.

Representative sample
>A sample in which every member of the defined population has a chance, and the same chance, of being selected to be part of the sample.

Response rate
>The proportion of the sample that completes the survey instrument (questionnaire or interview).

Role
>Culturally defined rights, obligations, and expectations that accompany a position or social status.

Role strain
>Can take the form of *overload,* which means that the demands of work and family roles are more than the person can handle, or *interference,* in which the demands of work call for one thing to be done while the demands of family call for another thing to be done.

Sample
>The portion of a defined population under investigation that a researcher actually studies.

Sanctions
>Social rewards for conforming behavior and punishments for deviant behavior.

Self
>The individual's sense of identity.

Sensorimotor stage
>According to Piaget, the first stage of human development, which begins at birth and lasts until about 2 years of age.

Serial monogamy
>One exclusive, legally sanctioned but relatively short-lived marriage after another.

Social class
>People who occupy the same layer in the social stratification system.

Social exchange perspective
>A perspective that seeks to explain individual and social behavior based on a reciprocity or balance between costs and rewards.

Social institution
>An established pattern of social relationships and behavior that structures a particular area of social life.

Social stratification
>The division of society into layers or strata.

Social structure
>The orderly and patterned ways in which people or groups interact with one another.

Social survey

A research method involving the use of standardized questionnaires, interviews, or both to gather data on large populations.

Socialization

The process whereby one acquires a sense of personal identity and learns what people in the surrounding culture believe and how they expect one to behave.

Sociological perspective

A perspective that examines groups and societies and how groups and societies influence individual social behavior.

Sororal polygyny

Marriage involving a man having more than one wife at one time and the wives are sisters.

Stem families

At least two generations living in a single residence. For example, a mother and father live in the same household with a married son, his wife, and children. The stem family differs from a classical extended family in that the mother and father choose to live with only one adult son, as compared to living with all adult children and their offspring.

Stress

Pressure or tension in the family system; a disturbance in the steady-state of the family.

Stressor (Stressor events)

Life events or changes in life circumstances that are of a significant magnitude to provoke a change in the family system.

Structure

The relatively stable and enduring patterns that organize social relationships and provide the basic framework for society (*see Social structure*).

Superego

According to Freud, the part of the personality that contains internalized representations of society's norms and values, especially as taught by parents.

Symbolic interaction framework

A perspective that stresses interaction between people as well as the social processes that occur within individuals made possible by language and internalized meanings.

Unilineal descent

Names, authority, and property are traced though one line, usually that of the father (*see Patrilineal descent*).

Values

Broad, abstract, shared standards of what is right, desirable, and worthy of respect.

■ Name Index

■ Subject Index

determinants of marital happiness in, 246

distinguishing features of, 144-145

economic disadvantage of, 145, 148-149, 159

exchange among, 7

historical legacy of slavery and, 145, 146-147, 159

impact of racism on, 145, 147-148, 159

sharing among, 7

structural forces that influenced form and function of, 145

See also African American families and African American family life, patterns of

Blended families, 413-418, 420

complexity of, 414

impact of on children, 416-418

stresses in, 414-416

See also Remarriage

"Broken homes," 419

Bundling, 173

Child abduction and divorce, 416-417

Child abuse, xxvii, 5, 46, 450, 451, 453, 454, 478

case of Mary Ellen Wilson, 454

extent of, 455-457

fathers as perpetrators of, 463

frequency of, 457

in single-parent families, 142

mothers as perpetrators of, 463

rates, 465

Child/adolescent employment, 330

Child care, 117, 511

Child homicide, 458

Child labor laws, 330

Childless couples, 6

Childlessness, 259

Child protection laws, 453

Child rearing, differences in, 310-312. See also Discipline

Children:

and remarriage of parents, 413-418

consequences of discipline on, 312-313

employment of, 330

historical view of images of, 306

impact of blended families on, 416-418

impact of divorce on, 408-410

impact of parental unemployment on, 346

murder of, 458

parental abduction of, 416-417

See also Child abuse and Child sexual abuse

Children of Divorce Project, 409

Child sexual abuse, xxvii, 5, 454, 458

factors associated with, 466

Four-Precondition Model of, 469-470, 478

Child support, 279, 415

Child-to-parent violence, 462, 478

China, childbearing in, 270

Cognitive development, Piaget's theory of, 299-301, 304, 314

concrete operational stage of, 300-301, 304, 314, 514

formal operational stage of, 301, 304, 314, 516

preoperational stage of, 300, 304, 314, 520

sensorimotor stage of, 300, 304, 314, 521

Cohabitation, 119, 120, 125, 176-178, 193, 486

and marital quality, 178

as socially acceptable, 176, 177

in Denmark and Sweden, 176

in future, 507

possible impact of on subsequent marriage, 178

Colonial families, 106-109

Chesapeake Bay/Virginia, 107-108

children and child rearing in, 108

divorce among, 108-109

European traditions and, 105-106

Plymouth Colony/Massachusetts, 106-107, 108

Common sense:

and family studies, 35-37

correctness of, 38

Communication, effective:

and marital quality, 242-243

Commuter marriages, 13, 342, 514

Comprehensive Child Development Bill, 25

Conceptual frameworks, 39-56, 69, 514

and family studies, 35

biosocial theory, 55, 94-95

conflict theory, 40, 69

definition of, 25

developmental, 39, 40, 69

family process, 39

feminist, 39, 55, 69

institutional, 39

interactional, 39

main, 39

radical critical theory, 55

situational, 39

social exchange theory, 40, 69

structural functional, 39, 40, 69, 516

symbolic interactional, 40, 69, 522

Conflict Tactics Scales, 56

Conflict theorists, questions asked by, 45-46

Conflict theory, 40, 44-46, 83, 131, 514

central assumptions of, 44-45

competition and, 45

conflict and, 45

consensus and, 45

critiques of, 46

force and aggression and, 45

key concepts of, 45

Marxian writings and, 44

negotiation and bargaining and, 45

power and influence and, 45

Conjugal family, characteristics of, 88

Conjugal relationship, 14

definition of, 514

Consanguine (blood) relationships, 14

definition of, 514

Control group, definition of, 65, 514

Coping, 426

among parents of children with cancer, 441

definition of, 429, 445, 514